EARLY BLAZON

GLOVER'S ROLL, St. George's version, copy *c*.
London, Society of Antiquaries, MS. 664, Roll 8, vol. i, fol. 23

EARLY BLAZON

HERALDIC TERMINOLOGY IN THE
TWELFTH AND THIRTEENTH CENTURIES
WITH SPECIAL REFERENCE TO
ARTHURIAN LITERATURE

BY

GERARD J. BRAULT

Professor of French
The Pennsylvania State University

OXFORD
AT THE CLARENDON PRESS
1972

Oxford University Press, Ely House, London W. 1

GLASGOW NEW YORK TORONTO MELBOURNE WELLINGTON
CAPE TOWN IBADAN NAIROBI DAR ES SALAAM LUSAKA ADDIS ABABA
DELHI BOMBAY CALCUTTA MADRAS KARACHI LAHORE DACCA
KUALA LUMPUR SINGAPORE HONG KONG TOKYO

PRINTED IN GREAT BRITAIN

TO JEANNE
AND FOR
FRANK
ANNE MARIE
AND SUE

PREFACE

THE present status of medieval heraldic studies is similar in many respects to the position occupied by Old English and Old French literary studies a hundred years ago. Of the nearly five score surviving English medieval rolls of arms, for example—a roll of arms is a list or book of painted or written descriptions (blazons) of coats of arms— less than half have ever been published. Only seventeen exist in medieval manuscripts, the remainder being known only through copies made in modern times, notably by sixteenth- and seventeenth-century heralds and scholars. Many of these rolls have survived in more than one variant version and most have been transmitted to us in several copies.

Until 1967, none of the forty-odd editions of the English rolls which had been published could be considered truly critical by modern standards. All but a few are simple transcriptions without any emendations of a single copy which only too often is not the best or most complete copy available to scholars today. While the first of these editions dates back to 1655, all but a dozen were published by the intrepid James Greenstreet in the last quarter of the nineteenth century. A number of other scholars have worked diligently at various times, compiling notes, transcripts, tricked and painted copies, and elaborate indices. The awesome product of these countless man-hours of painstaking labour lies gathering dust in neglected cartons and filing-trays preserved in such depositories as the Society of Antiquaries and the College of Arms in London.

A bright ray of light, however, has now pierced this gloom. In 1950, Sir Anthony Wagner, Garter King of Arms and foremost living heraldic expert, published his masterly *Catalogue of English Mediaeval Rolls of Arms* (*CEMRA* or *Aspilogia I*) which describes in minute detail, classifies, and dates all known manuscripts for the first time. Seventeen years later, another important break-through was achieved with the publication of *Aspilogia II*, a critical edition of three early rolls of arms, that is to say the Matthew Paris Shields, Glover's Roll, and Walford's Roll. This work, due to the collaboration of Sir Anthony Wagner, the late

Hugh Stanford London, and Thomas D. Tremlett, features transcripts of base manuscripts, variants selected from all known copies of the rolls in question, and—its chief merit—exceptionally fine historical and genealogical notes on the persons mentioned in the lists. *Aspilogia II* offers a commendable study of the language of the three rolls, but, unfortunately, only the sketchiest of glossaries. Since the recent untimely death of Dr. Paul Adam-Even, little if any progress is being made in compiling a catalogue of medieval French rolls or in editing these. On the other hand, good editions of the thirteenth-century Bigot, Chifflet–Prinet, and Wijnbergen Rolls exist.

The present volume, which has been more than seven years in the making, would have taken much longer to write, indeed would probably never have been begun, had it not been for the pioneering investigations of early blazon by Max Prinet (d. 1937), Hugh Stanford London (d. 1959), and Dr. Paul Adam-Even (d. 1964). These scholars each published numerous studies which greatly facilitated the gathering and analysis of the materials presented here. *CEMRA* and *Aspilogia II* have also been indispensable tools.

The author's interest in the subject dates back to 1957 when his doctoral research on the Old French poet Girart d'Amiens led to a study of the heraldry in the latter's romance *Escanor*. Many persons have been kind enough to encourage me in this work and I should like to take this opportunity to thank in particular Professor William Roach, my thesis supervisor at the University of Pennsylvania, Professor Emerita Ruth J. Dean of Mount Holyoke College, and Professor Allen M. Barstow of the University of Connecticut. The latter's Ph.D. dissertation (see List of Abbreviations), completed after the present volume was in press, extends beyond the period covered by this book to about the middle of the fourteenth century for Anglo-Norman rolls of arms.

This book has been made possible by research grants from the institutions with which I have had the honour of being associated: Bowdoin College, The University of Pennsylvania, and The Pennsylvania State University. Dr. James Stacy Coles, former President of Bowdoin College, and Dr. Thomas F. Magner, Associate Dean for Research and Graduate Studies at The Pennsylvania State University, gave invaluable moral as well as financial support. I have also been favoured by a Fulbright Fellowship and a number of grants-in-aid from the American Council of Learned Societies and the American Philosophical Society. While most of the time and travel afforded by these awards were devoted to other research projects, early blazon was one of my major concerns these past few years and steady progress in this connection was made on each of these various trips. I am indebted to Professors Raymond C. and Virginia A. La Charité of the University of Kentucky who aided me at the outset of this research project by compiling an index of persons named in the early rolls of arms while they were both graduate students at The University of Pennsylvania. I am grateful, too, for the editorial assistance provided in the final phases of this book by Mrs. Julie Burgoyne and Mr. Denis Jean, two graduate students at The Pennsylvania State University.

I should also like to take this opportunity to thank M. Jean Prinet, conservateur en chef de la Bibliothèque nationale, for granting me the use of his uncle's, Max Prinet's, apartment in Paris—including access to his private papers—for several days. The search I conducted there yielded some helpful bibliography and a fascinating glimpse of the working habits of a great scholar.

Finally, my wife and three children have shown extraordinary patience and good cheer all this time and I owe them a debt of gratitude which words alone cannot adequately express.

CONTENTS

PLATES

ABBREVIATIONS

T HIS list contains: (1) an alphabetical arrangement of the sources (rolls of arms and literary texts) cited in this work, and (2) the complete reference for the abbreviated titles of scholarly studies alluded to here. The editions used and, in the case of the rolls of arms, the manuscript copies collated by the author are also provided.

The dates for the English rolls of arms are those found in *CEMRA* and are considered to be relatively firm. However, slightly different dates for some of these lists have been proposed by Denholm-Young, *History and Heraldry*. Dating for the French rolls is provided by Dr. Adam-Even in various publications, notably in his editions and in his provisional 'Catalogue' (see Introduction, p. 1). In lexicography, one must always bear in mind, of course, that the manuscript copy occasionally contains scribal emendations and additions reflecting a later state of the text.

On the other hand, Old French literary texts are often very difficult to date with precision, and the chronology of the works cited here— those of Chrétien de Troyes, for example—is a continuing source of controversy. Nevertheless, many readers unfamiliar with the literature in question will doubtless find a guide useful and, consequently, dates are proposed here with the understanding that in many cases they are approximate at best. Somewhat different dates are at times listed in Raphael Levy, *Chronologie approximative de la littérature française du moyen âge* (Tübingen, 1957) [*Beihefte zur ZRPh.*, 98].

Adam-Even BA	Adam-Even's notes to his edition of *BA*.
Adam-Even CPA	Adam-Even's notes to his edition of *CPA*.
Adam-Even, '*Roman de Troie*'	Paul Adam-Even, 'Les usages héraldiques au milieu du XIIᵉ siècle d'après le *Roman de Troie* de Benoît de Sainte-Maure et la littérature contemporaine', *Archivum Heraldicum*, lxxvii (1963), 18–29.
Adam-Even, '*Tournoiement des Dames de Paris*'	Paul Adam-Even, 'Etudes d'héraldique médiévale. Armoiries des bourgeois de Paris au début du XIVᵉ siècle d'après le *Tournoiement des Dames de Paris* de Pierre Gencien', *Archives Héraldiques Suisses*, lxii (1948), 1–10. On the date, see below, s.v. *Tournoiement des Dames de Paris*.
Adam-Even WB	Adam-Even's notes to his edition of *WB*.
Adenet le Roi	*Les Œuvres d'Adenet le Roi*, ed. Albert Henry. I. *Biographie d'Adenet. La tradition manuscrite* (Bruges, 1951). II.

Buevon de Conmarchis (Bruges, 1953). III. *Les Enfances Ogier* (Bruges, 1956). [*Rijksuniversiteit te Gent. Werken uitgegeven door de Faculteit van de wijsbegeerte en letteren,* 109, 115, 121.] IV. *Berte aus grans piés* (Brussels, 1963). [*Université libre de Bruxelles. Travaux de la Faculté de philosophie et lettres,* 23.] *Li Roumans de Cléomadès, par Adenès li Rois,* ed. André van Hasselt (Brussels, 1865–6). 2 vols. Reference is also made to *Adenet le Roi's Berte aus grans piés,* ed. Urban T. Holmes, jun. (Chapel Hill, 1946). [*University of North Carolina Studies in the Romance Languages and Literatures,* 6.] Dates: 1269–85 for Adenet's entire literary production; *Buevon de Conmarchis* probably earliest, followed by *Les Enfances Ogier,* then *Berte aus grans piés* (after 1273) and *Cleomadés* (1285 at the latest).

AHS   *Archives Héraldiques Suisses.*

Aiol   *Aiol, chanson de geste,* edd. Jacques Normand and Gaston Raynaud (Paris, 1877). [*Société des Anciens Textes Français.*] Date: two parts, the first late twelfth century, the second early thirteenth century.

Alexandre de Lambert le Tort   *Li Romans d'Alixandre par Lambert li Tors et Alexandre de Bernay,* ed. Henri Michelant (Stuttgart, 1846). [*Bibliothek des Litterarischen Vereins in Stuttgart,* 13.] Date: *c.* 1170.

Aquin   *Le Roman d'Aquin ou la Conqueste de la Bretaigne par le roy Charlemaigne,* ed. F. Joüon des Longrais (Nantes, 1880). Date: 1170–90.

Armytage   See *B.*

Artus   *Le Livre d'Artus.* See Sommer.

Ashmolean Roll   Oxford, Bodleian Library, MS. Ashmole 15 A, unpublished (edition being prepared by Prof. Allen M. Barstow). Date: *c.* 1334.

Aspilogia II   *Aspilogia. Being Materials of Heraldry,* gen. ed. Sir Anthony Wagner. Vol. ii. *Rolls of Arms. Henry III. The Matthew Paris Shields, c. 1244–59,* ed. Thomas D. Tremlett. *Glover's Roll, c. 1253–8 and Walford's Roll, c. 1273,* ed. H. Stanford London. *Additions and Corrections to CEMRA,* by Sir Anthony Wagner (Oxford, 1967). Printed for the Society of Antiquaries of London.

Aspremont   *La Chanson d'Aspremont,* ed. Louis Brandin, 2nd edn. (Paris, 1923–4). 2 vols. [*Classiques Français du Moyen Age,* 19, 25.] Date: *c.* 1188.

Atre périlleux   *L'Atre périlleux, roman de la Table ronde,* ed. Brian Woledge (Paris, 1936). [*Classiques Français du Moyen Age,* 76.] Date: *c.* 1250.

Auberi le Bourgoing   *Le Roman d'Auberi le Bourgoing,* ed. P. Tarbé (Rheims, 1849). Date: *c.* 1250.

Aye d'Avignon   *Aye d'Avignon, chanson de geste anonyme,* ed. S. J. Borg (Geneva–Lille, 1967). [*Textes Littéraires Français,* 134.] Date: 1195–1205.

B   Glover's Roll, Harvy's version. London, College of Arms, MS. L. 14 (Miscellanea Curiosa), vol. i, fols. 38–42 (*Aspilogia II* = B II). Copy made in 1586.

References here are to *Ancient Rolls of Arms. Glover's Roll of the Reign of King Henry III*, ed. George J. Armytage (London, 1868). Date: in or soon after 1310, but items 1–211 (the only ones listed in our glossary) based on a copy of *Bl* (*c.* 1253).

B III
Portions of Glover's Roll (blazons of Somery and Audley arms) not found in *Bl*; see *Aspilogia II*, p. 159. Individual items listed here according to various manuscripts, viz. *Ba*, *Bb*, and *Bc*.

B IV
One blazon (Beauchamp of Emley arms) of Grimaldi's version of Glover's Roll not found in *Bl*; see *Aspilogia II*, p. 159. Believed to be derived from a lost original compiled *c.* 1240–5 (see *Aspilogia II*, pp. 91, 96). For other blazons from this roll, see *P*.

Ba
Glover's Roll, St. George's version, copy *a*. London, British Museum, Add. MS. 29796 (*Aspilogia II* = B III [a]). Copy made in the late sixteenth century; unpublished. Numbered here as in *B*; figures in brackets refer to London's numbering. Date: soon after 1258.

BA
Bigot Roll. Paris, Bibliothèque nationale, fonds français 18648, fols. 32–9. Copy made in the seventeenth century. Paul Adam-Even, 'Un armorial français du milieu du xiiie siècle. Le rôle d'armes Bigot — 1254', *Archives Héraldiques Suisses*, lxiii (1949), 15–22, 68–75, 115–21. Date: 1254.

Bangert
Friedrich Bangert, *Die Tiere im altfranzösischen Epos* (Marburg, 1885). [*Ausgaben und Abhandlungen aus dem Gebiete der romanischen Philologie*, 34.]

Barons' Letter
Some Feudal Lords and their Seals. The De Walden Library (London, 1904).

Barstow
Allen M. Barstow, *A Lexicographical Study of Heraldic Terms in Anglo-Norman Rolls of Arms, 1300–50*, unpublished University of Pennsylvania Ph.D. dissertation, 1970. Available on microfilm (University Microfilms, 300 N. Zeeb Road, Ann Arbor, Michigan 48106, U.S.A.).

Bataille de Caresme et de Charnage
La Bataille de Caresme et de Charnage, ed. Grégoire Lozinski (Paris, 1933). [*Bibliothèque de l'Ecole des Hautes Etudes*, 262.] Date: second half of the thirteenth century.

Bataille des VII Arts
The Battle of the Seven Arts, a French Poem by Henry d'Andeli, Trouvère of the Thirteenth Century, ed. L. J. Paetow (Berkeley, 1914). [*Memoirs of the University of California*, iv, no. 1, *History*, vol. i, no. 1.] Date: second quarter of the thirteenth century.

Baudouin de Sebourg
Li Romans de Bauduin de Sebourc, IIIᵉ roy de Jhérusalem; poème du xivᵉ siècle, ed. L. N. Boca, Valenciennes, 1841. 2 vols. Date: *c.* 1350.

Bayrav
S. Bayrav, *Symbolisme médiéval. Béroul, Marie, Chrétien* (Paris–Istanbul, 1957).

Bb
Glover's Roll, St. George's version, copy *b*. London, British Museum, MS. Harl. 6589, fol. 11 b (*Aspilogia II* = B III [b]). Copy made in the late sixteenth century; unpublished. Date: soon after 1258.

BBSIA   *Bulletin Bibliographique de la Société Internationale Arthurienne.*
Bc   Glover's Roll, St. George's version, copy *c* [Frontis-
                            piece]. London, Society of Antiquaries, MS. 664,
                            Roll 8, vol. i, fols. 23–4 (*Aspilogia II* = B III [c]).
                            Copy made *c*. 1640; unpublished. Numbered here as
                            in *B*; figures in brackets refer to London's numbering.
                            Date: soon after 1258.
BEC   *Bibliothèque de l'Ecole des Chartes.*
Bel Inconnu   *Renaut de Beaujeu. Le Bel Inconnu, roman d'aventures*, ed.
                            G. Perrie Williams (Paris, 1929) [*Classiques Français
                            du Moyen Age*, 38]. Date: 1185–90.
Berte   *Berte aus grans piés*. See Adenet le Roi.
Bl   Glover's Roll, Cooke's version, copy *a*. London, private
                            collection of Sir Anthony Wagner (formerly Wrest
                            Park MS. 16, fols. 10–16 *b*). Copy made in 1585.
                            References here are to London's edition in *Aspilogia II*,
                            pp. 115–59. Numbered here as in *B*; figures in brackets
                            refer to London's numbering. Date: *c*. 1253.
Blair   C. H. Hunter Blair, 'Armorials on English Seals from
                            the Twelfth to the Sixteenth Centuries', *Archaeologia*,
                            lxxxix (1943), 1–26.
Blancandin   *Blancandin et l'Orgueilleuse d'amour, roman d'aventures du
                            XIIIᵉ siècle*, ed. Franklin P. Sweetser (Geneva–Paris,
                            1964). [*Textes Littéraires Français*, 112.] Date: first third
                            of the thirteenth century.
B.N.   Paris, Bibliothèque nationale.
Bouly de Lesdain   L. Bouly de Lesdain,'Etudes héraldiques sur le XIIᵉ siècle',
                            Annuaire du Conseil héraldique de France, xx (1907), 185–
                            244.
Boutell   *Boutell's Heraldry*, rev. ed. by C. W. Scott-Giles and
                            J. P. Brooke-Little (London–New York, 1963).
Brault, 'Arthurian   Gerard J. Brault, 'Arthurian Heraldry and the Date of
  Heraldry'   *Escanor*', *BBSIA*, xi (1959), 81–8.
Brault, '*Cotice*'   Gerard J. Brault, 'The Old French Heraldic Term
                            Cotice "Narrow Bend"', *Romania*, lxxxvii (1966), 98–115.
Brault, '*de l'un en l'autre*' Gerard J. Brault, 'Ancien français *de l'un en l'autre*',
                            Romania, lxxxviii (1967), 84–91.
Brault K   Gerard J. Brault, 'Heraldic Terminology and Legendary
                            Material in the *Siege of Caerlaverock* (*c*. 1300)', *Romance
                            Studies in Memory of Edward Billings Ham*, ed. Urban T.
                            Holmes, jun. (Hayward, Cal., 1967), pp. 15–20. [*Califor-
                            nia State College Publications*, 2.]
Brault, 'The Chief'   Gerard J. Brault, 'The Chief in Early Blazon', *Notes and
                            Queries*, ccxi (1966), 82–6.
Brault, 'The Cross'   Gerard J. Brault, 'The Cross in Medieval Heraldry',
                            Antiquaries Journal, xlvii (1967), 214–23.
Brut   *Le Roman de Brut de Wace*, ed. Ivor Arnold (Paris, 1938–
                            40). 2 vols. [*Société des Anciens Textes Français*.] Date:
                            1155.
Buevon de Conmarchis   See Adenet le Roi.
*BW*⁴   Oscar Bloch and Walther von Wartburg, *Dictionnaire
                            étymologique de la langue française*, 4th edn. (Paris, 1964).

C Walford's Roll, Version I (Charles's). London, British Museum, MS. Harl. 6589, fols. 12–12 *b*. Copy made in 1607. W. S. Walford, 'A Roll of Arms of the Thirteenth Century', *Archaeologia*, xxxix (1864), 373–87. Date: *c.* 1275.

Cassidorus *Le Roman de Cassidorus*, ed. Joseph Palermo (Paris, 1963–4). 2 vols. [*Société des Anciens Textes Français*.] Date: *c.* 1270.

CC *Le Roman du Castelain de Couci et de la Dame de Fayel par Jakemes*, edd. John E. Matzke and Maurice Delbouille (Paris, 1936). [*Société des Anciens Textes Français*.] Date: *c.* 1300.

Cd Walford's Roll, Leland's version, copy *b*. Dublin, National Library of Ireland, Trinity College, MS. E 1–17, fols. 9–10 *b*. Copy made in the sixteenth century; unpublished. Numbered here as in *C*. Date: *c.* 1275.

CEMRA Sir Anthony Wagner, *Catalogue of English Mediaeval Rolls of Arms. Aspilogia I* (Oxford, 1950). Printed for the Society of Antiquaries of London.

Chanson d'Antioche *La Chanson d'Antioche, composée au commencement du XIIᵉ siècle par le pèlerin Richard, renouvelée sous le règne de Philippe Auguste par Graindor de Douay*, ed. Paulin Paris (Paris, 1848). 2 vols. [*Romans des douze Pairs*, 11–12.] Date: *c.* 1185 for the reworking of Graindor de Douai, early twelfth century for the *Chanson* by Richard le Pèlerin.

Charles's Roll See *F*.

Charrete *Le Chevalier de la Charrete*. See Chrétien de Troyes.

Chétifs *Les Chétifs* in appendix of *La Chanson du Chevalier au Cygne et de Godefroid de Bouillon*, ed. C. Hippeau (Paris, 1874–7), ii. 191–276. Date: middle of the twelfth century, reworked *c.* 1185.

Chevalier à la Manche *Dits et contes de Baudouin de Condé et de son fils Jean de Condé*, ed. Auguste Scheler, ii (Brussels, 1866), no. 23, pp. 167–242. Date: first half of the fourteenth century.

Chevalier au Cygne *La Chanson du Chevalier au Cygne et de Godefroid de Bouillon*, ed. C. Hippeau, i (Paris, 1874). Date: late twelfth century.

Chevalier au Lion *Le Chevalier au Lion (Yvain)*. See Chrétien de Troyes.

Chrétien de Troyes *Les Romans de Chrétien de Troyes*. I. *Erec et Enide*, ed. Mario Roques (Paris, 1952). II. *Cligés*, ed. Alexandre Micha (Paris, 1957). III. *Le Chevalier de la Charrete*, ed. Mario Roques (Paris, 1958). IV. *Le Chevalier au Lion (Yvain)*, ed. Mario Roques (Paris, 1960). [*Classiques Français du Moyen Age*, 80, 84, 86, 89.] *Chrétien de Troyes. Le Roman de Perceval ou le Conte du Graal*, ed. William Roach, 2nd edn. (Geneva–Paris, 1959). [*Textes Littéraires Français*, 71.] Dates: *Erec*, *c.* 1170; *Cligés*, *c.* 1176; *Yvain* and *Charrete*, 1177–81; *Perceval*, after 1181.

Cl Walford's Roll, Leland's version, copy *a*. Oxford, Bodleian Top. Gen. C. I (3117), Lelandi Collectanea, vol. i, pp. 897–905. Copy made about the middle of the sixteenth century. Edition by H. Stanford London in *Aspilogia II*, pp. 167–204. Numbered here as in *C*; figures in brackets refer to London's numbering. Date: *c.* 1275.

CL   Classical Latin.

Cleomadés   See Adenet le Roi.

Cligés   See Chrétien de Troyes.

Clipearius Teutonicorum   *Clipearius Teutonicorum* in Paul Ganz, *Geschichte der heraldischen Kunst in der Schweiz im XII. und XIII. Jahrhundert* (Frauenfeld, 1899), pp. 174–85. Date: third quarter of the thirteenth century.

Comte d'Anjou   *Jehan Maillart. Le Roman du Comte d'Anjou*, ed. Mario Roques (Paris, 1931). [*Classiques Français du Moyen Age*, 67.] Date: *c.* 1316.

Comte de Marsy   Le comte de Marsy, 'Le langage héraldique au XIIIᵉ siècle dans les poèmes d'Adenet le Roi', *Mémoires de la Société des antiquaires de France*, 5ᵉ série, xlii (1881), 169–212.

Couronnement de Louis   *Le Couronnement de Louis, chanson de geste du XIIᵉ siècle*, ed. Ernest Langlois, 2nd edn. (Paris, 1925). [*Classiques Français du Moyen Age*, 22.] Reprinted 1938. Date: *c.* 1130.

CP   Chifflet–Prinet Roll. Besançon, Bibliothèque municipale, Collection Chifflet, MS. 186, fols. 145–54. Copy made in the seventeenth century. Max Prinet, 'Armorial de France composé à la fin du XIIIᵉ siècle ou au commencement du XIVᵉ', *Le Moyen Age*, xxxi (1934), 1–49. Date: 1297.

CPA   Chifflet–Prinet Roll, Additions. Copy made at the end of the fifteenth century; formerly owned by the late Dr. Höfflinger of Vienna; present whereabouts unknown. Paul Adam-Even, 'Rôle d'armes de l'ost de Flandre (juin 1297)', *Archivum Heraldicum*, lxxiii (1959), 2–7. Date: 1297.

d.   died.

D   Camden Roll. London, British Museum, Cotton Roll XV. 8. [Plate 3.] Original manuscript; blazons on the dorse written in a late-thirteenth-century hand. James Greenstreet, 'The Original Camden Roll of Arms', *Journal of the British Archaeological Association*, xxxviii (1882), 309–28. See also *P*. Date: *c.* 1280.

Dauzat   Albert Dauzat, Jean Dubois, and Henri Mitterand, *Nouveau Dictionnaire étymologique et historique* (Paris, 1964).

DCELC   John Corominas, *Diccionario crítico etimológico de la lengua castellana* (Bern, 1954). 4 vols.

Dean Tract   'De Heraudie'. Cambridge, The University Library, MS. Ee. 4. 20, fols. 160 verso–161 verso. Copy made *c.* 1382. Ruth J. Dean, 'An Early Treatise on Heraldry in Anglo-Norman', *Romance Studies in Memory of Edward Billings Ham*, ed. Urban T. Holmes, jun. (Hayward, Cal., 1967), pp. 21–9. [*California State College Publications*, 2.]

	Date: possibly *c.* 1340 but including material drawn from *HE* (*c.* 1270–80).
Delbouille	See *CC* and *TC.*
Denholm-Young, *History and Heraldry*	N. Denholm-Young, *History and Heraldry 1254 to 1310. A Study of the Historical Value of the Rolls of Arms* (Oxford, 1965). See my review in *Speculum*, xli (1966), 318–20.
Denholm-Young K	N. Denholm-Young, 'The Song of Carlaverock and the Parliamentary Roll of Arms as Found in Cott. MS. Calig. A. xviii in the British Museum', *Proceedings of the British Academy*, xlvii (1962), 251–62.
Dering Roll	James Greenstreet and Charles Russell, 'Dering Roll', *Jewitt's Reliquary*, xvi (1875), 135–40, 237–40; xvii (1876), 11–16, 209–12; xviii (1877), 23–8, 89–92, 171–5. Date: *c.* 1275.
Des Deux Bordeors	*Des Deux Bordeors Ribauz* in *Recueil général et complet des fabliaux des XIIIe et XIVe siècles*, edd. Anatole de Montaiglon and Gaston Raynaud, i (Paris, 1872), 1–12. Date: thirteenth century.
Destruction de Rome	G. Gröber, '*La Destruction de Rome*, première branche de la chanson de geste *Fierabras*', *Romania*, ii (1873), 1–48. Date: late twelfth century.
D'Haucourt–Durivault	Geneviève d'Haucourt and Georges Durivault, *Le Blason* (Paris, 1949). [*Que sais-je?*, 336.]
Didot Perceval	*The Didot Perceval According to the Manuscripts of Modena and Paris*, ed. William Roach (Philadelphia, 1941). Date: *c.* 1202.
Du Cange	Charles du Fresne, sieur du Cange, *Glossarium Mediae et Infimae Latinitatis . . .*, ed. L. Favre (Paris, 1937–8). 10 vols.
Durmart	*Durmart le Galois. Roman arthurien du treizième siècle*, ed. Joseph Gildea, O.S.A. (Villanova, Pa., 1965–6). 2 vols. Date: *c.* 1200.
E.	English.
E	St. George's Roll. *Ancient Rolls of Arms. Charles' Roll of the Reigns of Henry III and Edward I*, ed. George J. Armytage (London, 1869). Date: *c.* 1285.
Elie de Saint-Gille	*Elie de Saint-Gille, chanson de geste*, ed. Gaston Raynaud (Paris, 1879). [*Société des Anciens Textes Français.*] Date: early thirteenth century.
Enéas	*Enéas, roman du XIIe siècle*, ed. J.-J. Salverda de Grave (Paris, 1925–9). [*Classiques Français du Moyen Age*, 44, 62.] 2 vols. Date: *c.* 1160.
EO	*Les Enfances Ogier.* See Adenet le Roi.
Enfances Vivien	*Les Enfances Vivien, chanson de geste*, edd. Carl Wahlund and Hugo von Feilitzen (Uppsala–Paris, 1895). Date: early thirteenth century.
Erec	*Erec et Enide.* See Chrétien de Troyes.
Escanor	*Der Roman von Escanor von Gerard von Amiens*, ed. Henri Michelant (Tübingen, 1886). [*Bibliothek des Litterarischen Vereins in Stuttgart*, 178.] Date: *c.* 1280.
Escoufle	*L'Escoufle, roman d'aventure*, edd. Henri Michelant and Paul Meyer (Paris, 1894). [*Société des Anciens Textes Français.*] Date: 1200–2.

Estoire	*L'Estoire del Saint Graal.* See Sommer.
F	Charles's Roll. W. S. Walford and C. S. Spencer, 'Two Rolls of Arms of the Reign of King Edward the First', *Archaeologia*, xxxix (1864), 389–91, 399–417, 441–6. Date: *c.* 1285.
Faits des Romains	*Li Fet des Romains*, edd. L. F. Flutre and K. Sneyders de Vogel (Paris–Groningen, n.d. and 1938). 2 vols. Date: 1213–14.
FCA, FCE, FCL, FCM, FCT	*The Continuations of the Old French Perceval of Chrétien de Troyes*, ed. William Roach. I. *The First Continuation. Redaction of MSS TVD* (Philadelphia, 1949). II. *The First Continuation. Redaction of MSS EMQU* (Philadelphia, 1950) (with the collaboration of Robert H. Ivy, jun.). III, Part I. *The First Continuation. Redaction of MSS ALPRS* (Philadelphia, 1952). See also Foulet, *Glossary of the First Continuation.* References here are to the various manuscripts (e.g. *FCA* = *First Continuation*, MS. *A*). Dates: there are several redactions, all of which were composed after Chrétien de Troyes's *Perceval* and at least some of which before the end of the twelfth century.
FEW	Walther von Wartburg, *Französisches etymologisches Wörterbuch*, i– (Bonn–Leipzig, 1922–).
f. fr.	Fonds français.
Fierabras	*Fierabras, chanson de geste*, edd. A. Kroeber and G. Servois (Paris, 1860). [*Anciens Poètes de la France*, 4.] Date: *c.* 1170.
Flinn	John Flinn, *Le Roman de Renart dans les littératures françaises et étrangères au Moyen Age* (Toronto, 1963).
Floire et Blancheflor	*Floire et Blanceflor*, ed. Edélestand du Méril (Paris, 1856). [*Bibliothèque elzévirienne.*] Date of the second redaction: last quarter of the twelfth century.
Flutre	Louis-Fernand Flutre, *Table des noms propres avec toutes leurs variantes figurant dans les romans du Moyen Age* (Poitiers, 1962). [*Publications du Centre d'études supérieures de civilisation médiévale*, 2.]
fol., fols.	Folio, folios.
Foulet, *Glossary of the First Continuation*	Lucien Foulet, *Glossary of the First Continuation*, vol. iii, Part II of *The Continuations of the Old French Perceval of Chrétien de Troyes*, ed. William Roach (Philadelphia, 1955).
Foulet, *Petite Syntaxe*	Lucien Foulet, *Petite Syntaxe de l'ancien français*, 3ᵉ éd. (Paris, 1930). [*Classiques Français du Moyen Age*, 21.]
Fouque de Candie	*Folque de Candie von Herbert le Duc de Danmartin*, ed. O. Schultz-Gora (Dresden–Jena, 1909–36). 3 vols. [*Gesellschaft für Romanische Literatur*, 21, 38, 49.] *Einleitung*, revised by Ulrich Mölk (Tübingen, 1966). [*Beihefte zur ZRPh.*, 111.] Date: early thirteenth century.
Fr.	French.
FS	*French Studies.*
G	Segar's Roll. James Greenstreet, 'The "Segar" Roll of Arms as an Ordinary', *The Genealogist*, iv (1880), 50–8, 90–7. Date: *c.* 1282.

G.	German.
Gaidon	*Gaydon, chanson de geste*, edd. F. Guessard and S. Luce (Paris, 1862). [*Anciens Poètes de la France*, 7.] Date: *c.* 1225.
Garin le Loherain	*Garin le Loheren*, ed. Josephine Vallerie (Ann Arbor, 1947). Date: late twelfth century.
Gaufrey	*Gaufrey, chanson de geste*, edd. F. Guessard and P. Chabaille (Paris, 1859). [*Anciens Poètes de la France*, 3.] Date: second half of the thirteenth century.
Gayre, *Heraldic Cadency*	Robert Gayre, *Heraldic Cadency* (London, 1961).
Gerbert's Continuation	Gerbert de Montreuil. *La Continuation de Perceval*, ed. Mary Williams (Paris, 1922–5). 2 vols. [*Classiques Français du Moyen Age*, 28, 50.] Date: 1226–30.
Girart d'Amiens	See *Escanor.*
Goddard	Eunice R. Goddard, *Women's Costume in French Texts of the Eleventh and Twelfth Centuries* (Baltimore–Paris, 1927). [*Johns Hopkins Studies in the Romance Literatures and Languages*, 7.]
Godefroy	Frédéric Godefroy, *Dictionnaire de l'ancienne langue française et de tous ses dialectes du IXe au XVe siècle* (Paris, 1881–1902). 10 vols.
Godefroid de Bouillon	*La Chanson du Chevalier au Cygne et de Godefroid de Bouillon*, ed. C. Hippeau, ii (Paris, 1877). Date: thirteenth century.
Gough H	Gough's notes to his edition of *H.*
Gough–Parker	Henry Gough and James Parker, *A Glossary of Terms Used in Heraldry* (Oxford and London, 1894). Reprinted by Gale Research Company, 1966.
Gr.	Greek.
Grandsaignes d'Hauterive	R. Grandsaignes d'Hauterive, *Dictionnaire d'ancien français, Moyen Age et Renaissance* (Paris, 1947).
Great Roll	See Parliamentary Roll.
Grimaldi's Roll	See *P.*
Guillaume	*La Chanson de Guillaume*, ed. Duncan McMillan (Paris, 1949–50). 2 vols. [*Société des Anciens Textes Français.*] Date: *c.* 1140.
Guillaume de Dole	*Jean Renart. Le Roman de la Rose ou de Guillaume de Dole*, ed. Félix Lecoy (Paris, 1962). [*Classiques Français du Moyen Age*, 91.] Date: 1212–13.
Guillim's Roll	James Greenstreet, '"Guillim's" Roll of Arms as an Ordinary', *The Genealogist*, i (1877), 323–7, 355–62. Date: *c.* 1295–1305.
H	Falkirk Roll, Thevet's version. London, British Museum, MS. Harl. 6589, fols. 9–9 *b.* Copy made in 1606. James Greenstreet, 'Falkirk Roll', *Jewitt's Reliquary*, xv (1875), 27–32, 68–74; see also *Hg.* Date: 1298.
Haidu	Peter Haidu, *Aesthetic Distance in Chrétien de Troyes: Irony and Comedy in Cligès and Perceval* (Geneva, 1968).
Hauptmann	Felix Hauptmann, 'Die Wappen in der *Historia Minor* des Matthäus Parisiensis', *Jahrbuch der K.K. Heraldischen Gesellschaft 'Adler'*, neue Folge, xix (1909), 20–55.
HE	Heralds' Roll, Fitzwilliam version. London, College of Arms, MS. Vincent 165, fols. 131–52 *b.* Copy made in

	1590. References here are to James Greenstreet, 'Planché's Roll', *The Genealogist*, new series, iii (1886), 148–55, 240–4; iv (1887), 17–22, 197–203; v (1888), 173–9. Date: *c.* 1270–80.
Hem	Sarrasin. *Le Roman du Hem*, ed. Albert Henry (Paris, 1939). [*Travaux de la Faculté de philosophie et lettres de l'Université de Bruxelles*, 9.] Date: 1278.
Heralds' Roll	See *HE.*
Hg	Falkirk Roll, Wrest Park version. London, private collection of Sir Anthony Wagner (formerly Wrest Park MS. 16, fols. 1–5). Copy made in 1585. References here are to Henry Gough, *Scotland in 1298* (Edinburgh, 1888), pp. 129–59 (edition of *H* and *Hg*). Numbered here as in *H*; figures in brackets refer to Gough's numbering. Date: 1298.
Hope	W. H. St. John Hope, *A Grammar of English Heraldry*, 2nd edn. revised by Sir Anthony Wagner (Cambridge, 1953).
Horn	*The Romance of Horn by Thomas. I. Text*, ed. Mildred K. Pope (Oxford, 1955). II. *Descriptive Introduction, Explicative Notes and Glossary*, by T. B. W. Reid (Oxford, 1964). [*Anglo-Norman Texts*, 9, 10, 12, 13.] Date: *c.* 1180.
Horrent, *Le Pèlerinage de Charlemagne*	Jules Horrent, *Le Pèlerinage de Charlemagne. Essai d'explication littéraire avec des notes de critique textuelle* (Paris, 1961). [*Bibliothèque de la Faculté de philosophie et lettres de l'Université de Liège*, 158.]
Hugues Capet	*Hugues Capet, chanson de geste*, ed. Le marquis de la Grange (Paris, 1864). [*Anciens Poètes de la France*, 8.] Date: 1359.
Hunbaut	*Hunbaut, altfranzösischer Artusroman des XIII. Jahrhunderts*, ed. Hermann Breuer (Dresden, 1914). [*Gesellschaft für Romanische Literatur*, 35.] Date: 1250–75.
Huon de Bordeaux	*Huon de Bordeaux*, ed. Pierre Ruelle (Paris–Brussels, 1960). [*Travaux de la Faculté de philosophie et lettres de l'Université Libre de Bruxelles*, 20.] Date: 1216–29.
Huon de Méry	See *TA.*
Ille et Galeron	*Ille et Galeron par Gautier d'Arras*, ed. Frederick A. G. Cowper (Paris, 1956). [*Société des Anciens Textes Français*.] Date: last quarter of the twelfth century.
Jakemes	See *TC.*
'Joli Buisson de Jonece (Le)'	*Œuvres de Froissart. Poésies*, ed. Auguste Scheler, ii (Brussels, 1871), 1–161. Date: 1373.
Joufroi	*Joufrois, roman français du XIIIᵉ siècle*, ed. Walter O. Streng-Renkonen (Turku, 1930). [*Annales Universitatis Aboensis, series B*, 12.] Date: middle of the thirteenth century.
Jourdain de Blaye	*Jourdain de Blaye (Jordains de Blaivies). Chanson de geste*, ed. Peter F. Dembowski (Chicago–London, 1969). Date: late twelfth or early thirteenth century.
K	Siege of Caerlaverock. London, British Museum, Cotton Caligula A. XVIII, fols. 23 *b*–30 *b*. Original manuscript. *The Siege of Caerlaverock, in the XXVIII Edward I, A.D.*

MCCC, ed. Nicholas Harris Nicolas (London, 1828). References here, except where otherwise noted, are to *The Roll of Arms of the Princes, Barons and Knights who Attended King Edward I to the Siege of Caerlaverock, in 1300*, ed. Thomas Wright (London, 1864). Date: *c.* 1300.

Lais de Marie de France (Les)   *Les Lais de Marie de France,* ed. Jean Rychner (Paris, 1966). [*Classiques Français du Moyen Age,* 93.] Date: 1160–70.

Lancelot propre   See Sommer.

Lat.   Latin.

Lathuillère   Roger Lathuillère, *Guiron le courtois. Etude de la tradition manuscrite et analyse critique* (Geneva, 1966). [*Publications Romanes et Françaises,* 86.] The prose romance in question is dated *c.* 1235.

Lejeune, *L'Œuvre de Jean Renart*   Rita Lejeune, *L'Œuvre de Jean Renart* (Paris–Liège, 1935). [*Bibliothèque de la Faculté de philosophie et lettres de l'Université de Liège,* 61.]

Lejeune–Stiennon, *La Légende de Roland*   Rita Lejeune and Jacques Stiennon, *La Légende de Roland dans l'art du Moyen Age* (Brussels, 1966). 2 vols.

Littré   Emile Littré, *Dictionnaire de la langue française* (Paris, 1873–7). 5 vols.

LL   Late Latin.

London, 'Notes and Reflections'   H. Stanford London, 'Notes and Reflections on Hope's *Grammar of English Heraldry', Coat of Arms,* ii (1953), 203–5.

London, 'Notes and Reflections, II'   H. Stanford London, 'Notes and Reflections on Hope's *Grammar of English Heraldry,* Part II', *Coat of Arms,* ii (1953), 270–3.

London, *Royal Beasts*   H. Stanford London, *Royal Beasts* (East Knoyle, Wiltshire, 1956).

London, 'Scintillatum Auro'   H. Stanford London, 'Scintillatum Auro. The Spark in Armory', *Coat of Arms,* ii (1952), 111–13.

London, 'Some Medieval Treatises'   H. Stanford London, 'Some Medieval Treatises on English Heraldry', *Antiquaries Journal,* xxxiii (1953), 169–83.

London, 'The Roundel'   H. Stanford London, 'The Heraldic Roundel or Rotund', *Notes and Queries,* cxcv (1950), 288–90, 310–11, 331–3, 354–6, 377–80.

Loomis, *Arthurian Legends*   Roger Sherman Loomis and Laura Hibbard Loomis, *Arthurian Legends in Medieval Art* (New York, 1938).

Loomis, *Arthurian Tradition*   Roger Sherman Loomis, *Arthurian Tradition and Chrétien de Troyes* (New York, 1949).

Löseth, *Le Roman en prose de Tristan*   Eilert Löseth, *Le Roman en prose de Tristan* (Paris, 1891).

Lot, *Etude sur le Lancelot en prose*   Ferdinand Lot, *Etude sur le Lancelot en prose* (Paris, 1918). [*Bibliothèque de l'Ecole des Hautes Etudes,* 226.]

M   Nativity Roll. London, British Museum, MS. Harl. 6589, fol. 10. Copy made in 1606. James Greenstreet, 'Nativity Roll', *Jewitt's Reliquary,* xv (1875), 228–30. Date: *c.* 1300.

Marsy   See Comte de Marsy.

Mathieu   Rémi Mathieu, *Le Système héraldique français* (Paris, 1946).

Matthew Paris Shields   See *Aspilogia II*.

McCulloch   Florence McCulloch, *Mediaeval Latin ana French Bestiaries* (Chapel Hill, 1962). [*University of North Carolina Studies in the Romance Languages and Literatures*, 33.]

MED   *Middle English Dictionary*, ed .Hans Kurath, i– (Ann Arbor, 1959–).

Meliador   *Méliador par Jean Froissart*, ed. Auguste Longnon (Paris, 1895–9). 3 vols. [*Société des Anciens Textes Français*.] Date: first redaction, *c.* 1365, second redaction, *c.* 1380.

Ménard   Philippe Ménard, *Le Rire et le sourire dans le roman courtois en France au moyen âge (1150–1250)* (Geneva, 1969). [*Publications Romanes et Françaises*, 105.]

Méraugis   *Méraugis von Portlesguez, altfranzösischer Abenteuerroman von Raoul von Houdenc*, ed. M. Friedwagner (Halle, 1897). Date: early thirteenth century.

MFr.   Modern French.

MLQ   *Modern Language Quarterly*.

MLR   *Modern Language Review*.

Mort Artu   *La Mort le roi Artu, roman du XIIIᵉ siècle*, ed. Jean Frappier, 2nd edn. (Geneva–Lille, 1956). [*Textes Littéraires Français*.] Date: *c.* 1230. See Sommer.

Mouskés   *Chronique rimée de Philippe Mouskés*, ed. Le baron F. de Reiffenberg (Brussels, 1836–8; *Supplément*, 1845). 3 vols. Date: 1265.

MS., MSS.   Manuscript, manuscripts.

Navarre   Armorial du héraut Navarre. L. C. Douët d'Arcq, 'Armorial de France de la fin du XIVᵉ siècle', *Le Cabinet historique*, v (1859), 10–23, 48–60, 89–94, 197–205, 249–57; vi (1860), 33–9, 116–22, 193–200, 225–32, 273–81. Paul Adam-Even, 'L'armorial du héraut Navarre. Partie inédite et corrections', *Nouvelle Revue Héraldique*, nouvelle série, i (1947), 49–68. Date: *c.* 1370.

Nicolas   See *K*.

OED   *The Oxford English Dictionary* (Oxford, 1933). 13 vols.

OFr.   Old French.

Ogier le Danois   *La Chevalerie d'Ogier de Danemarche*, ed. Mario Eusebi (Milan–Varese, 1963). [*Testi e Documenti di Letteratura Moderna*, 6.] Date: late twelfth or early thirteenth century.

Otinel   *Otinel, chanson de geste*, edd. F. Guessard and H. Michelant (Paris, 1859). [*Anciens Poètes de la France*, 1.] Date: late twelfth century.

Ott   André G. Ott, *Etude sur les couleurs en vieux français* (Paris, 1899). [*Inaugural-Dissertation*, Zurich.]

P   Grimaldi's Roll. Manchester, John Rylands Library, Western (French and Italian) MS. 88. Copy made in the early fifteenth century. 'Copy of a Roll of Arms (of the Reign of Edw. III) in the Possession of Stacey Grimaldi, Esq., F.S.A.', *Collectanea Topographica et Genealogica*, ii (1835), 320–8. Portions of this roll are drawn from a version of Glover's Roll (see *Aspilogia II*, pp. 90–1, 96 [= *B IV*]). Several blazons at the be-

	ginning of this roll are also plainly derived from a copy of the Camden Roll. Date: *c.* 1350.
Papworth's *Ordinary*	John Woody Papworth, *An Alphabetical Dictionary of Coats of Arms Belonging to Families in Great Britain and Ireland* (London, 1874) [edited from page 696 by Alfred W. Mourant]. Reprinted as *Papworth's Ordinary of British Armorials.* Introduction by G. D. Squibb and Sir Anthony Wagner (London, 1961).
Parliamentary Roll	Oswald Barron, 'The Parliamentary Roll of Arms', *The Genealogist,* N.S., xi (1885), 108–16, 174–82, 238–44; xii (1886), 59–62, 133–6, 206-11, 268–82. Also known as the Great Roll. Date: *c.* 1312.
Partonopeu	*Partonopeu de Blois. A French Romance of the Twelfth Century,* ed. Joseph Gildea, O.S.A. (Villanova, Penna., 1967– 70). 2 vols. Date: before 1188.
Payen	Jean-Charles Payen, *Le Motif du repentir dans la littérature française médiévale (Des Origines à 1230)* (Geneva, 1968). [*Publications Romanes et Françaises,* 98.]
Perceval	*Le Roman de Perceval ou le Conte du Graal.* See Chrétien de Troyes.
Perlesvaus	*Le Haut Livre du Graal: Perlesvaus,* edd. William A. Nitze and collaborators (Chicago, 1932–7). 2 vols. [*Modern Philology Monographs of the University of Chicago.*] Date: 1191–1212.
Pickford, 'The Three Crowns of King Arthur'	Cedric E. Pickford, 'The Three Crowns of King Arthur', *The Yorkshire Archaeological Journal,* xxxviii (1954), 373–82.
PMLA	*Publications of the Modern Language Association of America.*
Pope	Mildred K. Pope, *From Latin to Modern French with Especial Consideration of Anglo-Norman. Phonology and Morphology* (Manchester, 1934). Reprinted 1966.
Prinet CC	Max Prinet, 'Les armoiries dans le roman du *Châtelain de Coucy', Romania,* xlvi (1920), 161–79.
Prinet CP	Max Prinet's notes to his edition of *CP.*
Prinet K	Max Prinet, 'Les armoiries des Français dans le poème du *Siège de Carlaverock', Bibliothèque de l'Ecole des Chartes,* xcii (1931), 345–53.
Prinet TA	Max Prinet, 'Le langage héraldique dans le *Tournoiement Antechrist', Bibliothèque de l'Ecole des Chartes,* lxxxiii (1922), 43–53.
Prinet WR	Max Prinet, 'Armoiries françaises et allemandes décrites dans un ancien rôle d'armes anglais', *Le Moyen Age,* 2e série, xxv (1923), 223–60.
Prise d'Orange	Claude Régnier, *Les Rédactions en vers de la Prise d'Orange* (Paris, 1966). Date: *c.* 1200.
Pusikan	Major Oscar Göschen ('Pusikan'), 'Wappen aus den Werken des Mathias von Paris (†1259)', *Vierteljahrschrift für Heraldik, Sphragistik und Genealogie. Herausgegeben vom Verein 'Herold' zu Berlin,* ix (1881), 107–51.
Queste	*La Queste del Saint Graal, roman du XIIIe siècle,* ed. Albert Pauphilet, 2nd edn. (Paris, 1949). [*Classiques Français du Moyen Age,* 33.] Date: *c.* 1225. See Sommer.

Raoul de Cambrai	*Raoul de Cambrai, chanson de geste du XIIᵉ siècle*, edd. Paul Meyer and Auguste Longnon (Paris, 1882). [*Société des Anciens Textes Français.*] Date: last quarter of the twelfth century.
Réau	Louis Réau, *Iconographie de l'art chrétien* (Paris, 1955–9). 3 vols. (Vol. II in 2 parts, Vol. III in 3 parts).
Renart le Nouvel	*Renart le Nouvel par Jacquemart Gielee*, ed. Henri Roussel (Paris, 1961). [*Société des Anciens Textes Français.*] Date: c. 1288.
Rigomer	*Les Merveilles de Rigomer von Jehan, altfranzösischer Artusroman des XIII. Jahrhunderts*, ed. W. Foerster and H. Breuer (Dresden, 1908–15). [*Gesellschaft für Romanische Literatur*, 19, 39.] Date: last third of the thirteenth century.
Roland	*La Chanson de Roland*, ed. Joseph Bédier, 195ᵉ édition (Paris, 1955). Reference is also made to *La Chanson de Roland*, ed. T. Atkinson Jenkins (Boston, 1924). Date: c. 1100.
Roman de la Violette	*Le Roman de la Violette ou de Gerart de Nevers par Gerbert de Montreuil*, ed. Douglas Labaree Buffum (Paris, 1928). [*Société des Anciens Textes Français.*] Date: 1227–9.
Roman des Eles	Raoul de Houdenc. *Li Romans des Eles* in *Trouvères belges*, nouvelle série (Louvain, 1879), pp. 248–84. Date: first third of the thirteenth century.
RPh.	*Romance Philology.*
RR	*Romanic Review.*
St. George's Roll	See *E.*
Saisnes	*Jean Bodels Saxenlied*, edd. F. Menzel and E. Stengel (Marburg, 1906–9). 2 vols. [*Ausgaben und Abhandlungen aus dem Gebiete der romanischen Philologie*, 99, 100.] Date: last third of the twelfth century.
Schirling	Victor Schirling, *Die Verteidigungswaffen im altfranzösischen Epos* (Marburg, 1887). [*Ausgaben und Abhandlungen aus dem Gebiete der romanischen Philologie*, 69.]
SCK, SCM, SCP, SCQ, SCT, SCU	*The Second Continuation of the Old French Perceval of Chrétien de Troyes.* References here are to the various manuscripts (e.g. *SCK = Second Continuation*, MS. *K*) described in the introduction to Roach's edition of the *Continuations*; see above, s.v. *FCA, FCE*, etc. With a few exceptions, the citations are from an interpolation (second half of the thirteenth century) missing in the base manuscript used by Potvin in his edition. References followed by a verse number, however, are to Potvin's edition (see my Introduction, p. 39 n. 2). The *Second Continuation* itself has been preserved in several redactions, the earliest of which appears to date from the latter part of the twelfth century.
Schoepperle, *Tristan and Isolt*	Gertrude Schoepperle [Loomis], *Tristan and Isolt. A Study of the Sources of the Romance*, 2nd edn. revised by Roger Sherman Loomis (New York, 1960). 2 vols.
Schwan–Behrens	Eduard Schwan and Dietrich Behrens, *Grammaire de l'ancien français*, 3rd edn. (Leipzig, 1923).

Sommer	*The Vulgate Version of the Arthurian Romances*, ed. H. Oskar Sommer. I. *L'Estoire del Saint Graal* [=*Estoire*] (Washington, D.C., 1909). II. *L'Estoire de Merlin* [pp. 88–466 = *Vulgate Merlin Sequel*] (Washington, D.C., 1908). III. *Le Livre de Lancelot del Lac* [= *Lancelot propre*], Parts I, II, III (Washington, D.C., 1910–12 [each part is contained in a separate volume and is referred to here as *Lancelot propre*, III, IV, and V, respectively]). VI. *La Mort le roi Artus* [pp. 200–391] (Washington, D.C., 1913). Unless otherwise noted, references here are to Frappier's edition (see *Mort Artu*). VII. *Le Livre d'Artus* [= *Artus*] (Washington, D.C., 1913). 6 vols. [*Carnegie Institution of Washington, Publication no. 74.*] Dates: *Lancelot propre*, *Queste*, and *Mort Artu* were doubtless composed in that order in the period between 1215 and 1230; two other romances belonging to this cycle, *Estoire* and the *Vulgate Merlin Sequel*, as well as another compilation known as *Le Livre d'Artus*, were probably written after 1235.
Sone	*Sone von Nausay*, ed. M. Goldschmidt (Tübingen, 1899). [*Bibliothek des Litterarischen Vereins in Stuttgart*, 216.] Date: latter part of the thirteenth century.
SP	*Studies in Philology*.
Stalins	Baron A. Stalins, *Vocabulaire-Atlas héraldique en six langues* (Paris, 1952).
Sumberg	Lewis A. M. Sumberg, *La Chanson d'Antioche; étude historique et littéraire* (Paris, 1968).
Syn.	Synonym(s).
TA	*Li Tornoiemenz Antecrit von Huon de Mery*, ed. Georg Wimmer (Marburg, 1888). [*Ausgaben und Abhandlungen aus dem Gebiete der romanischen Philologie*, 76.] Date: *c.* 1234. For a slightly later date (1236–9), see Payen, p. 510 n. 82.
TC	*Jacques Bretel. Le Tournoi de Chauvency*, ed. Maurice Delbouille (Liège–Paris, 1932). [*Bibliothèque de la Faculté de philosophie et lettres de l'Université de Liège*, 49.] Date: 1285.
Thèbes	*Le Roman de Thèbes*, ed. Guy Raynaud de Lage (Paris, 1966–7). 2 vols. [*Classiques Français du Moyen Age*, 94, 96.] Reference is also made to *Le Roman de Thèbes*, ed. Léopold Constans (Paris, 1890). [*Société des Anciens Textes Français*.] 2 vols. Date: middle of the twelfth century.
Tobler–Lommatzsch	Adolf Tobler and Erhard Lommatzsch, *Altfranzösisches Wörterbuch*, i– (Berlin, 1925–).
Tournoi de Compiègne	F. V. Goethals, 'Les seigneurs artésiens au Tournoi de Compiègne (1238)', *Revue nobiliaire historique et biographique*, nouvelle série, ii (1866), 97–103; 'Les chevaliers normands au Tournoi de Compiègne (1238)', iii (1867), 97–103; 'Les Chevaliers français au Tournoi de Compiègne (1238)', 408–14; iv (1868), 73–81, 361–5. Date: *c.* 1270 (and not 1238).

Tournoiement des Dames	A. Jeanroy, 'Notes sur le *Tournoiement des Dames*', *Romania*, xxviii (1899), 232–44. Date: 1189.
Tournoiement des Dames de Paris	Mario Pelaez, '*Le Tornoiement as Dames de Paris*, poemetto in antico francese di Pierre Gencien', *Studi romanzi*, xiv (1917), 5–68. Date: early fourteenth century, according to Adam-Even, '*Tournoiement des Dames de Paris*'. See, however, François Maillard, 'Note sur *Le Tournoiement as Dames de Paris*', *Romania*, lxxxix (1968), 538–41, where an earlier date (*c.* 1270) is proposed.
Tristan de Béroul	*Béroul. Le Roman de Tristan, poème du XIIe siècle*, ed. Ernest Muret, 4th edn. revised by L. M. Defourques (Paris, 1967). [*Classiques Français du Moyen Age*, 12.] Date: latter part of the twelfth century.
Tristan de Thomas	*Le Roman de Tristan par Thomas, poème du XIIe siècle*, ed. Joseph Bédier (Paris, 1902–05). 2 vols. [*Société des Anciens Textes Français*.] Date: second half of the twelfth century.
Troie	*Le Roman de Troie par Benoît de Sainte-Maure*, ed. Léopold Constans (Paris, 1904–12). 6 vols. [*Société des Anciens Textes Français*.] Date: 1154–60.
Veyrin-Forrer	Théodore Veyrin-Forrer, *Précis d'héraldique* (Paris, 1951). [*Arts, styles et techniques*.]
VL	Vulgar Latin.
Vulgate Merlin Sequel	See Sommer.
Wagner, *CEMRA*	See *CEMRA*.
Wagner, *Heralds and Heraldry*	Sir Anthony Wagner, *Heralds and Heraldry in the Middle Ages*, 2nd edn. (Oxford, 1956).
Wagner, *Historic Heraldry*	Sir Anthony Wagner, *Historic Heraldry of Britain* (London–New York–Toronto, 1939).
WB	Wijnbergen Roll. Paul Adam-Even and Léon Jéquier, 'Un armorial français du XIIIe siècle, l'armorial Wijnbergen', *Archives Héraldiques Suisses*, lxv (1951), 49–62, 101–10; lxvi (1952), 28–36, 64–8, 103–11; lxviii (1954), 55–80. Date: 1265–70.
West	G. D. West, *An Index of Proper Names in French Arthurian Verse Romances 1150–1300* (Toronto, 1969). [*University of Toronto Romance Series*, 15.]
Wright	See *K*.
ZFSL	*Zeitschrift für französische Sprache und Literatur*.
ZRPh.	*Zeitschrift für romanische Philologie*.

INTRODUCTION

IN this book, we have endeavoured to provide a useful research tool for scholars of heraldry, genealogy, literature, philology, history, and art, more or less in that order.

We have assumed a rudimentary knowledge of heraldry on the part of the reader. However, rapid perusal of Oswald Barron's article entitled 'Heraldry' in the *Encyclopaedia Britannica* (11th edn.) should afford adequate background information. Without seeking to recommend any manual in particular, we have found the revision by C. W. Scott-Giles and J. P. Brooke-Little of *Boutell's Heraldry* (London, 1963) to be a useful guide for modern English usage. Numerous allusions to French terms as defined by Théodore Veyrin-Forrer in his handy *Précis d'héraldique* (Paris, 1951) are also made here. Hugh Stanford London's pamphlet, *The Right Road for the Study of Heraldry*, 2nd edn. revised by Cecil R. Humphery-Smith (East Knoyle, Wiltshire, 1960), is a brief but judicious guide to manuals and reference works in the English language. A basic bibliography for French heraldry was similarly compiled by Dr. Paul Adam-Even in his article 'Jalons pour l'étude de l'héraldique. II. L'héraldique française', *Archives Héraldiques Suisses*, lxvii (1953), 34–5. See also his 'Catalogue des armoriaux français imprimés', *Nouvelle Revue Héraldique*, nouvelle série, i (1946), 19–29.

Our purpose here is to trace the evolution of blazon from the earliest times down to about the year 1300. No glossary of medieval heraldry has ever been published. The more reliable manuals available today are sadly lacking in this respect and, ignoring, for the most part, the semantic evolution of the terms and phrases which have survived in modern blazon, can seriously mislead even the specialist.

The present work, so far as thirteenth-century French and Anglo-Norman rolls of arms are concerned, is based upon the best available copies of all the known blazoned rolls, collated, whenever possible, upon photographs of the originals. Other published and unpublished painted and blazoned rolls for the period in question and later centuries were also studied as they shed much light upon the meanings of various heraldic terms.

As quasi-heraldic descriptions and blazons abound in Old French literature, a representative number of these has been incorporated in our glossary. The reasons for this are many. Numerous terms appearing in later rolls but missing from the thirteenth-century lists are found in literary contexts of a heraldic nature. Other attestations in Old French epics and romances antedate the earliest uses in the rolls by a century or more. The symbolic value attached to certain tinctures and charges, often a source of considerable speculation today, is frequently clarified in Old French literature, though only a sampling of such information could be provided here. The emergence of fictitious arms for historical personages (e.g. Harold and William the Conqueror in Matthew Paris), the consistent use of certain armorial bearings for literary characters (e.g. Roland in the Heralds' Roll, Gawain in the Arthurian romances), the bearing of legendary arms at Round Tables and other fashionable spectacles and even their adoption by certain individuals are still further indications that the line between reality and imagination is often blurred in the period being studied. Finally, Old French literature provides us with numerous expressions relating to heraldry but not actually used to blazon a coat of arms (e.g. *pour amour de*).

This book is descriptive and not in the least bit prescriptive. It seeks to provide accurate definitions for each term and phrase encountered, noting, when appropriate, synonyms and significant differences in modern uses of the same expressions. No reforms in terminology are proposed, though, conceivably, others desiring 'a return to first principles' may wish to use these materials for this purpose.

It is hoped that our research has resulted in the sort of reference work which Max Prinet had announced for the *Classiques Français du Moyen Age* series before his death in 1937. Prinet, who was the author of numerous important publications concerning heraldry and who taught a course in heraldry and sigillography at the Ecole des Chartes, does not appear to have written the manual in question. At any rate, his voluminous private papers, which I was able to examine through the courtesy of his nephew in Paris, failed to yield any draft of the projected work.

The author is acutely aware of the fact that much more remains to be said about early blazon, especially from a philological and literary point of view. Contemporary Latin and German terminology, too, fully deserves to be studied independently, though it was largely influenced by French blazon. The language of each roll of arms could also be the subject of separate articles and monographs. The year 1300 has served as a convenient cut-off date for our purposes, but the choice of that year is, to be sure, somewhat arbitrary. On the other hand, by the end of the thirteenth century, the language of heraldry had become relatively fixed and was to remain largely unchanged for the next two centuries when, under the growing influence of certain teachers and treatise-writers, it entered into a phase marked by unnecessary elaborateness and hermeticism. Others may wish to determine exactly how and under what circumstances this phenomenon occurred.

These materials, then, it is hoped, will assist scholars seeking to interpret texts, will suggest possible relationships and tend to disprove others, and will lead to a better understanding of medieval language and culture.

(2) THE STUDY OF EARLY BLAZON[1]

In sharp contrast with the gratifying advances which have been made by scholars over the past century in tracing back the evolution of true heraldry (i.e. 'the systematic use of hereditary devices centred on the shield')[2] to the second quarter of the twelfth century through the study of armorial seals, little progress has been made in the analysis of verbal descriptions of arms, or blazon.

In recent years, a number of excellent articles and notes have shed much light on the original meaning and semantic evolution of individual lexical items, but no definition of what it is exactly which distinguishes classic heraldic blazon from other forms of description in Old French and its various dialects has ever been put forward.

The study of this aspect of heraldry has been greatly hampered by medieval and Tudor categorizations. The early rolls of arms were arranged hierarchically and regionally for the most part, and provide no classification according to terminology. Cooke's version of Glover's Roll (*c.* 1253), for example, begins with the King and his eldest son, followed by twenty English earls (items 3–22) and lords and knights (items 23–215).[3] The Bigot Roll (*c.* 1254) features notations by the scribe indicating successive groupings of 'Alemans', 'Ruyers' (i.e. inhabitants of the region which lies between the Meuse and Rhine

[1] Sections (2) and (4) are expanded versions of articles first published under the titles 'The Emergence of the Heraldic Phrase in the Thirteenth Century', *Coat of Arms*, viii (1961), 186–92, and 'On the Nature and Diversity of Separators in Early Blazon', *Coat of Arms*, ix (1966), 54–9. [2] Wagner, *Heralds and Heraldry*, p. 12.
[3] *CEMRA*, p. 4; *Aspilogia II*, p. 91. Denholm-Young, *History and Heraldry*, believes that Glover's Roll was compiled and preserved at Kenilworth for Simon de Monfort, Earl of Leicester and Steward of England, and represents 'the heraldic situation in or prior to 1252' (p. 42).

Rivers), 'Hasbinons', 'Ardenois', 'Braibanchons', 'Holandois', etc. The Falkirk Roll, on the other hand, the oldest known English occasional roll, groups the knights who participated in the battle of that name in 1298 by divisional commands.

Cooke's Ordinary (*c.* 1340) was the first attempt anywhere to present heraldry as such in a systematic way.[1] The original of this roll, which has been preserved, shows the painted shields of English lords and knights arranged in rows but grouped according to the principal figure depicted thereon. Interestingly enough, the arrangement does provide a reflection of medieval values in that crosses appear first—surely out of respect for the Christian symbol *par excellence*—followed by lions and eagles, the noblest of beasts and birds. This pattern is also found at the beginning of Cotgrave's Ordinary, blazoned and illustrated about the same date.[2] Lions and eagles begin William Jenyn's Ordinary (composed some forty years later) and Thomas Jenyn's Book (about 1410).[3] It was formerly believed that ordinaries were produced only in England during the Middle Ages.[4] Dr. Paul Adam-Even, however, pointed out that the mid-fifteenth-century compilation known as 'Le Grand Livre Armorial' is a French ordinary.[5]

Medieval treatises adopted a similar format in their discussions of heraldic terminology and rules[6] and it was not until Tudor times that the classification of devices into ordinaries (here with the new meaning of a certain group of linear figures, said to be the most ancient), subordinaries, and other charges was evolved.

The notion that the earliest heraldic figures are accounted for in the traditional list of ordinaries is, of course, erroneous, for the lion and several other devices generally omitted from this grouping are attested at the dawn of heraldry.

Though the latter system may have its advantages since it does group objects which are similar (to the eye, at any rate) in a convenient

[1] *CEMRA*, pp. 58–9.   [2] *CEMRA*, p. 60.
[3] *CEMRA*, pp. 69–71, 73–8; *Aspilogia II*, p. 270.
[4] *CEMRA*, p. xv: 'the whole continent of Europe can apparently show no single mediaeval ordinary'.
[5] Paris, Bibliothèque nationale, fonds français 5931, 'Le Livre du héraut Orléans'. According to the *Catalogue des manuscrits français. Ancien fonds*, v (Paris, 1902), 180, it was earlier attributed to Jean Le Feron. See also H. S. London in *Coat of Arms*, v (1958), 29.
[6] See, for example, the *Boke of St. Albans* (1486). For the best discussion of such works, consult London, 'Some Medieval Treatises'. The *Dean Tract* arranges ordinaries and charges according to such irrelevant features as the number of tinctures involved. For one of the few examples of 'rationalizing' in early blazon (*escuçon vuidié* = escutcheon), see Brault K, pp. 15–16. In general, the compilers of rolls of arms in the Middle Ages steered clear of treatise writers. The latter's influence was greatly felt, however, wherever the theory (as opposed to the practice) of heraldry was taught.

fashion, it leads to a classification of terms which is based exclusively upon visual criteria. Now the classification of things according to their purely exterior aspect not infrequently proves unsatisfactory upon scientific investigation. This system, which has been dutifully carried over in most manuals in circulation today, provides the standard heraldic frame of reference. It is, in point of fact, as inadequate to the modern linguist as the superficial descriptions of animals and precious stones found in medieval bestiaries and lapidaries are to present-day zoologists and gemmologists.

(3) HERALDIC ART AND PRE-CLASSIC BLAZON

The more one studies the conventions used in depicting heraldic shields and in describing them verbally, the more one realizes that both derive in great part from the clichés of earlier artists and craftsmen. In other words, first came medieval artistic tradition with its characteristic style and various ornamental motifs. Then, in the early twelfth century, when artists and craftsmen were called upon to paint heraldic shields and cut armorial seals, they merely adapted these conventions to the new surface. Bezants, billets, chevrons, crosslets, lozenges, saltires, and so forth, are all widely attested in Romanesque ornamental borders. The manner of representing ermine and diapering is an old stereotype and the shapes and attitudes of many of the heraldic animals derive ultimately from Byzantine art.

We must banish, therefore, the persistent but wholly erroneous notion that the heralds *invented* many of the terms used in blazon and borrowed the rest from the *everyday* lexicon of terms relative to architecture, armour, clothing, etc. Heraldic terminology is derived, for the most part, from the specialized language of artists. Thus *besant* does not mean a Byzantine coin, *chevron* a rafter, *cotice* a leather thong, and *manche* a sleeve, but the stylized bezant, chevron, cotice, and maunch of artistic tradition. Information about the linguistic conventions of art is admittedly sparse for the period in question, but the existence in medieval painting and sculpture of prototypes for the principal elements of heraldic art is undeniable and confirms our proposed chronology.

(4) THE FORMULATION OF CLASSIC BLAZON

There can be little doubt, however, that something important happened about 1250 to bring about an altogether different kind of stylization of blazon.

The Latin descriptions found in certain copies of the Matthew Paris Shields *c.* 1244 are a precious documentary source of information about the state of blazon on the eve of the classic period, but they 'are the work of a clerk, a keen and accurate observer, but one who looked at heraldry from the outside'.[1] Matthew's blazon, a curious blend of Latin and French (e.g. 'Hugonis Dispensatoris, album ubi benda nigra, aliud gules a or freté'),[2] appears at times to be a crude but successful attempt to describe armorial bearings according to classic standards. At other times, however, it in no way suggests familiarity with the style which emerges with the other thirteenth-century rolls of arms. The fact that the author chose to write in Latin will doubtless continue to foil all attempts to discover a completely French blazon behind these descriptions.

We shall probably never know where classic blazon originated, for French was, of course, in widespread use on both sides of the Channel when heraldry came into being.

The sudden refinement in blazon about 1250 doubtless resulted, in part, at any rate, from the realization that precision in heraldry had legal consequences. The *Siege of Caerlaverock* in 1300 mentions a legal dispute (*chalonge* or *chalenge*) over the right to bear a certain coat of arms:

> Le beau Brian le Filz Aleyn,
> De courtoisie et de honnour pleyn,
> I vi o baniere barree,
> De or et de goules bien paree;
> Dont de chalenge estoit li poinz,
> Par entre li e Hue Poinz,
> Ki portoit tel ne plus ne meins,
> Dont merveille avoit meinte e meins.[3]

We know also that the language of the law was becoming more and more technical at precisely this moment in history.[4] A detailed study of this matter is beyond the scope of this book, but would, no doubt,

---

[1] *Aspilogia II*, p. ix.

[2] *Aspilogia II*, p. 48, item 58 (the manuscript reads *freté*, as I have given it here, however, not *fretté*). On the language of this copy of the Matthew Paris Shields, see Tremlett's observations in *Aspilogia II*, p. 7 ('Matthew's descriptions are certainly not the technical blazon of [Glover's Roll and Walford's Roll]').

[3] *K*, vv. 353–60. On this passage, see Wagner, *Heralds and Heraldry*, pp. 18–19, 122, and ESTRE DE CHALENGE PAR ENTRE . . . ET . . ., *Note*.

[4] See G. E. Woodbine, 'The Language of English Law', *Speculum*, xviii (1943), 395–436, and, especially, R. J. Schoeck, 'Law French: Its Problems and the Status of the Scholarship', *Kentucky Foreign Language Quarterly*, vi (1959), 132–9. See also above, p. 4 n. 6.

reveal many interesting parallel developments, though several funda-
mental differences must also be recognized.

The standardization of blazon beginning with the early rolls of arms
in the thirteenth century was chiefly brought about, however, for the
purpose of answering to the heralds' needs for a mnemonic system to
assist them in the execution of their professional duties. There can
be little doubt that these patterns, once agreed upon, made the task
of learning and remembering how to blazon a large number of shields
properly much easier. It was a particularly far-sighted development
as far as England was concerned, for the knowledge of French there
was to wane rapidly in the generations to come.

It is a serious mistake to imagine that thirteenth-century heralds or
other persons knowledgeable about heraldry could not have managed,
had they so desired, to describe armorial bearings in a manner approxi-
mating that of present-day blazon. There is no inherent flaw in
thirteenth-century French preventing this and the language is quite
capable of expressing rather sophisticated concepts with great precision. Early blazon is at times incomplete or imprecise because heraldry
itself was a good deal less specific than it was later to become. When,
for example, an early-thirteenth-century writer describes a shield as
having a cross upon it, the particular shape of this charge evidently
mattered little to him and this lack of concern is matched by the
variations we find in the crosses depicted upon the armorial seals and
monuments of the day.

We should not, however, unduly emphasize the parallelism between
sigillographic or monumental heraldry on the one hand, and contemporary blazon on the other, because there was evidently a considerable lag in the latter regard. New data may one day reveal the
existence of classic blazon at a much earlier date, but it now appears
that the disposition of charges upon the shield and the charges themselves became stylized long before it became customary to blazon these
arrangements and devices in the manner referred to here as classic.

How can we explain this lag?

We have generally associated heraldry with heralds, that is with the
class of professional criers who, among other duties, identified knights
at tournaments and other public occasions. Though heralds were later
to be charged with devising coats of arms and supervising their proper
depiction upon seals, shields, and monuments, it is by no means certain
that they were assigned this task in the beginning. Heralds, like
jongleurs, were held in low esteem in the twelfth century and it is

unlikely that they would have been given such responsibility.[1] This type
of work, on the other hand, would quite naturally have been performed
by clerks in the entourage of kings and nobles. By the middle of the
thirteenth century, heralds, like jongleurs, became attached to noble
households and either prevailed upon the clerks to maintain heraldic
records, i.e. rolls of arms, for them or began compiling these themselves.
This, then, could very well explain the relatively late emergence, about
1250, of classic blazon more than a century after the birth of heraldry.

Did an oral tradition exist before the first blazons were set down to
constitute the thirteenth-century rolls of arms? The sudden emergence
of classic blazon about 1250 poses the same problem as the surprising
appearance of the *Song of Roland* in French literature a century and
a half earlier and the solution of both problems may never be found.
It seems reasonable to suppose, however, that the heralds followed the
example of the jongleurs who made use of materials no doubt originally
composed by clerks. The latter co-operated with the jongleurs and the
heralds by utilizing formulaic language.

For if classic blazon is typified by the sort of orderliness and tele-
graphic concision which would appeal to clerks, it is also a prime
example of formulaic diction. The mnemonic requirements of effective
oral delivery have always fostered stereotyped expressions and phrasing.
The early French epics, which were designed for oral delivery, are
replete with clichés which made the jongleurs' task easier.[2] The same
need for a system based upon readily assimilated patterns clearly
played a key rôle in the development of blazon.

Stereotyping, however, does not mean uniformity. There is often
a good deal of variation in terminology and style from one compilation
to another and even from one copy of the same roll to another. But this
flexibility stays, nevertheless, within a rigid framework of convention.

The first blazoned rolls of arms, which appear simultaneously in
France and England shortly after the middle of the thirteenth century,
provide a remarkable increase in the number and disposition of charges
being named for the first time in descriptions of shields. Few, if indeed
any, of the terms are peculiar to heraldry, however, and those attested
here for the first time anywhere in French were doubtless in current use
in other connections (e.g. wearing-apparel, architecture) if not in
descriptions of shields.

[1] See Ménard, p. 168 (bibliography in n. 119).
[2] The bibliography on formulas in Old French epics is extensive. The basic study, however, remains that of Jean Rychner, *La Chanson de geste. Essai sur l'art épique des jongleurs* (Geneva
and Lille, 1955).

A rather surprising number of heraldic terms, the testimony of Old French literature proves beyond any doubt, were used to describe shields in the twelfth century while many others make their appearance before the middle of the following century. A mere increase in the number of attested lexical items, therefore, noteworthy though it may be, does not constitute the essential originality of the blazon found in the earliest rolls of arms.

Of considerably greater import is the frequently-cited rule that blazon must begin with the field, then the principal charge, followed by secondary charges. This rule is, to be sure, in force in the thirteenth-century rolls of arms but it is important to note that there are antecedents in this respect in the manner of describing shields found in Old French literature before 1250. The exigencies of versification are such, however, that the rule is often violated in literature and there are a number of such infractions in the celebrated *Siege of Caerlaverock*, the authenticity of whose blazon is never questioned. For instance:

> E Guillems li Marescaus,
> Dont en Irlande ot la baillie,
> La bende de or engreellie
> Portoit en la rouge baniere.[1]

> Edewars, sires de Irois,
>
> .   .   .   .   .
>
> En sa banier trois lupart,
> De or fin estoient mis en rouge.[2]

We must look elsewhere, consequently, for the essential trait which characterizes classic style.

The single most important innovation in blazon about 1250 has not, to my knowledge, received any attention from scholars. It consists in what I shall henceforth refer to as the *heraldic phrase*, which was developed to specify the nature of certain charges and lines and, above all, to indicate the position of all charges.

The authors of thirteenth-century rolls of arms occasionally neglected to provide us with as precise a blazon as we should like as to the exact charge and line which was intended, but they recognized the importance of indicating very clearly the position of the charge. In the vast majority of cases, both needs were satisfied concisely and clearly. Though there are a few isolated instances of the heraldic phrase in Old French literature before 1250, and though there are many synonymous heraldic

[1] *K*, vv. 48–51.   [2] *K*, vv. 213, 220–1.

phrases in use after that date, the emergence of this element of blazon provides the key to classic style.

Two types of heraldic phrases appear with the thirteenth-century rolls of arms: (1) the *descriptive* phrase; and (2) the *positioning* phrase.

Examples of descriptive phrases are italicized in the following blazons from Harvy's version of Glover's Roll:

> B 8: Le counte de Winchester, de goules a six *mascles* d'or *voydés du champ.*
>
> B 13: Le counte d'Aumarle, de goules ung *croiz paté* de verre.
>
> B 61: Hamon Creveceuer, d'or ung *faulx crois* de goules.
>
> B 76: William de Vescy, goules a ung *croix patonce* d'argent.

It will be observed that the descriptive phrase is made up of a *free* form (the word *mascles* in B 8 above, for example) and one or more *bound* forms, i.e. lexical items which are never used alone in a blazon (the words *voydés du champ* in the same example).

In the following blazons, again drawn from the same version of Glover's Roll, note how the *positioning* phrase consists of a *free* form and a *bound* locution, the latter containing a term which may appear elsewhere or in the same blazon as a *free* form (the word *quartier* in the bound locution *en le quartier devant*, for example, in the first item below).

> B 11: Le conte de Oxford, quartelé d'or et de goules ung *molet* d'argent *en le quartier devant.*
>
> B 45: William de Evereus, de goules ove ung fesse d'argent et trois *torteaulx* d'argent *en le cheif.*
>
> B 208: William de Mongomery, d'ermyne a la bordure de goules et *les fers en la bordure.*

A variation on the positioning phrase involves two free forms joined by a preposition. Citing again the same roll:

> B 141: Ernaud de Mounteney, d'azur ung *bend entre* six *merlots* d'or.
>
> B 182: Walter le Fitz Robert, d'or ung *fece entre* deux *cheverons* de goules.

Another refinement in the art of expressing position in classic blazon involves two free forms once again, but relies on order of items only. In the following example from Glover's Roll, the item in italics is to be placed upon the preceding charge (i.e. the chief):

> B 102: Simon de Genevill, noir a trois breys d'or au cheif d'argent ung *demi lion* de goules.

It is evident, then, that the proper classification of heraldic terms from a linguistic point of view must take phraseology into account. In other words, it matters not so much whether a charge be an ordinary, an animal, a monster, a celestial object, or what have you; what counts, linguistically speaking, is whether it appears as a free form (e.g. *bende, lionceaus, quartier*) or as part of a heraldic phrase (e.g. descriptive: *bende engreslee, lionceaus rampanz, quartier devant*; positioning: *bende ou merletes, lionceaus en la bordure, quartier a un croissant*).

All other terms in thirteenth-century blazon, except those we shall class separately below, are *field designators*. By *field* is meant here the entire surface of the shield, of its parts, or of its charges. The term field designator encompasses all tinctures, partitions, powdering and diapering. It may appear either as a *simple* form (e.g. the tinctures) or as a *locution*, i.e. a form calling for a certain preposition (e.g. *semé de*) or pair of co-ordinated prepositions (e.g. *burelé de . . . et de . . .; esquartelé de . . . et de . . .; ondé de . . . et de . . .; parti de . . . et de . . .*). Just as genders and plurals receive rather brutal treatment in the hands of post-thirteenth-century scribes, late copies of the early rolls often reveal a dismaying lack of consistency in the use of prepositions whether employed singly or in pairs.

The only exceptions to this system based upon free forms, phrases, and field designators are *numbers* and *separators*. The latter function as commas and are interspersed more or less regularly throughout the blazon to isolate its component parts.

There are a large number of synonymous expressions in early blazon but only two ways of composing the heraldic description: with or without separators. In the following examples, note how the italicized separators are entirely omitted in another version of the same roll of arms:

B 1: Le roy d'Angleterre porte goules trois lupards d'or.

Bl 1: Le roy d'Angleterre port l'escu de gules *ove* trois lupards d'or.

B 3: Le conte de Cornewail, argent ung lion de goulz coronné or ung borde de sable besanté d'or.

Bl 3: Le comte de Cornewaill, d'argent *ou* un leon de gules coronné d'or *ove* le bordure noir besanté d'or.

C 14: Le roy d'Ermeny, un leon rampant gulez un border gulez indentee.

Cl 14: Le roy d'Ermenye, d'or *a* un liun rampant de goule *a* un bordure de goule endenté.

C 23: Le contee de Bretaigne, chequy d'or et d'azure un canton
d'ermin un border gulez.

Cl 23: Le counte de Bretaine, eschekeré d'or e d'azur *a* une kantelle
d'ermine *a* un bordure de goule.

The same preposition may be used as a separator and as part of
a phrase. In the following examples, the same preposition functions
as a separator in the first group of blazons, as part of a locution in the
second, from the same roll:

BA 256: Renax de Pressingny, l'escu contrebendé d'or et d'azur
a .i. escuchon d'argent *au* kief estakié *as* cornés geronnés. Baneres
et de Toraine.

B 197: Walter de Faucombe, noir ung quintefueile d'argent *et* les
merlotts d'argent entour.

H 1: Henry de Lacy, counte de Nichole, chevetaigne de la premier
bataille, porte d'or *ou* ung leoun rampaund de purpure.

BA 8: Le comte Aioul des Mans, l'escu blanc a un lyon de gueulles
a la keue forkie au lablel d'asur. Alemans.

B 185: Henry de Boun, d'azur six leonceux d'or a ung bend d'argent
et deux cotises goules.

H 2: Humfray de Boun, counte de Hereford, conestable de Engleterre, porte d'azur ou ung bende d'argent *ou* .vi. leonceux d'or
ou deux cotises d'or.

A separator generally indicates that a new category is being introduced. At times, however, a kind of link is actually constituted, resulting
in a situation halfway between that of a separator and a connecting
word in a locution. Thus in the following blazon, the first *ou* merely
serves to separate the principal charge from the field, whereas the
second *ou* may be said to relate the former to the secondary charge:

H 72: Sr John Badeham port d'argent *ou* la croys de gulez *ou* .v.
molets d'or en la croys.

A number of different separators were in use in the thirteenth century.
Scribes usually utilized three or four of these rather consistently, but
a few copyists show a complete disregard for uniformity in this respect.

The earliest known French roll of arms, the Bigot Roll, dated 1254,
regularly uses the separator *a*, which corresponds to the Modern French
preposition *à*:

BA 53: Guautiers de Hoingreng, l'escu d'azur *au* kief d'argent *a* la
bordeure de geules endentee. Braibanchon.

BA 282: Li visquens de Perrigort, l'escu d'argent *a* .i. fer de molin vert *a* le bordeure de geules besandé d'or.

The same preposition is also used in positioning phrases and descriptive phrases:

BA 236: Le sires de Clincamp, l'escu noir a une bende d'argent *a* .ii. listiax d'argent. Mansel.

BA 251: Esteilles de Mauny, l'escu noir a une croix blanque eslaisie *a* box a .i. baston de geules en beslive. De Torayne.

A similar situation obtains for the only other French roll prior to 1300 which is blazoned and not painted. The Chifflet–Prinet Roll, dated 1297 by the late Dr. Paul Adam-Even, at times, however, deviates slightly from this practice by using the conjunctions *et* or the combination *et a* as separators:

CP 24: Mesire Ansel de Schoisel porte les armes noir au fleurs de lis d'or semees *et* une bande d'argent.

CP 76: Mesire Joffroi de Vendome porte les armes d'argent au chef de gheules a un lion d'asur *et a* une fleur de lis d'or en l'espaule du lion.

The earliest English roll of arms, Glover's Roll, uses a profusion of terms as separators. The copy of Cooke's version in the possession of Sir Anthony Wagner which is believed to represent an original compiled about 1253 prefers *od* and *ove*, but *a*, *al*, *au*, *et*, and *ou* are also found. Harvy's version of the same roll, probably compiled about 1310 or soon after, reduces the number of separators somewhat to *a et*, *ou*, and *ove*, while copies of St. George's version (*c.* 1258) use various combinations of these terms.

To indicate that a coat of arms was the same as the one blazoned in the preceding item in the roll, with or without differencing, scribes used various expressions such as *autel*, *autretel*, and *mesme*, with or without a following separator:

B 31: Roger de Clifford, *autiel ove* ung fesse de goulz.

B 154: Thomas de Moulton le Forestier, *autiel* ung label noire.

BA 25: Le conte de Viane le porte *autretel*. Ruyer.

B 133: Thomas le Fitz William port *mesme*.

In Harvy's version of Glover's Roll only, in the thirteenth century, a separator, corresponding to Modern French *avec*, which appears nowhere else in the roll, is used in this connection:

B 2: Son fitz, teile *ovecque* ung labell d'azur.

B 112: Nicholas son filz, mesmes *oveque* la labell goulez.

In Charles's version of Walford's Roll (*c.* 1275), only two separators are found, *a* and *et*:

C 17: Le roy de Man, gulez *a* trois jambes armés argent.

C 122: Ernauld de Boyes, d'argent a deux barres *et* un canton gulez.

Ove is used as a linking word in certain phrases of this copy (*C* 60: Le countee de Musoin, gulez un leopard rampand *ove* la cowe furché d'or), but this term does not appear at all either in Leland's version or in the Trinity College manuscript.

The only separators used in the Camden Roll (*c.* 1280) are *a* and *od*. Here, as in some of the other rolls of the period, the scribe used both forms indiscriminately, at times even in the same blazon:

D 8: Le rey de Cezile, l'escu de azur floretté d'or *a* un label de gules.

D 12: Le rey de Griffonie, l'escu de azur *od* un griffun d'or.

D 32: Cunte de Seynt Pol, l'escu palé de veir et de gules *od* le chef de or *a* un label de azur.

By far the most frequently used separator in Thevet's version of the Falkirk Roll (1298), on the other hand, is *ou*, though the copyist occasionally employed *e(t)*, *o*, and *od* in this connection:

H 106: Sʳ Rauff Pipart porte d'argent ou ung feez et demy feez *et* le cantell d'azure et en le cantell quintfoyl d'or.

H 65: Sir le Fitz Payn port de gules ou .iii. leons passauntz d'argent *o* ung baston d'azure.

H 7: Sʳ Robert Tatershall port eschequeré d'or et de gulez *od* le chief de hermyn.

H 6: Sʳ Roger le Fitz Wauter port d'or *ou* deux cheverons de gulez *ou* ung fez de gulez.

In the Nativity Roll (*c.* 1300), *ou* is once again the most widely used separator with only occasional use being made of *et*:

M 1: Sʳ Richard Archat porte d'argent *ou* la bend de gulez *ou* .iii. florettz d'or *ou* .ii. lytteg' de gulez *ou* la bordure de gulez.

M 53: Sʳ Phillip de Mowbray d'Escoce port de gulez ou ung lyon d'argent *et* ung bend engrelé de sable.

This roll, however, also contains several examples of the curious form *odve*, which is derived, like *ove* and *ove(c)que*, from the blending of *o(d)* (< Lat. *apud*) and *avuec*, *avoec* (< Vulgar Lat. **abhoc*):[1]

---

[1] On these prepositions, consult G. Löfgren, *Etude sur les prépositions françaises od, atout, avec, depuis les origines jusqu'au XVIᵉ siècle* (Uppsala, 1944).

M 25: Sr Nicholas de Gray porte barré d'azure et d'argent *odve* la bend d'or et de gulez goboné.

M 71: Sr Robert Tillyolf por de gules *odve* leon d'argent le baston d'azure.

Finally, the *Siege of Caerlaverock* (*c.* 1300) makes frequent use of *a, e, o,* and *ove* singly and in various combinations:

K, vv. 160–3: Robert le Fiz Paien sievable
Ot sa baner flanc a flanc
Rouge *a* passans lyons de blanc
Trois, de un bastoun bleu surgettez.

K, vv. 296–9: Le roi son bon seignour connoie
Sa baniere mout honouree,
De or e de asur eschequeré,
O une fesse vermellette.

K, vv. 70–1: Baniere avoit en asure teinte,
Ove un lyon rampant d'argent.[1]

K, vv. 181–4: Rogers de la Ware ovec eus,
Uns chevalers sagis e preus,
Ki les armes ot vermellettis
O blonc lyoun *e* croissellettes.

K, vv. 710–13: Henri de Graham unes armes
Avoit vermeilles cumme sanc,
O un sautour *e au* chief blanc,
Ou ot trois vermeilles cokilles.

The use of the separator *à* in modern French blazon is an excellent example of heraldic continuity in that language. As for modern English practice, some continue to make generous use of 'ands' and 'withs' while others prefer a terser style omitting all separators. This, too, represents a faithful tradition, for, as we have seen, there is a precedent for both manners of blazon in the earliest rolls of arms.

(5) FURTHER CHARACTERISTICS OF CLASSIC BLAZON

Classic blazon is generally more precise and detailed than the descriptions which preceded it. Ambiguities persist, however. These are

---

[1] I have given here the reading of this verse found in College of Arms, MS. Arundel LXII, fols. 4–34, as published in Nicolas's edition of *K*, p. 8; the British Museum MS. reads: 'O un lyoun rampant de argent' and omits the preceding verse altogether.

inherent in any technical language of a bygone day: meanings for certain expressions have changed, numerous synonyms and pleonasms must be taken into account, dialectal and orthographical peculiarities compound the confusion. Above all, there are surprising omissions and inconsistencies which would not be tolerated today.

It is often difficult to determine whether a particular blazon is the result of an error or lack of information on the part of the compiler (or copyist), or merely an illustration of looser contemporary practices. The recurrence of certain usages often confirms the latter interpretation. Thus a compiler may specify that a lion has a forked tail but neglect to add that the latter is also crossed in saltire. When the charges are numerous, he may provide only an approximate figure, or list them as a semy pattern. Crosses are described as *fourchiee* or *patee* with apparent indifference. A flower may be termed a sixfoil in one roll and appear as a cinquefoil in another. Blazons such as these, unacceptable today, were evidently tolerated in the thirteenth century. Sometimes, however, the situation is far from clear as when, for example, Walford's Roll violates the rule about order of items in a blazon, suggesting that the charge is in the field rather than on the chief. Errors do exist, of course, and the latter case is doubtless an instance of it.

While classicism was achieved in the second half of the thirteenth century, the period in question is also a transitional one characterized by a number of archaisms (e.g. *bende de belic*), pleonasms (*escuçon par mi*), and much experimentation. In general, lengthy circumlocutions have been eliminated but survivals are particularly noticeable in literary contexts. There is increasing specialization (e.g. *liste*) but still hesitation in the meaning ascribed to such terms as *baston* and *bende*. Many distinctions such as *besant | gastel | rondel | tourtel*; *bordure | orle*; *endenté | engreslé*; *estoile | molete*; *losengié | masclé*; *pal | pile*; and even *liepart | lion* have yet to be made. There are some important exceptions, but, as a rule, no indication is given as to the number of stripes in a barry, bendy, or paly field or as to the number of points in an indented bend or fess (i.e. what we would today blazon as lozenges or fusils in bend or in fess). Such distinctions became necessary with the proliferation of arms, but they were also a product of a later tendency to split hairs.

Above all, many synonymous expressions in widespread use were destined to be eliminated. Classic blazon is unconcerned about the abundance of synonyms which are a source of considerable confusion to us. As a matter of fact, the author of the *Siege of Caerlaverock* seems to use synonyms whenever possible, probably to vary his narrative, but also, no doubt, to display his heraldic virtuosity. The latter work also contains an interesting example—the earliest attested thus far—of the nefarious effect of rationalizing (*escuçon vuidié* = escutcheon) which will characterize the later treatises and which, unfortunately, still plagues us today.

While diminutives (e.g. *eglel* vs. *egle*; *liepardel* vs. *liepart*; *lioncel* vs. *lion*) are reserved for multiple charges, the simplex is also employed for this purpose and there was as yet no fixed rule governing the use of the former. We also find a few examples of *barre* in the singular and *fesse* in the plural.

When not otherwise specified, the disposition of three charges in present-day heraldry is always 2 and 1, that is, two above and one below, conforming to the shape of the shield. An in pale disposition, i.e. an arrangement of charges along a vertical line, must always be indicated. This is generally true of early blazon also, but a person was somehow expected to know that certain charges such as horse-brays (*broies*) and hamaides (*hamedes*) naturally were arranged in pale and that pikes (*luz*) faced upwards.

While today it is still not a firm rule of heraldry that canting arms be blazoned with terms indicating, whenever possible, the pun in question, the practice is much more generalized in our day than it was in the thirteenth century. At times, of course, the original play on words was no more evident to the herald than it is today. Versification enters into the picture, too, no doubt. For one of these reasons, or perhaps more than one, the author of the *Siege of Caerlaverock* blazoned the Scales arms with *coquilles* rather than the punning escallops.

No examples of crests have been noted in early blazon, though the ancestor of the motto, the *cri de guerre*, appears frequently in thirteenth century accounts of tournaments, a fashionable literary genre.

In a few isolated instances (e.g. *barre*, *cotice*), there would appear to be a distinction between insular and continental practice, but any attempt to generalize on the basis of the sparse indications we have been able to gather would be unwise, for there are simply no systematic differences here. On the contrary, cross-fertilization, fostered by much cross-Channel traffic on the part of the heralds, doubtless played an important role in standardizing thirteenth-century heraldry.[1]

A certain amount of vocabulary appears only in blazons recorded in literature as opposed to those listed in the rolls. Some terms are frequently used in literary contexts only (e.g. *sinople*), others are unique

---

[1] See Brault K, pp. 5–7.

(e.g. *vaironé*). There is a certain amount of overlapping in this regard, as when the author of the *Siege of Caerlaverock* uses the term *vermeil*. The latter work straddles the line between literature and a roll of arms. Much more emphasis is accorded to heraldry, as a matter of fact, than to aesthetic matters. There are numerous items of incidental interest in the *Siege of Caerlaverock*, but the poem was obviously written primarily for the purpose of leaving to posterity an accurate description of the arms borne by certain individuals on that occasion.

Once again, however, it is important to recognize the unity of blazon in the classic period, whether it be found in England or in France, in a roll of arms or in a contemporary work of literature, and to understand that the transformation which occurred about 1250, while it was a major and even a revolutionary one, was based upon terms and phrasing already existing in the language.

(6) LITERATURE AND HERALDRY

Twelfth-century French literature has been studied by a number of heraldists but almost exclusively with a view to complementing the sigillographic evidence of early heraldic practice and not with the intention of establishing the chronological development of verbal blazon. The most comprehensive study is still that of L. Bouly de Lesdain,[1] who analysed many of the early French poems, largely, however, with the former view in mind. Of interest, too, is Jean Marchand's study of the vocabulary of the *Song of Roland*,[2] which establishes the fact that several of the terms which later appear in blazon are already attested in this earliest of the French *chansons de geste*.

More recently, Dr. Paul Adam-Even has brought together numerous descriptions of shields in twelfth-century romances and pointed to the value of Benoît de Sainte-Maure's *Roman de Troie* for the study of heraldry.[3] Bouly de Lesdain had noted that twelfth-century French authors generally adhered to the rule that metal may not appear on metal, nor colour on colour, a custom respected by Benoît.[4] Whereas contemporary poets frequently did not hesitate to ascribe different shields and banners to the same character and rarely indicated family

[1] 'Etudes héraldiques sur le XIIᵉ siècle', *Annuaire du Conseil héraldique de France*, xx (1907), 185–244.
[2] Jean Marchand, 'L'art héraldique d'après la littérature du Moyen Age. Les Origines: la *Chanson de Roland*', *Le Moyen Age*, xlvii (1937), 37–43.
[3] Adam-Even, '*Roman de Troie*,' pp. 18–29.
[4] Bouly de Lesdain, p. 232, listing two exceptions; Adam-Even, '*Roman de Troie*', p. 24. Cf. *Aspilogia II*, p. 107, and see CROIS[1], *Note*; SOR, *Note*.

relationships heraldically, Dr. Adam-Even was persuaded that Benoît made an effort to individualize his coats of arms and may even, in the case of at least two of Priam's sons, have indicated kinship by heraldic differencing. The arms borne by Hector and Troilus do, as a matter of fact, both feature a field of gold and a lion, the first brother's charge being gules, the second's azure. A third brother, Paris, carries a shield bearing a leopard, but the tinctures are not mentioned. The late French scholar's views are subject to reservations here, however, since other family relationships in Benoît's romance are not so indicated while a lion is borne by several other characters, in one case on a field of gold. Benoît does not specifically name his patroness, but there is little doubt that the long poem was composed *c.* 1160 with an eye to pleasing Eleanor of Aquitaine, wife of King Henry II of England.[1]

We note, then, numerous mentions in twelfth-century French epics and romances of shields painted in various colours and bearing many of the animals which later figure prominently in heraldry.[2] It is an incontrovertible fact that heraldry did exist at the time when most of these works were written, but it is doubtful whether much heraldic significance may be attached to these early descriptions of arms. Virtually all the shields and banners mentioned in passing in twelfth-century French literature, in particular the scores of *escuz bendés*, *escuz a lion*, and *escuz a quartiers*, are purely decorative. There are, however, some notable allusions to historical arms.

(7) HERALDIC FLATTERY

The oldest extant French version of the famous romance of Tristan and Isolt was written by a poet named Thomas who was also in the entourage of King Henry II. The sole surviving copy of this work is preserved in several fragments totalling about 3,150 verses. Only one coat of arms is mentioned, that of a minor character named Tristan

---

[1] Adam-Even, '*Roman de Troie*', p. 18; Rita Lejeune, 'Rôle littéraire d'Aliénor d'Aquitaine et de sa famille', *Cultura Neolatina*, xiv (1954), pp. 22–4.

[2] Consult Bangert, items 511 (Adler), 597 (Drache), 305 (Eber), 593 (Greif), 410 (Hund), 443 (Leopard), 430–5 (Löwe), 569 (Schlange); Volkmar Bach, *Angriffswaffen in den altfranzösischen Artus- und Abenteuer-Romanen* (Marburg, 1887) [*Ausgaben und Abhandlungen aus dem Gebiete der romanischen Philologie*, 70]; Schirling, pp. 5–30. For an excellent discussion of quasi-heraldic illustrations in a manuscript dated *c.* 1109, see P. Gras, 'Aux origines de l'héraldique', *BEC*, cix (1951), 198–208. For similar devices on shields in a manuscript dated 1130–40, see *The Bodleian Library. Heraldry. Catalogue of an Exhibition held in Connection with the English Heraldry Society, 1967* (Oxford, 1967), p. 14, item 1, and Plate I. Cf. also the shields in the Bayeux Tapestry.

le Nain (Tristan the Dwarf), whom the hero encounters toward the end of the poem. Thomas describes his arms as follows:

> Escu ot d'or a vair freté,
> De meime le teint ot la lance,
> Le penun e la conisance.[1]

Bédier, relying on the testimony of an early German translation of Thomas' poem by Gottfried of Strasbourg, believed that Tristan's arms featured a boar.[2] Roger Sherman Loomis, however, noting that the Old Norse Tristan *Saga* mentions gold lions on a red field on the trappings of the hero's horse, that the Middle English *Sir Tristrem* makes use of the word *lyoun* in this connection, and that the Chertsey tiles twice represent Tristan bearing a single lion rampant, all three illustrations of the story being closely related in several other respects to Thomas' version, conjectured that the missing portion of the latter's poem described the hero's arms as featuring *a lion rampant or on a field of gules*.[3] Loomis believed that these arms constituted a clear allusion

---

[1] *Tristan de Thomas*, i. vv. 2182–4. On the date (possibly before 1160), see Rita Lejeune, 'Rôle littéraire de la famille d'Aliénor d'Aquitaine', *Cahiers de civilisation médiévale*, i (1958), 334. The knight in question is discussed by Bédier in *Tristan de Thomas*, ii. 282–3; Schoepperle, *Tristan and Isolt*, pp. 124–8, 249–50. In Béroul's romance (*Tristan de Béroul*, vv. 3999–4004), Tristan appears as the Black Knight, his horse being covered with black and his lance bearing a black pennant given to him by 'la bele'; cf. Gawain in the *First Continuation* (see below, p. 42 n. 7). Giflet in vv. 4015–16 refers to him as 'Li Noirs de la Montaigne'.

[2] *Tristan de Thomas*, i. 61, and note 1. See also J. Loth, 'Contributions à l'étude des Romans de la Table Ronde. II. Le Bouclier de Tristan', *Revue celtique*, xxxii (1911), 296–8; George L. Hamilton, 'Tristram's Coat of Arms', *MLR*, xv (1920), 425–9.

[3] Loomis developed his theory, based upon a suggestion of Prof. W. R. Lethaby, in a series of publications: *Illustrations of Medieval Romance on Tiles from Chertsey Abbey* (*University of Illinois Studies in Language and Literature*, ii. 2 [Urbana, 1916]), pp. 50–5; 'A Sidelight on the *Tristan* of Thomas', *MLR*, x (1915), 307–8; 'Notes on the *Tristan* of Thomas', *MLR*, xiv (1919), 39; and, especially, 'Tristan and the House of Anjou', *MLR*, xvii (1922), 24–30 (see also 'Problems of the Tristan Legend', *Romania*, liii [1927], 100, and his *Arthurian Legends in Medieval Art* [in collaboration with Laura Hibbard Loomis], [New York, 1938], p. 47 [item 19]). Opposition to Loomis's theory was voiced in the article by Hamilton cited above in n. 2 and by Lucy M. Gay, 'Heraldry and the "Tristan" of Thomas', *MLR*, xxiii (1928), 472–5. In general, however, Loomis's views have been accepted by scholars; see, for example, René Louis, *Girart, comte de Vienne dans les chansons de geste* (Auxerre, 1947), i. 349–51, and Professor Lejeune's article cited above, p. 19 n. 1 (p. 32). Loomis mentions briefly Tristan's coat of arms in the fifteenth-century Arthurian rolls (*vert, a lion rampant or armed and langued gules*). These arms are attested in the following sources: (1) *manuscript illuminations*: Chantilly, MS. 645, frontispiece, fols. 89 recto, 106 verso, 175 verso; MS. 646, fols. 82 verso, 115 verso, 119 recto, 128 recto; MS. 647, fols. 31 verso, 72 verso, 88 recto, 150 verso, 252 recto, 279 recto; Condé, MS. 315, frontispiece; Paris, Bibliothèque nationale, fonds français 5233, fol. 3 verso; fonds français 5939, fol. 14 recto; fonds français 14357, fol. 24 recto; (2) *Arthurian rolls of arms*: Paris, Bibliothèque nationale, fonds français 1435, fol. 32 recto; fonds français 1436, fols. 15 recto, 61 recto; fonds français 1437, fol. 57 verso; fonds français 1438, fol. 23 verso; fonds français 5233, fol. 3 verso; fonds français 5937, fol. 21 verso; fonds français 5939, fol. 14 recto; fonds français 12597, fol. 27 recto; fonds français 23,999, fol. 4 recto; Chantilly, MS. 642, fol. 5 recto.

to those of Henry II. While no direct evidence of the arms borne by this monarch (1154–89) has been preserved, it is a highly plausible conjecture that Henry bore one or more lions on his shield and that the tinctures were those which became firmly established in the Royal Arms of England (*gules, three leopards or*) with King Richard I in 1198 and which appear in the reconstructed arms of Tristan.

Dr. Adam-Even, who does not appear to have taken cognizance of the Loomis theory, suggested a similar instance of heraldic flattery in another work by Benoît de Sainte-Maure commissioned by Henry II *c.* 1174.[1] This lengthy chronicle narrates the history of Henry's Norman ancestors including William the Conqueror. Benoît doubtless had the English king's arms in mind when he devised a heraldic device for William in the following passage:

> Dites, fait il, vostre seignor
> Qu'en un cheval blanc comme flor
> Serai armez, forz e isnieaus,
> Si ert mis escuz od leonceaus
> D'or, en azur faiz et assis.
> Por ce mes armes li devis
> Teu me connoisse e teu m'avra.[2]

Medieval authors not infrequently mistook or deliberately altered elements of a coat of arms, so the substitution of an azure field for one of gules does not in the least rule out the French scholar's interesting suggestion.

In at least two other early French romances, the Royal Arms of England are associated with fictitious kings. In *Durmart le Galois*, which is believed by its most recent editor to have been composed in the early years of the thirteenth century, the hero's arms are blazoned *gules, two leopards or crowned argent*, a coat also ascribed to his father, King Jozefent.[3] Two leopards appear in the arms of several members of the English royal family in the latter part of the twelfth century. Before his accession to the throne, King John is known to have borne such a coat in 1177, as did his illegitimate son Richard de Varenne, his elder sister

---

[1] Adam-Even, '*Roman de Troie*', p. 19. On the date, see Lejeune, 'Rôle littéraire d'Aliénor d'Aquitaine et de sa famille', p. 26.

[2] *Chronique des ducs de Normandie par Benoît*, ed. Carin Fahlin, ii (Uppsala–Wiesbaden–The Hague–Geneva, 1954), vv. 36941–7. In the Matthew Paris Shields, William also bears the three leopards of England; see *Aspilogia II*, p. 11, item 2. The two-leopard coat now associated with the Duchy of Normandy is attested only much later.

[3] *Durmart*, vv. 1278–9, 1408–10 (the leopards have silver crowns), 1415–16, 2630, 9253–4, 9275–6, 9344–6, 10100–1, 11143, 11799–800, 12370, 12916–18 (the leopards have silver crowns), 13048–9, 13157, 13613, 13902, 14415–16 for Durmart; vv. 9256–8, 9717 for Jozefent.

Maud, and her son Henry, Count Palatine of the Rhine in 1195.[1] As we have said above, *three* leopards became the distinctive feature of the Royal Arms of England only in 1195. The same writer ascribes the well-known arms of France Ancient (*azure, semy of fleurs-de-lis or*) to the Roi des Isles, a stock character in the Arthurian romances of the day.[2]

In *Durmart*, the hero is said to be the son of the King of Wales (*Gales*) and of Denmark who is also King Arthur's cousin. To be sure, *Gales* need not necessarily be equated with England, but the convergence of arms seems more than fortuitous. A second instance of such association tends to confirm this. In MS. *K* (second half of the thirteenth century) of the *Second Continuation*, King Arthur's shield is blazoned *three leopards passant or*.[3] There seems little doubt here that the inventor of these arms wished to link the then reigning monarch (Edward I, in view of his known Arthurianism,[4] strikes us as being a logical candidate) to his fabled ancestor, King Arthur.

Another example of heraldic flattery may be recorded in *Le Bel Inconnu*, an Arthurian romance composed between 1185 and 1190 by Renaut de Beaujeu. Guinglain, who is the 'Fair Unknown' of the title, turns out to be Sir Gawain's son. He bears a shield described in the following terms:

> Et ses escus d'asur estoit,
> D'ermine un lion i avoit.[5]

Later these arms are confirmed by the author:

> Un chevalier i ai veü
> Que i porte un escu d'azon,
> U d'ermine a un blanc lion.[6]

---

[1] London, *Royal Beasts*, Ch. III.   [2] *Durmart*, vv. 8557–62.

[3] *SCK*, fol. 106 *f.* In *Sone*, vv. 14937–9, the hero's arms are blazoned *or, a lion rampant crowned gules*, differenced from those of his ancestors said to have borne *gules, three lioncels rampant crowned or* (vv. 9867–9). Numerous other coats are borne by Sone, however; see, for example, p. 40 n. 1.

[4] See R. S. Loomis, 'Edward I, Arthurian Enthusiast', *Speculum*, xxviii (1953), 114–27.

[5] *Bel Inconnu*, vv. 73–5.

[6] *Bel Inconnu*, vv. 5920–2. Williams's identification of these arms is on page viii of his Introduction. For the unflattering device on Duke William IX of Aquitaine's shield, see my note s.v. JAMBES DE S'AMIE. The Emperor's arms in *Guillaume de Dole*, vv. 68–71, are evidently an allusion to one of Jean Renart's contemporaries; see my note s.v. DEMI². For possible heraldic flattery in the lion device ascribed to the hero of Conrad's German translation of the *Roland*, consult Lejeune–Stiennon, *La Légende de Roland*, i. 115–16. Finally, Professor Mary Giffin, 'The Date of the "Dream of Rhonabwy"', *Cymmrodorion Society. Transactions* (1959), 33–40 (summary in *BBSIA*, ix [1957], 119–20), argues that 'The arms and trappings of the "Dream" resemble in a similar way those of [*K*]' (p. 35) and, consequently, that the former may be dated *c.* 1300. Heraldic flattery occurs in art, too, of course; see, for example, Loomis, *Arthurian Legends*, p. 63 (Tristan's shield bears the three horns of the Guicciardini family).

G. Perrie Williams, who edited the romance for the *Classiques Français du Moyen Age* series in 1929, believed that these arms were analogous to those borne by members of the Baugé family, neighbours of the Beaujeus. The Baugé arms feature the same ermine lion rampant, but this charge was placed upon a field of gules, not azure.

(8) CANTING AND SYMBOLIC ARMS

Armes parlantes, i.e. canting arms or devices which involve a pun on the individual's name or occupation, appear rarely in twelfth-century blazon. The only possible example which has come to our attention is the dragon on King Arthur's helmet and standard according to Geoffrey of Monmouth, a device which some may consider to be heraldic in view of the fact that Arthur's father is also said to have carried such a banner. The passage referring to Arthur's helmet in Geoffrey's *Historia Regum Britanniae* (c. 1136) reads as follows: 'Ipse vero Arturus, lorica tanto rege digna indutus, auream galeam simulacro draconis insculptam capiti adaptat.'[1] Wace, whose translation of the *Historia* is dated before 1155, specified that the monarch's father had owned the helmet before his son:

> Helme ot en sun chief cler luisant,
> D'or fu tut li nasels devant
> E d'or li cercles envirun;
> Desus ot purtrait un dragun;
> El helme ot mainte piere clere,
> Il ot esté Uther, sun pere.[2]

If we now recall that Arthur's father's full name was Uther Pendragon, we may interpret the dragon as a pun on the latter's name. While in no way ruling out the possibility of canting arms here, it seems more likely that in Geoffrey's mind a dragon was associated with Arthur and Uther simply because this was a traditional symbol of the Saxons.[3] Henry of Huntington, whom Geoffrey had read, specifically mentions the dragon of the West Saxons.[4]

---

[1] Edmond Faral, *La Légende arthurienne. Etudes et documents* (Paris, 1929), iii. 233.

[2] *Brut*, vv. 9283–8.

[3] J. S. P. Tatlock, 'The Dragons of Wessex and Wales', *Speculum*, viii (1933), 223–35; Wagner, *Historic Heraldry*, p. 57; William N. Ferris, 'Arthur's Golden Dragon', *Romance Notes*, i (1959), 69–71; Karl H. Göller, 'Die Wappen König Arthurs in der Hs. Lansdowne 882', *Anglia*, lxxix (1962), 264–6. In literature, a dragon is frequently associated with Arthur: *Lancelot propre*, iv. 22; *Vulgate Merlin Sequel*, pp. 143, 264–5, 383, 437; *Artus*, p. 14; *TA*, vv. 1978–81; Paris, Bibliothèque nationale, fonds français 18651, fol. 1 recto.

[4] Robert Huntington Fletcher, *The Arthurian Material in the Chronicles especially those of Great Britain and France* (Boston, 1906), p. 72 (*Harvard Studies and Notes in Philology and Literature*, x).

Arms featuring symbolic and in particular religious devices are much more widely attested in twelfth-century blazon. As a matter of fact, crosses appear on shields and banners as early as Constantine's day.[1] The *vexillum* which Pope Alexander II gave to William the Conqueror bore a yellow or a red cross on a white field and, of course, the cross was adopted as an emblem by the Crusaders following Pope Urban II's eloquent appeal at the Council of Clermont in November 1095.[2] In heraldry, the plain cross of Savoy appears on the armorial seals of Counts Amadeus and Humbert in 1143 and 1151, respectively.[3]

The earliest mention in literature of religious symbolism on a shield is Geoffrey of Monmouth's description of the image of the Virgin Mary on King Arthur's shield in the passage immediately following the one cited above concerning the dragon device: 'humeris quoque suis clypeum vocabulo Pridwen, in quo imago sanctae Mariae Dei genitricis inpicta ipsam in memoriam ipsius saepissime revocabat.'[4] Wace translates as follows:

> Sur un cheval munta mult bel
> E fort e curant e isnel,
> Pridwen, sun escu, a sun col.
> Ne sembla pas cuart ne fol.
> Dedenz l'escu fu par maistrie
> De ma dame sainte Marie
> Purtraite e peinte la semblance,
> Pur enur e pur remembrance.[5]

Mention is made of the Virgin device on Arthur's shield in Geoffrey's presumed source, the anonymous *Historia Britonum*, but there is also a similar passage ('fretus imagine Dominicae matris, quam armis suis insuerat', i.e. aided by the image of the mother of the Lord, which he had sewn on his arms) in the earlier (1125) *Gesta regum Anglorum* by William of Malmesbury.[6] The ultimate source of the allusion is apparently the following statement in Nennius' early-ninth-century *Historia Britonum*: 'Arthur portavit imaginem sanctae Mariae perpetuae virginis super humeros suos', in which the image of the Virgin

---

[1] See, for example, the article 'Labarum' in Dom Fernand Cabrol and Dom Henri Leclercq, *Dictionnaire d'archéologie chrétienne et de liturgie*, VIII, 1 (Paris, 1928), cols. 927–62.

[2] C.G.P.J., 'Further Notes on the Arms of the Kingdom of Jerusalem', *Coat of Arms*, i (1950), 47; Kenneth M. Setton, *A History of the Crusades*, i (Philadelphia, 1955), 239–40, 246–7; John A. Goodall, 'The Origins of the Arms and Badge of the Order of St. John of Jerusalem', *Coat of Arms*, v (1958), 373–4. A number of Romanesque sculptures, believed to represent Roland, feature a shield bearing a cross; see Lejeune–Stiennon, *La Légende de Roland*, ii, plates 11, 56, 62, 66, 154A.

[3] *Aspilogia II*, p. 66, note to item 40.   [4] See above, p. 23 n. 1.

[5] *Brut*, vv. 9289–96.   [6] Fletcher, p. 32; Faral, i. 247, note 1.

does not appear on Arthur's shield but is carried instead on his shoulders.[1] It was long ago pointed out, however, that the story was doubtless first recorded in Old Welsh and that the word for shield in that language (*ysgwydd* or *iscuit*) was simply mistaken for the word for shoulder (*ysgwyd* or *iscuid*) in Nennius' source.[2]

Another early mention of religious symbolism on a shield is the portrait of *Mahomet*, or Mohammed, the Prophet of Islam, taken here, as in other French poems of the day, as one of the pagan deities: 'Mahomes estoit pains el senestre quartier.'[3] The verse in question is from the mid-twelfth-century crusade epic *Chétifs* and the shield is that of the Saracen Cornumaran. A picture of *Apolin*, or Apollo, similarly regarded as a pagan god, is cited in the following passage from *Fierabras*, an epic composed about 1170:

> A son col a pendu son fort escu listé;
> Quatre lionchiaus d'or i avoit painturé.
> L'image d'Apolin fu desous le boucler,
> Et de fer et d'acier estoit entour listés.[4]

On the other hand, Garnier, Christian hero of the epic *Aye d'Avignon*, written *c.* 1200, bears a shield depicting Christ raising Lazarus from the dead:

> En l'escu de son col ot paint .i. gent miracle,
> Ainssi con Nostre Sire resuscita saint Ladre.[5]

In the *Lancelot propre*, mention is made of two shields, the first purely symbolic, the second partly symbolic and partly magic.

A company of Arthur's knights arrives at the Fountain of the Pine just as a squire is hanging a shield upon the tree. The shield is black semy of argent drops ('si estoit li escus noirs, d'argent goutés menuement').[6] Another knight, later identified as Hector, arrives upon the scene and, seeing the shield, immediately begins to weep and lament. This grief, however, promptly turns to joy only to change back again to sorrow. The process is repeated several times before Arthur's knights learn that the gouté shield symbolizes Hector's sorrow and tears ('li noirs senefie duel et les goutes d'argent senefient larmes')[7] over the fact

---

[1] Faral, iii. 38.

[2] Bibliography in Fletcher, p. 32 n. 6; see also Loomis, *Arthurian Tradition*, p. 49, para. 13.

[3] *Chétifs*, p. 276; see also *Gaufrey*, vv. 3011–12.

[4] *Fierabras*, vv. 666–9; see also *Aiol*, vv. 9995, 10010.   [5] *Aye d'Avignon*, vv. 2736–7.

[6] *Lancelot propre*, iii. 278.

[7] *Lancelot propre*, iii. 284. Cf. *Lancelot propre*, v. 403, where Lancelot has Pelles make him a black shield charged with the picture of 'une royne d'argent' with a knight kneeling before her as if imploring mercy. Lancelot goes daily before this shield to lament. The scene is

that he was forced to vow to his true love, the niece of an unidentified dwarf, that he would not fight Segurade who hates the damsel for refusing to marry him.

In another part of the same work, the Damsel of the Lake sends Guenevere a shield which is cleft in the middle thus separating an armed knight and a beautiful lady who would be depicted as embracing each other were the two sections joined.[1] When the knight has gained the lady's complete love, the shield will close up. One night, when Lancelot has given adequate proof of his undying affection for the Queen, Guenevere rises at midnight and, feeling the mended shield in the dark, is finally satisfied that her lover will remain faithful to her forever ('si taste sans alumer si le trueve tout entier sans fendure. Si en est moult lie car ore seit ele que ele est la miex amee de nule autre amie').[2]

The vogue for symbolic arms reached its high point with the *Tournoiement Antecrit*, an allegorical poem composed *c.* 1234 by Huon de Méry which tells of an imaginary tournament between the forces of good and of evil.[3] Each vice and each virtue bears arms laden with heavy symbolism, which makes the work rather tedious to read today. The poem is important from our point of view, however, because it shows better than any other source the broad potentialities of blazon on the eve of the classic era.[4]

(9) ALLUSIVE ARMS

The Tournament of Noauz episode in Chrétien de Troyes's *Charrete* (*c.* 1180) contains the first illustration of the practice of referring heraldically to a prior literary event. This passage records the conversation of the knights who have not entered the lists because 'prison ou croisié se erent' (they were prisoners or had taken the crusader's vows) and who are watching the jousting in the company of Queen Guenevere and her female entourage. The men blazon the shields of the knights whom they most admire in the following terms:

> Antr'ax dïent: 'Veez vos or
> Celui a cele bande d'or

illustrated in British Museum, Add. MS. 10, 293, fol. 381 recto. For use of the latter motif in Malory and Tennyson, consult C. W. Scott-Giles, 'The Heraldry of Romance', *Coat of Arms*, ii (1953), 259.

[1] *Lancelot propre*, iii. 305.

[2] *Lancelot propre*, iii. 411. Galahad's red-cross shield is magic, too, or, rather, miraculous as it has healing properties (*Queste*, p. 33).   [3] See Prinet TA, pp. 43–53.

[4] Other examples of symbolic arms include the shields of the Faith and of the Soul in Matthew Paris (*Aspilogia II*, p. 61, items 8 and 9); cf. *Otinel*, vv. 300–6 (signs of the Zodiac).

Par mi cel escu de bernic?
C'est Governauz de Roberdic.
Et veez vos celui aprés,
Qui an son escu pres a pres
A mise une aigle et un dragon?
C'est li filz le roi d'Arragon
Qui venuz est an ceste terre
Por pris et por enor conquerre.
Et veez vos celui dejoste
Qui si bien point et si bien joste
A cel escu vert d'une part,
S'a sor le vert point un liepart,
Et d'azur est l'autre mitiez:
C'est Ignaures li covoitiez,
Li amoreus et li pleisanz.
Et cil qui porte les feisanz
An son escu poinz bec a bec?
C'est Coguillanz de Mautirec.
Et veez vos ces deus delez
A ces deus chevax pomelez
As escuz d'or as lÿons bis?
Li uns a non Semiramis
Et li autres est ses conpainz,
S'ont d'un sanblant lor escuz tainz.
Et veez vos celui qui porte
An son escu pointe une porte?
Si sanble qu'il s'an isse uns cers.
Par foi, ce est li rois Yders.'

.   .   .   .   .

'Et cil autres si est de l'uevre
D'Engleterre, et fu fez a Londres,
Ou vos veez ces deus arondres
Qui sanblent que voler s'an doivent,
Mes ne se muevent, ainz reçoivent
Mainz cos des aciers poitevins:
Sel porte Thoas li meschins.'
Ensi devisent et deboissent
Les armes de ces qu'il conoissent.[1]

The King of Aragon, whose son's arms are blazoned here, is a stock character in Arthurian romance and was doubtless associated with Spain only in the vaguest sort of way in Chrétien's mind. At any rate, the eagle preying on (?) the dragon on this shield has nothing whatsoever to do with the Royal Arms of Aragon (*or, four pales gules*) attested on the seal of Ramon Berengar IV of Aragon in 1157.[2] The observation

---

[1] *Charrete*, vv. 5773–5802, 5816–24.   [2] *Aspilogia II*, p. 168, note to item 9.

that Semiramis bears a shield identical with that of his companion in arms finds a clear parallel in historical fact: in 1173, William Marshal bore the Tancarville arms when he spent some time at the latter court.[1] Dr. Adam-Even also cites numerous early historical and literary instances, beginning with the *Roman de Troie*, where the men in a knight's retinue all bore his coat of arms.[2]

The same passage in Chrétien describes the shield of King Ider as bearing a stag issuing from a gate. If this person is identical with the knight Yder, son of Nut, mentioned in Chrétien's earlier romance *Erec*, the arms in question doubtless allude to the famous White Stag episode in that romance.[3] According to a time-honoured custom, the knight who succeeded in slaying a white stag was obliged to kiss the fairest maiden at court, come what may. During the hunt organized by King Arthur for this purpose, Erec encounters Yder who allows a dwarf to affront Queen Guenevere. Erec subsequently avenges this insult and wins the hand of Enide who, brought back to Arthur's court, is declared the fairest damsel of all. Versions of the White Stag episode appear in the *Second Continuation*, the *Didot Perceval*, and *Durmart le Galois*, but it is a striking parallel in the *Perlesvaus* which lends support to our hypothesis. In the latter romance, the hero is recognized by a white stag painted on his shield, plainly an allusion to the episode as told in the *Second Continuation*.[4]

While Ider's shield in Chrétien's *Charrete* would appear to be a reference, then, to the White Stag episode in the same author's *Erec*, the peculiar attitude of the stag issuing from a gate is strangely identical with the arms associated with Ireland since the end of the thirteenth century.[5] A ray of light suggesting the possible reason why the stag is depicted as issuing from a gate in the latter tradition is shed by this allusion in Chrétien, but the evidence is, of course, more tantalizing than conclusive.

---

[1] Bouly de Lesdain, p. 221.   [2] Adam-Even, '*Roman de Troie*', p. 28.

[3] On this episode, see R. Harris, 'The White Stag in Chrétien's *Erec et Enide*', *FS*, x (1956), 55–61.

[4] *Perlesvaus*, ii. 224, 231, notes to lines 510, 627. Cf., on the other hand, King Yder's banner (white with red stripes) in *Lancelot propre*, iii. 413. In the fifteenth- and sixteenth-century Arthurian rolls, King Yder bears *gules, three lions' heads or armed and langued sable*.

[5] See S. M. Collins, 'Some English, Scottish, Welsh and Irish Arms in Medieval Continental Rolls', *Antiquaries Journal*, xxi (1941), 209–10. Add Paris, Bibliothèque nationale, f. fr. 18651, fol. 103 recto, and Paris, Bibliothèque de l'Arsenal, MS. 5027, fol. 190 recto: 'Roy Belsors d'Irlande', *azure, a stag gules issuing from a gate argent*.

(10) PLAIN ARMS[1]

Though no rule of heraldry forbids it, few historical personages have borne plain arms, i.e. a shield consisting of a single tincture.[2] The rarity of this practice has, as a matter of fact, resulted in distinctive armorial bearings in the few recorded instances of plain arms. In the thirteenth century, Robert de Beauchamp, Hugh de Ferrers, and Robert de la Ward bore vair, vairy gold and gules, and vairy argent and sable respectively, while Amanieu d'Albret, a relative of King Edward I of England, carried a shield of plain gules.[3] Surely the most celebrated case, however, is that of Brittany whose arms since the fourteenth century have been plain ermine.

Before providing an explanation of the origin of the latter coat of arms which, as we shall see, is related to the Tristan legend, it is well to note that plain arms are frequently found in Old French literature. The *Song of Roland*, which antedates the first examples of true heraldry, mentions shields of plain gules and plain argent: 'L'escut vermeill li freint, de col li portet';[4] 'Cuntre le coer li fruisset l'escut blanc'.[5] Numerous other early epics and romances cite shields of a single tincture, notably gold, silver, red, and green, with no apparent significance being attached to this.[6] Modern scholars are very prone to reading symbolism into any use of colour in literature, but such is certainly not the case in the vast majority of instances of plain arms in Old French literature. Since we know that shields of a single tincture were a rarity in actual practice from the beginning of heraldry, the literary use of plain arms merely served in most cases to create an atmosphere suggesting a time long since past and the opulence and splendour of the universe of epic and romance. A valuable clue in this connection is provided by Geoffrey of Monmouth, writing at the dawn of heraldry (*c.* 1136). Wishing to extol the virtues of the Arthurian age, the author of the *Historia Regum Britanniae* states that in those days knights worthy of the name wore clothing and bore arms of a single colour, implying

---

[1] This section and the one following the next are a revised form of an article entitled 'The Use of Plain Arms in Arthurian Literature and the Origin of the Arms of Brittany', *BBSIA*, xviii (1966), 117–23.

[2] Not to be confused with *armes pleines* 'undifferenced arms' borne only by the chief of the line; see Robert Gayre, *Heraldic Cadency* (London, 1961), p. 19. On the confusion between *armes plaines* and *armes pleines*, consult Mathieu, p. 99 n. 2.

[3] *B* 95: 'Robert de Beauchamp, de vairree'; 139: 'Hughe de Ferrers, vairré de argent et d'azur'; *D* 154: 'Munsire Robert de la Warde, l'escu verré d'argent et de sable'; *K*, vv. 261–2: 'Mes Eumenions de la Brette / La baner ot tout rougette.' On the latter arms, see below, p. 54 n. 4.   [4] *Roland*, v. 1619.   [5] *Roland*, v. 3465.

[6] On the numerous epic formulas involving plain arms to express the idea of a blow received on the shield or the result of such a blow, consult Rychner, pp. 143–6.

no doubt that twelfth-century heraldic ornamentation contained an element of pretence: 'Quicumque vero famosus probitate miles in eadem erat, unius coloris vestibus atque armis utebatur.'[1]

Chrétien de Troyes, however, introduced a second use of plain arms in his *Cligés*. The hero of this Arthurian romance, wishing to remain incognito at the Tournament of Osenefort (Oxford), enters the lists on three successive days bearing first plain black, then plain green, and finally plain red arms, defeating in turn Sagremor, Lancelot, and Perceval.[2] A variation on this theme is found in Chrétien's *Charrete* at the Tournament of Noauz, i.e. in the same passage as the one noted above containing the allusive arms of King Ider. In this famous episode, Lancelot obeys Guenevere's command first to play the coward, then, on the following day, to do his best. As we have seen, other less celebrated knights at the tournament carry shields charged with various devices. Lancelot, however, wishing to remain incognito, bears plain red arms.[3] Plain arms thereafter become a favourite device in Arthurian literature used whenever an author needs to disguise a character or involve him in a case of mistaken identity.[4]

Finally, in Chrétien's last romance, Perceval defeats the Red Knight in an early encounter and thereafter carries the latter's plain red shield, arms which are associated with Perceval throughout the Middle Ages.[5] Since the latter was regarded as *nice* ('simple-minded') and uncouth when he acquired these arms, a greenness he was to lose thanks to Gornemant de Gohort's tutoring, this is probably the reason why thirteenth-century Arthurian romances frequently ascribe plain arms to unproven knights (*chevaliers nouveaus*).[6]

[1] Faral, iii. 246.

[2] *Cligés*, vv. 4543–833. On the fourth day, Cligés, bearing the plain white arms given to him earlier (v. 3988) by his uncle Alis, Emperor of Constantinople, fights Gawain to a draw (vv. 4855–927). See Haidu, pp. 88–9, Ménard, p. 631. In a typical imitation of this motif, Arthur in a three-day tournament in *Perlesvaus* appears first as a Golden Knight (p. 289), then as a Blue Knight (p. 292), and finally as a Red Knight (line 6943).

[3] *Charrete*, vv. 5575–6058. Lancelot's red shield belongs to Meleagant who holds him imprisoned; the latter's wife allows him to leave the prison upon his word that he will return after the tournament and she lets him borrow her husband's armour and steed (vv. 5498–501). For this reason and for the one outlined below in the section entitled 'Black Knights, Green Knights, Red Knights, etc.', I do not believe that Lancelot's red arms in this romance have the significance attached to them by Loomis, *Arthurian Tradition*, pp. 192, 194.

[4] Thus in the *Didot Perceval*, pp. 145–8, Perceval bears red arms sent to him as a disguise by Gawain's sister Elaine; and Kay, in *Lancelot propre*, v. 315, is mistaken for Lancelot when he arrives at court with the latter's red arms. On the recurrence of this motif, see *Cligés*, p. xvi, and, especially, *Arthurian Literature in the Middle Ages. A Collaborative History*, ed. R. S. Loomis (Oxford, 1959), p. 358 (includes bibliography, note 2) and Ménard, pp. 343–5.

[5] See below, section entitled 'Arthurian Heraldry'; p. 48; and also p. 33 n. 2.

[6] e.g. *Lancelot propre*, iii. 299 (Gawain borrows Helain de Taningues's shield): 'et li escus ous blans comme nois si comme a chel tans estoit coustume que chevaliers noviax portoit

(11) BLACK KNIGHTS, GREEN KNIGHTS, RED KNIGHTS, ETC.

We have stated that no symbolism is involved in most instances of plain arms in Old French literature. One of the most important literary uses of such shields, however, remains to be commented upon, for Black Knights, Green Knights, Red Knights, etc., are forever emerging from the forest to challenge the heroes of Arthurian romances. These mysterious adversaries are often evil-doers and the urge to give sinister connotations to their arms is well-nigh irresistible. On the other hand, when the knights turn out to be friends or relatives, the tendency is to turn to Celtic myth or Christian ritual for an appropriate interpretation. Some of these views are no doubt valid, but, unquestionably, many of the tinctures were simply chosen at random. A comprehensive study of these arms is very much needed. Meanwhile, the following sampling will serve to give an idea of the scope and complexity of the problem.

1. *Black Knights*

Cligés, vv. 4677, 4706.

Tristan de Béroul, vv. 3999–4004 (Tristan); vv. 4015–16 (li Noirs de la Montaigne = Tristan); his companion, Governal, is the Vair Knight in v. 4017.

Didot Perceval, p. 173.

Perlesvaus, pp. 38–40, 55.

Lancelot propre, iii. 181 (Exiles); 231 (Meliadus); 283 (unidentified knight); 283, 290 n. 2, 316 (Lancelot); v. 87 (Lancelot, but his shield is *sable, a lion rampant argent* here); 89 (Terican); 212 (Hector is a White Knight but he carries a black shield); 231 (Lancelot); 237, 286 (Bohort); 253 (Belias le Noir); 263 (Briade, the latter's brother); 286 (Hector), 294, 306 (unidentified knight).

Mort Artu, p. 63 (Lancelot).

West, s.v. 'Noir Chevalier, le', lists six different knights by that name in addition to those cited here. In the Matthew Paris Shields, plain sable, dimidiated by England, constitutes the arms of Henry the young

escu d'un seul taint le premier an que il l'estoit'; Löseth, *Le Roman en prose de Tristan*, p. 98: 'mais Tristan, à cause de son écu d'un seul taint, est pris pour un chevalier nouveau'; see also p. 100 (Tristan and Persides, wearing plain arms, are taken for new knights); *Mort Artu*, p. 8 (Lancelot takes the plain red shield of a new knight in order to disguise himself); *Escanor*, vv. 3482–3: 'Kez ot unes armes vermeilles / Simples, con chevaliers nouviauz'. In the latter romance, vv. 3755–63, Girart d'Amiens goes on to explain that in those days it was the custom for new knights to bear plain arms 'de vermeil, / De noir ou de tel apareil / Qu'en plaines armes doit avoir' the first year. For other plain arms ('tables d'attente'), see *Tournoiement des Dames de Paris*, vv. 214–18 (*plain sable*), 271 (*plain gules*), 1576–7 (*plain or*). At times the expression has ironic overtones; see Ménard, pp. 579–80.

King, no doubt as a sign of mourning.[1] In the fourteenth century, Sir Thomas Holand bore plain sable (see below) and, of course, Edward, Prince of Wales (1330–76), was known as the Black Prince, though the reason for this is obscure (see, however, Boutell, p. 164).

2. *Blue Knights*

Erec, v. 2130 (Randuraz, 'Filz la Vielle de Tergalo' [v. 2129]).
Fouque de Candie, v. 10404 (Girart de Comarcis).
Perlesvaus, pp. 207–8.

Froissart is the author of a 'Dit dou Bleu Chevalier' (1361–7); see *Œuvres de Froissart. Poésies*, ed. Auguste Scheler, i (Brussels, 1870), 348–62; Normand R. Cartier, 'Le Bleu Chevalier', *Romania*, lxxxvii (1966), 289–314.

3. *Green Knights*

Troie, v. 7878.
Cligés, v. 4715.
Fouque de Candie, v. 10407 (Guischart).
Durmart, vv. 10000–5 (Gladoin le Vert).
Perlesvaus, p. 126 (he is said to bear the same arms as his brother Gladoin; on p. 301, Lancelot bears a green shield as a sign of love for the Green Knight).

A good deal more has been written about the Green Knight than any other such character because of the importance of the Middle English romance *Gawain and the Green Knight*. On the Old French sources of the Green Knight theme, consult Nitze's note in *Perlesvaus*, ii. 281. Brutus Green Shield (*Brutus Viride Scutum*; in Wace's *Brut: Brutus Vert Escu*) is the name of a fictitious king of England in Geoffrey of Monmouth. In the fifteenth-century Arthurian rolls, it is King Meliadus who bears a plain green shield. Plain green is ascribed to Gawain's mother, on the other hand, in Strangways' Book (*c.* 1454); see London, 'Some Medieval Treatises', pp. 181–2. As for the association of green with Wales, see Major Francis Jones, 'The Colours of Wales', *Coat of Arms*, vi (1960), 141–4.

4. *Motley Knights*

Perlesvaus, p. 79.
Lancelot propre, iii. 407 (Gawain bearing the shield of Galain); iv. 186 (Meloos de Lambale); 264 (Bohort); v. 431 (Appendix) (Bohort).

---

[1] *Aspilogia II*, p. 59, items 11, 13; see also p. 8.

Vulgate Merlin Sequel, p. 195 (King Urien's household); p. 404 (Merlin).

Artus, p. 7 (Galesguinan's army); p. 13 (Arthur); p. 62 (Madoc le Noir and his nephew Plares).

5. *Red Knights*

Thèbes, v. 5033 (Amphiaraüs).

Troie, v. 7998 (Dolon).[1]

Erec, v. 5849 (Mabonagrain).

Cligés, v. 4816.

Perceval, vv. 871-2 (Red Knight of the Forest of Quinqueroi).

Fouque de Candie, vv. 9949, 9981 (Povre Veü).

Perlesvaus, p. 43 (Red Knight); p. 356 (Red Knight of the Deep Forest).

Didot Perceval, p. 145 (arms sent to Perceval by Elaine, Gawain's sister); p. 158 (Orguelleus de le Lande).

Lancelot propre, iii. 319 (unidentified knight); iv. 226, 281 (Argondras le Rous); 283 (Atramant le Gros); 308 (unidentified knight); 337 (Hector); 351 (Marigart le Rous); v. 100 (Gawain); 171, 218 (Lancelot); 185 (Bohort); 201 (Mauduit the Giant); 286 (Lancelot).

Vulgate Merlin Sequel, p. 374 (Belias).

Artus, p. 61 (Raolais); p. 166 (Oriol the Dane); p. 293 (Kaol Sans Douceur).

Atre périlleux, v. 1517 (Gawain); v. 5124 (Perceval); v. 6017 (Gawain).

Joufroi, vv. 901, 991, 1060.

Partonopeu, v. 7803 (Gaudin le Bloi).

Red shields are also found in *Roland*, v. 1619 and *Couronnement de Louis*, v. 411 (William) and v. 911 (Corsolt). Plainly one of the most popular figures in Arthurian literature (see Nitze, *Perlesvaus*, ii. 167–8, 221–4; West, s.v. 'Chevalier Vermeil, le' and 'Chevalier Vermel, le'), the Red Knight also makes an appearance in *Alice in Wonderland* (he fights the White Knight) and may even be said to be the ancestor, in a manner of speaking, of Germany's First World War ace, the Red Baron (Manfred von Richtofen).[2]

---

[1] Adam-Even, '*Roman de Troie*', p. 26: 'ce qui laisse supposer que même les fils de grands dynastes ne pouvaient alors user d'armoiries qu'après avoir été investis d'un fief les plaçant à la tête d'un contingent important et explique l'usage, par de nombreux jeunes gens, d'écus seulement unis, ainsi qu'il sera signalé longtemps encore par la littérature du xiiie siècle.'

[2] Among the many symbolic interpretations of the Red Knight's arms, I note that suggested by Loomis, *Arthurian Tradition*, p. 165, and the completely different proposal by Bayrav, pp. 173–4, 209, 211. For a historical Red Knight (Amanieu d'Albret), see p. 29 n. 3 and p. 54 n. 4.

6. White Knights

Cligés, v. 4899; cf. also v. 1146 (Alixandre).

Fouque de Candie, vv. 2320, 10527 (Fouque).

Perlesvaus, p. 43; p. 154 (Meliot de Logres); as of line 4549, the hero himself.

Gerbert's Continuation, v. 1139 (Gaudin au Blanc Escu); v. 4183 (Gosengos).

Didot Perceval, p. 231 (Gawain); Appendix B, p. 310 (Perceval).

Lancelot propre, iii. 118 (Lancelot); 362 (Gawain); iv. 215, 271 (Bohort); 233 (Hector and Lionel); 279 (Lancelot); 359 (unidentified knight); v. 97 (Galehodin); 100 (Lancelot); 173 (Gawain and Bohort); 184 (Lancelot); 212 (Hector, but his shield is black here); 286 (Mordred); 307 (unidentified knight); 319 (Brumant); 393 (Bliant); 427 (Appendix) (Bohort, but his shield is *argent, a lion rampant gules* here).

Queste, p. 29.

Estoire, p. 62.

Partonopeu, v. 7743 (Partonopeu).

See also West, s.v. 'Blanc Chevalier, le' and 'Blans Chevaliers, li'. The most celebrated White Knight, of course, is Lancelot who receives his white armour and white horse from the Lady of the Lake in the *Lancelot propre*, iii. 118.[1] His traditional arms, however, are quite different (see the section below on 'Arthurian Heraldry'). A white shield is mentioned in *Roland*, v. 3465, but the most intriguing prototype of the White Knights of literary tradition is to be found in the narratives of the First Crusade. On 20 June 1098 the Crusaders were greatly assisted in their battle against Kerboga before the city of Antioch by a vision of St. George, St. Demetrius, and St. Mercurius, wearing white armour and riding white horses, accompanied by an army of white knights.[2] The phantom cavalry made another appearance at the Battle of Montgisard against Saladin on 25 November 1177.[3] These incidents caused a great sensation and are

---

[1] Lot, *Etude sur le Lancelot en prose*, p. 167: 'Même dans le détail l'influence du [*Lanzelet*] se fait sentir à chaque instant. Le récit du départ de Lancelot tout vêtu de blanc pour la cour d'Arthur lui est emprunté pour le fonds.' For this and other symbolism of the arms in *Lancelot propre*, see Lot, pp. 97–9, Bayrav, p. 211.

[2] Setton, i. 323; Paul Deschamps and Marc Thibout, *La Peinture murale en France. Le Haut Moyen Age et l'époque romane* (Paris, 1951), pp. 124–5; Sumberg, p. 336.

[3] Deschamps–Thibout, p. 125 n. 3. For similar visions in the course of earlier campaigns against the Moslems in Spain, see P. Boissonnade, *Du nouveau sur la Chanson de Roland* (Paris, 1923), pp. 37, 284, 288 (and n. 1); Réau, iii². 693; Barton Sholod, *Charlemagne in Spain: the Cultural Legacy of Roncesvalles* (Geneva, 1966), p. 69.

depicted in a number of Romanesque murals which have survived.[1] These show White Knights battling Red Knights, the latter representing Saracens. In the late-twelfth-century romance *Robert le Diable* (ed. E. Löseth [Paris, 1903] [*Société des Anciens Textes Français*]), vv. 1788 ff., a celestial messenger appears in the guise of a White Knight and triumphs over the Turks on three occasions. Robert himself wears these arms and the Seneschal disguises himself in the same way, vv. 4127 ff. In the first half of the fourteenth century, Jean de Condé is the author of 'Li Lays dou Blanc Chevalier'; see *Dits et Contes de Baudouin de Condé et de son fils Jean de Condé*, ed. Auguste Scheler, ii (Brussels, 1866), 1–48.

7. *Yellow (or Golden) Knights*

Erec, v. 3603 (Galoain).

Perceval, v. 4106 (Arthur wishes to give Perceval 'Unes armes totes dorees', but the latter prefers to keep instead the arms of his vanquished foe, the Red Knight).

Durmart, v. 1821 (Grant Chevalier).

Perlesvaus, p. 191 (Perlesvaus), p. 289 (Arthur), p. 294 (Gawain).

In the fifteenth-century Arthurian rolls of arms, plain or is borne by Guiron le Courtois. These arms are attested in the prose romance dated *c.* 1235 which bears this character's name (see Lathuillère, pp. 240 [listed here s.v. SANS AUTRE TAINT], 495).

Quite frequently in Arthurian romances, the character's name suggests plain arms of a certain tincture to the writer, or vice versa. To add to our sampling, we examined the first three letters of Flutre's *Table des noms propres* and found that of the 43 knights whose name involved a colour (e.g. Alain le Blanc, Brunor le Noir, Caulas le Roux) nearly three out of four were either 'the Red' or 'the Black'. The figures are as follows: Red 16, Black 13, Blue 5, Yellow 4, White 3, Green 2.

(12) THE ARMS OF BRITTANY

Round Tables and other imitations of Arthurian romances were the height of fashion in the thirteenth century and for a long time afterward.[2] Evidence that plain arms were actually used by historical

---

[1] Deschamps–Thibout, pp. 124–6. St. Theodore was also at times represented as a White Knight in medieval art; Réau, i. 309. See also below, s.v. CIGNE (the Swan Knight).

[2] See R. S. Loomis, 'Arthurian Influence on Sport and Spectacle', in *Arthurian Literature in the Middle Ages*, pp. 553–9. Add to the list of Round Tables provided by Loomis, p. 554, another mention in *TA*, v. 1145: 'A Bar, a la table roonde'.

personages is scant, but one well-documented instance lends support to the view that these literary conventions exerted a greater influence than is generally recognized. Sir Thomas Holand (1320–60), who between the years 1341 and 1343 bore the Holand family arms (*azure fleuretty a leopard rampant argent*), later abandoned these for a plain black shield, as attested by his armorial seals dated 1354 and 1357 and by the Antiquaries' Roll, no. 106 (*c.* 1360). Blair, p. 10, who cites this interesting case, conjectures quite plausibly: 'perhaps it was in imitation of the "unknown knight" of medieval romance, or perhaps it was a "tournament" shield'.

We may safely assume considerable familiarity with these conventions and other Arthuriana on the part of the Dukes of Brittany, three of whom were named Arthur,[1] for Brittany was the locale for many of the Arthurian stories. Throughout the thirteenth century, the Dukes bore variations on the checky or and azure coat of arms of the Dreux family.[2] John of Brittany, nephew of Edward I, served his uncle at Falkirk and Caerlaverock and bore these arms differenced by a bordure gules charged with golden leopards (for England) and a canton ermine.[3] His father[4] was succeeded by Arthur II who bore the bordure engrailed. When the latter died in 1312, his son, John III, became Duke and saw fit to abandon the Dreux family arms in favour of the distinctive coat which has remained to this day the arms of Brittany.

It has long been assumed that the plain ermine was derived from the canton ermine of John III's arms. It appears much more likely, however, that a pun was intended and that plain ermine constitutes canting arms for *Ermenie*, Tristan's legendary homeland and one of the names for Brittany in Old French and Middle English literature.[5]

An interesting parallel may be seen in the late-thirteenth-century Camden and Heralds' Rolls.[6] The arms of Lesser Armenia, a kingdom

---

[1] Arthur I (1187–1203), Arthur II (1262–1312), Arthur III (1393–1458).

[2] Prinet WR, pp. 227–8; *Aspilogia II*, p. 172.

[3] *H* 51: 'Sʳ John de Bretaigne porte eschekeré d'or et d'azure ou le cantell d'ermyne ou la bordure de gulez poudré ou leopars d'or'; *K*, vv. 245–8: 'Baniere avoit cointe e paree, / De or e de asur eschequeré, / A rouge ourle o jaunes lupars, / De ermine estoit la quart pars.'

[4] John II, Duke of Brittany, 1286–1305; *WB* 922.

[5] Flutre, p. 251, s.v. *Hermanie*; Robert W. Ackerman, *An Index of Arthurian Names in Middle English* (Stanford–London, 1952), p. 83, s.v. *Ermonie*. The discussions concerning the ultimate origin of this place-name, which may be primitively insular, in no way alter the fact that in the twelfth and thirteenth centuries, *Ermenie*, when used in a literary context, meant Brittany or a port in Brittany. See Ernst Brugger, 'Almain and Ermonie as Tristan's Home', *Modern Philology*, xxv (1928), 269–90. Cf. ORLURE DE L'ENCHAMPURE A ROSES, *Note*.

[6] On the Arthurian aspect of the latter roll, see Denholm-Young, *History and Heraldry*, pp. 45–54.

whose name is homonymic with Tristan's homeland in Old French and Middle English,[1] regularly feature a lion rampant in contemporary rolls of arms.[2] The Camden Roll, however, substitutes a field of ermine as the distinctive characteristic, a trait also found in the identical blazon of the Heralds' Roll.[3] The author of this substitution was no doubt influenced by the name *Ermenie* 'Lesser Armenia' just as the originator of the modern arms for Brittany (plain ermine) had in mind the other *Ermenie* of literary tradition.

(13) ARTHURIAN HERALDRY

In 1944, Edouard Sandoz published an edition of a fifteenth-century treatise on Arthurian tournaments which is followed in certain manuscripts by an illustrated list of the coats of arms of one hundred and fifty—in other manuscripts by as many as one hundred and seventy-five—knights of the Round Table.[4] Scholars have tended to assume that this fifteenth-century tradition provides the only consistent Arthurian roll of arms. There was, however, an earlier and distinct phase to Arthurian heraldry which is represented in three main sources: *Durmart, Escanor,* and certain manuscripts of the *Second Continuation.*

Sometime after the year 1200, an anonymous author wrote the Arthurian romance entitled *Durmart le Galois.*[5] It tells the story of Durmart, the son of Jozefent, King of Wales and Denmark, the monarch also being Arthur's cousin. After falling in love with the young wife of his father's seneschal, Durmart decides to mend his ways and search for the ideal bride. She is Fenise, Queen of Ireland, whom he finds and weds in a manner strongly reminiscent of the White Stag episode in the *Second Continuation.* The tale, then, is the familiar Bride Quest with

[1] Flutre, p. 198, s.v. *Armenie*; Ackerman, p. 83, s.v. *Ermonye*; West, p. 56, s.v. *Ermenie*.

[2] *C* 14: 'Le roy d'Ermeny, un leon rampant gulez un border gulez indentee'; *WB* 1269: 'le roy d'Ermenie' (the painted shield shows *a lion rampant gules on a field of gold*); *G* 140: 'Rey de Ermenye' (the painted shield is *azure, a lion rampant argent*).

[3] *D* 14: 'Le rey de Ermenie, l'escu de ermine a une croiz de goules, od une corone d'or'; *HE* 15: 'Le roy d'Ermenie' (the painted shield is *ermine, on a cross gules, a crown or*). Denholm-Young, *History and Heraldry*, p. 48: 'The coat of arms of the King of Armenia [in the Heralds' Roll] reminds us that his envoys were received on 28 May 1277 and Tartar envoys at Easter.' Same remark, p. 63, apropos of the same arms in the Camden Roll.

[4] 'Tourneys in the Arthurian Tradition', *Speculum*, xix (1944), 389–420; see also Harold Bowditch, 'Another Printed Version of the Arms of the Knights of the Round Table', *Speculum*, xxi (1946), 490–92. Mr. Michael Maclagan, Slains Pursuivant, kindly allowed me to read the manuscript of an unpublished paper on 'Arthurian Heraldry', dealing in particular with fifteenth-century coats of arms.

[5] *Durmart le Galois. Roman arthurien du treizième siècle.* Publié par Joseph Gildea, O.S.A. (Villanova, Pa.). Tome I, *Texte*, 1965. Tome II, *Etude*, 1966. See my review in *RR*, lx (1969), 54–7.

moralistic overtones and the author probably drew most of his material from Chrétien de Troyes's *Perceval* and its first two *Continuations*.

We have already noted (in the section entitled 'Heraldic Flattery') the evident connection between the arms of King Jozefent and his son and the Royal Arms of England on the one hand, and between the coat borne by the Roi des Isles and the arms known as France Ancient. As a matter of fact, heraldry is used extensively throughout *Durmart le Galois*. Several family relationships are indicated by differencing, e.g. the Roi des Mores (*or semy of eaglets azure*; vv. 7731–2) and his two nephews Cardroin (*gules, an eagle argent*; v. 2348) and Brun de Morois (*gules, an eagle or*; vv. 4666–7). It is the arms of the sons of King Loth, viz. Gawain and his brothers, which interest us most here, however.

Gawain's arms (*argent, a canton gules*; v. 8409) are related by tincture to those of his brothers Guerehet (*argent semy of eaglets gules*; v. 8415) and Agravain (*argent, a lion rampant gules and a peacock's tail* [*position not indicated*]; vv. 8483–4). Mordret le Petit, Gawain's half-brother, is dressed in red samite interwoven with an ornamental silver design (vv. 8418–19), evidently participating in the same heraldic tradition. On the other hand, the arms attributed to Gawain's other brother Gaheriet (*plain ermine*; v. 8413) constitute a jarring note. The problem here is not the identity of Gaheriet's arms with those of Brittany—the latter, as we have seen, only appear in the fourteenth century—but rather the lack of any connection with his brothers' arms. Other coats in *Durmart* will interest us, but in order to elucidate the matter of Gaheriet's arms, we shall proceed immediately to a consideration of the Arthurian lists in *Escanor* and the *Second Continuation*.

Girart d'Amiens, the author of the romance *Meliacin* (or *Cheval de fust*) and the lengthy epic *Charlemagne*, neither of which has ever been published, dedicated his Arthurian romance *Escanor* to Eleanor of Castile, wife of King Edward I of England. There are twenty-one coats of arms described by Girart as worn by the participants in the tournament before *Bauborc* (Bamborough in Northumberland) for the hand of Andrivete. The arms attributed to the King of Scotland and to the King of Wales correspond to the historical arms of King Alexander III of Scotland and Llywelyn ap Gruffydd, Prince of Wales, and the fact that the latter is shown in a favourable light means that Girart's romance was composed about 1280 during the brief period when the rebel prince enjoyed singular favour at the court of Edward I.[1]

---

[1] See Brault, 'Arthurian Heraldry', pp. 6–8; cf. also above, s.v. 'Heraldic Flattery', and

In *Escanor*, the arms of King Loth's progeny are blazoned as follows: Gawain, *argent, a canton gules*;[1] Guerehet, *argent, three eaglets gules* (vv. 4954–7); Agravain, *argent, three lioncels rampant gules* (vv. 5001–5); and Gaheriet, *argent, a canton gules semy of eaglets argent* (vv. 5218–20, 5578–80). The correspondence between these arms in *Escanor* and *Durmart* is great enough to enable us to correct Gaheriet's coat in the latter romance since the blazon in Girart's poem is obviously more consistent with that of the knight's brothers. The error in *Durmart* becomes apparent when we note that plain ermine is ascribed to the Lait Hardi in *Escanor*, vv. 3568–71. The correctness of the arms for Gawain and his brothers in Girart d'Amiens is further confirmed by the roll in the *Second Continuation*.

Chrétien's *Perceval* (or *Conte del Graal*), begun about 1180 or 1181, was never finished by him. Four lengthy continuations were composed before 1230 and it is the second one of these, as yet unavailable in a modern edition, which interests us here.[2] The Arthurian roll of arms does not appear in all the manuscripts of the *Second Continuation* and would seem to be a later interpolation, probably second half of the thirteenth century, the date of the manuscripts in question. There are

below, s.v. 'History, Heraldry, and Literature'. Heraldic flattery is surely involved in the case of 'le roi d'Escoce' and 'le roi de Gales'; is it also involved in the following arms in *Escanor* which are identical with contemporary historical coats (see also below, pp. 53–4)?

(1) De la Mare: *gules, a maunch argent* (E 579).

> Espinogre, vv. 4122–3:
> Et ot unes armes vermeilles
> A une mance toute blanche.

(2) Irthington: *gyronny or and sable* (E 88).

> Sagremor, vv. 4992–3:
> D'or et de seble gironnees
> Portoit li unz les armes plaines.

(3) Stuteville: *buruly argent and gules, a lion rampant sable* (*Aspilogia II*, p. 154, item 200).

> Hector des Mares, vv. 3598–600:
> Burelé d'argent et de geules
> R'aloit Hector l'escu portant
> Au noir demi lion rampant.

(4) Tony: *argent, a maunch gules* (*Aspilogia II*, p. 24, item 57).

> Gontier, v. 4929–3:
> Sour le blanc la mance vermeille.

(5) Turberville: *argent, a lion rampant gules* (F 35).

> Le Beau Mauvais, vv. 3966–7:
> Et portoit un escu d'argent
> A un lion rampant vermeil.

[1] Gawain's arms are not blazoned in *Escanor*, but may be inferred from the descriptions of his brothers' armorial bearings.

[2] I am indebted to Professor William Roach for the use of Xerox copies of his transcript of the manuscripts in question. The section containing the Arthurian roll of arms in the *Second Continuation* is missing in the manuscript used by Charles Potvin as the basis for his edition (*Perceval le Gallois ou le Conte du Graal publié d'après les manuscrits originaux*, 2e partie [Mons, 1866–71]). In MS. *K*, the passage is interpolated between Potvin, vv. 29164 and 29165; in MSS. *TV*, it occurs between 29354 and 29355. Professor Roach is preparing a new edition of the *Second Continuation*.

variations in the list found in the three copies of the interpolation, but all three include the arms of Gawain and his brothers Guerehet, Agravain, and Gaheriet. Their arms are blazoned as follows: Gawain, *argent, a canton gules*; Guerehet, *argent, three eaglets gules*; Agravain, *argent, two lions rampant gules*; Gaheriet, *argent, a canton gules semy of eaglets or*.

In the same roll of arms found in the *Second Continuation*, Giglain, Gawain's son, is said to bear *ermine, a canton gules*, a coat obviously patterned after Gawain's (*argent, a canton gules*). The latter arms for Gawain are further attested in Adenet le Roi's *Enfances Ogier*, vv. 5092–7, an epic composed in the decade before *Escanor*. In Adenet's poem, Gawain's coat is identical with that of his cousin Hoel of Nantes.[1]

Illustrators of medieval manuscripts were not always accurate in their depictions of the arms borne by literary characters and often decorated shields with purely conventional devices. On the other hand, many illustrations follow the text very closely and render armorial bearings with great precision whenever they are mentioned. Of even greater interest to us here, however, are the medieval manuscripts providing correct painted shields for Arthurian characters where the accompanying text offers absolutely no guidance in this regard. Such is the case for Gawain's arms (*argent, a canton gules*) in a number of illuminated manuscripts of the Prose Lancelot cycle. No mention of these particular arms has been found in any part of that vast compilation, yet this is the shield he carries in the following illustrations:

British Museum Add. MS. 10, 292, fols. 167 recto and 174 recto.

British Museum Add. MS. 10, 293, fols. 87 recto, 92 recto, 92 verso, 93 recto, 93 verso, 107 recto, 118 verso, 177 verso, 179 recto, 190 verso, 191 recto, 191 verso; also 95 recto, but here erroneously labelled 'Lancelot'.

British Museum Add. MS. 10, 294, fols. 29 verso and 55 verso; also 84 recto, but here the canton is fretty gules.

British Museum Royal E. 3, fols. 97 verso, 115 recto, 125 recto, 142 verso.

Paris, Bibliothèque nationale, fonds français 770, fol. 169 recto; in fols. 199 recto and 264 recto, the arms for Gawain are reversed, i.e. *gules, a canton argent*.

In the fifteenth- and sixteenth-century manuscripts providing the

---

[1] See Comte de Marsy, pp. 197–8, items 12 and 13. On Hoel, see Fletcher, p. 82; West, s.v. *Hoel* (includes bibliography). The hero of *Sone* also bears, on occasion (vv. 9045–6, 9152–3), *argent, a canton gules*; see above, however, p. 22 n. 3. Finally, two more characters are associated with these arms in *Meliador*; see Longnon, iii. 354, 357.

Arthurian roll of arms we have mentioned at the beginning of this section, Gawain bears *purpure, a double-headed eagle or, beaked and membered azure*, for example:[1]

Chantilly, MS. 642, fol. 4.

Paris, Bibliothèque nationale, fonds français 1435, fol. 30 recto.

Paris, Bibliothèque nationale, fonds français 1436, fols. 15 recto and 59 recto.

Paris, Bibliothèque nationale, fonds français 1437, fol. 54 recto.

Paris, Bibliothèque nationale, fonds français 1438, fols. 22 verso and 23 recto.

Paris, Bibliothèque nationale, fonds français 5233, fol. 3 verso.

Paris, Bibliothèque nationale, fonds français 5937, fol. 20 verso.

Paris, Bibliothèque nationale, fonds français 5939, fol. 14 recto.

Paris, Bibliothèque nationale, fonds français 12597, fol. 25 recto.

Paris, Bibliothèque nationale, fonds français 14357, fol. 20 verso.

On the other hand, a variant Arthurian roll of arms preserved in at least the two following sixteenth-century manuscripts maintains the older blazon for Gawain, i.e. *argent, a canton gules*:

Paris, Bibliothèque de l'Arsenal, MS. 5027, fol. 192 verso.

Paris, Bibliothèque nationale, fonds français 18651, fol. 105 recto.

As we shall see below, there is an explanation—a pun on the name or an allusion to some incident in prior literary tradition involving them—for the arms associated with many Arthurian heroes. What is the significance, then, of Gawain's older arms?

The first mention of Arthur's nephew is in William of Malmesbury, *De Gestis Regum Anglorum* (*c.* 1125).[2] Geoffrey of Monmouth added many new particulars to Gawain's biography including the fact that he was for a time during his youth in the care of Pope Sulpicius who gave him his arms: 'Erat tunc Walwanius, filius praedicti Loth, XII annorum

---

[1] See also Gawain's arms in the fifteenth-century illustration of the French school described by Loomis, *Arthurian Legends*, p. 107 (fig. 286). In a private communication to me dated 22 January 1959, Mlle Edith Brayer of the Institut de Recherche et d'Histoire des Textes in Paris informed me of the following other Arthurian rolls of arms, doubtless similar to, if not identical with, those I list above: Milan, Biblioteca Trivulziana 1395; Lille, Bibliothèque municipale 513; Paris, Bibliothèque nationale, fonds français 23,999. None of these manuscripts dates from before the fifteenth century. There were also printed versions of these rolls in the sixteenth century.

[2] *Willelmi Malmesbiriensis Monachi. De Gestis Regum Anglorum*, ed. William Stubbs, ii (London, 1889), 342 (para. 287). Gawain's name, or a variant thereof, begins appearing in cartularies about the year 1100, suggesting birth dates *c.* 1085–90; see Pierre Galais, 'Bleheri, la cour de Poitiers et la diffusion des récits arthuriens sur le continent', *Actes du VIIᵉ Congrès national de Littérature comparée (Poitiers, 1965)* (Paris, 1967), pp. 62–70, 75–9.

juvenis, obsequio Sulpicii papae ab avunculo traditus, a quo arma recepit.'[1] There are numerous descriptions of Gawain's arms in the early romances—in the majority of cases, there is no significant pattern to be seen in these shields charged with various devices or in the fact that they are plain arms—but none seem to allude to the papal gift, that is heraldically speaking.[2] In the *Perlesvaus*, on the other hand, Gawain is associated with Pope Gregory the Great[3] and he bears a shield blazoned as *gules, an eagle or* said to have belonged to Judas Maccabaeus.[3] He also appears as the Golden Knight, however (*li Chevalier as Armes d'Or*), in a later passage of the same work.[5] We note in passing, finally, Gawain's arms in the *Tournoiement Antecrit* where they are associated first with murder and cruelty (vv. 930–41), then with prowess and courtesy (vv. 1982–5).

Gawain inherited the Kingdom of Orcanie from his father King Loth,[6] but the arms of the Orkney Islands, which appear to be the source of this legendary place-name, feature a ship at least as early as the end of the thirteenth century (*WB* 1282). Our hero's strength reaches its peak at high noon but no allusion to this trait is made in his arms. In German heraldry, names ending in *-ecke* or *-eg* (e.g. *Hochenecke*) are often associated with a canton, G. *Ecke* 'corner' suggesting an obvious pun. No such play on words seems likely in Gawain's case.

A satisfactory explanation for Gawain's arms cannot be given at the present time. In the *First Continuation*, the Demoiselle de Lis sends her *ami* Gawain a pennant embroidered with her arms.[7] *Lis* implies white which is the colour of the arms borne by Gawain in the *Didot Perceval* (p. 231) and many other early romances. The canton may simply constitute differencing of one sort or another. These suggestions, we repeat, are mere conjectures. It is hoped that more light will someday be thrown on this vexing matter.

---

[1] Faral, iii. 239; *Brut*, ii, vv. 9853–8.

[2] On the papal gift of a pennant, see *La Chanson de Roland*, ed. T. Atkinson Jenkins (Boston–New York–Chicago–London, 1924), note to vv. 3093–5; see also above, p. 24.

[3] *Perlesvaus*, ii. 327, note to line 7300.

[4] *Perlesvaus*, lines 784–5, 1185–6, 1520–1; see Nitze's note to line 784 in ii. 234 (also discussion of the variant *angle* vs. *aigle* and of the allusion to the eagle).

[5] *Perlesvaus*, lines 6940–1.

[6] In a fifteenth-century roll listing 'Les armes du roy Gallhot et des .xxx. roys qu'il conquesta' (Paris, Bibliothèque nationale, fonds français 18651, fol. 103 recto), Loth d'Orcanie bears *argent, a canton gules* (in the other late Arthurian rolls, he always bears *purpure, a double-headed eagle or membered azure*), but these arms are obviously derived from those of Gawain.

[7] This passage is discussed and the complete references to the various versions of the episode are provided by Jean Frappier, 'Le personnage de Gauvain dans la *Première Continuation de Perceval (Conte du Graal)*', *RPh.*, xi (1957–8), 336–7. Cf. Tristan, p. 20 n. 1 above.

Meanwhile, another early shield ascribed to Gawain is worthy of special note. In the Heralds' Roll (*c.* 1270–80), which Professor Denholm-Young fittingly refers to as the Eleanor Roll of Arms because it is the only roll featuring ladies and because Eleanor of Castile's Spanish parents figure in it, a shield *sable fretty or* is captioned 'Sire Gawyn Mautrevers' (*HE* 60). Wagner (*CEMRA*, pp. 10, 11) and Denholm-Young (*History and Heraldry*, p. 52), having noted the fact that these arms are followed by two other shields belonging to fictitious characters (Roland and Sir Bevis), have identified the Gawain in *HE* 60 as the Gawain of Arthurian romance. This view is strongly supported by the recurrence of the same arms in the fourteenth-century *Dean Tract*, this time, however, linked to the name Gawain alone, without the surname.

The arms, nevertheless, are unquestionably those of the Mautravers or Maltravers family (*Aspilogia II*, p. 155, item 203: 'John Mautravers, noir fretté d'or'). According to an old theory, the Maltravers fretty constitutes canting arms representing 'something *hard to pass*'.[1] Was John Maltravers in some way associated with Gawain (his contemporaries, the members of the Tony family, fancied themselves descendants of the Swan Knight)? Or do the three fictitious names in the Heralds' Roll furnish us with some sort of a record of a Round Table at which one of the Maltravers masqueraded as Gawain? We know that Edward I was a great Arthurian enthusiast[2] and that Round Tables at which high-placed persons played the part of Arthurian knights were held in 1279, 1281, 1284, 1287, 1299, and 1302 at the very least during this period. I know of no member of the Maltravers family named Gawain but a relative, Marmaduke de Thweng (*c.* 1282), had a son who bore that name.[3]

Having established the fact that a thirteenth-century tradition did exist for the arms of Gawain and his brothers, we may now pass in review the arms associated with a number of other Arthurian characters during this period.

---

[1] C. W. Scott-Giles, *The Romance of Heraldry* (London and Toronto, 1929), p. 5; *Aspilogia II*, p. 108.

[2] See above, p. 22 n. 4 and p. 35 n. 2.

[3] *Complete Peerage*, xii (London, 1953), 739, note *b*. John Maltravers married Agnes Nereford of Leicestershire; her arms show the Thweng parrots. The bibliography relative to Gawain's shield in the Middle English *Gawain and the Green Knight* is very extensive. Recent items include Robert W. Ackerman, 'Gawain's Shield: Penitential Doctrine in *Gawain and the Green Knight*', *Anglia*, lxxvi (1958), 254–65; Richard H. Green, 'Gawain's Shield and the Quest for Perfection', *English Literary History*, xxix (1962), 121–39; and Donald R. Howard, 'Structure and Symmetry in *Sir Gawain*', *Speculum*, xxxix (1964), 425–33. Finally, the double-headed eagle on Gawain's shield in the fifteenth-century Arthurian rolls suggests a connection with the emblem of the Holy Roman Empire.

We have already mentioned three heraldic devices connected with King Arthur himself, viz. leopards (see 'Heraldic Flattery'), a dragon, and the Virgin (see 'Canting and Symbolic Arms'). In the second half of the thirteenth century, a fourth and by far the most widely-attested coat of arms for Arthur appeared: *azure, three crowns or*. We find these arms, for example, with occasional variations in tincture and in the number and position of the crowns, in the following illuminations of early manuscripts of the Prose Lancelot cycle:

British Museum Add. MS. 10, 292, fols. 102 recto (*azure, two crowns argent*), 170 recto (*azure, three crowns argent*), 170 verso (*azure, two crowns argent*).

British Museum Add. MS. 10, 294, fols. 73 recto (*gules, two crowns argent*), 75 verso (*azure, three crowns argent*), 76 recto (*azure, three crowns argent*) [Plate 2], 87 verso (*azure, four crowns argent*), 93 recto and 94 recto (*azure, two crowns argent*).

Paris, Bibliothèque nationale, fonds français 749, fols. 177 verso, 181 verso, 191 recto, 193 verso, 195 verso, 199 recto, 230 recto, 234 recto, 239 recto, 247 verso, 249 verso, 265 verso (in all these illustrations, Arthur's arms are *or, three crowns gules*).

Paris, Bibliothèque nationale, fonds français 770, fols. 208 verso (*gules, three crowns or*), 221 verso (*azure, three crowns argent*), 304 verso (*gules, three crowns argent*).

It is worth noting that these are the same manuscripts where we had found illustrations of Gawain's arms (*argent, a canton gules*) and that Arthur's coat, as in the case of his nephew's, has no textual basis.[1]

We do not know the origin of the triple-crown symbol for King Arthur. A number of relevant facts have been assembled, however, in prior investigations:

1. Identical arms are associated in English heraldic tradition with other pre-Norman kings, notably St. Edmund.[2]

---

[1] Cf. *Meliador*, vv. 28985–6: 'ses armes vermeilles / A .iii. couronnes d'or dessus'; Longnon's commentary is in iii. 354; see also A. H. Diverres, 'Froissart's *Meliador* and Edward III's Policy Towards Scotland', *Mélanges offerts à Rita Lejeune*, ii (Gembloux, 1969), 1408 n. 1. Illustrations of the three-crown device for Arthur are to be found in certain fifteenth-century Arthurian rolls only (cf. p. 46 n. 4 below): Paris, Bibliothèque nationale, fonds français 5233, fols. 3 recto and 20 recto; fonds français 5937, fol. 5 recto; Paris, Bibliothèque de l'Arsenal, MS. 5027, fol. 192 verso. A number of these illustrations are commented upon by Pickford, 'The Three Crowns of King Arthur'. See also John Bromley, 'Two Armorial Seal-Bags of the 14th Century', *Coat of Arms*, v (1959), 177–9.

[2] For St. Edmund, see Wagner, *Historic Heraldry*, p. 53. On the saints and their symbols in medieval heraldry, consult Max Prinet, 'Les caractéristiques des saints dans les armoiries familiales', *Revue de l'art chrétien*, lxii (1912), 417–26; H. S. London, 'Les armoiries de saint

PLATE 2

KING ARTHUR
London, British Museum, MS. Additional 10294, fol. 76

2. Three crowns were frequently an allusion to the Three Wise Men whose relics were brought by Frederick I Barbarossa from Milan to Cologne in 1164. Commemorating this event, three crowns are featured in the arms of the City of Cologne dating from the end of the thirteenth century as well as on the seal of the University of Cologne from 1392 onwards.[1]

3. The triple-crown device has been traced in Sweden to the seal of King Magnus Ladulås as early as 1275 and was introduced as the Swedish coat of arms by Albrecht of Mecklenburg in 1364.[2]

4. A legend relates that it was Helen of Colchester, spouse of the Roman Emperor Constantius and mother of Constantine the Great, who introduced the three-crown symbol to England.[3]

5. Edward I granted certain privileges to a number of towns and this fact is symbolized by the presence of three crowns in the arms of these localities.[4] Finally, royal patronage also probably accounts for the three crowns in the coat of arms of Oxford University[5] and on the seal of the King of Arms in England, beginning in 1276.[6]

Once adopted, at any rate, the triple-crown device lent itself readily to all sorts of symbolic interpretations. Matthew Paris had earlier provided the following inscription for the three crowns drawn as an illustration of his account of the death of Emperor Frederick II in 1250:

Josse et de quelques autres saints', *AHS* (1930), 3–8. See also London's letter to the editor calling for an 'Armorial of the Saints' in the *Coat of Arms*, iii (1955), 291–2, and the letter by John A. Goodall in iii (1955), 334–5. John P. Harthan in the *Coat of Arms*, iv (1956), 130, notes that there is a three-volume manuscript entitled 'Heraldry of the Saints' by George Arthur Bouvier in the Victoria and Albert Museum in London.

[1] The most exhaustive study of the three-crown device in European heraldry is that of Heribert Seitz, *De Tre Kronorna. Det Svenska Riksvapnet i Sitt Europeiska Sammanhang* (Stockholm, 1961). See also the latter's 'De Tre Kronorna. Symbolens Väg till Vårt Land', *Livrustkammaren (Journal of the Royal Armoury, Stockholm)*, viii (1959), 119–40 (English summary, pp. 141–4); 'Trekronorssymbolen Under 1300-Talet. Några Jämförande Iakttagelser', *Livrustkammaren*, viii (1960), 199–212 (English summary, pp. 213–14). In the English language, see Arvid Berghman, 'The Origin of the Three Crowns of Sweden', *Coat of Arms*, iii (1954), 7–10; C. G. V. Scheffer, 'The Coats of Arms of Sweden. Genesis and Development', *Coat of Arms*, viii (1965), 273–9. Cf. Adrian de Freston, 'The Three Kings of Cologne', *Coat of Arms*, viii (1965), 302.

[2] Seitz, 'De Tre Kronorna. Symbolens Väg till Vårt Land', pp. 122–6.

[3] John Whitehead, *Guardian of the Grail. A New Light on the Arthurian Legend* (London, 1959), pp. 256–66. For other saints associated with three crowns (Elizabeth of Hungary and Sophia), see Réau, iii³. 1509, and, especially, John A. Goodall, 'Heraldry and Iconography. A Study of the Arms Granted to the Drapers' Company of London', *Coat of Arms*, iv (1957), 171–83.

[4] C. W. Scott-Giles, *Civic Heraldry of England and Wales*, rev. ed. (London, 1953), pp. 403–6; Pickford, 'The Three Crowns of King Arthur'.

[5] Wagner, *Historic Heraldry*, p. 54 (includes bibliography); J. P. Brooke-Little, 'The Arms of Oxford University and its Colleges', *Coat of Arms*, i (1950), 158–61, 198–200, 235–8.

[6] Denholm-Young, *History and Heraldry*, p. 61. See also FLEUR DE LIS TOUT EN MILIEU, *Note*.

Triplici corona coronatur imperator Romanorum: Aurea ratione imperii
Romani quod quasi aurum toti mundo. Argentea, ratione Alemannie, quae
nummismata argentea ditatur, et habundat commerciis. Necnon est famosa,
unde vulgariter dicitur imperator Alemannie. Argenteum enim sonorum est.
Ferrea ratione Italie, quae armis et cominu urbibus roboratur ferrum nam-
que pro armis accipitur, scilicet materia pro materiato.[1]

Finally, in the north portico of the Cathedral of Chartres, a number of
shields representing the Virtues are sculptured in stone. One of them,
dating from the thirteenth century, features two crowns and is captioned LIBERTAS.

Arthur's three crowns were popularized in the numerous illustrations
of the Nine Worthies beginning with the *Voeux du paon*, a poem written
by Jacques de Longuyon about 1310.[2] Already by the end of the
thirteenth century, however, the number of crowns increases to
thirteen (and even thirty!),[3] symbolizing the kingdoms conquered by
Arthur.[4] It is interesting to note, finally, that crowns are featured in
a pennant belonging to Arthur's spouse, Queen Guenevere, in the
Lancelot propre (iii. 421): 'et le camp del pignon estoit d'aisur a .iii.
corones d'or et a une seule aigle et des corones tant que l'en i pooit
metre.'[5]

When the Lady of the Lake brings Lancelot to the court of King
Arthur in one of the early episodes of the *Lancelot propre*, she insists that
he wear her livery. She gives him a white horse, white armour, 'et escu
tout blanc comme noif a boucle d'argent moult bele'.[6] Arthur replies
that all his knights wear armour provided by him, but Yvain argues
that in this case it is more important to have this new recruit than to
stand on a principle. Arthur is convinced and Lancelot bears white
arms in his first adventures. Later, however, the damsel at the castle
called the Dolorous Garde, who turns out to be a friend of the Lady
of the Lake, shows Lancelot three magic shields. All are white, but the

---

[1] *Aspilogia II*, p. 34, item 96; John A. Goodall, 'Heraldry and Iconography', *Coat of Arms*,
iv (1957), 174.

[2] Loomis, *Arthurian Legends*, pp. 37–40; Göller, p. 261.

[3] British Museum, Royal MS. 20 A II, fol. 4 recto; Pickford, p. 377.

[4] Göller, p. 264. In addition to the illustrations of the thirteen-crown device for Arthur
cited by the latter, p. 264, n. 3, see also the following fifteenth-century Arthurian rolls
(cf. p. 44 n. 1 above): Paris, Bibliothèque nationale, fonds français 1435, fol. 2 verso; fonds
français 1436, fols. 15 recto and 33 recto; fonds français 1438, fol. 1 verso, fonds français
5937, fol. 14 recto; fonds français 14357, fol. 24 recto; Chantilly, MS. 642, fol. 1 recto. In
Paris, Bibliothèque nationale, fonds français 5937, fol. 20 verso, there are eleven crowns in
the painted shield as well as in the blazoned arms ('unze').

[5] Göller, p. 263, cites a similar passage from the French *Roman de Merlin* and the English
Merlin, or The Early History of King Arthur.

[6] iii. 118. See Lot, *Etude sur le Lancelot en prose*, p. 98 n. 4 and p. 167.

first, which has the power to impart to its owner the strength of one man, has a *single* bend; the second has *two* bends representing the power of two men; the third has *three* bends, for the strength of three men.[1] Henceforth, Lancelot's shield is blazoned *argent, three bends gules* more often than not in Old French literature and medieval art.[2] Like other characters in Arthurian romances, he will, of course, carry a variety of other shields, often as a disguise, but the three-bend device is associated with him with unusual regularity after this episode in the *Lancelot propre*. We are somewhat taken aback, then, to find Lancelot's correct arms in *Durmart le Galois*, vv. 8435–9, 8441 (*argent, three bends gules*), a romance believed to antedate the *Lancelot propre*. This suggests that the relative chronology of these works is in error or, more likely, that Lancelot's traditional arms—and the three-magic-shields motif from which they are derived—date back at least to about the year 1200. There is, finally, a possible hint connecting Lancelot and Guenevere in Galehot's shield ('l'escu d'or a corounes d'aisur') borne by Lancelot in *Lancelot propre*, iii. 402, when we recall the blue field and golden crowns of Guenevere's pennant (see preceding paragraph).

[1] iii. 147.

[2] These traditional arms for Lancelot appear in the following passages (at times, the variant shields are disguises): *Lancelot propre*, iii. 150 (*argent, a bend gules*), same page (*two bends*), 151 (*three bends*), 165 (*one bend*), 168 (*argent, two bends gules*), same page (*three bends*), 170 (*argent, three bends gules*), 174 (*three bends*), same page (*gules, a bend argent*), 192 (*argent, a bend sable*), 194 (*argent, a bend sable*), 259 (*argent, a bend* ['*bare . . . de bellic*'] *gules*), same page (*two bends gules, three bends gules*), 395 (*sable, a bend argent*), 407 (*sable, a bend argent*), 424 (*sable, a bend argent*); iv. 104 (var.) (*argent, a bend gules* [cf. below, p. 49 n. 3]); 133 (*argent, a bend sable*), 149 (*a bend argent*), 160 (*gules, a bend argent*), 220 (*gules, three bends argent*); *Mort Artu*, pp. 78 (*argent, three bends gules*), 97 (*argent, a bend*), 103 (*argent, a bend gules*). For Lancelot's symbolic shield in v. 403, see above, p. 25 n. 7. In the early manuscript illuminations, I note a similar heraldic tradition for Lancelot: British Museum, Add. MS. 10293, fols. 195 verso, 196 recto, 197 verso (*or, a bend sable*); fols. 200 recto, 205 verso, 206 recto, 280 recto, 288 verso, 322 verso, 337 recto, 338 recto, 342 recto and verso, 355 verso, 356 verso (*argent, three bends gules*); fol. 207 recto (*argent, three bends sable*); fol. 352 recto (*argent, a bend gules*); Add. MS. 10294 fols. 67 verso, 68 recto, 84 recto, 85 recto (*argent, four bends gules*); Royal 14 E. 3, fol. 156 verso (*argent, three bends gules*). Later illustrations include: Chantilly, MS. 645, frontispiece and fols. 210 recto, 222 recto, 236 recto (*argent, three bends gules*); MS. 646, fols. 13 verso, 39 verso, 59 recto, 128 recto (*argent, three bends gules*); MS. 647, frontispiece and fols. 119 recto, 150 verso, 204 recto (*argent, three bends gules*); Condé, MS. 315, frontispiece (*argent, three bends gules*). In the following fifteenth- and sixteenth-century Arthurian rolls, Lancelot always bears *argent, three bends gules*: Paris, Bibliothèque nationale, fonds français 1435, fol. 29 recto; fonds français 1436, fols. 15 recto and 57 verso; fonds français 1437, fol. 51 verso; fonds français 1438, fol. 20 recto; fonds français 5233, fol. 3 recto; fonds français 5937, fol. 20 recto; fonds français 5939, fol. 14 recto; fonds français 12597, fol. 24 recto; fonds français 18651, fol. 105 recto; fonds français 23,999, fol. 4 recto; Chantilly, MS. 642, fol. 2 recto (the bends are azure); Bibliothèque de l'Arsenal, MS. 5027, fol. 192 verso. See also Loomis, *Arthurian Legends*, pp. 107, 111. In the *Pas d'armes de la Belle-Pèlerine* held near Saint-Omer in 1449, Lancelot's shield was *argent, a bend gules*; see Max Prinet, 'Armoiries familiales et armoiries de roman au xvᵉ siècle', *Romania*, lviii (1932), 571, note 2: 'Ordinairement, l'écu de Lancelot est donné comme portant non pas *une* bande mais *trois* bandes de gueules.'

Perceval, we have said (see 'Plain Arms'), assumes the Red Knight's arms and armour beginning with Chrétien de Troyes' *Perceval*, or *Conte del Graal*. In the *Tournoiement Antecrit*, Huon de Méry confirms this tradition:

> Perceval ot armes vermeilles,
> Qu'il toli jadis en Illande
> Au Vermeil de la Rouge Lande,
> Quand il fu chevaliers noviax.[1]

These arms are also to be found in *Durmart le Galois*, vv. 8445–6 ('L'enseigne de vermel cendal, / C'est la baniere Perceval') and in certain late Arthurian rolls of arms.[2] The most popular fifteenth- and sixteenth-century Arthurian list, however, provides an entirely new coat of arms for Perceval: *purpure crusily or*.[3]

The Arthurian roll in certain manuscripts of the *Second Continuation* provides arms for the following characters:

MS. *K*	MSS. *TV*
Gawain	Gawain
Giglain	Giglain
Gaheriet	Gaheriet
Guerehet	Guerehet
Agravain	Agravain
Sagremor	**Yvain[1]
*Tor	Sagremor
*Arthur	**Bran de Lis
	**Yvain[2]

* does not appear in MSS. *TV*
** does not appear in MS. *K*

Yvain[1] is readily blazoned *or, two lions rampant gules*, but Yvain[2] poses a slight problem. The latter appears as follows in the two manuscripts in question (*TV*):

> A l'escu qu'il voit paleté
> Et as lions vermaus (*V*: vermals) et pains
> Conut que c'est mesire Yvains.

When the number of charges is not specified, this usually means that the field is semy. In this passage, then, the field which is gold-spangled (*paleté*), i.e. or, is apparently semy of lioncels rampant gules. When we

---

[1] *TA*, vv. 2004–7.

[2] British Museum, Add. MS. 10294, fol. 14 verso; Paris, Bibliothèque nationale, fonds français 18651, fol. 105 recto; Bibliothèque de l'Arsenal, MS. 5027, fol. 192 verso.

[3] Paris, Bibliothèque nationale, fonds français 1435, fol. 25 verso; fonds français 1436, fols. 15 recto and 54 recto; fonds français 1437, fol. 48 recto; fonds français 1438, fol. 16 verso; fonds français 5233, fol. 4 recto (*a canton argent charged with a six-pointed mullet sable*); fonds français 5937, fol. 20 recto; fonds français 5939, fol. 14 recto; fonds français 12597, fol. 21 recto; fonds français 23,999, fol. 4 recto.

compare this blazon with that for Yvain[1], however, we are inclined to interpret *as lions* as merely a loose term for two lioncels rampant. Whatever construction we give to this expression, however, it is clear that lions are involved here and that the allusion is to Chrétien's romance.

In Chrétien de Troyes, Yvain is, of course, known as *Le Chevalier au Lion* in the romance of the same name. Nowhere in the latter work, however, does the hero bear a shield decorated with a lion device. Nevertheless, the fact that Yvain rescued a lion from a fiery serpent and that the grateful animal became the hero's companion and protector in this story resulted in traditional arms featuring a lion. In *Durmart le Galois*, for example, Yvain and all his retinue bear arms alluding to this event:

Cele autre baniere doree
A cel vermel lion ranpant
N'est mie sens saignor vaillant,
Car ele est monsaignor Yvain
Qui de bonté a le cuer plain.
Tote cele rote a lions
Que nos si plainement veons
Conois je molt grant piech'a,
Certes bon chevaliers i a.
De tos ceaz vos sai je bien dire,
Que mesire Yvains en est sire.[1]

In his poem composed about 1234, Huon de Méry added a symbolic interpretation to the lion:

Ivains ert en sa compaignie,
Qui ot escu de bele guise
Parti d'amour et de franchise,
A .i. lïoncel de proesce,
A meins overtes de largesce,
C'orent Cligés et Lancelot
Et tuit li enfant le roi Lot,
Qui s'entresembloient de vis.[2]

Other examples of the lion device for Yvain may be found in the *Lancelot propre*, iv. 93 (*a lion gules*),[3] and in the fifteenth-century Arthurian lists (*azure, a lion rampant or armed and langued gules*).[4] Finally, the un-

---

[1] *Durmart*, vv. 8424-34. [2] *TA*, vv. 1986-93.

[3] Cf. iii. 271, note 1 (var.) and iv. 393 (Appendix) where Yvain is said to carry a lion skin on his shield. In iv. 104 (var.), Yvain bears *gules, a bend argent* 'pur amur de Lancelot qui lo portoit blanc a .i. bende vermeille de bellic'. See above, p. 47 n. 2.

[4] Paris, Bibliothèque nationale, fonds français 1435, fol. 36 verso; fonds français 1436, fols. 15 recto and 65 recto; fonds français 1437, fol. 65 recto; fonds français 5233, fol. 4 verso;

identified knight in *Escanor*, vv. 5565–7 ('Mais dites moi se connoissiez / Cel escu d'or a .iii. lyonz/ De geules') is probably Yvain.

In the *Perlesvaus*, one of the hero's shields features a plain red cross.[1] The author states that the shield originally belonged to Joseph of Arimathea who placed the cross upon it following Christ's death. In the *Queste del Saint Graal*, written some years later, the dying Josephe traces a cross on a white shield with blood flowing from his nose and presents it to Mordrain as something by which to remember him.[2] The shield is ultimately destined for Galahad whose white shield generally bears a red cross in manuscript illuminations following this episode and always bears one in fifteenth-century Arthurian rolls of arms.[3]

In *Durmart le Galois*, *Escanor*, and the *Second Continuation*, Arthur's knight called Sagremor bears gyronny arms.[4] We do not know why

fonds français 5937, fol. 21 recto; fonds français 12597, fol. 31 recto; fonds français 23,999, fol. 5 recto; Chantilly, MS. 642, fol. 11 recto.

[1] *Perlesvaus*, line 610: 'un escu . . . bendé d'argent e d'azur e une croiz vermeille e une bocle d'or'. See Nitze's note, ii. 230. The symbolism is explained in lines 9566–8. See also lines 4549–50.

[2] Bibliography in Nitze's note, ii. 230. The scene is illustrated in Paris, Bibliothèque nationale, fonds français 95, fol. 108 recto; British Museum, Add. MS. 10292, fol. 73 recto; Royal 14 E. 3, fol. 85 verso.

[3] The red-cross shield is cited in the following passages: *Lancelot propre*, iv. 175 (King Galahad, i.e. an ancestor of the knight of the Round Table); *Estoire*, p. 93 (Red Cross Ship); *Vulgate Merlin Sequel*, pp. 376 (Leonce and Pharien), 384 (Clarion), 389 (Christian Princes), 400 (people of Clarence identify Red Cross Knights as help sent from Christ). Josephe, Mordrain, or Galahad bear a red-cross shield in the following early manuscript illuminations: Paris, Bibliothèque nationale, fonds français 95, fols. 25 verso, 44 verso; fonds français 749, fols. 118 recto, 121 recto; fonds français 770, fol. 31 recto; British Museum, Add. MS. 10292, fols. 25 recto (Red Cross Ship), 76 recto; Royal 14 E. 3, fols. 85 verso, 94 recto and verso, 95 recto, 97 recto, 98 verso, 125 recto. Later manuscript illuminations include: Chantilly, Condé MS. 315; Chantilly, MS. 645, frontispiece; MS. 647, frontispiece and fols. 67 recto, 204 recto, 279 recto. Illustrations of Galahad's red-cross arms in the fifteenth- and sixteenth-century Arthurian rolls: Paris, Bibliothèque nationale, fonds français 1435, fol. 25 recto; fonds français 1436, fols. 15 recto and 53 verso; fonds français 1437, fol. 47 recto; fonds français 1438, fol. 16 recto; fonds français 5233, fol. 4 recto; fonds français 5937, fol. 20 recto; fonds français 5939, fol. 14 recto; fonds français 12597, fol. 20 verso; fonds français 14357, fol. 20 verso; fonds français 23,999, fol. 4 recto; Chantilly, MS. 642, fol. 62 recto. On the late-fourteenth-century legend of the origins of the arms of Catalonia said to recall the bars of the Cross, see Martín de Riquer in *Annalecta Sacra Tarraconensia* (*Barcelona*), xxii (1949), 227 ff., who believes this is a reminiscence of Galahad's shield; see, however, the critique by Pere Bohigas, 'La matière de Bretagne en Catalogne', *BBSIA*, xiii (1961), 88–9. The history of the red-cross device in literature has been studied in detail by Roland M. Smith, 'Origines Arthurianae: The Two Crosses of Spenser's Red Cross Knight', *Journal of English and Germanic Philology*, liv (1955), 670–83. On the symbolism of the colour red in Galahad's shield, see Lot, *Etude sur le Lancelot en prose*, p. 192.

[4] *Durmart*, vv. 8480–2; *Escanor*, vv. 4992–3; *Second Continuation*, MS. *K*, fol. 106 *f*; MS. *T*, fol. 126 *e*; MS. *V*, fol. 93 *a*. In Paris, Bibliothèque nationale, fonds français 18651, a sixteenth-century Arthurian roll, only five of the twenty-one painted shields are captioned; there is every reason to believe, however, that shield no. 17 (*or, gyronny of six sable*) is for Sagremor. In all the other fifteenth- and sixteenth-century Arthurian rolls, however, this knight bears *sable, two mullets or, on a canton argent a mullet sable*, or a variant thereof.

this character, whose name means 'sycamore' in Old French, was given the epithet *le Desreé* 'the Madman' by Chrétien de Troyes,[1] but we may safely assume that the latter designation suggested the 'rays' of Sagremor's canting arms (OFr. *desreé* < OFr. *des-* [< Latin *dis-*]+*reer* [< Latin *radiare* < *radium* 'ray']).

The Lait Hardi's arms in *Durmart le Galois* provide one of the rare instances of a positioning phrase attested before the classic period. Though the chief is found charged as early as the twelfth century (e.g. Robert Brus, who added a leopard on the chief of the Bruce arms [seal dated *c.* 1195], an augmentation for his lordship of Annandale), Old French literature offers only scant information as to how this or any other positioning was described.[2] In *Durmart*, Arthur's seneschal, Sir Kay, is given arms which may be blazoned *sable, a chief argent*:

> Lors le conoissent mainte gent
> A l'escu noir al chief d'argent
> Que mesire Kez porte bel
> Par les enarmes en chantel.[3]

In the following verses, Kay's nephew, the Lait Hardi, is said to bear the same arms as the seneschal but with the addition of a lioncel courant gules on the chief:

> Ces noires banieres parans
> As chiés d'argent resplendissans,
> Celes sont Ke le seneschal.
> Je le voi sor un grant cheval;
> De ses armes est acesmés.
> Ce est iloc mesires Kes
> Cil qui la vient devant sa gent
> A l'escu noir al chief d'argent,
> Et cil qui porte el chief devant
> Le vermel lioncel corant
> Ce est ses niés li Lais Hardis.[4]

The phrase *el chief devant* indicating the position of the lioncel in Kay's nephew's arms is nowhere else to be found in early blazon. Analagous

---

[1] The name appears, for example, in *Erec*, vv. 1701, 2175, and *Cligés*, v. 4612; see also *Lancelot propre*, iii. 339, 381; iv. 313; *Artus*, pp. 46, 318. On the name, see Lot, *Etude sur le Lancelot en prose*, p. 174 n. 2; Loomis, *Arthurian Tradition*, p. 490; Loomis, *Arthurian Literature in the Middle Ages*, p. 323. Sagremor is an ancient name as it appears in an Italian cartulary dated 1148; see Lejeune–Stiennon, *La Légende de Roland*, i. 89. For a discussion of an important characteristic of *le desreé* in literature, consult Payen, ch. iv. Scott-Giles, 'The Heraldry of Romance', p. 259, notes that in the *Morte Arthure* Sir Jerante bears a gyronny (*jerownde*) shield, plainly another instance of canting arms. See *MED*, s.v. *gerone*.

[2] See Brault, 'The Chief', p. 83.   [3] *Durmart*, vv. 7009–12.

[4] *Durmart*, vv. 8467–77.

use of *devant*, however, indicates quite clearly that the phrase means 'in dexter point of the chief', i.e. on the right side of the chief viewed, as is customary in heraldry, from behind the shield.[1]

Two other allusions to Kay's arms in early texts reflect upon his character reputed to be rather unsavoury:

> Cil qui portoit un escucel
> Des armes Keu le seneschal
> En son escu bouclé d'archal
> En ot erroment grant envie.
> Il fut toz les jors de sa vie
> Assez plus fel que ne fu Keus.[2]
>
> Misire Quiex li senesciaus,
> Sans fere autre descrepcïon,
> Ot les armes detraccïon,
> Endentees de felonie,
> A ramposnes de vilenie,
> A .iii. tourteaus fez et farsiz
> De ramposnes et de mesdiz.[3]

In the fifteenth-century Arthurian rolls, the allusion in Kay's arms will be to his function as a seneschal: *azure, two keys argent*.[4] Girart d'Amiens, in a similar vein, ascribes arms featuring butts to Lucan, King Arthur's butler:

> Lucanz les ot a .v. bouchiauz
> D'argent par desuz le vermeil.[5]

(14) HISTORY, HERALDRY, AND LITERATURE

In a recent book,[6] Professor Denholm-Young has amply demonstrated that the thirteenth-century rolls of arms yield a wealth oj information concerning the composition of the Edwardian cavalry and the functions of constable, marshal, knight of the shire, and sheriff. This important study also sheds considerable light on the rôle of the

---

[1] Brault, 'The Chief', p. 84 n. 12. [2] *Guillaume de Dole*, vv. 3159–64.
[3] *TA*, vv. 2008–14.

[4] Paris, Bibliothèque nationale, fonds français 1435, fol. 36 recto; fonds français 1436, fols. 15 recto and 64 verso; fonds français 1437, fol. 64 recto; fonds français 1438, fol. 26 recto; fonds français 5937, fol. 21 recto; fonds français 5939, fol. 14 verso; fonds français 12597, fol. 30 verso; fonds français 23,999, fol. 5 recto. Keys figure in the canting arms of Philip and William Chamberlain in the thirteenth century.

[5] *Escanor*, vv. 3484–5. Cf. the canting arms (cups) of Sir John le Botiler in *Mediaeval England*, ed. H. W. C. Davis (Oxford, 1924), p. 209 and fig. 213. On Lucan, see *Perlesvaus*, ii. 226–7, note to line 592. In the fifteenth- and sixteenth-century Arthurian rolls, Lucan's arms (*or, a lion rampant gules armed sable*) do not allude to his function; on the other hand, another member of Arthur's household, Bedoier le Conestable, bears *or, a gonfanon gules*.

[6] N. Denholm-Young, *History and Heraldry, 1254 to 1310. A Study of the Historical Value of the Rolls of Arms* (Oxford–New York, 1965). See my review in *Speculum*, xli (1966), 318–20.

heralds and on the circumstances surrounding the compiling of rolls of arms.

We have endeavoured to show in the preceding paragraphs that literature, too, is intimately associated with history and heraldry. It is very difficult at times, as a matter of fact, to distinguish between fact and fancy in the thirteenth century.

Edward I and Eleanor of Castile systematically promoted Arthurianism in their entourage and, in England as well as on the Continent, masquerading as legendary and, notably, literary characters was a favourite pastime.[1] Further characterizing this era are the fanciful arms which are invented for pre-Norman kings (the Matthew Paris Shields, for example, include arms for Edmund Ironside, Canute, and Harold)[2] and other illustrious persons in history and legend (e.g. King Arthur and his Knights of the Round Table, Charlemagne, Roland, and Prester John),[3] for far-away lands (e.g. Cyprus in the Camden Roll and Poland in the Wijnbergen Roll), and even for Christ, the Saints, the Vices and Virtues.[4]

We should not be surprised, therefore, to find historical arms in literary works at times associated with fictitious counterparts (King Alexander III of Scotland's arms for 'le roi d'Escoce' and those of Prince Llywelyn ap Gruffydd of Wales for 'le roi de Gales' in *Escanor*), at other times as a flattering identification with a hero of romance (Henry II's arms for Tristan in Thomas's poem).

The reverse phenomenon has been accorded less attention but is none the less prevalent in the thirteenth century. We have provided evidence, for instance, of a connection between Gawain's arms in the Heralds' Roll, on the one hand, and those of the Maltravers family, on the other. The same roll lists a shield for Roland which may be blazoned *or, a lion rampant gules within a bordure engrailed sable* (*HE* 61), arms which Jean de Gavre adopted before his death in 1297 to commemorate the family legend which relates that one of his ancestors, having lost his own shield at the battle before Luiserne, was given that of Charlemagne's

---

[1] Royal and noble personages commissioned and owned copies of many literary works throughout the Middle Ages.

[2] *Aspilogia II*, pp. 79, 83, 85. Harold and a number of pre-Norman English kings also appear in the Heralds' Roll. The earliest roll of fictitious kings is in *WB* 1257–1312; see Adam-Even WB, p. 73 n. 1.

[3] See Louis Carolus-Barré and Paul Adam-Even, 'Les armes de Charlemagne dans l'héraldique et l'iconographie médiévales', *Mémorial d'un voyage d'études de la Société nationale des antiquaires de France en Rhénanie (juillet 1951)* (Paris, 1953), pp. 289–308. Roland's arms are discussed in Lejeune–Stiennon, *La Légende de Roland*, i. 319, 348, notes 13 and 14. For Prester John's arms, see *HE* 1; Gough-Parker, p. 476; Boutell, p. 61.

[4] See, notably, the *Tournoiement Antecrit*.

nephew.[1] A similar legend is doubtless involved in the connection between Simon le Voier's arms in *Berte aus grans piés* and those of one of Adenet le Roi's contemporaries.[2] We know also that at this time members of the Tony family fancied themselves descendants of the Swan Knight.[3] Does the plain gules of the La Brette or Albret family, one of whom distinguished himself at Caerlaverock in 1300, allude to Perceval's arms?[4] Brian FitzAlan, Lord of Bedale (d. 1306), once owned the Oxford MS. of the *Perlesvaus* and may have liked to think of himself as the Brien des Illes of that and other romances.[5] In the fourteenth century, the Dukes of Brittany assumed plain ermine arms, no doubt referring to the fact that *Ermenie* was a name for Brittany in the romances, and Sir Thomas Holand abandoned his family arms in favour of the Black Knight's plain sable. In the fifteenth century, finally, Regnier Pot adopted the arms of another hero of romance, Palamedes.[6]

While the 'tournament' as a literary genre featuring historical personages bearing authentic coats of arms reaches its apogee in such late-thirteenth-century works as the *Tournoi de Chauvency* and the *Roman du Hem*, heraldic flattery in literature persisted until the end of the Middle Ages. Certain well-known chroniclers, notably Jacques de Hemricourt and Froissart,[7] devoted considerable space to record historical coats of arms and the fifteenth-century romance entitled *Jehan de Saintré* includes a roll of arms remarkable for its length and for its correctness.[8]

[1] Max Prinet, 'Un armorial inachevé du Bailliage de Senlis (xive siècle)', *BEC*, xc (1929), 323–4; Lejeune–Stiennon, *La Légende de Roland*, i. 317–19.

[2] See FLEUR DE LIS TOUT EN MILIEU, *Note.*

[3] Matthew Paris states that Ralph de Tony (d. 1239) was descended from the knights 'qui a Cigni nomine intitulantur' (*Aspilogia II*, p. 25, note to item 57). The Tony seal affixed to the Barons' Letter (1301) specifically claims the same descent. See CIGNE, *Note.*

[4] The name La Brette evoked strong literary associations in the thirteenth century (OFr. *Bret* [= the Trojan Brutus, supposed ancestor of the Bretons; see Flutre, p. 37]). In Geoffrey of Monmouth, Brutus is the name of a fictitious king of England who supposedly bore a green shield (*Brutus Viride Scutum*). *Le Bret* or *Brait* is also another name for the *Prose Tristan*; see C. E. Pickford, 'Le Roman du Bret', in *Dictionnaire des lettres françaises*, ed. Cardinal Georges Grente, i. *Le Moyen Age*, ed. Robert Bossuat (Paris, 1964), 650–1. Finally, a number of English families bear coats of arms ascribed to Arthurian characters in the contemporary romance *Escanor* (see p. 38 n. 1). Cf. also ORLURE DE L'ENCHAMPURE A ROSES, *Note.*

[5] See Nitze, ii. 3–8, 100–1; Denholm-Young, *History and Heraldry*, p. 23 n. 4.

[6] Max Prinet, 'Armoiries familiales et armoiries de roman au xve siècle', *Romania*, lviii (1932), 569–73. 'A la fin du Moyen Age, on a si souvent emprunté les noms des chevaliers de la Table Ronde, qu'il n'est pas surprenant qu'on ait parfois emprunté leurs armoiries' (p. 573).

[7] L. Bouly de Lesdain, 'L'héraldique dans Henricourt', *Revue du Nord*, iv (1913), 324–39; Max Prinet, 'Les usages héraldiques au xive siècle d'après les Chroniques de Froissart', *Annuaire-Bulletin de la Société de l'histoire de France*, liii, 2e partie (1916), 141–55.

[8] Antoine de La Salle, *Jehan de Saintré*, edd. Jean Misrahi and Charles Knudson (Geneva, 1965).

(15) ARRANGEMENT OF ITEMS IN THE PRESENT GLOSSARY

This glossary is arranged alphabetically and includes each individual term encountered (except articles, numbers, and separators) and the descriptive and positioning phrases in which it occurs.

Entries, other than mere cross-references, provide the following information:

1. Definition in English.
2. All known examples except where the item is preceded by an asterisk (*).[1]
3. Synonyms.
4. Notes concerning historical and philological data, textual problems, present-day equivalents in French and English blazon, bibliography, etc.

Citations are necessarily brief and the full blazon has been provided only when particularly significant. We have resisted the temptation to invent new phrases by combining known elements. On the other hand, we have included a substantial number of terms which do not fit into the traditional categories but which are definitely related to heraldry (see Table I. X. General). It is obvious that many terms and phrases which do not appear here were known to early blazon. Also, a few of our entries may contain doubtful blazons as a result of defective source material. A number of such items, known to have been caused by scribal error, are labelled *ghost words*.

As a rule, our data consist of blazons of shields, but a few examples of descriptions of armorial banners and horse bardings have also been included.

The listing of synonyms under a particular heading does not necessarily mean that the latter was the principal term. In general, however, we have tried to find the word in most widespread use for this purpose or the one which was destined to survive. The choice of a heading to enter synonyms of positioning phrases, on the other hand, is completely arbitrary.

We debated for a long time whether to distinguish material drawn from the rolls from that found in literature, and items belonging to the period before 1250 from those attested after that date. The line which

---

[1] The present work originally featured a complete concordance of the copies of every thirteenth-century roll of arms cited in the Abbreviations. For reasons of economy, it was necessary to condense the following entries, many of which covered several pages: ARGENT, AZUR, BLANC, CHEVRON, CHIEF[1], ESCHEQUERÉ DE . . . ET DE . . ., ESCU[1], ESCUÇON[1], FESSE, GEULES, LABEL[1], LION[1], LION RAMPANT, NOIR, OR, SABLE, and VERMEIL.

separates these categories is so fine, however, and the overlapping so great that the distinctions would very likely have been artificial and misleading. Finally, we have included a number of examples of quasi-heraldic terminology, it being extremely difficult to distinguish between these and bona fide blazons.

(16) ORTHOGRAPHICAL AND GRAMMATICAL CONSIDERATIONS

Orthographical variants have everywhere been preserved in transcribing source material. A certain amount of standardization was needed, however, for entry headings. This was necessary in view of the great variation encountered in dialectal forms and in scribal habits.

Since the French language evolved considerably in the period under study (e.g. *goles* > *geules*), we have adopted for headings an orthography in widespread use in France in the second half of the thirteenth century. Our guide in this rather complex matter has been Mildred K. Pope, *From Latin to Modern French With Especial Consideration of Anglo-Norman. Phonology and Morphology* (Manchester, 1934).

Whenever a choice was possible, we have used a form more apt to be recognized by persons familiar with present-day French and English heraldic terms, e.g. *bordure*, rather than *bordeure* (Pope, para. 377–8); *beuf*, *bleu*, and *meule*, rather than *buef*, *bloe*, or *moele* (Pope, para. 542, 551, 714); *treçoir*, rather than *treçouer* (Pope, para. 518–20); but *vuivre* rather than *vivre*. The most misleading spellings are listed alphabetically in our glossary with a reference to the appropriate entry.

A number of conventions are adhered to in editing Old French texts. Accordingly, the reader will find that all diacritical marks have been omitted except the acute accent indicating a stressed final *e* (*besanté*, *vuidié*) and the cedilla to mark an *s*-sound (*escuçon*). Since most of our citations are prose, use of the diaeresis to show a diphthong was felt to be unnecessary when transcribing words such as *bordeure* (= *bordeüre*), except, of course, in poetry.

Only a few terms listed in the present study are not recorded, in one manner or another, in either Godefroy or Tobler–Lommatzsch and the reader will doubtless wish to avail himself of the latter dictionaries for additional information about genders, orthographical variations, other meanings, etc. On the other hand, we have provided numerous earlier attestations and heraldic meanings for a substantial group of terms listed in these standard reference works.

The following observations will appear elementary to students of Old French but may prove helpful for non-specialists.

Old French had a nominative as well as an oblique form, e.g.:

Nom. sing. *li murs*	Nom. pl. *li mur*
Obl. sing. *le mur*	Obl. pl. *les murs*

This paradigm which features a final *-s* in the nominative singular and no final *-s* in the nominative plural—a frequent source of confusion for persons not used to reading Old French—applies to masculine nouns only. As is customary, we have listed all initial entries in the oblique singular, even when the terms are attested only in the plural in blazon (e.g. *besant*).

Final *-s* may be a reduction of an etymological *-z* (i.e. a *ts*-sound). Thus *egles* may be the plural of *egle* or represent *eglez*, the plural of *eglet* (Pope, para. 194–5, 796).

Words ending in *-al* and, in certain cases, *-el* vocalized to *-au* / *-eau* before *-s*, as in *chapel* / *chapeaus* (Pope, para. 814).

Final *-x* usually represents *-us*, as in *aniax* = *aneaus*, the plural of *anel*. However, *-x* as the sign of the plural in such words as *aux* and *chapeaux* occurs systematically only much later than 1300.

Old French almost always had a single consonant where Modern French has a double letter, e.g. OFr. *nule* vs. MFr. *nulle*, but cf. *esquar-tillié*.

We have preferred the orthography *ie* to *e* in such words as *chief*, *fessié*, and *fourchié*, but pronunciation varied according to region (Pope, para. 510, 512).

The most common orthographical variants encountered in manuscript sources were:

c, k, / *ch*	e.g. *escalope* = *eschalope*
c / *qu*	e.g. *escartelé* = *esquartelé*
e / *ai*	e.g. *chaisne* = *chesne*

The most frequent abbreviations were:

&	= *et*
6 or *u, v*	= *en le*
9	= *con-, com-,* or *-aus, -us*
~	= *n, un*

The abbreviation *6* (= *en le*) in *Cl* 47, 120, 131, 135, 136, 140, 153, 159, and 170, was solved inconsistently by London as *al, en, en le,* and *sur le* in *Aspilogia II.*

There was, finally, a problem in the interpretation of two final letters:

(*a*) an *s*-shaped squiggle extending below the line, and (*b*) an elongated
-*e*, the bottom loop likewise extending below the line. In Nicholas
Charles's copy of Walford's Roll (*C*), I have rendered the *s*-shaped
squiggle as a final -*s* (Walford: -*es*). In John Leland's copy of the same
roll (*Cl*), I believe that the elongated -*e* was meant to represent a final
-*e* (Hearne, London: -*es*).

Numbers have been uniformly cited in lower-case Roman numerals
(.*i*.; .*ii*.; etc.) except where spelled out in the text itself and in the entry
headings.

Many instances of masculine/feminine words (e.g. *egle*) are to be
found in Old French. For entry purposes here, we have arbitrarily
used only one form. In a few instances where separate words are
apparently involved (e.g. *molet* / *molete*; *cornier* / *corniere*), individual
entries have been made. Attestations such as *une lion* are merely the
result of scribal ignorance or indifference.

Feminine adjectives derived from Latin two-termination forms (e.g.
grandis > *grant*; *talis* > *tel*) did not regularly add the analogical -*e*
(*grande*, *tele*) until the Middle French period, i.e. after 1300 (Pope,
para. 770, 773, 780), although examples are encountered in the
materials we have provided. The reader should not be surprised to find
exceptions from time to time to other rules cited here.

The special rules governing Anglo-Norman versification are far too
complex to outline here. The reader seeking information on this subject
will be greatly assisted by the discussions and bibliography in *Les
Œuvres de Simund de Freine*, ed. John E. Matzske (Paris, 1909) [*Société
des Anciens Textes Français*], pp. xliii–lx; Joseph Bédier, *La Chanson de
Roland commentée* (Paris, 1927; reprinted 1968), pp. 263 ff.; and *Guillaume*, ii. 46–57.

Words have been divided according to the following system: *parmi* =
preposition; *par mi* = prepositional phrase. It would have been
possible to standardize all prepositions (*a* instead of *o*, *od*, etc.) as well
as word order in the entry headings. Our object here, however, was
to rewrite as little as possible and faithfully to record the many variations in early blazon.

In the blazons cited in this book, the parenthetical readings are those
of the editors of the published rolls named in the List of Abbreviations.
For example, *K*, v. 190: *Jaune o crois noire egreellie* (W: *engreelie*) means
that Wright, the editor of the *Siege of Caerlaverock*, misread the word in
question.

TABLE I

CHIEF TERMS LISTED IN THE PRESENT GLOSSARY

N.B. This table provides in synoptic form, and according to the traditional classification, the principal English heraldic terms (in roman type) corresponding to the twelfth- and thirteenth-century French words listed here (in capitals). For synonyms and phrases, consult the individual entries in the glossary.

The illustrations are the work of C. W. Scott-Giles, Fitzalan Pursuivant of Arms. Only the terms and phrasing which can be related to authentic arms of the period have been included, no attempt being made to illustrate fanciful devices. The reader should appreciate the fact that while a certain stylistic uniformity was achieved in depicting armorial shields in the thirteenth century, many individual variations are also to be found.

I. THE SHIELD

According to Boutell, p. 21, the modern heraldic shield has thirteen points (Fig. 1):

A Dexter side	F Sinister chief	L Honour point
B Sinister side	G Middle chief	M Fess point
C Chief	H Dexter base	N Nombril or Navel
D Base	J Sinister base	point
E Dexter chief	K Middle base	

Early blazon apparently concerned itself with only the following five points (Fig. 2):

C Chief, see CHIEF[2]	F Sinister chief, see CORNIERE[3]
D Base, see PIÉ[2]	M Fess point, see MILIEU
E Dexter chief, see DEVANT[3]	

Each of the three points ('corners') of the shield, see CORNIERE[2] (Fig. 134)
Edge of the shield, see ENCHAMPURE
Lower part of the shield, see FONT
Sinister, see SENESTRE

II. TINCTURES

The chief tinctures found in present-day blazon are all attested during the period under consideration.

Argent (white), see ARGENT
Or (yellow), see OR
    To colour or (yellow), see DORER

Azure (blue), see AZUR
Gules (red), see GEULES
Purpure (purple), see POURPRE
Sable (black), see SABLE
Vert (green), see VERT

Grey, see GRIS
Greyish-brown, see BIS
Ivory, see IVOIRE
Russet-red, see ROUS

Ermine, see ERMINE (Fig. 3)
Vair, see VAIR (Fig. 4)
Vairy, see VAIRIÉ DE . . . ET DE . . . (Fig. 4)
    To be vairy, see ESTRE VAIRIÉ DE . . . ET DE . . . (Fig. 4)

We also find the following other terms relating to tincture:

Tincture, see TAINT[1]
    Of the same tincture, see DEL MESME
    To have no other tincture underneath (?), see N'AVOIR NULE AUTRE TAINT
        DESOUS
Tinctured, see TAINT[2]

III. LINES

The lines known to early blazon are relatively few in number.

Bretessé (embattled on both sides), see ENCHASTELÉ (Fig. 58)
Dancetty, see DANCIÉ (Figs. 6, 78)
Indented (a continuous sawtooth line), see ENDENTÉ[1] (Figs. 24, 28, 70, 115)
Indented (two continuous sawtooth edges), see ENDENTÉ[2] (Figs. 64, 84, 93,
    105)
Undy (see IV. FIELDS) (Figs. 7, 20)

Ornamented with triangular points, see ENDENTÉ[3] (Fig. 108)

IV. FIELDS

The principal fields of modern heraldry are all attested in early blazon.

Barry, barruly, see BARRÉ DE . . . ET DE . . .[1] (Fig. 5)
  Barry dancetty, see DANCIÉ A DANCES (Fig. 6)
  Barry undy, see ONDÉ DE . . . ET DE . . . (Fig. 7)
Bendy, see BENDÉ DE . . . ET DE . . .[1] (Fig. 8)
Checky, see ESCHEQUÉ DE . . . ET DE . . . (Fig. 9)
Chevronny, see CHEVRONÉ DE . . . ET DE . . . (Fig. 10)
Compony, gobony, see COUPONÉ DE . . . ET DE . . . (Fig. 12)
Concentric rings of alternating tinctures covering the whole field, see ROUELÉ
  DE . . . ET DE . . . (Fig. 11)
Fretty, see FRETÉ (Fig. 13)
Gyronny (field), see GIRONÉ DE . . . ET DE . . .[1] (Fig. 14)
Gyronny (corners), see GIRONÉ DE . . . ET DE . . .[2] (Fig. 15)
Lozengy, see LOSENGIÉ DE . . . ET DE . . .[1] (Fig. 16)
  Lozengy in bend, see BENDÉ DE . . . ET DE . . . ENDENTÉ L'UN EN L'AUTRE
  (Fig. 17)
Masculy, see OD LES LOSENGES PERCIEES (Fig. 18)
Paly, see PALÉ DE . . . ET DE . . . (Fig. 19)
  Paly undy, see ONDÉ DE LONC DE . . . ET DE . . . (Fig. 20)
Party per pale, see PARTI DE . . . ET DE . . . (Fig. 21)
  Half of a party field, see DEMI[2]
  One side of a party field, see PART
  The other side, the other half of a party field, see D'AUTRE PART
Party per pale and barry counterchanged, see FESSIÉ DE . . . ET DE . . . ET
  CONTREFESSIÉ (Fig. 22)
Party per pale and bendy counterchanged, see BENDÉ CONTREBENDÉ DE . . .
  ET DE . . . (Fig. 23)
Party per pale indented, see PARTI ENDENTÉ DE . . . ET DE . . . (Fig. 24)
Quarterly, see ESQUARTELÉ DE . . . ET DE . . . (Fig. 25)
  In certain quarters of a quarterly field, see EN LES QUARTIERS DE . . . EN
  LES QUARTIERS DE . . .
  In the first quarter of a quarterly field, see EN LE QUARTIER DEVANT
  (Fig. 26)
  In the . . . quarter of a quarterly field, see OU QUARTIER DE . . .
Quarterly per fess indented, see ESQUARTELÉ DE . . . ET DE . . . ENDENTÉ
  (Fig. 28)

Field, see ESCU[1]
  On the field, see EL CHAMP
Traversed by multiple stripes (direction not indicated), see A BENDES
  BENDÉ

V. SEMY AND DECORATIVE PATTERNS

Many locutions are used in early blazon to designate powdered fields (see POUDRÉ). The charges appearing in such a pattern consist of the following:

Bezants, see BESANTÉ (Fig. 29)

Billets, see BILLETÉ (Fig. 30)

Castles, see CHASTELÉ[1] (Fig. 31)

Choughs (?), see OD LES COUWES (Fig. 32)

Cinquefoils, see QUINTEFEUILLES OU . . . (Fig. 33)

Crescents, see OD LES CROISSANZ (Fig. 34)

Crosslets, see CROISELÉ (Fig. 35)

    To be crusily, see ESTRE CROISILLIÉ (Fig. 35)

Crowns, see A COURONES (Fig. 36)

Drops, see GOUTÉ DE . . . ET DE . . . (Fig. 37)

    One of the drops of a goutté pattern, see GOUTE (Fig. 37)

Eaglets, see A EGLEAUS SEMÉ (Fig. 38)

Escallops, see A COQUILLES SEMÉ (Fig. 39)

Eyes (i.e. the markings on a peacock's tail), see D'IEUZ DE PAON OEILLETÉ

Fleurs-de-lis, see FLEURETÉ[1] (Fig. 40)

Garbs, see JARBES EN LA CROIS

Leopards, see SEMÉ DE LIEPARDEAUS (Fig. 41)

Lioncels rampant, see SEMÉ DE LIONCEAUS (Fig. 42)

Magpies, see OU LES PIES (Fig. 43)

Martlets, see A MERLOZ (Fig. 44)

Mascles (see FIELDS)

Mullets, see A MOLETES SEMÉ (Fig. 45)

Nails, see FERRETÉ (Fig. 46)

Roses (heraldic), see SEMÉ DE ROSETES (Fig. 47)

Small saltires, see SAUTOIRS EN L'OR (Fig. 94)

Sparks, see ESTENCELÉ (Fig. 48)

Tiny lozenges, see SEMÉ DE GRAINS (Fig. 49)

Trefoils, see SEMÉ DE TREFLES (Fig. 50)

A number of ornamental patterns were also known to the early heralds:

Diapered, see DIASPRÉ (Fig. 51)

    To diaper, see DIASPRER

Gold-spangled, see PALETÉ (Fig. 52)

Scaly, see PAPELONÉ (Fig. 53)

Decorated with an ornamental pattern, see FALLOLÉ

Ornamented with letters, an arabesque, or other design, see LETRÉ DE . . .
    ET DE . . .

Ornamented with a wheel-like or flowery design, see TOUT ROUÉ

Scattered all over the field but not over the principal charge, see ENVIRON[2] (2)

VI. ORDINARIES

Modern heraldic manuals group together a number of simple charges and term them ordinaries. While this classification was unknown in the period in question, we provide it here for the sake of convenience.

Bar, see BARRE[1] (Fig. 54)
    Bar over all, see BARRE SOR LE TOUT (Fig. 55)
    Barrulet, see JUMEAUS[2] (Fig. 56)
    Bars gemelles, see JUMELES[1] (Fig. 56)
    Demi-fess (i.e. bar) embattled on both sides, see FESSIEL ENCHASTELÉ DESOUS
        ET DESUS (Fig. 58)
    Triple bars, see JUMELES[2] (Fig. 59)
Bend, see BENDE[1] (Fig. 60)
    Bend cotised, see BENDE[1] (2) (Fig. 61)
    Bend over all, see SORJETÉ D'UN BASTON (Fig. 62)
    Bendwise, see DE BELIC
    Fimbriated bend, see BENDE ENLISTEE A DEUS BASTONS ENCOSTE (Fig. 63)
    Fusils conjoined in bend, see BENDE ENGRESLEE (Fig. 64)
    On the bend, see BENDE[1] (3) (Fig. 65)
Chevron, see CHEVRON (Fig. 66)
    On the chevron, see EN LE CHEVRON (Fig. 67)
    Twin chevrons, see CHEVRONS JUMEAUS (Fig. 68)
Chief, see CHIEF[1] (Fig. 69)
    Chief indented, see CHIEF ENDENTÉ (Fig. 70)
    Dexter chief, see DEVANT[3] (Fig. 2)
    Dexter point of the chief, see DEVANT[2] (Fig. 71)
    In chief, see EN LE CHIEF[2] (Fig. 72)
    In dexter chief, see OU CHANTEL DEVANT, QUARTIER DEVANT[2] (Fig. 73)
    In sinister chief, see EN LA CORNIERE (Fig. 74)
    On the chief, see EN LE CHIEF[1] (Fig. 75)
    Sinister chief, see CORNIERE[3] (Fig. 2)
Cotice, see COTICE (Fig. 76)
    Cotice ornamented with fleurs-de-lis, see LISTE FLEURETEE (Fig. 77)
    Cotised, see COTICIÉ (Figs. 61, 82)
    Double cotice, see LISTE[3] (Fig. 83)
Daunce (fess dancetty), see DANCE (Fig. 78)
    Daunce over all, see SORJETÉ O UNE DANCE (Fig. 79)
Fess, see FESSE (Fig. 80)
    Demi-fess, see DEMI FESSE (Fig. 81)
    Fess cotised, see FESSE A DEUS LISTEAUS UN DESOUS ET L'AUTRE DESOR (Fig. 82)
    Fess dancetty, see Daunce
    Fess double-cotised, see FESSE A DEUS LISTES (Fig. 83)

Fesswise, see DE TRAVERS
Fusils conjoined in fess, see FESSE ENDENTEE (Fig. 84)
On the fess, see FESSE (1) B. (Fig. 85)
Fusil, see Bend, Fess
Lozenge, see LOSENGE[1] (Fig. 86)
Lozenges conjoined in cross, see CROIS ENDENTEE[1] (Fig. 105)
Tiny lozenge, see GRAIN (Fig. 49)
Mascle, see FAUSE LOSENGE (Fig. 87)
Pale, see PAL (Fig. 88)
In pale, see L'UN DESOUS ET L'AUTRE DESUS (Fig. 89)
Pallet, see PELET (Fig. 90)
Pallet couped, see PEL RECOUPÉ (Fig. 15)
Per pale, see EN LONC[1]
To impale, see PARTIR DE . . . ET DE . . .
Pile, see PILE (Fig. 91)
Saltire, see SAUTOIR[1] (Fig. 92)
Saltire cantoned with multiple charges, see ENTRE, *Note*
Saltire engrailed, see SAUTOIR ENGRESLÉ (Fig. 93)
Small saltire, see SAUTOIR[2] (Fig. 94)

Traversed by a single diagonal stripe (a bend), see BENDÉ[1] (Fig. 60)
Traversed by a single horizontal stripe (a fess), see FESSIÉ (Fig. 80)
Voided, see FAUS (Fig. 87)

VII. THE CROSS

Beginning with the Classic Period of medieval heraldry, the terminology of the cross is both varied and extensive.

Cross couped, see CROIS[2] (Fig. 95)
Cross flory, see CROIS FLEURETEE (Fig. 96)
Cross formy, see CROIS FORMEE (Fig. 97)
Cross formy throughout, see CROIS ESLAISIEE AUS BOUZ (Fig. 98)
Cross fourchy, see CROIS FOURCHIEE[2] (Fig. 101)
Cross gringolé, see FER DE MOULIN A TESTES DE SERPENZ AU FER DE MOULIN
(Fig. 99)
Crosslet, see CROISELE (Fig. 100)
Cross moline, see CROIS RECERCELEE (Fig. 101)
Cross patonce, see CROIS ESLARGIE PAR LES BOUZ (Fig. 102)
On the cross patonce, see EN LA CROIS[1] (2)
Cross potent, see CROIS BILLETEE (Fig. 103)
Cross voided, see CROIS PERCIEE (Fig. 104)
Lozenges conjoined in cross, see CROIS ENDENTEE[1] (Fig. 105)
Plain cross, see CROIS[1] (Fig. 106)

Cantoned, see EN LE CHANTEL[3] (Fig. 107)

Plain cross cantoned with multiple charges, see EN LES QUATRE QUARTIERS (Fig. 27)

    On the plain cross, see EN LA CROIS[1] (1)

Plain cross ornamented with triangular points, see CROIS ENDENTEE[2] (Fig. 108)

Small cross, see CROIS[3] (Fig. 140)

Toulouse cross, see CROIS PATEE ET PERCIEE (Fig. 109)

Botonny, see BOUTONÉ (Fig. 109)

End, tip, see BOUT

    At the ends, see AUS BOUZ, PAR LES BOUZ

Formy, see FORMÉ

Formy throughout, see ESLAISIÉ

Fourchy, see FOURCHIÉ[4]

In cross, see CROIS[4] (Fig. 110)

Moline, see RECERCELÉ

Patonce, see ESLARGI[2]

Plain, see PASSANT[2]

Potent, see BILLETÉ[2]

Voided, see FAUS (Fig. 104)

VIII. SUBORDINARIES

This classification is as arbitrary and as late as that of the ordinaries. It will serve, however, to assist persons seeking to find charges customarily listed under this heading.

Annulet, see ANEL (Fig. 111)

Bezant (roundel, torteau, etc.), see BESANT (Fig. 112)

    To charge with bezants, see BESANTER

Billet, see BILLETE (Fig. 113)

Bordure, see BORDURE[1] (Fig. 114)

    Along the line of a bordure or an orle, see ENVIRON[1]

    Bordure indented, see BORDURE ENDENTEE (Fig. 115)

    On the bordure, see BORDURE[1] (2), (3) (Fig. 116)

    With a bordure, see BORDÉ[1]

Canton, quarter, see CHANTEL[1] (Fig. 117)

    Cantoned with = cross or saltire between multiple charges (see VI. ORDINARIES and VII. THE CROSS)

    On the canton, see EN LE QUARTIER[1] (Fig. 118)

Corner, see CORNIER (Fig. 15)

Escutcheon, see ESCUÇON[1] (Fig. 119)

    Small escutcheon, see ESCUÇON[2] (Fig. 74)

    Small shield consisting of the field inside an orle, see ESCU[3] (Fig. 120)

Gyron, see Corner

Label, see LABEL¹ (Fig. 121)
  On the label, see EN LE LABEL (Fig. 122)
  Pendant, point, see LABEL² (Fig. 123)
Orle, see FAUS ESCUÇON (Fig. 124)
  In orle, see BORDURE² (Fig. 125)
  Small shield consisting of the field inside an orle, see Escutcheon
Quarter, see Canton
Roundel, see Bezant
Tressure, see TREÇOIR (Fig. 126)
  Double tressure, see BORDURE³
  Double tressure flory counterflory, see BORDURE FLEURETEE (Fig. 127)

IX. CHARGES

A. DIVINE BEINGS

Angel, see MESSAGE
  Angel's wings, see ELES DE MESSAGE
  Charged with an angel's wings, see ENPENÉ
  Small angel, see ANGELOT (Fig. 128)
Apollo (here regarded as a pagan deity), see APOLIN
Lazarus, see SAINT LAZARE
Mohammed (here regarded as a pagan deity), see MAHOMET
Our Lord upon the Cross, see HOME QUI ESTOIT CRUCEFIÉ (Fig. 129)
Small devil, see DIABLEL
  Orle of small devils, see BORDÉ DE DIABLEAUS (Fig. 130)
Virgin (the), see MADAME SAINTE MARIE (Fig. 131)
  The Virgin's shift, see CHEMISE NOSTRE DAME (Fig. 132)

B. HUMAN BEINGS

Damsel, see DAMOISELE
Hand (dexter), see MEIN (Fig. 133)
  Grasping hand, see MEIN CROCHUE
  Open hand, see MEIN OUVERTE
His sweetheart's legs, see JAMBES DE S'AMIE
Mailed legs embowed and conjoined at the thighs, see JAMBES ARMEES (Fig. 134)
Sanctimonious person, hypocrite, see PAPELART
Thigh, see CUISSE
Tongue with edges, see LANGUE A TRANCHANZ

C. THE LION

Lioncel courant, see LIONCEL COURANT (Fig. 71)
Lioncels rampant in pale, see LIONCEAUS RAMPANZ L'UN DESOUS ET L'AUTRE
  DESUS (Fig. 89)

Lion passant = leopard (see D. OTHER BEASTS)

Lion rampant, see LION[1] (Fig. 135)

    Collared lion rampant, see LION A UN COLIER (Fig. 136)

    Crined lion rampant, see LION CRESTÉ (Fig. 137)

    Crowned lion rampant, see LION COURONÉ (Fig. 138)

    Crowned lion rampant langued grasping a maunch in its mouth with a sword pommelled and hilted cutting the lion in half, see LION RAMPANT COURONÉ A LA LANGUE A UNE MANCHE EN LA GEULE DU LION A UNE ESPEE AU PONG ET AU HELT QUI TRANCHE LE LION PAR MI (Fig. 139)

    Crowned lion rampant shouldering a small cross, see LION COURONÉ A UNE CROIS SOR L'ESPAULE (Fig. 140)

    Crowned lion rampant statant on a mount, see LION RAMPANT COURONÉ ESTANT SUS UNE MOTE (Fig. 141)

    Crowned lion rampant with a forked tail, see LION RAMPANT COURONÉ O DOUBLE COUE (Fig. 142)

    Crowned lion rampant with a forked tail crossed in saltire, see LION COURONÉ LA COUE FOURCHIEE (Fig. 143)

    Demi-lion rampant, see DEMI LION (Fig. 144)

    Lion rampant holding an axe in its paws, see LION RAMPANT OD UNE HACHE (Fig. 145)

    Lion rampant with a forked tail, see LION RAMPANT A LA COUE FOURCHIEE[1] (Fig. 146)

    Lion rampant with a forked tail crossed in saltire, see LION RAMPANT A LA COUE FOURCHIEE[2] (Fig. 147)

    Lion rampant with a shoulder charged with a cinquefoil, see LION RAMPANT ET EN LES ESPAULES DU LION UNE QUINTEFEUILLE (Fig. 148)

    Lion rampant with a shoulder charged with a fleur-de-lis, see LION RAMPANT A UNE FLEUR EN L'ESPAULE DU LION (Fig. 149)

    Lions rampant addorsed, see LIONS ADOSSÉS (Fig. 150)

Referring to a shield charged with a lion, see LIONEL

D. OTHER BEASTS

Boar, see SANGLIER (Fig. 151)

Bruin (animal character [a bear] in the *Roman de Renart*), see BRUN (Fig. 152)

Cat, see CHAT (Fig. 153)

Cow, see VACHE (Fig. 154)

Dog, see Greyhound, Kennet, Mastiff

Elephant, see OLIFANT (Fig. 155)

Ewe passant, see OEILLE PASSANT (Fig. 156)

Greyhound (collared), see LEVRIER OU LE COLIER (Fig. 157)

Hare rampant, see LIEVRE RAMPANT (Fig. 158)

Hind, doe, see BISSE (Fig. 159)

Horse (saddled), see CHEVAL SELLÉ (Fig. 160)

Kennet, small hunting-dog, see CHIENET (Fig. 161)

Lamb, see MOUTON

  Lamb's head, see TESTE DE MOUTON

Leopard (lion passant), see LIEPART (Fig. 162)

  Crowned leopard, see LIEPART COURONÉ (Fig. 163)

  Crowned leopard courant, see LIEPART COURANT ET COURONÉ (Fig. 164)

  Demi-leopard (= demi-lion rampant), see DEMI LIEPART (Fig. 144)

  Leopard courant, see LIEPART COURANT (Fig. 166)

  Leopards facing each other, see LIONCEAUS PASSANZ L'UN CONTRE L'AUTRE EN CHIEF (Fig. 165)

  Leopard's head jessant-de-lis, see FLEUR DE LIS CROISSANT HORS DE LA TESTE DU LIEPART (Fig. 167)

  Leopard with a lamb's head, see LION PASSANT A TESTE DE MOUTON

Mastiff, see MASTIN (Fig. 168)

  Mastiff's head, see CHIEF DE MASTIN (Fig. 169)

  Mastiff with bared teeth, see MASTIN RECHIGNIÉ (Fig. 170)

Mule, see MULE

  Mule's ear, see OREILLE D'UNE MULE

Noble (animal character [a lion] in the *Roman de Renart*), see NOBLE

Ox, see BEUF (Fig. 171)

Stag, see CERF (Fig. 172)

  Stag issuing from a gate, see ISSIR (Fig. 256)

  Stag's attire, or antler, see PERCHE DE DAIM (Fig. 173)

Tiger (heraldic), see TIGRE (Fig. 174)

Wolf, see LEU

  Wolf's head, see TESTE DE LEU (Fig. 175)

Collared, see COLERÉ

Courant, see COURANT

Crested, crined, see CRESTÉ

Facing each other, see L'UN CONTRE L'AUTRE

Gorged, see ENGORGIÉ

Jaws, mouth, see GEULE

  In the mouth, see EN LA GEULE

  With bared teeth, see RECHIGNIÉ

  With gaping jaws, see ENGOULÉ

Passant, see PASSANT[1]

Rampant, see RAMPANT

Salient (?), see PASSANT[4]

Shoulder, see ESPAULE

  On the shoulder, see EN L'ESPAULE (Figs. 148, 149)

  Shouldering, see SOR L'ESPAULE (Fig. 140)

Statant, see ESTANT
Tail, see COUE
    Forked tail, see COUE FOURCHIEE[1]
    Forked tail crossed in saltire, see COUE CROISIEE
    Tip (of the tail), see SOM[1]
        At the tip (of the tail), see EN SOM
    To spread out in a fork, see SOI ESPANDRE EN DOUBLE
Tongue, see LANGUE

E. BIRDS

Bird's wing (here part of a vol), see PENART (Fig. 176)
Bittern (a kind of heron), see BUTOR (Fig. 177)
Chough (?), see COUWE (Fig. 178)
Cock, see COC (Fig. 179)
Crow, see CORNEILLE (Fig. 180)
Eagle, see EGLE (Fig. 181)
    Beak, see BEC
    Crowned eagle, see EGLE COURONEE (Fig. 182)
    Demi-eagle, see DEMI EGLE (Fig. 183)
    Double-headed eagle, see EGLE A DEUS TESTES (Fig. 184)
    Eagle charged with a crescent on its breast, see EGLE A UN CROISSANT EN
        LA POITRINE (Fig. 185)
    Eagle preying on (?) a dragon, see PRES A PRES UNE EGLE ET UN DRAGON
        (Fig. 186)
    Eaglet, see EGLEL (Fig. 187)
    Eagle volant, see EGLE VOLANT (Fig. 188)
    Membered eagle, see EGLE . . . LE BEC ET LES PIÉS
    Orle of eaglets, see BORDURE D'EGLES (Fig. 189)
    To fly, see VOLER
Falcon, see ANOT (Fig. 203)
    Orle of falcons, see ANOZ ENTOUR (Fig. 190)
Hawk, see Sparrow-hawk
Hen, see GELINE (Fig. 191)
    Hen statant on a mount, see GELINE DESUS LE PUI (Fig. 192)
Heron, see HERON (Fig. 193)
    Membered heron, see HERONS PETIZ BEESTEZ
Magpie, see PIE (Fig. 194)
Martlet, see MERLETE[1] (Fig. 195)
    Orle of martlets, see BORDURE DE MERLETES (Fig. 125)
Nightingale, see ROSSIGNOL (Fig. 196)
Oriole, see ORIOL (Fig. 197)
Peacock, see PAON
    Peacock's tail, see ROUE DE PAON (Fig. 198)

Pheasant, see FESAN (Fig. 199)
  Pheasants face to face, see FESANZ BEC A BEC (Fig. 200)
Popinjay (parrot), see PAPEGAI (Fig. 201)
Raven, see CORBEAU (Fig. 202)
Sparrow-hawk, see ESPREVIER (Fig. 203)
  Sparrow-hawk volant, see ESPREVIER QUI DE VOLER NE SE REPOSE (Fig. 204)
Swallow volant, see ARONDE (Fig. 205)
Swan, see CIGNE (Fig. 206)
Vol, see Bird's wing
Woodcock, see WITECOC
  Orle of woodcocks, see ORLE DE WITECOCS (Fig. 207)

Close, see SOI REPOSER DE VOLER
Statant, see DESUS (1)
Volant, see VOLANT

F. FISH

Barbel, see BARBEL (Fig. 208)
Dace (a kind of carp), see DARS (Fig. 209)
Dolphin, see DAUFIN (Fig. 210)
Escallop, see ESCHALOPE (Fig. 211)
  Escallops in cross, see CROIS DE COQUILLES (Fig. 110)
  Orle of escallops, see ESCHALOPES BORDANZ (Fig. 212)
Fish, see POISSON
Herring, see HARENC (Fig. 213)
Pike, see LUZ (Fig. 214)
Salmon, see SAUMON (Fig. 215)
Sea-perch, sea-wolf, see BAR
  Sea-perch addorsed, see BARS SINANZ (Fig. 216)

G. REPTILES

Serpent, see SERPENT (Fig. 217)
  Serpent's ear, see OREILLE
  Serpent's foot, see PIÉ[1]
  Serpent's head, see TESTE DE SERPENT (Fig. 99)
Tortoise, see TORTUE (Fig. 218)

H. MONSTERS

COQUEFABUE
Dragon, see DRAGON (Fig. 219)
  Crested dragon's head, see TESTE D'UN DRAGON CRESTÉ (Fig. 220)
  Dragon's head, see CHIEF DEL DRAGON (Fig. 220)
Eagle preying on (?) a dragon, see PRES A PRES UNE EGLE ET UN DRAGON
    (Fig. 186)

Griffin, see GRIFON (Fig. 221)
   Griffin rampant, see GRIFON RAMPANT (Fig. 222)
   Griffin volant, see GRIFON VOLANT (Fig. 223)

I. CELESTIAL OBJECTS

Clouds, see TENEBRES
Crescent, see CROISSANT[1] (Fig. 224)
Star (estoile, mullet, rowel), see ESTOILE (Fig. 225)
   Pierced mullet, see MOLETE PERCIEE[1] (Fig. 226)
   Small mullet, see ESTENCELE[1] (Fig. 240)
Sun in his splendour, see RAI DE SOLEIL (Fig. 227)

J. TREES AND PLANTS

Garb, see JARBE (Fig. 228)
Hot pepper volant, see POIVRE CHAUT O LES PENARZ
Oak, see CHESNE (Fig. 229)
Oats, see Garb
Pear, see POIRE
   Orle of pears, see ORLE DE POIRES (Fig. 230)
Tree, see ARBRE (Fig. 231)

K. FLOWERS

Angemme, see ANGEMME
   Orle of angemmes, see ANGEGNIES EN L'ESCU (Fig. 232)
Chaplet, garland of heraldic roses, see CHAPEL (Fig. 233)
Cinquefoil, see CINCFEUILLE (Fig. 234)
Fleur-de-lis, see FLEUR (Fig. 235)
   Blossoming, open, see ESPART
   Demi-fleur-de-lis, see DEMI FLEUR DE GLAIEUL (Fig. 236)
   Fleur-de-lis couped (i.e. 'nourri'), see FLEUR DE LIS EN LONC (Fig. 237)
   Flory-counter-flory, see FLEURETÉ[3] (Fig. 127)
   Halved, see DEMI[1]
   Jessant, see CROISSANT[2]
   Ornamented with fleurs-de-lis, see FLEURETÉ[2]
Hollyhock, see PASSEROSE (Fig. 238)
Lime-blossom, see TRUMEL (Fig. 239)
Rose (heraldic), see ROSE[1] (Fig. 47)
   Heraldic rose slipped, see ROSE[2] (Fig. 241)
   Stem of a heraldic rose slipped, see ROSIER (Fig. 241)
Rose (heraldic, but here part of a chaplet), see ROSE[3] (Fig. 233)
Sixfoil, see SISFEUILLE (Fig. 242)
Trefoil, see TIERCEFEUILLE (Fig. 243)

L. INANIMATE OBJECTS

Axe, see HACHE (Fig. 244)
Barge, galley, see BARGE (Fig. 245)
Barnacle, horse-bray, see BROIE (Fig. 144)
Buckle, see FERMAIL (Fig. 246)
Butt, see BOUCEL PAR DESUS LE . . . (Fig. 247)
Carbuncle, see CHARBOUCLE FLEURETÉ (Fig. 248)
    Carbuncle pommy and conjoined, see CHARBOUCLE BESANCIÉ (Fig. 249)
    Demi-carbuncle, see DEMI CHARBOUCLE (Fig. 250)
Castle, see CHASTEL¹ (Fig. 251)
Checkerboard, see ESCHEQUIER
Cheese, see FROMAGE
    Cheese in a small basket, see FROMAGE EN FEISSELE
Collar, see COLIER (Figs. 136, 157)
Crown, see COURONE (Fig. 252)
Cup, see COUPE (Fig. 253)
    Foot (and stem) of a cup, see PIÉ DE HANAP
Die (i.e. the singular of dice), see DE (Fig. 254)
Door, gate, see PORTE (Fig. 255)
    Stag issuing from a gate, see ISSIR (Fig. 256)
Fer-de-moline (see Cross moline s.v. THE CROSS)
Glove, see GANT (Fig. 257)
    Glove with the fingers upwards, see GANT LES DOIZ DESOR (Fig. 258)
Gonfanon, see FANON (Fig. 259)
Gospel, see EVANGILE (Fig. 260)
Hamaide, humet, see HAMEDE (Fig. 261)
Hammer, mallet, see MARTEL (Fig. 262)
    Hammer bendwise, see MARTEL EN BELIC (Fig. 263)
Hook, see Iron hook
Horse-bray, see Barnacle
Horseshoe, see FER¹ (Fig. 264)
    Orle of horseshoes, see BORDURE DE FERS A CHEVAL (Fig. 265)
Hunting-horn, see COR (Fig. 266)
Iron hook, see CROCHET DE FER (Fig. 267)
Key, see CLEF (Fig. 268)
Maunch, see MANCHE¹ (Fig. 269)
Mount, see MOTE (Figs. 141, 192)
Pillar, see PILIER (Fig. 270)
Pitcher, see PICHIER (Fig. 271)
Rake, see RASTEL¹ (Fig. 272)
Sleeve, see MANCHE² (Fig. 132)
Spark, see ESTENCELE² (Fig. 48)

Stirrup, see ESTRIER (Fig. 273)
Sword, see ESPEE (Fig. 274)
   Handle, grip, see PONG (Fig. 139)
   Hilt, see HELT (Fig. 139)
Trumpet, see TROMPE (Fig. 275)
Water-bouget, see BOUGE (Fig. 276)
Wooden horse hanging from a gallows, see CHEVAL FUST APENDU D'UNES
   FOURCHES

X. GENERAL

A. TERMS USED IN BLAZON

Above, see DESUS
Above and below, see DESOUS ET DESOR
Alone, see SEUL
Arms, see ARMES
   Different arms, see D'AUTRE SEMBLANCE
   The same arms, see AUTEL[1]
   The same arms as, see AUTELS ARMES COM
   The same arms, differenced by, see AUTEL[2]
   The same arms, without, see AUTEL SANS
As a difference, see PAR DESCONOISSANCE
As a distinctive device, see PAR CONOISSANCE[1]
Assume, see PRENDRE
Be, see ESTRE
Bear, see PORTER
   Bear . . . instead of, see EN LIEU DE . . . METRE
Below, see DESOUS
Between, see ENTRE
   Placed between, see ENTREALÉ
But, except, see MES
Call, give a name to, see DIRE
Charge, see ENSEIGNE[2]
   Remaining charges, what needs to be added to complete the blazon, see
      SORPLUS
Come out of, see ISSIR
Completely, all, see TOUT[5]
Concerning which, whose, see DONT
Conjoined, see JOINT
Counterchanged, see DE L'UN EN L'AUTRE[1]
Difference, see DESCONOISSANCE[2]
   To differentiate, see DESCONOISTRE[1]
   To have no other difference between, see N'AVOIR NULE AUTRE DIVERSITÉ
   D'ARMES ENTRE

Different, see DIVERS

Different, distinct, see DESPAREIL[2]

Different from, see AUTREMENT QUE

Distinctive device, see CONOISSANCE[1]

Downward, see CONTREVAL

Each, see CHASCUN

Except, see FORS

  Except that, see FORS QUE

Field, see ESCU[1]

  On the field, see EL CHAMP

Full, see PLEIN

Full, complete, referring to a charge as it appears in its simple or normal
    form, without any adornment or modification, see ENTIER[2]

Have, see AVOIR

Identical with, see AINSI COM

Inside, see ENZ

Instead of, see EN LIEU DE

In the middle, see ENMI

Less, see MOINS

Middle, see MILIEU

On, see SOR

On each side (of a bend), see AU DEHORS

Only, see SEULEMENT

Or, see OU[4]

Other, see AUTRE

Out of, see HORS

Over all, see SOR LE TOUT

  Over all and straddling the lines, see DE L'UN EN L'AUTRE[4]

  To place a charge over all the others on the shield, see JETER SOR

Perhaps, see FORSE

Piece, see POINT[1]

Placed, situated, see ASIS

  To be placed, see SEIR

  To place upon, see METRE

Plain arms, i.e. shield of a single tincture, see ARMES PURES SANS NULE AUTRE
    DESCONOISSANCE

  Plain arms, except that, see D'UNE COULEUR FORS

Small, see MENU

These things, see CEZ CHOSES

Unaccustomed, different arms (as a disguise), see ESTRANGES ARMES

Undifferenced arms, see ARMES PLAINES[1]

  Undifferenced arms, except that, see TOUT PLAIN FORS TANT QUE

Where, see OU[3]

Which, see QUI
Whole, see TOUT[3]
Wide, large, see GROS
With, see AVUEC
With the exception of, see FORS DE
With the exception that, see FORS QUE
Without, see SANS
Without any other charge, see SANS NULE AUTRE ENSEIGNE

B. MISCELLANEOUS

Abandon, relinquish (arms), see JETER PUER
Bear arms, see AVOIR UNES ARMES
    All bearing the same arms, see TOUT ENSEIGNIÉ D'UNE MANIERE
    To bear another person's arms as a sign of love for or alliance with him,
       see POUR AMOUR DE
Bestow one's own arms upon someone as a sign of love for or alliance with
       him, see POUR L'AMOUR DE
    To bestow one's undifferenced arms upon someone, see CHARGIER SES ARMES A
Blazon (a), see DEVIS
Blazon (to), see DEVISER[1]
Carved, cut into, see ENTAILLIÉ
Challenge, see CHALENGE
    To be the subject of a challenge, see ESTRE DE CHALENGE PAR ENTRE . . . ET . . .
Change arms (as a disguise), see ARMES CHANGIER
    Arms changed (as a disguise), see DESGUISIÉ[1]
    To change one's arms (as a disguise), see CHANGIER SES ARMES
Charge (to), see ESTRE MIS EN . . .
Complex, bizarre (arms), see DESGUISIÉ[2]
Disguise one's arms, see SOI DESCONOISTRE
Herald, see HIRAUT
His own arms, his proper arms, see SES PROPRES ARMES
Illustrate, represent symbolically by means of arms, see DEVISER[3]
Invent a coat of arms, see DEVISER[2]
King of arms, see ROI HIRAUT
Make similar arms, see CONTREFAIRE
Meaning, symbolism (of a coat of arms), see SENEFIANCE
Misappropriated (arms), see CONTREFAIT
Recognize (arms), see CONOISTRE
    To recognize one another's arms, see SOI ENTRECONOISTRE
Represent, symbolize, see SENEFIER
True, correct arms, see DROIT[1]
War-cry, see ENSEIGNE[3]
    To utter a war-cry, see ESCRIER

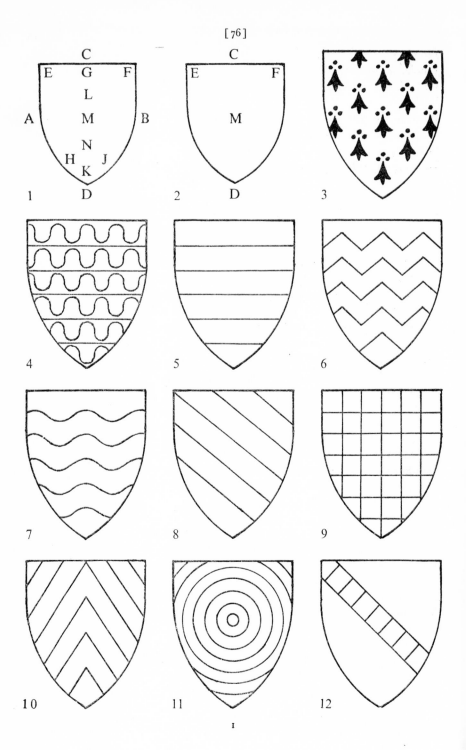

1

2

3

4

5

6

7

8

9

10

11

12

13

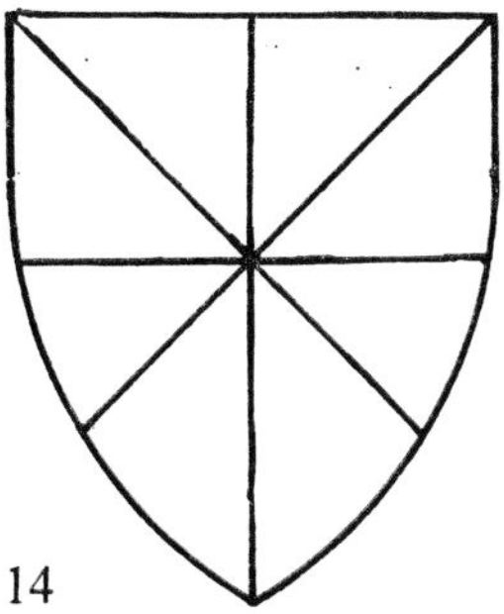

14

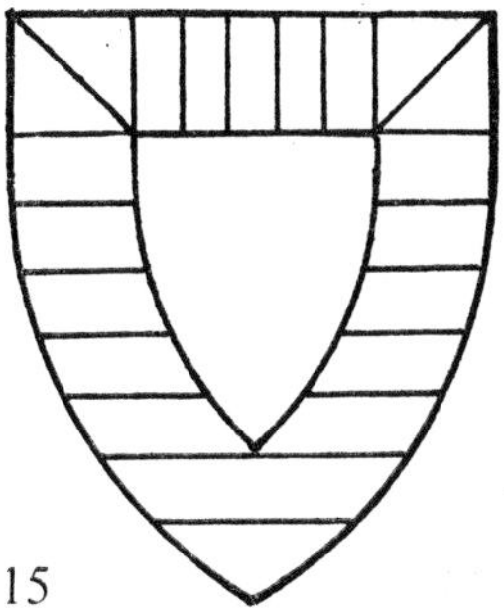

15

16

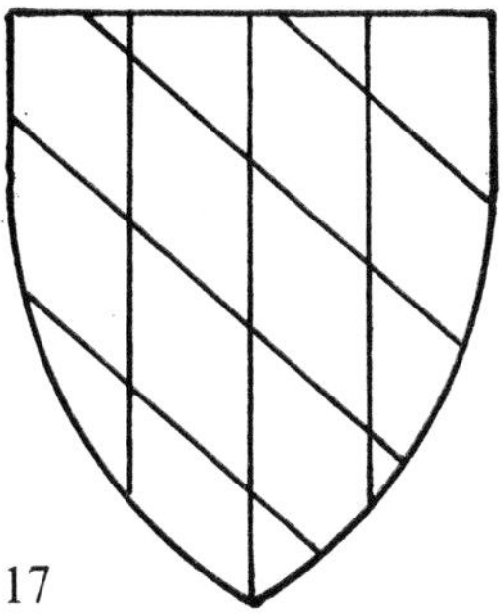

17

18

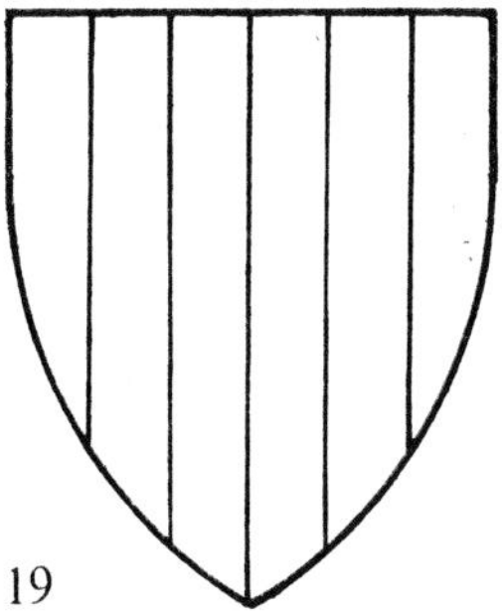

19

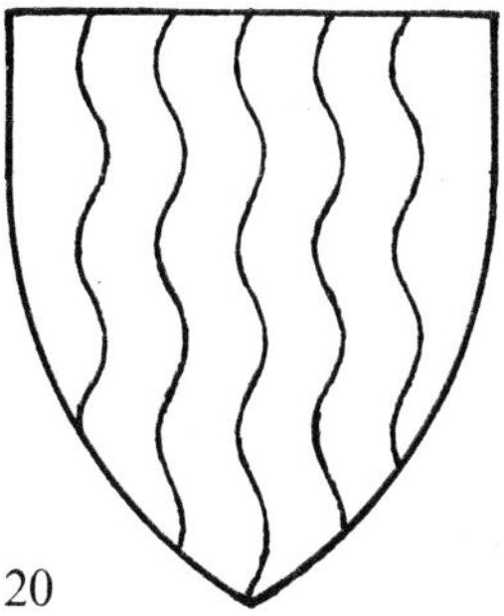

20

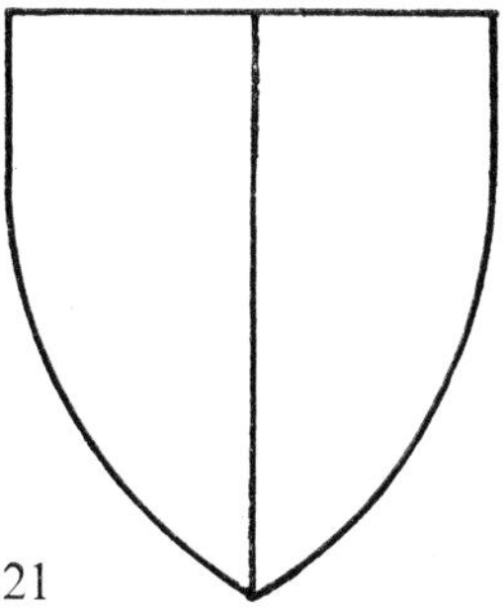

21

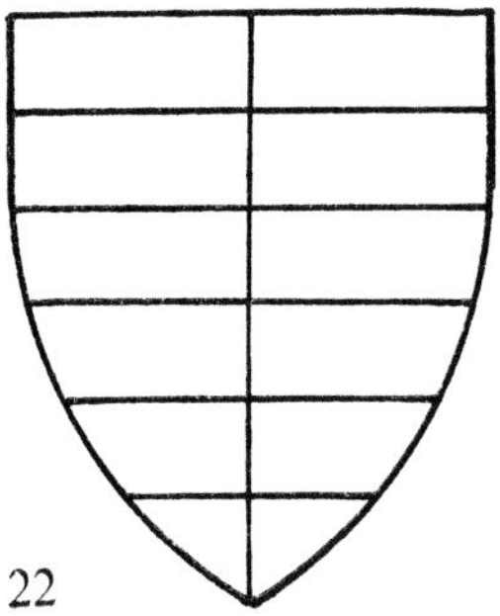

22

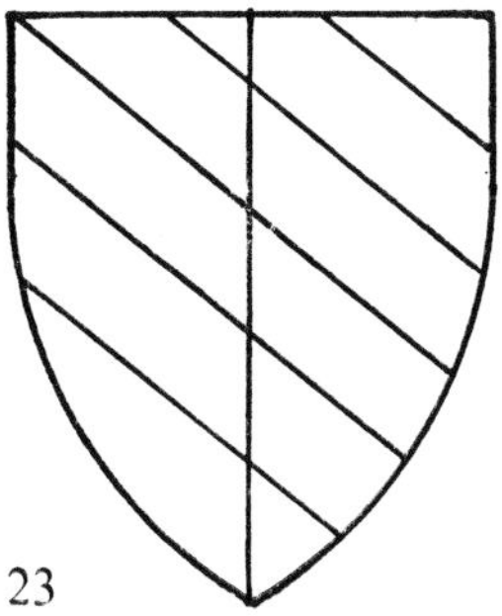

23

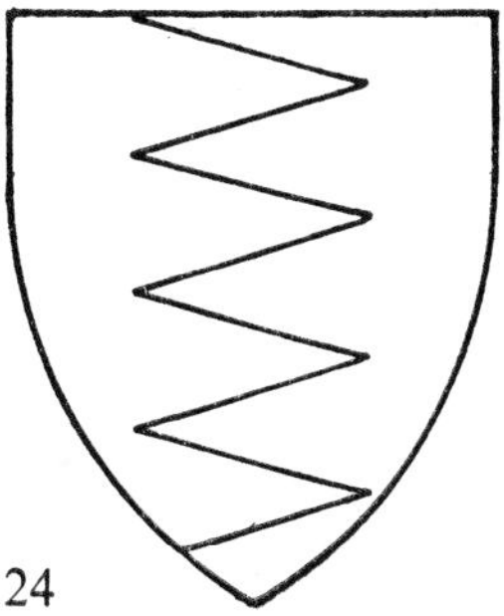

24

25

26

27

28

29

30

31

32

33

34

35

36

3

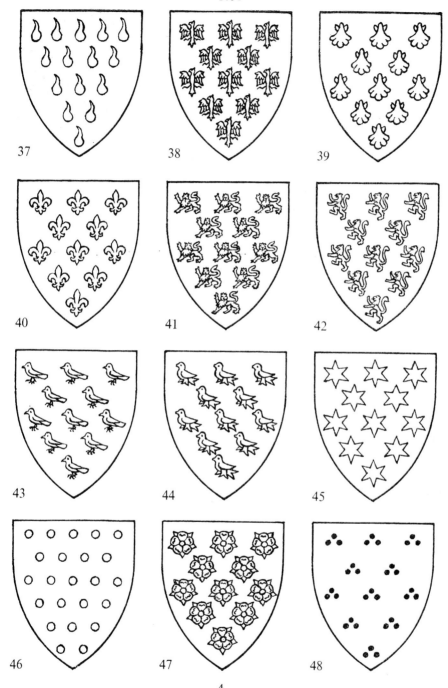

37

38

39

40

41

42

43

44

45

46

47

48

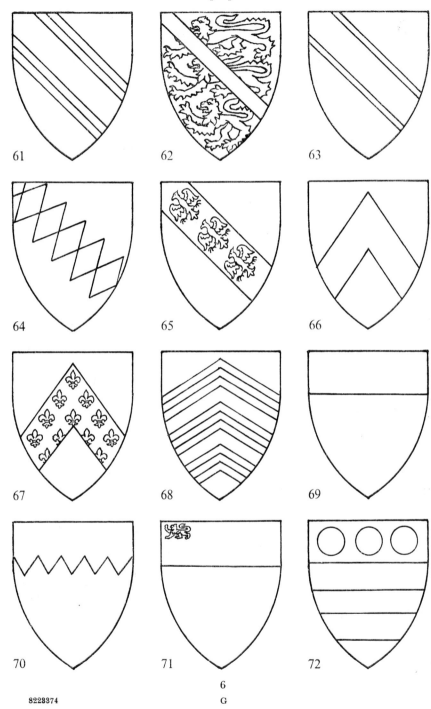

61

62

63

64

65

66

67

68

69

70

71

72

8228374

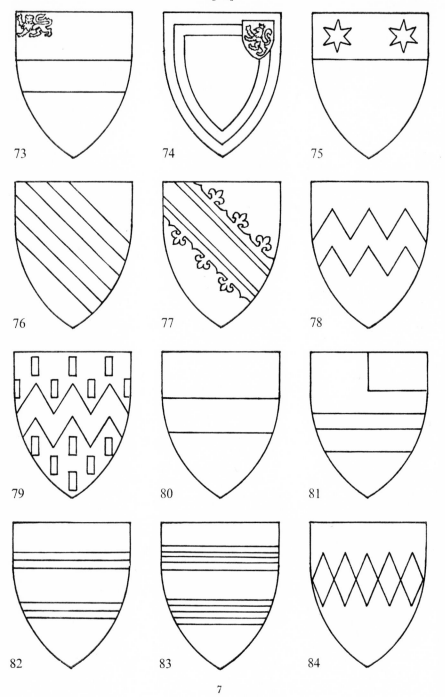

73

74

75

76

77

78

79

80

81

82

83

84

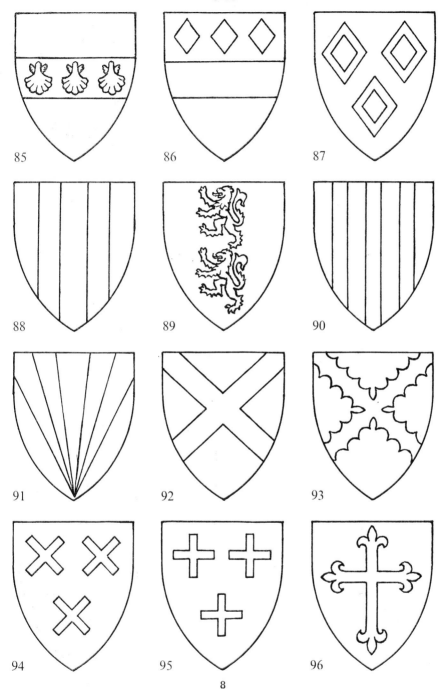

85

86

87

88

89

90

91

92

93

94

95

96

8

97

98

99

100

101

102

103

104

105

106

107

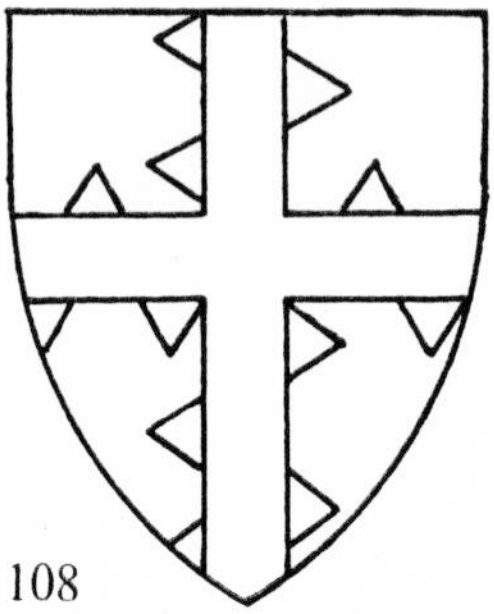

108

109

110

111

112

113

114

115

116

117

118

119

120

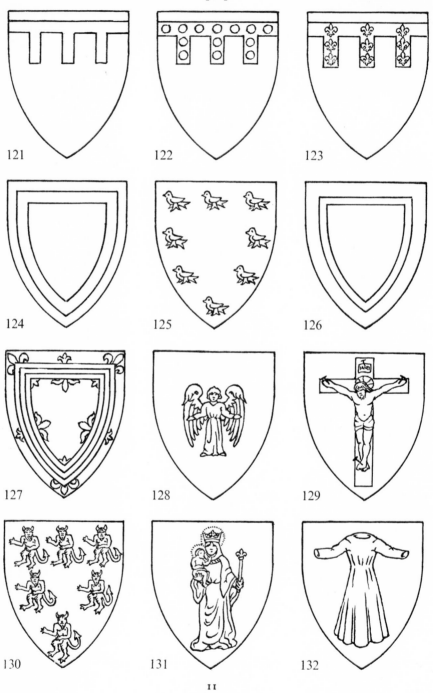

133

134

135

136

137

138

139

140

141

142

143

144

12

145   146   147

148   149   150

151   152   153

154   155   156

157

158

159

160

161

162

163

164

165

166

167

168

169

170

171

172

173

174

175

176

177

178

179

180

181 182 183

184 185 186

187 188 189

190 191 192

193

194

195

196

197

198

199

200

201

202

203

204

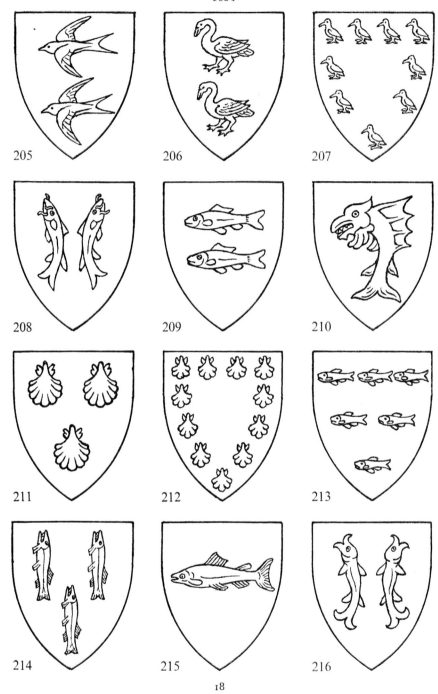

205

206

207

208

209

210

211

212

213

214

215

216

217   218   219

220   221   222

223   224   225

226   227   228

229   230   231

232   233   234

235   236   237

238   239   240

241

242

243

244

245

246

247

248

249

250

251

252

253

254

255

256

257

258

259

260

261

262

263

264

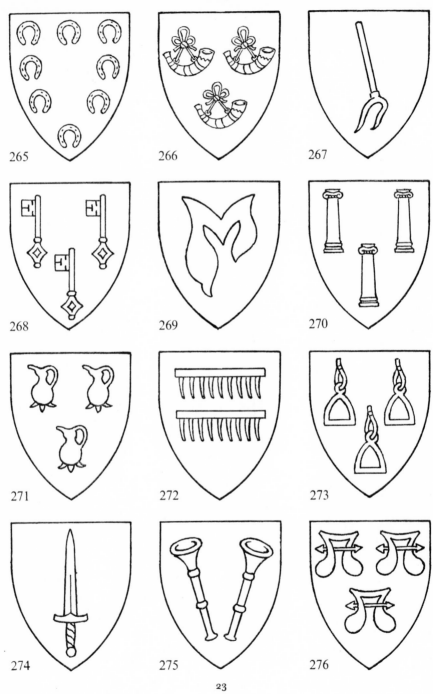

265

266

267

268

269

270

271

272

273

274

275

276

TABLE II

ADDITIONAL FRENCH AND ENGLISH TERMS PROVIDED IN THE NOTES

French heraldic terms are indicated in italics, English in roman type. A certain number of these French terms (e.g. *bretessé*) are, of course, used in English blazon.

Addorsed, see BAR
Affronté, see COMBATRE; LIONCEAUS PASSANZ L'UN CONTRE L'AUTRE EN CHIEF
Affronted, see LIONCEAUS PASSANZ L'UN CONTRE L'AUTRE EN CHIEF
Alésé, see ESLAISIÉ
Anelet percié, see MEULET PERCIÉ
Anelete perciee, see MEULET PERCIÉ
Angenne, see ANGEGNIES EN L'ESCU
Angevine, see ANGEGNIES EN L'ESCU
Bande vivrée, see DANCE EN BELIC A OISEAUS
Bar, see FESSE
Bar sinister, see BARRE[1]
Barre, see BARRÉ DE . . . ET DE . . .[1]
Bastillé, see ENCHASTELÉ
Baston, see BASTON[1]
Baston couped, see BASTON[1]
Bâton, see AUTRETEL
Bâton alaisé (or *alésé*), see BASTON[1]
Bâton en bande, see BASTON[1]
Bâton en barre, see BASTON[1]
Bâton péri, see BASTON[1]
Baucent, '*Beau Séant*', see CROIS FORMEE, CROIS PASSANT
Bend sinister, see BARRE[1]; BASTON[1]
Bendy sinister, see BARRÉ DE . . . ET DE . . .[1]
Bois de cerf, see PERCHE DE DAIM
Bordé, see BORDÉ ENVIRON; ORLÉ
Boutoné, see BOUTONÉ
Bras (*d'un sautoir*), see SAUTOIR[1]
Bretessé, see ENCHASTELÉ
Burelle, see FESSE
Burellé, see FESSIÉ DE . . . ET DE . . .[1]
Cane, see CROIS FOURCHIEE AU KANEE
Cannette, see MERLETE[1]

Canton (sinister), see Sinister canton

Chapel, see CHAPEL

Chefs fleurettés (les), see CROIS FOURCHIEE AU KANEE

Chevet (d'une croix), see CROIS FOURCHIEE AU KANEE

Combattant, see LIONCEAUS PASSANZ L'UN CONTRE L'AUTRE EN CHIEF

Combed, see CRESTÉ

Contre-bastillé, see ENCHASTELÉ

Contre-rampant, see COMBATRE

Cornière, see CORNIERE[1]

Cotice, see AUTRETEL

Coue, see CROIS FOURCHIEE AU KANEE

Counter-rampant, see COMBATRE

Crenelé, see ENCHASTELÉ

Crêté, see CRESTÉ

Crined, see CRESTÉ

Crois a les degrees, see BARGE

Crois martelee, see BARGE

Crois recoupee, see CROIS ENDENTEE[2]

Croix fleurdelysée, see FLEURETÉ[2]

Croix hendée, see CROIS FOURCHIEE AU KANEE

Croix pattée, see CROIS PATEE

Cross botonny, see BOUTONÉ; CROIS RECROISELEE

Cross Calvary, see BARGE

Cross couped, see CROIS ENDENTEE[2]

Cross couped trebel fitchy, see CROIS FOURCHIEE[1]

Cross crosslet, see CROIS RECROISELEE

Cross floretty, see FLEURETÉ[2]

Cross flory, see FLEURETÉ[2]

Cross ('headless'), see 'Headless' cross

Cross humetty, see CROIS ENDENTEE[2]

Cross (moline), see Moline cross

Cross potent, see BARGE; CROIS[1]; CROIS BILLETEE

Cross raguly, see CROIS ENDENTEE[2]

Dancetty, see VUIVRE DE TRAVERS EL CHIEF

Dimidiation, see PARTI DE . . . ET DE . . .

Displayed, see EGLE; ESPANI

Dot, see ESTENCELÉ

Du même, see DEL MESME

En cœur, see ESCUÇON[1]

Ends (of a cross), see BOUT

Engoulé, see BISSE

Ployé, see ESPANI

Escarboucle accolée en orle, see CHARBOCLE

Escarboucle fermée et pommetée, see CHARBOCLE

Etincelle, see ANGEGNIES EN L'ESCU

Etoilé, see SEMÉ DE TENCELES

Extrémités (d'une croix), see BOUT

Fasce, see FESSE; FESSIÉ DE . . . ET DE . . .[1]

Fascé, see FESSIÉ DE . . . ET DE . . .[1]

Fasce vivrée, see DANCE

Feathered, see ENPENÉ

Fess fusilly, see DANCE

Fimbriated, see BORDÉ ENVIRON

Flames (semy of), see ESTENCELÉ

Flanchis, see SAUTOIR[2]

Fleur de lis à pied coupé, see FLEUR DE LIS EN LONG

Fleur de lis à pied nourri, see FLEUR DE LIS EN LONG

Fleur de lis du pied nourry, see FLEUR DE LIS EN LONG

Frestel, see COTICE

Fretel, see AUTRETEL

Fuseau, see FESSIEL ENCHASTELÉ DESOUS ET DESOR

Fusel, see FESSIEL ENCHASTELÉ DESOUS ET DESOR

Fusele, see FESSIEL ENCHASTELÉ DESOUS ET DESOR

Gante, see GANT

Gemelle, see JUMEAUS[2]

Giron, see GIRONÉ DE . . . ET DE . . .[2]

Goose (wild), see Wild goose

Grain, see BESANT

Greneté, see SEMÉ DE GRAINS

Guivre, see DE FUIRES

Gurge, see ROUELÉ DE . . . ET DE . . .

Hauriant, see BAR

'Headless' cross, see CROIS ENDENTEE[2]

Hearts (semy of), see ESTENCELÉ

Hempbray, see BROIE

Huchet, see COR

Impalement, see PARTI DE . . . ET DE . . .

Issant, see BISSE; NAISSANT

Issuant, see NAISSANT

Jante, see GANT

Leaves (semy of), see ESTENCELÉ

Léopard lionné, see LION PASSANT

Lion léopardé, see LION PASSANT

Lion passant guardant, see LIEPART

Lune, see LUNETE

Lunel, see LUNETE

Même (du), see *Du même*
Mi-parti, see PARTI DE . . . ET DE . . .
Mi-partition, see PARTI DE . . . ET DE . . .
Moline cross, see CROIS FOURCHIEE AU KANEE
Nebuly, see ONDÉ DE . . . ET DE . . .
Of the same, see DEL MESME
Oueille, see OUISSE
Pard, see LIEPART
Partition, see PARTI DE . . . ET DE . . .
Patriarchal cross, see CROIS[3]
Pellet, see PELOTE
Penne, see CHIEF[2]
Penned, see ENPENÉ
Per pall, see GIRONÉ DE . . . ET DE . . .[2]
Pièce, see PEL
Pleine lune, see LUNETE
Pois, see BESANT
Potence, see FOURCHES
Quatrefoil, see ESTENCELÉ
Queue, see CROIS FOURCHIEE AU KANEE
Quintefeuille angemmée, see ANGEGNIES EN L'ESCU
Quintefeuille percée, see ANGEGNIES EN L'ESCU
Raie de soleil, see ANGEGNIES EN L'ESCU
Rais, see ANGEGNIES EN L'ESCU
Ramure, see PERCHE DE DAIM
Rose, see ANGEGNIES EN L'ESCU
Rose trémière, see PASSEROSE
Rowel, see ESTOILE
Same (of the), see Of the same
Seax, see HACHE
Sinister canton, see CHANTEL[4]
Sinople, see VERT
Spark, see ANGEGNIES EN L'ESCU
Sun in his splendour, see ANGEGNIES EN L'ESCU
Swallow, see MERLETE[1]
Swallowing, see ENGOULÉ
Terrace in base, see CHAMPAIGNE
Tiercé en pairle, see GIRONÉ DE . . . ET DE . . .[2]
Tiercefeuille angemmée, see ANGEGNIES EN L'ESCU
Tiercefeuille percée, see ANGEGNIES EN L'ESCU
Tower, see CHASTEL[1]
Traverse, see BASTON[1]
Turret, see CHASTEL[1]

PLATE 3

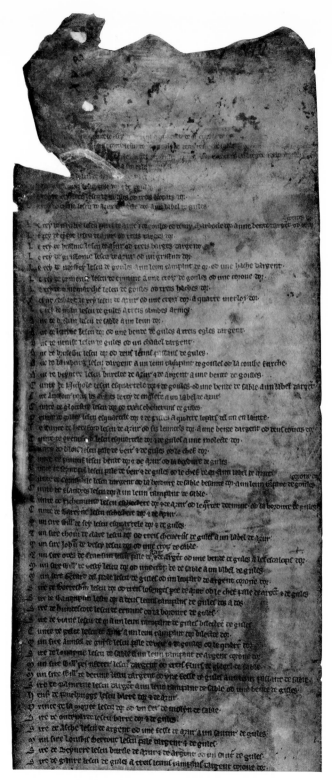

BEGINNING OF THE CAMDEN ROLL
London, British Museum, Cotton Roll XV. 8

Vivre, see DANCE; DE FUIRES

Vivré, see DE FUIRES; VUIVRE DE TRAVERS EL CHIEF

Vouivre, see DE FUIRES

Wavy, see ONDÉ DE . . . ET DE . . .

Wild goose, see GANT

Wivern, wyver, wyvern, see VUIVRE DE TRAVERS EL CHIEF

A GLOSSARY OF HERALDIC TERMS AND PHRASES IN THE THIRTEENTH-CENTURY FRENCH AND ANGLO-NORMAN ROLLS OF ARMS

TOGETHER WITH A LIST OF SUCH EXPRESSIONS FOUND IN A REPRESENTATIVE NUMBER OF TWELFTH- AND THIRTEENTH-CENTURY FRENCH LITERARY TEXTS

a bendes, *bendy* (Fig. 8). *Raoul de Cambrai,* v. 508: A bendes d'or fu la boucle. *Syn.:* see BENDÉ DE . . . ET DE . . .[1].

a bendes bendé, *traversed by multiple stripes (direction not indicated).Aye d'Avignon,* v. 2970: A .iiii. bendes d'or sont bendez lor escus. *Syn.:* BENDÉ DE BENDES, DE BENDES PAR MI LISTÉ, LISTÉ DE . . . ET DE . . . *Note:* see BENDE[1], *Note;* BENDÉ[2].

a bendes de belic, *bendy* (Fig. 8). *Vulgate Merlin Sequel,* p. 119: a menues bendes . . . de belic si menuement com pot faire. *Syn.:* see BENDÉ DE . . . ET DE . . .[1].

a bendes en travers, *barry* (Fig. 5). *Vulgate Merlin Sequel,* p. 120: et a bendes en travers. *Syn.:* see BARRÉ DE . . . ET DE . . .[1].

a billetes semé, *billety* (Fig. 30). *BA* 30: a bilettes . . . semees; 118: a billettes . . . semee (A: semees); 15, 117 (A: billette), 128: a billettes . . . semees. *Syn.:* see BILLETÉ[1].

achon, see AZON.

a coquilles semé, *semy of escallops* (Fig. 39). *BA* 35: a cokilles . . . semees. *Syn.:* AUS ESCHALOPES, CHAMP PLEIN D'ESCHALOPES, OD LES ESCHALOPES. *Note:* cf. ESCHALOPES BORDANZ.

a courones, *semy of crowns* (Fig. 36). *Lancelot propre,* iii. 402: a corounes; *Vulgate Merlin Sequel,* p. 120: a courounes; p. 143: a corounes; p. 316: a ces courounes. *Syn.:* DES COURONES TANT QUE L'ON I POUVOIT METRE.

a croiseles, *crusily* (Fig. 35). *Bl* 71: a croisseles (*B* 71, see A CROISELEZ). *Syn.:* see CROISELÉ.

a croiseles poudré, see POUDRÉ A CROI-SELES·

a croiseles semé, *crusily* (Fig. 35). *Bb* 55: [a crosslet tricked] . . . semmy (*B/Bl* 55, see CROISELÉ; *Ba* 55, see POUDRÉ A CROI-

SELES; *Bc* 55, see A CROISILLES POUDRÉ A L'ESCU). *Syn.:* see CROISELÉ.

a croiselez, *crusily* (Fig. 35). *B* 71: a croi-selets (*Bl* 71, see A CROISELES). *Syn.:* see CROISELÉ.

a croisetes semé, *crusily* (Fig. 35). *BA* 41: a croisettes . . . semees. *Syn.:* see CROISELÉ.

a croisilles poudré a l'escu, *crusily* (Fig. 35). *Bc* 55: a crusile . . . poudré al le escu (*B/Bl* 55, see CROISELÉ; *Ba* 55, see POUDRÉ A CROISELES; *Bb* 55, see A CROISELES SEMÉ). *Syn.:* see CROISELÉ. *Note:* on this locution, see *Aspilogia II,* p. 95.

adossé, *addorsed (back to back).* See LIONS ADOSSÉS. *Syn.:* DOS A DOS, SINANT.

a droit, *true, correct (arms).* See ARMES A DROIT. *Syn.:* see DROIT[1].

a egleaus, *semy of eaglets* (Fig. 38). *Troie,* v. 7828: a aigleaus; *FCT,* v. 4882: a ces aigliax; *TA,* v. 1384: a egleaus. *Syn.:* see A EGLEAUS SEMÉ.

a egleaus semé, *semy of eaglets* (Fig. 38). *EO,* v. 5144: D'armes vermeilles a aigliaus d'or semés. *Syn.:* A EGLEAUS, A EGLES, A EGLEZ, AUS EGLES, POUDRÉ D'EGLEZ, SEMEN-CIÉ D'EGLES.

a egles, *semy of eaglets* (Fig. 38). *Durmart,* v. 7732: A aigles. *Syn.:* see A EGLEAUS SEMÉ.

a eglez, *semy of eaglets* (Fig. 38). *Durmart,* v. 8415: a . . . aigliés. *Syn.:* see A EGLEAUS SEMÉ.

a eschequier, *checky* (Fig. 9). *Chétifs,* p. 276: A son col pent la targe qui fu a eschequier; *Lancelot propre,* iv. 310: d'unes armes paintes a eskequier. *Syn.:* see ESCHEQUÉ DE . . . ET DE . . .

a fleuretes, *semy of fleurs-de-lis* (Fig. 40). *Floire et Blancheflor,* p. 153, v. 960: A floretes. *Syn.:* see FLEURETÉ[1]. *Note:* second redaction only. On floral symbolism in the earlier (third quarter of the twelfth century) version, consult W. C. Calin, 'Flower Imagery in *Floire et Blancheflor*', *FS*, xviii (1964), 103–11.

a fleuretes semé, *semy of fleurs-de-lis* (Fig. 40). *BA* 232: a florette (A: florettes) . . . semees. *Syn.*: see FLEURETÉ[1].

a fleurs, *semy of fleurs-de-lis* (Fig. 40). *Roland*, v. 1810: E cil escuz, ki ben sunt peinz a flurs; *Thèbes*, v. 2989: Escuz a or bien painz a flors; *Troie*, v. 17136: l'escu peint a flor; *Chevalier au Cygne*, v. 3276: escus pains a flor; *Saisnes*, v. 5121: escuz painz a flor; *SCU*, fo. 168 *d*: a fleurs; *TA*, v. 1718: l'escu paint a flour. *Syn.*: see FLEURETÉ[1]. *Note*: numerous other early examples of *escu a fleurs* and its variants are provided by Bouly de Lesdain, pp. 191, 195; Schirling, pp. 21–2; Tobler–Lommatzsch, iii. 1936.

a fleurs de lis, *semy of fleurs-de-lis* (Fig. 40). *Durmart*, v. 8558: A flors de lis. *Syn.*: see FLEURETÉ[1].

a fleurs de lis semé, *semy of fleurs-de-lis* (Fig. 40). *BA* 238, 246: a fleurs de lis . . . semees; *CP* 24: au fleurs de lis . . . semees; 134: au fleur de lis . . . semees; *CPA* 1, 150: a fleurs de lis . . . semees. *Syn.*: see FLEURETÉ[1].

a fleurs de l'un a l'autre, *fleurs-de-lis counterchanged. Escoufle*, vv. 1136–7:

Ses escus ert d'azur et d'or,
Bendés a flors de l'un a l'autre.

Syn.: see FLEURÉ DE L'UN EN L'AUTRE. *Note*: on this locution, see Brault, '*de l'un en l'autre*', p. 85. Add C. D. Rouillard, *The Turk in French History, Thought, and Literature 1520–1660* (Paris, 1938), p. 49.

agegnie, see ANGEGNIES EN L'ESCU.

a geules freté, *descriptive phrase referring to the gules stripes of a barry field.* The complete blazon reads as follows: *Cd* 89: Hernold de la Wede, barré d'or e de gules, a goules fretté argent. *Note*: cf. FRETÉ EN LE GEULES, SAUTOIRS EN L'OR. *Aspilogia II*, p. 183, note to item 77: '[*Cd* 89's blazon] makes it clear that only the red bars are fretty, or as L'Espinoy blazons it charged with five saltires.'

aigle, aiglel, aiglet, aiglete, aiglier, see EGLE, EGLEL, EGLET, EGLETE, EGLIER.

ainsi som, *identical with. TC*, v. 3160: Ainsi vermoilles comme feu.

airiant, *hauriant*. See LUCET AIRIANT.

aisur, see AZUR.

al = **a le,** *equivalent of MFr. 'au'*.

al croisel, see AUS CROISEAUS.

a l'escu, *pleonasm.* See A CROISILLES POUDRÉ A L'ESCU. *Note*: refers to ESCU[1].

a losenges, *lozengy* (Fig. 16). *TA*, v. 2312: l'escu portret a losenge. *Syn.*: see LOSENGIÉ DE . . . ET DE . . .[1].

a losenges de . . . et de . . . losengié, *lozengy* (Fig. 16). *TA*, vv. 1958–9:

Que a losenges de concorde
Et d'amour ierent losengié.

Syn.: see LOSENGIÉ DE . . . ET DE . . .[1].

al som, *in chief* (Fig. 72). See EGLET AL SOM. *Syn.*: see EN LE CHIEF[2].

altretel, see AUTRETEL.

a merloz, *semy of martlets* (Fig. 44). *K*, vv. 339–40:

Thouchez, chevaliers de bon los,
Le ot vermeille a jaunes merlos.

Syn.: POUDRÉ DE MERLOZ. *Note*: in MS. Cotton Caligula A. XVIII, the word *Emlam* has been added above the name *Thouchez* by a different hand. Nicolas, p. 209, points out that a 'Sire William Thochet' bearing the same arms ('de goules a les merelos de or') is mentioned in the Parliamentary Roll. Papworth's *Ordinary* lists numerous other attestations, s.v. *birds* (*gules, six* [*ten*, or *semy of*] *martlets or* [also *gules, seven sheldrakes or* and *gules, ten martlets argent*]), for the family named Thochett, Tochett, Touchet, Touchett, Tuchet, Tuckett, and Duche or Duchet.

amie, see JAMBES DE S'AMIE.

a moletes semé, *semy of mullets* (Fig. 45). *BA* 287: a molette . . . semees (A: semmees). *Syn.*: ESTELÉ, ESTENCELÉ, ESTENCELÉ DE . . . ET DE . . ., MOLETES EN LE . . ., SEMÉ DE TENCELES, TOUT ESTELÉ.

amont, see LION AMONT RAMPANT, LION RAMPANT AMONT. *Syn.*: CONTREMONT.

amont rampant, see LION AMONT RAMPANT.

amour, see POUR AMOUR DE, POUR L'AMOUR DE, POUR L'AMOUR QU'OT A.

an, *the English indefinite article.* See examples s.v. EGLE, ORLE OF MERLOZ.

and, *the English conjunction.* See CHEQUÉ DE . . . ET DE . . .

aneaus, *annulets.* See ANEL.

aneaus de l'un en l'autre, *referring to a*

*barry field with annulets of a different tincture
over all and straddling the lines. BA* 280:
a .v. enniax (A: a semiax) . . . de l'un en
l'autre, see BENDÉ DE . . . ET DE . . .². *Note*:
for these arms, see *WB* 904. Refers to DE
L'UN EN L'AUTRE⁴.

anel, *annulet* (Fig. 111). *BA* 198, 228: a .vi.
aniax; 274: a .x. aniax (A: ainiax); 275:
a .x. aniax (A: ainax); *TC*, v. 455: a cinq
annés; v. 649: a trois aniaus. *Syn.*: ANELET,
ANELETE, FAUSE ROUELE, FAUS RONDELET,
MEULETE PERCIEE, MEULET PERCIÉ. See also
CERCLE and cf. ANEAUS DE L'UN EN L'AUTRE.
Note: the plural form is *aneaus.*

anelet, *annulet* (Fig. 111). *M* 14: ou .vi.
aneletz. For another use, see ANELET EN LA
FESSE. *Syn.*: see ANEL. *Note*: *anelet* is a
diminutive of OFr. *anel*. The plural form is
anelez. For the canting arms of the Colet
family, see Wagner, *Historic Heraldry*, p. 68.

anelete, *annulet* (Fig. 110). *M* 76: ou .vi.
anelettez; 77: odve seez anelettez. *Syn.*:
see ANEL. *Note*: *P* 88 (= *B* 99, see FAUS
RONDELET) reads: 'a sys anelettes'.

anelet en la fesse, *on a fess an annulet. CP*
96: a trois annelets . . . en la fesse.

anelete perciee, *ghost word.* See MEULET
PERCIÉ.

anelez, *annulets.* See ANELET.

angegnies en l'escu, *orle of angemmes*
(Fig. 232). *CP* 77: Li camberlains de Tan-
carvile porte les armes de [lacuna in MS.]
a un escusson d'argent parmi, agegnies d'or
en l'escu. *Note*: cf. ANGEVINE, ENGEIGNIE.
Prinet CP, p. 26, no. 3, identifies these
arms as those of Robert de Tancarville,
Chamberlain of Normandy, whose seal
features an inescutcheon 'à la bordure
d'*angemmes* (fleurs à six pétales)'. Littré
defines *angemme* or *angenne*, a feminine
substantive, as follows: 'Terme de blason. Fleur imaginaire à feuilles arrondies,
tantôt au nombre de cinq comme dans la
quinte-feuille, tantôt au nombre de six.
— *Etym.* Origine inconnue'. D'Haucourt–
Durivault, p. 92: 'Si les pétales sont ar-
rondis et le cœur percé, laissant voir le
champ, l'on a respectivement la *tiercefeuille percée* ou *angemmée* (trois pétales),
l'*angemme* (quatre pétales), la *quinte-feuille
percée* ou *angemmée*.' London, 'Scintillatum
Auro', p. 113, states: 'The fact is that the
spark, in common with the *angemme* or

angevine and the *rais* or *raie de soleil*, was
peculiar to Normandy and was little known
even in other provinces of France. Moreover it was apt to vary both in the number
and in the shape of the points. These however are often, though not invariably,
separate as in St. George's Roll, and the
only treatise which attempts to distinguish
clearly between the *angemme*, *étincelle* and
rais, a 15th-century manuscript known as
L'Ordre des hérauts, gives that as the distinctive mark of the *étincelle.*' London adds
that 'for an authoritative study of the
étincelle, the *angemme* and the *rais* we must
await the essay which Dr. Adam-Even is
writing for the *Archives Héraldiques Suisses*'.
London, 'Notes and Reflections, II', p. 270,
again returns to this subject: 'The *rey de
soleil* or *rais* was a Norman speciality like
the *étincelle* and the *angemme* or *angevin* [*sic*]
(pp. 67–8). It was represented as a star-like
object with many long straight rays [here
London adds, in a footnote: 'In France
the *rais* sometimes assumed a more floral
character, barely distinguishable from the
angemme, but I have not found that in
England'], a much more pleasing charge
than the ungainly sun in splendour of
modern armory.' The parenthetical page
numbers refer to Hope, pp. 67–8, where we
read the following quotation from a grant
of arms of King Henry VI, dated 11 March
1444–5, to Bernard Angevin, one of the
King's counsellors in Aquitaine: 'Quorum
quidem armorum campus est de asura cum
uno leone ungulato et linguato de goules
ac cum decem floribus per circuitum
vocatis *Angevins* de argento.' To my knowledge, Dr. Adam-Even never published the
study alluded to by London, though he
referred to the charge in question on at
least one occasion: 'Parmi la flore on peut
distinguer les *roses*, très rares (Nº 69, etc.),
et les *angemmes*, spéciales à la Normandie
(Nº 361, etc.), qui ont 6 pétales' (Adam-
Even WB, p. 56). Angemmes are blazoned
in *WB* 361, 407, and 441, and illustrated
by Dr. Adam-Even in figs. 52 and 87.
Huon de Méry makes interesting use of this
association between the angemme and
Normandy in the *Tournoiement Antecrit.* He
indicates first (vv. 636–41, 651–2) that the
Normans are notorious braggarts:

Bobenz parmi le fonz d'un brueil
Au vent desploie sa baniere,
Qui ert de trop plesant maniere
Por ce qu'el est de Vanterie:
D'un drap dont cil de Normendie
Se vestent tuit communement.

.   .   .   .

Et Veinegloire et Vanterie,
Qui est dame de Normendie.

Then he provides the following arms for
Orgeil and her retinue among which
Vanterie (Bragging) figures prominently
(vv. 654–9):

De ceste gent dire vos veil,
Qui portoient l'escu tot plein
De Vanterie et de Desdaing
Bien connëu en totes places
A .i. sautëoir de menaces,
A l'*angevine* de dangier.

Variants of the latter verse provide the
readings *l'enguegine*, *l'angeignie*, and *l'an-*
guegnie. In the same poem, Hypocrisy
bears a shield 'A l'engeignie de faintié'
among other charges (v. 862). Wimmer's
critical apparatus provides the following
variants: *angevine*, *anguegine*, and *engeignie*.
Whatever the ultimate etymon of our word
may be, it was clearly influenced by OFr.
engigne 'ruse, trick', a derivative of Late
Lat. *ingenium* in this sense.

angelot, *small angel* (Fig. 128). *TA*, v. 2075:
As angeloz. *Note*: cf. MESSAGE.

angemme, *angemme*, *angenne*. See ANGE-
GNIES EN L'ESCU, ANGEVINE, ENGEIGNIE.

angevine, *angemme* (?) (Fig. 232). *TA*,
v. 659: A l'angevine. *Note*: see ANGEGNIES
EN L'ESCU.

Angletere, *England*. See ARMES LE ROI
D'ANGLETERE A, D'ANGLETERE A, ESTRE DE
SES ARMES TEL D'ANGLETERE A.

anot, *kind of falcon* (Fig. 203). See ANOZ
ENTOUR. *Syn.*: see ESPREVIER. *Note*: on the
confusion between falcons and hawks in
heraldry, see ESPREVIER, *Note*.

anoz entour, *orle of falcons* (Fig. 190). The
complete blazon reads as follows: *Bl* 197:
Walt' de Fauconberg, noir od un quintefoill d'argent et les avoz [*sic*] d'argent
entour. *Note*: arms of Sir Walter de
Fauconberge of Rise and Withernwick in
Holderness, Yorks., evidently a descendant

of the Châtelains of Saint-Omer (Pas-de-
Calais), lords of Fauquembergues. This
information is provided by *Aspilogia II*,
p. 155, note to item 201. London, misled
by the reading *avoz* and by the lack of
supporting evidence in the other copies of
Glover's Roll and in *C/Cl/Cd* 129 (see MER-
LOZ BORDANZ), states (p. 154): 'one would
have expected falcons as cant.' The glossary, p. 228, adds: '*Avoz* (L. *avis*) = birds'.
Such a derivation, however, is phono-
logically impossible. *Avoz* is a scribal error
(or a misreading [the letters *n* and *u*
(for *v*) are often indistinguishable in
thirteenth-century script]) for *anoz*, plural
of OFr. *anot*, a hapax but a term for which
there is much evidence. Its etymon is ultimately Lat. *anas* 'duck' which yielded
OFr. *ane* 'duck' from which the diminutive
anet 'duckling' was derived. In a private
communication to me dated 21 May 1968,
Professor Gunnar Tilander, the leading
authority on Romance hunting terms, suggests a possible explanation: '*Anoz* has the
same relation to *anez* as *merloz* to Fr. *mer-*
lette. Bengt Hasselrot has solidly studied the
alternation of the suffix -*ot* and -*et* in his
Etudes sur la formation diminutive dans les
langues romanes (Uppsala, 1957). *Merloz*,
anoz and *anez* are plurals and correspond
to the singular forms *merlot*, *anot*, *anet*.
Anet exists: annet, provincial name for the
kittiwake, Montagu, *Ornithological Diction-*
ary, 1802 (*New English Dictionary*); annet,
the common gull, Larus canus, Joseph
Wright, *The English Dialect Dictionary* . . . I
have no idea if annet is the same word as
OFr. *anet* "duckling" but it does not seem to
me quite unlikely. The couple *anet* : *anot* is
parallel to *merlot* : *merlette*. If *avoz* is to be read
anoz, *anot* may be the same word as OFr. *anet*
"duckling".' Cf. TESTE D'AUNE A LA TESTE
COURONEE D'UNE COURONE, *Note*. Plausible
as this explanation may be, the fact remains
that a duck is hardly a falcon. After writing
to Professor Tilander, a recent study by Professor Dafydd Evans (*Lanier, histoire d'un*
mot [Geneva, 1967] [*Publications Romanes*
et Françaises, 93]) attracted my attention. Evans, developing an earlier study
by E. G. Lindfors-Nordin ('Lanier, Lane-
ret, Lanette', *ZFSL*, lx [1935–7], 164–70;
appendix by E. Gamillscheg, pp. 170–2),

shows that terms for the various species of diurnal predatory birds used for hunting purposes were first developed in German. The neologisms were composed of two elements, the first of which denoted the prey. Thus *cranoh* (Mod. G. *Kranich*) 'crane', *cans* (Mod. G. *Gans*) 'goose', *anot* (Mod. G. *Ente*) 'duck', and **sparwa* 'little bird' (Mod. G. *Sperling* 'sparrow') were part of the etyma for terms (*cranohari, canshapuh, anothapuh,* and *sparuuarius*) designating hawks trained to hunt cranes, geese, ducks, and sparrows, respectively. E. *goshawk* and *sparrow-hawk* and OFr. *esprevier* (MFr. *épervier*), among other terms, show related developments. OFr. *anot*, the term used to blazon the falcons in the Fauconberge arms, is plainly akin to Lat. *anas* and, more specifically, to its Germanic derivative *anothapuh* 'duck-hawk'. It seems clear, however, that *anot* was a dialectal variant, for the term in most widespread use in Old French was the kindred word *lanier*, a derivative of the hypothetical form **anier* (< *ane* 'duck'+*-ier*+agglutinated article).

anulete, *ghost word*. See MEULET PERCIÉ.

apareil, see ARMES DE TEL APAREIL.

apendu, *hanging*. See CHEVAL FUST APENDU D'UNES FOURCHES.

Apolin, *Apollo (here regarded as a pagan deity)*. *Fierabras*, v. 668: L'image d'Apolin fu desous le boucler; *Aiol*, v. 9995: En la targe le roi est escris Apolins; v. 10010: Il saisi la grant targe u fu poins Apolins. *Note*: see Introduction, p. 25.

a quartiers, see ESCU A QUARTIERS. *Note*: see QUARTIERS.

a quartiers de . . . et de . . ., *quarterly* (Fig. 25). The complete blazon reads as follows. *Partonopeu*, v. 6901: D'or et de sinople a quartiers. *Syn.*: see ESQUARTELÉ DE . . . ET DE . . . *Note*: arms of Partonopeu; cf. v. 6913 ('De quartier sunt les covertures') and v. 6915 ('A quartiers sunt li gonfannon'), both referring to the same character. See also QUARTIERS, *Note*.

arbre, *tree* (Fig. 231). *CPA* 148: a un arbre; 178: a l'arbre.

*argent, *argent (white)*. Very frequent in literary sources, e.g. *Thèbes*, v. 10286: d'argent; *Troie*, vv. 7469, 7918: d'argent; *Bel Inconnu*, v. 330: d'argent; v. 1711: a argent; *Berte*, v. 3227: d'argent; *TC,*

vv. 650, 669: d'argent. Extremely frequent in the rolls where, except for two thirteenth-century sources (see BLANC), it is the only term used, e.g. *BA* 1, 6: d'argent; *B* 4 (*Ba/Bc* 4: de argent; *Bb* 4: d'argent), 10, 44, 62 (*Ba/Bc/Bl* 62, see ERMINE), 184: d'argent (*Bl* 4, 10, 44, 184, see BLANC); *C* 6, 10: d'argent; *M* 1-6: d'argent. For other uses, see EN ARGENT, EN L'ARGENT, SOR L'ARGENT. *Syn.*: BLANC, BLANCHET, SORARGENTÉ. *Note*: Matthew Paris uses the term *d'argent* four times; see Pusikan, pp. 122, 123, 150, 151. Gough H, p. 136, note to item 34: 'The word *d'argent* in [*H* 33] should, no doubt, have been erased'; idem, p. 130, note to item 2: 'The blazon in [*Hg* 2] differs from all other authorities' [substitute *d'or* for *d'argent*].

armé, *armed (mailed)*. See JAMBES ARMEES, JAMBES ARMEES O TOUTES LES CUISSES CHASCUNE CUISSE JOINTE AUS AUTRES ET EN CHASCUNE CORNIERE SEIT UN PIÉ, JAMBES ARMEES O TOUTES LES CUISSES ET EN CHASCUNE CORNIERE SEIT UN PIÉ.

armes, *arms*. The general term for a coat of arms whether on a shield, tunic, caparison, etc. See also AVOIR UNES ARMES, CELES ARMES A, CEZ MESMES ARMES A, CONOISTRE, DEVISER, ESCUÇON DES ARMES DE, ESTRE DE SES ARMES TELS D'ANGLETERE A, HIRAUT D'ARMES, MESMES LES ARMES MES, MESMES LES ARMES OU, PORTER LES ARMES, PROPRES ARMES, TOUT DE PLAIN LES ARMES FORS QUE, etc. See also the following items. *Syn.*: ENSEIGNE, ESCU[1]. *Note*: for the English equivalent, see the *MED*, i. 385-6, s.v. *armes 3*.

armes a droit, *true, correct arms*. *Artus*, p. 169: se vos portez voz armes a droit, car autrement ne vos reconois. *Syn.*: VRAI. *Note*: cf. DROITES ARMES, SES PROPRES ARMES, SOIES ARMES MESMES.

armes a Nostre Seigneur, *Our Lord's arms*. *Didot Perceval*, p. 183: armes a nostre Segnor. *Syn.*: ARMES NOSTRE SEIGNEUR.

armes a son pere, *his father's arms*. *Ille et Galeron*, vv. 363-5:

Il voient que li fix lor frere
Porte les armes a son pere,
Tolt altreteles conissances;

Saisnes, v. 1791: Des armes a som pere ot ansaigne en l'escu. *Syn.*: AUTELS ARMES COM

SON PERE, AUTRETEL COM SON PERE. *Note*: cf.
ARMES SON PERE A, PORTER DE PAR SON PERE.

armes celes mesmes a, *the same arms,*
differenced by. CP 12: porte celles mesmes a.
Syn.: see AUTEL².

armes changier, *to change arms (as a dis-*
guise). Cligés, vv. 4849–50: Demain au
chevalier estrange, / Qui chascun jor ses
armes change; v. 4992: voz armes chan-
giez; *Perlesvaus,* p. 195: li chevaliers n'est
mie aesius a conoistre, car il a ses armes
changiees; *Mort Artu,* p. 15: mes il ne le
connurent pas li uns l'autre, por ce qu'il
avoient leur armes changiees par plus
couvertement venir au tornoiement; *Lance-*
lot propre, iv. 274: il lez puet bien avoir
cangiés; v. 171: quar il avoit sez armes cangiés; 187: pour les armes qu'il avoit cangiés;
441: pour les armes qu'il avoit changees;
463: Car ilz changent si souvent leurs
armes qu'a pene pourroient estre congneuz
seullement par veoir; *Artus,* p. 227: quar
il avoient lor armes changiees; *Sone,*
vv. 9168, 13218, 13410, 13811: ses armes
cangier; 9864: mes armes cangerai; 12993:
vos armes cangier; 13419: armes canga;
15192: ses armes qu'il ot cangié. *Syn.*:
ARMES MUER, CHANGIER LA CONOISSANCE,
RENOUVELER ARMES. *Note*: cf. CHANGIER
SES ARMES, COUVERTURES CHANGIER, DES-
CONOISTRE², DESCONOISTRE (SOI), DESGUISIÉ¹,
ESTRANGES ARMES, MUER SON ESCU. The
reference in *Lancelot propre,* v. 463, is to
Hector's remark apropos of the Knights
of the Round Table; cf. Gawain's observation, s.v. MUER SON ESCU.

armes de Blois a, *arms of Blois, differenced*
by. CP 61: porte les armes de Blois a.

armes de Brienne, *arms of Brienne.* See
ESCUÇON DES ARMES DE BRIENNE.

armes de Douai, *arms of Douai. TC,*
v. 1995: Parti des armes de Douai. *Note*:
see PARTI DE . . . ET DE . . ., *Note*.

armes de France a, *France Ancient, differ-*
enced by. CP 53, 106: porte les armes de
France a.

armes de plain . . . fors qu'el quartier
avoit egletes par desconoissance, *the*
full coat, but the canton semy of eaglets.
Escanor, vv. 5217–20 (referring to Gaheriet):

Et portoit les armes de plain
Son frere monseingnor Gavain,

Fors qu'el quartier avoit aigletes
Par desconoissance blanchetes.

Syn.: TEL COM . . . FORS QU'AU CRESTEL
EGLES AVOIT, TEL COM . . . FORS QU'EL
CRESTEL EGLES AVOIT, TEL COM . . . FORS
QU'EL QUARTIER EGLEZ AVOIT, TOUT DE
PLAIN LES ARMES . . . FORS QU'EL QUARTIER
A EGLES. *Note*: cf. AUTEL². On Gawain's
arms and those of his brothers, see Brault,
'Arthurian Heraldry', p. 85.

armes de Sainte Eglise, *arms of the Holy*
Church. Queste, p. 62: armes de Sainte
Eglise. *Syn.*: see ARMES NOSTRE SEIGNEUR.

armes de son pere a, *his father's arms,*
differenced by. CP 17: porte les armes de son
pere a; *K,* vv. 488–91:

Johans de Seint Johan son hoir
Lour ot baillie a compaignon,
Ki de son pere avoit le non,
E les armes au bleu label.

Syn.: ARMES SON PERE A, ARMES SON PERE
OD, ARMES SON PERE OU. *Note*: cf. ARMES
A SON PERE, PORTER DE PAR SON PERE.

armes despareilles, *different, distinct arms.*
Cligés, vv. 4555–7:

Trois peires d'armes desparoilles,
Unes noires, autres vermoilles,
Les tierces verz . . .

Note: refers to DESPAREIL².

armes de tel apareil, *the same arms. Hem,*
vv. 1122–3:

. . . un chevalier, qui porte
Ses armes de tel appareil.

Syn.: see AUTEL¹.

armes du duc de Bourgogne, *arms of the*
Duke of Burgundy. See ESCUÇON DES ARMES
DU DUC DE BOURGOGNE EN LA BORDURE.

armes du roi de France a, *France Ancient,*
differenced by. C 90: lez armes du roy de
France a (*Cl* 90, see ARMES LE ROI DE
FRANCE A; *Cd* 90: les armes du roy de
France). *Syn.*: see DE FRANCE A.

armes le conte, *arms of the Count.* (1)
indicating one half of a party shield. Bl 107
[109]: les armes le comte de Garenne.
Note: on these arms, see *Aspilogia II,*
p. 136, note to item 109. (2) *locution used*
in differencing, order of items only indicating
this fact. The complete blazon reads as
follows: *CPA* 15: Pierre de Bretaigne: les
armes le conte [i.e. the Duke of Brittany

listed in a preceding blazon], la bordure besantee d'argent.

armes le conte de Dreux, *arms of the Count of Dreux, differenced by.* CPA 20: les armes le conte de Dreux. *Note:* word order only indicates differencing.

armes le conte od, *arms of the Earl, differenced by.* The complete blazon reads as follows: *Hg,* Dunbar [36]: Patrike de Dunebarre porte les armes le counte Patrike od le lambel d'asur. *Note: CEMRA,* p. 29, omits the *e* in both cases where Gough reads *Patrike.*

armes le roi, *arms of the King. Guillaume de Dole,* v. 2603: Un penon des armes le roi.

armes le roi avuec, *England, differenced by.* H 50: lez armez le roy ovec (*Hg* 50 [52]: les armes le roy ovec). *Syn.:* see D'ANGLE-TERE A.

armes le roi d'Angletere a, *England, differenced by.* D 25: les armes le rey de Engletere a. *Syn.:* see D'ANGLETERE A.

armes le roi de France, *France Ancient.* See FLEUR.

armes le roi de France a, *France Ancient, differenced by.* Cl 90: les armes le roy de Fraunce a (C/Cd 90, see ARMES DU ROI DE FRANCE A). *Syn.:* see DE FRANCE A.

armes le roi son pere o, *the same arms as his father, the King, differenced by.* K, vv. 408–9:

> E portoit, o un bleu label,
> Les armes le bon roi son pere.

armes muer, *to change arms (as a disguise). Sone,* vv. 10061–3:

> 'Quelz armes soloit il porter?'
> 'Dame, souvent les wet müer,
> Pour ce que il ne soit connus.'

Syn.: see ARMES CHANGIER.

armes Nostre Seigneur, *Our Lord's arms. Queste,* pp. 81–2, 142, 234: armes Nostre Seignor. *Syn.:* ARMES A NOSTRE SEIGNEUR, ARMES DE SAINTE EGLISE. *Note:* while these arms are not blazoned, it seems clear that *argent, a plain cross gules* is intended. Cf. Middle English *Cristes armes, armes of Our Lord, armes of the Passion,* cited in the *MED,* i. 386, s.v. *armes 3.* On the quasi-heraldic display of the instruments of the Passion known as the Arma Christi, see Réau, ii². 508–9 (bibliography, p. 512).

armes plaines¹, *undifferenced arms. Escanor,* vv. 4992–3:

> D'or et de seble gironnees
> Portoit li unz les armes plaines.

Syn.: DROITES ARMES, ENTIER¹, PLAIN.¹ *Note:* on these arms, see Brault, 'Arthurian Heraldry', pp. 84–5. The meaning of 'plain' arms here is clear: 'the full coat, undifferenced arms'. In the expressions ARMES DE PLAIN . . . FORS QU'EL QUARTIER AVOIT EGLETES PAR DESCONOISSANCE, TOUT DE PLAIN LES ARMES . . . FORS QU'EL QUARTIER A EGLES, TOUT PLAIN FORS TANT QUE, however, the locutions *de plain, tout de plain,* and *tout plain* are used in phrases in which differencing is indicated. For an elliptical expression, see CHARGIER SES ARMES A. On the confusion between *armes plaines* and *armes pleines,* consult Mathieu, p. 99 n. 2.

armes plaines², *plain arms, i.e. shield of a single tincture.* See PLAINES ARMES.

armes pures sans nule autre desconoissance, *plain arms, i.e. shield of a single tincture.* CC, vv. 3255–7:

> Si s'est armés hasteement
> D'unes armes pures d'argent,
> Sans nulle autre desconnissance.

Syn.: ARMES SIMPLES, D'UN SEUL TAINT, PLAIN³, PLAINES ARMES, PUR, SANS AUTRE CONOISSANCE, SANS AUTRE TAINT, SANS CONOISSANCE NULE, TOUT¹, TOUT D'UNE COULEUR, TOUT D'UN TAINT, TOUT PUR. *Note:* cf. D'UNE COULEUR FORS, D'UNE COULEUR FORS TANT QUE, ENTIER³, ENTIERE-MENT A, TOUT², TOUT⁵, TOUT . . . FORS SEULEMENT. A similar use is found in the fourteenth-century *Tournoiement des Dames de Paris,* vv. 214–18:

> Couvert de couvertures noires,
> Sans nulle autre desconnoisance:
> Elle a fait par senefiance
> C'onques encore son seignor
> N'avoit eu armes nul jor.

According to Adam-Even, '*Tournoiement des Dames de Paris*', p. 10, a shield of a single tincture indicates that the bearer—here a woman—is not yet entitled to a coat of arms: 'L'emploi du champ plain, simple table d'attente par ceux qui n'ont pas encore d'armoiries'. See TOUT PUR, *Note.* For other instances of historical and literary shields of a single tincture, see Introduction.

armes simples, *plain arms, i.e. shield of a single tincture.* Escanor, vv. 3482–3:

> Kez ot unes armes vermeilles
> Simples, con chevaliers nouviaux.

Syn.: see ARMES PURES SANS NULE AUTRE DESCONOISSANCE.

armes son cousin germain, *his first cousin's arms.* TA, v. 1136: armes son cosin germein.

armes son frere a . . . sans, *his brother's arms, differenced by . . . without . . .* K, vv. 466–7:

> E portoit les armes son frere,
> Au bleu bastoun sanz le label.

Note: cf. AUTEL SANS.

armes son pere a, *his father's arms, differenced by.* Cleomadés, v. 535: Les armes son pere a label. *Syn.:* see ARMES DE SON PERE A.

armes son pere od, *his father's arms, differenced by.* Hg 4 (H 4, see ARMES SON PERE OU), 109 [110]: les armes son pere od. *Syn.:* see ARMES DE SON PERE A.

armes son pere ou, *his father's arms, differenced by.* H 4: lez armez son pere ou (Hg 4, see ARMES SON PERE OD). *Syn.:* see ARMES DE SON PERE A.

armes tels . . . a, *the same arms, differenced by.* See TELS ARMES A.

armes tels com . . . mes que, *the same arms, differenced by.* Mouskés, vv. 7855–7:

> Et cil autres est Baligans;
> A ces armes teus com ses frere,
> Mais que la bordure est dentee.

Syn.: see AUTEL². *Note:* see BORDURE DENTEE.

aronde, *swallow volant* (Fig. 205). Charrete, vv. 5818–20:

> Ou vos veez ces deus arondres
> Qui sanblent que voler s'an doivent,
> Mes ne se muevent . . .

a rosetes, *semy of heraldic roses* (Fig. 47). K, v. 352: Le ot noire a rosettes de argent. *Syn.:* see SEMÉ DE ROSETES.

a rosetes semé, *semy of heraldic roses* (Fig. 47). BA 187: a rosettes . . . semees (A: semee). *Syn.:* see SEMÉ DE ROSETES.

as = aus, *equivalent of MFr. 'aux'.*

as fesanz, see FESAN.

asis, *placed, situated.* See BENDE ENTREALEE DE DEUS COTICES LIONCEAUS EN RAMPANT ASIS AU DEHORS. *Note:* cf. example cited s.v. ESTACHIÉ EN BELIC DE . . . ET DE . . .

asis en, see EN . . . ASIS.

asis sor, *on a field of.* TA, v. 1269: Asise sor; v. 1727: Asise sour. *Syn.:* ASIS SUS, EN . . . ASIS. *Note:* cf. ASIS.

asis sus, *on a field of.* TA, vv. 675, 1159 1211: Asis sus. *Syn.:* see ASIS SOR.

as lions, see LION (1) and *Note.*

asor, see AZUR.

asur, *azure.* See AZUR.

au = a le, *equivalent of MFr. 'au'.* Note, however, the distinction established in the following items.

au chief, *on the chief* (Fig. 75). See CHIEF A UN DEMI LION ET COURONE AU CHIEF, OISELET AU CHIEF. *Syn.:* see EN LE CHIEF¹.

au crestel, see TEL COM . . . FORS QU'AU CRESTEL EGLES AVOIT.

au dehors, *on each side (of a bend cotised).* See BENDE ENTREALEE DE DEUS COTICES LIONCEAUS EN RAMPANT ASIS AU DEHORS.

au desous de la crois, see DRAGON AU DESOUS DE LA CROIS.

au kanee, *meaning obscure.* See CROIS FOURCHIEE AU KANEE.

aune, *meaning obscure.* See TESTE D'AUNE ET LA TESTE COURONEE D'UNE COURONE. *Note:* see ANOZ ENTOUR, *Note.*

au quartier, *on the canton* (Fig. 118). See ESPEE AU QUARTIER. *Syn.:* see EN LE QUARTIER¹.

aus, *equivalent of MFr. 'aux'.* See also AS.

aus bouz, *at the ends, referring to a cross formy throughout.* See CROIS ESLAISIEE AUS BOUZ. *Syn.:* see PAR LES BOUZ.

aus claveaus, *cloué (ornamented with a pattern of nails)* (Fig. 46). Fouque de Candie, v. 10400: as blans clavelx assis. *Syn.:* FERRETÉ. *Note:* see POINT².

aus croiseaus, *crusily* (Fig. 35). Bl 40: al croisel (B 40, see CROISELÉ). *Syn.:* see CROISELÉ.

aus egles, *semy of eaglets* (Fig. 38). SCT, fol. 127 a / SCV, fol. 93 b: as aigles. *Syn.:* see A EGLEAUS SEMÉ.

aus eschalopes, *semy of escallops* (Fig. 39). See BENDE AUS ESCHALOPES. *Syn.:* see A COQUILLES SEMÉ.

aus fleurs de lis, *semy of fleurs de lis* (Fig. 40). Fouque de Candie, appendix I, c, vv. 422–3:

> Tibaus le reconut, qui i mist son avis,
> A l'escu d'asur paint et as flors d'or de lis.

Syn.: see FLEURETÉ¹. *Note:* arms of King Louis, son of Charlemagne.

autant de l'un com de l'autre, see
BENDES DE . . . ET DE . . . AUTANT DE L'UN
COM DE L'AUTRE.

autel[1]**,** *the same arms.* B 191: autiel (*Bl* 191
[195]: autiel); *Bl* 81, 89 (*B* 89, see AUTEL
MES), St. John [111]: autiel. *Syn.*: ARMES
DE TEL APAREIL, AUTRETEL, AUTRETELS
CONOISSANCES, CONOISSANCES AUTRETELS,
DE MESME[1], DE MESME LE TAINT, D'ICELE
FAÇON, ITELS ARMES, PORTER ITEL, MESMES
PORTER ARMES, PORTER MESME, PORTER
SIFAIT ESCU, PORTER TELS ARMES, TOUT
AUTEL. *Note*: cf. D'UNE MANIERE.

autel[2]**,** *the same arms, differenced by.* B 67
(*Ba/Bb/Bc* 67, see AUTEL A; *Bl* 67, see AUTEL
OD), 154, 162 (*Bl* 154 [158], 162 [166],
see AUTEL OD): autiel. *Syn.*: ARMES CELES
MESMES A, ARMES TELS COM . . . MES QUE,
AUTEL A, AUTEL MES, AUTEL OD, AUTEL OU,
AUTEL OVE, AUTEL SANS, CELES ARMES A,
CELES MESMES A, CEZ MESMES ARMES A, DE
MESME[2], DE MESME A, DE MESME LE TAINT,
LE MESME A, MESMES ARMES, MESMES AVUEC,
MESMES LES ARMES MES, MESMES LES ARMES
OU, NE LA PORTER DIVERSE FORS DE,
N'ESTRE DIVERS DE RIEN NON FORS DE . . .
SEULEMENT, PORTER TEL, PORTER TELS
ARMES SANS, TEL AVUEC, TEL COM, TELS
ARMES A, TELS (ARMES) . . . MES QUE, TELS
(ARMES) QUE . . . MES POUR DESCOMPAROISON,
TOUT AUTEL A. *Note*: locution used in
differencing. Cf. ARMES DE PLAIN . . . FORS
QU'EL QUARTIER AVOIT EGLETES PAR
DESCONOISSANCE and its synonyms; also
BANIERE SON PERE A . . . POUR, PAR
DESCONOISSANCE, PORTER AUTREMENT QUE,
TELS ARMES MES QU'EN LIEU D'UNE BARRE
MEINS, TOUT[2].

autel a, *the same arms, differenced by.* B/Bl 71:
autiel a; *Ba/Bc* 37: autel a (*B* 37, see AUTEL
OVE; *Bl* 37, see AUTEL OD); *Ba/Bb/Bc* 67:
autel a (*B* 67, see AUTEL[2]; *Bl* 67, see AUTEL
OD); *C/Cl* 88: autel a (*Cd* 88, see LE MESME
A). *Syn.*: see AUTEL[2].

autel com, *with the same arms as. Lancelot
propre,* v. 205: li chevaliers en avoit fait
contrefaire .i. autel comme Lioniaus portoit. *Syn.*: AUTRETEL COM.

autel mes, *the same arms, differenced by.*
B 89: autiel mais (*Bl* 89, see AUTEL[1]).
Syn.: see AUTEL[2].

autel od, *the same arms, differenced by.*
Ba/Bb/Bc 31: autel od (*B/Bl* 31, see AUTEL

OVE); *Bl* 37 (*B* 37, see AUTEL OVE; *Ba/Bc*
37, see AUTEL A), 38 (*B* 38, see AUTEL OU),
43 (*B* 43, see AUTEL OVE), 67 (*B* 67, see
AUTEL[2]; *Ba/Bb/Bc* 67, see AUTEL A), 144 (*B*
144, see AUTEL OVE), 154, 166 (*B* 154, 166,
see AUTEL[2]): autiel od. *Syn.*: see AUTEL[3].

autel ou, *the same arms, differenced by.* B 38:
auteil ou (*Bl* 38, see AUTEL OD). *Syn.*: see
AUTEL[2].

autel ove, *the same arms, differenced by.*
B/Bl 31 (*Ba/Bb/Bc* 31, see AUTEL OD), 37
(*Ba/Bc* 37, see AUTEL A), 43 (*Bl* 43, see
AUTEL OD), 144 (*Bl* 144 [148], see AUTEL
OD): autiel ove; *Bl* 2: autiel ove (*B* 2, see
TEL AVUEC). *Syn.*: see AUTEL[2].

autel sans, *the same arms, without.* B 29:
autiel sans (*Bl* 29: autiel sanz). *Syn.*:
PORTER TELS ARMES SANS. *Note*: locution
used in differencing when an omission is
to be indicated.

autels armes com, *the same arms as. TA,*
v. 933: autiex armes com il ot. *Syn.*:
AUTRETELS CONOISSANCES COM, ITEL SI
COM.

autels armes com son pere, *the same
arms as his father. Mort Artu,* p. 256: autiex
armes comme ses peres souloit fere. *Syn.*:
see ARMES A SON PERE.

autre, *other.* See AUTANT DE L'UN COM DE
L'AUTRE, CHASCUNE CUISSE JOINTE AUS
AUTRES, D'AUTRE SEMBLANCE, DE L'UN A
L'AUTRE, DE L'UNE ET DE L'AUTRE, DE L'UN
EN L'AUTRE, DE L'UN ET DE L'AUTRE, DE
L'UN ET L'AUTRE, EN UN EN L'AUTRE, FESSE
A DEUS LISTEAUS UN DESOUS ET L'AUTRE
DESOR, L'AUTRE MOITIÉ, L'UN DESOUS ET
L'AUTRE DESUS, LIONCEAUS PASSANZ L'UN
CONTRE L'AUTRE EN CHIEF, L'UN EN L'AUTRE,
N'AVOIR NUL AUTRE TAINT DESOUS, N'AVOIR
NULE AUTRE DIVERSITÉ D'ARMES ENTRE,
PARTI DE . . . ET DE . . . PAR LE . . . L'AUTRE,
SANS AUTRE CONOISSANCE, SANS AUTRE TAINT,
SANS NULE AUTRE DESCONOISSANCE, SANS
NULE AUTRE ENSEIGNE.

autrement que, *different from.* See PORTER
AUTREMENT QUE.

autretel, *the same arms. Perlesvaus,* p. 38:
escu autretel; *Lancelot propre,* iii. 231:
covertures autreteles; *Mort Artu,* p. 27:
couvertures autreteles; *BA* 25: Le conte
de Viane le porte autretel (A: au fretel).
Rujers (A: Ruyer). For other uses, see
AUTRETELS CONOISSANCES, CONOISSANCES

AUTRETELS. *Syn.*: see AUTEL[1]. *Note*: in his glossary, p. 20, Dr. Adam-Even provides the following definition, s.v. *tretel* [*sic*], with a reference to *BA* 25: 'cotice ou bâton; peut-être de tret: petite corde "bâton gresle comme cotice"'. See also p. 17: '*baton* (24) ou *fretel* (25)'. Dr. Adam-Even was doubtless thinking of OFr. *fretel* attested later in this meaning. See COTICE, *Note*. The arms, which are those of the Count of Vianden, are here said to be identical with those immediately preceding in this roll (*BA* 24: Vualerans ses freres de Vilers [A: Viliers] le porte a .i. baston de geules en beslive. Baneres [A: Banneret] et Rujers [A: Ruyers]) the field being gold as in *BA* 23 (Le comte [A: conte] de Vilers, l'escu d'or au lion noir rampant a la keu forqie. Rujers [A: Ruyer]), thus constituting a differencing of the Vianden arms as blazoned in *BA* 44 and *WB* 1184 (gules, a fess argent).

autretel com, *with the same arms as*. *Perlesvaus*, p. 126: un chevalier qui porte .i. vert escu autretel comme je faz; p. 208: .i. escu autretel com il vit avoir Perceval a la premiere foiz. *Syn.*: AUTEL COM.

autretel com son pere, *with the same arms as his father*. *Perlesvaus*, p. 144: un escu vermel autretel com fist ses pere. *Syn.*: see ARMES A SON PERE.

autretels conoissances, *the same arms*. *Troie*, v. 8067: Autreteus sont ses conoissances; *Ille et Galeron*, v. 365: Tolt altreteles conissances. *Syn.*: see AUTEL[1].

autretels conoissances com, *the same arms as*. *Durmart*, vv. 5778–80:

> Ce sunt autretels conissances
> Come cil a dont vos oëz
> Qui mes compaingnons a tüez.

Syn.: see AUTELS ARMES COM.

aveine, *oats*. See JARBE D'AVEINE.

avoir, *to have*. Appears frequently in metrical blazons, e.g. *CC*, vv. 1316–18:

> Ses escus avoit le cief d'or,
> Et saciés qu'il avoit encor,
> El cief, une mierle de sable.

This verb is listed here only when it is needed for the intelligence of the blazon. The items in the preceding passage, for example, are entered under the tinctures, under CHIEF[1], and under MERLE EL CHIEF

(with a cross-reference to MERLE). Cf., however, the heraldic phrase ARMES DE PLAIN . . . FORS QU'EL QUARTIER AVOIT EGLETES PAR DESCONOISSANCE.

avoir unes armes, *to bear arms*. *Hem* vv. 1072–3:

> Tu vois c'unes armes d'or ai,
> A coquefabues vermeilles;

K, vv. 710–13:

> Henri de Graham unes armes
> Avoit vermeilles cumme sanc,
> O un sautour e au chief blanc,
> Ou ot trois vermeilles cokilles.

avot, see AVOZ ENTOUR.

avoz entour, see ANOZ ENTOUR.

avuec, *with*. See ARMES LE ROI AVUEC, MESMES AVUEC, TEL AVUEC.

azon, *azure* (*blue*). *Bel Inconnu*, v. 5921: un escu d'azon; *Joufroi*, v. 408: a achon. *Syn.*: see AZUR. *Note*: *Bel Inconnu*, v. 5603, mentions lances 'Paintes a or et a ason'.

azor, see AZUR.

***azur**, *azure* (*blue*). Very frequent in literary sources, e.g. *Thèbes*, vv. 6267, 9041: d'azur; *Troie*, vv. 7715, 7745: d'azur; *Erec*, v. 2100: D'azur; *Gaidon*, vv. 1070, 7141: d'azur; *Blancandin*, v. 4387: d'azur; *Berte*, v. 3223: D'asur; *Escanor*, v. 3642: d'asur; *K*, v. 70: asure; vv. 66, 152, 171: de asur. Extremely frequent in the rolls where it is the only term used, e.g. *BA* 7, 12: d'azur; *B* 2, 7: azure; *C* 5, 8: d'azure; *Cl* 6 [4]: d'azur (*C*/*Cd* 6, see POURPRE); *CP* 1, 26: d'azur; *M* 4, 5: d'azure. *Syn.*: AZON, AZUR BIS, AZURIN, BLEU, INDE, PERS. For other uses, see EN AZUR, EN L'AZUR, L'AZUR, SOR AZUR, SOR L'AZUR. *Note*: cf. *Perlesvaus*, p. 292: '.i. bloues armes autresi comme d'azur'. For *azur* and *d'azur* in Matthew Paris, see Pusikan, pp. 128, 145. In *Bb*, the conventional letter *B* is used to indicate azure in most items. In *Bl* 128 [132] and 152 [156], *d'azur* is an error for *d'argent*. In *Cl* 170, *dazure* is a scribal error for *danse*. See FESSE ET UNE DANCE EN LE CHIEF. So, too, *d'asur* in *CP* 124; see FLEUR DE LIS. *H* 31 is a conflated blazon and omits the tincture azure. MS. Cotton Caligula A. XVIII omits *K*, v. 70. According to Ott, p. 98: 'En vieux français ce vocable [i.e. *azur*] ne désigne que la nuance *claire* de la couleur qui nous

occupe.' See also Grandsaignes d'Hauterive, s.v. *bloi*: 'N'indique pas une couleur
bien définie: blême, verdâtre; bleu, blond;
pâle.' Though a great variety of shades
were used for all the tinctures in medieval
heraldry (see Hope, pp. 13–14), OFr. *azur*
here always meant 'blue'.

azur bis, *azure (blue)*. *Saisnes*, v. 719 (var.):
d'azur bis; *Huon de Bordeaux*, v. 1745:
d'asur bis. *Syn.*: see AZUR. *Note*: Bouly de
Lesdain, p. 230: 's'agit-il ici d'un bleu plus
foncé?' In the glossary of his edition of
Huon de Bordeaux, p. 443, Ruelle defines
bis as 'sombre, foncé'.

azurin, *azure (blue)*. *K*, vv. 309–12:

> Del bon Hue de Courtenay
> La baniere oubliee ne ay,
> De or fin o trois rouges rondeaus,
> E asurins fu li labeaus.

Syn.: see AZUR. *Note*: on this term, see Ott,
p. 99.

bande, see BENDE.

baniere o besanz, *bezanty banner*. *K*, vv.
496–500:

> Aleyn de la Souche tresor
> Signefioit, ke fust brisans
> Sa rouge baniere o besans;
> Kar bien sai ke il a despendu
> Tresour plus ke en bourse pendu.

Syn.: see BESANTÉ.

baniere son pere a . . . pour, *his father's
banner (i.e. arms), differenced by . . . because of.*
K, vv. 121–4:

> Cil ot la baner son pere,
> Au label rouge por son frere,
> Johan, ki li ainsnez estoit,
> E ki entiere la portoit.

Note: locution used for differencing. Cf.
AUTEL[2]. On banners and bannerets, consult Denholm-Young, *History and Heraldry*,
pp. 22–5, 112. Cf. ENSEIGNE[3], *Note*.

bar, *sea-perch, sea-wolf (a kind of fish)* (Fig.
216). *TC*, v. 3161: a deus bar; vv. 3976–7:
Soufri cil as armes vermoilles / Ou li bar
d'or estoient point; *La Bataille de Caresme et
de Charnage*, v. 300 (var.): En sa baniere ot
un grant bar; *CP* 41, 42: a deus bars; *Hg*
52 [54]: od deux bars (*H* 52, see BARBEL);
CC, v. 1205: a deus bars; *K*, vv. 249–52:

> Johans de Bar iluec estoit,
> Ke en la baner inde portoit

Deuz bars de or, e fu croissilie,
O la rouge ourle engreellie
                    (W: engreelie).

Syn.: BAR DE MER, BARS SINANZ, VAIRON.
Note: in these examples there are usually
two sea-perch and they are addorsed and
hauriant (back to back and palewise with
the head upwards). On the device in *La
Bataille de Caresme et de Charnage* and on the
sea-perch itself, consult G. Lozinski's note,
pp. 129–30, no. 12, s.v. *bar*. OFr. *bar* is
derived from Dutch *baers* and has often
been confused with OFr. *barbel* (MFr.
barbeau) 'barbel' (a fresh-water fish distinguished by the four barbs attached to
its upper jaws) < VL *barbellus* < Late
Latin *barbulus* (CL *barbus*) 'bearded'. See
below, s.v. BARBEL. The confusion is not
only lexical but pictorial as well, for the
sea-perch in medieval heraldic illustrations was often drawn with barbs. See, for
example, the illustration for Count Henry
II of Bar in Matthew Paris (Hauptmann,
Table II, fig. 36). Part of the confusion may
stem from the fact that the sea-perch was
sometimes depicted with protruding lips
curving outwards, giving the impression
of hooks. See Adam-Even WB, figs. 94–8.
On the canting arms of Sir John of Bar,
see Prinet *K*, pp. 347–8. For the early
history of this device, consult *Aspilogia II*,
p. 25, note to item 25 (Bar arms).

barbeaus, barbes, *barbels*. See BARBEL.

barbel, *barbel* (Fig. 208). The complete
blazon reads as follows: *H* 52: Sr John de
Bare porte d'azure ou .ii. barbes d'or
croiselé d'or ou la bordure endenté de
gules (*Hg* 52, see BAR). *Note*: in this blazon,
the heraldic sea-perch (OFr. *bar*) has been
confused with another kind of fish, the
barbel. See above, s.v. BAR, *Note*, and *La
Bataille de Caresme et de Charnage*, ed. G.
Lozinski, p. 130, no. 13, s.v. *barbue*. The
plural of OFr. *barbel* is *barbeaus*. See
Navarre 617: 'Le comte de Montheliart [*sic*,
for Montbeliart], de gueules a trois bar-
beaux d'or'.

bar de mer, *sea-perch, sea-wolf (a kind of
fish)* (Fig. 216). *Cl* 29a: a deus bars de mere
(*Cd* 29b: a .ii. bars de mer). *Syn.*: see BAR.
Note: *C* 29, due to haplography, is a fusion
of two blazons which are here listed in the
two other MSS. as *Cl* 29a and *Cl* 29b,

and *Cd* 29a and *Cd* 29b respectively. On OFr. *bar de mer*, consult Prinet WR, p. 230, item 14.

barge, *barge, galley* (Fig. 245). The complete blazon reads as follows: *D* 11: 'Le rey de Bealme, l'escu de azur od treis barges d'argent. *Note*: cf. *P* 27: 'Le roy de Boeme porte d'azur ove trois barges d'argent.' *Bealme* has been interpreted to mean 'Bethlehem' (by Richard Kimbey, temp. Elizabeth I, who made a copy of the Camden Roll; see James Greenstreet, 'The Original Camden Roll of Arms', *Journal of the British Archaeological Society*, xxxviii [1882], 311: 'Kimbey erred in judgment when he rendered "Bealme" in his copy "Bedlme", explaining by a note that it meant Bethlehem'; see also Denholm-Young, *History and Heraldry*, p. 46 n. 1: '"Bealme" is perhaps Bethlehem, for Jerusalem'. Greenstreet, however, lists these arms in his Index of Names, p. 325, s.v. *King of Bohemia*. Neither explanation is satisfactory, for the arms blazoned here correspond neither to those of Jerusalem (correctly given, moreover, in *D* 1: '... rlm porte le escu de argent a une croiz de or cruselé de or'; cf. *P* 11: 'Le roy de Jherusalem porte d'argent ove une croice martellee d'or et poudree de croicelettes d'or'; see also *WB* 1259) nor to those of Bohemia (gules, a lion rampant double-queued and crossed in saltire argent, crowned or; see *WB* 1266 and consult Jiří Louda, 'Arms of Sovereignty in the Czechoslovak Republic and in the Former Kingdom of Bohemia', *Coat of Arms*, vii [1963], no. 53, 192–7; cf. also Prinet WR, pp. 226–7, item 6 [= *Cl* 10: 'Le roy de Boesme, de argent a un lion de sable coroné de or a un croyz d'or sur l'espaule']). As noted by Denholm-Young, the arms blazoned here are also to be found in *HE* 18, a painted roll, with the caption 'Le roy de ...' Similar arms, however, are ascribed to King Haakon of Norway in Matthew Paris; see Hauptmann, pp. 35 (item no. 98), 50–1; Table IV, fig. 68; *Aspilogia II*, p. 35, item 100; p. 72, item 73 (cf. pp. 79–80, item 4 [Canute]): gules, three barges or, in middle chief a crosslet formy argent (the crosslet symbolizes the fact that he took the cross in 1250). For

the ship on a seal of Harald, King of Man in 1246, see *Aspilogia II*, p. 171, note to item 19. Hauptmann, p. 51, notes that these are not the arms of Norway found in other sources (e.g. *D* 13: 'Le rey de Norwey, l'escu de goules a un leun rampant de or od une hache d'argent'; *WB* 1275, the same, but the axe or) and suggests a connection with the arms of the city of Bergen which feature a ship. For other uses of barges in the arms of Norway, see *Aspilogia II*, p. 35, note to item 100. There are many discrepancies in the early rolls as to the arms of foreign or fictitious kings. Significant in this respect are the arms of Cyprus which immediately precede the arms in question in the Camden Roll (*D* 10): 'Le rey de Cypre, l'escu de azur od treis targes d'or'. On similarly un-attested arms for Cyprus in Walford's Roll, see *Aspilogia II*, p. 170, note to item 16. The painted shields for both 'Bealme' and 'Cypres' in the Camden Roll are erased. In the thirteenth century, Cyprus was a kingdom ruled by the Lusignans and, consequently, its arms were derived from those of that family (barruly argent and azure; see *Aspilogia II*, p. 32, item 86; p. 182, item 71) differenced by a lion rampant gules crowned or (*WB* 1276; *HE* 26; *Navarre* 1257; *P* 12). Note that the author of the Camden Roll has ascribed strikingly similar arms to Cyprus and 'Bealme': in each case the field is azure, the charge is or, and it is made up of three pieces. The charge itself (*targes, barges*) varies orthographically in the initial letter only. In thirteenth-century script, the letters *t* and *b* resemble each other and the original blazons may have been inverted. This would provide canting arms for Cyprus, since the pronunciation of the latter word in Old French, as borne out by the most common orthography (*Chipre, Chyppre, Chippres*; see Flutre, p. 223; cf. also MFr. *Chypre*), sounds like E. *ship*. OFr. *eschipre* 'sailor' does not lend itself to this pun as readily and *esquif* is a word attested only in 1497 in French (*BW*4, s.v.). *Escuçon*, not *targe*, was the heraldic term for shield (see ESCUÇON[1]; the term does appear, however, in *Meliador*, v. 4524 [arms of Agaiant]). Examples of similar Anglo-French punning in medieval English heraldry are numerous (see Wagner, *Historic Heraldry*, p. 32; *Aspilogia II*, pp. 8, 108). In the Camden Roll, punning is evident in the fictitious arms provided for *D* 12, *Griffonie* (= Greece, see GRIFON, *Note*), *D* 14, *Ermenie* (= Lesser Armenia, see ERMINE, *Note*), and *D* 15 *Denemarche* (= Denmark, see HACHE, *Note*). The fact that the compiler of Grimaldi's Roll, which is closely related to the Camden Roll as well as Glover's Roll, corrected his blazon corresponding to *D* 12 (*P* 19: 'Le roy de Grece porte d'argent ove une croice d'une pee de goules'; the latter, incidentally, is probably another instance of canting arms; cf. the parallel examples cited in the discussion of the *Dean Tract's croice a les degrees* 'cross Calvary' in Brault, 'The Cross', p. 221), *D* 15 (*P* 13: 'Le roy de Danemark porte d'or ove trois leopardes passantz d'azure'), and here in *D* 10 (*P* 12: 'Le roy de Cipres port burelee d'argent et d'azure ove un leon rampant de goules coroné d'or'; see above) is a strong argument in support of the explanation we propose for *barge* in *D* 11, a spurious item followed by *P* 27.

barre[1], *bar (horizontal stripe)* (Fig. 54). (1) *alone on the shield.* B 65 (*Ba/Bc* 65: a deus barres; *Bb* 65: 2 barres; *Bl* 65: od deus barres): a deus barres; 69 (*Ba/Bc* 69: a deus barres; *Bb* 69: 2 barres; *Bl* 69: od deus barres), 198 (*Bl* 198 [202]: od deux barres): a deux barres; 153: a trois barres (*Bl* 153 [157]: od trois barres); *Bb* 25 (*B* 25, see BARRÉ DE . . . ET DE . . .[1]; *Bb* 25, see: BENDÉ DE . . . ET DE . . .[2]): ou 2 barres; *C* 121 (*Cl* 121: a deus barres; *Cd* 121: a .ii. barres), 168 (*Cl* 168: a deus barres; *Cd* 168: a .ii. barres): a deux barres; 103 (*Cl* 103: a treis barres; *Cd* 103: a 3 barres): trois barres; *D* 80, 144, 145: a deus barres; *H* 40, 76 (*Hg* 40 [41]: od deux barres; *Hg* 76 [88]: od deus barres): ou .ii. barrez (G: barres); 42 (*Hg* 42 [43]: od deux barres): ou .ii. barrez; *M* 47, 78: ou .ii. barres; *K*, v. 75: o treis barres. (2) *the top bar sets off a 'chief' which is charged.* A. *referring to* EN CHIEF[2] *or* EN LE CHIEF[2]. *Bb* 51: 2 barres (*B* 51, see BARRE OVE UN TOURTEL EN LE CHIEF; *Ba* 51, see FESSE A UN TOURTEL EN CHIEF), see TOURTEL EN CHIEF. See also

BARRE A UN MEULET EN LE CHIEF, BARRE OD UNE ESTOILE EN LE CHIEF, BARRE OD UN TOURTEL EN CHIEF, BARRE OD UN TOUR-TEL EN LE CHIEF, BARRE OU UN TOURTEL EN LE CHIEF, BARRE OVE UNE MEULE EN LE CHIEF. B. *a locution other than* EN CHIEF[2] *or* EN LE CHIEF[2] *is used.* See BARRE OD UNE PELOTE. *Syn.*: see FESSE A UNE ROUELE EN LE CHIEF, FESSE A UN TOURTEL EN CHIEF. *Note*: see CHIEF[2], *Note*. (3) *the word* CHIEF *is used and designates an area of the shield completely distinct from the bars* (i.e. CHIEF[1]). *M* 48: ou deux barres, see CHIEF[1] (1). *Note*: see JUMEAUS[1] (2) [*H* 77] and JUMELES[1] (1) A. [*B* 121]; cf. also JUMEAUS DE L'UN EN L'AUTRE, JUMEAUS DE L'UN ET DE L'AUTRE. (4) *the bars are used in conjunction with a canton.* B 49: a deux barre, see LIEPART EN LE QUARTIER; 105: deux barres (for *Bl* 49 and 105, see BASTON[3]); *C* 122: deux barres; *D* 133: od deu[s] barres. For other uses, see BARRE ENGRES-LEE, BARRE SOR LE TOUT, FESSIÉ D'UNE BARRE ET OU CHIEF UN LIONCEL PASSANT, TELS ARMES MES QU'EN LIEU D'UNE BARRE MEINS. *Syn.*: BASTON[3], BASTON DE TRAVERS, BENDE[2], BENDE DE TRAVERS, FESSE (2), FESSE DE TRAVERS, FESSE EN MI, JUMEAUS[2], ROIE[2] (?). *Note*: *P* 126 and 124, corresponding to *B* 65 and 69 respectively, read *deux fesses* instead of *deus/deux barres*. Like its participial counterpart, *barré de . . . et de . . .*[1], *barre* appears only in English rolls of arms during this period. The bars are always in multiples (see Prinet WR, p. 109 n. 4) and are never charged, though in *C* 103 the bars are diapered ('Le counte de le Ille, gules trois barres d'or diasprés'). This usage corresponds essentially to modern English heraldic practice. In two literary instances, one French, one English, OFr. *barre* is used in the singular. See FESSIÉ D'UNE BARRE ET OU CHIEF UN LIONCEL PASSANT and TELS ARMES MES QU'EN LIEU D'UNE BARRE MEINS. On the meaning of *barre* in *CC*, see BARRÉ DE . . . ET DE . . .[2]. In modern French heraldry, *barre* has come to mean 'bend sinister', i.e. a stripe travers-ing the shield from right to left (from sinister chief to dexter base, technically speaking). Cf. BARRÉ DE . . . ET DE . . .[1]. On the popular but spurious heraldic term 'bar sinister', consult Julian Franklyn,

'A Note on Bar Sinister', *Coat of Arms*, i (1951), no. 5, pp. 155–6; see also the letters to the editor, i, no. 6, p. 212, no. 7, pp. 246–7; and ii (1952), no. 10, p. 79. Differencing arms for bastardy is discussed in detail by Mathieu, pp. 115–23, and by Gayre, *Heraldic Cadency*, chs. xx and xxv.

barré[2], *bend* (Fig. 60). See BARRE DE BELIC. *Syn.*: see BENDE[1].

barre a un meulet en le chief, *bar, in chief a roundel*. B 83: a deux barres . . . a trois molets en le chief (*Bl* 83, see BARRE OVE UNE MEULE EN LE CHIEF). *Syn.*: see FESSE A UN TOURTEL EN CHIEF.

barre de belic, *bend* (Fig. 60). *Lancelot propre*, iii. 259: a une bare . . . de bellic. *Syn.*: see BENDE[1].

barré de . . . et de . . .[1], *barry, barruly* (Fig. 5). B 25 (*Ba* 25, see BENDÉ DE . . . ET DE . . .[2]; *Bb* 25, see BARRE; *Bl* 25: barrés de . . . et de . . .): barrés de . . . et de . . .; 32: barré . . . de . . . et de . . . (*Bl* 32, see BENDÉ DE . . . ET DE . . .[2]); 72 (*Ba/Bc* 72: barré de . . . e de . . .; *Bb* 72: barré . . . et . . .; *Bl* 72: barré de . . . et de . . .), 135, 137, 187, 196 (*Bl* 135 [139], 137 [141], 187 [191]: barré de . . . et de . . .; 196 [200], see BURELÉ DE . . . ET DE . . .): barree de . . . et de . . .; 42 (*Bl* 42: barré de . . . et de . . .): barry de . . . et de . . .; *Bb* 23 (*B/Ba* 23, see BURELÉ DE . . . ET DE . . .); 56: barry . . . et . . . (*B/Ba* 56, see BURELÉ DE . . . ET DE . . .); C 43 (*Cl* 43: barré de . . . et de . . .; *Cd* 43: barré . . . e . . .), 89 (*Cl/Cd* 89: barré de . . . e de . . .): barry de . . . et . . .; 71 (*Cl/Cd* 71: barré de . . . et de . . .), 128 (*Cl* 128: barrey de . . . et de . . .; *Cd* 128: barré de . . . e de . . .), 158 (*Cl* 158: barré de . . . e de . . .; *Cd* 158: barré de . . . et . . .): barry de . . . et de . . .; 125 (*Cl* 125: barré de . . . e de . . .; *Cd* 125: barré de . . . e . . .): barré de . . . et de . . .; 126 (*Cl* 126: barry de . . . et de . . .; *Cd* 126: bar . . . de . . . e . . .), 142 (*Cl* 142: barré de . . . et de . . .; *Cd* 142: barré de . . . e . . .), 175 (*Cl* 175: barré de . . . e de . . .): barry de . . . et de . . .; D 53, 55, 97, 118, 159: barré de . . . et de . . .; H 16 (*Hg* 16, see PIECES DE . . . ET DE . . .), 30, 36 (*Hg* 36, see PIECES DE . . . ET DE . . .), 44, 67, 107 (*Hg* 30, 44 [45], 107: barré de . . . et de . . .; 67 [68]: de

. . . et de . . . barré): barré de . . . et de . . .; M 25, 26: barré de . . . et de . . .; K, vv. 355–6, 382–3: barree / De . . . e de . . .; vv. 438, 440: barré . . . / De . . . e de . . . *Syn.*: A BENDES EN TRAVERS, BARRÉ DE . . . POINZ DE . . . ET DE . . ., BENDÉ DE . . . ET DE . . ., BENDÉ DE . . . ET DE . . . DE TRAVERS, BURELÉ DE . . . ET DE . . ., DE . . . PIECES BARRÉ DE . . . ET DE . . ., DE-TRENCHIÉ, FESSIÉ DE . . . ET DE . . .[1], FESSIÉ DE . . . ET DE . . . A . . . PIECES, PIECES DE . . . ET DE . . . *Note*: P 76 (= B 25) reads *bendees de . . . et de . . .* In the only other instance where Grimaldi's Roll provides a blazon corresponding to one in which Glover's Roll uses this expression (B 72), P 102 provides an identical reading: *barree de . . . et de . . .* P 76, then, is probably simply an error having nothing to do with BARRÉ DE . . . ET DE . . .[2], though conceivably confusion of the two meanings for *barré* may have been involved. The distinction between *barré de . . . et de . . .* as used here ('barry') and the modern French heraldic locution which it resembles (meaning 'bendy-sinister') parallels the contrasting uses we have noted above, s.v. BARRE[1]. See Prinet WR, p. 235. The number of bars which make up this ordinary is never noted except in the locutions which are given below. As a rule, barry applies only to the field of the shield proper or of the escutcheon. In C 43, however, it refers to that of a lion rampant. On the modern distinction between *barry* and *barruly*, see BURELÉ DE . . . ET DE . . ., *Note*.

barré de . . . et de . . .[2], *bendy (or, possibly, 'striped [in general]'; see Note)* (Fig. 8). CC, vv. 1227–30:

> L'uns fu Aubiers de Longeval:
> En lui avoit moult biel armé.
> Il portoit un escu baré,
> Bien sai, de geules et de vair.

Syn.: see BENDÉ DE . . . ET DE . . .[1]. *Note*: for a possible confusion between BARRÉ DE . . . ET DE . . .[1] and BARRÉ DE . . . ET DE . . .[2] in Grimaldi's Roll (P 76), see BARRÉ DE . . . ET DE . . .[1], *Note*. According to Prinet CC, pp. 170, 179, Jakemes's use of barry here is an error for bendy. The latter, however, may simply be using *baré* as a designation for any kind of stripe. This view is

supported by his use of *barre* in the locution
FESSIÉ D'UNE BARRE ET OU CHIEF UN LIONCEL
PASSANT in which *fessié* is clearly the part
of the phrase which indicates the direction
of the stripe. In any case, Delbouille's use
of the modern French heraldic term *barré*
(p. 282), which means 'bendy-sinister', to
define Jakemes's use of the word which
resembles it in Old French is misleading.
The same may be said for his definition
('barre [hérald.]') of OFr. *barre* on the
same page of his glossary. See FESSIÉ D'UNE
BARRE ET OU CHIEF UN LIONCEL PASSANT.

barré de . . . pieces de . . . et de . . .,
see DE . . . PIECES BARRÉ DE . . . ET DE . . .

barré de . . . poinz de . . . et de . . .,
*barry of . . . (the number of pieces, i.e. stripes,
is indicated)* (Fig. 5). *K*, vv. 203–5:

> E la baniere Hue Poinz (W: Pointz)
> Estoit barree de .viii. (W and MS.: .viiij.)
>   poinz,
> De or e de goules ovelment.

Syn.: see BARRÉ DE . . . ET DE . . .[1].

barre engreslee, *fusils conjoined in fess*
(Fig. 84). *C* 148: trois barres . . . engrellés
(*Cl* 148: a treys barres . . . engrellé; *Cd*
148: .iii. barres ingrelé). *Syn.*: see FESSE
ENDENTEE. *Note*: see ENGRESLÉ[2] and consult Prinet WR, p. 242. *Aspilogia II*,
p. 188, note to item 108, referring to *Cl*
148 [108]: 'The [Crespin] arms were
variously drawn as two or three bars of
fusils or as lozengy . . .'

barre od une estoile en le chief, *bar, in
chief a mullet*. The complete blazon reads
as follows: *Bl*, Gaddesden [108]: Gaddesden, d'argent a deux barres noir od trois
estoilles noir en le chief. *Syn.*: see FESSE
A UNE ROUELE EN LE CHIEF. *Note*: refers
to BARRE[1] (2) A., ESTOILE EN LE CHIEF[2].

barre od une pelote, *bar, in chief a roundel*.
D 95: a deus barres . . . od treis pelotes.
Syn.: see FESSE A UN TOURTEL EN CHIEF.

barre od un tourtel en chief, *bar, in chief
a roundel*. *Bl* 51: deux barres . . . od trois
turteux . . . en chief (*B* 51, see BARRE OVE
UN TOURTEL EN LE CHIEF; *Ba* 51, see FESSE
A UN TOURTEL EN CHIEF; *Bb* 51, see BARRE[1]
[2] A.). *Syn.*: see FESSE A UN TOURTEL EN
CHIEF. *Note*: refers to BARRE[1] (2) A., EN
CHIEF[2].

barre od un tourtel en le chief, *bar, in*

chief a roundel. Hg 61 [62]: od deux barres
. . . od trois tourteaux . . . en le chef (*H* 61,
see BARRE OU UN TOURTEL EN LE CHIEF).
Syn.: see FESSE A UN TOURTEL EN CHIEF.
Note: refers to BARRE[1] (2) A., EN LE CHIEF[2].

barre ou un tourtel en le chief, *bar, in
chief a roundel. H* 61: ou .ii. barrez . . . od
.iii. turteus . . . en le chef (*Hg* 61 [62], see
BARRE OD UN TOURTEL EN LE CHIEF). *Syn.*:
see FESSE A UN TOURTEL EN CHIEF.

barre ove une meule en le chief, *bar,
in chief a roundel. Bl* 83: od deux barres . . .
ove trois moeles . . . en le chief (*B* 83, see
BARRE A UN MEULET EN LE CHIEF). *Syn.*:
see FESSE A UN TOURTEL EN CHIEF.

barre ove un tourtel en le chief, *bar,
in chief a roundel. B* 51: a deulx barres . . .
ove trois torteux . . . en le cheif (*Ba* 51,
see FESSE A UN TOURTEL EN CHIEF; *Bb* 51,
see BARRE (2) A.; *Bl* 51, see BARRE OD UN
TOURTEL EN CHIEF). *Syn.*: see FESSE A UN
TOURTEL EN CHIEF.

barre sor le tout, *bar over all. Bl* 107
[109]: deux barres . . . sur le tout. *Note*:
for complete blazon, see PARTI DE . . .
ET DE . . .

bars sinanz, *sea-perch addorsed* (Fig. 216).
The complete blazon reads as follows: *BA*
156: Gerars (A: Gerart) de Fornewil (A:
Foveil), de geules (A: gueules) a .ii. bars
d'or sinans. Hannuiers (A: Hainnuier).
Note: according to Adam-Even's note, p. 75,
these are the arms of Gerard of Solre,
Lord of Beaumont in 1305. In the glossary,
p. 20, the French scholar defines *sinans* as
follows: 'attribut du bar, qui se trouve dans
Urfé: adossé'. 'Urfé' is the name given by
Adam-Even to a treatise (Bibliothèque
nationale, MS. f. fr. 32753) dated by him
c. 1440, which has, erroneously, it would
seem, been attributed to Jean Courtois
('Sicile'), sometime herald to Alfonso,
King of Aragon and Sicily. See Adam-
Even, 'Les armoiries étrangères du moyen âge', *Hidal-
guía*, iii (1955), 793, 796–7. Cf. LUCET
AIRIANT.

baston[1], *bend (diagonal stripe from dexter
chief to sinister base)* (Fig. 60). *TA*, v. 1628:
A .i. baston; *TC*, v. 2039: A un baston;
v. 2062: au baston; v. 2245: Celui au
baston troncenei; *CP* 3, 98, 124, 145: a un
baston; *CPA* 3, 4, 146: au baton; 149:

a .ii. batons; *H* 5: ou ung baston (*Hg* 5: a un baston); 36, 54 (*Hg* 36 [37], 54 [55] od le baston): ou le baston; 50: ovec ung baston (*Hg* 50: ovec un baston); 65: o ung baston (*Hg* 65 [66]: od un baston); *Hg* 17: a un baston; *CC*, v. 1111: Au baston; v. 1404: un baston; *M* 4, 55: ou ung baston; 5: ou le baston; 19, 71: le baston; 27: et ung baston; *K*, v. 467: Au . . . bastoun (see ARMES SON FRERE A . . . SANS). *Syn.*: see BENDE[1] and cf. BASTON JETÉ SOR. For other uses, see EL BASTON, SORJETÉ D'UN BASTON. *Note*: although merely a synonym for the bend in the thirteenth century, the baston was later felt to be a charge, not an ordinary, and was shortened to resemble more closely the stick it depicted. In modern English usage, the baston is always shown *couped*, i.e. cut short so as not to touch the edges of the shield. French heraldry, however, continues to use the term *bâton* to designate a narrow bend or bend sinister, sometimes adding the words *en bande* or *en barre* to specify the direction of the diagonal. MFr. *traverse* is a synonym for *bâton en barre*. The equivalent of E. *baston* in modern French heraldry is *bâton alaisé* (sometimes spelled *alésé*), although the adjective is frequently omitted even when the ends of the stick are cut short. On this charge and the term *bâton péri*, consult Veyrin-Forrer, p. 37.

baston[2], *pale* (*vertical stripe*) (Fig. 88). The complete blazon reads as follows: *CC*, vv. 1316–21:

> Ses escus avoit le cief d'or,
> Et saciés qu'il avoit encor,
> El cief, une mierle de sable,
> Ce n'est ne mencongne ne fable,
> Et de geules estoit li fons,
> S'i ot trois vaironnés bastons.

Syn.: see PAL. *Note*: Prinet CC, pp. 171–2, 178–9, points out that the term is improperly used by Jakemes here.

baston[3], *fess* (*horizontal stripe*) (Fig. 80). *BA* 146, 147: a .ii. bastons; *B* 53: ou deux bastons (*Ba/Bc* 53: a deus bastuns; *Bb* 53: a deux bastiones; *Bl* 53: od deus bastons); *Bl* 49: od deus bastons (*B* 49, see BARRE [4]); 105: od deux bastons (*B* 105, see BARRE [4]). For other uses see BASTON DE TRAVERS and cf. BASTON DE FUIRES; see also

Note (for *Bc*). *Syn.*: see BARRE[1]. *Note*: in the Bigot Roll, fol. 32 recto, after *BA* 179, a number of partial blazons including the fragment . . . *aston*, obviously for *baston*, were not included by Adam-Even in his edition. *Baston* is the only one of the four synonyms listed here which is ever charged; in *B* 53, the bastons are bezanty. On the meaning of this term in Glover's Roll, see *Aspilogia II*, pp. 108; 124, note to item 49; 125, note to item 53. Wagner, *CEMRA*, p. 4, states that *Bl* 49, 53, and 105 contain examples of *baston* in this sense, a use 'found in no other English roll of arms and only one early French roll, the "Bigot"'; on pp. 5–6, he does not note its appearance in Harvy's version (see above, *B* 53) and, on p. 7, he erroneously asserts that it is not found in St. George's version either (see above *Ba/Bb/Bc* 53). On the meaning of the term in the Bigot Roll, see Adam-Even BA, glossary, p. 19: 'fasce'.

baston[4], *fimbriation* (*narrow edging* [*here, of a bend*] *of a different tincture*). See BENDE ENLISTEE A DEUS BASTONS ENCOSTE.

baston de fuires, *fess dancetty, daunce* (Fig. 78). The complete blazon reads as follows: *BA* 4: Gerars (A: Gerart) de Quepeni (A: Quepen), l'escu d'or a .ii. bastons de gueules (A: gueules) de fuires au lambel vert. Baneres (A: Banneret) et Alemans. *Syn.*: see DANCE. Cf. also DANCE EN LE CHIEF, VUIVRE DE TRAVERS EN LE CHIEF.

baston de travers, *fess* (*horizontal stripe*) (Fig. 80). *BA* 28: a 2 bastons . . . de travers ou triers (A: ou tu ers); 215: a .ii. batons . . . de travers (A: en travers); 259: a .ii. bastons . . . de travers. *Syn.*: see BARRE[1]. *Note*: *BA* 28 actually reads: 'a 2 bastons noirs de (Travers) ou triers'.

baston de travers el chief, *on a chief a fess*. *BA* 206: a .i. baston . . . de travers el (A: es) kief. *Note*: refers to EN LE CHIEF[1]; cf. BASTON[3], BASTON DE TRAVERS OU CHIEF.

baston de travers ou chief, *in chief a fess*. *BA* 209: a .iii. batons (A: bastons) . . . de travers u kief; 229: a .iii. batons . . . u kief de travers. *Note*: refers to OU CHIEF[1]; cf. BASTON[3], BASTON DE TRAVERS EL CHIEF.

baston en belic, *bend* (Fig. 60). *BA* 24, 42, 127, 173, 234, 251, 257, 260: a .i. baston . . . en beslive; 173: a un baston . . . beslive

live (A: en beslive); 226: a .i. baton . . . en
beslive. *Syn.*: see BENDE[1]. *Note*: cf. BASTON[1],
BENDE EN BELIC.

baston endenté en belic, *fusils conjoined
in bend* (Fig. 64). *BA* 136: a .i. baston
endenté en beslive. *Syn.*: BENDE ENGRESLEE.
Note: see ENDENTÉ[2].

baston en travers, *ghost word.* See BASTON
DE TRAVERS.

baston jeté sor, *bend (the quarters involved
are specified).* The complete blazon reads
as follows: *K*, vv. 303–8:

> Du bon Hue le Despensier,
> Ki vassaument sur le coursier
> Savoit desrompre une mellee,
> Fu la baniere esquartelee
> De une noir bastoun sur blanc getté,
> E de vermeil jaune fretté.

Note: cf. BASTON[1]. The concision of this
remarkable blazon in no wise detracts
from its precision. Heralds had not as yet
evolved the system for numbering the
quarters, yet by indicating the tinctures
crossed by the bend, the author was able
to be quite specific in this respect. Cf. his
uses of SORALÉ DE BENDE O EGLEAUS, SOR-
JETÉ D'UN BASTON, and SORJETÉ O UNE
DANCE.

bayes, see BROIE.

bec, *beak.* See EGLE . . . LE BEC ET LES PIÉS,
FESANZ BEC A BEC. Cf. also HERONS PETIZ
BEESTEZ.

beestez, see HERONS PETIZ BEESTEZ.

bek, beke, see EGLE . . . LE BEC ET LES PIÉS.

belic, belif, belive, bellin, bellinc, see
DE BELIC, EN BELIC. *Note*: this expression
has confused a number of scholars since
Godefroy, viii. 313–14, s.v. *belif* (cf., however, i. 616, s.v. *belif, belin*, where the correct definition is provided), erroneously
defined it as a term meaning red; see, for
example, Ott, p. 131 (correction by Gaston
Paris in *Romania*, xxix [1900], 478); Bouly
de Lesdain, pp. 230–1; and Mario Roques
in the glossary of his edition of *Charrete*,
p. 234, s.v. *bernic*. For the correct definition
and etymology of OFr. *belic*, consult
FEW, vii. 270–1, s.v. *obliquus*, and Tobler–
Lommatzsch, i. 941–2, s.v. *beslic* (but cf.
i. 912–13, s.v. *bellic* 'rote Farbe'!).

bende[1], *bend* (Fig. 60). (1) *the bend bears
no charge.* Perceval, v. 4752: Une bende;

v. 4753: Li tiers de l'escu fu la bende;
Elie de Saint-Gille, v. 325: la bende; v. 413:
les bendes; v. 457: le bende; *Lancelot propre*,
iii. 147: .ii. . . . .iii. [bendes] . . . .ii. bendes
. . . .iii. bendes . . . a une seule bende; 168:
as .ii. . . . a .iii. bendes; 150 (2), 168: as .ii.
bendes; 151, 161, 174: as .iii. bendes; 162,
194: a le bende; 165: chil a la seule bende;
170: a .iii. bendes; 176, 192: a une bende;
259: .ii. bendes; iv. 104 (var.): a la bende;
220: a trois bendes; v. 368: a .ii. bendes;
437: a quatre bandes; *TA*, v. 859: A une
bende d'eresie; *BA* 167, 199: a la bende;
177: une bende (A: bande) (on these three
items, see *Note*); *B* 9 (*Bl* 9: ove une bende),
33, 110 (*Bl* 110 [114]: od un bend): ung
bend; 14 (*Bl* 14: ove une bend), 30 (*Ba/Bc*
30: a une bende; *Bl* 30: ove une bende),
54 (*Ba* 54: un bende; *Bc* 54: a une bende;
Bl 54: od un bend), 72 (*Ba* 72: a un bend;
Bc 72: a une bende; *Bl* 72: od une bende),
165, 166 (*Bl* 165 [169], 166 [170]: od un
bend), 168 (*Bl* 168 [172]: od une bende),
174 (*Bl* 174 [178]: od un bend): ung bende;
Ba/Bc 73: a treis bendes (*B* 73, see BENDE
EN BELIC; *Bb* 73: a 3 bends, see *Note*);
C 53 (*Cl/Cd* 53: a une bende), 55 (*Cl* 55:
a un bende; *Cd* 55: a bend), 69 (*Cl/Cd* 69:
a une bende), 70 (*Cl* 70: a un bende; *Cd*
70: a une bende), 125 (*Cl* 125: a un bende;
Cd 125, see BORDURE[1], *Note*), 169 (*Cl/Cd*
169: a une bende), 175 (*Cl* 175: et une
bende): un bend; 117: und bend (*Cl* 117:
a un bende; *Cd* 117: a une bende); *D* 23,
74, 83, 84, 131: a une bende; 24, 52, 160,
176, 177: od une bende; *CP* 4: a trois
bandes; 24: une bande; 25, 59, 63, 103:
a une bande; *CPA* 152: a une bande; 153,
166, 172: a la bande; *H* 26: ou ung bende
(*Hg* 26: a une bende); *M* 9: ou .iii. bendez;
23, 46, 50, 60: ou la bend; 25: odve la
bend; 49: la bend; *K*, v. 97: O un bende.
Note: in *Bb/Bc* 33, the bend is omitted from
the blazon; in *Bb* 30, 54, 72, the bend is
tricked; in *Bb* 73, the bend is tricked but
the words *a 3 bends* are added at the end of
the blazon. In *Cl* 178 [183], *a une bende* is
a scribal error for *a un lion*. See LION RAM-
PANT A LA COUE FOURCHIEE[2]. (2) *the bend
bears no charge and is cotised* (Fig. 61). A. *the
term* LISTES *or* LISTEAUS *is used.* See BENDE
A DEUS LISTEAUS (1), BENDE A LISTES,
BENDE A LISTES FLEURETEES, BENDE OU

FLEURETES OU DEUS LISTEAUS, LIONCEAUS A UNE BENDE LES LISTES. B. *the term* COTICE *is used.* See BENDE A COTICES, BENDE A LIONCEAUS A DEUS COTICES, BENDE ENTREALEE DE DEUS COTICES LIONCEAUS EN RAMPANT ASIS AU DEHORS, BENDE ET A DEUS COTICES, BENDE OD DEUS COTICES, BENDE OU LIONCEAUS OU DEUS COTICES, LIONCEAUS A UNE BENDE A DEUS COTICES, LIONCEAUS A UNE BENDE ET DEUS COTICES, LIONCEAUS A UNE BENDE OD DEUS COTICES, LIONCEAUS OD UNE BENDE ET DEUS COTICES, LIONCEAUS OU UNE BENDE ET A DEUS COTICES, LIONCEAUS OVE UNE BENDE A DEUS COTICES. C. *the term* COTICIÉ *is used.* See BENDE COTICIEE, BENDE COTICIEE ENTRE LIONCEAUS. *Note*: cf. BENDE ENLISTEE A DEUS BASTONS ENCOSTE. (3) *the bend is charged.* A. *the locution* EN LA BENDE *is used.* BA 39: a une bende, see COQUILLE EN LA BENDE; *C* 77: un bend (*Cl* 77: a une bende; *Cd* 77: une bende), see EGLET EN LA BENDE; *CP* 6: a une bande, see ESCUÇON DES ARMES DU DUC DE BOURGOGNE EN LA BORDURE; 92: a une bande, see EGLE EN LA BENDE; *H* 89: ou la bende, see EN LA BENDE UNE EGLETE (*Hg* 89 [87]: od la bende, see EN LA BENDE UNE EGLE); *M* 15: ou la bend, see EN LA BENDE UNE ESCHALOPE; 64: ou le bend, see EN LA BENDE UN LIONCEL. For another use, see EN UNE BENDE. B. *the word* BENDE *is used alone, order of items only indicating that the bend is charged. Hem,* v. 3092: A une bende, see COQUILLE (3) B. For other uses, see BENDE A UNE EGLE, BENDE AUS ESCHALOPES, SORALÉ DE BENDE O UN EGLEL. C. *the bend is cotised.* See BENDE A DEUS LISTEAUS[1]. D. *the bend is cotised and charged.* See BENDE OU UNE FLEURETE OU DEUS LISTEAUS. *Note*: on the position of charges on a bend, see Dr. Harold Bowditch's letter to the editor, *Coat of Arms*, vii (1962), 172–3; B. Tennberg, 'Charges on a Bend', *Coat of Arms*, ix (1966), 157. (4) *the bend separates multiple charges.* A. *the bend is cotised.* See BENDE A LIONCEAUS A DEUS COTICES, BENDE COTICIEE ENTRE LIONCEAUS, BENDE ENTREALEE DE DEUS COTICES LIONCEAUS EN RAMPANT ASIS AU DEHORS, BENDE OU LIONCEAUS OU DEUS COTICES, LIONCEAUS A UNE BENDE A DEUS COTICES, LIONCEAUS A UNE BENDE ET DEUS COTICES, LIONCEAUS A UNE BENDE LES

LISTES, LIONCEAUS A UNE BENDE OD DEUS COTICES, LIONCEAUS OD UNE BENDE ET DEUS COTICES, LIONCEAUS OU UNE BENDE A DEUS COTICES, LIONCEAUS OVE UNE BENDE A DEUS COTICES. B. *the bend is not cotised.* See BENDE A LIONCEAUS RAMPANZ, BENDE A LIONS RAMPANZ, BENDE A MERLETES, BENDE A MERLOZ, BENDE A OISELEZ, BENDE ENTRE MERLOZ, BENDE ET LIONS RAMPANZ, BENDE ET MERLETES, BENDE ET MERLOZ, BENDE OD ESMERLOZ, BENDE OD MERLOZ, BENDE OU CROISSANZ, BENDE OU MERLETES, BENDE OU MERLEZ, MERLOZ ET BENDE, MERLOZ ET UNE BENDE. For other uses see A BENDES, BENDÉ A BENDES, BENDÉ A UNE BENDE, BENDÉ DE BENDES, BENDÉ D'UNE BENDE, EN UNE BENDE. *Syn.*: BARRE DE BELIC, BARRE EN BELIC, BASTON[1], BASTON EN BELIC, BASTON JETÉ SOR, BENDE DE BELIC, BENDE EN BELIC, BENDE PARMI DE BELIC, BENDE TOUTE SEULE, COTICE (2), LOIER. *Note*: on the combination of martlets and a bend, see MERLETE[1], *Note*. Bouly de Lesdain, pp. 205–6, observes apropos of the use of *bende* and *bendé* in twelfth-century French literature: 'Faut-il voir dans ces bandes la propre figure héraldique qui a gardé ce nom et traverse diagonalement l'écu? Nous ne le croyons pas . . . et nous ne voyons dans ces pièces que des bandes au sens vulgaire du mot, c'est-à-dire des pièces métalliques plus longues que larges, appliquées en sens divers sur l'écu pour le renforcer.' Bouly de Lesdain goes on to cite several passages in Old French literature where *bendé* designates the metal bands around huntinghorns, axe-handles, and clubs. That a heraldic stripe was intended in most if not all of the twelfth-century examples cited here is evident, it seems to me, however, although the direction of the bend sometimes varied even in classic blazon. Matthew Paris confuses BENDE[1] and BENDE[2]. In the blazons for the Earl of Hereford ('Scutum azureum, leones aurei, benda album', Pusikan, p. 140), the Earl of Warwick ('Scutum eschekeratum d'or et d'azur, bende . . .', Pusikan, p. 141), and the Earl of Lincoln ('Cantel anterior d'or et correspondens, alia cantella de gules, benda nigra, quae gallice sable dicitur', Pusikan, p. 144), *benda* or *bende* corresponds to BENDE[1]. However, in the shields ascribed to Giffard and Hussey ('Scutum d'ermine, III bendes de gules', Pusikan, p. 123; *Aspilogia II*, pp. 7, 47, item 56) and to Roger de Huntingfield ('Scutum d'or, benda de gules a III gasteos de blanc', Pusikan, p. 145; *Aspilogia II*, p. 40, item 23), the same term must be listed under BENDE², as clearly indicated by the accompanying painted shields. Cf. FESSE, *Note*. The Sierck family arms (*BA* 39) are known to feature a bend charged with escallops (see BENDE A UNE COQUILLETE). For other synonyms, see BENDE A DEUS LISTEAUS¹, BENDE AUS ESCHALOPES. The term *bende*, however, sometimes refers to a horizontal stripe in the Bigot Roll (see BENDE², BENDE A DEUS LISTEAUS², and cf. BENDÉ DE . . . ET DE . . .²) and *BA* 167, 177, and 199, for lack of supporting evidence, are listed here only provisionally. Finally, *Ba/Bb/Bc/Bl* 33 and *P* 98 (corresponding to *B* 33) omit the bend.

bende², *fess* (Fig. 80). See BENDE A DEUS LISTEAUS², BENDE DE TRAVERS, BENDE EN TRAVERS. *Syn.*: see BARRE¹. *Note*: see BENDE¹, *Note*, and cf. BENDÉ DE . . . ET DE . . .². On the meaning 'fess' for *bende* in *P* 93 ('Roger de Clifforde porte eschequeré d'or et d'azure a une bende de goules', corresponding to *B* 31 [see FESSE (1), *Note*]), see *Aspilogia II*, pp. 108, 121, note to item 31; same meaning in the *Dean Tract*, p. 28, l. 128 (cf. BENDÉ DE . . . ET DE . . .², *Note*).

bendé¹, *traversed by a single diagonal stripe (a bend)* (Fig. 60). *Troie*, v. 7715: bendé; v. 12244: bendez; v. 22710: bendee; *Aiol*, v. 698: bendees; *Elie de Saint-Gille*, v. 1072: bendé; *Huon de Bordeaux*, v. 1870: bendés; v. 7760: bendé; *Enfances Vivien*, v. 3697: bandei; *SCU*, fol. 185 *c*: bendé; *TA*, vv. 900, 922, 1094, 1118, 1591, 1698, 1700, 1827: bendé; vv. 1048, 1212, 1518: bendez; *Vulgate Merlin Sequel*, p. 192: bendee. For another use, see BENDÉ A UNE COQUILLETE. *Syn.*: BENDÉ A UNE BENDE, BENDÉ D'UNE BENDE. *Note*: cf. FESSIÉ. The term may in certain cases be synonymous with BENDÉ DE . . . ET DE . . .¹. On this problem, see Prinet TA, p. 45: 'Parmi les grandes pièces héraldiques, c'est la *bande* qui est le plus fréquemment nommée . . . Souvent, la bande est répétée dans un écu *bandé*. Le blason de Convoitise est "bandé

de termes et d'usure", celui de Sapience "bandez d'onour et de conseil". Mais le mot "bendé" ne désigne pas uniquement, comme dans le blason moderne, un champ couvert de bandes d'émaux alternés; il désigne également un champ chargé d'une seule bande. Les écus d'Aumône, de Pitié, de Leauté et de Vérité "d'une bende d'aliance erent bendé".' While shields traversed by a single bend may have been commonplace in early French literature, arms *azure, a bend or* became the subject of a famous controversy between Sir Richard Le Scrope and Sir Robert Grosvenor in the fourteenth century. According to Boutell, pp. 106–7: 'The proceedings in the Court of Chivalry . . . began on the 17th August, 1385, and the final judgment of the King himself on the appeal of the defendant against the finding of the Court was not pronounced until the 27th May, 1390. On the 15th May, 1389, the judgment of the Court assigned *Azure, a bend or*, to Sir Richard Le Scrope; and to Sir Robert Grosvenor these arms: *Azure, a bend or within a plain bordure argent*. Thus the Court confirmed to Le Scrope the right to bear the ordinary alone; and at the same time it was decided that these arms of Scrope should be differenced with a bordure in order that they might become the arms of Grosvenor. Appeal being made to the Sovereign, Richard II determined that a plain bordure argent was a mark of cadency, perfectly sufficient as a difference "between cousin and cousin in blood", but "not a sufficient difference in arms between two strangers in blood in one kingdom". The King therefore cancelled and annuled the sentence of the Court of Chivalry, and in so doing gave a very clear definition of the distinction to be observed between cadency and differencing. Grosvenor therefore adopted the arms *Azure, a garb or*.' Further details are provided by Geoffrey Scrope in an article entitled 'The Scrope and Grosvenor Roll', *Coat of Arms*, ii (1952), 83–6.

bendé², *bendy* (Fig. 8). *Durmart*, v. 8441: tot cil as escus bendés. See also A BENDES BENDÉ, BENDÉ A . . . ET A . . ., BENDÉ DE BENDES. *Syn.*: see BENDÉ DE . . . ET DE . . .¹. *Note*: the shields mentioned in *Durmart* belong to the knights in Lancelot's retinue. Lancelot's arms are described as *argent, three bends gules* in vv. 8435–9. For an illustration of the vestimentary origin of this term, see ENTIER[2], *Note*.

bendé[3], *gyronny* (?) (Fig. 14). *SCK*, fol. 107 *a*:

> Li rois d'Irlande, ce me sanble,
> Ala joster a Sagremor
> Si que l'escu bendé a or
> Li a par mi frait et fendu.

Syn.: GIRONÉ DE . . . ET DE . . .[1] (?). *Note*: in an earlier passage, Sagremor's arms are described as gyronny sable and or (*SCK*, fol. 106 *f*):

> Aprés recoisi Sagremor
> Qui banieres de noir et d'or
> Portoit, ce sanbloit, gironees.

On Sagremor's gyronny arms, see Introduction, p. 50.

bendé[4], *paly* (?) (Fig. 19). See DE LONC EN LONC BENDÉ. *Syn.*: see PALÉ DE . . . ET DE . . .

bendé a bendes, see A BENDES BENDÉ.

bende a cotices, *bend cotised* (Fig. 61). *C* 40: un bend . . . cousteces (*Cl* 40: a une bende . . . a custeres; *Cd* 40: a une bende . . . a clistires). *Syn.*: see BENDE[1] (2). *Note*: the cotices are diapered. See *Aspilogia II*, Appendix II, pp. 164–6: 'the Champagne cotices were at one time, probably in the thirteenth century, made of, or represented as though made of, gold brocade, the "custeces diaprez" of Walford's Roll. The pattern was, doubtless, of a simple, geometric character, and after a few decades was stereotyped as the potent-counter-potent of the later blazons' (p. 166).

bende a deus listeaus[1], *bend cotised* (Fig. 61). *BA* 286: a une bande (A: bende) . . . a .iii. listiax, see MOLETE EN LA BENDE. *Syn.*: see BENDE[1] (2), BENDE[1] (3) C. *Note*: '.iii.' is doubtless a scribal error for '.ii.', for the arms (here ascribed to 'Jehans de Sansuerre' [A: Sansuere]) are known to be those of Jean I of Sancerre whose seal, as noted by Adam-Even BA, p. 120, bore a bend cotised. See also *CP* 8: 'Li contes de Sansoire porte les armes d'asur a une bande d'or et a deus cotices d'argent.'

bende a deus listeaus[2], *fess cotised* (Fig. 82). *BA* 236: a une bende . . . a .ii. listiax. *Syn.*: FESSE A DEUX LISTEAUS UN DESOUS ET

L'AUTRE DESOR. *Note*: incorrectly defined as a *bend cotised* in Brault, '*Cotice*', p. 114 (also, the blazon should read 'Le sire*s* de Clincamp'). On the arms in question, see Dr. Adam-Even's note, p. 117. See also BENDE[2], *Note*.

bendé a . . . et a . . ., *bendy* (Fig. 8). *Joufroi*, v. 408: A or bendé et a achon. *Syn.*: see BENDÉ DE . . . ET DE . . .[1].

bende a les eschalopes, see BENDE AUS ESCHALOPES.

bende a lionceaus a deus cotices, *bend cotised between lioncels rampant*. *Hg* 2: a une bende . . . a sis leonseaux . . . a deux costiz (*H* 2, see BENDE OU LIONCEAUS OU DEUS COTICES). *Syn.*: see BENDE[1] (4) A.

bende a lionceaus rampanz, *bend between lioncels rampant*. *C* 45: un bend . . . deux leonceux rampanz (W: rampant; MS.: ramp.) (*Cl* 45: a un bende . . . a deus liuncels . . . raumpante; *Cd* 45: a bend . . . a .ii. lionceus rampant). *Syn.*: see BENDE A LIONS RAMPANZ.

bende a lions rampanz, *bend between lions rampant*. *Cl* 62: a un bend . . . a .ii. liuns rampant (*C* 62, see BENDE ET LIONS RAMPANZ; *Cd* 62: a bend . . . a .ii. lions rampant). *Syn.*: BENDE A LIONCEAUS RAMPANZ, BENDE ET LIONS RAMPANZ.

bende a listes, *bend cotised* (but see *Note*). The complete blazon reads as follows: *C* 44: Le countee de Guerd, gulez un bend d'argent a listes d'or (*Cl/Cd* 44, see BENDE A LISTES FLEURETEES). *Note*: at first glance, the bend cotised here would appear to be identical with the others listed s.v. BENDE[1] (2), i.e. as in Fig. 61. See, however, the corresponding blazon in the next item.

bende a listes fleuretees, *bend cotised, the cotices ornamented with fleurs-de-lis* (Fig. 77). The complete blazon reads as follows: *Cl* 44: Le counte de Guerd, de gules a un bende d'argent a litte d'or fluretés; (*Cd* 44: Le conte de Guerde, gules a une bende argent a lytte d'or floretés; *C* 44, see BENDE A LISTES). *Note*: cf. preceding item. Prinet WR, p. 237, item 35 (referring to *Cl* 44), states: 'L'écu décrit est *de gueules à la bande d'argent cotoyée de deux cotices fleuronnées d'or*. Ce sont les armes des comtes de Werd (ou Wœrth), qui furent landgraves de Basse-Alsace de 1196 au milieu du XIVe siècle. Elles sont restées l'emblème héraldique du landgraviat et de la Basse-Alsace jusqu'à nos jours.' *Aspilogia II*, p. 179, note to item 52: 'Usually . . . the cotices are flory on the outside only.' The best discussion of these arms is by Paul Martin, 'Les armoiries de l'Alsace', *AHS*, lxvii (Annuaire 1953), 31–46.

bende a merletes, *bend between martlets. BA* 91 (A: bande), 92, 94: a une bende . . . a .vi. mellettes. *Syn.*: BENDE A MERLOZ, BENDE A OISELEZ, BENDE ENTRE MERLOZ, BENDE ET MERLETES, BENDE ET MERLOZ, BENDE OD ESMERLOZ, BENDE OD MERLOZ, BENDE OU MERLETES, BENDE OU MERLEZ, MERLOZ ET BENDE, MERLOZ ET UNE BENDE. Cf. MERLOZ A UNE BENDE ENGRESLEE, MERLOZ ET UNE BENDE ENGRESLEE. *Note*: refers to BENDE[1] (4) B., the martlets always being separated by the bend, 3 and 3.

bende a merloz, *bend between martlets. Cl* 93: a un bende . . . a sis merlor (*C* 93, see BENDE ET MERLOZ: *Cd* 93, see BENDE ET MERLETES). *Syn.*: see BENDE A MERLETES.

bende a oiselez, *bend between martlets. BA* 194: a une bende (A: a bende) . . . a .vi. oiselés. *Syn.*: see BENDE A MERLETES.

bendé a une bende, *traversed by a single diagonal stripe (a bend)* (Fig. 60). *TA*, vv. 774–5:

Targe d'or bendee d'argent
A une bende besantee.

Syn.: BENDÉ[1].

bendé a une coquillete, *on a bend an escallop. TC*, vv. 668–9: Bendés . . . / A trois coquilletes. *Syn.*: COQUILLE (3) B., COQUILLE EN LA BENDE, EN LA BENDE UNE ESCHALOPE. *Note*: refers to BENDE[1]. Cf. BENDE AUS ESCHALOPES. On this term in *TC*, consult Delbouille, pp. xxix, xcii. For the arms in question (Sierck), see *BA* 39 (s.v. COQUILLE EN LA BENDE) and *WB* 531.

bende a une egle, *on a bend an eagle. D* 19: une bende . . . a treis egles. *Syn.*: see EGLE EN LA BENDE.

bende aus eschalopes, *bend semy of escallops. D* 40: od une bende . . . a les escalops. *Note*: Grandison arms. Though the escallops are erased on the corresponding painted shield (no. 41), the correct blazon is provided by *F* 118. For a similar locution in *D*, see BENDE A UNE EGLE; cf., however, BENDE ENGRESLEE A ESCHALOPES.

bendé contrebendé de . . . et de . . ., *party per pale and bendy counterchanged (the tinctures of the bends are reversed as they cross the middle part of the shield resulting in a party and varied field)* (Fig. 23). See FESSIÉ DE . . . ET DE . . . ET CONTREFESSIÉ. *Note*: evidently an error for *palé de . . . et de . . .*, but cf. CONTREBENDÉ DE . . . ET DE . . .

bende coticiee, *bend cotised* (Fig. 61). *TA*, vv. 827–8:

A une bende de faintié
Contichiee d'ennemistié.

Syn.: see BENDE[1] (2).

bende coticiee entre lionceaus, *bend cotised between lioncels rampant.* See BENDE ENTRE LIONCEAUS COTICIEE.

bende de belic, *bend* (Fig. 60). *Troie*, v. 7919: O une bende de besli; *Lancelot propre*, iii. 147: une bende . . . de bellic; 150, 174, 395, 424: a une bende . . . de bellic; 259: a .iii. bendes de bellic; 407: a le bende . . . de bellic; iv. 104 (var.): a .i. bende . . . de bellic; 149: a une bende . . . de bellinc; *Mort Artu*, p. 78: a trois bendes de bellic; p. 97: a une bende de bellic; p. 103: une bende de bellic; *Artus*, p. 67: et une bende . . . de besengnis; p. 307: a une bende . . . de bellic. For another use, see A BENDES DE BELIC. *Syn.*: see BENDE[1].

bendé de bendes, *traversed by multiple stripes (direction not indicated). Thèbes*, vv. 6229–30:

D'ermin ot entresaing bendé
De longues bendes de cendé.

Syn.: see A BENDES BENDÉ. *Note*: see BENDE[1], *Note*; BENDÉ[2].

bendé de . . . et de . . .[1], *bendy* (Fig. 8). *Perlesvaus*, pp. 49, 64: bendé de . . . e de . . .; p. 145: bandé de . . . et de . . .; pp. 190, 191, 219: bendé de . . . et de . . .; *Escoufle*, vv. 1136–7: Ses escus ert d'azur et d'or, / Bendés a flors de l'un a l'autre; *TA*, v. 779: Bendé de . . . et de . . .; vv. 995, 1879: Bendez de . . . et de . . .; *B* 113: bendé de . . . et de . . . (*Bl* 113 [117]: bendé de . . . et de . . .); *C* 72: bendy de . . . et de . . . (*Cl/Cd* 72: bendé de . . . e de . . .); *D* 31, 104, 116, 149: bendé de . . . et de . . .; *CPA* 12: bandé de . . . et de . . . *Syn.*: A BENDES, A BENDES DE BELIC, BARRÉ DE . . . ET DE . . .[2], BENDÉ[2], BENDÉ A . . .

ET A . . ., BENDÉ DE . . . ET DE . . . EN
BELIC, BENDES DE . . . ET DE . . . AUTANT DE
L'UN COM DE L'AUTRE, ESTACHIÉ EN BELIC
DE . . . ET DE . . . *Note*: for *P* 76 (*bendees
de . . . et de . . .*), see BARRÉ DE . . . ET DE . . .[1],
Note. On the blazon in *Escoufle*, see Brault,
'*de l'un en l'autre*', p. 85.

bendé de . . . et de . . .[2], *barry, barruly*
(Fig. 5). *BA* 95, 103, 104, 157 (95, 157,
see MOLETES EN LE . . .), 280 (see ANEAUS
DE L'UN EN L'AUTRE): bendé de . . .
et de . . .; *Ba/Bc* 25: bendez de . . . e
de . . . (*B* 25, see BARRÉ de . . . ET DE . . .[1];
Bb 25, see BARRE); *Bl* 32: bendé [de . . .
et de] (*B* 32, see BARRÉ DE . . . ET DE . . .[1]).
TC, v. 2197: bendéz. For another use, see
BENDÉ DE . . . ET DE . . . DE TRAVERS and
cf. BENDÉ CONTREBENDÉ DE . . . ET DE . . .
(see FESSIÉ de . . . ET DE . . . ET CONTRE-
FESSIÉ, *Note*) and CONTREBENDÉ DE . . .
ET DE . . . *Syn.*: see BARRÉ DE . . . ET DE . . .[1].
Note: proof that *bendé de . . . et de . . .* has
this meaning in *BA* 95, 157, and 280 is
provided by the painted shields of *WB* 811
(corresponding to the first two items in *BA*)
and *WB* 904. For *BA* 103 and 104, see
J. T. de Raadt, *Sceaux armoriés des Pays-Bas*,
iv (1900), 393, barry shield on seal dated
1397. Also cf. BENDE[2]. On the use of this
term in *Ba* and *TC*, consult *Aspilogia II*,
pp. 108; 119, note to item 25; 121, note
to item 32; and Delbouille, pp. lxxxv–
lxxxvi. This meaning is also found in the
Dean Tract, p. 26, l. 36; p. 27, l. 64; p. 28,
l. 128 (cf. BENDE[2], *Note*).

bendé de . . . et de . . .[3], *lozengy in bend*
(Fig. 17). See BENDÉ DE . . . ET DE . . .
ENDENTÉ L'UN EN L'AUTRE. *Note*: cf. FESSIÉ
DE . . . ET DE . . .[2].

bendé de . . . et de . . . de travers, *barry,
barruly* (Fig. 5). *BA* 62, 63, 69, 102, 152,
222: bendé de . . . et de . . . de travers.
Syn.: see BARRÉ DE . . . ET DE . . .[1]. *Note*:
refers to BENDÉ DE . . . ET DE . . .[2]. Cf.
BENDE DE TRAVERS. In *BA* 62, alternative
stripes are charged with small saltires.
See EN L'OR.

bendé de . . . et de . . . en belic, *bendy*
(Fig. 8). *BA* 61, 141, 185, 279: bendé de
. . . et de . . . en beslive. *Syn.*: see BENDÉ
DE . . . ET DE . . .[1]. *Note*: cf. BENDE EN BELIC.

**bendé de . . . et de . . . endenté l'un en
l'autre,** *lozengy in bend* (Fig. 17). *BA* 247:

bendé de . . . et de . . . endenté l'un en
l'autre. *Syn.*: MASCLÉ DE . . . ET DE . . .[2].
Note: refers to BENDÉ DE . . . ET DE . . .[3];
cf. FESSIÉ DE . . . ET DE . . . ENDENTÉ
DE L'UN A L'AUTRE, LOSENGIÉ DE . . . ET
DE . . .[1]. The arms in question (Foulques
de Daon) are known from an armorial
seal; see Adam-Even BA, p. 118, note to
item 247.

bendé de . . . pieces de . . . et de . . .,
*bendy of . . . (the number of pieces, i.e. stripes,
is indicated)* (Fig. 8). *EO*, vv. 5152–3:
De . . . et de . . . bendés / De douze pieces.

bende de travers, *bar* (Fig. 54). *FCE*,
vv. 12188–9: D'or fin a une bande fu /
D'azur qui aloit de travers; *BA* 1: a 3
bandes . . . de travers; 76, 201, 203: a .iii.
bendes . . . de travers; 202: a trois bendes
. . . de travers. *Syn.*: see BARRE. *Note*: cf.
BENDÉ DE . . . ET DE . . . DE TRAVERS.

bendé d'une bende, *traversed by a single
diagonal stripe (a bend)* (Fig. 60). *TA*,
vv. 1956–7: Car d'une bende d'aliance /
Erent bendé. *Syn.*: see BENDÉ[1].

bende en belic, *bend* (Fig. 60). *Lancelot
propre*, iv. 133: a une bende . . . en bellinc;
Vulgate Merlin Sequel, p. 388: une bende en
belic; *Durmart*, vv. 8437–8: Troi bendes
vermelles i sont / Qui totes troi en bellin
vont; *B* 73: a trois bendes . . . embelief
(*Ba/Bb* 73, see BENDE[1] [1]; *Bl* 73: od trois
bendes . . . en beliff). *Syn.*: see BENDE[1].
Note: cf. BENDÉ DE . . . ET DE . . . EN BELIC.
For *P* 50, see EN BELIC, *Note*.

bende engreslee, *fusils conjoined in bend*
(Fig. 64). (1) *the ordinary is alone on the
shield. B* 152: ung bend engrelé (*Bl* 152
[156]: od un bend engrelé); *C* 173: un
bend engrelé (*Cl* 173: a un bende . . .
engrallé); *D* 114: a une bende engraslé;
CP 60: a une bande . . . engrelee; *K*, v. 50:
La bende . . . engreellie; v. 384: O bende
. . . engreellie. (2) *a lion is debruised by the
ordinary.* *M* 53: et ung bend engrelé. (3)
the ordinary separates charges into two groups.
A. *martlets, 3 and 3.* See MERLOZ A UNE
BENDE ENGRESLEE, MERLOZ ET UNE BENDE
ENGRESLEE. B. *escallops, 3 and 3.* See BENDE
ENGRESLEE A ESCHALOPES. *Syn.*: BASTON
ENDENTÉ EN BELIC. For another use, see
ESTRE ENGRESLÉ. *Note*: on this ordinary,
see ENGRESLÉ[2] and consult Prinet WR,
p. 253, and Prinet CP, p. 21 n. 3. *Bende*

engreslee in Walford's Roll is *preceded* in one instance by the multiple charges it separates (in the phrases MERLOZ A UNE BENDE ENGRESLEE, MERLOZ ET UNE BENDE ENGRESLEE) and *followed* by them in another (in the phrase BENDE ENGRESLEE A ESCHALOPES). Gough H, p. 138, note to item 37: 'In [*K*, v. 384, John Grey's] bend is described as *engrailed*, which seems to be merely an error of the rhymer.'

bende engreslee a eschalopes, *fusils conjoined in bend between escallops. C* 174: un bend . . . engrelé six escallops (*Cl* 174: a une bende . . . engrallé a sis escalopes). *Note*: see BENDE ENGRESLEE (3) B.

bende enlistee a deus bastons encoste, *fimbriated bend (the bend is ornamented with a narrow edging of a different tincture)* (Fig. 63). The complete blazon reads as follows: *TC*, vv. 2218–21:

> Vallés, c'est cist as armes d'or,
> A celle bende troncenee
> D'argent et d'azur enlistee
> A deus bastons vermaus encoste.

Note: refers to BASTON[4]; cf. BENDE[1] (2) C. I have omitted the comma placed after the word *enlistee* (v. 2220) in Delbouille's edition. See Brault, *'Cotice'*, p. 114. These verses are referred to in *Aspilogia II*, p. 194, note to item 128. For *celle*, see CELE, CELES.

bende en travers, see A BENDES EN TRAVERS.

bende entrealee de deus cotices lionceaus en rampant asis au dehors, *bend cotised between lioncels rampant. K*, vv. 108–12:

> Baniere out de inde cendal fort,
> O une blanche bende lee,
> De deus costices entrealee,
> De or fin, dont au dehors asis
> Ot en rampant lyonceaus sis.

Syn.: see BENDE[1] (4) A. *Note*: Wright joins the words *bende lee* 'wide bend' together forming the ghost word *bendelee*. Though there is no indication of this in Wright's edition, the base manuscript utilized by the latter (British Museum MS. Cotton Caligula A. xviii, fols. 23 *b*–30 *b*) omits the last verse quoted above. Wright inserted the line either from Nicolas's earlier edition or from College of Arms MS. Arundel lxii, fols. 4–34 used by the latter.

bende entre lionceaus coticiee, *bend cotised between lioncels rampant. B* 184: ung bend . . . entre six leonceux . . . cotisee (*Bl* 184 [188], see LIONCEAUS OD UNE BENDE ET DEUS COTICES). *Syn.*: see BENDE[1] (4) A.

bende entre merloz, *bend between martlets. B* 141, 143, 145: ung bend entre six merlots (*Bl* 141 [145], 143 [147], 145 [149], see MERLOZ ET UNE BENDE). *Syn.*: see BENDE A MERLETES.

bende et a deus cotices, *bend cotised* (Fig. 61). *CP* 8: a une bande . . . et a deux cotices. *Syn.*: see BENDE[1] (2).

bende et lions rampanz, *bend between lions rampant. C* 62: un bend et deux leons rampanz (W: rampant; MS.: ramp.) (*Cl/Cd* 62, see BENDE A LIONS RAMPANZ). *Syn.*: see BENDE A LIONS RAMPANZ.

bende et merlez, *bend between martlets. Cd* 93: a bend . . . e 6 merlets (*C* 93, see BENDE ET MERLOZ; *Cl* 93, see BENDE A MERLOZ). *Syn.*: see BENDE A MERLETES.

bende et merloz, *bend between martlets. C* 93: un bend et siz merloz (*Cl* 93, see BENDE A MERLOZ; *Cd* 93, see BENDE ET MERLETES). *Syn.*: see BENDE A MERLETES.

bende fleuretee, see FLEURETÉ[1], *Note.*

bendelee, see BENDE ENTREALEE DE DEUS COTICES LIONCEAUS EN RAMPANT ASIS AU DEHORS.

bende od deus cotices, *bend cotised* (Fig. 61). *D* 9: a une bende . . . od deus cotices. *Syn.*: see BENDE[1] (2). *Note*: as this is a party field, only the dexter half of the charge appears. See DEMI CHARBOUCLE.

bende od esmerloz, *bend between martlets. D* 65: a une bende . . . od sis esmerloz. *Syn.*: see BENDE A MERLETES.

bende od merloz, *bend between martlets. Hg* 68 [69]: od la bende . . . od .vi. merlous (*H* 68, see BENDE OU MERLETES). *Syn.*: see BENDE A MERLETES.

bende ou croissanz, *bend between crescents. M* 24: ou la bende . . . ou .vi. cressannts (G: cressaunts). *Note*: see BENDE[1] (4) B.

bende ou lionceaus ou deus cotices, *bend cotised between lioncels rampant. H* 2: ou ung bende . . . ou .vi. leonceux . . . ou deux cotises (*Hg* 2, see BENDE A LIONCEAUS A DEUS COTICES). *Syn.*: see BENDE[1] (4) A.

bende ou merletes, *bend between martlets. H* 68: ou la bende . . . ou .vi. marletez (*Hg* 68, see BENDE OD MERLOZ). *Syn.*: see BENDE A MERLETES.

bende ou merlez, *bend between martlets.*
M 43: ou la bend . . . ou .vi. merletts.
Syn.: see BENDE A MERLETES.

bende ou une fleurete ou deus listeaus,
bend cotised, on the bend a fleur-de-lis. M 1:
ou la bend . . . ou .iii. florettz (G: floretez)
. . . ou .ii. lytteaus (G and MS.: lytteg').
Note: see BENDE[1] (3) D. The 'g' at the end
of the word *lytteg'* (i.e. *lytteaus*) in this
manuscript of the Nativity Roll is simply a
common abbreviation (actually resembling
a *g* more than a *g*) for the suffix *-us* or *-aus*
in medieval French manuscripts. On this
symbol, consult Pope, p. 288, para. 733.

bende parmi de belic, *bend* (Fig. 60).
Charrete, vv. 5774–5:

Celui a cele bande d'or
Parmi cel escu de bernic?

Syn.: see BENDE[1].

**bendes de . . . et de . . . autant de l'un
com de l'autre,** *bendy* (Fig. 8). *Lancelot
propre,* iii. 291: si ot une cote armoire
vestue a bendes d'or et d'aisur autant de
l'un comme de l'autre. *Syn.*: see BENDÉ DE
. . . ET DE . . .[1].

bendes losengiees de . . . et de . . .,
lozengy (Fig. 16). *TA,* vv. 668–9:

A .iiii. bendes losengiees
De vaine gloire et d'arogance.

Syn.: see LOSENGIÉ DE . . . ET DE . . .[1].
Note: cf. BASTON ENDENTÉ EN BELIC, BENDE
ENGRESLEE 'lozenges conjoined in (a single)
bend'. While the four bends here may conceivably be charged with lozenges, this
does not appear very likely.

bende toute seule, *bend* (Fig. 60). *Escanor,*
vv. 3594–7:

Li fix le roy l'escu d'argent
Portoit a .i. demi lyon
Vermeil bordé d'or environ
A .ii. bendes vers toutes seules.

Syn.: see BENDE[1].

bernic, see BELIC.

besancié, *ornamented with bezants.* See CHAR-
BOUCLE and cf. BESANTÉ.

besant, *bezant* (Fig. 112). (1) *the bezants
charge alternating stripes of a barry undy field.*
The complete blazon reads as follows: *BA*
84: Alebert de Leuch, l'escu ondé d'or et de
geules as besans (A: a V besans) d'argent en

le (A: es) geules, see EN LE GEULES[2]. (2) *a field
semy of bezants* (Fig. 29). *EO,* vv. 4819–21:

Androines ot armes moult acesmans
Qui erent verdes semees de besans,
Li besant erent d'or qui ert flamboians.

(3) *bordure bezanty.* See BESANZ EN L'ORLE.
(4) *a single bezant in each of the four quarters*
(Fig. 27). See CROIS PASSANT A BESANZ EN
LES QUATRE QUARTIERS EN CHASCUN BESANT
UNE CROISILLE. For other uses, see BANIERE
O BESANZ, EN CHASCUN BESANT UNE CROI-
SILLE and cf. MOLET[2], MOLETE[2]. *Syn.*:
BESANTEL, GASTEL, MEULE, MEULET, MEU-
LETE, MIREOR, PELOTE, RONDEL, RONDELET,
TOURTEL. *Note*: cf. BESANCIÉ, BESANTÉ, BE-
SANTER. The bezant is sometimes charged;
see BEZANZ EN LES QUATRE QUARTIERS, RON-
DEAUS EN LES QUATRE QUARTIERS. The
heraldic term bezant, its various synonyms
and uses, and their relative frequencies in
medieval rolls of arms, have been studied
by H. S. London in a masterly article entitled 'The Heraldic Roundel or Rotund',
Notes and Queries, cxcv (1950), 288–90,
310–11, 331–3, 354–6, 377–80. See also
the latter's 'The Roundel', *Coat of Arms,*
i (1951), 171–2, and the letters to the
editor in this regard, i. 205–6; ii (1952),
37–8. In the *Notes and Queries* article,
p. 310, London points out that Matthew
Paris's Latin blazon includes the terms
besantes (= OFr. *besanz* [in the arms of
Richard, Earl of Cornwall; see below]) and
turtelli (= OFr. *tourteaus*) as well as *gasteus*
and its cognate *vastelli* (= OFr. *gasteaus*).
See Pusikan, pp. 127, 128, 135, 145. London omits any mention of OFr. *grains*
which Prinet CP, p. 30 n. 2, considered to
be a synonym of *besanz.* In the illustration
for *WB* 441 (fig. 87), however, Adam-
Even shows that the *grains* were actually
tiny lozenges. See SEMÉ DE GRAINS. A long
tradition holds that bezants in a coat of
arms was an indication that the knight
had been to Palestine. See, for instance,
Littré, s.v. *besant,* Schirling, p. 21, and
Grandsaignes d'Hauterive, p. 62. As
pointed out by Bouly de Lesdain, however,
bezants appear on the shields of the
Bayeux Tapestry and would therefore
seem to be purely ornamental in origin.
See also the shield borne by Avarice in

TA and the explanation provided in the passage cited s.v. BANIERE O BESANZ. Bezants, during this period, are never numbered. Cf. *Navarre* 799 ('a trois besans d'or sur la bende'), 987 ('a .iii. besans d'or sur la bende'). The bezants in the bordure of the famous arms of Richard, Earl of Cornwall and Count of Poitou, were termed *pois* ('peas') by J. R. Planché, *The Pursuivant of Arms* (London, 1873), p. 171, the latter theorizing that the charge alluded to Poitou. See, however, Wagner's negative appraisal of this assertion in *Historic Heraldry*, p. 43. Adam-Even, 'Les armoiries des comtes de Poitiers — leur groupe héraldique', *Revue française d'héraldique et de sigillographie*, viii (1952), 3–11 (this, incidentally, is the article referred to in *Aspilogia II*, p. 20, note to item 38 [Cornwall], as 'privately printed, *c.* 1950'), has shown how the bordure in question, primitively a mode of differencing, was later assumed to be the distinctive element in the arms of Cornwall. See also Gayre, *Heraldic Cadency*, p. 94.

besanté, *bezanty, semy of bezants* (Fig. 29). (1) *a field semy of bezants. B* 85: besantee (*Bl* 85: besanté); 86: besanté (*Bl* 86: besanté); *C* 13 (*Cl* 13: besanté; *Cd* 13: besannté), 133 (*Cl* 133: bezantié; *Cd* 133: bessanté): besantee; *D* 90, 92: besanté; *H* 9: besanté (*Hg* 9 [8], see OD LES TOURTEAUS). (2) *bars bezanty. B* 53: besanté (*Ba/Bb/Bc* 53: besanté), see BASTON³. (3) *bend bezanty. TA*, vv. 775, 2368: besantee. *BA* 226: besandé, see BASTON EN BELIC. *Note*: the arms in *TA* are ascribed to Avarice and given as *or, a bend argent bezanty* (*or*), apparently a double case of metal upon metal. (4) *bordure bezanty.* A. *the term* BORDE *is used. B* 3: besanté (*Bl* 3, see below, item B.), see BORDE¹. B. *the term* BORDURE *is used. BA* 282: besandé; *Bl* 3: besanté (*B* 3, see above, item A.); *C* 99: besantee (*Cl* 99: besanté; *Cd* 99: bessannté); 167: besanté (*Cl* 167: besanté; *Cd* 167: bessannté); *D* 33: besanté; *CP* 44: besantee; *CPA* 15: besantee; *H/Hg* 59: besanté; *H* 90: besaunté (*Hg* 90 [89]: besanté). C. *the term* ORLE *is used. EO* 976: besentee. (5) *chevron bezanty. B* 52: besantee (*Ba/Bb/Bc* 52: besanté; *Bl* 52: besandé). (6) *label bezanty. BA* 90, (A: bezandé), 110, 125, 138,

146, 166, 184, 291: besandé; *TC*, v. 2198: besantéz; *CP* 34, 110: besanté; *CPA* 8: besanté; *M* 38: besanté, see EN LE LABEL. *Syn.*: BESANTÉ DE PETIZ BESANTEAUS, BESANZ EN L'ORLE, OD LES TOURTEAUS, SEMÉ DE BESANZ. *Note*: cf. BESANTER and see BESANT. For SEMÉ DE GRAINS, see below. The bezants are always gold except when a bordure (*CPA* 15) or a label (*BA* 90, 110, 166, 184; *CP* 110; *CPA* 8) are involved, when they may be silver. In *C* 13 ('Le roy de Cypre, vert besantee un crois passant d'or'), the bezants are presumably gold, but *Cl* ('besanté de goules') and *Cd* ('besannté de g.') give them as gules.

besanteaus, *bezants.* See BESANTEL.

besanté de petiz besanteaus, *bezanty* (Fig. 29). *Cleomadés*, vv. 8663–70:

> Quels armes ot rois Primonus
> Vous deviserai. Ses escus
> Ert d'or a .i. noir olifant
> A .i. ourle moult bien seant
> De gueules qui ert endentee ;
> Et li ourle estoit besentee
> De petis besentiaus d'argent
> Qui moult i erent bel et gent.

Syn.: see BESANTÉ. *Note*: see ORLE ENDENTÉ.

besantel, *bezant.* See BESANTÉ DE PETIZ BESANTEAUS. *Note*: besantel (plural: besanteaus) is the diminutive form of OFr. *besant*.

besanter, *to charge with bezants. Berte*, v. 3227: Le label au mainsné d'argent on besenta. *Note*: cf. BESANCIÉ, BESANTÉ, BESANT.

besanz en les quatre quartiers, see CROIS PASSANT A BESANZ EN LES QUATRE QUARTIERS EN CHASCUN BESANT UNE CROISILLE.

besanz en l'orle, *bordure bezanty. K*, v. 688: En le ourle noire li besant. *Syn.*: see BESANTÉ (4). *Note*: cf. SAUTOIRS EN L'ORLE. Refers to EN L'ORLE¹.

besengnis, see BELIC.

beslic, beslif, beslive, see DE BELIC, EN BELIC.

beuf, *ox* (Fig. 171). *C* 15: un beauff (*Cl* 15: a un beuf; *Cd* 15: a une beuff). *Note*: on the ox in heraldry, consult London, *Royal Beasts*, pp. 25–7.

beuf el chief, *on a chief an ox.* The complete blazon reads as follows: *CPA* 161: Ernou Berart, d'azur au chef d'or au lion d'argent et un boeuf de gueules et [*sic*, for el] chef.

bezanz, *bezants.* See BESANT.

biche, *hind, doe.* See BISSE.

billete, *billet (oblong figure set upright)* (Fig. 30). *K*, vv. 874–7:

> Cil ki porte dance e bilettes
> De or en asur, al assaut court,
> Johans avoit a non Daincourt,
> Ki mult bien i fist son devoir.

For other uses, see A BILLETES SEMÉ, SEMÉ DE BILLETES. *Note:* OFr. *billete* is a derivative of VL *bilia* 'tree trunk'. The term is probably architectural in origin as the device is by far the most common ornament of the Romanesque period. 'Sa vogue ne commence à baisser que dans le second quart du XIIe siècle, encore persiste-t-elle longtemps dans les provinces où l'architecture gothique fut lente à pénétrer', R. de Lasteyrie, *L'Architecture religieuse en France à l'époque romane* (Paris, 1929), p. 574.

billeté¹, *billety* (Fig. 30). *TA*, vv. 1703, 2072: billeté; *BA* 115: billeté; 145, 176, 179: billetté; *B* 106 (*Bl* 106 [107]: et billetés), 177 (*Bl* 177 [181]: billetés), 205: billety (*Bl* 205 [209]: billetté); 116: billeté (*Bl* 116 [120]: billetté); *C* 27 (*Cl* 27: billeté; *Cd* 27: belletté), 149 (*Cl* 149: byleté; *Cd* 149, see SEMÉ DE BILLETES): billeté; 53 (*Cl* 53: byleté; *Cd* 53: bileté): billetté; *D* 46, 47: bilettee; 70: bileté; *CP* 1, 23, 101, 119, 139: billeté; *CPA* 11: billeté; *H* 45: byletté (*Hg* 45 [46]: billetté); *M* 8: billetté (G: billettee); 18: byletté; *K*, v. 565: De inde coulour (W: colour) de or billetee. *Syn.:* A BILLETES SEMÉ, BILLETES POUDREES EN L'ESCU, SEMÉ DE BILLETES. *Note:* generally followed by *de*. In the blazon for Acre in *Cl*/*Cd*, and in *Cd* 27, however, the preposition is omitted.

billeté², *potent* (Fig. 103). See CROIS BILLETEE.

billetes poudrees en l'escu, *billety* (Fig. 30). *P* 91: ove billetz d'or poudrés en l'escu. *Syn.:* see BILLETÉ¹. *Note:* corresponds to *B* 106 (see BILLETÉ¹).

bis, *greyish brown. Troie,* vv. 8784, 20968, 23924: bis; *Charrete,* v. 5795: bis; *Gaidon,* v. 2129: bis; *Fouque de Candie,* vv. 1531, 3431: bis; *Saisnes,* v. 1228: bise; v. 2011: bis; *Raoul de Cambrai,* v. 2533: escu bis; *EO*, v. 3781: Qui estoit d'or a trois lionciaus bis; *SCT*, fol. 127 *a* / *SCV*, fol. 93 *b*: bis. For

another use, see AZUR BIS. *Note:* cf. GRIS. Ott, p. 40, derives the term from Lat. *byssus* 'cotton', the meaning having theoretically evolved from an adjective meaning 'colour of cotton'. This view has not generally been accepted and etymological dictionaries list its origin as obscure.

bisse, *hind, doe* (Fig. 159). *C* 65: un bysse (*Cl* 65: a un byse; *Cd* 65: a une byse). *Syn.:* OUISSE. *Note:* according to Prinet WR, p. 247, the hind should properly be statant on a three-peaked mountain; *Aspilogia II*, p. 192, note to item 120. OFr. *bisse* (the modern French pronunciation *biche* is attested as early as the twelfth century and is believed to result from Norman or Picard influence) is derived from VL *bistia* (CL *bestia*). For the male of the species, see CERF. On the hind in the crest of the arms of Sir Edward Bysshe, consult H. Gladstone, 'Heraldic Terms (Bysshe)', *Notes and Queries*, clxxxi (1941), 13; see also London, 'Notes and Reflections, II', 271 (*teste de bis* 'hind's head' in the Parliamentary Roll). The Latin etymon of OFr. *bisse* apparently also yielded a homograph with the meaning 'serpent-monster' 'facilement reconnaissable à ce qu'elle *engoule* un enfant *issuant* de sa gueule' (Veyrin-Forrer, p. 116). E. G. Lindfors-Nordin, '*Issant de Bisse*'. *Terme héraldique. Etude historique et étymologique* (Stockholm, 1952), has conjectured that the latter is derived from Gr. *ábyssos*, but this view has been opposed by Stephen Ullmann in his review of the monograph in question in *RPh.*, ix (1955–6), 399.

*blanc, *argent (white).* Very frequent in literary sources, e.g. *Thèbes*, v. 5513: blanc; *Cligés*, v. 4857: blanc; *Otinel*, v. 367: Blanc; *Didot Perceval*, pp. 231, 310: blanc; *Estoire*, p. 62: blanc; *Atre périlleux*, v. 5531: blances; *Hem*, v. 1124: Blances; *CC*, v. 1409: blance, but attested in only two thirteenth-century rolls of arms, viz. *BA* 3, 8, 16, 27 (A: blan), 34, 35, 50, 58, 65, 73, 85, 88, 99, 108, 111, 113, 117, 119, 120, 128, 134, 141, 146, 147, 162, 165, 167, 182, 187, 189, 197, 198, 205, 230, 234, 264, 265, 272, 274, 289, 294 (A: blan), 712, 836, 872: blanc; 9, 13, 14, 22: blan; 33: blans; 54, 177, 251: blanque; 68: blanques; 96: bl . . .; *B*/*Bl* 87: blank; *Bl* 4 (*B*/*Ba*/*Bb* 4, see ARGENT), 44: blank; *Bl* 10, 184 [188]: blanche (*B*/*Ba*/*Bb* 10 and *B* 184, see ARGENT). Cf. also *K*, vv. 109, 260, 270, 343, 350 (W: blance), 375, 419, 424, 581: blanche; vv. 162, 168, 487: de blanc; vv. 342, 419, 576: blanc; vv. 416, 572: blancs; v. 184: blonc. For other uses, see EN BLANC, SOR BLANC, SOR LE BLANC, TOUT BLANC. *Syn.*: see ARGENT. *Note*: cf. ERMINE BLANC. For *Lancelot propre*, v. 136 n. 2, see GOUTÉ[1], *Note*. Wagner, *CEMRA*, p. 4, mentions the five instances of *blank* for 'argent' in Cooke's version of Glover's Roll, a feature described as archaic and 'found in no other English roll of arms'. Wagner also mentions, p. 4, the Bigot Roll in this connection. It should be added, however, that Harvy's version of Glover's Roll contains a further example of *blank*; see above (*B* 87). Finally, Matthew Paris also makes use of *blanc* in his blazon of Roger de Huntingfield's arms (quoted in full above, s.v. BENDE[1], *Note*).

blanchet, *argent (white). Escanor,* v. 5220: blanchetes. Complete blazon provided above, s.v. ARMES DE PLAIN . . . FORS QU'EL QUARTIER AVOIT EGLETES PAR DESCONOIS-SANCE. *Syn.*: see ARGENT.

blason, *shield.* Numerous attestations from the earliest times in this sense. See Godefroy, i. 659; Tobler–Lommatzsch, i. 993. *Note*: in the thirteenth century, a *blasonier* is a shield maker, *blasonerie* is his trade (Godefroy, i. 659; Tobler–Lommatzsch, i. 995). By the fifteenth century, English *blasoun* had come to mean a coat of arms (*MED*, i. 996), *blasen*, a verb meaning to inscribe with armorial bearings, to identify armorial bearings, and to describe in heraldic terms (*MED*, i. 954). The transition from a word designating a shield (OFr. *blason*) to the term signifying a coat of arms (Modern French *blason*) seems apparent in a passage such as this in *Hugues Capet* (1359), vv. 3833–4:

Chil laisserent le prinche quant virent le blason
Dez fleur de lis de France qui furent roy Charlon.

See Schirling, pp. 9, 22.

bleu, *azure (blue). Fouque de Candie,* v. 10404: Cil a ces bloies armes; *Perlesvaus,* p. 208: li chevaliers as bleues armes; p. 292: .i.

bloues armes autresi comme d'azur; p. 293: celui as armes bloues; *Saisnes,* v. 5283 (var.): la targe bloie; *Blancandin,* vv. 1917, 2076: blaus; *EO,* v. 5070: Armes ot bleues, s'i ot d'or trois croissans; *Cleomadés,* v. 630: Mais que labiaus bleus i avoit; vv. 732–3: et bleues oreilles;/ Et ot aussi la teste bleue; v. 9881: bleu; *K,* vv. 158, 163, 408, 467, 491, 832: bleu; v. 363: bleus. *Syn.*: see AZUR. *Note*: cf. *Erec,* v. 2130 (Randuraz): Et fu coverz d'un cendal blo. *Note*: on this term, consult Emmanuel Walberg, 'Sur *blou, bloi* en ancien français', *Uppsatser i romansk Filologi tillägnade Professor P.A. Geijer på hans Sextioårsdag den 9. April 1901* (Uppsala, 1901), pp. 83–98.

Blois, see ARMES DE BLOIS A.

bod, see BORDURE ENDENTEE.

bordant, *in orle* (Fig. 125). See ESCHALOPES BORDANZ, MERLOZ BORDANZ. *Syn.*: see BORDURE[2].

borde[1], *bordure* (Fig. 114). The complete blazon reads as follows: *B* 3: Le conte de Cornewaile, argent ung lion de goulz coronné or ung borde de sable besanté d'or (*Bl* 3, see BORDURE[1] [2]). *Syn.*: see BORDURE[1]. *Note*: OFr. *borde* is a feminine substantive.

borde[2], *double tressure.* See BORDE FLEURETEE. *Syn.*: BORDURE[3].

bordé[1], *with a bordure. FCT,* v. 4877: Cil a cel escu broudé d'or; *TA,* v. 1049: Bordez d'abominaciön. *Syn.*: LISTÉ, ORLÉ, ORLÉ ENVIRON, ORLÉ PAR CONOISSANCE D'UNE ENBORDURE. *Note*: cf. BORDURE[1]. The arms in *TA* are ascribed to Avoltire (Adultery). This is probably a pun relating to the fact that the shield is made from a brothel door (v. 1040: 'Une targe d'uis de bordel'; see also v. 2522: 'la targe d'uis de bordel'). The meaning 'brothel' for this word, rare in Old French, is, nevertheless, attested at the end of the twelfth century (see Dauzat, pp. 97–8, s.v. *bordel*). For a sixteenth-century French derivative, see R. Marichal, 'Border, broder, bourder, et "Autant pour le brodeur"', *Etudes rabelaisiennes,* vi (1965), 89–112.

bordé[2], *in orle.* See BORDÉ DE DIABLEAUS. *Syn.*: see BORDURE[2].

bordeaud, see MERLOZ BORDANZ.

bordé de diableaus, *orle of small devils* (Fig. 130). *TA,* v. 540: Car bordez ert de dëableaus.

bordé environ, *with a bordure. Escanor,* vv. 3594-7:

> Li fix le roy l'escu d'argent
> Portoit a .i. demi lyon
> Vermeil bordé d'or environ
> A .ii. bendes vers toutes seules.

Syn.: see BORDÉ[1]. *Note*: cf. BORDURE[1]. Not to be confused with the modern French heraldic term *bordé* used to designate a charge, such as a bend or a pale, ornamented with a narrow border of a different tincture. The corresponding English term is *fimbriated.* See ENLISTÉ.

borde fleuretee, *double tressure flory counterflory* (Fig. 127). The complete blazon reads as follows: *C* 11: Le roy d'Escoce, d'or un lion rampant et un borde floretté de gulez (*Cl/Cd* 11, see BORDURE FLEURETEE). *Syn.*: see BORDURE FLEURETEE.

border, *bordure.* See BORDURE.

bordeur, *bordure.* See BORDURE.

bordon, see CANTON.

bordure[1], *bordure (border outlining the edge of the shield)* (Fig. 114). (1) *the bordure bears no charge. FCT,* v. 4347: A une bordeüre (= *FCE,* v. 8113, see ORLURE); *BA* 77, 210 (A: bordure): a la bordeure; 86, 282 (A: a bordeure): a le bordeure; 174 (A: a la bordeure), 294 (A: a la): a le bordeure; 228: a la bordeure; *B* 28 (*Ba* 28: od la bordur; *Bb* 28: un bordur; *Bc* 28: od la bordeure; *Bl* 28: ove la bordure): a la bordur; 68 (*Ba/Bc* 68: a la bordur; *Bb* 68: a border; *Bl* 68: et la bordure), 123, 189 (*Bl* 123 [127], 189 [193]: od la bordure): a la bordure; *C* 23 (*Cl* 23: a un bordure; *Cd* 23: a une bourdour), 25 (*Cl* 25: a une bordeur; *Cd* 25: a bourdure), 39 (*Cl* 39: a une bordure; *Cd* 39: une bourdure), 63 (*Cl* 63: a un bordure; *Cd* 63: a une bourdure), 71 (*Cl* 71: a une bordre; *Cd* 71: a bourdour); 72 (*Cl* 72: a une bordure; *Cd* 72: a bourdour): un border; *Cd* 125: a bordor ... (*C/Cl* 125, see BENDE[1]); *D* 31, 35, 45, 72, 75, 136: od la bordure; *CP* 4: et a (P: et) une bordure; 31, 33, 39, 43, 95: a une bordure; *CPA* 2: a bordure; 12, 13, 18: a une bordure; *M* 1: ou la bordure. (2) *the bordure is charged and two separate tinctures are specified for the ordinary and its charge. BA* 282: a le bordeure (A: a bordeure); *B* 29: le bordure (*Bl* 29:

le bordure); 118: ung bordure (*Bl* 118 [122]: od un bordure); 135: a la bordur (*Bl* 135 [139]: od la bordure), see MERLOZ EN LA BORDURE; *Bl* 3: ove le bordure (*B* 3, see BORDE[1]); *C* 99: border (*Cl* 99: a une bordure; *Cd* 99: a une bourdure); 167 (*Cl* 167: a une bordure; *Cd* 167: a un bourdour): un border; *Cd* 51: a bourdur; *D* 33: od la bordure; *CP* 44: a la bordure; *CPA* 6: a la bordure; 15: la bordure; *H* 51: ou la bordure (*Hg* 51 [53]: et la bordure); 59: ou le bordoure (*Hg* 59: od la bordure); 90: ou le bordour (*Hg* 90 [89]: od la bordure). For other uses, see BORDURE OD LES FERS, LIONCEAUS EN LA BORDURE, MERLOZ EN LA BORDURE. (3) *the bordure is charged, but only one tincture is provided, that of the bordure. B* 208: a la bordure (*Bl* 208 [212]: od la bordure), see FERS EN LA BORDURE; *Hg* 23: od la bordure, see POUDRÉ DE ROSES (*H* 23, see BORDURE DE ROSES). For another use, see BORDURE DE ROSES and cf. BESANZ EN L'ORLE. *Syn.*: BORDE[1], BORDURE ENTIERE, ENBORDURE, LISTE[4], ORLE[1], ORLE ENTIER, ORLURE, ORLURE DE L'ENCHAMPURE. See also BORDÉ[1], BORDÉ ENVIRON, EN LA BORDURE[1], ESCUÇON[1], ORLÉ D'UNE ENBORDURE ENVIRON, and cf. BORDURE DENTEE, BORDURE ENDENTEE, BORDURE ENGRESLEE. *Note*: once again, Matthew Paris uses a heraldic term in two different meanings. In the following blazon of the Daubeny arms (Pusikan, p. 145), *bordura* corresponds to BORDURE[1] (1): 'Scutum de dor [*sic*], cheveruns (P: chevers) cum bordura [MS.: b'd'a] de gules'. In his description (Pusikan, p. 150) of the armorial bearings of Ralph FitzNichol, however, the same word, or its Old French equivalent (the term is abbreviated *bord*', making it impossible to determine which form was intended; cf., however, preceding item), refers to the remaining area of the field around the principal charge which is semy of escallops: 'Scutum de gules, pentafolium d'or, bord' escal' d'argent'. The two reproductions which I have examined of the arms in question (plates in Pusikan and *CEMRA*) do not show the escallops very clearly and it may be that their disposition is actually that described below, s.v. BORDURE[2]. Cf. EN L'ESCU and, especially, ESCHALOPES BORDANZ.

bordure², *in orle* (Fig. 125). See BORDÉ², BORDURE D'EGLES, BORDURE D'EGLETES, BORDURE DE FERS A CHEVAL, BORDURE DE MERLES, BORDURE DE MERLETES, BORDURE DE MERLOZ, BORDURE DE MERLOZ PORALEE TOUT ENTOUR, BORDURE D'OISELEZ. See also BORDURE DANTELEE. *Syn.*: BORDANT, EN L'ORLE², ENTOUR, ORLE², TOUT ENTOUR; see also ENVIRON¹, MERLETE¹, *Note*, and MERLOT (5). *Note*: position only is indicated, the charges being placed parallel to but not touching the edge of the shield. Powdering, i.e. scattering charges over a field, often had the same effect as placing them in orle; see ANGEGNIES EN L'ESCU, *Note*; MERLETE¹, *Note*, and cf. POUDRÉ.

bordure³, *double tressure*. See BORDURE FLEURETEE. *Syn.*: BORDE². *Note*: cf. TREÇOIR, TREÇOIR ENVIRON, TREÇON.

bordure⁴, *error for* BENDE. See ESCUÇON DES ARMES DU DUC DE BOURGOGNE EN LA BORDURE.

bordure dantelee, *error for* BORDURE D'EGLETES. *CP* 62: a une bordure dantelee. *Note*: ostensibly a variant of BORDURE ENDENTEE and interpreted in that way by Prinet CP, p. 22 n. 2, the locution is now known to contain the ghost word *dantelee* representing *d'egletes*. See BORDURE D'EGLETES and consult Adam-Even CPA, p. 5, item 62 *bis* and note.

bordure de fers a cheval, *orle of horseshoes* (Fig. 265). *CP* 75: a une bordure de fers a ceval. *Syn.*: cf. FERRETÉ. *Note*: refers to BORDURE². Not to be confused with BORDURE OD LES FERS, FER¹, FERS EN LA BORDURE.

bordure d'egles, *orle of eaglets* (Fig. 189). *BA* 255: a le bordure (A: la bordeure) d'aigles. *Syn.*: BORDURE D'EGLETES. See also BORDURE DANTELEE. *Note*: refers to BORDURE².

bordure d'egletes, *orle of eaglets* (Fig. 189). *CPA* 62 *bis*: a une bordure d'aiglettes. *Syn.*: BORDURE D'EGLES. *Note*: refers to BORDURE². See also BORDURE DANTELEE which is a scribal error in *CP* 62 for BORDURE D'EGLETES.

bordure de merles, *orle of martlets* (Fig. 125). *CP* 108: a une bordure de merles. *Syn.*: see BORDURE DE MERLETES. *Note*: refers to BORDURE².

bordure de merletes, *orle of martlets* (Fig. 125). *BA* 267: a le bordeure de mellets (A: mellettes); 270: a le bordure de mellettes (A: a la bordure de mellettes). *Syn.*: BORDURE DE MERLES, BORDURE DE MERLOZ, BORDURE DE MERLOZ PORALEE TOUT ENTOUR, BORDURE D'OISELEZ, LES MERLOZ, MERLOZ BORDANZ, MERLOZ EN L'ORLE, MERLOZ ENTOUR, OD MERLOZ, OD LES MERLOZ, ODVE LES MERLETES, OISELEZ ENTOUR, ORLE DE MERLOZ, ORLE OF MERLOZ. *Note*: refers to BORDURE²; cf. MERLOZ EN LA BORDURE (refers to BORDURE¹).

bordure de merloz, *orle of martlets* (Fig. 125). *Bl* 23: ove la bordure des merloz (*B/Bb* 23, see ORLE DE MERLOZ; *Ba* 23, see LES MERLOZ; *Bc* 23: a la bordure de merloz). *Syn.*: see BORDURE DE MERLETES. *Note*: refers to BORDURE².

bordure de merloz poralee tout entour, *orle of martlets* (Fig. 125). *K*, vv. 169–73:

> De Walence Aymars li vaillans
> Bele baniere i fu baillans,
> De argent e de asur burelee,
> O la bordure poralee
> Tout entour de rouges merlos.

Syn.: see BORDURE DE MERLETES. *Note*: refers to BORDURE².

bordure dentee, *bordure indented* (Fig. 115). *Mouskés*, v. 7857: la bordure est dentee; *Hg* 52 [54]: od la bordure denté (*H* 52, see BORDURE ENDENTEE). *Syn.*: see BORDURE ENDENTEE. *Note*: for complete blazon in *Mouskés*, see ARMES TELS COM . . . MES QUE.

bordure de roses, *bordure semy of heraldic roses*. The complete blazon reads as follows: *H* 23: Le counte Patrik porte de gulez ou ung leon d'argent ou le bordure d'argent de roses (*Hg* 23, see BORDURE¹ [3], POUDRÉ DE ROSES). *Syn.*: ORLURE DE L'ENCHAMPURE A ROSES. *Note*: refers to BORDURE¹ (3).

bordure d'oiselez, *orle of martlets* (Fig. 125). *BA* 230: a le bordures d'oiselés (A: a la bordure d'oiselers); *CP* 18, 67: a une bordure d'oiselés; 122, 123: a une bordure d'oiselets; *CPA* 152: a la bordure d'oiselets; 155: a la bordure d'oisets [*sic*, for oiselets?]. *Syn.*: see BORDURE DE MERLETES. *Note*: refers to BORDURE².

bordure endentee, *bordure indented* (Fig. 115). *BA* 53: a la bordeure . . . endentee; 141: a le (A: la) bordeure . . . endentee; *C* 14: un border . . . indentee (*Cl* 14: a un bordure . . . endenté; *Cd* 14: a une bourdoure . . . endentit); 80: un border indenté de . . . et de . . . (*Cl* 80: a un bordure endenté de . . . e de . . .; *Cd* 80: a une bordoure endentit . . . et . . .); 141: un border . . . indentez (*Cl* 141: a une bod [*sic*] . . . endenté; *Cd* 141: a bourdous . . . indentit); *D* 77: od la bordure . . . endentee; *CPA* 149: a une bordure . . . endentee; *H* 52: ou la bordure endenté; *M* 2: ou le bordour endenté; 27: ou le bordure . . . endenté; *K*, v. 798: Cil portoit bordure endentee. *Syn.*: BORDURE DENTEE, BORDURE ENGRESLEE, ORLE ENDENTÉ, ORLE ENDENTÉ ENVIRON, ORLE ENGRESLÉ. *Note*: refers to ENDENTÉ[1]. For *C*/*Cl*/*Cd* 80, however, see ENDENTÉ DE . . . ET DE . . .

bordure engreslee, *bordure indented* (Fig. 115). *CPA* 14, 20: la bordure engreslee. *Syn.*: see BORDURE ENDENTEE. *Note*: refers to ENGRESLÉ[1].

bordure entiere, *bordure* (Fig. 114). *C* 36: un border entere (*Cl* 36: a une bordure entere; *Cd* 36: a bourdoure entere). *Syn.*: see BORDURE[1]. *Note*: on these arms, consult Prinet WR, pp. 232–3, and Prinet CC, p. 176.

bordure fleuretee, *double tressure flory counterflory* (Fig. 127). The complete blazon reads as follows: *Cl* 11: Le roy d'Eschosce, d'or a un lion de goules a un bordure d'or fluretté de goules (*Cd* 11: Le roy d'Eschosce, d'or a .i. lion de g. a .i. bordur d'or floretté g.; *C* 11, see BORDE FLEURETEE). *Syn.*: BORDE FLEURETEE, DOUBLE TREÇON. *Note*: cf. TREÇOIR, TREÇOIR ENVIRON. The Royal Arms of Scotland appear first on the Great Seal of Alexander II (1214–49). Consult Wagner, *Historic Heraldry*, p. 48, item 48, and see also *WB* 777, 1272. The Scottish tressure first appears, however, in Matthew Paris; see *Aspilogia II*, p. 32, note to item 32 (cf. the single tressure in another copy of the Matthew Paris Shields, p. 45, note to item 48). The same arms are also painted in the earliest version (*c.* 1285) of St. George's Roll, item 3 (ed. Armytage) which a fifteenth-century version blazons as follows: 'Le roy d'Escosse porte d'or a ung lyon rampant et un double trace fleureté de gueules' (Wagner, *CEMRA*, pp. 20–1; *Historic Heraldry*, p. 48). Cf. also Girart d'Amiens's blazon of these arms s.v. DOUBLE TREÇON; *Tournoi de Compiègne*, p. 75, item 7;

and consult John A. Stewart, 'The Royal Banner of Scotland', *Coat of Arms*, ii (1953), no. 14, 228–9, the letters to the editor of this journal by C. Campbell, iii (1955), 278, 323, and the latter's article entitled 'The Royal Arms in the Grünenberg Roll', *The Scottish Genealogist*, xiii (1966), 39–46. In each case, the double tressure is *gules* (as it is, as a matter of fact, in *C* 11; see BORDE FLEURETEE), not *or*. According to Veyrin-Forrer, p. 39: 'Le trescheur est théoriquement un orle réduit des deux tiers; en fait, on ne rencontre jamais que le *double-trescheur*'; see, however, TREÇOIR and TREÇOIR ENVIRON. The double tressure in the Royal Arms of Scotland is customarily ornamented with fleurs-de-lis in a design described as flory counterflory, 'i.e. the heads of the fleurs-de-lis point alternately outwards and inwards, but the fleurs-de-lis are broken at the centre, the space between the two concentric parts of the double-tressure being voided throughout' (Boutell, p. 55). Variant patterns appear, however, in the Matthew Paris shields, where demi-fleurs-de-lis, heads pointing outwards, charge a bordure or on one shield (Hauptmann, p. 31, item 83; Table 4, fig. 56), and where demi-fleurs-de-lis, heads pointing inwards, overlap a bordure gules on another (Pusikan, p. 121).

bordure od les fers, *bordure semy of horseshoes* (Fig. 264). The complete blazon reads as follows: *D* 147: Munsire William de Ferers, l'escu verré d'or et de gules, od la bordure de sable, od les fers d'argent. *Syn.*: FERS EN LA BORDURE (1). See also FER[1]. *Note*: refers to BORDURE[1] (2). Not to be confused with BORDURE DE FERS A CHEVAL.

borel, see BURELÉ DE . . . ET DE . . .

bot, see BOUT.

bouceaus, see BOUCEL PAR DESUS LE . . .

boucel par desus le . . . , *butt, vessel made of wood or hide, used as a container for liquids* (Fig. 247). *Escanor*, vv. 3484–5:

Lucanz les ot a .v. bouchiauz
D'argent par desuz le vermeil.

Note: on these canting arms, see Introduction, p. 52. For the confusion of OFr. *boucel* (< Lat. *butticellum*) 'keg' and OFr. *bouchel* (< Lat. *buccalem*) 'vessel made of hide', consult Paul Barbier, 'Miscellanea Lexicographica, VIII', *Proc. Leeds Phil.*

and Lit. Soc., Lit. and Hist. Sec., ii (1928), 383–7. Cf. BOUGE and, especially, BUSSEL, *Note.*

bouge, *water-bouget* (Fig. 276). *B* 66: a trois bouges (*Ba* 66: treis boous; *Bb* 66, see BOUGES DEUS ET UNE; *Bc* 66: a treis boous; *Bl* 66: a trois bouz); 169: trois bouges (*Bl* 169 [173]: od trois bouz); *C* 83: trois bousses (*Cl* 83: a treys buz; *Cd* 83: a 3 buz); 105: a troiz buzes (*Cl* 105: a treis buz; *Cd* 105: a 3 buges); *H* 31: a .iiii. bousses (*Hg* 31, see BUSSEL); *K*, v. 202: o trois bouz. For other uses, see BOUGES DEUS ET UNE, FESSE ET BOUGES. Cf. also BOUCEL PAR DESUS LE . . ., BUSSEL. *Syn.*: BOUGES DEUS ET UNE, BUSSEL. *Note*: Gough H, p. 136, note to item 32: '[*H* 31] erroneously reads "iiii" [for "iii"].' OFr. *bouge,* a derivative of Lat. *bulga* 'bag, pouch' (and in no way related to Fr. *bout,* as suggested in *Aspilogia II,* glossary, p. 228), is feminine and is stylized in heraldry as a pair of large skins or bags joined together with a wooden cross-piece by which they were carried over the shoulder. See D'Haucourt–Durivault, p. 108, fig. 467. Matthew Paris uses the Latin equivalent *utres* (plural of Lat. *uter*) in his blazon of the arms of Robert de Ros (Pusikan, p. 123): 'Scutum de gules, tres utres d'argent'. On this charge, consult George H. Viner, 'Water-bougets and the Garde Bras', *Coat of Arms,* i (1950), no. 2, 63–4; *Aspilogia II,* p. 47, note to item 55.

bouges deus et une, *water-bougets, 2 and 1. Bb* 66: 3 (a water-bouget tricked) 2 et 1 (*B/Ba* 66, see BOUGE). *Syn.*: see BOUGE. *Note*: the phrase *deus et une* refers to the relative position of the charges in question, two of which are placed above the third. Such notation has always been considered superfluous in the case of three objects charging a field, as this is their normal position.

bourdous, see BORDURE ENDENTEE.

Bourgogne, see ARMES DU DUC DE BOURGOGNE.

bousse, see BOUGE.

bout, *end (referring to the tips of a cross).* See CROIS ESLAISIEE AUS BOUZ, CROIS ESLARGIE PAR LES BOUZ, CROIS O BOUZ FLEURETÉS. *Note*: *bouz* is the plural of OFr. *bout.* Modern French prefers *les extrémités* when referring

to the ends of a cross. For a fourteenth-century synonym, see CHIEF[5] and CROIS FOURCHIEE AU KANEE, *Note.* Cf. SOM[1].

boutoné, *botonny (referring to the Toulouse cross whose splayed limbs are adorned with three isolated knobs, actually stylized buds)* (Fig. 109). See CROIS PERCIEE ET PATEE ET BOUTONEE. *Syn.*: POMELÉ. *Note*: not to be confused with the modern *cross botony* whose limbs end in trefoils. OFr. *boutoné* is derived from OFr. *bouton* 'bud, burgeon'. In medieval iconography, St. Joseph, for example, is frequently depicted holding a flowering staff in his hand, alluding to a legend concerning the selection of a spouse for Mary. Compare the heraldic term *boutoné* with the following passage from the *Chevalier au Cygne,* vv. 3537–8:

De celui vint Joseph qui fu a l'asamblee,
En qui main fu la verge florie et botonee.

bouz[1], *water-bougets.* See BOUGE.

bouz[2], *ends (referring to the tips of a cross).* See BOUT.

bowe, see LION RAMPANT A LA COUE CROISIEE ET COURONÉ.

bresses, see EN LE . . . UNE BROIE.

breteles, see ESCU A BRETELES.

brey, see BROIE.

Brienne, see ARMES DE BRIENNE.

broie, *barnacle, horse-bray* (Fig. 144). *B* 102, 103: a trois breys (*Bl* 102, 103: od treis breys); *D* 156: od treis bayes. For other uses, see BROIE SOR LE . . .; EN LE . . . UNE BROIE. *Note*: for an illustration of this charge, see Adam-Even WB, p. 67, fig. 100. OFr. *broie* is feminine and its modern French heraldic equivalent is sometimes spelled *broye* (D'Haucourt–Durivault, p. 106; Veyrin-Forrer, p. 95). Long confused with the *hempbray* (illustrated in Boutell, p. 289, fig. 437), the charge in question has been shown to be a stylized *horse-bray* or *barnacle,* 'an instrument consisting of two pieces of notched wood hinged together at one end', used for curbing horses. See London, 'Notes and Reflections, II', p. 271, and, especially, the latter's definitive study entitled 'The Geneville Brays', *Coat of Arms,* iii (1954), no. 19, 84–7. See also *Aspilogia II,* p. 135, note to item 103: 'The brays of Geneville were taken from the canting arms of Simon de Broye, first husband of Felicity de Brienne (fl. *c.* 1140), though the Genevilles were descended from Felicity's second husband and had no connexion with Broyes.'

broie sor le . . ., *horse-bray charging the . . .* The complete blazon reads as follows: *CP* 40: Mesire Jehan de Genville porte les armes d'asur au chief d'ermine a un demi lion de gheules et couronne d'or au chief et a trois broies d'or sor l'asur. For other uses, see BROIE. *Syn.:* EN LE . . . UNE BROIE. *Note*: see CHIEF[1] (2) B. These arms, like those of the Mortimer and Pressigny families (see FESSIÉ DE . . . ET DE . . . ET CONTREFESSIÉ) were considered difficult to blazon. They are the first to be blazoned in the *Dean Tract* (vv. 13–18):

> Ore vuille comencer, par seint Gyle,
> As armes my sire de Geneville:
> A un leon recoupee de gules;
> Ces .iii. choses ne sount pas souls,
> Unquore y ad, je me recorde,
> Al chief desuz .iii. braz d'or.

On the latter, see CEZ CHOSES, *Note.*
broudé, see BORDÉ[1].
brulé, see BURELÉ DE . . . ET DE . . .
Brun, *Bruin* (*animal character* [*a bear*] *in the* '*Roman de Renart*') (Fig. 152). The complete blazon reads as follows: *TA*, vv. 700–5:

> Felonie, qui het Pitié,
> Avoit Bourgaignons a plenté
> Et portoit l'escu endenté
> A .i. rous mastin rechignié;
> Par mi rampoit Bruns sans pitié
> Pour bien demostrer felonie.

Note: on this allusion, see Prinet TA, p. 49: 'Félonie, la cruauté, était désignée par les images du chien et de l'ours du *Roman de Renart*'; see also Flinn, pp. 124–5. Cf. NOBLE. A recurring character in the Old French Arthurian romances is also called Brun Sans Pitié; see Flutre, p. 37; West, p. 28.

buef, *ox.* See BEUF.
buelé, see BURELÉ DE . . . ET DE . . .
buge, see BOUGE.
bullé, see BURELÉ DE . . . ET DE . . .
burelé de . . . et de . . ., *barruly* (Fig. 5). *TA*, v. 986: De . . . et de . . . burelees; *BA* 17, 38, 56, 64, 87, 164, 207, 212, 231, 239, 269, 270: burelé de . . . et de . . .; 31:

burelé de . . . et . . .; 214: buelé de . . . et de . . .; *B* 23: burelee de . . . et de . . . (*Ba/Bc* 23: burlé de . . . e de . . .; *Bb* 23, see BARRÉ DE . . . ET DE . . .[1]; *Bl* 23: burlé de . . . et de . . .); 56 (*Ba/Bc* 56: burlé de . . . e de . . .; *Bb* 56, see BARRÉ DE . . . ET DE . . .[1]; *Bl* 56: burlé de . . . et de . . .), 167: burelé de . . . et de . . . (*Bl* 167: burlé de . . . et de . . .); *Bl* 196 [200]: burlé de . . . et de . . . (*B* 196, see BARRÉ DE . . . ET DE . . .[1]); *C* 30: burulé de . . . et de . . . (*Cl/Cd* 30, see BURELÉ D'UNE GROSSE BURELURE DE . . . ET DE . . .); 33: burulee de . . . et . . . (*Cl/Cd* 33, see BURELÉ D'UNE MENUE BURELURE DE . . . ET DE . . .); 57: burullé de . . . et de . . . (*Cl* 57: burlé de . . . et de . . .; *Cd* 57: burlé de . . . e de . . .); 59: burulee de . . . et de . . . (*Cl* 59: burlé de . . . e de . . .; *Cd* 59: burlé de . . . e . . .); 97: burellé de . . . et de . . . (*Cl* 97: burlé de . . . e de . . .; *Cd* 97: burlé . . . e . . .); *Hem*, vv. 3090–1: bullé / De . . . et de . . .; *D* 23: burelee de . . . et de . . .; 58, 132: burelé de . . . et de . . .; *Escanor*, v. 3598: Burelé de . . . et de . . .; *TC*, v. 1873: De . . . et de . . . burelé; v. 3216: de . . . bureleies (complete blazon provided s.v. DETRENCHIÉ); *CP* 5: burelé de . . . et de . . .; 114: burelé de . . .; *CPA* 153, 166: burelé de . . . et de . . .; *CC*, vv. 1165, 1519: brullé; vv. 1402–3: brullet / De . . . et de . . .; *H* 39: borel de . . . et de . . . (*Hg* 39 [40]: burlee de . . . et de . . .); *Hg*, Valence [98]: burel de . . . et de . . .; *M* 21: burellé de . . . et de . . .; *K*, v. 171: De . . . e de . . . burelee. For other uses, see BURELÉ D'UNE GROSSE BURELURE DE . . . ET DE . . ., BURELÉ D'UNE MENUE BURELURE DE . . . ET DE . . . *Syn.:* see BARRÉ DE . . . ET DE . . .[1]. *Note*: Matthew Paris provides the following example of OFr. *burelé de . . . et de . . .*: 'Comitis de Marchia. Scutum burelé de azuro e argento, quot lineas vis, primam tamen de argento' (Pusikan, p. 126). English heraldry today restricts this term to a field consisting of numerous (say, ten) bars, a lesser number of horizontal stripes producing the varied field called barry. In early blazon, the terms were interchangeable, though a distinction is established in Walford's Roll (see below) between a *grosse burelure* and a *menue burelure*. The etymology of OFr. *burelé* is a matter of conjecture, though the term is seemingly related to OFr. *burel* 'kind of rough woollen cloth, brownish in colour'. On the latter, consult W. Rothwell, 'Bureau', *Medium Ævum*, xxix (1960), 102–14. The English form *barruly*, doubtless influenced by BARRÉ DE . . . ET DE . . .[1], is late (*OED*: 1562).

burelé d'une grosse burelure de . . . et de . . ., *barry* (Fig. 5). *Cl* 30: burlé de une grosse burlure de . . . et de . . . (*Cd* 30: burlé de un grosse burlure . . . e . . .; *C* 30, see BURELÉ DE . . . ET DE . . .). *Note*: Prinet WR, p. 231 n. 1: 'Par "grosse burlure", il faut entendre un burelé de peu de pièces; un burelé de pièces plus nombreuses formant la "menue burlure" que notre héraut attribue au comte de Grandpré et à d'autres. Sur les sceaux et les monnaies, le nombre des burelles varie, dans les armes de Vaudémont: 8, 10 ou 12.' For these arms, see also *WB* 530. Though the author of Walford's Roll specifies that the field here is made up of 'wide' stripes (*grosse burelure*), modern English as well as French heraldry would blazon a field of ten or twelve stripes *barruly*, of eight or less, *barry*. Here once again, early blazon is less rigorous, as *burelé* is used indiscriminately in conjunction with the smaller as well as with the greater number of bars.

burelé d'une menue burelure de . . . et de . . ., *barruly* (Fig.5). *C* 56: burulee de . . . et de . . . de un menue burules (*Cl/Cd* 56: burlé de une menue burlure de . . . e de . . .); 169: burelé de un menue burlure de . . . et de . . . (*Cl* 169: burlé de une menue burlure de . . . et de . . .; *Cd* 169: burlé de une menue burlure de . . . e de . . .). *Syn.*: MENUE BURELURE DE . . . ET DE . . . *Note*: see preceding item.

burelure, see BURELÉ D'UNE GROSSE BURELURE DE . . . ET DE . . ., BURELÉ D'UNE MENUE BURELURE DE . . . ET DE . . ., MENUE BURELURE DE . . . ET DE . . .

burlé, see BURELÉ DE . . . ET DE . . .

burlure, see BURELURE.

burule, see BURELURE.

busseaus, see BUSSEL.

bussel, *water-bouget* (*but see Note*) (Fig. 276). The complete blazons read as follows: *D* 180: Munsire Robert de Ros, l'escu de gules a treis bussels d'argent; *Hg* 31 [32]:

Willam de Ros porte de goules a troys busseaux d'argent (*H* 31, see BOUGE). *Syn.*: see BOUGE. *Note*: though there can be no doubt that water-bougets were intended here (see *Aspilogia II*, p. 47, note to item 55), the form *bussel* (plural *busseaus*) suggests a confusion with OFr. *boucel* 'butt, vessel made of wood or hide'; see BOUCEL PAR DESUS LE . . ., *Note*.

butor, *bittern* (*a kind of heron*) (Fig. 177). See EN MILIEU UN BUTOR. *Note*: cf. HERON.

çaintour, *saltire*. See SAUTOIR.

campaigne, see CHAMPAIGNE.

cantel, see CHANTEL.

canton, *canton, quarter* (Fig. 117). (1) *the canton bears no charge*. B 105: ung canton (*Bl* 105, see QUARTIER[1]); *C* 23 (*Cd* 23: a une canton; *Cl* 23, see CHANTEL[1]), 122 (*Cl* 122, see CHANTEL[1]): un canton; *Cd* 88: a canton (*C/Cl* 88, see CHANTEL[1]); *CP* 122: a un bordon [*sic*, for canton]. (2) *the canton bears a charge*. *Cd* 131: a canton, see EN LE CANTON UNE CROIS PATEE (*C* 131, see EN UN CHANTEL UNE CROIS PATEE; *Cl* 131, see CHANTEL[1]). *Syn.*: see CHANTEL[1] (but see *Note*). *Note*: for the reading in *CP*, consult Prinet CP, p. 40 n. 2. *Canton* is used interchangeably with CHANTEL[1] and QUARTIER[1] during this period. Unlike these two terms, however, it is never used to designate the first quarter of a quarterly partition (see also QUART PART). In modern French and English heraldry, *canton* designates a subordinary occupying less than a quarter of the shield.

canz, see GANT.

carboncle, *carbuncle*. See CHARBOUCLE.

cartier, see QUARTIER.

castel, *castle*. See CHASTEL.

castelé, see CHASTELÉ[2].

catele, see CHASTELÉ[2].

cele, celes, see ARMES CELES MESMES A, BENDE ENLISTEE A DEUS BASTONS ENCOSTE, CELES ARMES A, CELES MESMES A. *Note*: *cele* and *celes* are the feminine accusative singular and plural of the Old French demonstrative adjective. For paradigms in the twelfth century and later periods, consult Pope, pp. 325–6, paragraphs 845–6. For the alternate form, see CEZ CHOSES, *Note*. On these two demonstratives, consult Foulet, *Petite Syntaxe*, paragraphs 236–46.

celes armes a, *the same arms, differenced by.* *CP* 16, 135: celles armes a. *Syn.*: see AUTEL².

celes mesmes a, *the same arms, differenced by.* *CP* 3, 19, 22, 44, 66, 73, 98, 99: celles mesmes a; 28, 89: celes mesmes a. *Syn.*: see AUTEL².

cendal, *red cloth.* *Queste,* p. 32: un escu ou il fist une croiz de cendal. *Note:* cf. GEULES.

cercle, see POUDRÉ A CERCLES.

cerf, *stag* (Figs. 172, 256). *Charrete,* vv. 5799–5802:

> Et veez vos celui qui porte
> An son escu pointe une porte?
> Si sanble qu'il s'an isse uns cers.
> Par foi, ce est li rois Yders;

Perlesvaus, pp. 44, 49, 142: a .i. cerf; pp. 179, 185: au cerf; *C* 67: un cheif (*Cl/Cd* 67: a un cherf). *Syn.*: DAIM. *Note:* for the female deer, see BISSE. On the stag symbolism in *Perlesvaus,* reminiscent of the White Stag and Hound episode in the *First Continuation* of Chrétien de Troyes's *Perceval,* consult Nitze's note to l. 510 in ii. 224. The stag on King Yder's shield in *Charrete,* on the other hand, probably alludes to the Stag episode in Chrétien's earlier romance *Erec*; see Introduction. The stag as a symbol in medieval art and Old French literature has intrigued scholars. Among the recent publications in this connection, the following are worthy of mention: R. Harris, 'The White Stag in Chrétien's "Erec and Enide"', *FS,* x (1956), 55–61; J. Frappier, *Chrétien de Troyes* (Paris, 1957), p. 93; Bayrav, pp. 117, 184, 203–4; J. Wathelet-Willem, 'Le mystère chez Marie de France', *Revue belge de philologie et d'histoire,* xxxix (1961), 667 n. 1; Lejeune–Stiennon, *La Légende de Roland,* i. 38, 41 (notes 44–8); and J. Rathofer, 'Der "wunderbare Hirsch" der Minnegrotte', *Zeitschrift für deutsches Altertum,* xcv (1966), 27–42. On the arms in *C,* consult Prinet WR, p. 248, item 59.

cez choses, *these things.* *CC,* vv. 1425–9:

> Ses escus fu couviers d'argent,
> S'i avoit une crois de geules;
> Ces coses n'i furent pas seules,
> Car en le crois avoit encor
> Cinq cokillettes de fin or.

Note: loose term for any part of the coat of arms, here the tincture of the field and the principal charge. Cf. SORPLUS. On these arms, consult Prinet CC, p. 173. The same expression is used in the *Dean Tract* (complete blazon provided s.v. BROIE SOR LE . . .), but it is not clear what 'three things' are referred to (also the tinctures of the field [azure] and of the chief [ermine] are omitted; on the Joinville or Geneville arms, see BROIE, *Note.* Compare, on the other hand, the use of this locution in the early-fourteenth-century *Tournoiement des Dames de Paris,* this time plainly alluding to: (1) the field or; (2) the semy of eaglets azure; and (3) the bend gules (vv. 419–32):

> Elle portoit une baniere
> Qui moult estoit et noble et chiere,
> Fort et diverse a deviser,
> Grant paine mis au raviser:
> Le champ fu d'or fin esmerez,
> D'aigles d'azur menu semez
> A une belingue de gueules;
> Ces trois choses n'i sont pas seules,
> Quar la bellingue ot .iii. escus
> Un poi grandes d'argent batus;
> Es trois escus ot trois chastiaus,
> Petis, bien fais, cointes et biaus,
> De sinople non pas de pierre;
> De chascun ist un arbre d'ierre.

According to Adam-Even, 'Tournoiement des Dames de Paris', pp. 4–5, the arms are those of the wife of Jehan d'Yerre. *Cez* is the feminine accusative plural of the alternate Old French demonstrative adjective; see CELE, CELES.

cez mesmes armes a, *the same arms, differenced by.* *CP* 29: ces mesmes armes a. *Syn.*: see AUTEL².

chaisne, *oak.* See CHESNE.

chalenge, *challenge (dispute about the right to bear a certain coat of arms).* See ESTRE DE CHALENGE PAR ENTRE . . . ET . . .

chalonge, see CHALENGE.

champ, *field of the shield.* *Lancelot propre,* iii. 309: si estoit le camp d'or; 421: le camp del pignon estoit d'aisur; *Vulgate Merlin Sequel,* p. 143: li champ; pp. 143, 423: le champ; p. 383: le camp; *Artus,* p. 19: li chans; p. 67: le champ. For other uses, see EN LE CHAMP, LE CHAMP PLEIN DE, VUIDIÉ DU CHAMP. *Syn.*: see ESCU¹.

champaigne, *field. Saisnes,* v. 1792: la champaingne ert blanche au lion d'or batu; *Lancelot propre,* iii. 413 (2): la campaigne. *Syn.:* see ESCU[1]. *Note:* for complete *Lancelot propre* reference, see ROIE. Godefroy, ix. 34, provides the following definition: 'terme de blason, l'espace, en bas, du tiers de l'escu', which is the meaning of the modern French heraldic term (see Veyrin-Forrer, p. 39, and Table IX, fig. 1), corresponding to E. *terrace in base* (Stalins, item 169). Godefroy's fourteenth-century examples, however, drawn from Froissart and *Perceforest,* actually illustrate the meaning 'field' as does the example from *Baudouin de Sebourg* (c. 1350) cited by Tobler–Lommatzsch, ii. 200, s.v. *champagne.*

champ plein d'eschalopes, *semy of escallops* (Fig. 39). *B* 150: le champ pleyn des escallopes (*Bl* 150 [154], see ESCHALOPES ENTOUR). *Syn.:* see A COQUILLES SEMÉ. *Note: Aspilogia II,* p. 105 n. 1: '[B] replaces the Fitz Nichol *scalops entour* by *le champ pleyn des escallopes,* which at least to a modern armorist is not the same thing.'

changier, see ARMES CHANGIER, COUVERTURES CHANGIER.

changier la conoissance, *to change arms (as a disguise). Cligés,* v. 1815: Chanjons, fet il, noz conuissances; *Perlesvaus,* p. 404: Onques la connoissance ne voust changier, kar tele la porta ses peres. *Syn.:* see ARMES CHANGIER.

changier ses armes, *to change one's arms (as a disguise). Destruction de Rome,* vv. 1003–4:

Si changerons nos armes et nos escus
    bouclers,
Les contrefaites armes vesterons del cité.

Syn.: MUER SON ESCU. *Note:* cf. ARMES CHANGIER.

chantel[1], *canton, quarter* (Fig. 117). (1) *the canton bears no charge. Thèbes,* v. 6267: a un grant chantel; *C* 88: a un cantell (*Cl* 88: a une cauntel; *Cd* 88, see CANTON); *Cl* 23: a une kantelle (*C*/*Cd* 23, see CANTON); 122: a une kantel (*C* 122, see CANTON); *Cd* 121: a un cantell; *H* 29, 51 (*Hg* 29, 51 [53]: od le cauntel): ou le cantell; 59: ou le cantel (*Hg* 59: od le cantel); *M* 7: le cauntel. (2) *the canton bears a charge.* A. *positioning of the charge on the canton is indicated by order of items only. C* 180: a un cantell

(*Cl* 180: a une cauntel), see ROUELE[1]. B. *the word* CHANTEL *is used twice, positioning of the charge on the canton being indicated by the locution* EN LE CHANTEL. *Cl* 131: a une cantel, see CROIS PATEE EN LE CHANTEL (*C* 131, see EN UN CHANTEL UNE CROIS PATEE; *Cd* 131, see EN LE CANTON UNE CROIS PATEE); *H* 106: le cantell (*Hg* 106: et le cauntel), see EN LE CHANTEL UNE QUINTEFEUILLE. *Syn.:* CANTON, CRESTEL, QUARTIER[1], QUART PART. *Note:* on the blending of the top bar with the canton in the Pipart arms, see FESSE ET UNE DEMI FESSE, *Note.* In his glossary (ii. 169), Prof. G. Raynaud de Lage defines *chantel* in *Thèbes,* v. 6267, as follows: 'lisière', bord'. Cf., however, Tobler–Lommatzsch, ii. 227, citing the corresponding word in Constans' ed. (v. 6579: o un blanc chantel).

chantel[2], *first quarter of a quarterly field.* See EN LE CHANTEL[2]. *Syn.:* QUARTIER[2], QUARTIER DEVANT[1]. *Note:* cf. DEVANT, OU QUARTIER DE, ESQUARTELÉ DE . . . ET DE (2) F.; see also Matthew Paris's blazon of the Earl of Lincoln's arms (quoted in full above, s.v. BENDE[1], *Note*) where OFr. *chantel* and its Latin equivalent are used to designate any one of the four quarters of a quarterly shield. See also ESQUARTELÉ DE . . . ET DE . . . UN LION PASSANT EN LE PRE . . ., *Note.*

chantel[3], *dexter chief set off by the upper part of a plain cross.* See CROIS PASSANT EN LE CHANTEL UNE MERLETE. *Note:* refers to EN LE CHANTEL[3], indicating position only. Cf. CHANTEL DEVANT, QUARTIER[5].

chantel[4], *corner* (Fig. 15). The complete blazon reads as follows: *C* 142: Roger de Mortymer, barry d'or et d'azure al cheif palee al cantel geronné un escocheon d'argent (*Cl* 142: Roger de Mortymer, barré d'or et d'azur al chef palé al chantel geroné a un esbochon d'argent; *Cd* 142: Roger de Mortimer, barré d'or e azure al cheif palee al cantel geroné a n'yn eschochon d'argent). *Syn.:* see CORNIER. *Note:* though *chantel* is used in the singular here, the arms in question actually feature a canton as well as a sinister canton, which, in this case, may more properly be referred to as the *corners* of the chief.

chantel[5], *dexter chief* (Fig. 2). See CHANTEL DEVANT, EL CHANTEL DEVANT UNE FLEUR, EN CHANTEL DE DEVANT UN LION, LIONCEL

RAMPANT EL CHANTEL. *Syn.*: see CHANTEL DEVANT. *Note*: refers to position only. On the locution *l'escu en chantel* 'the shield in a defensive position', consult H. Petersen Dyggve, *Neuphilologische Mitteilungen*, xxxix (1938), 299.

chantel devant, *dexter chief* (Fig. 2). See LIONCEL PASSANT OU CHANTEL DEVANT. *Syn.*: CHANTEL[5], CHIEF[3], QUARTIER[3], QUARTIER DEVANT[2]. *Note*: refers to position only. In *D* 51, the lion passant is in dexter chief without any indication of this positioning. See FESSE A UN LION PASSANT.

chapeau, *chaplet, garland of heraldic roses*. See CHAPEL.

chapeau de roses, *chaplet, garland of heraldic roses*. See CHAPEL DE ROSES.

chapel, *chaplet, garland of heraldic roses* (Fig. 233). *Durmart*, v. 8374: C'est cil a ces vermauz chapeaz; v. 8634: cil as chapeaz; vv. 8731–2: Li blans chevaliers fait mervelles / As chapeaz de roses vermelles; *H* 39: ou .iii. chapeus (*Hg* 39 [40]: od troys chapeaux). *Syn.*: CHAPEL DE ROSES. *Note*: not to be confused with the cognate term *chapel* 'hat', the heraldic chaplet or wreath is generally depicted as a broad ring carrying any one of a variety of charges. In the Falkirk Roll, however, the wreath bears roses and the term is therefore synonymous with the following item.

chapel de roses, *chaplet, garland of heraldic roses* (Fig. 233). *Durmart*, vv. 8292–303:

Chapeax de roses li atachent
Par tote sa cote a armer;
Ne pas n'i vulent oblïer
Les covertures del destrier,
Ains i font chapeaz atachier
L'un aprés l'autre espessement,
Et par tot l'escu ensement.
Sor blanc dyaspre tot novel
Sunt bien atachié li chapel.
Li elmes est tos frex dorés
Et par deseure est coronés
De vermelles roses mout beles;

M 21: ou .iii. chapaus de roses; *K*, v. 199: Trois chapeaus de rosis. *Syn.*: CHAPEL. *Note*: in the items listed here and s.v. CHAPEL, the wreaths are all gules. The roses here are heraldic roses but they refer to ROSE[3] (cf. ROSE[1] and ROSE[2]). While it is

evident from the context in *Durmart* that the chaplets are real garlands of flowers attached to the tunic, shield, helm, and horse bardings of the knight, these insignia serve at least a quasi-heraldic function in this romance, for the hero is later identified as the (White) Knight of the (Red) Chaplets; see CHAPEL; cf. also MANCHE. Major T. R. Davies, 'The Label', *Coat of Arms*, ix (1967), 306–7, cites similar evidence from a German source dated *c.* 1300. In the *Vulgate Merlin Sequel*, p. 228, King Rion's mantle is described as 'covertures toutes plaines de barbes et de courones'— here real beards and crowns borne as tokens of victory over royal adversaries— and he expresses a desire to add King Arthur's beard to these trophies; see also p. 412. The motif of a cloak made of beards of vanquished kings has been traced to Geoffrey of Monmouth; for a discussion and bibliography, see *Perlesvaus*, ii. 277–8, note to line 2714, to which add an allusion in Jacques de Longuyon's *Vœux du paon* (1312); see Pickford, 'The Three Crowns of King Arthur', p. 374; Ménard, pp. 384–5.

charbocle, charboncle, charboucle, *carbuncle pommy and conjoined* (see *Note*) (Fig. 249). *C* 9: un carbuncle (*Cl/Cd* 9, see CHARBOUCLE BESANCIÉ). *Syn.*: CHARBOUCLE BESANCIÉ. *Note*: for another use, see DEMI CHARBOUCLE. The heraldic carbuncle, it is generally held, was an outgrowth of the *umbo* or ornamental knob in the centre of the shield, a connection supported, to be sure, by the Old French term for the boss in question (OFr. *bocle, boucle* < Lat. *buccula*, a diminutive of Lat. *bucca* 'mouth'). The charge is essentially, however, a stylized representation of the precious stone of the same name (OFr. *carboncle, charboncle, charboucle, escarboncle, escarboucle, escharbocle* < Lat. *carbunculus*, a diminutive of Lat. *carbo* 'coal'), originally masculine in gender but becoming feminine by association with OFr. *bocle, boucle* (see above). The carbuncle's luminous qualities held the men of the Middle Ages in awe; see Arthur R. Harden, 'The Carbuncle in Medieval Literature', *Romance Notes*, ii (1960), 58–62. Its ordinary appearance in heraldry is described s.v. CHARBOUCLE FLEURETÉ. Here in Walford's Roll, however, it designates the distinctive carbuncle in the arms of the Kingdom of Navarre. Instead of having sceptre-like rays ending in fleurs-de-lis (Fig. 248; see Boutell, p. 92), the eight rays are tipped with roundels or bezants (whence the synonymous term *charboucle besancié*) which are conjoined with cross-pieces in the form of a square. In modern French heraldry, this charge is blazoned *fermée et pommetée* (cf. *accolée en orle*, Veyrin-Forrer, p. 48), the word *escarboucle* being feminine. On these arms and their modern counterpart (the carbuncle has become an interlocking chain), consult Prinet WR, p. 226, item 5. See also *WB* 1271.

charboucle besancié, *carbuncle pommy and conjoined* (Fig. 249). *Cl* 9: a un charbucle . . . lesance (*Cd* 9: a .i. scharbucle . . . lozence; *C* 9, see CHARBOUCLE). *Syn.*: CHARBOUCLE. *Note*: for a discussion of the arms in *Cl* 9, consult Prinet WR, p. 226, item 5; *Aspilogia II*, pp. 167–8, note to item 6. See also CHARBOUCLE, *Note*. London, *Aspilogia II*, pp. 168, 228, suggests a possible connection between *lesance* and lozengy, but this relationship is unlikely.

charboucle fleureté, *carbuncle* (Fig. 248). *C* 58: un carbuncle . . . flurté (*Cl* 58: a un charbocle . . . flurté; *Cd* 58, see ESCHARBOUCLE FLEURETÉ). *Syn.*: ESCHARBOUCLE EN LA BOUCLE, ESCHARBOUCLE FLEURETÉ. *Note*: the carbuncle blazoned here is the ordinary one, with sceptre-like rays, usually eight in number, radiating like spokes from a hub, the rays tipped with fleurs-de-lis. In the arms of the Cleves family, which are those blazoned here in Walford's Roll, an escutcheon occupies the central part of the shield, blocking out all but the tips of the carbuncle which form a kind of orle of fleurs-de-lis around the escutcheon. On these arms, see Prinet WR, p. 244, item 50, and *WB* 632, fig. 150. *Aspilogia II*, p. 190, note to item 113, points out, however, that the counterseal of Count Thierry VI of Cleves (1202–60) 'shows a charbocle overlying the scocheon', in other words reversed positions for the two charges.

chargier ses armes a, *to bestow one's* (*undifferenced*) *arms upon* (*someone*). *EO*, vv. 2537–9:

Et dist Ogiers: 'De ce sui moult joians,
Moult en doi estre envers vous mercians
Quant si preudons m'est ses armes
    carchans';

Berte, v. 3229: Pour l'amour k'ot a aus ces armes lor charcha. *Note*: on the concept of undifferenced arms, see ARMES PLAINES[1], *Note*. In *Berte*, the reading *ces* = *ses* (supported by the variant in MS. R) is preferable although not absolutely necessary. On the arms in question in both these passages, see the notes to DROITES ARMES, ORLE ENDENTÉ, POUR L'AMOUR QU'OT A. For another possible use of OFr. *chargier*, see HARGE.

charmin, *gules* (*red*). *Troie*, vv. 7877–8:

Heaumes, haubers, escuz d'or fin,
De vert, d'azur e de charmin;

Fouque de Candie, v. 10476: l'escu charmin. *Syn.*: see GEULES.

chascun, *each*. See EN CHASCUN BESANT UNE CROISILLE, EN CHASCUNE CORNIERE SEIT UN PIÉ, EN CHASCUN LABEL UNE FLEUR DE LIS, EN CHASCUN RONDEL UN CROISIÉ, EN CHASCUN RONDEL UNE CROISILLE, ROSIERS SOR CHASCUN ROSIER UNE ROSE, CHASCUN ROSIER. *Note*: the use of the alternate adjectival form *chaque*, though attested as early as the twelfth century (*BW*[4], s.v. *chacun*), is rare in French before the sixteenth century. See Foulet, *Petite Syntaxe*, para. 273.

chascune cuisse jointe aus autres, see JAMBES ARMEES O TOUTES LES CUISSES CHASCUNE CUISSE JOINTE AUS AUTRES ET EN CHASCUNE CORNIERE SEIT UN PIÉ.

chastel[1], *castle* (Fig. 251). (1) *the castle is alone on the shield*. Castile (new item in *Cd* and *Cl* [7]), *Cl*: a un chastel; *Cd*: a chastel; *Hem*, v. 1124: a un castel; *D* 20: od un chastel; *H* 57: ou ung chastel (*Hg* 57 [58]: a un chastel). (2) *a castle in the first and fourth quarters*. *Cd* 6: .i. chasteaus. See also ESQUARTILLIÉ DE . . . ET DE . . . A CHASTEAUS EN LES QUARTIERS DE . . ., A LIONCEAUS EN LES QUARTIERS DE . . ., ESQUARTILLIÉ DE . . . UN CHASTEL, ET DE . . . UN LION RAMPANT. (3) *semy of castles*. See POUDRÉ A CERCLES. *Syn.*: TOUR, TOURELES, TOURETES. *Note*: Matthew Paris, blazoning the arms of Castile and León, twice uses the Latin equivalent *castrum*. See Pusikan, pp. 129–

30. *Cd* 6, a defective blazon, omits mention of the quarterly partition. Contrary to modern heraldic practice, which distinguishes between castles, towers, and turrets, the first of these having at least two towers, early blazon used all three terms interchangeably.

chastel². *In the following blazons, 'castel' is a ghost word*: (1) *for 'gastel'*. *Cd* 120: Rauff de Camoylet, or a cheif de gules a 3 casteles argent en le chief, see GASTEL EN LE CHIEF; (2) *for 'rastel'*. *Cd* 41: Le conte Restel, gules a 3 castels d'or, see RASTEL and RASTELE. *Note*: cf. CHASTELÉ², ENCHASTELÉ, POUDRÉ A CERCLES.

chastelé¹, *semy of castles* (Fig. 31). The complete blazon reads as follows: *CPA* 7: Le conte d'Artoys, de Franche au lambel de gueules castellé d'or. *Syn.*: POUDRÉ A TOURELES, POUDRÉ A TOURETES. See also POUDRÉ A CERCLES.

chastelé². *In the following blazon, 'chastelé' is a ghost word for 'masclé'*: *Cd* 75: Le ducke de Baviere, castelé azure argent [*sic*], see MASCLÉ DE . . . ET DE . . .². *Note*: *Aspilogia II*, p. 178, note to item 48: '[*Cd* 75] blazons this "catele az. ar.", a term which is still to be explained.'

chat, *cat* (Fig. 153). *Des Deux Bordeors*, p. 9, vv. 13–14:

Si connois Renaut Brise-teste,
Qui porte un chat en son escu.

Note: on this charge in heraldry, see Julian Franklyn, 'A Musion (or Catte)', *Coat of Arms*, i (1950), 45–6; idem, 'The Cat in Heraldry', *Coat of Arms*, i (1951), 265–8. See also, ii (1952), 117.

chaut, *hot*. See POIVRE CHAUT O LES PENNARZ.

chemise Nostre Dame, *the Virgin's shift* (Fig. 132). See ESCHARBOUCLE ENTRE EVANGILES EN DEUS MANCHES DE LA CHEMISE NOSTRE DAME. *Note*: on this relic, preserved at Aix-la-Chapelle, Chartres, Compiègne, and Laon, consult Goddard, pp. 96–7; Horrent, *Le Pèlerinage de Charlemagne*, p. 40; Louis Réau, *Iconographie de l'art chrétien*, i (Paris, 1955), 377 n. 1; ii² (Paris, 1957), 61–2.

chequé de . . . et de . . ., *checky* (Fig. 9). *B* 20: chequy de . . . et de . . . (*Ba/Bc* 20, see ESCHEQUERÉ DE . . . ET DE . . .; *Bb* 20:

chequy . . . and . . .; *Bl* 20, see ESCHEQUERÉ DE . . . ET DE . . .); *Bb* 30 (*B* 30, see ESCHEQUÉ DE . . . ET DE . . .: *Ba/Bc/Bl* 30, see ESCHEQUERÉ DE . . . ET DE . . .), 33 (*B* 33, see ESCHEQUÉ DE . . . ET DE . . .; *Ba/Bc/Bl* 33, see ESCHEQUERÉ DE . . . ET DE . . .), 50 (*B* 50, see ESCHEQUÉ DE . . . ET DE . . .; *Ba/Bc/Bl* 50, see ESCHEQUERÉ DE . . . ET DE . . .): chequy . . . et . . .; *C* 23 (*Cl/Cd* 23, see ESCHEQUERÉ DE . . . ET DE . . .), 25 (*Cl/Cd* 25, see ESCHEQUERÉ DE . . . ET DE . . .), 160 (*Cl/Cd* 160, see ESCHEQUERÉ DE . . . ET DE . . .): chequy de . . . et de . . .; 138 (*Cl/Cd* 138, see ESCHEQUERÉ DE . . . ET DE . . .): cheky de . . . et . . .; 147 (*Cl/Cd* 147, see ESCHEQUERÉ DE . . . ET DE . . .): cheky de . . . et de . . . *Syn.*: see ESCHEQUÉ DE . . . ET DE . . .

chequeré de . . . et de . . ., *checky* (Fig. 9). *H/Hg* 55 [56]: chekeré de . . . et de . . .; *Hg* 51 [53]: chekeré de . . . et de . . . (*H* 51, see ESCHEQUERÉ DE . . . ET DE . . .); *M* 5: chekeré de . . . et de . . . *Syn.*: see ESCHEQUÉ DE . . . ET DE . . . *Note*: Pusikan, p. 139, errs in his reading of the following blazon: 'Comitis de Warenni. *Cheketé* de auro et azuro'. The MS. clearly reads *chekeré* (see Wagner, *CEMRA*, Plate I; *Aspilogia II*, p. 37, item 7).

cherf, *stag*. See CERF.

chesne, *oak* (Fig. 229). *B* 156: ung kene (*Bl* 156 [160]: od un kene). *Note*: Hope, *A Grammar of English Heraldry*, p. 54, incorrectly interprets this charge as an *ox*. The correct blazon is provided by H. S. London, *Coat of Arms*, ii (1953), no. 15, 270. On the velar *k*, see CROIS FOURCHIEE AU KANEE, *Note*.

cheval, *horse*. See FER A CHEVAL.

cheval fust apendu d'unes fourches, *wooden horse hanging from a gallows*. *TA*, vv. 924–5:

Et d'unes forches apendu
Ot en l'escu .i. cheval fust.

Note: the 'wooden horse' in the arms of Larrecin (Larceny) is probably the instrument of torture used for racking prisoners.

cheval sellé, *saddled horse* (Fig. 160). *C* 16: un chivall . . . sellé (*Cl* 16: a un chevald . . . sellé; *Cd* 16: a .i. shaivall . . . sellé). *Note*: on the heraldic horse, see *Coat of Arms*, i (1950), 38, 102–3; London, *Royal Beasts*, pp. 51–5; *Aspilogia II*, pp. 169–70, note to item 17.

chevet, chevez, see CROIS FOURCHIEE AU KANEE.

*chevron, *chevron* (Fig. 66). One literary example only before *c.* 1250, viz. *Saisnes*, v. 2966: a un . . . chavron (cf. var., p. 187, v. 4: au . . . chevron); however, several attestations in literature after that date, e.g. *EO*, v. 5132: a un vert cheveron; *TC*, v. 1462: A chevrons; *K*, v. 59: o un cheveron; v. 478: o trois chiverons; v. 576: o un chievron. Very frequent in the rolls: (1) *alone on the shield.* A. *the chevron bears no charge,* e.g. *BA* 29, 168: a .iii. kevrons; *B* 5: a trois cheverons (*Bl* 5: ove trois cheverons); *H* 81: ou .ii. cheverons (*Hg* 81, see CHEVRONS ET UNE FESSE). B. *the chevron is charged,* e.g. *B* 148: a ung cheveron (*Bl* 148 [152]: ove un chevron), see FLEURETES EN LE CHEVRON. *Syn.:* CHEVRON EN MI. *Note:* cf. CHEVRONS OD LA FESSE, *Note*; FESSE, *Note*. (2) *the chevron separates multiple charges. M* 44: ou ung cheveron, see FEUILLE. For other uses, see CHEVRON A OISELEZ, CHEVRON ET TOURTEAUS, CHEVRON O MOLETES, CHEVRON OD MOLETES, MEULETES OD UN CHEVRON. (3) *the chevron is on a chief.* See CHEVRON EN LE CHIEF, CHEVRON SOR LE CHIEF. (4) *fess between two chevrons.* See CHEVRONS A LA FESSE, CHEVRONS A UNE FESSE, CHEVRONS ET UNE FESSE, CHEVRONS OD LA FESSE, CHEVRONS OU UNE FESSE, FESSE A CHEVRONS, FESSE ENTRE CHEVRONS, FESSE ET CHEVRONS, FESSE OD CHEVRONS. *Note:* Pusikan, pp. 137, 145, and 148, provides unnecessarily diverse readings for the five blazons in Matthew Paris featuring chevrons, viz. *chevrons, chevers, chevrons, cheveruns,* and *chevrunes.* Actually, every single mention is an abbreviation (*ch', chev's, cheũs, chev'ũs, chev's*) which may uniformly be solved *cheveruns.* In *Bb* 20 and *Bb* 52, the chevron is tricked. The arms of Hugues Beckart de Maisey, mentioned in *TC*, vv. 1461–3 (the complete blazon reads as follows: 'Estoit arméz d'armez vermoilles / A chevrons d'or, et a mervoilles / Fu de dames le jor prisiéz') contain a single chevron; see *WB* 565. Gough H, p. 146, note to item 81: '[*H* 81] seems to be erroneous . . .' (see CHEVRONS ET UNE FESSE). OFr. *chevron* 'rafters joined together to form a gable'

seems to be the origin of this term (Oswald Barron, article 'Heraldry' in *Encyclopaedia Britannica*; Wagner, *Historic Heraldry*, p. 105). OFr. *chevron* is a diminutive of OFr. *chevre* (< Lat. *capra*) 'goat', a derivation doubtless suggested by the fact that rafters resemble a 'little goat' the way a saw-horse resembles a 'little horse' (cf. OFr. and MFr. *chevalet* and E. *easel* < Dutch *ezel* 'ass, donkey'). This architectural interpretation is supported by Conrad of Mure's use of the Latin term *tactus* (for CL *tectum* 'roof') in this meaning in the *Clipearius Teutonicorum* (third quarter of the thirteenth century). See also *chevroné* in *TA*. Chevrons appear at the dawn of heraldry (1141–6) in the arms of the Clare family. See Wagner, *Historic Heraldry*, pp. 36–7, item 4; *Aspilogia II*, p. 22, note to item 46. On the position of the fess between chevrons, see CHEVRONS OD LA FESSE, *Note*; FESSE, *Note*.

chevron a oiselez, *chevron between martlets.* *CPA* 169: au quevron . . . a .iii. oiselets. *Note:* refers to CHEVRON (2).

chevroné de . . . et de . . ., *chevronny* (Fig. 10). *TA*, v. 1519: Chevronnez de festes anniex; *C* 38: cheveronnee de . . . et de . . . (*Cl* 38: cheveroné de . . . e de . . .; *Cd* 38: cheveroné . . . e . . .); *CP* 86: chevronné de . . . et de . . . *Note:* in *Guillaume de Dole*, vv. 236–9, fur surcoats and mantles are described as made of ermine and squirrel decorated with a chevronny design of black sable:

> Orent et cotes et manteaus,
> A penes fresches bien ovrees,
> D'ermine et de gris chevronees,
> A sables noirs, soëf flerans.

See also *Blancandin*, v. 4735: Et la cote fu chevronee.

chevron en le chief, *on a chief a chevron.* *Cl* 47: a une chefrune . . . en le chef (*C*/*Cd* 47, see CHEVRON SOR LE CHIEF). *Syn.:* CHEVRON SOR LE CHIEF. *Note:* refers to CHEVRON (3). For the abbreviation 6 (= *en le*), see Introduction, p. 57.

chevron en mi, *chevron* (Fig. 66). *K*, vv. 423–5:

> Baniere ot Henris li Tyois
> Plus blanche de un poli lyois,
> O un chievron vermeil en mi.

Syn.: CHEVRON. *Note*: refers to CHEVRON (1).

chevron et tourteaus, *chevron between torteaux. B* 179: ung chevron et trois torteux *(Bl* 179 [183], see MEULETES ET UN CHEVRON). *Syn.*: MEULETES OD UN CHEVRON. *Note*: refers to CHEVRON (2). On the position of the charges, see *Aspilogia II*, pp. 104, 150, note to item 183.

chevron o moletes, *chevron between mullets. K*, vv. 872–3:

En son blanc escu ot fait teindre
Un chievron rouge o trois molettes.

Syn.: CHEVRON OD MOLETES. *Note*: refers to CHEVRON (2).

chevron od moletes, *chevron between mullets. D* 137: a un cheverun . . . od treis molettes. *Syn.*: CHEVRON O MOLETES. *Note*: refers to CHEVRON (2).

chevrons a la fesse, *fess between chevrons. Ba* 60: a deus cheveruns . . . a la fesse *(B* 60, see CHEVRONS ET UNE FESSE; *Bb* 60: 2 cheverons . . . a fesse; *Bc* 60: a deus cheveruns . . . a la feses; *Bl* 60, see CHEVRONS OD LA FESSE). *Syn.*: see CHEVRON (4).

chevrons a une fesse, *fess between chevrons. Hg* 6: a deus cheverons . . . a un fesse *(H* 6, see CHEVRONS OU UNE FESSE). *Syn.*: see CHEVRON (4).

chevrons et une fesse, *fess between chevrons. B* 60: a deux cheverons et ung fece *(Ba/Bb* 60, see CHEVRONS A LA FESSE; *Bl* 60, see CHEVRONS OD LA FESSE); *Hg* 81: a deux cheverons et un fesse *(H* 81, see CHEVRON [1] A.). *Syn.*: see CHEVRON (4). *Note*: *P* 92 (= *B* 182 [see FESSE ENTRE CHEVRONS]) reads: 'a deux cheverons et une fesse'. For *H* 81, see CHEVRON, *Note.*

chevrons jumeaus, *twin chevrons (chevronels placed together to form a pair)* (Fig. 68). *BA* 183: a .iii. kevrons . . . jumiax. *Note*: refers to JUMEAUS[1]. The modern French equivalent is *chevrons jumelés.* See *Navarre* 913: 'M. Guiffroy de Clect, d'or a trois quevrons jumelés d'azur'.

chevrons od la fesse, *fess between chevrons. Bl* 60 *(B* 60, see CHEVRONS ET UNE FESSE; *Ba/Bb* 60, see CHEVRONS A LA FESSE), 182 [186] *(B* 182, see FESSE ENTRE CHEVRONS): od deus cheverons . . . od la fesse. *Syn.*: see CHEVRON (4). *Note*: *Aspilogia II*, p. 105: 'The fact that the Monmouth fess is over all, [*Bl*] 92, is not expressed, and the use

of exactly the same phrasing to blazon Pecche, [*Bl*] 60, and FitzWalter, [*Bl* 182 (186)], suggests that the fess in those coats was originally over rather than between the two chevrons.' For *B/Bl* 92, see FESSE (1).

chevron sor le chief, *on a chief a chevron. C* 47: un cheverone . . . sur le cheif *(Cl* 47, see CHEVRON EN LE CHIEF; *Cd* 47: a un cheveron . . . sur le chef). *Syn.*: CHEVRON EN LE CHIEF. *Note*: refers to CHEVRON (3).

chevrons ou une fesse, *fess between chevrons. H* 6: ou deux cheverouns . . . ou ung fez *(Hg* 6, see CHEVRONS A UNE FESSE). *Syn.*: see CHEVRON (4).

***chief**[1], *chief (the ordinary, i.e. the upper part of the shield set off from the field by a horizontal line and a different tincture)* (Fig. 69). Frequent in literary sources, very frequent in the rolls. (1) *the chief bears no charge,* e.g. *Bel Inconnu,* v. 330: Li ciés fu d'or, li piés d'argent; *FCL,* v. 789: Escu ot d'or, el cief vermel; *FCT,* v. 822: od le chief; *BA* 45, 53: au kief; *B* 32: a cheif *(Bl* 32: a chief); 195: ung cheff *(Bl* 195 [199], see CHIEF[1] [2]); *Bl* 134 [138]: et le chief *(B* 134, see FRETÉ EN LE CHIEF); *Cl* 171: al cheif *(C* 171, see CHIEF[1] [2], *Note; Cd* 171: a chief); *H* 77: ou le chef *(Hg* 77 [76]: et le chef, see JUMEAUS[1] [2] and *Note); M* 48: ou le chef (see BARRE[1] [3]). *Note: C* 67 (un cheif) and *CP* 93 (au chef) are scribal errors; see CERF and CLEF. For *B/Bl* 121, *H* 77, and *M* 48 (chief used in conjunction with bars gemelles), see BARRE[1] (3), *Note.* (2) *the chief bears a charge.* A. *the word* CHIEF *is used twice, one of which is in the locution* AU CHIEF, EL CHIEF, EN CHIEF[1], EN LE CHIEF[1], *or* SOR LE CHIEF. *BA* 205, 206: au kief, see VUIVRE DE TRAVERS EL CHIEF, BASTON DE TRAVERS EL CHIEF; St. John (new item in *Bl* [110]): od chief, see ESTOILE EN LE CHIEF[1]; *Bl* 195 [199]: au chief, see MIREOR EN LE CHIEF *(B* 195, see CHIEF[1] [1]); *C* 47 *(Cl* 47: al chef, see CHEVRON EN LE CHIEF; *Cd* 47: al cheif, see CHEVRON SOR LE CHIEF): un cheif, see CHEVRON SOR LE CHIEF; 159 *(Cl* 159: a chef; *Cd* 159: au cheif): a cheif, see ROUELE EN CHIEF[1]; *Cl* 120 *(Cd* 120: a cheif; *C* 120, see paragraph B. below): al chef, see GASTEL EN LE CHIEF; *CP* 12: see OISELET AU CHIEF; 40: au chief, see DEMI LION ET COURONÉ AU CHIEF (see also paragraph B. 3. below); 109: au chief, see LIONCEAUS

PASSANZ L'UN CONTRE L'AUTRE EN CHIEF; *CPA* 161: au chef, see BEUF EL CHIEF; *CC*, v. 1316: le cief, see MERLE EL CHIEF; *H* 102: ou le chef, see MOLETE EN LE CHIEF (*Hg* 102: od le chef, see MOLET EN LE CHIEF). For a different use of EN LE CHIEF in this connection, see FRETÉ EN LE CHIEF. B. *the word* CHIEF *is used only once. 1. order of items alone indicates that the charge is on the chief.* *Ba* 64: a chefe, see TOURTEL (2) (*B/Bc* 64, see CHIEF A UN TOURTEL; *Bb* 64: a cheife; *Bl* 64: a chief, see TOURTEL EL CHIEF); 102 (*Bl* 102, see CHIEF OD UN DEMI LION), 103 (*Bl* 103, see CHIEF ET UN DEMI LION): au cheif; *C* 120 (*Cl/Cd* 120, see paragraph A. above), 176 (*Cl* 176, see CHIEF A UNE FLEURETE RECOUPEE): al cheif. For other uses, see CHIEF A UN COR, CHIEF A UN DEMI LION, CHIEF A UNE FLEURETE RECOUPEE, CHIEF A UN LION RECOUPÉ, CHIEF A UN MARTEL, CHIEF A UN MARTEL EN BELIC, CHIEF ET UN DEMI LION, CHIEF OD DEMI FLEUR DE GLAIEUL, CHIEF OD UN DEMI LION, CHIEF OD UNE MERLETE, CHIEF O UN GASTEL, CHIEF OU OT UNE COQUILLE. *Note: Bl* 195 [199] listed here s.v. CHIEF¹ (2) A. 'omits the bezants, probably by inadvertence' (*Aspilogia II*, p. 154, note to item 199); cf. *B* 195, s.v. CHIEF¹ (1). In the following blazons, the charges are in the field, not on the chief, in spite of the order of items. (1) *C* 19: Le auntient de Temple, d'argent un chief sable un crois gulez passant (*Cl* 19: Le baucent del Temple, d'argent al chef de sable a un croyz de goule passant; *Cd* 19: Le baron del Temple, d'argent le cheif de sable a une croiss de gules passant). For a discussion of the early banner and arms of the Knights Templars and the position of the cross, see CROIS PASSANT, *Note*. (2) *C* 171: Robert de Cresignes, d'azure al chief d'or et trois gemells d'or (*Cl* 171 [176]: Robert de Creseques, d'azur al chef d'or a treis gemelle d'or; *Cd* 171: Robert de Creseques, d'azur a chief d'or a 3 gemes d'or). On these arms, consult Prinet WR, p. 252, item 68. See also JUMELES². (3) *D* 129: Munsire Robert de Brus, l'escu d'or od le chef de gules a un sautur de gules od une molette d'argent. The accompanying painted shield (no. 143) is blazoned as follows by Greenstreet: 'Or, a saltire gules, and in sinister point

of a chief of the second, a mullet of six points . . .' Cf. CHIEF³, *Note*. (4) *CPA* 163: Ytier de Magnac, de gueules au chef d'or a .ii. pans [*sic*, for paus; see PAL] vaires. Adam-Even notes: 'Les pals sont sous le chef.' (5) See JUMEAUS DE L'UN EN L'AUTRE, JUMEAUS DE L'UN ET DE L'AUTRE. 2. *order of items alone indicates that the charge (here a lion rampant) is 'over all', i.e. overlaps the field as well as the chief.* *C* 32: Le countee Wandome, d'argent un cheif d'azure un leon rampant gules (*Cl/Cd* 32, see *Note*). *Note*: in the following blazons, the locutions CHIEF A UN LION and CHIEF A UN LION RAMPANT are used in the same meaning. *BA* 264: Li quens de Vendosme (A: Vendome), l'escu blanc au kief de geules (A: gueules) a .i. lion rampant [*sic*, no tincture indicated]. De Torrainne (A: Toraine); *Cl* 32: Le counte de Wandome, d'argent al chef d'azur a une lion raumpant de goule (*C* 32, see above; *Cd* 32: Le conte de Wandom, argent cheif azure une lion rampant gules); *CP* 76: Mesire Joffroi de Vendome porte les armes d'argent au chef de gheules a un lion d'asur et a une fleur de lis d'or en l'espaule du lion. On the Vendôme arms, consult Prinet WR, pp. 231–2, item 18, who blazons the lion as 'brochant sur un chef'; see also *Aspilogia II*, p. 175, note to item 34. 3. *the tincture of the field is repeated to indicate that the charge is placed in it, not on the chief.* The complete blazons read as follows: *C* 146: Geffrey Genevile, d'azure al cheif d'ermine un lion recoupé de gulez, en le azure trois bresses d'or (*Cl* 146: Geffrey de Genevile, d'azur al chef d'ermine a un leun recoupé de goule, en l'azur .iii. bresser d'or; *Cd* 146: Geffrey de Genvylle, d'azur al cheif d'ermyne a un lion recoupé de gules, in l'azur bresers d'or); *CP* 40: Mesire Jehan de Genville porte les armes d'asur au chief d'ermine a un demi lion de gheules et couronné d'or au chief, et a trois broies d'or sor l'asur (see para. A. above). For other uses, see AU CHIEF, EL CHIEF, EN CHIEF¹, EN LE CHIEF¹, EN LE CHIEF³, SOR LE CHIEF. *Note*: cf. PIÉ². On the various uses of OFr. *chief*, consult Brault, 'The Chief'. Add the meanings cited here s.v. EL CHANTEL, to p. 84 n. 12, and s.v. LABEL², *Note*, to pp. 82–3 n. 1.

chief[2], *chief* (*position only, i.e. the upper part of the shield set off from the field by the horizontal line of an ordinary*) (Fig. 72). See EN CHIEF[2], EN LE CHIEF[2], OU CHIEF[1]. *Syn.*: SOM. *Note*: in MOLETE EN CHIEF, the chief is constituted by the arms of a saltire. The word *chief* is omitted entirely, but the blazon still indicates that a charge is found in chief in a number of instances involving horizontal stripes. See BARRE (2), FESSE (1) C., JUMEAUS[1] (3), JUMELES[1] (1) B., LISTE[2]. On the other hand, there is no horizontal line involved in the use of the term *som*; see EGLET AL SOM. There was, finally, another term used in the meaning 'upper part of the shield' in Old French, viz. *penne*. See, for example, *TC*, v. 2007: 'Desus les pennes des escus'; v. 2057: 'Bas le quartier, avant la penne'; *Hem*, v. 4306: 'Haut en l'escu, deseur la penne'. While I have not found any examples in early blazon, the term is used in *Navarre* 285 in the same meaning: '284. M. Jehan des Moustiers, d'argent a une bende d'azur frecté d'or. — 285. M. Jehan des Moustiers d'Asie, semblablement, a .i. lionceau de gheules en la penne de l'escu'.

chief[3], *dexter chief* (Fig. 2). See FESSIÉ D'UNE BARRE ET OU CHIEF UN LIONCEL PASSANT. *Syn.*: see CHANTEL DEVANT. *Note*: refers to position only. Cf. QUARTIER DEVANT[2]. For the sinister chief, see CORNIERE[3].

chief[4], *head*. See CHIEF DEL DRAGON, CHIEF DE MASTIN, CHIEF DU DRAGON, LION LI CHIEF COURONÉ COUE FOURCHIEE. *Syn.*: TESTE.

chief[5], *end* (*referring to the tips of a cross*). See CROIS FOURCHIEE AU KANEE, *Note*. *Syn.*: BOUT.

chief[6], *pendant, point* (*of a label*). See LABEL[2], *Note*.

chief a un cor, *on a chief a hunting-horn*. *Escanor*, v. 3642: Au chief d'asur a .i. blanc cor. *Note*: for complete blazon, see COR.

chief a un demi lion, *on a chief a demi-lion rampant issuant*. *BA* 111: au kief . . . a .i. demy lion. *Syn.*: CHIEF A UN LION RECOUPÉ, CHIEF ET UN DEMI LION, CHIEF OD UN DEMI LION. *Note*: see also CHIEF[1] (2) B. 1. and 3. Cf. DEMI LION ET COURONÉ AU CHIEF.

chief a un demi lion et couroné au chief, *on a chief a crowned demi-lion rampant*. Complete blazon (*CP* 40) given s.v. CHIEF[1]

(2) B. 3. *Note*: on the meaning of the second *chief* in this locution, see AU CHIEF, a phrase which counterbalances SOR L'ASUR in this blazon. For the crown in the Joinville arms, see H. S. London, 'The Geneville Brays', *Coat of Arms*, iii (1954), 85.

chief a une fleurete recoupee, *on a chief a demi-fleur-de-lis*. *Cl* 176: al chef . . . a une flurette . . . recoupé (*C* 176, see CHIEF[1] (2) B. 1. and FLEURETE[2]). *Syn.*: CHIEF OD UNE DEMI FLEUR DE GLAIEUL. See also FLEUR DE LIS ISSANT and FLEURETE[2].

chief a un lion, *chief with a lion rampant over all*. See CHIEF[1] (2) B. 2., *Note*, and FLEUR DE LIS EN L'ESPAULE DU LION.

chief a un lion rampant, *chief with a lion rampant over all*. See CHIEF[1] (2) B. 2., *Note*.

chief a un lion recoupé, *on a chief a demi-lion rampant issuant*. *Cl* 146: al chef . . . a un lion recoupé (*C* 146, see CHIEF[1] (2) B. 3.; *Cd* 146: al cheif . . . a un lion recoupé); *D* 156: od le chef . . . a un leun recoupé. *Syn.*: see CHIEF A UN DEMI LION.

chief a un martel, *on a chief a hammer*. *BA* 114: au kief . . . a .iii. martiax.

chief a un martel en belic, *on a chief a hammer bendwise*. *BA* 113: au kief . . . a .iii. martiax (A: martiaux) . . . en beslive.

chief a un tourtel, *on a chief a roundel*. *B* 64: ung cheif . . . a trois torteux (*Ba* 64, see CHIEF[1] [1] 2. B. 1.; TOURTEL [2]; *Bb* 64, the torteaux are tricked; *Bc* 64: a chef . . . a treis turteus; *Bl* 64, see TOURTEL EL CHIEF). *Syn.*: see GASTEL EN LE CHIEF.

chief del dragon, *dragon's head* (Fig. 220). *Perlesvaus*, p. 252 (2): le chief del dragon. *Syn.*: CHIEF DU DRAGON, EN MILIEU OU LA TESTE DEL DRAGON ESTOIT, TESTE DEL DRAGON, TESTE DEL DRAGON EN MI. *Note*: cf. TESTE D'UN DRAGON CRESTÉ.

chief de mastin, *mastiff's head* (Fig. 169). *Garin le Loherain*, v. 501: Ou es alez tu, al chief de mastin? *Note*: see MASTIN.

chief devant, see EL CHIEF DEVANT LE LIONCEL COURANT.

chief du dragon, *dragon's head* (Fig. 219). *Perlesvaus*, p. 259: au chevalier anemi qui le cief dou dragon portoit en son escu, qui jetoit fou e flamme. *Syn.*: see CHIEF DEL DRAGON.

chief endenté, *chief indented* (Fig. 70). *BA* 109, 164, 197: au kief . . . endenté; *B* 136: ung cheif . . . endenté (*Bl* 136 [140]: od le chief . . . endenté); *D* 151 : od les endenté [*sic*, for od le chef endenté?]. *Note*: refers to ENDENTÉ[1]. The chief bears no charge. In the Camden Roll, the corresponding painted shield (no. 167) shows a chief indented.

chief endenté enté d'une coquille, *on a chief indented an escallop.* See CHIEF ENDENTÉ ENTÉ D'UNE MOLETE.

chief endenté enté d'une molete, *on a chief indented a mullet.* The complete blazon reads as follows: *K*, vv. 881–5:

> E li .ii. frere Basset ausi,
> Dont li ainsnez portoit ensi,
> De ermine au chief rouge endenté
> De trois molettes de or enté;
> Li autres de cokilles trois.

chief et un demi lion, *on a chief a demi-lion rampant issuant. Bl* 103 : od un chief . . . et un demi lion (*B* 103, see CHIEF[1] [2] B. 1.). *Syn.*: see CHIEF A UN DEMI LION.

chief od un demi lion, *on a chief a demi-lion rampant issuant. Bl* 102 : al chief . . . od un demi leon (*B* 102, see CHIEF[1] [2] B. 1.). *Syn.*: see CHIEF A UN DEMI LION.

chief od une demi fleur de glaieul, *on a chief a demi-fleur-de-lis. D* 73 : od le chef . . . od demy flur de glag[el]. *Syn.*: see CHIEF A UNE FLEURETE RECOUPEE.

chief od une molete, *on a chief a mullet. D* 105 : od le chef . . . od deus molettes. *Syn.*: see ESTOILE EN LE CHIEF[1].

chief o un gastel, *on a chief a roundel. K*, vv. 313–16:

> E le Amauri de Saint Amant,
> Ki va prouesce (W: provesté) reclamant,
> De or e de noir fretté, au chief
> O trois gasteaus de or derechief.

Syn.: see GASTEL EN LE CHIEF. *Note*: refers to CHIEF[1] (2) B. 1. See also the variant form CHIEF O UN RONDEL.

chief o un rondel, *on a chief a roundel. K*, vv. 315–16:

> De or et de noir fretté, a chief
> O troi rondeaus de or derechief.

Syn.: see GASTEL EN LE CHIEF. *Note*: refers to CHIEF[1] (2) B. 1. This is the form provided by College of Arms MS. Arundel LXII, as edited by Nicolas. Cf. CHIEF O UN GASTEL.

chief ou ot une coquille, *on a chief an escallop.* The complete blazon reads as follows: *K*, vv. 710–13:

> Henri de Graham unes armes
> Avoit vermeilles cumme sanc,
> O un sautour e au chief blanc,
> Ou ot trois vermeilles cokilles.

chienet, *kennet, small hunting-dog* (Fig. 161). *Note*: only in Matthew Paris (Pusikan, p. 121): 'Scutum N. de Kenetz. Scutum de gules, caniculi de argento'. On these canting arms, see *Aspilogia II*, p. 46, note to item 50, and cf. MASTIN, MASTIN RECHIGNIÉ, LEVRIER OD LE COLIER, LEVRIER OU LE COLIER.

chose, *thing. EO*, v. 2544: Encore y a chose moult avenans. For another use, see CEZ CHOSES. *Note*: loose term for any part of the coat of arms, here the bordure. For the complete blazon, see ORLE ENDENTÉ.

choue, see COUWE.

cigne, *swan* (Fig. 206). *TA*, v. 1942: a .ii. cignes. *Note*: on the symbolism of the swan, the Swan Knight, and the Feast of the Swans at Whitsuntide in 1306, see N. Denholm-Young, 'The Tournament in the Thirteenth Century', *Studies in Medieval History Presented to F. M. Powicke* (Oxford, 1948), p. 266; R. S. Loomis, 'Edward I, Arthurian Enthusiast', *Speculum*, xxviii (1953), 114–27; A. R. Wagner, 'The Swan Badge and the Swan Knight', *Archaeologia*, xcvii (1959), 127–38; R. L. Schurfranz, 'The French Swan-Knight Legend', unpublished University of North Carolina doctoral dissertation (Chapel Hill, 1959); F. M. Powicke, *The Thirteenth Century 1216–1307*, 2nd ed. (Oxford, 1962), pp. 515–16; Denholm-Young K, pp. 251–62; Denholm-Young, *History and Heraldry*, pp. 13, 26, and *passim*; Brault K, pp. 16–18; and Valentina A. Cohn, 'The Image of the Swan in French Literature', unpublished Stanford University doctoral dissertation (Stanford, 1968). 'The symbolism of the swan, a persistent but obscure thread in thirteenth-century epic literature, was associated in real life with the Tony or Thony family. Matthew Paris remarks that Roger de Thony was descended from those famous knights *qui a Cignis nomine intitulantur* and promises further information about them which in fact he never gives' (Denholm-Young K, p. 254 n. 1). The fashionable ceremony of taking an oath on a bird is commemorated in a number of Middle French poems, e.g. *Vœux du paon*, *Vœux de l'épervier*, *Vœux du héron*; see P. Zumthor, *Histoire littéraire de la France médiévale (VIe–XIVe siècles)* (Paris, 1954), pp. 289, 297. On the manner of preparing and serving the swan, consult *La Bataille de Caresme et de Charnage*, ed. G. Lozinski, pp. 137–8, no. 32.

cincfeuille, *cinquefoil* (Fig. 234). *Bb* 70: 3 cinquefoyles (*B/Ba* 70, see QUINTE-FEUILLE); *Cd* 96: a une cynquefole (*C/Cl* 96, see QUINTEFEUILLE); 110: a 3 cinque-foles (*C/Cl* 110, see QUINTEFEUILLE); 111: a 3 cinquefoyeles (*C/Cl* 111, see QUINTE-FEUILLE); 129: a une cinquefoele (*C/Cl*, see QUINTEFEUILLE); 162: a 3 cinquefoles (*C/Cl* 162, see QUINTEFEUILLE). *Syn.*: QUIN-TEFEUILLE, RAI, ROSE[1], ROSETE. *Note*: see ESTOILE, *Note*. Matthew Paris blazons the cinquefoil in the FitzNichol arms as a *penta-folium* (*Aspilogia II*, p. 44, item 39). In *Cd* 110, 111, 129, and 162, the first part of the word is abbreviated with the number 5 (e.g. *Cd* 110: a 3 5 foles). On this charge, consult A. C. Fox-Davies, 'The Heraldic Cinquefoil', *Genealogical Magazine*, vii (1903), 207–10. See also SISTEFEUILLE, *Note*.

cinquefeuille, *cinquefoil*. See CINCFEUILLE.

circle, see CERCLE.

cisne, see CIGNE.

clavel, *nail*. See AUS CLAVEAUS. *Syn.*: POINT[2].

clef, *key* (Fig. 268). *D* 166: od treis clefs; *CP* 93: au chef [*sic*, for a la clef]. *Note*: on the error in *CP*, consult Prinet CP, p. 31 n. 1.

clistire, see BENDE A COTICES.

cloué de poinz el baston, *the bend orna-mented with nails*. *TA*, vv. 1628–31:

> A .i. baston de penitance,
> Cloé par grant devocïon
> De dous poinz par componcïon
> El baston, qui bien i avint.

Note: cf. AUS CLAVEAUS, FERRETÉ.

coc, *cock* (Fig. 179). *B* 167: a trois cockes (*Bl* 167 [171]: od trois coks); *Cl/Cd* 97: a .iii. cos (*C* 97, see LION RAMPANT). *Note*: *Aspilogia II*, p. 184, note to item 85: 'cos [in *Cd/Cl* 97 (85)] . . . may be meant for

lions as in [*C* 97], but . . . seems nearer to the cocks which [*B* 167 (171)] attributes to William de Stuteville.' *P* 109 (= *C* 97) reads 'ove un leon rampant' instead of three cocks. For the female of the species, see GELINE.

coc ou quartier devant, *in dexter chief a cock*. *BA* 103 (A: coke), 104: a .i. cokes . . . u quartier devant. *Note*: refers to position only; see QUARTIER DEVANT[2].

coe, *tail*. See COUE.

coignet, *corner* (Fig. 15). The complete blazon reads as follows: *CP* 38: Mesire Renaut de Prechenig porte les armes fessié d'or et d'asur et contrefescié et bandé au coigniet gironné et a un escuchon d'argent ou milieu. *Syn.*: see CORNIER. *Note*: on the Pressigny arms, consult Prinet CP, p. 15 n. 2, and cf. *BA* 256, 257; *WB* 511. OFr. *coignet* is a derivative of Lat. *cuneus* 'wedge, corner' + the diminutive suffix *-ittum*.

coleré, *collared*. See LION COLERÉ.

colier, *collar* (Figs. 136, 157). See LEVRIER OD LE COLIER, LEVRIER OU LE COLIER, LION A UN COLIER, LION ET A UN COLIER, LION RAMPANT A UN COLIER, LION RAMPANT OD UN COLIER. *Note*: cf. COLERÉ.

collered, *collared*. See LION COLERÉ.

colour, *tincture*. See COULEUR.

com, *as, like*. See AINSI COM, ARMES TELS COM . . . MES QUE, AUTANT DE L'UN COM DE L'AUTRE, AUTEL COM, AUTELS ARMES COM, AUTELS ARMES COM SON PERE, AUTRETEL COM, AUTRETEL COM SON PERE, AUTRETELS CONOISSANCES COM, ITEL SI COM, TEL COM . . . FORS QU'AU CRESTEL EGLES AVOIT, TEL COM . . . FORS QU'EL CRESTEL EGLES AVOIT, TEL COM . . . FORS QU'EL QUARTIER EGLEZ AVOIT.

combatre, *to fight*. *TA*, vv. 568–9:

> .I. dëablel et .i. sarpent
> Vi combatre enmi la baniere.

Note: contemporary French heraldists pre-fer *affronté*. E. *counter-rampant* is a synonym for *combatant*; Fr. *contre-rampant*, however, today describes two animals which are ad-dorsed (see ADOSSÉ); cf. LIONCEAUS PASSANZ L'UN CONTRE L'AUTRE EN CHIEF.

comte, see ARMES LE CONTE.

conoissance[1], *arms or distinctive device on a heraldic shield*. See AUTRETELS CONOISSANCES,

AUTRETELS CONOISSANCES COM, CHANGIER LA CONOISSANCE, PAR CONOISSANCE[1], SANS AUTRE CONOISSANCE, SANS CONOISSANCE NULE. *Syn.*: DESCONOISSANCE[1]. *Note*: cf. DESPAREIL[2]. Used frequently in both the singular and the plural since the earliest times, e.g. *Roland*, v. 3090: 'Escuz unt genz, de multes cunoisances'. On this term, consult Bouly de Lesdain, p. 196; Schirling, p. 21. On protoheraldic terminology in the *Roland*, see J. Marchand, 'L'art héraldique d'après la littérature du Moyen Age. Les origines: la *Chanson de Roland*', *Moyen Age*, xlvii (1937), 37–43; for the term under consideration here, see, especially, J. Harris, '"Munjoie" and "Reconuisance" in *Chanson de Roland*, l. 3620', *RPh.*, x (1957), 168–73. The various meanings ascribed to OFr. *conoissance* are also listed in Tobler–Lommatzsch, ii. 703–4. In *Lancelot propre*, iii. 407, the red silk pennant which Guenevere sent Lancelot is said to have been 'la premiere connoissance qui onques fust portee au tans le roi Artu sor hiaume'; cf. MANCHE, *Note*. According to Wagner, *Heralds and Heraldry*, p. 158: 'H. Ellis Tomlinson in an unpublished thesis on "the historical development of heraldic terms with especial consideration of armes parlantes", 1942, shows by a series of quotations that *enseigne* and *conoissance* originally meant lance flag and much the same as *gunfainun* and *penuncel.*'

conoissance[2], *difference*. See PAR CONOISSANCE[2]. *Syn.*: see DESCONOISSANCE[2].

conoissances autretels, *the same arms.* *Perlesvaus*, p. 196: a conoissances autretex. *Syn.*: see AUTEL[1]. *Note*: cf. AUTRETELS CONOISSANCES.

conoistre, *to recognize.* (1) *a coat of arms.* *Charrete*, vv. 5823–4:

> Ensi devisent et deboissent
> Les armes de ces qu'il conoissent;

Partonopeu, appendix II, v. 292: Et par les armes conneü; *Durmart*, vv. 6884–6:

> Bon chevalier d'ancise pris
> Et qui des armes conissoient
> Delés les dames se seoient;

Lancelot propre, iii. 259: Ches enseignes connois je bien; *Sone*, v. 1389: les escus

connistera; v. 9024: connissoit son escu; v. 13251: Ces escus nous connisterés; *Escanor*, vv. 5565–7:

> Mais dites moi se connoissiez
> Cel escu d'or a .iii. lyonz
> De geules . . .

Syn.: RECONOISTRE. (2) *a person by his coat of arms.* *Cligés*, v. 3488: Qui por les armes nel conoissent; *Horn*, v. 4485: Bien i ad conu Horn al gripun del escu; *Durmart*, v. 7009: Lors le conoissent mainte gent; *Perlesvaus*, pp. 195, 198: conoistre; p. 289: je ne voil mie que vos soiez coneüz as armes; *Lancelot propre*, iii. 166: Je le connois bien as armes; *Queste*, p. 52: conoissent; p. 56: connurent; *Mort Artu*, p. 15: il ne connurent pas li uns l'autre; pp. 75, 78, 97: connoistre; p. 256: connut; *Cassidorus*, i. 255: et congnut Cassidorus a l'enseigne de son glaive; *Sone*, v. 15242: As armes bien se connissoit; *Des Deux Bordeors*, vv. 2–4, 7–8, 13–14:

> Ge connois monseignor Hunaut
> Et monseignor Rogier Ertaut,
> Qui porte un escu a quartiers;
> .   .   .   .   .   .
> Ge connois monseignor Begu,
> Qui porte un escu a breteles;
> .   .   .   .   .   .
> Si connois Renaut Brise-teste,
> Qui porte un chat en son escu;

TC, v. 1974: A ses armez bien le cognois; *CC*, vv. 710–11:

> As armes vous connisterons.
> Dou connoistre estons asseür.

(3) *an armorial banner.* *K*, vv. 296–7, 341–4:

> Le roi son bon seignour connoie
> Sa baniere mout honouree.
> .   .   .   .   .   .
> Cele au conte de Laönois
> Rouge o un blanc lyoun conois
> E blanche en estoit le ourleüre
> A roses de l'enchampeüre.

Note: I am indebted to Prof. Richard F. O'Gorman of the University of Iowa for pointing out the reference to *Des Deux Bordeors Ribauz* to me.

conte, see ARMES LE CONTE, ARMES LE CONTE OD.

conte de Dreux, see ARMES LE CONTE DE DREUX.

contichié, see COTICIÉ.

contre, see L'UN CONTRE L'AUTRE.

contrebendé de . . . et de . . ., *party per pale and barry counterchanged (the tinctures of the bars are reversed as they cross the middle of the shield resulting in a party and varied field)* (Fig. 22). The complete blazon reads as follows: *BA* 256: Renax de Pressingny (A: Pressigny), l'escu contrebendé d'or et d'azur a .i. escuchon d'argent au kief estakié as cornés geronnés. Baneres (A: Banneret) et de Toraine (A: de Torayne). *Syn.*: see FESSIÉ DE . . . ET DE . . . ET CONTREFESSIÉ. *Note*: cf. BENDÉ DE . . . ET DE . . .[2] and see FESSIÉ DE . . . ET DE . . . ET CONTREFESSIÉ.

contrefaire, *to make similar arms.* Lancelot propre, v. 205: li chevaliers en avoit fait contrefaire .i. autel comme Lioniaus portoit.

contrefait, *referring to misappropriated arms.* Destruction de Rome, vv. 1003–4:

Si changerons nos armes et nos escus
    bouclers,
Les contrefaites armes vesterons del
    cité.

contrefessié, see FESSIÉ DE . . . ET DE . . . ET CONTREFESSIÉ.

contremont, *upward.* See LION RAMPANT CONTREMONT. *Syn.*: AMONT. *Note*: pleonasm; cf. CONTREVAL.

contreval, *downward.* See ESTACHIÉ CONTREVAL DE . . . ET DE . . . *Note*: antonym of CONTREMONT, but here a pleonasm.

coponé de . . . et de . . ., *compony, gobony.* See COUPONÉ DE . . . ET DE . . .

coquefabue, *fictitious animal.* Hem, vv. 1068–75:

'Se tu veus mes armes aprendre
A deviser, eles sont d'or,
Et se tu veus sonner ce cor,
Le surplus t'en deviserai.
Tu vois c'unes armes d'or ai,
A coquefabues vermeilles.
— Par foi, or oi ge grans merveilles',
Fait li vallés, 'vous me mokiés'.

Note: these verses blazon an imaginary shield which Count Robert II of Artois pretends in jest to be carrying. OFr.

coquefabue, a hapax, is doubtless related to the family of words designating fictitious animals, chief among which is *coquecigrue,* said to be a kind of bird. The term is first attested in 1532 in Rabelais's *Pantagruel* (ed. V. L. Saulnier [Paris, 1946], p. 65) and was translated by Urquhart as *cocklicrane.* See Hem, pp. xxxv and 146. Godefroy, ii. 293, cites a heraldic use of the related term *coqbasile* in the fourteenth-century Arthurian romance *Perceforest.* The Count of Artois, who in *Hem* disguises himself as the Chevalier au Lion, bore in reality *azure semy of fleurs-de-lis or, a label gules semy of castles or*; see *WB* 760 and Prinet WR, p. 230, item 15. Henry, p. 134, note to verse 1073, omits mention of the label.

coquille, *escallop* (Fig. 211). (1) *position of the escallop is specified.* See CHIEF ENDENTÉ ENTÉ D'UNE COQUILLE, CHIEF OU OT UNE COQUILLE, COQUILLE EN LA BENDE, COQUILLE EN LA CROIS, COQUILLE EN LA FESSE. (2) *semy of escallops* (Fig. 39). See A COQUILLES SEMÉ. (3) *position or number of escallops not specified.* A. *escallop is the only charge.* CP 27: a trois coquilles; *K,* v. 338: o cokilles. B. *on a bend an escallop.* Hem, v. 3093: a cinc quoquilles, see BENDE[1] (3) B. *Syn.*: see BENDÉ A UNE COQUILLETE. C. *on a saltire an escallop.* CC, v. 1529: cinq cokilles, see SAUTOIR. D. *escallops in cross* (Fig. 110). See CROIS DE COQUILLES. *Syn.*: see ESCHALOPE.

coquille en la bende, *on a bend an escallop.* BA 39: a .iii. koquilles . . . en le bende. *Syn.*: see BENDÉ A UNE COQUILLETE. *Note*: refers to BENDE[1] (3) A.

coquille en la crois, *on a cross an escallop.* BA 242: a .v. cokilles . . . en le croix (A: crois); *TC,* vv. 759–61:

Un escu d'or a la crois noire,
Et en la crois, si com j'espoire,
Avoit cinq coquilles d'argent;

CP 36: a cinq coquilles . . . en la crois, see EGLES ES QUATRE QUARTIERS; 49: a cinq coquilles . . . en la croix; 50, 51: a cinq coquilles . . . en la crois. *Syn.*: COQUILLETE EN LA CROIS, ESCHALOPES EN LA CROIS. *Note*: cf. CROIS DE COQUILLES, indicating position only.

coquille en la fesse, *on a fess an escallop.* BA 46, 105 (A: la), 160 (A: la): a .iii.

cokilles . . . en le faisse. *Note*: cf. FESSE OU
ESCHALOPES.

coquillete, *escallop* (Fig. 211). See BENDÉ
A UNE COQUILLETE, COQUILLETE EN LA CROIS.
Syn.: see COQUILLE.

coquillete en la crois, *on a cross an
escallop*. *CC*, vv. 1428–9: en le crois . . . / Cinq
cokillettes. *Syn.*: see COQUILLE EN LA CROIS.
Note: for complete blazon, see CEZ CHOSES.

cor, *hunting-horn* (Fig. 266). (1) *alone on the
field*. *BA* 119: a .iii. cors. (2) *on a chief*.
Escanor, vv. 3637–42:

> Li rois de Serre, jones honz,
> Qui hardis ers come lyonz
> Et avoit armes mult diverses:
> Les droites armes des Traverses,
> Vermeilles a .ii. vaches d'or
> Au chief d'asur a .i. blanc cor.

Note: see OLIFANT. The modern French
heraldic equivalent is *huchet*. *Escanor*, v. 3642,
refers to CHIEF A UN COR.

corbeau, *raven* (Fig. 202). *B* 194: deux cor-
beaux (*Bl* 194 [198]: od deux corbeux).
Syn.: CORBIN.

corbin, *raven* (Fig. 202). *D* 62: a deus cor-
byns; *H* 27: ou deux corbins (*Hg* 27:
a trois corbins). *Syn.*: CORBEAU. *Note*:
H 27 (not *Hg* 27) is correct; Corbet's seal
shows two ravens in pale (Gough H,
p. 134, note to item 27; *Aspilogia II*, p. 154,
note to item 198). OFr. *corbin* (< Lat.
corvinum) is a diminutive of OFr. *corbeau*.

corneille, *crow* (Fig. 180). *Cleomadés*, vv.
11323–5 (alluding to the arms of Bleo-
patris):

> Qui erent d'or a trois corneilles
> Noires; s'orent testes vermeilles
> Les corneilles, çai entendu.

cornet, *corner* (Fig. 15). *BA* 256: as cornés.
For complete blazon, see CONTREBENDÉ
DE . . . ET DE . . . *Syn.*: see CORNIER.

cornier, *corner* (Fig. 15). The complete
blazons read as follows: *B* 32: Roger de
Mortimer, barré a cheif palee a corners
geroné d'or et d'azur a ung escuchon
d'argent (*Bl* 32, see CORNIERE[1]); *H* 67:
Sr Roger de Mortymer port barré d'or et
d'azure ou le chef palee et les corners geruné ou ung eschuchun d'ermyne (*Hg* 67
[68]: Roger de Mortimer porte d'or et

d'asure barré od le chef palé et les corners
geruné a un escuchonn d'erminn). *Syn.*:
CHANTEL[4], COIGNET, CORNET, CORNIERE[1].
Note: *P* 73 (= *B* 32): 'Roger Mortymer
port d'azure ove troys barres d'or ove
trois pens [*sic*, for peus] recopez deux
d'azure un d'or ove les cornors gerunés
ove un escuchon d'argent.'

corniere[1], *corner* (Fig. 15). The complete
blazons read as follows: *Bl* 32: Roger de
Mortymer bendé a chief palé a corneres
geronné [d'or et d'azur] ove un escucheon
[d'argent] (*B* 32, see CORNIER). *K*, vv. 435–
42:

> E puis Rogiers de Mortemer,
> Ki deça mer et dela mer,
> A porté quel part ke ait alé
> L'escu barré au chief palé,
> E les cornieres gyronnees,
> De or et de asur enluminees,
> O le escuchon vuidié de ermine,
> Ovoec les autres se achemine.

Syn.: see CORNIER. *Note*: *corniere* is the feminine form of OFr. *cornier* 'corner, angle',
a derivative of VL **corna* (< CL *cornua*,
the neuter plural form of *cornu* 'horn',
taken for a feminine singular), not Fr.
cornée 'cornea', as suggested by *Aspilogia II*,
glossary, p. 228. It refers to the canton and
sinister canton, i.e. subordinaries set off
from the field by right angles, and should
not be confused with the modern French
heraldic term *cornière* which designates the
rare horseshoe-shaped charge with curved
ends believed by some to represent a kettle-
handle (Veyrin-Forrer, p. 95). According
to the *Larousse du XXᵉ siècle*, the only
instance of the latter charge occurs in the
arms of the Villiers de l'Isle-Adam family
where it is used for differencing.

corniere[2], *corner* (Fig. 134). See EN CHAS-
CUNE CORNIERE SEIT UN PIÉ. *Note*: refers to
position only, viz. the three points of the
shield in the dexter chief, sinister chief,
and base respectively.

corniere[3], *sinister chief* (Fig. 2). See ESCUÇON
OVE UN LION COURONÉ EN LA CORNIERE,
ESCUÇON OVE UN LION RAMPANT COURONÉ
EN LA CORNIERE. *Syn.*: CHIEF[1] (2) B. I.,
Note (3), QUARTIER[4]. *Note*: for the dexter
chief, see CHIEF[3].

cotice, *cotice*, *narrow bend*. (1) *used in pairs*,

one on either side of a bend (Fig. 61). See
BENDE A COTICES, BENDE ENTREALEE DE
DEUS COTICES LIONCEAUS EN RAMPANT ASIS
AU DEHORS, BENDE ET A DEUS COTICES,
BENDE OD DEUS COTICES, BENDE OU LION-
CEAUS OU DEUS COTICES, LIONCEAUS A UNE
BENDE A DEUS COTICES, LIONCEAUS A UNE
BENDE ET DEUS COTICES, LIONCEAUS A UNE
BENDE OD DEUS COTICES, LIONCEAUS OD
UNE BENDE ET DEUS COTICES, LIONCEAUS
OU UNE BENDE ET A DEUS COTICES, LION-
CEAUS OVE UNE BENDE A DEUS COTICES. (2)
used in multiples as the principal charge (Fig.
76). The complete blazons read as follows:
CP 32: Mesire Gui de la Roche porte les
armes d'or a cinq cotices d'asur et a une
bordure de gueulles; 104: Mesire de
Denisi porte les armes d'or a trois cotices
noires. *Syn.*: for (1), LISTE[1], LISTEL (cf. also
COTICIÉ); for (2), see BENDE[1]. *Note*: cf.
BENDE ENLISTEE A DEUS BASTONS ENCOSTE.
For the double cotice, see JUMEAUS[1].
Heralds in England restricted the term
cotice to denote the narrow stripes placed
on either side of a bend, while their counterparts in France also used it to describe
narrow bends without any accompanying
charge. LISTEL (in *BA*) is the only term
used to designate a *fess* cotised; see BENDE
A DEUS LISTEAUS[2]. For a fess *double-cotised*,
however, see JUMEAUS[1] and LISTE[3]. The
double cotice is used only with the fess in
our examples. OFr. *cotice* 'leather thong'
(used as a shoe-lace, a whip, or for tying
various objects) is attested as early as 1213–
14 (*Faits des Romains*, i. 736), and it is clear
that the heraldic cotice is merely a stylized
leather band. The traditional derivation
from Lat. *costa* 'side' or 'rib' suggested by
the meaning listed above under paragraph
(1) should be discarded in favour of the
hypothetical Latin form **cuticia* (< Lat.
cutis 'skin, leather') 'leather thong' modelled
on Lat. *pellicia* (< Lat. *pellis* 'animal
skin') > OFr. *pelice* 'fur coat'. See Brault,
'Cotice', and cf. LOIER. For OFr. *frestel*
'ribbon' in this sense, see *Navarre* 603:
Le comte de Champaigne, d'azur a une
bende d'argent a .ii. fresteaux d'or poten-
chiez'. See also AUTRETEL, *Note*. Cotices
may be diapered (see BENDE A COTICES) or
ornamented with a stylized flower (see
BENDE A LISTES FLEURETEES).

coticié, *cotised*. See BENDE COTICIEE, BENDE
ENTRE LIONCEAUS COTICIEE. *Note*: cf. CO-
TICE (1).

cotrises, see LIONCEAUS OU UNE BENDE A
DEUS COTICES.

coue, *tail*. *TA*, vv. 616–17:

> Par mi rampoit misires Nobles
> A une queue bobenciere.

For another use, see DOUBLE COUE. *Note*:
see CROIS FOURCHIEE AU KANEE, *Note*.

coue croisiee, *forked tail crossed in saltire*. See
LION RAMPANT A LA COUE CROISIEE COURONÉ,
LION RAMPANT A LA COUE CROISIEE
ET COURONÉ. *Syn.*: COUE FOURCHIEE[2], COUE
FOURCHIEE EN SOM, COUE FOURCHUE.

coue double, *forked tail*. See LION DONT
DIOMS LA COUE DOUBLE. *Syn.*: see COUE
FOURCHIEE[1].

coue en double, *forked tail*. See LION RAM-
PANT DONT LA COUE S'ESPANT EN DOUBLE.
Syn.: see COUE FOURCHIEE[1].

coue fourchiee[1], *forked tail*. See LION A LA
COUE FOURCHIEE[1], LION ET LA COUE FOUR-
CHIEE, LION LI CHIEF COURONÉ COUE FOUR-
CHIEE, LION RAMPANT A LA COUE FOUR-
CHIEE[1], LION RAMPANT ET LA COUE
FOURCHIEE, LION RAMPANT OD LA COUE
FOURCHIEE[1]. *Syn.*: COUE DOUBLE, COUE EN
DOUBLE, DOUBLE COUE. *Note*: early blazons, whether describing shields verbally
or depicting them visually, frequently pay
little attention to the tail. Thus, a beast
described as a *lion rampant* may or may not
have a forked tail and the phrase *lion
rampant a la coue fourchiee* may refer to a lion
rampant whose tail is not only forked but
also crossed in saltire. See, for example,
the diversity in the blazons of the lion in
the arms of the Dukes of Limburg (Prinet
CC, p. 164 n. 7; cf. *WB* 619).

coue fourchiee[2], *forked tail crossed in saltire*.
See LIEPART RAMPANT A LA COUE FOUR-
CHIEE, LIEPART RAMPANT OVE LA COUE
FOURCHIEE, LION A LA COUE FOURCHIEE[2],
LION COURONÉ LA COUE FOURCHIEE, LION
RAMPANT A LA COUE FOURCHIEE[2], LION
RAMPANT OD LA COUE FOURCHIEE[2]. For
another use, see COUE FOURCHIEE EN SOM.
Syn.: see COUE CROISIEE.

coue fourchiee en som, *forked tail crossed
in saltire*. See LION A LA COUE FOURCHIEE
EN SOM. *Syn.*: see COUE CROISIEE.

coue fourchue, *forked tail crossed in saltire.* See LION A LA COUE FOURCHUE. *Syn.*: see COUE CROISIEE.

couleur, *tincture. Cligés,* v. 3987: Ne n'i ot color ne pointure; *K,* v. 188: Baner ot de rouge colour; v. 565: De inde coulour (W: colour). For other uses, see D'UNE COULEUR, D'UNE COULEUR FORS, D'UNE COULEUR FORS TANT QUE, ESQUARTELÉ DE QUATRE COULEURS DE . . . ET DE . . . ET DE . . . ET DE . . . *Syn.*: TAINT. *Note*: cf. the following pleonastic use in *Joufroi,* v. 2525: A dous aigles de verz colors.

couleuré, *tinctured. K,* vv. 167–8:

> Cil ot baner eschequeree,
> De blanc e rouge coulouré.

Syn.: TAINT².

coulouré, *tinctured.* See COULEURÉ.

coupe, *cup (large covered goblet with stem and foot)* (Fig. 253). *D* 140: a treis cupes. *Syn.*: HANAP. *Note*: Matthew Paris (Pusikan, p. 149) blazons the arms of the same family (Argentine) as follows: 'Scutum de gules, cuppae argenteae'.

couponé de . . . et de . . ., *compony, gobony (referring to a baston or bend cut into square sections of alternating tinctures)* (Fig. 12). *BA* 173: couponné (incomplete blazon); *C* 69: gobony de . . . et de . . . (*Cl/Cd* 69: goboné de . . . et de . . .); *CPA* 3: coponé de . . . et de . . .; 146: coponné de . . . et de . . .; *M* 4, 25: de . . . et de . . . goboné; 19: goboné de . . . et de . . .; 49: de . . . et de . . . goubonez. *Syn.*: TRONÇONÉ DE . . . ET DE . . . *Note*: of the many etymologies proposed (e.g. *OED,* s.v. *gobony*: 'OFr. *gobon,* an unrecorded form'; Littré, i. 702, s.v. *componé*: 'le latin *componere,* disposer'; Dauzat, s.v. *compon*: 'subst. verbal de l'anc. fr. *compondre* [XIVe s.], disposer, régler [du Lat. *componere,* v. COMPOTE], peut-être avec infl. de *coupon*'), that provided by W. von Wartburg (*FEW,* iv. 180), i.e. VL *colpus* > OFr. *cop* 'blow' > OFr. *couper* 'to cut' > OFr. *coupon* 'tailored piece of cloth' > OFr. *couponer* 'to cut into squares', is clearly the only acceptable explanation.

courant, *running.* See LIEPART COURANT, LIEPART COURANT ET COURONÉ, LIONCEL COURANT. *Note*: cf. PASSANT¹.

courone, *crown* (Fig. 252). *Lancelot propre,* iii. 421: a .iii. corones . . . et des corones tant que l'en i pooit metre; *BA* 132: a une coronne; *Cleomadés,* v. 737: a trois coronnes noires. For other uses, see A COURONES, COURONÉ D'UNE COURONE, CROIS OD UNE COURONE, DES COURONES TANT QUE L'ON I POUVOIT METRE, LION RAMPANT ET COURONE. *Note*: for an example of real crowns borne as quasi-heraldic arms, see CHAPEL DE ROSES, *Note.*

couroné, *crowned.* See CHIEF A UN DEMI LION ET COURONÉ AU CHIEF, EGLE COURONEE, ESCUÇON OVE UN LION RAMPANT COURONÉ EN LA CORNIERE, LIEPART COURONÉ, LIEPART COURANT ET COURONÉ, LIEPART PASSANT COURONÉ, LIONCEL COURONÉ RAMPANT, LIONCEL RAMPANT COURONÉ, LION COURONÉ, LION COURONÉ LA COUE FOURCHIEE, LION COURONÉ A UNE CROIS SOR L'ESPAULE, LION LI CHIEF COURONÉ COUE FOURCHIEE, LION PASSANT COURONÉ, LION RAMPANT A LA COUE CROISIEE COURONÉ, LION RAMPANT A LA COUE CROISIEE ET COURONÉ, LION RAMPANT COURONÉ, LION RAMPANT COURONÉ A LA LANGUE A UNE MANCHE EN LA GEULE DU LION A UNE ESPEE AU PONG AU HELT QUI TRANCHE LE LION PAR MI, LION RAMPANT COURONÉ ESTANT SUS UNE MOTE, LION RAMPANT COURONÉ O DOUBLE COUE, LION RAMPANT COURONÉ SUS UNE MOTE, LION RAMPANT ET COURONÉ, RAMPANT LION COURONÉ. *Syn.*: COURONÉ D'UNE COURONE.

couroné d'une courone, *crowned.* See TESTE D'AUNE ET LA TESTE COURONEE D'UNE COURONE. *Syn.*: COURONÉ.

couvertures changier, *to change arms (as a disguise). Sone,* v. 9180: ses couvretures cangier; v. 12999: pour couvretures cangier. *Syn.*: see ARMES CHANGIER. *Note*: OFr. *couvertures* refers here to the horse-cloths which are ornamented with armorial bearings.

couwe, *chough* (?) (Fig. 178). See OD LES COUWES. *Syn.*: PIE.

cresté, *crested, crined.* See DRAGON CRESTÉ, LION CRESTÉ. *Note*: on the meaning of this term, see TESTE D'UN DRAGON CRESTÉ, *Note.* In modern heraldic terminology, Fr. *crêté* is used when a cock or dolphin has a comb of a different tincture. English heraldry utilizes the kindred expression *crested* (or *combed*) when referring to the cock, *crined* when to a lion's mane, a boar's bristles, or to various other protuberances from the head, such as a dragon's crest.

cresteaus, see CRESTEL.

crestel, *canton* (Fig. 117). See TEL COM . . . FORS QU'AU CRESTEL EGLES AVOIT, TEL COM . . . FORS QU'EL CRESTEL EGLES AVOIT. *Syn.*: see CHANTEL[1]. *Note*: the corresponding blazon in *SCK* provides the reading *quartiers*; see TEL COM . . . FORS QU'EL QUARTIER EGLEZ AVOIT. *Crestel* in *SCT/SCV* may be related to OFr. *crestel* 'crenel (one of the square openings alternating with the merlons in a battlement)'. A canton does bear a certain resemblance to a crenel. The original reading, however, may simply have been *chantel*.

creté, see CRESTÉ.

crochet, *(iron)* hook (Fig. 267). *TA*, v. 541: A .i. crochet de dampnement. *Syn.*: CROCHET DE FER.

crochet de fer, *iron hook* (Fig. 267). *TA*, v. 595: a crochet de fer. *Syn.*: CROCHET. *Note*: refers to FER[2]. Here a devil's instrument (illustration based on medieval iconography only; for the chief varieties of heraldic hooks, consult Gough–Parker, pp. 330–1).

crochu, *grasping.* See MEIN CROCHUE.

crois[1], *plain cross* (Fig. 106). (1) *the cross bears no charge. Fouque de Candie*, v. 10402: Et cele croiz; *Perlesvaus*, pp. 49: e une croiz; pp. 64, 140, 190 (2), 191, 199, 208: a une croiz; p. 110: Li escuz ou la . . . croiz estoit; pp. 145, 191, 201, 209: a la croiz; p. 201 (var.): a une crois; p. 262: la croiz en l'escu Perlesvaus; p. 371: la croiz en son escu; p. 374: la croiz . . . que il portoit en son escu; p. 387: la croiz; *Lancelot propre*, iv. 175: a une . . . crois; *Queste*, p. 28: a une croiz; p. 32: une croiz; pp. 51, 196: a la croiz; *Estoire*, p. 48: une crois; p. 62: a une . . . crois; *Vulgate Merlin Sequel*, p. 383: a la crois, see DRAGON AU DESOUS DE LA CROIS; p. 384: et une crois; p. 390: as . . . crois; *Chevalier au Cygne*, v. 1407: Qu'il ne fiere en la crois ou la coulors rougie; v. 1515: en la crois; v. 1946: a crois; v. 2180: a la crois; *TA*, v. 1268: A une grant croiz; v. 1627: A une croiz de pacïence; *BA* 41, 107, 266: a une croix; 186: et le crois (A: a la crois); *B* 6: a ung crois (*Bl* 6: ove une croix); 128: a la croix (*Bl* 128 [132]: od la crois); 101: ung

crois (*Bl* 101: ove une crois); *Bl*, Upsale [106]: croix; *C* 91 (*Cl* 91: a un croiz; *Cd* 91: a une crosse), 151 (*Cl* 151: a une croyz; *Cd* 151, see CROIS ENTRE EGLEZ): un crois; *D* 1, 110: a une croiz; 39, 41, 184: od une croiz; *TC*, vv. 1098, 1410, 1975: a la crois; v. 1583: une crois; v. 3237: A une crois; *CP* 23: a une crois; 136, a crois (see *Note*); *CC*, v. 1409: a le . . . crois; v. 1432: a une crois. (2) *the cross bears no charge but separates multiple charges. B* 46: la croix (*Ba* 46: a la croiz; *Bb* 46: a crosse; *Bc* 46, see CROIS A LIONCEAUS; *Bl* 46, see CROIS ET LIONCEAUS), see LIONCEL; *C* 150: un crois, see LION RAMPANT (*Cl* 150, see CROIS A LIONS RAMPANZ; *Cd* 150, see CROIS A EGLES); Chevreuse (addition in *Cd* [110] only): a crosse, see LIONS RAMPANZ ON THE QUARTERS OF THE FIELD; *CP* 10: a une crois, see EGLES ES QUATRE QUARTIERS; 13: a une crois, see EGLES ES QUATRE QUARTIERS; 20: a une crois, see LIONS ES QUATRE QUARTIERS; *CPA* 151: a la crois, see LION[1]. For other uses, see CROIS A EGLES, CROIS A MERLOZ, CROIS ENTRE EGLEZ. *Syn.*: EN LES QUATRE QUARTIERS. *Note*: see ENTRE, *Note*. (3) *the cross bears a charge. B* 193: ung crois (*Bl* 193 [197]: od trois croix), see ESCHALOPE EN LA CROIS; *TC*, v. 759: a la crois, see COQUILLE EN LA CROIS; *CP* 49–51: a une crois, see COQUILLE EN LA CROIS; *CC*, v. 1426: une crois, see COQUILLETE EN LA CROIS; *H* 72: ou la croys (*Hg* 72 [73]: od la croyz), see MOLET EN LA CROIS. *Note*: the locution EN LA CROIS is always used. For another use, see CROIS OD UNE COURONE. On the erroneous blazon in *Bl* 193 [197], see *Aspilogia II*, p. 154, note to item 197: 'probably in taking the item from the 1240 collection the 1253 compiler misread *un* as *iij* and therefore wrote *trois*. A similar mistake may well account for William Sarren's unsatisfactory *trois croix*' (see CROIS[2], *Note*). (4) *the cross is charged and separates multiple charges. BA* 242: a .i. croix, see COQUILLE EN LA CROIS, CROIS A EGLES; *CP* 36: a une crois, see COQUILLE EN LA CROIS, EGLES ES QUATRE QUARTIERS. *Syn.*: CROIS EL MILIEU, CROIS PAR LE MILIEU, CROIS PASSANT, CROIS PLAINE, CROIS SANS PLUS. *Note*: on the terminology of the cross, see Brault, 'The Cross'. The cross appears at the dawn of heraldry in the arms of Savoy; see *Aspilogia II*, p. 66, note to item 40. The complete blazon for *D* 1, which is defective, reads as follows: '. . . rlm porte le escu de argent a une croiz de or cruselé de or.' The painted shield corresponding to this blazon is erased except for the caption 'Le rey de Ier'l'm', making it impossible to determine the form of the cross. The arms of Jerusalem are usually given as *argent, a cross potent between four crosslets or*. On the origin of these arms, the shape of the cross, and the unorthodox use here of metal on metal (see above, p. 18 n. 4, and below, s.v. SOR, *Note*; *Aspilogia II*, p. 107; *Dean Tract*, p. 27), see G. Bellew, 'The Arms of the Kingdom of Jerusalem', *Coat of Arms*, i (1950), 25–6; C. G. P. J., 'Further Notes on the Arms of the Kingdom of Jerusalem', i. 47–8, and (same title) by A. W. B. Messenger, i (1951), 195; the discussion was continued in letters to the editor by H. P. Cotman, i (1951), 246; C. H. Hunter Blair, i. 287–8; and S. C. Kaines Smith, ii (1952), 38. I should merely like to add that the earliest illustration of the arms of Jerusalem is not, as C. H. Hunter Blair maintains, on the episcopal seal of Louis de Beaumont, Bishop of Durham (1318–30), but in the thirteenth-century rolls. Since the type of cross has intrigued scholars, I note a plain cross in the Matthew Paris Shields (Hauptmann, pp. 45–6, figs. 6, 69, 85; later examples discussed on p. 47 and illustrated in figs. 89–90; *Aspilogia II*, pp. 12–13, items 6, 7, 12; p. 15, item 20; p. 23, item 53; p. 36, items 101 and 1), a cross crosslet in *WB* 1259, and a cross potent in *HE* 2 and *G* 70. For the earliest attestation of the cross potent in blazon, see CROIS BILLETEE. According to Prinet CP, p. 44 n. 3, the blazon for Joffroi le Bornie (*CP* 136) is incomplete; the cross should properly be charged with escallops. Entry would then appear here in paragraph (3). For the crosspiece or horizontal part of the cross, see PASSANT[3]; the ends or tips of the charge are termed BOUZ. See also CROIS FOURCHIEE AU KANEE, *Note*. For another locution for a plain cross in the *Dean Tract* (*crois entiere sans nule diversité*), see ENTIER[2], *Note*.

crois[2], *small cross, cross couped* (Fig. 95). *Huon de Bordeaux*, vv. 4791–6:

> Les armes voit dont il ert adoubés:
> Une crois d'or de grant nobilité;
> Trois en i ot, ce saciés par vreté,
> Dedens ses armes, moult ricement
>   ouvré.
> Si tost qel voit la pucele au vis cler,
> Sot bien qu'il ert de France le rené;

B 160: a trois crois (*Bl* 160 [164]: od trois croix). *Syn.*: FER DE MOULIN.[2] *Note*: on the significance of the arms in *Huon de Bordeaux*, see my review of Ruelle's edition in *RR*, lv (1964), 207. On the Sarren arms (*B* 160), see *Aspilogia II*, p. 147, note to item 164: 'Neither version specifies the pattern of the crosses nor does the coat seem to occur elsewhere. Possibly *trois* is a mistake, *un* being misread as *iij*.' London mentions the erroneous blazon of *Bl* 193 [197] in this regard; see CROIS[1] (3), *Note*. For similar scribal errors in *M* 56 and *M* 65, see FESSE OU ESCHALOPES and QUARTELÉ DE . . . ET DE . . . EN LE CHANTEL DE . . . UNE MOLETE.

crois[3], *small cross* (Fig. 140). See LION COURONÉ A UNE CROIS SOR L'ESPAULE. *Note*: Prinet WR, pp. 226–7, item 6, and p. 227 n. 1, has suggested that the arms in question (Bohemia) resemble those borne by the descendants of Przemyslaw I of Poland, rulers of Bohemia in the thirteenth century. Prinet notes, however, that the latter bore *gules, a lion double-queued crossed in saltire argent* (to the evidence cited by Prinet in this connection, add *Navarre* 1260 ['Le roy de Brehaingne, de gueules a un lion d'argent rampant a la queue noire (*sic*, for nouee) et fourchie'] and *WB* 1266 [Adam-Even's blazon for *Le roy de Boeme*: 'De gueules au lion d'argent à la queue fourchée, passée en sautoir et nouée, couronnée d'or']), while Walford's Roll blazons the field as argent, the lion, sable. As we mentioned above, s.v. COUE FOURCHIEE[1], the tail is often neglected in early blazons and tinctures are occasionally reversed. What is notable about the description here is the addition of a cross which suggests a connection with the arms of Armenia, as in *WB* 1301 (fig. 109), blazoned by Adam-Even as follows: 'De gueules au léopard lionné couronné d'or, une croix patriarchale mouvant de son dos'. On the patriarchal cross in heraldry, see *Coat of Arms*, i (1951), 228, 284. See also CROIS A DEUS PASSANZ.

crois⁴, *in cross* (Fig. 110). See CROIS DE COQUILLES, LOSENGES EN LA CROIS. See also CROIS ENDENTEE[1], CROIS ENGRESLEE. *Syn.*: EN LA CROIS[2]. *Note*: refers to position only, multiple charges forming a cross.

crois⁵, *cross patonce* (Fig. 102). *Ba* 13: a une croyx (*B* 13, see CROIS PATEE; *Bb* 13, see below, *Note*; *Bc/Bl* 13: ove un croix); *Ba/Bc* 76: a une croiz (*B* 76, see CROIS PATONCE; *Bb* 76, see CROIS PLAINE; *Bl* 76, see CROIS FOURCHIEE[1]); *Cl* 50: a une croyz (*C* 50, see CROIS PATEE; *Cd* 50: a crosse). *Syn.*: see CROIS ESLARGIE PAR LES BOUZ. *Note*: *Bb* 13 features a trick which may be interpreted as either a cross patonce or a cross flory. On these arms (Earl of Aumale), see *Aspilogia II*, p. 117, note to item 13, and, especially, H. S. London, 'Pattee, Patonce and Formee', *Coat of Arms*, v (1958), no. 33, 359. The Vescy arms (*B* 76) are also discussed on that page, in v (1958), no. 34, 31, and see *Aspilogia II*, p. 129, item 76 (see CROIS FOURCHIEE[1]).

crois a deus passanz, *ghost word*. The complete blazon reads as follows: *C* 12: Le roy de Hungrey, d'or estenzelé a deux passans d'azure (*Cl* 12: Le roy de Hongerye, de or estenzelé a deus passanz d'azur; *Cd* 12: Le roy de Hugarie, de or estenzelé de gules a .ii. passanz roron [*sic*]). *Note*: cf. CROIS³. London, 'Scintillatum Auro', p. 112, notes that the patriarchal cross has been associated with Hungary since the early thirteenth century and emends *C* 12 to read as follows: 'd'or estenzelé *un crois* a deux passans d'azure'. In Brault, 'The Cross', p. 220, consequently, I recorded this example as an early expression for the patriarchal cross. In *Aspilogia II*, p. 169, note to item 11, however, London reverses his opinion, accepting a suggestion by Adam-Even that 'the missing word must be *leons* and that the blazon is really that of Denmark'. Since the arms of that kingdom (*or semy of hearts gules, three lions passant azure*) are attested as early as *c.* 1190, I concur with London who characterized Dr. Adam-Even's suggestion as 'certainly correct'. London emends *Cl* 12 to read 'estenzelé a deus leons passans [the MS.

actually provides the reading *passanz*]'. I suggest, however, that *deus* is a garbled form of *leuns* and that the missing word is *treis* 'three', a reading which conforms more exactly with the correct blazon, the only missing element now being the tincture (gules) of the sparks. In the *Aspilogia II* note, London has also suggested that the word after *passanz* in *Cd* 12 should be interpreted as *rormy*, possibly for *formy*. The term formy is rare in early blazon, however (see CROIS FORMEE, *Note*), and the word looks to me more like *roron* (for *coroné*?).

crois a egles, *cross cantoned with eagles*. *Cd* 150: a une crosse . . . a .iiii. egles (*C* 150, see CROIS[1] [2]; *Cl* 150, see CROIS A LIONS RAMPANZ). *Syn.*: CROIS ENTRE EGLEZ, EGLES ES QUATRE QUARTIERS. *Note*: cf. CROIS[1] (2), EGLE (2).

crois a lionceaus, *cross cantoned with lioncels rampant*. *Bc* 46: a la croyz . . . a quatre lionceus (*B/Ba/Bb* 46, see CROIS[1] [2]; *Bl* 46, see CROIS ET LIONCEAUS). *Syn.*: see CROIS[1] (2).

crois a lions rampanz, *cross cantoned with lions rampant*. *Cl* 150: a un croyz . . . a quatre liuns rampant (*C* 150, see CROIS[1] [2]; *Cd* 150, see CROIS A EGLES). *Syn.*: see CROIS[1] (2).

crois a merloz, *cross cantoned with martlets*. *D* 16: od une croiz . . . a quatre merloz. *Note*: refers to CROIS[1] (2).

crois billetee, *cross potent* (Fig. 103). *Cl*, Acre [14]: a une croyz . . . bylletté; *Cd*, Acre: a .i. croys . . . bylletté. *Note*: omitted in Brault, 'The Cross', this charge is correctly blazoned for the first time by London in *Aspilogia II*, pp. 169–70, item 14; see also p. 12, item 6. See CROIS[1], *Note*. The cross potent is blazoned as such in the *Dean Tract* (complete blazon provided s.v. BARGE).

crois de coquilles, *escallops in cross (the charges form a cross)* (Fig. 110). *BA* 108: a une croix de cokilles. *Note*: refers to CROIS⁴, indicating position only. Contrast with COQUILLE EN LA CROIS, COQUILLETE EN LA CROIS, ESCHALOPE EN LA CROIS.

croisel, see AUS CROISEAUS. *Syn.*: see CROISELE.

croisele, *crosslet* (Fig. 99). The complete blazon reads as follows: *B* 174: John de Nevill le Forrestier, d'or ung bende de goules croiselles noire (*Bl* 174 [178], see OD CROISELES). For other uses, see A CROISELES, A CROISELES SEMÉ, OD CROISELES, POUDRÉ A CROISELES. *Syn.*: CROISEL, CROISE-LET, CROISELETE, CROISETE, CROISIÉ[1], CROI-SILLE, PETITE CROISETE. *Note*: this term and its synonyms always refer to a semy field. Modern heraldry distinguishes between *plain crosslets* and the variants involved in fields blazoned *crusily botonny, crusily fitchy,* etc., where the ends of the crosslets are variously ornamented. No such distinction was drawn in early blazon which was indifferent to the considerable variety of crosses found in the earliest sources (compare, for example, *WB* 413, 519, 614, and 1208). Prinet WR, p. 230 n. 3: 'Il semble que le seul mot "croisile", ou "crusile", ait suffi à désigner la *croisette recroisetée au pied fiché* (et non une croisette quelconque).' See also Roger F. Pye, 'A Return to First Principles. V—Heraldry Eternal', *Coat of Arms*, vii (1963), no. 56, 338–9.

croiselé, *crusily* (Fig. 35). *B* 40: crusulé (*Bl* 40, see AUS CROISEAUS); 55 (*Ba* 55, see POUDRÉ A CROISELES; *Bb* 55, see A CROISELES SEMÉ; *Bc* 55, see A CROISILLES POUDRÉ A L'ESCU; *Bl* 55: croiselez), 140: croiselé (*Bl* 140 [144], see OD CROISELEZ); *C* 2: crusuly (*Cl/Cd* 2, see POUDRÉ A CROI-SILLES); *D* 1: cruselé; *H* 52, 53 (*Hg* 52 [54], 53 [51]: crosulé): croiselé; 62, 63: croyselé; 109: croyselee; *Hg*, Brewes [31], Engaine [64]: crosulé; *M* 42: crusulé. *Syn.*: A CROISELES, A CROISELES SEMÉ, A CROISELEZ, A CROISETES SEMÉ, A CROISILLES POUDRÉ A L'ESCU, AUS CROISEAUS, CROISETTÉ, CROI-SETTES OU . . ., CROISILLIÉ, CROISILLIÉ TOUT ENVIRON, ESTRE CROISILLIÉ, OD CROISELES, OD CROISELEZ, OD CROISILLES, OD LES CROISILLES, OU LES CROISELETES, POUDRÉ A CROISELES, POUDRÉ A CROISILLES, SEMÉ DE CROISETES. *Note*: generally followed by *de*; in *H* 62, 63, however, the preposition is omitted. Matthew Paris blazons a crusily field as 'multae cruces in campo' (Pusikan, p. 122). For *Hg*, Brewes, see AZUR, *Note*. Gough H, p. 144, note to item 63: 'The addition "croysele" in [*H* 62] is erroneous.'

croiselet, *crosslet* (Fig. 100). *B* 71: a croiselets. See A CROISELEZ, OD CROISELEZ. *Syn.*: see CROISELE.

croiselete, *crosslet* (Fig. 100). *H* 38: ou .iii.

cruselettez (*Hg* 38 [39], see ROSE[1]); *K*, vv. 181–4:

> Rogers de la Ware ovec eus,
> Uns chevalers sagis e preus,
> Ki les armes ot vermellettis
> O blonc lyoun e croissellettes.

For another use see OU LES CROISELETES. *Syn.*: see CROISELE. *Note*: Gough H, p. 138, note to item 39: 'The word "cruselettez" in [*H* 38] is an error'; see ROSE[1].

croiseleté, *crusily* (Fig. 35). *B* 175: crois-seletté (*Bl* 175 [179], see OD CROISILLES). *Syn.*: see CROISELÉ.

crois el milieu, *plain cross* (Fig. 106). *Vulgate Merlin Sequel,* p. 389: en chascune ot une crois vermeille el milieu. *Syn.*: see CROIS[1].

crois endentee[1], *lozenges conjoined in cross (the charges form a cross)* (Fig. 105). *BA* 74, 140 (A: endente): a une croix . . . endentee; 79, 80: a la crois . . . endentee. *Syn.*: CROIS ENGRESLEE, LOZENGES EN LA CROIS.

crois endentee[2], *plain cross ornamented with triangular points jutting from the edges forming an unbalanced and discontinuous line* (Fig. 108). *TC,* vv. 1766–9:

> De ce sui je bien sovenans
> Que ses escus d'azur estoit
> Et li atours que il vestoit,
> A une crois d'or endentee.

Note: refers to ENDENTÉ[3]. The miniaturist, who everywhere else is remarkably accurate in his blazons, doubtless erred in his rendering of this cross (see reproduction in Delbouille, Plate VIII, miniature 9). Delbouille, pp. xcvi–xcvii, saw in the fact that modern blazons of the arms of the Gymnich family specified a cross *engrailed* reason enough to place in doubt identification of the knight in question with this family. The terms *crois endentee* and *crois engreslee,* however, were synonymous in this period; the Gymnich arms, moreover, feature a *crois endentee* in the Bigot Roll (*BA* 79, 80; see above, s.v. CROIS ENDENTEE[1]). See also *WB* 662. A similar confusion doubtless accounts for the origin of the 'headless' cross and the cross raguly in the medieval treatises. The original blazon in Johannes de Bado Aureo, *Tractatus de Armis* (c. 1394, ed. Evan John Jones in

Medieval Heraldry [Cardiff, 1943], p. 125) specified a *crux truncata* or *crois recoupie* [= *recoupee*], i.e. a cross couped, one whose limbs do not touch the edge of the shield like the plain cross, but are cut short (this charge is sometimes referred to as a cross humetty). Certain illuminators, however, mistakenly showed this charge as a T-shaped or headless cross, while others depicted the limbs as tree-trunks with the branches couped, resulting in a cross raguly (Jones, Plate I, figs. *c* and *d*).

crois engreslee, *lozenges conjoined in cross (the charges form a cross)* (Fig. 105). *C* 94: un crois engrelé (*Cl* 94: a une croyz . . . engarlé; *Cd* 94: a crosse . . . engrelé); *D* 85: a une croiz engraslé; *CPA* 179, 180: a la crois . . . engreslee; *H* 74: ou la crois engrelee (*Hg* 74 [75]: od la croyz engreylee); 111: ou ung croys engrelé (*Hg* 111 [109]: a une croiz engreilé); *K*, v. 190: o crois . . . egreellie (W: engreelie); v. 803: O la crois . . . engreellie. *Syn.*: see CROIS ENDENTEE[1]. *Note*: on this term, see Brault, 'The Cross', pp. 218–19.

crois entre eglez, *cross cantoned with eagles*. *Cd* 151: une crosse . . . inter 6 [*sic*, for 16] aiglets (*C/Cl* 151, see POUDRÉ D'EGLES). *Syn.*: see CROIS A EGLES.

crois eslaisiee aus bouz, *cross formy throughout* (Fig. 98). The complete blazon reads as follows: *BA* 251: Esteilles de Mauny, l'escu noir a une croix blanche eslaisie a box a .i. baston de geules en beslive. De Torayne. *Syn.*: see CROIS ESLARGIE. *Note*: cf. CROIS FORMEE. Adam-Even identified the knight in question with a certain Etudes de Malo-Nido cited in a cartulary dated 1235, but provides no definition of the cross in these arms. OFr. *eslaisier* (< Lat. **exlatiare* < Lat. *latus* 'wide'), however, meant 'to widen, to expand', suggesting a connection with the two following items, especially the first, *Navarre* 750: 'Le sire de Roigie, de gueules a une croiz d'argent patee et *eslesee*'; 785: 'M. Boabbes de Rougie, de gueules a une croix d'argent *eslaisie* et empatee a un baton d'azur'. *BA* 251 is not mentioned by H. S. London in his important article entitled 'Pattee, Patonce, and Formee', *Coat of Arms*, v (1958), no. 33, 358–64; v (1958), no. 34, 26–33.

crois eslargie, *cross formy throughout* (Fig. 98). The complete blazon reads as follows: *CP* 142: Mesire de Rouchi porte les armes de gheules a une crois d'argent eslargie. *Syn.*: CROIS ESLAISIEE AUS BOUZ. *Note*: cf. CROIS FORMEE. On the Rougé family arms, see *Navarre* 750 (cf. also 785); Prinet CP, p. 46 n. 1; *WB* 954; and especially H. S. London, 'Pattee, Patonce, and Formee', *Coat of Arms*, v (1958), no. 34, 29–30.

crois eslargie par les bouz, *cross patonce* (Fig. 102). The complete blazon reads as follows: *CP* 107: Mesire Hardoin de la Haye porte les armes de gheules a une crois d'ermine eslargie par les bous. *Syn.*: CROIS[5], CROIS FOURCHIEE[1], CROIS FOURCHIEE AU KANEE, CROIS PATEE, CROIS PATONCE. See also CROIS FLEURETEE, *Note*. *Note*: on the De la Haie arms, consult Prinet CP, p. 35 n. 3, and especially London, 'Pattee, Patonce, and Formee', *Coat of Arms*, v (1958), no. 34, 29–30.

croisete, *crosslet* (Fig. 100). See A CROISETES SEMÉ, CROISETES EN LE . . ., CROISETES OU . . ., PETITE CROISETE, SEMÉ DE CROISETES. *Syn.*: see CROISELE.

croiseté, *crusily* (Fig. 35). *BA* 130 (A: a croisette), 144: croisetté. *Syn.*: see CROISELÉ.

croisetes en le . . ., *crosslets charging the . . .* (Fig. 35). See next item.

croisetes ou . . ., *crosslets charging the . . .* (Fig. 35). The complete blazons read as follows: *BA* 70: Rojers (A: Rouers) de Enghien (A: d'Enghien), gheronné d'argent et de noir croisette d'or u noir (MS.: *le*, read: *en le = ou = u*; A: sur le noir) Banneret et Brabanchon (A: Braibanchon), see OU NOIR; 72: Gherars d'Ainghien (A: d'Enghien) ses freres, l'escu gheronné d'or et de geules croisette d'or en le (MS.: *les*; A: en) gueules. Baneres (A: Banneret) et Braibanchon, see EN LE GEULES. *Syn.*: see CROISELÉ. *Note*: see ES GEULES, *Note*.

crois et lionceaus, *cross cantoned with lioncels rampant*. *Bl*/46: od la crois . . . et quartier lentes (*B/Ba Bb* 46, see CROIS[1] [2]; *Bc* 46, see CROIS A LIONCEAUS). *Syn.*: see CROIS[1] (2). *Note*: Dakeny arms. *Aspilogia II*, p. 124, item 46, has been emended to read *quartier leunces*. London notes: 'The arms are correctly given in [*Bb*] *A cross between four* *lions or.* In [*Bl*] Glover wrote *quartier lentes* and in [*B*] *quartires leonceus. Lentes* must be a misreading of *leuces,* i.e. leunces or leon-ceux, while *quartier* and *quartires* are ob-viously meant for *quatre.*' See QUARTIER⁵.

crois fleuretee, *cross flory* (Fig. 96). *D* 157: od une croiz . . . floretté; *H* 78: ou ung croys florettez (*Hg* 78: a .vii. crois flerté). *Syn.:* CROIS O BOUZ FLEURETÉS. *Note:* cf. also CROIS⁵. Gough H, p. 146, note to item 78: 'For ".vii." in [*Hg* 78], read "un".' H. S. London, 'Pattee, Patonce, and For-mee', *Coat of Arms,* v (1958), no. 34, 33: 'As for the flory cross it is clear that for the medieval herald this was indistinguishable from the cross patonce. Modern practice however regards it as a distinct variety. It may as well be called flory.' London had earlier noted, however (*Coat of Arms,* no. 33, p. 361), that the Siward arms, cited here in both the Camden Roll and the Falkirk Roll, feature a cross flory-at-the-ends in the thirteenth-century painted version of St. George's Roll.

crois formee, *cross formy* (Fig. 97). The complete blazon reads as follows: *C* 20: Le auntient del Hospitall, gules un crois formy d'argent (*Cl* 20: Le baucent del Hospitale, de goule a un croyz d'argent fourmé; *Cd* 20: Le baucent del Hospital, de gules a une croiss d'argent formé). *Note:* cf. CROIS ESLAISIEE AUS BOUZ, CROIS ESLARGIE. The cross formy characteristic-ally appears couped in England, through-out in France; see London, *Coat of Arms,* no. 34, p. 28. The charge appears here in the Hospitalers' arms; on the other forms of the Hospitalers' cross, consult Hauptmann, p. 54 and Table III, fig. 37; John A. Goodall, 'The Origin of the Arms and Badge of the Order of St. John of Jerusalem', *Coat of Arms,* v (1958), no. 33, 372–8; *Aspilogia II,* pp. 25–6, note to item 61; p. 109 ('the term does not appear again in any roll of arms for more than half a century'); p. 172, note to item 22 ('This seems to be the earliest occurrence of that term'). On the banner called *bau-cent,* see CROIS PASSANT, *Note.* For a possible use of 'formy' in *Cd,* see CROIS A DEUS PASSANZ, *Note.*

crois fourchiee¹, *cross patonce* (Fig. 102). *Bl* 76: od une crois . . . furchee (*B* 76, see

CROIS PATONCE; *Ba/Bc* 76, see CROIS⁵; *Bb* 76, see CROIS PLAINE). *Syn.:* see CROIS ESLARGIE PAR LES BOUZ. *Note:* cf. CROIS FOURCHIEE AU KANEE. On the Vescy arms, see *Aspilogia II,* p. 17, note to item 76 (see CROIS PATONCE, *Note*), and CROIS⁵. The sense ascribed here to *crois fourchiee* is not to be confused with the *croix fourchée* of modern French heraldry (cross couped treble-fitchy; see Veyrin-Forrer, p. 63, fig. 1, and especially London, *Coat of Arms,* no. 34, p. 31) or the *cross fourchée* or *fourchy* of modern English textbooks (see CROIS FOURCHIEE²).

crois fourchiee², *cross fourchée,* or *fourchy* (Fig. 101). *B* 202: ung croix fourché (*Bl* 202 [206]: ove une crois furché). *Note:* cf. CROIS RECERCELEE, CROIS RECROISELEE, FER DE MOULIN¹. London, 'Pattee, Patonce, and Formee', *Coat of Arms,* v (1958), no. 34, 31: 'In English blazon from the middle of the fifteenth century it has been applied either to the moline or millrind cross or, more often, to a variant thereof in which the points are cut off.' For the meaning of the term in modern French heraldry, see CROIS FOURCHIEE¹, *Note.* London's article did not mention this example in his dis-cussion of the term *fourché* and, following his lead, I listed it as an illustration of the various terms for cross patonce in Brault, 'The Cross', p. 220. In *Aspilogia II,* how-ever, London defines the cross in question (Vale arms) as a cross fourchy (p. 155, note to item 206; see also p. 215), thus contradicting the statement quoted above in this note as to the late appearance of this meaning in English blazon. The illustrations of this blazon in the earliest copies of Glover's Roll show: (1) a blank shield and (2) a cross moline, and the matter is further complicated by a seal of Robert de Vale *c.* 1200–10 showing a plain cross. London concludes: 'The fourchy cross of this roll may be a cadency dif-ference, but it is more likely that it merely shows the fluidity of arms at this time' (*Aspilogia II,* p. 155, note to item 206).

crois fourchiee au kanee, *cross patonce* (Fig. 102). The complete blazon reads as follows: *B* 151: John de Lexington, d'argent ung crois d'azur fourché au kanee (*Bl* 151 [155]: Joh'n de Lexington, d'argent od une croix d'azure furchee au kauee [?kanee]). *Syn.*: see CROIS ESLARGIE PAR LES BOUZ. *Note*: characterized in *Aspilogia II*, p. 145, note to item 155, as 'one of the outstanding problems of this roll', no explanation provided thus far for this locution is entirely convincing. Pusikan, p. 125, suggested that the correct reading was *au kouee*, the second word being a form of OFr. *coue* 'tail'. In his important article entitled 'Pattee, Patonce, and Formee', *Coat of Arms*, v (1958), no. 33, 359, London noted that in 'the original, 1253, version of Glover's Roll' (i.e. the copy we have designated here as *Bl*), the Lexington cross patonce is blazoned *furchee au kanee* (London also reads *B* 151 as *furchee* [not *fourche*, as in Armytage] *au kanee*) and that 'the 1310 editor [i.e. the compiler of *B*] was evidently unable to interpret the old term and therefore left it unchanged'. In the same article (*Coat of Arms*, no. 34, pp. 31–2), London pointed out that Matthew Paris drew the Lexington shield 'as a moline cross with a small point in the angle of the ends' (cf. D'Haucourt–Durivault, p. 71, fig. 179, blazoned, p. 66, as a *croix hendée*). Relying on this evidence, London concluded that 'we may safely read the Glover's Roll blazon *furchee au kanee* as *fourchee avec une cane*, *cane* being an Old French word for tooth'. London added the following: 'In the manuscripts the third letter of the last word could also be read as *u*, in which case the word would be *kauee*, i.e. *coue* or *queue*, tail. Dr. Adam-Even, however, considers *kanee* the more likely reading and that is my own feeling.' The chief objection to both the *coue* and the *cane* hypotheses is that no other example has been found linking either term to a cross. No one, to my knowledge, has noted the suggestive use of OFr. *chief* in this connection in the Parliamentary Roll (*c.* 1312) where the flowered ends of a cross flory are blazoned *les chefs fleurettés* (see Hope, p. 60). The ends of a cross, then, are known to have been referred to as 'chiefs' about this time (cf. BOUT) and it is but a short semantic step from a derivative of Lat. *caput* (> OFr. *chief*, *chef*) to a derivative of the related Latin term *capitium* (> OFr. *chevez*, *chevais*, MFr.

chevet) and what is doubtless the most plausible explanation of the locution under consideration. For another use of OFr. *chief* in early blazon, see LABEL², *Note*. London, in *Aspilogia II*, p. 103, observes briefly that 'the language of [Glover's Roll] is French and resembles that of the northern French (Picard) roll known as the *Armorial Bigot* [= *BA*]'. The velar *k* (cf. *B*/*Bl* 156 [160]: *kene*; see CHESNE) and retention of *a* countertonic are characteristics of dialects of the northern French region including Picard; see Pope, para. 417 and p. 487. The thirteenth-century form *li cavés* is attested (see Grandsaignes d'Hauterive, p. 107, s.v. *chevez*) in the meaning 'head of a bed', bringing us very close indeed, the orthographical peculiarities of Glover's Roll being taken into account, to *furchee au kanee* (read *kauee* or *kavee*, the letter *v* not being distinguished from *u* in thirteenth-century script). In our view, the original doubtless represented a form of OFr. *crois fourchiee aus chevez* (or *au chevet*).

croisié¹, *crosslet* (Fig. 100). See CROIS PASSANT A RONDEAUS EN LES QUATRE QUARTIERS ET EN CHASCUN RONDEL UN CROISIÉ. *Syn.*: see CROISELE.

croisié², *forked and crossed in saltire (referring to a lion's tail)*. See COUE CROISIEE. *Syn.*: FOURCHIÉ², FOURCHIÉ EN SOM, FOURCHU. *Note*: cf. ESCU A BRETELES, SAUTOIR¹.

croisille, *crosslet* (Fig. 100). See A CROISILLES POUDRÉ A L'ESCU, CROIS PASSANT A BESANZ EN LES QUATRE QUARTIERS EN CHASCUN BESANT UNE CROISILLE, CROIS PASSANT A RONDEAUS EN LES QUATRE QUARTIERS EN CHASCUN RONDEL UNE CROISILLE, OD LES CROISILLES, POUDRÉ A CROISILLES, SEMÉ DE CROISILLES.

croisillié, *crusily* (Fig. 35). *D* 79, 99, 101, 103, 106, 134, 139, 178, 183: crusilé; *H* 24: croisilé; *M* 37: crusilé; *K*, vv. 188–9, 317–18, 575–6:

> Baner ot de rouge colour,
> O fesse de or e croissillie.
>
> · · · · · ·
>
> Johans de Engaigne le ot jolie,
> Rouge dance de or croissillie.
>
> · · · · · ·
>
> Baniere ot vermeille cum sanc,
> Croissillie o un chievron blanc.

Syn.: see CROISELÉ.

croisillié tout environ, *crusily* (Fig. 35).
K, vv. 58–60:

> Phelippe (W: Phellipe) le seignur
>   (W: seigneur) de Kyme,
> Ky portoit rouge o un cheveron,
> De or croissillie tot environ.

Syn.: see CROISELÉ. *Note*: refers to ENVIRON[2]
(2).

crois o bouz fleuretés, *cross flory* (Fig. 96).
K, vv. 348–50:

> Richart Suwart, ke o eus converse,
> Noire baniere ot aprestee,
> O crois blanche (W: blance) o bouz
> flouretee.

Syn.: CROIS FLEURETEE.

crois od une couronne, *on a plain cross
a crown.* The complete blazon reads as
follows: *D* 14: Le rey de Ermenie, l'escu
de ermine a une croiz de goules od une
corone d'or. *Note*: refers to CROIS[1] (3).

crois ou milieu, *plain cross* (Fig. 105).
Vulgate Merlin Sequel, p. 389: une crois . . .
el milieu. *Syn.*: see CROIS[1].

crois par le milieu, *plain cross* (Fig. 106).
Artus, p. 19: croiz . . . par le mileu. *Syn.*:
see CROIS[1].

crois passant, *plain cross* (Fig. 106). (1) *the
cross bears no charge. C* 13 (*Cl* 13: a un croyz
. . . passant; *Cd* 13: .i. croyz . . . passant),
19 (*Cl* 19: a un croyz . . . passant; *Cd* 19:
a une croiss . . . passant), 152 (*Cl* 152:
a une croyz passant; *Cd* 152: a une croyes
passant), 164 (*Cl* 164: a une croyz . . .
passant, see ESQUARTILLIÉ DE . . . ET DE . . .;
Cd 164: a une croise . . . parssannt, see
ESQUARTELÉ DE . . . ET DE . . .): un crois
passant; *M* 74: ou ung croys passens (G:
passeur), see CROIS PASSEUR. (2) *the cross
bears a charge. M* 61: ou la crois passaunt,
see EN LA CROIS UNE MOLETE. (3) *the upper
part of the cross delineates a canton in dexter
chief* (Fig. 107). See CROIS PASSANT EN LE
CHANTEL UNE MERLETE. *Syn.*: see CROIS[1].
Note: in *C* 19 (the complete blazon reads as
follows: 'Le auntient de Temple, d'argent un cheif sable un crois gulez passant'
[*Cl* 19 (21): Le baucent del Temple, d'argent al chef de sable a un croyz de goule
passant; *Cd* 19: Le baron del Temple,
d'argent le cheif de sable a une croiss de

gules passant]), the order of items is misleading. The cross should be named immediately after the tincture of the field
in order not to appear to be on the chief
as in *C* 120 (Raffe de Camois, d'or al cheif
gulez trois gastells d'argent) and *C* 176
(Robert de Basseger, paly de verry et de
gulez al cheif d'or un florete de sable); see
CHIEF[1] (2) B. 1., *Note*. On the Templars'
banner (OFr. *baucent* < VL **balteanus*,
a derivative of Lat. *balteus* 'belt'), thus
designated because of its black and white
colours (the name spread to other banners;
see CROIS FORMEE), consult Hauptmann,
pp. 52–4, and Tables III, fig. 38, VI,
fig. 96; see also *Aspilogia II*, pp. 79, 172,
notes to items 21 and 22. Through folk
etymology, the banner of the Templars
became known as 'Beau Séant', which
was also their war-cry (Boutell, p. 191).
According to *Aspilogia II*, p. 26, note to
item 62, the banner of the Templars was
regularly *argent, a chief sable* (cf., however,
Aspilogia II, p. 82, note to item 19, where
it is *per fess sable and argent*), but in *Cl* 19
[21] 'it is surcharged with a red cross', by
which I assume that London meant that
the cross was over all. On p. 214, however,
the same banner is blazoned 'Argent, on
a chief sable a cross patonce gules'. Two
illustrations of the Templars' arms are
provided by G. R. Gayre, *The Heraldry of
the Knights of St. John* (Allahabad, 1956);
p. 2, fig. 9, shows a shield *argent, a plain
cross gules*, but fig. 10 depicts another *argent, a plain cross [gules?], a chief sable*. In
a note, Gayre explains that while fig. 9
represents the 'usual arms' of the Templars,
the coat in fig. 10 'is sometimes attributed
to them'.

**crois passant a besanz en les quatre
quartiers en chascun besant une croisille,** *plain cross cantoned with bezants charged
with plain crosslets* (Fig. 27). The complete
blazon reads as follows: *Cd* 2: L'empereur
de Constantinoble, de gules poudré a
crosyle d'or a ung croyz or passant a .iiii.
bessannts in .iiii. quarteres in cheschun
bessannt ung croshylle gules (*C* 2, see
CROIS PASSANT A RONDEAUS EN LES QUATRE
QUARTIERS ET EN CHASCUN RONDEL UN
CROISIÉ; *Cl* 2, see CROIS PASSANT A RONDEAUS
EN LES QUATRE QUARTIERS ET EN CHASCUN

RONDEL UNE CROISILLE). *Syn.*: CROIS PASSANT A RONDEAS EN LES QUATRE QUARTIERS ET EN CHASCUN RONDEL UN CROISIÉ, CROIS PASSANT A RONDEAS EN LES QUATRE QUARTIERS ET EN CHASCUN RONDEL UNE CROISILLE. *Note*: on the arms of Constantinople, consult Max Prinet, 'Les armoiries des empereurs latins de Constantinople', *Revue numismatique* (1911), 250–6. Bezants are canting arms for Byzantium, the earlier name of Constantinople. For a seal with these arms dated 1280, see Prinet, p. 251, fig. 1; see also *WB*, Plate VIII, blazoned as follows by Dr. Adam-Even in *WB* 1273: 'De gueules à la croix d'or cantonnée de 4 annelets et 20 croisettes de même'. Gough-Parker, p. 59, s.v. *bezant*: 'It is said that this money, once current, had no device whatsoever stamped on it.' However, one class of the so-called Saracenic bezants, which circulated in France and England in the thirteenth century, had a cross at the centre of a ring on one side (see U. T. Holmes, jun., 'Coins of Old French Literature', *Speculum*, xxi [1956], 317 and Plate I [10]; R. A. G. Carson, *Coins of the World* [New York, 1962], p. 223 and Plate 426) and bore a striking resemblance to the charge in question. See also note to next item.

crois passant a rondeaus en les quatre quartiers en chascun rondel une croisille, *plain cross cantoned with bezants charged with plain crosslets* (Fig. 27). The complete blazon reads as follows: *Cl* 2 [12]: L'emperour de Constantinople, de goule poudré a crosyle d'or a un croyz d'or passaunt a quatre roundeles d'or en quatre quarteres e en chekun roundelle un croysille (*C* 2, see CROIS PASSANT A RONDEAUS ET EN CHASCUN RONDEL UN CROISIÉ; *Cd* 2, see CROIS PASSANT A BESANZ EN LES QUATRE QUARTIERS EN CHASCUN BESANT UNE CROISILLE). *Syn.*: see CROIS PASSANT A BESANZ EN LES QUATRE QUARTIERS EN CHASCUN BESANT UNE CROISILLE. *Note*: in *Aspilogia II*, p. 169, note to item 12, London suggests that since the earliest illustrations of the arms of Constantinople show annulets, not roundels, the blazon in *Cd/Cl* 2 [12] was probably intended for *pierced* roundels, i.e. annulets. However, the corresponding blazon in *Cd* suggests canting arms

(bezants = Byzantium); see CROIS PASSANT A BESANZ EN LES QUATRE QUARTIERS EN CHASCUN BESANT UNE CROISILLE, *Note*.

crois passant a rondeaus en les quatre quartiers et en chascun rondel un croisié, *plain cross cantoned with bezants charged with plain crosslets* (Fig. 27). The complete blazon reads as follows: *C* 2: L'empereur de Constantinople, gules crusuly d'or un crois passant d'or a 4 rondells d'or in les 4 quarters et in chescun rondell un croisee (*Cl* 2, see CROIS PASSANT A RONDEAUS EN LES QUATRE QUARTIERS ET EN CHASCUN RONDEL UNE CROISILLE; *Cd* 2: CROIS PASSANT A BESANZ EN LES QUATRE QUARTIERS EN CHASCUN BESANT UNE CROISILLE). *Syn.*: see CROIS PASSANT A BESANZ EN LES QUATRE QUARTIERS EN CHASCUN BESANT UNE CROISILLE.

crois passant en le chantel une merlete, *plain cross a martlet cantoned* (Fig. 107). *M* 28: ou la croys . . . passant en la cantel (G: cantell) une merlettz. *Note*: refers to CHANTEL[3], indicating position only.

crois passeur, *ghost word.* See CROIS PASSANT (1). *Note*: erroneous reading by Greenstreet.

crois patee, *cross patonce* (Fig. 102). *B* 13: ung croiz paté (*Ba/Bb/Bc/Bl* 13, see CROIS[5]); *C* 50: un crois patee (*Cl/Cd* 50, see CROIS[5]); *D* 128: od une croiz patee; *H* 62 (*Hg* 62 [63]: od la croyz patee), 63: ou la croys paté; 103: ou ung crois patee (*Hg* 103 [104]: a un croys patee, see JARBES EN LA CROIS); *M* 3: ou ung croys paté; 38: ou la croys paté; 40: ou la crois paté; 70: croys patté; *K*, vv. 426–30:

> Prouesce ke avoit fait ami
> De Guilleme le Latimier,
> Ki la crois patee de or mier
> Portoit, en rouge bien pourtraite,
> Sa baniere ot cele part traite.

Syn.: see CROIS ESLARGIE PAR LES BOUZ. *Note*: for other uses, see CROIS PATEE ET PERCIEE, CROIS PERCIEE ET PATEE ET BOUTONEE. Also, not to be confused with the meaning attached to *croix pattée* in all French rolls and most English rolls since the middle of the fifteenth century, viz. 'cross formy'. See H. S. London, 'Paty and Formy', *Coat of Arms*, iii (1955), 285–6, superseded by the latter's 'Pattee, Patonce,

M

and Formee', *Coat of Arms*, v (1958), no. 33, 358–64; v (1958), no. 34, 26–33.

crois patee en le chantel, *on a canton a cross patonce*. *Cl* 131 [92]: a une croys . . . patee en le cantelle (*C* 131, see EN UN CHANTEL UNE CROIS PATEE; *Cd* 131, see EN LE CANTON UNE CROIS PATEE). *Syn.*: EN LE CANTON UNE CROIS PATEE, EN UN CHANTEL UNE CROIS PATEE. *Note*: refers to EN LE CHANTEL[1]. On the arms in question (Basset), consult H. S. London, 'Pattee, Patonce, and Formee', *Coat of Arms*, v (1958), no. 33, 359–60.

crois patee et perciee, *Toulouse cross (cross clechy, voided and botonny)* (Fig. 109). *C* 39: un crois patee percee (*Cl* 39: a un croyz . . . paté et persé; *Cd* 39: a crosse patté e percee). *Syn.*: CROIS PERCIEE ET PATEE ET BOUTONEE, FAUSE CROIS POMMELEE. *Note*: on the Toulouse cross and its variants, see Prinet WR, p. 234, item 25, D'Haucourt–Durivault, p. 66, and p. 71, fig. 189; and especially H. S. London, 'Pattee, Patonce, and Formee', *Coat of Arms*, v (1958), no. 33, 359–60. The Matthew Paris Shields feature a fine example of the Toulouse cross, blazoned simply as follows, however: 'Scutum de gules, crux aurea' (Pusikan, p. 151). *Aspilogia II*, p. 109: 'C's use of *paté* for the Toulouse cross is important, for it points to the word's derivation from the Latin *patens* "spreading", rather than from *patte* "a paw".' I rather conclude that the term was originally derived from OFr. *patte* 'paw' but later associated, through false learned etymology, with Latin *patens*. On the latter process, consult G. Gougenheim, 'La fausse étymologie savante', *RPh.*, i (1948), 277–86.

crois patonce, *cross patonce* (Fig. 102). *B* 76: a ung croix patonce (*Ba/Bc* 76, see CROIS[5]; *Bb* 76, see CROIS PLAINE; *Bl* 76, see CROIS FOURCHIEE[1]). *Syn.*: see CROIS ESLARGIE PAR LES BOUZ. *Note*: on this charge, see H. S. London, 'Pattee, Patonce, and Formee', *Coat of Arms*, v (1958), no. 33, 359–64; v (1958), no. 34, 28–33; *Aspilogia II*, p. 109: '*patonce* . . . is probably Glover's mistake for *furchee* or some other, perhaps illegible, word'; cf. p. 129, note to item 76: 'that term [i.e. patonce in *B* 76] is otherwise unknown before the sixteenth

century and it may be Glover's translation of patee.'

crois perciee, *cross voided* (Fig. 104). *Ba* 61: une croiz percé (*B/Bl* 61, see FAUSE CROIS; *Bb* 61, see CROIS VUIDIEE; *Bc* 61: a une croyz percé); *D* 127: od une croiz percé. *Syn.*: CROIS VUIDIEE, FAUSE CROIS.

crois perciee et patee et boutonee, *Toulouse cross (cross clechy, voided and botonny)* (Fig. 109). *H* 87: la croys percé et patee et botonee. *Syn.*: see CROIS PATEE ET PERCIEE.

crois plaine, *plain cross* (Fig. 106). *Bb* 76: a crosse . . . playne (*B* 76, see CROIS PATONCE; *Ba/Bc* 76, see CROIS[5]; *Bl* 76, see CROIS FOURCHIEE[1]). *Syn.*: see CROIS[1]. *Note*: the blazon here is an error for cross patonce.

crois recercelee, *cross moline* (Fig. 101). *C* 157: un crois . . . reserscelé (*Cl* 157: a un croys . . . rescerselé; *Cd* 157, see CROIS RECROISELEE); 172: un crois . . . resercelé (*Cl* 172: a une croyz . . . recerselé; *Cd* 172: a une crosse). *Syn.*: CROIS RECROISELEE, FER DE MOULIN. *Note*: cf. CROIS FOURCHIEE[2]. On this charge, see Prinet WR, p. 252, item 69; Prinet CP, p. 23 n. 1; *Aspilogia II*, p. 198, note to item 160. Cf. FER DE MOULIN A TESTES DE SERPENZ AU FER DE MOULIN.

crois recroiselee, *cross moline* (Fig. 101). *Cd* 157: a une crois . . . recrosselé (*C/Cl* 157, see CROIS RECERCELEE). *Syn.*: see CROIS RECERCELEE. *Note*: not to be confused with cross crosslet, the ends of whose limbs are squared and crossed or treflé. On the modern distinction between cross crosslet and cross botonny, see R. F. Pye, 'A Return to First Principles. V', *Coat of Arms*, vii (1963), 337–40. According to *Aspilogia II*, p. 198, note to item 160, *Cd*'s '*recrosselé* is more suggestive of a cross crosslet or *recroisetee*. The Paveley cross is generally given either as patonce or as flory at the ends . . . [but] it is possible that the variation in the cross is a difference.'

crois sans plus, *plain cross* (Fig. 106). *Vulgate Merlin Sequel*, p. 376: et qu'il i ait une crois vermeille sans plus. *Syn.*: see CROIS[1].

croissant[1], *crescent* (Fig. 224). *TA*, vv. 1594–5:

> Croissant en argent foilleté
> I ot portret de demi ris;

BA 130, 143, 144: a .i. croissant; *B* 186: ung croissant (*Bl* 186 [190]: od un cressant); *C* 165: trois cressants (W: cressantes) (*Cl* 165: treis cresçantz; *Cd* 165: a 3 cresannts); *EO*, v. 5070: Armes ot bleues, s'i ot d'or trois croissans; *Sone*, v. 13947: a trois croissans; *K*, vv. 367–9:

Guilleme de Ridre i estoit,
Ke en la baniere inde portoit
Les croissans de or enluminez.

For other uses, see BENDE OU CROISSANZ, EGLE A UN CROISSANT EN LA POITRINE, OD LES CROISSANZ, OU LES CROISSANZ. *Syn.*: CROISSANTE, LUNETE.

croissant², *jessant* (Fig. 167). See FESSE OD FLEURS DE LIS CROISSANZ HORS DE TESTES DE LIEPARZ, FESSE OU FLEURS CROISSANZ HORS DE LA TESTE DU LIEPART, FLEUR DE LIS CROISSANT HORS DE LA TESTE DU LIEPART. *Syn.*: NAISSANT. *Note*: while CROISSANT² and NAISSANT are synonymous in that they refer to a fleur-de-lis depicted as growing out of the mouth of a leopard's head, ISSANT indicates that the fleur-de-lis is couped, placed on the chief, and appears to be rising out of the lower section of the shield. See DEMI.

croissante, *crescent* (Fig. 224). *D* 139: od treis cressantes. For another use, see QUARTIER A UNE CROISSANTE. *Syn.*: see CROISSANT¹. *Note*: feminine form of OFr. *croissant*.

crois sor l'espaule, see LION COURONÉ A UNE CROIS SOR L'ESPAULE.

crois vuidiee, *cross voided* (Fig. 104). *Bb* 61: un crois voydé (*B/Bl* 61, see FAUSE CROIS; *Ba* 61, see CROIS PERCIEE). *Syn.*: see CROIS PERCIEE.

crosille, see CROISILLE.

crosule, see CROISELÉ.

crounnet, see LION RAMPANT COURONÉ.

crucefié, *crucified*. See HOME QUI ESTOIT CRUCEFIÉ, OU MILIEU UN HOME CRUCEFIÉ QUI TOUT ESTOIT SANGLANT.

cruselé, *crusily*. See CROISELÉ.

cuisse, *thigh*. See JAMBES ARMEES O TOUTES LES CUISSES CHASCUNE CUISSE JOINTE AUS AUTRES ET EN CHASCUNE CORNIERE SEIT UN PIÉ, JAMBES ARMEES O TOUTES LES CUISSES ET EN CHASCUNE CORNIERE SEIT UN PIÉ.

cupe, *cup*. See COUPE.

custere, see BENDE A COTICES.

cygne, see CIGNE.

daim, *stag, deer, buck*. See PERCHE DE DAIM.

Dame, see NOSTRE DAME.

damoisele, *damsel*. *Note*: according to *Thèbes*, ed. Léopold Constans, ii. 343, note to vv. 6585–6: 'Dans *Troie* (v. 8165 sqq.), le grec Palamides porte un écu où est peinte une "damoiselle".' The passage in question in *Troie*, however, does not mention Palamedes' arms which are blazoned as follows in v. 7469: 'A goles ot escu d'argent'. Nowhere else does this character bear a damsel on his shield to my knowledge. In the fourteenth-century *Meliador*, vv. 26301–2, Sagremor's arms feature a lady ('dedens une targe blance/ . . . une blewe dame'; for other shields charged with this device in this romance, see Longnon, iii. 354–6) and Oliver's coat often bore a damsel's head; see Lejeune–Stiennon, *La Légende de Roland*, i. 320–3; 349 n. 11; 354, 387–8; Plate LV; ii, figs. 372–5, 431, 472, 474. Cf. JAMBES DE S'AMIE. Additional bibliography in Ménard, p. 292 n. 513.

dance, *daunce, fess dancetty* (Fig. 78). *TA*, v. 1719: a une dance; *B* 106: ung danse (*Bl* 106 [107]: od le daunce); *H* 18: ou ung daunse (*Hg* 18: a une dance); 45: ou ung daunce; (*Hg* 45 [46]: a un daunce); *Hg*, Engaine [64]: od un dance; *M* 18: odve la daunce; 75: ou ung daunse. *K*, vv. 85–6, 317–21, 874–6:

Baner avoit ben conoissable,
De or fyn o la dance de sable.

· · · · · ·

Johans de Engaigne le ot jolie,
Rouge dance de or croissillie.
Puis i ot Watiers de Beauchamp
Sis merlos de or el rouge champ,
O une fesse en lieu de dance.

· · · · · ·

Cil ki porte dance e bilettes
De or en asur, al assaut court,
Johans avoit a non Daincourt.

For other uses, see DANCE EN BELIC A OISEAUS, DANCE EN CHIEF, DANCE EN LE CHIEF, DANCIÉ A DANCES, FESSE ET UNE DANCE EN CHIEF, FESSE ET UNE DANCE EN LE CHIEF, SORJETÉ O UNE DANCE. *Syn.*: BASTON DE FUIRES, DANTE, FESSE DANCIEE, SORJETÉ O UNE DANCE. Cf. also VUIVRE DE TRAVERS EL CHIEF. *Note*: on this charge, consult H. S. London, 'Dancetty and

Indented', *Coat of Arms*, i (1950), 93–4; R. F. Pye, 'A Return to First Principles, IV', *Coat of Arms*, vii (1963), 293–4. For definitions, see Prinet WR, p. 251: 'nom de la fasce vivrée, ou vivre'; Prinet CP, p. 21 n. 1: 'C'est l'un des noms de la vivre ou fasce vivrée'; Adam-Even BA, p. 19: 'la dance est une fasce vivrée.' Hope, p. 16: 'A fesse that zigzagged across the field was called a daunce or dance, perhaps because its points "danced" up and down, and cotises were often drawn as zigzags or dancetty.' The correct etymology is provided by W. von Wartburg, *FEW*, iii. 43, s.v. *denticatus*. The gender of OFr. *dance* is feminine except in Anglo-Norman sources, where it may be either masculine or feminine. On the confusion of daunce and fess fusilly in painted blazons, see *Aspilogia II*, p. 123, note to item 43. Prinet TA, p. 48: 'Ailleurs, l'idée symbolique naît d'un calembour. Ainsi, les *dances* de l'écu de Cointise rappellent les *danses* qu'aiment les coquets et les coquettes.'

dance en belic a oiseaus, *bend dancetty between martlets.* BA 182: a une danche . . . en beslive a .vi. oisel. *Note*: Adam-Even BA, p. 19, defines the locution *dance en belic* as 'une bande vivrée'.

dance en chief, *in chief a fess dancetty.* C 135: ung dansee . . . en cheif (*Cl/Cd* 135, see DANCE EN LE CHIEF). For another use, see FESSE ET UNE DANCE EN CHIEF. *Syn.*: DANCE EN LE CHIEF. *Note*: refers to EN CHIEF[2].

dance en le chief, *in chief a fess dancetty.* *Cl* 135: a une dans . . . en le chefe (*C* 135, see DANCE EN CHIEF; *Cd* 135: a une danz . . . en le cheif). For another use, see FESSE ET UNE DANCE EN LE CHIEF. *Syn.*: DANCE EN CHIEF. *Note*: refers to EN LE CHIEF[2].

dancié, *dancetty* (Fig. 78). See FESSE DANCIEE. *Note*: cf. DANCIÉ A DANCES.

dancié a dances, *barry dancetty* (Fig. 6). *TA*, v. 667: A dances d'or en vert danciees. *Note*: cf. DANCIÉ.

d'Angletere a, *England, differenced by.* K, v. 461: De Engletere, au label de France. *Syn.*: ARMES LE ROI, ARMES LE ROI D'ANGLE-TERE A, ESTRE DE SES ARMES TEL D'ANGLE-TERE A. *Note*: complete blazon provided s.v. DE FRANCE.

dante, *daunce, fess dancetty* (Fig. 78). CP 58: a une dante. *Syn.*: see DANCE. *Note*: Prinet

CP, p. 21 n. 1: 'Le mot *dante* doit être lu *dance*. C'est l'un des noms de la vivre ou fasce vivrée.' The term is listed separately here since the author (or scribe) may have been influenced by Lat. *dentem*. The first attested use of OFr. *dent* in a heraldic sense occurs in *Fouke Fitz Warin* early in the fourteenth century (ed. Louis Brandin [Paris, 1930], p. 85: 'En l'escu sunt douze dentz / De goules e de argentz').

dantelee, see BORDURE DANTELEE.

dars, *dace (a kind of carp)* (Fig. 209). See SAUMON ENTRE DARS. *Note*: for OFr. *dars*, sometimes attested as *dart* (under the influence of OFr. *dart* [MFr. *dard*] 'dart'?), see Godefroy, ix. 224, s.v. *dart* ('nom populaire de la vandoise [E. *dace*] qui saute, se lance brusquement'), *FEW*, iii. 18, s.v. *darsus*, and Tobler–Lommatzsch, ii. 1196, s.v. *dars*. The latter provides a bibliography of studies relating to this term.

daufin, *dolfin* (Fig. 210). Cd 35: a dolfin (*C/Cl* 35, see DAUFIN DE MER); *CP* 7: a un daufin. *Syn.*: DAUFIN DE MER. *Note*: on this charge, see Prinet CP, pp. 673–4.

daufin de mer, *dolfin* (Fig. 210). *C* 35: un dolphin del mere (*Cl* 35: a un dauffin de mer; *Cd* 35, see DAUFIN). *Syn.*: DAUFIN. *Note*: for an illustration of the heraldic dolfin, see *WB* 1164, fig. 80.

d'autre semblance, *different arms.* Perlesvaus, p. 201 (var.): unes armes d'autre sanblance. *Note*: cf. D'UNE SEMBLANCE.

de, *die (i.e. the singular of dice)* (Fig. 254). *TA*, vv. 1118–19:

> Escu bendé de larrecin
> Ot Hasarz a .iii. dez du meins.

de, *the preposition 'of'.* The standard particle used, notably, to introduce words denoting tincture.

deableau, deablel, see DIABLEL.

debat, see EN DEBAT.

de belic, *bendwise.* See BARRE DE BELIC, BENDE DE BELIC, BENDE PARMI DE BELIC. *Syn.*: EN BELIC.

de bendes par mi listé, *traversed by multiple stripes.* Enéas, v. 4458: De trois bandes par mi listez. *Syn.*: see A BENDES BENDÉ.

deboissier, *to blazon.* Charrete, vv. 5823–4:

> Ensi devisent et deboissent
> Les armes de ces qu'il conoissent.

Syn.: DEVISER. *Note*: the primitive sense of this verb is 'to sculpture, to carve out of wood'.

dedenz, *in. EO*, v. 5005: Dedenz l'azur flours de lis d'or avoit. *Syn.*: see SOR. *Note*: complete blazon provided s.v. PARTI DE . . . ET DE . . . DEDENZ LE . . . ET . . . SOR LE . . . See also EN AZUR. Cf. *P* 127: 'Hugh Baillol de Bywelle porte de goules ove un escuchon voidé d'argent et dedenz un escu d'azure ove un leon rampant d'argent coroné d'or.' The latter is an erroneous blazon; see ESCU³, ESCUÇON OVE UN LION RAMPANT COURONÉ EN LA CORNIERE, *Note*.

de . . . et de . . .¹, *barry undy* (Fig. 7). The complete blazon reads as follows: *B* 93: Phelip Bassett, d'or et de goules (*Bl* 93, see ONDÉ DE . . . ET DE . . .). *Syn.*: see ONDÉ DE . . . ET DE . . . *Note*: elsewhere, *B* uses the locution *ondé de . . . et de . . . P* 106 (= *B* 93) reads: 'Phillip Basset porte oundee d'or et de goules.' In his commentary on the Basset arms in Matthew Paris, Pusikan, p. 148, notes: 'In der Gloverrolle ist "Phelip Basset, d'or et de goules" mit Hinweglassung des Näheren.'

de . . . et de . . .², *paly* (Fig. 19). The complete blazon reads as follows: *H* 59: Sᵣ captan de Bucher port d'or et de gules ou le cantel d'ermyne ou le bordoure de sable besanté d'or (*Hg* 59, see PALÉ DE . . . ET DE . . .). *Syn.*: PALÉ DE . . . ET DE . . .

de . . . et de . . .³, *party per pale* (?) (Fig. 21). The complete blazon reads as follows: *Vulgate Merlin Sequel*, p. 316: a cel escu d'or et d'asur al lyon rampant a cele fasse de travers a ces couronnes d'argent. *Note*: cf. PARTI DE . . . ET DE . . . Since these arms are fictitious and nowhere else attested to my knowledge it is difficult to determine the meaning of this expression which may, as a matter of fact, be the same as either DE . . . ET DE . . .¹ or DE . . . ET DE . . .².

de . . . et de . . . a quartiers, see A QUARTIERS DE . . . ET DE . . .

de France, *France Ancient.* (1) *referring to a bordure. CPA* 6: de Franche. (2) *referring to a label. K,* vv. 459–61:

Thomas de Langcastre estoit contes;
Se est de ses armes teus li contes,
De Engleterre, au label de France.

Note: azure semy of fleurs-de-lis or.

de France a, *France Ancient, differenced by. CPA* 5: de France a; 7, 8: de Franche au. *Syn.*: ARMES DU ROI DE FRANCE A, ARMES LE ROI DE FRANCE A. Cf. DE FRANCE.

de fuires, *dancetty.* See BASTON DE FUIRES. *Note*: probably akin to OFr. *guivre, vuivre* 'serpent' < VL **wipera* < Lat. *vipera*. See *BW*⁴, s.v. *guivre*, and cf. VUIVRE DE TRAVERS EL CHIEF. The *-s* in *de fuires* was a regular characteristic of Old French adverbs and adverbial locutions. See Pope, p. 215, paragraph 597. Modern French heraldry has two representatives of the latter term: *guivre, vivre, vouivre,* a kind of serpent monster swallowing a child (Veyrin-Forrer, p. 118), and *vivré,* referring to a zigzag line or ordinary (Veyrin-Forrer, pp. 26, 57).

dehors, *on each side (of a bend cotised).* See AU DEHORS.

delice, see FLEUR DE LIS.

del mesme, *of the same tincture.* The complete blazon reads as follows: *P* 110: Ernalde de Boys porte d'argent a deux barres de goules ove un quarter de le mesme. *Note*: refers to MESME² and corresponds to *B/Bl* 105 which omit this expression. *De+le* should normally be contracted to the enclitic forms *del* or *du*; the former is provided here rather arbitrarily. Foulet, *Petite Syntaxe*, para. 65, however, observes that while certain dialects confuse the masculine and feminine articles, using the oblique form *le* before words of both genders, the contractions *del* or *du* do not occur when *le* precedes a feminine noun, but rather the separate words *de le* are invariably attested. It may be, then, that *mesme* refers to the feminine noun *couleur* which could be understood here, though no mention of any word for tincture is made in this roll. Pope, para. 1253 (iii), finally, notes that the replacement of the enclitic form *del* by the separate words *de le* is a characteristic of Later Anglo-Norman, the dialect of *P*. At any rate, if *P* 110 records an authentic thirteenth-century blazon, this is the earliest attestation of what many now consider to be the old-fashioned custom of referring to the last-mentioned tincture by the expression 'of the same'. Modern French blazon, on the other hand, still uses *du même* in this sense (Veyrin-Forrer, p. 21): 'Lorsqu'un émail a déjà été mentionné, on évite de le répéter; on dit alors: . . . *du même* (si c'est l'émail qu'on vient de nommer).'

de lonc, *per pale.* See ONDÉ DE LONC DE . . . ET DE . . . *Syn.*: DE LONC EN LONC, EN LONC[1].

de lonc en lonc, *per pale.* See DE LONC EN LONC BENDÉ. *Syn.*: see DE LONC.

de lonc en lonc bendé, *paly* (?) (Fig. 19). *Fouque de Candie*, vv. 6868–9:

Porte une enseigne de lonc en lonc bendee,
Ynde et vermeille, en sa hanste fermee.

Syn.: see PALÉ DE . . . ET DE . . . *Note*: arms of Mauduit.

de l'un a l'autre, *pleonasm.* See FESSIÉ DE . . . ET DE . . . ENDENTÉ DE L'UN A L'AUTRE, FLEURÉ DE L'UN A L'AUTRE, FLEURS DE L'UN A L'AUTRE. *Syn.*: see DE L'UN EN L'AUTRE[2].

de l'une a l'autre, *counterchanged.* See FLEURS DE LIS DE L'UNE A L'AUTRE. *Syn.*: see DE L'UN EN L'AUTRE[1].

de l'une et de l'autre, *counterchanged.* See FLEURÉ DE L'UNE ET DE L'AUTRE, FLEURETÉ DE L'UNE ET DE L'AUTRE. *Syn.*: see DE L'UN EN L'AUTRE[1].

de l'un en l'autre[1], *counterchanged.* See FLEURÉ DE L'UN EN L'AUTRE, FLEURS DE GLAIEUL DE L'UN EN L'AUTRE, LIEPARDEAUS DE L'UN EN L'AUTRE, LIEPARZ DE L'UN EN L'AUTRE. *Syn.*: DE L'UNE A L'AUTRE, DE L'UNE ET DE L'AUTRE, DE L'UN ET DE L'AUTRE[1], DE L'UN ET L'AUTRE, EN UN EN L'AUTRE. *Note*: the charges are always multiple and are placed on a party or varied field, or involve one of the ordinaries. Cf. DE . . . SOR LE . . . ET DE . . . SOR LE . . . On the various meanings ascribed to this locution and its variants, see Brault, '*de l'un en l'autre*'.

de l'un en l'autre[2], *pleonasm.* See ESQUARTELÉ DE . . . ET DE . . . ENDENTÉ DE L'UN EN L'AUTRE. *Syn.*: DE L'UN A L'AUTRE, DE L'UN ET DE L'AUTRE[2], L'UN EN L'AUTRE. *Note*: in the cross reference and in each one of its synonyms, the word *endenté* is used, and it is clear that *de l'un en l'autre* (also *de l'un a l'autre, l'un en l'autre, de l'un et de l'autre*) merely reiterates the idea of interlocking, already indicated by *endenté*.

de l'un en l'autre[3], *pleonasm.* See JUMEAUS DE L'UN EN L'AUTRE. *Syn.*: DE L'UN ET DE L'AUTRE[3]. *Note*: the complete blazon reads as follows: *B* 209: 'Roand le connestable

de Richemund, de goules a ung chief d'or a deus gemeus de l'un en l'autre d'or'. Here the locution *de l'un en l'autre* underscores the alternation of tinctures only. In other words, the bars gemells or on a field of gules constitute, roughly, a series of horizontal bars where the tinctures are *alternately* gules and or.

de l'un en l'autre[4], *referring to a barry field with annulets of a different tincture over all and straddling the lines.* The complete blazon reads as follows: *BA* 280: Payens d'Orliens, l'escu bendé d'argent (A: d'or) et de vert a .v. enniax (A: a semiax) de geules (A: gueules) de l'un en l'autre. Baneres et Angevins (A: Banneret Angevin). *Note*: Adam-Even *WB* 904 refers to *BA* 280 and blazons the same arms (Orléans-Cléry) as follows: 'Fascé d'argent et de sinople à six annelets de gueules brochant sur les traits'. See his illustration, fig. 33.

de l'un et de l'autre[1], *counterchanged.* See FLEURETÉ DE L'UN ET DE L'AUTRE. *Syn.*: see DE L'UN EN L'AUTRE[1].

de l'un et de l'autre[2], *pleonasm.* See ESQUARTELÉ DE . . . ET DE . . . ENDENTÉ DE L'UN ET DE L'AUTRE. *Syn.*: see DE L'UN EN L'AUTRE[2].

de l'un et de l'autre[3], *pleonasm.* See JUMEAUS DE L'UN ET DE L'AUTRE. *Syn.*: see DE L'UN EN L'AUTRE[3].

de l'un et l'autre, *counterchanged.* See ESQUARTELÉ DE . . . ET DE . . . LIONS DE L'UN ET L'AUTRE, ESQUARTILLIÉ DE . . . ET DE . . . A LIEPARZ DE L'UN ET L'AUTRE, FLEURETÉ DE L'UN ET L'AUTRE, FLEURETES DE L'UN ET L'AUTRE.

de mesme[1], *the same arms.* Bb 65: William Maudet port de mesme. *Syn.*: see AUTEL[1].

de mesme[2], *the same arms, differenced by.* CPA 14: de meme la bordure engreslee. *Syn.*: see AUTEL[2].

de mesme a, *the same arms, differenced by.* CPA 2–4, 19: de meme a; 177: de mesme a. *Syn.*: see AUTEL[2].

de mesme le taint, *the same arms. Tristan de Thomas*, vv. 2182–4:

Escu ot d'or a vair freté,
De meime le taint ot la lance,
Le penun e la conisance.

Syn.: see AUTEL[1]. *Note*: see TAINT[1], *Note*.

demi[1], *halved. Syn.*: ISSANT, RECOUPÉ. *Note*: cf. CROISSANT[2], EN LONC[2].

demi², *half (of a party field)*. *Guillaume de Dole*, vv. 68–71:

> Et si portoit l'escu demi
> Au gentil conte de Clermont,
> Au lïon rampant contremont
> D'or et d'azur . . .

Syn.: D'UNE PART, L'AUTRE MOITIÉ. *Note*: cf. DEMI . . . ET DEMI . . ., MOITIÉ, PART (1), PARTI DE . . . ET DE . . . On this blazon, consult Lejeune, *L'Œuvre de Jean Renart*, pp. 115–19; *Guillaume de Dole*, p. 189; Anthime Fourrier, 'Les armoiries de l'empereur dans *Guillaume de Dole*', *Mélanges offerts à Rita Lejeune*, ii (Gembloux, 1969), 1211–26.

demi charboucle, *demi-carbuncle* (Fig. 250). *D* 9: od demy charbocle. *Note*: the field is party, with a line dividing the carbuncle palewise, only the dexter half appearing on the shield. See Mathieu, opposite p. 160, fig. 36, and BENDE OD DEUS COTICES.

demi egle, *demi-eagle* (Fig. 183). *EO*, v. 5006: Et demi aigle noire sor l'or seoit. *Note*: complete blazon provided s.v. PARTI . . . DE . . . ET DE . . . DEDENZ LE . . . ET . . . SOR LE . . . The field is party, with a line dividing the eagle palewise, only the sinister half appearing on the shield.

demi . . . et demi . . ., *party per pale* (Fig. 21). *Thèbes*, vv. 5513–14:

> D'yvoire ot escu demi blanc
> Et demi rouge conme sanc.

Syn.: see PARTI DE . . . ET DE . . . *Note*: cf. DEMI². See also PAR ESCHEQUIERS, *Note*.

demi fesse, *demi-fess* (Fig. 81). See FESSE ET DEMI FESSE. *Note:* cf. FESSIEL.

demi fleur de glaieul, *demi-fleur-de-lis* (Fig. 236). See CHIEF OD UNE DEMI FLEUR DE GLAIEUL. *Syn.*: FLEUR DE LIS ISSANT, FLEURETE², FLEURETE RECOUPEE. *Note*: cf. FLEUR DE LIS EN LONC. In this coat of arms and in those listed under the synonyms provided here, the demi-fleur-de-lis is on a chief and, consequently, appears to be 'issuing' from the bottom half of the shield. On this fleur-de-lis, which is couped just below the horizontal band at its middle, only the upper part remaining, consult Prinet WR, p. 254; Prinet CP, p. 34 n. 1. For illustrations of this charge which in our examples is always on a chief, see *WB* 881, fig. 29; 1175, fig. 82.

demi liepart, *demi-leopard* (= *demi-lion rampant*) (Fig. 144). *Escanor*, v. 3817: D'or au demi liepart de geules. *Note*: the leopard is doubtless rampant and couped at the middle, only the upper part remaining. Cf. DEMI LION.

demi lion, *demi-lion rampant* (Fig. 144). (1) *on a chief a demi-lion rampant*. *B* 102: ung demi lion; 103: ung demy lion. For other uses, see CHIEF A UN DEMI LION, CHIEF ET UN DEMI LION, CHIEF OD UN DEMI LION. (2) *the demi-lion rampant charges the field*. *Escanor*, vv. 3594–7, 3650–1:

> Li fix le roy l'escu d'argent
> Portoit a .i. demi lyon
> Vermeil bordé d'or environ
> A .ii. bendes vers toutes seules.
>
> .   .   .   .   .   .
>
> Ses armes furent totes blanches
> A un vermeil demi lyon;

CP 53, 106: a un demi lyon. *Syn.*: DEMI LIEPART, DEMI LION RAMPANT, LION RECOUPÉ. *Note*: the demi-lion is always rampant and couped at the middle, only the upper part remaining. The demi-lion in *CP* 106 is an error, 'le lion étant entier pour les armes des Beaumont au Maine' (Adam-Even CPA, p. 3).

demi lion et couroné au chief, *on a chief a crowned demi-lion rampant*. See CHIEF A UN DEMI LION ET COURONÉ AU CHIEF.

demi lion rampant, *demi-lion rampant* (Fig. 144). *Escanor*, vv. 3598–600:

> Burelé d'argent et de geules
> R'aloit Hector l'escu portant
> Au noir demi lion rampant.

Syn.: see DEMI LION.

denté, *indented*. See BORDURE DENTEE. *Syn.*: see ENDENTÉ¹.

de par, see PORTER DE PAR SON PERE.

de . . . pieces barré de . . . et de . . ., *barry of . . . (the number of pieces, i.e. stripes, is indicated)* (Fig. 5). *K*, vv. 64–6:

> Banier avoit, e par droit conte,
> De sis pecys la vous mesur,
> Barree de argent e de asur.

Syn.: see BARRÉ DE . . . ET DE . . .¹.

de plain, *undifferenced (arms)*. See ARMES DE PLAIN . . . FORS QU'EL QUARTIER AVOIT EGLETES PAR DESCONOISSANCE, TOUT DE

PLAIN LES ARMES . . . FORS QU'EL QUARTIER
A EGLES. *Syn.*: see ARMES PLAINES[1].

descomparoison, *difference.* See POUR DES-
COMPAROISON. *Syn.*: see DESCONOISSANCE[2].

desconoissance[1], *arms or distinctive device on
a heraldic shield.* See SANS NULE AUTRE
DESCONOISSANCE. *Syn.*: CONOISSANCE[1]. *Note*:
cf. the following non-heraldic use where
the locution *par desconoissance* means 'as
a distinctive sign'; *TC*, vv. 4516–17:

> Blanche corroie et blanc cordel
> Avoient per deconissance.

Cf. PAR DESCONOISSANCE. In *CC*, v. 3270,
desconoissance also means 'distinctive sign':

> La veïssiés tant garniment
> D'or et de samis et de soie
> Que li paÿs en reflamboie,
> Et maint pyngnon et mainte mance
> Et mainte autre desconnissance.

desconoissance[2], *difference.* See PAR DES-
CONOISSANCE. *Syn.*: CONOISSANCE[2], DES-
COMPAROISON, DESPAREIL[1], DESPAREILLE,
RECONOISSANCE. *Note*: see DESCONOISTRE[1]
and cf. CONOISSANCE[1]. A difference is a variation in a coat assuring distinctiveness
from related armorial bearings. On differencing, consult Robert Gayre, *Heraldic
Cadency* (London, 1961).

desconoistre[1], *to differentiate* (*arms*). *EO*,
vv. 4833–8:

> Li rois Corsubles l'uitisme conduisoit,
> C'ert la plus grande, car raisons
>   l'enseignoit;
> Armes bendees d'or et de noir portoit,
> Et Danemons ses fieus teles avoit,
> Mais que une ourle qui les
>   descounoissoit
> I ot de gueules qui bien y avenoit.

Note: cf. DESCONOISSANCE[2]. Henry, iii. 360,
note to v. 4837: '*Descounoistre*: "distinguer, faire reconnaître"; ce sens manque à
God[efroi], et T[obler]–L[ommatzsch] ne
connaît que notre seul exemple.'

desconoistre[2], *to disguise* (*one's arms*).
Perlesvaus, p. 198: il desconoist son escu et
ses armes; *Lancelot propre*, v. 185: pour
estre desconneus. *Syn.*: DESCONOISTRE (SOI).
Note: cf. ARMES CHANGIER.

desconoistre (**soi**), *to disguise one's arms.*
Perlesvaus, p. 194: il se veult desconoistre
de cestui; *Lancelot propre*, iii. 276: Et por

chou que nous nous desconnoisons li .i. des
autres, si gardés que chascuns ait pendu
son escu a son col che dedens defors. *Syn.*:
DESCONOISTRE[2]. *Note*: cf. ARMES CHANGIER.

**des courones tant que l'on i pouvoit
metre,** *semy of crowns* (Fig. 36). *Lancelot
propre*, iii. 421: et des corones tant que l'en
i pooit metre. *Syn.*: A COURONES.

desguisié[1], (*arms*) *changed* (*as a disguise*).
Vulgate Merlin Sequel, p. 378: deguisés de
lor armes. *Note*: cf. ARMES CHANGIER, ES-
TRANGES ARMES.

desguisié[2], *complex, bizarre* (*arms*). *Cleomadés*, v. 727: Armes portoit moult desgui-
sees. *Note*: complete blazon provided s.v.
SERPENT.

de son pere, *his father's* (*arms*). See ARMES
DE SON PERE A.

desor, *above, upwards.* See DESOUS ET DESOR,
DEUS DESOR ET UN DESOUS, GANT LES DOIZ
DESOR, MEIN DESOR, UN DESOUS ET L'AUTRE
DESOR. *Syn.*: see DESUS. *Note*: cf. SOR and see
example from *Sone* cited in *Note*.

de . . . sor le . . . et de . . . sor le . . . ,
see PARTI DE . . . ET DE . . . , DE . . . SOR
LE . . . ET DE . . . SOR LE . . . *Note*: cf. DE
L'UN EN L'AUTRE[1]. See also EN AZUR.

desous, *below.* See AU DESOUS DE LA CROIS,
L'UN DESOUS ET L'AUTRE DESUS, N'AVOIR NUL
AUTRE TAINT DESOUS, UN DESOUS ET L'AUTRE
DESOR.

desous et desor, *below and above.* See
FESSIEL ENCHASTELÉ DESOUS ET DESOR.

desous et l'autre desor, *below and above.*
See LISTEAUS UN DESOUS ET L'AUTRE DESOR.

despareil[1], *difference.* See PAR DESPAREIL.
Syn.: see DESCONOISSANCE[2].

despareil[2], *different, distinct.* See ARMES DES-
PAREILLES.

despareille, *difference.* See POUR DESPA-
REILLE. *Syn.*: see DESCONOISSANCE[2].

desparoil, *difference.* See DESPAREIL.

desploié, *displayed.* See EGLE DESPLOIEE.
Syn.: see EGLE.

desus, *on, thereon.* (1) *preposition.* See FLEU-
RETÉ DESUS LE . . . , GELINE DESUS LE PUI.
(2) *adverb.* *TC*, vv. 3231–7:

> Joifrois d'Aspremont vint premiers,
> Si ne sambla pas pautonniers.
> N'avoit chapel ni esclavine,
> Tous fu covert de soie fine

Si riche que trop me mervoil,
Ca ce fu d'un samis vermoil
A une crois d'argent desus.

For other uses, see DEUS DESOR ET UN
DESOUS, L'UN DESOUS ET L'AUTRE DESUS,
PAR DESUS LE . . . *Syn.*: DESOR, SUS. *Note*:
on the arms of Joffroi d'Aspremont,
consult Delbouille, pp. lxxvi, lxxxii.

de tel apareil, *same* (*arms*). See ARMES DE
TEL APAREIL.

de travers, *fessewise*. See BASTON DE TRAVERS,
BENDÉ DE . . . ET DE . . . DE TRAVERS, BENDE
DE TRAVERS, FESSE DE TRAVERS, VUIVRE DE
TRAVERS EL CHIEF. *Syn.*: EN TRAVERS.

detrenchié, *barry, barruly* (Fig. 5). *TC*,
vv. 3213–16:

Arméz estoit, par grant cointise,
De riches armez a devise,
Detranchies et ferreteies
D'argent, de guelles bureleies.

Syn.: see BARRÉ DE . . . ET DE . . .[1]. *Note*:
Delbouille, glossary, p. 171: 'detranchies
3215, *découpées en bandes étroites,* — et
ferreteies = *burelées*'. See, however, FER-
RETÉ.

deus, *two*. See BAR, BASTON[4], COTICE, EGLE
A DEUS TESTES, LIONS RAMPANZ DOS A DOS,
LISTE[3], LISTEL, SAUMON, and synonyms.

deus desor et un desous, *2 and 1*. See
SAUTOIRS DEUS DESOR ET UN DESOUS. *Syn.*:
DEUS ET UNE.

deus et une, *2 and 1*. See BOUGES DEUS
ET UNE. *Syn.*: DEUS DESOR ET UN DESOUS.

deus . . . un . . ., *2 (of one tincture) and
1 (of another)*. See PEUS RECOUPÉS DEUS . . .
UN . . .

devant[1], *referring to the first quarter of a
quarterly shield*. See DEVANT UNE ESTOILE,
EN LE QUARTIER DEVANT. *Syn.*: PREMERAIN
QUARTIER, PREMIER QUARTIER. *Note*: in
Matthew Paris's blazon of the arms of
William of Mandeville (Pusikan, p. 145:
'Ad quatre quartiers, quartier devant d'or
cum suo pari'), *quartier devant* may be taken
to refer to the third as well as to the first
quarter. Elsewhere, Matthew Paris uses
Lat. *ante* (Pusikan, p. 33: 'de Berners.
Quarteré d'or et viridi, auro ante) and
anterior (Pusikan, p. 147: 'Willelmi de
Bellocampo. Quartier d'or anterior cum
suo pari, alia de gules, la fesse de gules';

'Hugonis de Novilli. Anterior quartier
[P: quartena] cum suo pari') in a similar
way. Cf. his use of *cantel anterior* in his
blazon of the Earl of Lincoln's arms quoted
in full above, s.v. BENDE[1]. Finally, in yet
another blazon, *ante* refers to the front half
of the lion charging a party field, the tincture here being the same as the other half
of the lion (Pusikan, p. 143: 'Comitis
Marescalli. Medieta [*sic*; P: medietas]
viridis, alia au̅r [P: aurea; *Aspilogia II*,
p. 39, item 18: aurei] leo gules, ante leo-
nem gules'). Cf. also EN LE PRE . . .

devant[2], *referring to the dexter point of a chie*
(Fig. 71). See EL CHIEF DEVANT LE LIONCEL
COURANT.

devant[3], *referring to the dexter chief* (Fig. 2).
See EL CHANTEL DEVANT UNE FLEUR, EN
CHANTEL DE DEVANT UN LION. *Note*: cf.
QUARTIER[4].

devant une estoile, *in the first quarter
a mullet*. See ESQUARTELÉ DE . . . ET DE . . .
ET DEVANT UNE ESTOILE. *Syn.*: see MOLET EN
LE QUARTIER DEVANT. *Note*: refers to
DEVANT[1].

devis, *blazon*. See DIRE LE DEVIS. *Syn.*:
DEVISION.

deviser[1], *to blazon*. Most common term to
denote the action of describing a coat of
arms. For example, *Charrete*, vv. 5771–2,
5823–4:

Et cil lor armes lor devisent
Des chevaliers que il plus prisent.

. . . .

Ensi devisent et deboissent
Les armes de ces qu'il conoissent;

FCT, v. 4344: Or deviserai lor escus;
Durmart, v. 1407: Bien vos sai l'escu
deviser; v. 12195: Ne deviserai pas chascune; *Perlesvaus*, p. 209: tel escu com vos
devisez; p. 405: e connut l'escu tel com
en li ot devisé; *Lancelot propre*, iii. 173: mon
escu li devisés . . . si li devise son escu;
Mort Artu, p. 19: devisent; p. 27: com vos
avez devisé; p. 79: devise; p. 97: devisees;
Hem, vv. 1068–71:

Se tu veus mes armes aprendre
A deviser, eles sont d'or,
Et se tu veus sonner ce cor,
Le surplus t'en deviserai.

Syn.: DEVISER LA FAÇON DE L'ESCU, DEVISER LA FAÇON DES ARMES, DIRE LE DEVIS. *Note*: for another example, see SERPENT.

deviser², *to devise, i.e. invent a coat of arms.* Berte, vv. 3221–4:

La devienent si home, chascun en foi baisa;
Les armes qu'il porterent li rois les devisa
D'asur, mais que de blanc un poi les
        dyaspra
Li maistres qui les fist, car on li conmanda.

Note: for discussion, see DIASPRER, *Note*, and FLEUR DE LIS TOUT EN MILIEU, *Note*.

deviser³, *to illustrate, to represent symbolically (by means of arms).* Mort Artu, p. 63: le jor qu'il porta les armes noires et qu'il vein-qui l'assemblee de vos deus, einsi comme la portreture que vos veez ici le devise. *Note*: cf. SENEFIANCE.

deviser la façon de l'escu, *to blazon.* Lancelot propre, v. 12: un tel escu. Si li devise la fachon. *Syn.*: see DEVISER¹.

deviser la façon des armes, *to blazon.* Lancelot propre, iv. 236: Et il li devise des armes la fachon; . . . la fachon des armes que li chevaliers li devise. *Syn.*: see DEVISER¹.

division, *blazon. EO*, vv. 5023–7:

Quels armes ot Charlos, li fieus
        Charlon,
Deviserai, car ce me samble bon.
Teles, dont j'ai fait la devision,
K'ot li rois Charles o le flori grenon
Portoit Charlos ses fieus . . .

Syn.: DEVIS.

diablel, *small devil. TA*, vv. 568–9:

.I. dëablel et .i. sarpent
Vi combatre enmi la baniere.

For another use, see BORDÉ DE DIABLEAUS.

diaspré (de . . . et de . . .), *diapered* (Fig. 51). (1) *the tincture of the diapering is not specified. C* 40: diaprés (*Cl* 40: diasprez; *Cd* 40: erasrer [*sic*]); 103: diasprés (*Cl* 103: diasprez; *Cd* 103: diasprés); *CC*, vv. 1598–9:

S'i ot une fasse endentee
De geules qui fu diaspree.

(2) *the tincture of the diapering is specified. Cleomadés*, vv. 712–14 (complete blazon provided s.v. TESTE D'AUNE):

Garsianis portoit l'escu
Dyaspré de vert et de jaune,
A une noire teste d'aune;

CP 100: d'argent a une fesse d'asur diapree d'or. *Syn.*: PAILLIÉ. *Note*: cf. LETRÉ DE . . . ET DE . . ., PALETÉ. The diapering here covers cotices, bars, fusils conjoined in fess, the field, and a fess respectively. OFr. *diaspre* (< Medieval Lat. *diasprum* 'flowered cloth' < Lat. *jaspis* 'jasper [the stone]') was the name of a kind of precious cloth ornamented with flowers or arabesques; the term, however, was also used to designate precious cloth generally. In the following passages, for example, the latter sense is intended and no diapering as such is involved (*Escanor*, vv. 3643–4):

Suz .i. cheval sist fort et aspre
Qui couvers fu d'un blanc dyaspre.

Elsewhere, the arms of this horse's rider, who is identified as Melian de Lis, are blazoned 'totes blanches / A un vermeil demi lyon' (*Escanor*, vv. 3650–1). Cf. *Cleomadés*, vv. 533–9:

Cleomadés sor .i. destrier
Seoit fin et fort et legier;
Les armes son pere a label
Portoit, qui moult li sirent bel;
Et estoient d'un vert dyaspre
Li label, et moult trouvoit aspre
Le cheval sor quoi il seoit.

In medieval heraldry, diapering is usually represented as a pattern of golden rings enclosing alternately an eagle and a lion on a green or blue background. See Prinet WR, p. 234; Prinet CP, p. 33 n. 3; Prinet K, p. 350, *Aspilogia II*, appendix II, pp. 164–6 (but see BENDE A COTICES, *Note*). Cf. *Aspilogia II*, p. 51, note to item 71, and ESTENCELÉ, *Note*. There is a fine example of 'heraldic' diapering on the walls of the Sainte-Chapelle in Paris (ground floor); the intention here was to represent the precious cloth. For modern varieties, see Boutell, pp. 36–7, Veyrin-Forrer, pp. 20–1.

diasprer, *to diaper. Berte*, v. 3223: un poi les dyaspra. *Note*: for complete blazon and discussion, see DEVISER² and FLEUR DE LIS TOUT EN MILIEU, *Note*. Professor Urban T. Holmes, jun., in his edition of *Berte*, p. 80, note to vv. 3221–4, states that the diapering here corresponds to the two styles extending from the fleurs-de-lis in the Boschier family arms which he believes are alluded to in this passage. For a discussion of heraldic diapering, however, see DIASPRÉ, *Note*.

d'icele façon, *with the same arms*. *Saisnes*, vv. 2966–7:

Ses escuz ert d'azur a un hermin chavron,
Baniere et coverture ot d'icele façon.

Syn.: see AUTEL[1].

d'ieuz de paon oeilleté, *semy of 'eyes' (i.e. the markings on a peacock's tail)*. *TA*, v. 1894: d'euz de paon oilleté. *Syn.*: OEILLETÉ.

dioms, *first person plural indicative present of* DIRE. *Note*: on this form, consult Pope, p. 363, paragraph 961. Though the analogical variant *disons* appeared as early as the thirteenth century, the etymological form *dioms* (CL *dicimus* > OFr. *dimes*, *dioms*), attested in the twelfth century, persisted until the seventeenth century.

dire, *to call, to give a name to*. See LION DONT DIOMS LA COUE DOUBLE.

dire le devis, *to blazon*. *Hem*, vv. 1064–5:

Et des armes que vous portés,
Sire, dites moi le devis.

Syn.: see DEVISER[1].

divers, *different*. See NE LA PORTER DIVERSE FORS DE, N'ESTRE DIVERS DE RIEN NON FORS DE . . . SEULEMENT. *Note*: for another meaning ('difficult [to blazon]'), see CEZ CHOSES, *Note*.

diversité, see N'AVOIR NULE AUTRE DIVERSITÉ D'ARMES ENTRE.

do[1], *ghost word*. The complete blazon reads as follows: *H* 25: Sr John de Wake porte d'or ou .ii. fesses de gulez ou .iii. tortous do en le chief (*Hg* 25: Johan de Wake porte d'or a deus fesses de goules od troys tourteaux de goules en le chef). *Note*: Gough H, p. 134, note to item 25: 'In [*H* 25], for "do", read "de gulez".'

do[2], *ghost word*. The complete blazon reads as follows: *Bc* 10: Le c. de Hereford, de azur a sis leonceus de or do une bende de argent a deus cotinces de or (*B/Ba/Bb* 10, see LIONCEAUS OU UNE BENDE A DEUS COTICES; *Bl* 10, see LIONCEAUS OVE UNE BENDE A DEUS COTICES).

doit, *finger (of a glove)*. See GANT LES DOIZ DESOR.

doiz, see DOIT.

dont, *concerning which, whose*. See LION DONT DIOMS LA COUE DOUBLE, LION RAMPANT DONT LA COUE S'ESPANT EN DOUBLE. See also BENDE ENTREALEE DE DEUS COTICES LIONCEAUS EN RAMPANT ASIS AU DEHORS, LION LI CHIEF COURONÉ COUE FOURCHIEE.

doré, *or (yellow)*. *Aquin*, v. 742: en son escu porte un leon doré; *Durmart*, v. 8424: doree; v. 3999: dorees; vv. 11143, 11800, 12370, 13049, 13157, 13902: dorés; v. 12917: doré; *Jourdain de Blaye*, vv. 1066, 1091: en la doree targe; *Chevalier au Cygne*, v. 6200: doré; *TA*, v. 1943: Doré; *Atre périlleux*, v. 2814: escu doré; *CC*, v. 1863: Tous semenciés d'aigles dorés; *Sone*, v. 13883: doré; v. 13923: Dorét. For another use, see TOUT DORÉ. *Note*: cf. DORER.

dorer, *to colour or (i.e. yellow)*. *TA*, vv. 848–51:

Plesant escu ot Loberie,
Car trop sembla le traïson
Fors d'itant, que Detractïon
Le dora de faintes parolles.

Note: cf. DORÉ.

dos a dos, *addorsed (back to back)*. See LIONS RAMPANZ DOS A DOS. *Syn.*: see ADOSSÉ.

Douai, see ARMES DE DOUAI.

double, *double, in two (referring to a forked tail)*. See COUE DOUBLE, EN DOUBLE. *Syn.*: see FOURCHIÉ[1].

double coue, *forked tail*. See LION RAMPANT COURONÉ O DOUBLE COUE. *Syn.*: see COUE FOURCHIEE[1].

double treçon, *double tressure (flory counterflory)* (Fig. 127). *Escanor*, vv. 3692–7:

Le roi d'Escoce qui bien pris
S'ert garde de son couvenant
Point envers lui tot maintenant,
Bien armez sor le cheval sor,
.I. lyon de geules sour l'or
A .i. double treçon vermeil.

Syn.: see BORDURE FLEURETEE. *Note*: though the tressure here is not blazoned as flory counterflory, the arms in question are plainly those of Scotland. See Brault, 'Arthurian Heraldry', pp. 86–7.

dragon, *dragon* (Fig. 219). *Aquin*, vv. 68–9:

Thehart de Rennes qui portoit ung dragon
En son escu vermail comme leyon;

Aye d'Avignon, v. 943: si porte le dragon; *TA*, v. 1980: au dragon. For other uses, see CHIEF DEL DRAGON, CHIEF DU DRAGON,

EN LIEU OU LA TESTE DEL DRAGON ESTOIT, PRES A PRES UNE EGLE ET UN DRAGON, TESTE DEL DRAGON, TESTE DEL DRAGON EN MI. *Syn.*: DRAGON CRESTÉ. *Note*: on the dragon as a device on Christian as well as pagan banners, consult Bangert, pp. 231–2, no. 596. The heraldic dragon is discussed by George Bellew, 'Three Dragons', *Coat of Arms*, ii (1952), 5–7; see also the letter to the editor, ii (1953), 77. The best account, however, is in London, *Royal Beasts*, pp. 43–6.

dragon au desous de la crois, *dragon below the cross. Vulgate Merlin Sequel*, p. 383: la grant ensegne a la crois vermeille dont le camp estoit plus blans que noef et li dragons estoit al desous de la crois.

dragon cresté, see TESTE D'UN DRAGON CRESTÉ. *Syn.*: DRAGON.

Dreux, see ARMES LE CONTE DE DREUX.

droit[1], *true, correct (arms).* See A DROIT. *Syn.*: VRAI.

droit[2], *undifferenced (arms).* See DROITES ARMES. *Syn.*: see PLAIN[1].

droites armes, *undifferenced arms. Durmart*, vv. 9270–1:

> En son cuer est mout esjoïs
> De ses droites armes qu'il a;

EO, v. 2536: Mes droites armes; *Escanor*, v. 3640: Les droites armes des Traverses. *Syn.*: ARMES PLAINES[1]. *Note*: cf. ARMES A DROIT, SES PROPRES ARMES, SOIES ARMES MESMES. In his note to *EO*, v. 2536 (p. 351), A. Henry states that Tobler–Lommatzsch translates *droit* as 'eigen' (i.e. 'own'), giving only this example in *EO* as an illustration. He goes on to say: 'Mais par "propre", il faut comprendre, je pense: mes armes telles quelles (sans aucun signe distinctif en surcharge, par exemple, un lambel); il ne s'agit donc pas d'un sens spécial de *droit*, mais d'une acception particulière de *droit*, "juste, vrai".' Professor Henry's interpretation is correct, for the context makes it clear that Ogier refuses to bear his uncle's arms without any differencing (as the latter offers to allow), choosing a coat with a bordure which is full instead of being indented like Naimes'. See ORLE ENTIER and cf. ORLE ENDENTÉ ENVIRON where the indented bordure in *EO*, v. 5029 is said to be *pour descomparison*

(see TELS ARMES QUE . . . MES POUR DESCOMPAROISON). The passage in question is cited in full s.v. ORLE ENDENTÉ. See also POUR L'AMOUR DE, *Note*; POUR L'AMOUR QU'OT A.

duc de Bourgogne, see ARMES DU DUC DE BOURGOGNE.

du mesme, see DEL MESME.

d'une barre fessié, see FESSIÉ D'UNE BARRE.

d'une couleur, *(arms) of the same tincture (for recognition). Troie*, vv. 6721–6:

> Armes ont fresches e noveles,
> Heaumes, haubers, escuz e seles
> Totes d'un teint, d'une color,
> Qu'ensi plaiseit a lor seignour,
> Por ço qu'il s'entreconeüssent
> Es granz batailles ou il fussent.

Note: the locution is listed here merely because it resembles the expression TOUT D'UNE COULEUR ('plain arms, i.e. shield of a single tincture'); see also D'UNE COULEUR FORS, D'UNE COULEUR FORS TANT QUE. From the context, however, it is clear that the men are dressed and armed alike so that they may recognize one another in battle. Cf. TOUT D'UN TAINT.

d'une couleur fors, *plain arms (i.e. shield of a single tincture) except that. Alexandre de Lambert le Tort*, p. 121, vv. 33–4:

> Ses escu fu a or, entrais d'une coulour
> Fors el cantiel devant ot asise une flor.

Syn.: D'UNE COULEUR FORS TANT QUE, ENTIER[3], ENTIEREMENT A, TOUT[2], TOUT . . . A, TOUT . . . FORS SEULEMENT. *Note*: pleonasm. On the concept of plain arms, see ARMES PURES SANS NULE AUTRE DESCONOISSANCE, *Note*.

d'une couleur fors tant que, *plain arms (i.e. shield of a single tincture) except that. Durmart*, vv. 8546–8:

> Ses armes sont d'une color
> Vermeille comme graine fine;
> Fors tant que li ciés sont d'ermine.

Syn.: see D'UNE COULEUR FORS. *Note*: pleonasm.

d'une maniere, *with the same arms. Mort Artu*, p. 12: couvertures d'une maniere; p. 31: armes d'une maniere. For another use, see TOUT ENSEIGNIÉ D'UNE MANIERE.

Syn.: D'UNE SEMBLANCE, D'UN SEMBLANT, D'UN SEMBLANT TAINT. *Note*: cf. AUTEL[1].

d'une part, *one side, one half (of a party field).* *Charrete,* v. 5785: A cel escu vert d'une part. *Syn.*: see DEMI[2].

d'une semblance, *with the same arms.* *Artus,* p. 19: [banieres] toutes d'unes semblances. *Syn.*: see D'UNE MANIERE. *Note*: cf. D'AUTRE SEMBLANCE, LION RAMPANT CONTREMONT.

d'un semblant, *with the same arms.* *Mort Artu,* p. 31: armes . . . d'un semblant. *Syn.*: see D'UNE MANIERE.

d'un semblant taint, *with the same arms.* *Charrete,* vv. 5796–8:

> Li uns a non Semiramis
> Et li autres est ses conpainz,
> S'ont d'un sanblant lor escuz tainz.

Syn.: see D'UNE MANIERE. *Note*: refers to TAINT[2].

d'un seul taint, *plain arms, i.e. shield of a single tincture.* *Lancelot propre,* iii. 299: li escus tous blans comme nois si comme a chel tans estoit coustume que chevaliers noviax portoit escu d'un seul taint le premier an que il l'estoit. *Syn.*: see ARMES PURES SANS NULE AUTRE DESCONOISSANCE.

d'un taint, see TOUT D'UN TAINT.

e, *the conjunction 'and'.* See ET.

ebarquelé, see ESQUARTELÉ DE . . . ET DE . . .

ebartilé, see ESQUARTILLIÉ DE . . . ET DE . . .

edenté, *indented* (?). The complete blazon, which is defective, reads as follows: *BA* 178: geules (A: gueules) edentee au lablel d'azur. *Note*: probably akin to *endenté* which is, however, a bound form varying in meaning according to the term with which it is used.

egle, *eagle* (Fig. 181). (1) *the number of eagles is specified.* A. *the eagle is the principle charge.* *FCE,* v. 8470: a l'aigle; *Perlesvaus,* p. 56: .i. escu vermeill o avoit escrit .i. aigle d'or; p. 71: e al aigle; pp. 84, 207: a un aigle; pp. 197, 209: a l'egle; *Lancelot propre,* iii. 421: a une seule aigle; *Durmart,* v. 2348: a une aigle; *Joufroi,* v. 2525: A dous aigles; *BA* 3, 10, 12, 16, 99: a l'aigle; 13, 110: a une aigle; *B* 84: a trois egles (*Bl* 84: ove trois egles); *Mouskés,* v. 22036: a l'aigle; *C* 42 (*Cl* 42: a une egle; *Cd* 42: an egle),

48 (*Cl* 48: a une egle; *Cd* 48: an eigle), 63 (*Cl* 63: a un egle; *Cd* 63: a un eigle): un egle; *Cl* 3: a un egle (*C* 3, see EGLE DESPLOIEE; *Cd* 3: a .i. egle); 68: a une egle (*C* 68, see EGLE ESPANIE; *Cd* 68: a un egle); *D* 4: [a un egle]; 19: a treis egles; *CP* 111: a une egle; *CPA* 170: A une aigle; 157: a .iii. aigles; *H* 95: ou ung egle (*Hg* 95: a un egle); *Sone,* v. 13792: a un aigle; vv. 13883, 13899, 13922: a l'aigle; *K,* v. 482: le egle. *Syn.*: EGLE DESPLOIEE, EGLE ESPANIE. B. *a cross separates the eagles into four groups.* *BA* 242: a .xvi. aigles, see COQUILLE EN LA CROIS, CROIS A EGLES. *Syn.*: CROIS ENTRE EGLEZ, EGLES ES QUATRE QUARTIERS. (2) *semy* (Fig. 38). See A EGLES, AUS EGLES, BORDURE D'EGLES, SEMENCIÉ D'EGLES, TEL COM . . . FORS QU'AU CRESTEL EGLES AVOIT, TEL COM . . . FORS QU'EL CRESTEL EGLES AVOIT, TOUT DE PLAIN LES ARMES . . . FORS QU'EL QUARTIER A EGLES. For other uses, see BENDE A UNE EGLE, EGLE EN LA BENDE, EN LA BENDE UNE EGLE, PRES A PRES UNE EGLE ET UN DRAGON. *Note*: cf. EGLE VOLANT. *Aspilogia II,* p. 168, note to item 8: 'In [*Cd* 3], a four or five-letter word has been scrawled through after "s" [i.e. the abbreviation for *sable*]. This may have been "doubl" as, unlike [other versions of Walford's Roll, *Cd*] gives the single eagle to the Emperor.' The word in question is crossed out and illegible but was more likely a tincture designation beginning with the word *de* or *d'*. The eagle, in medieval as well as in modern heraldry, is normally *displayed*, i.e. has its legs and wings spread out on each side. The heraldic term *aigle* is feminine in Modern French, either masculine or feminine in Old French. For a discussion of this charge in heraldry, consult London, *Royal Beasts,* pp. 61–3.

egle a deus testes, *double-headed eagle* (Fig. 184). *BA* 7: a l'aigle . . . a 2 testes; 258, 269: a .i. aigle . . . a .ii. testes; *Cl* 1: a un egle . . . a deus testes (*C* 1, see EGLE ESPANIE OVE DEUS TESTES; *Cd* 1, see EGLE A UNE TESTE). *Syn.*: EGLE DE DEUS TESTES, EGLE ESPANIE OVE DEUS TESTES. *Note*: the word immediately following *egle* in *Cl* 1 is *peyr* (according to the printed version by Thomas Hearne in 1770) and it was emended to *neyr* (= *noir*) by Prinet WR,

p. 225 (see NOIR). *Aspilogia II*, p. 166, item 1, however, substitutes *espany*, a reading provided by *C* 1 (see EGLE ESPANIE OVE DEUS TESTES). The corner of the page where this word appeared in the MS. is now missing. London also adds the word *sable* at the end of this blazon. The double-headed eagle as the symbol of the Holy Roman Empire appears in Matthew Paris: 'Scutum Imperatoris Romae. Scutum aureum, aquila biceps nigra vel moniceps' (Pusikan, pp. 119–20; *Aspilogia II*, pp. 15–16, item 21). For Matthew Paris's explanation, see *Aspilogia II*, p. 34, item 96. Richard le Poitevin, however, used a similar expression to address Eleanor of Aquitaine in exile in 1173–84, alluding to the crowns of Aquitaine and England which she wore: 'Dic, Aquila bispertita, dic: ubi eras quando pulli tui, de nidulo suo avolantes, ausi sunt levare calcaneum suum contra regem Aquilonis?' (Rita Lejeune, 'Rôle littéraire d'Aliénor d'Aquitaine et de sa famille', *Cultura Neolatina*, xiv [1954], 46–7 and n. 134). The adoption of the double-headed eagle by the grand prince of Muscovy in the 1490s, usually said to symbolize Byzantine influence, has recently been explained as an imitation of the use of this device by the Habsburg rulers of the Holy Roman Empire; see Gustave Alef, 'The Adoption of the Muscovite Two-headed Eagle: a Discordant View', *Speculum*, xli (1966), 1–21.

egle a un croissant en la poitrine, *eagle charged with a crescent on its breast* (Fig. 185). *C* 76: un egle . . . un cresçant in le petrine (*Cl* 76: a un egle . . . a une cressant en la petryne; *Cd* 76: a une aigle . . . a cressannt in la first [?]). *Note: Aspilogia II*, p. 178, note to item 49, apropos of *first* in *Cd* 76: 'This looks like a mis-hearing of *breast* or the German *Brust*.' The arms, here attributed to Poland, are actually those of Lower Silesia. The crescent, according to London, 'is usually ensigned with a cross'.

egle a une teste, *eagle* (Fig. 181). *Cd* 1: a .i. egle a .i. teste (*C* 1, see EGLE ESPANIE OVE DEUS TESTES; *Cl* 1, see EGLE A DEUS TESTES). *Note:* apparently an error for a double-headed eagle. The arms are those of the Holy Roman Empire.

egleaus, *eaglets.* See EGLEL.

egle couronee, *crowned eagle* (Fig. 182). *D* 165: a un egle . . . coroné.

egle de deus testes, *double-headed eagle* (Fig. 184). *D* 2: [. . . gle de deus testes]. *Syn.:* see EGLE A DEUS TESTES.

egle desploiee, *displayed eagle* (Fig. 181). *C* 3: un egle displayé (*Cl/Cd* 3, see EGLE). *Syn.:* see EGLE.

egle en la bende, *on a bend an eagle. Cl* 77: a treis egles . . . en la bende (*C* 77, see EGLEZ EN LA BENDE; *Cd* 77: a 3 eigles . . . in le bende); *CP* 92: a trois egles . . . en la bende. *Syn.:* BENDE A UNE EGLE, EGLET EN LA BENDE, EN LA BENDE UNE EGLE, EN LA BENDE UNE EGLETE, SORALÉ DE BENDE O UN EGLEL. *Note:* for illustrations, see *WB* 517, fig. 92; Gayre, *Heraldic Cadency*, p. 39, fig. 57.

egle espanie, *displayed eagle* (Fig. 181). *C* 68: un egle espany (*Cl/Cd* 68, see EGLE). *Syn.:* see EGLE.

egle espanie ove deus testes, *double-headed eagle* (Fig. 184). *C* 1: ung egle espany ove deux testes (*Cl* 1, see EGLE A DEUS TESTES; *Cd* 1, see EGLE A UNE TESTE). *Syn.:* see EGLE A DEUS TESTES.

egle et un dragon pres a pres, see PRES A PRES UNE EGLE ET UN DRAGON.

eglel, *eaglet* (Fig. 187). (1) *the number of eaglets is specified. SCU*, v. 32488: trois aigliaus (*SCM:* un aiglel; *SCQ*, see EGLIER). For another use, see SORALÉ DE BENDE O UN EGLEL. (2) *semy* (Fig. 38). See A EGLEAUS, A EGLEAUS SEMÉ. *Syn.:* EGLET, EGLETE, EGLIER. *Note: eglel* is a diminutive of OFr. *egle.* The plural form is *egleaus.*

egle . . . le bec et les piés, *membered eagle (the tincture of the beak and legs is indicated). B* 200: ung egle . . . beke et les pees (*Bl* 200 [204]: od un egle . . . le bek et les pees). *Note:* cf. *P* 134: 'Jernegan Fitz Hugh de Tanfelde port d'or ove trois fees d'azure chargez d'un egle desplaié de goules beck et pees d'or'; *Navarre* 194: 'Le sire d'Aunouf, d'argent a une fesse de gueule a trois egletes de gueules a pié et bec d'azur'. Cf. HERONS PETIZ BEESTEZ.

egle qui de voler faisoit semblant, *eagle volant* (Fig. 188). *FCE*, vv. 8119–20:

A un aigle d'ermine blanc
Qui de voler faisoit samblant.

Syn.: see EGLE VOLANT.

egles es quatre quartiers, *cross cantoned with eaglets.* (1) *there is one eaglet in each canton. CP* 13: a quatre egles . . . es quatre quartiers. (2) *there are four eaglets in each canton. CP* 10: a seize egles . . . es quatre cartiers; 36: et a .xvi. egles . . . es quatre cartiers, see COQUILLE EN LA CROIS. *Syn.:* see CROIS A EGLES. *Note:* see CROIS[1].

eglet, *eaglet* (Fig. 187). (1) *the number of eaglets is specified. SCK,* fol 106 *e / SCT,* fol. 126 *d / SCV,* fol. 92 *e:* a trois aiglés. For other uses, see CROIS ENTRE EGLEZ, EGLET EN LA BENDE. (2) *semy* (Fig. 38). See A EGLEZ, POUDRÉ D'EGLEZ, TEL COM . . . FORS QU'EL QUARTIER EGLEZ AVOIT. *Syn.:* see EGLEL. *Note: eglet* is a masculine diminutive of OFr. *egle.* The plural form is *eglez.* Cf. the feminine form EGLETE.

eglet al som, *in chief an eaglet. Blancandin,* v. 1118: Ou li ayglez sïent al son.

eglete, *eaglet* (Fig. 187). (1) *the number of eaglets is specified.* See EGLETE EN LA BENDE, EN LA BENDE UNE EGLETE. (2) *semy* (Fig. 38). See ARMES DE PLAIN . . . FORS QU'EL QUARTIER AVOIT EGLETES PAR DESCO-NOISSANCE, BORDURE D'EGLETES. *Syn.:* see EGLEL.

eglet en la bende, *on a bend an eaglet. C* 77: troiz egletts (W: eglettes) . . . in le bend (*Cl* 77: a treis eglés . . . en la bende; *Cd* 77: a 3 eiglés . . . in le bende). *Syn.:* see EGLE EN LA BENDE.

egle volant, *eagle volant* (Fig. 188). *Godefroi de Bouillon,* v. 1721: Une ensaigne i ot riche et .iii. aygles volans. *Syn.:* EGLE QUI DE VOLER FAISOIT SEMBLANT, EN MILIEU UNE EGLE QUI DE VOLER FAISOIT SEMBLANT.

eglier, *eaglet* (Fig. 187). *SCQ,* v. 32488: deus aigliers (*SCU/SCM,* see EGLEL). *Syn.:* see EGLEL.

Eglise, see SAINTE EGLISE.

el = en le. *Syn.:* OU[1].

el baston, see CLOUÉ DE POINZ EL BASTON.

el champ, *on the field.* See MERLOZ EL CHAMP O UNE FESSE. *Syn.:* EL ESCU, EN L'ESCU, EN SON ESCU. *Note:* in the following blazon, Wright, p. 25, translates *Blanche banier avoit el champ* as: 'Bore a banner with a white ground' following Nicolas (p. 59: 'bore a banner with a yellow ground' [the latter's *yellow* translates the variant *jaune* found in his base MS.]). *Champ* here, however, is not a heraldic term referring to the

field of the shield. It alludes to the battle-field; *K,* vv. 579–82:

> Mes Allissandres de Bailloel,
> Ke a tout bien faire gettoit le oel,
> Blanche banier (W: baniere) avoit
> el champ,
> Al rouge escu voidié du champ.

el chantel, *in dexter chief* (Fig. 73). See LIONCEL RAMPANT EL CHANTEL. *Note:* the locutions *el chantel, el chantel devant,* and *en chantel de devant* are synonymous with OU CHANTEL DEVANT and its synonyms. In the case of OU CHANTEL DEVANT and its synonyms, however, note that in all but one of the latter expressions (OU QUARTIER DEVANT), a 'chief' is set off with a fess. One might even argue that the barry field in the exception provides a horizontal stripe at the line of the chief, although no true chief is actually being constituted. Cf. EL PREMERAIN QUARTIER.

el chantel devant une fleur, *in dexter chief a fleur-de-lis. Alexandre de Lambert le Tort,* p. 121, vv. 33–4:

> Ses escu fu a or, entrais d'une coulour
> Fors el cantiel devant ot asise une flor.

Note: refers to DEVANT[3].

el chief, *on the chief* (Fig. 75). See BASTON DE TRAVERS EL CHIEF, BEUF EL CHIEF, MERLE EL CHIEF, TOURTEL EL CHIEF, VUIVRE DE TRAVERS EL CHIEF. *Syn.:* see EN LE CHIEF[1].

el chief devant le lioncel courant, *in dexter point of the chief a lioncel courant. Durmart,* vv. 8467–77:

> Ces noires banieres parans
> As chiés d'argent resplendissans,
> Celes sont Ke le seneschal.
> Je le voi sor un grant cheval;
> De ses armes est acesmés.
> Ce est iloc mesires Kes
> Cil qui la vient devant sa gent
> A l'escu noir al chief d'argent;
> Et cil qui porte el chief devant
> Le vermel lioncel corant
> Ce est ses niés li Lais Hardis.

Note: refers to DEVANT[2]. On this blazon, see Brault, 'The Chief', pp. 83–4. Cf. also LIONCEL RAMPANT EL CHANTEL.

el chief une molete, *on a chief a mullet. K,* v. 417: El chief . . . deus molectes. *Syn.:* see ESTOILE EN LE CHIEF[1].

el crestel, see TEL COM . . . FORS QU'EL
CRESTEL EGLES AVOIT.

el escu, *on the field. K,* vv. 385–90:

> E Guillemes de Cantelo,
> Ke je par ceste raison lo,
> Ke en honnour a touz tens vescu;
> Fesse vaire ot el rouge escu,
> De trois flours de lis de or espars
> Naissans de testes de lupars.

Syn.: see EL CHAMP.

eles de message, *angel's wings.* See ENPENÉ
D'ELES DE MESSAGE.

el milieu, see CROIS EL MILIEU.

el premerain quartier, *in the first quarter
of a quarterly field.* Aspremont, vv. 2284–6,
2386, 5670:

> Sus en la targe, el premerain quartier,
> Le feri si dus Namles li Baivier
> Que il li fist et fendre et trespercier.

> .   .   .   .

> Desos la boucle, el premerain quartier,

> .   .   .   .

> Sus en la targe el premerain quartier.

Syn.: see EN LE QUARTIER DEVANT. *Note:*
refers to QUARTIER². Cf. ESQUARTELÉ DE . . .
ET DE . . . (2).

el quartier, *on the canton* (Fig. 118). See
ARMES DE PLAIN . . . FORS QU'EL QUARTIER
AVOIT EGLETES PAR DESCONOISSANCE, TEL
COM . . . FORS QU'EL QUARTIER EGLEZ AVOIT,
TOUT DE PLAIN LES ARMES . . . FORS QU'EL
QUARTIER A EGLES. *Syn.:* see EN LE QUAR-
TIER¹.

el senestre quartier, *in sinister chief* (Fig.
74). See MAHOMET EL SENESTRE QUARTIER.
Syn.: EN LA CORNIERE.

embelis, see EN BELIC.

en, see EL. *Syn.:* see SOR.

en argent, *on a field of argent. TA,* vv. 1594–
5:

> Croissant en argent foilleté
> I ot portret de demi ris.

Syn.: EN BLANC, SOR ARGENT¹, SOR L'ARGENT.

en . . . asis, *on a field of. Troie,* vv. 7756–7,
7828–9:

> Armes aveit a leonceaus
> D'azur en or vermeil asis.

> .   .   .   .   .

> Ses armes erent a aigleaus
> D'or esmeré en vert asis;

TA, v. 1385: en . . . assis; vv. 1465, 1981:
en . . . asis. *Syn.:* see ASIS SOR.

en azur, *on a field of azure. K,* vv. 52–5:

> Hue Bardoul de grant maniere,
> Riches homs e preus e cortois.
> En asur quintfullez trois
> Portoit de fin or esmeré;

v. 875: en asur (complete blazon provided
S.V. DANCE). *Syn.:* EN INDE, SOR AZUR.
Note: for parallel uses of the preposition
en in positioning phrases, see EN ARGENT,
EN BLANC, EN OR, EN ROUGE, EN SABLE, EN
VERT. In all these phrases, the tincture,
which is that of the field, is mentioned
only once. The preposition *sor* is similar-
ly employed in BASTON JETÉ SOR, SOR LE
BLANC. In the following locutions, on the
other hand, the same tincture is mentioned
twice, first as a field designator, then as
part of a positioning phrase: PARTI DE . . .
ET DE . . ., DEDENZ LE . . . ET . . . SOR LE
. . .; PARTI DE . . . ET DE . . . DE . . . SOR LE
. . . ET DE . . . SOR LE . . .; PARTI DE . . .
ET DE . . . LE . . . LE . . .; PARTI DE . . . ET
DE . . . PAR LE . . . L'AUTRE . . .; PARTI DE
. . . ET DE . . . PER LE . . . LE . . ., SOR LE . . .;
TOUT . . . MES SOR LE . . . PAR CONOISSANCE,
LION RAMPANT CONTREMONT. See also
EN L'ARGENT, EN LE GEULES¹, which refer
to the countercoloured sections of the same
quarterly shield (*D* 3).

en belic, *bendwise.* See BASTON EN BELIC,
BASTON ENDENTÉ EN BELIC, BENDÉ DE . . .
ET DE . . . EN BELIC, BENDE EN BELIC, DANCE
EN BELIC A OISEAUS, ESTACHIÉ EN BELIC DE
. . . ET DE . . ., MARTEL EN BELIC. *Syn.:* DE
BELIC. *Note:* P 50 (= *B* 10; see LIONCEAUS
OU UNE BENDE A DEUS COTICES), reads:
'Le conte de Hereford port d'azure ove
une bende d'argent ove deus coustices d'or
et sys leonceaux rampantz embelis d'or.'
A first reading suggests that it is the lioncels rampant which are 'embelis', but
comparison with other blazons argues in
favour of relating this phrase to *bende.* In
other words, the phrase is *bende en belic*
here, not *lionceaus rampanz en belic.* Wagner,
CEMRA, p. 4, states that the lion of Hugh
le Bigod in two tricked copies of Glover's
Roll preserved in the College of Arms is
drawn '"embelief" (i.e. in bend), though
it is not so blazoned'; see also *Aspilogia*

II, p. 132, note to item 89. I have not encountered this phrase anywhere else; cf., however, the 'lion rampant bendways' mentioned in connection with the seal of Ralph, Earl of Chester, in *Aspilogia II*, p. 23, note to item 48.

en belif, *bendwise.* See EN BELIC.

en bellin, en bellinc, *bendwise.* See EN BELIC.

en blanc, *on a field of argent. K*, vv. 830–3:

> Badelsmere, ki tout le jour
> Iluec se contint bien e bel,
> Portoit en blanc, au bleu label,
> Fesse rouge entre deuz jumeaus.

Syn.: see EN ARGENT. *Note*: see EN AZUR.

enbordure, *bordure.* See ORLÉ PAR CONOISSANCE D'UNE ENBORDURE. *Syn.*: see BORDURE[1].

encastelé, see ENCHASTELÉ.

enchampure, *edge of the shield.* See ORLURE DE L'ENCHAMPURE A ROSES.

en chantel de devant un lion, *in dexter chief a lion rampant. Alexandre de Lambert le Tort*, p. 120, vv. 30–1:

> Lor escut sunt vermel; en cantiel de
> devant
> Ot cescuns .i. lion a fin or reluisant.

Syn.: LIONCEL RAMPANT EL CHANTEL. *Note*: refers to DEVANT[3]. See EL CHANTEL, *Note*.

en chascun besant une croisille, see CROIS PASSANT A BESANZ EN LES QUATRE QUARTIERS EN CHASCUN BESANT UNE CROISILLE. *Syn.*: EN CHASCUN RONDEL UN CROISIÉ, EN CHASCUN RONDEL UNE CROISILLE.

en chascun corniere seit un pié, see JAMBES ARMEES O TOUTES LES CUISSES CHASCUNE CUISSE JOINTE AUS AUTRES ET EN CHASCUNE CORNIERE SEIT UN PIÉ, JAMBES ARMEES O TOUTES LES CUISSES ET EN CHASCUNE CORNIERE SEIT UN PIÉ.

en chascun label une fleur de lis, *on each pendant (of a label) a fleur-de-lis.* See LABEL EN CHASCUN LABEL UNE FLEUR DE LIS. *Note*: first label refers to LABEL[1], second to LABEL[2].

en chascun rondel un croisié, see CROIS PASSANT A RONDEAUS EN LES QUATRE QUARTIERS ET EN CHASCUN RONDEL UN CROISIÉ. *Syn.*: see EN CHASCUN BESANT UNE CROISILLE.

en chascun rondel une croisille, see CROIS PASSANT A RONDEAUS EN LES QUATRE QUARTIERS EN CHASCUN RONDEL UNE CROISILLE. *Syn.*: see EN CHASCUN BESANT UNE CROISILLE.

enchastelé, *bretessé (embattled on both sides)* (Fig. 58). See FESSIEL ENCHASTELÉ DESOUS ET DESOR. *Note*: the modern French heraldic term is *bretessé*, but note the following distinctions: 'Une fasce pourvue de créneaux sur le bord supérieur est *crénelée*; si les *créneaux* sont sur le bord inférieur, elle est *bastillée*; si elle en porte sur chaque bord, elle est *bretessée* lorsque les créneaux d'un côté répondent à ceux de l'autre, et *contre-bretessée* si chaque créneau répond sur l'autre côté à une embrasure' (Veyrin-Forrer, pp. 57–8).

en chief[1], *on the chief* (Fig. 75). See LIONCEAUS PASSANT L'UN CONTRE L'AUTRE EN CHIEF, ROUELE EN CHIEF[1]. *Syn.*: see EN LE CHIEF[1].

en chief[2], *in chief* (Fig. 72). See DANCE EN CHIEF, FESSE A UN TOURTEL EN CHIEF, JUMELES ET UN LIEPART EN CHIEF, MOLETE EN CHIEF, TOURTEL EN CHIEF, ROUELE EN CHIEF[2]. *Syn.*: see EN LE CHIEF[2]. *Note*: refers to CHIEF[2], indicating position only.

encoste, *alongside (describing the position of the edging in a fimbriated bend).* See BENDE ENLISTEE A DEUS BASTONS ENCOSTE.

en debat, see ESTRE DE CHALENGE ENTRE . . . ET . . ., *Note*.

endenté[1], *indented, continuous sawtooth line* (Figs. 24, 28, 70, 115). See BORDURE ENDENTEE, CHIEF ENDENTÉ, CHIEF ENDENTÉ ENTÉ D'UNE COQUILLE, CHIEF ENDENTÉ ENTÉ D'UNE MOLETE, ESQUARTELÉ DE . . . ET DE . . . ENDENTÉ, ESQUARTELÉ DE . . . ET DE . . . ENDENTÉ DE L'UN EN L'AUTRE, ESQUARTELÉ DE . . . ET DE . . . ENDENTÉ DE L'UN ET DE L'AUTRE, ESQUARTILLIÉ DE . . . ET DE . . . ENDENTÉ, ORLE ENDENTÉ, ORLE ENDENTÉ ENVIRON, PARTI ENDENTÉ DE . . . ET DE . . ., PARTI DE . . . ET DE . . . ENDENTÉ L'UN EN L'AUTRE. *Syn.*: DENTÉ, ENGRESLÉ[1]. *Note*: see also EDENTÉ.

endenté[2], *indented, referring to an ordinary made up of lozenges or fusils and presenting two continuous sawtooth edges* (Figs. 64, 84, 93, 105). See BASTON ENDENTÉ EN BELIC, BENDÉ DE . . . ET DE . . . ENDENTÉ L'UN EN L'AUTRE, CROIS ENDENTEE[1], FESSE ENDENTEE, FESSIÉ DE . . . ET DE . . . ENDENTÉ DE L'UN A L'AUTRE, SAUTOIR ENDENTÉ. *Syn.*: ENGRESLÉ[2], ESTRE ENGRESLÉ.

endenté³, *referring to a plain cross ornamented with triangular points jutting from the edges forming an unbalanced and discontinuous line* (Fig. 108). See CROIS ENDENTEE².

endenté⁴, *party per pale indented* (Fig. 24). *TA,* v. 702: endenté; v. 2011: endentees; *SCK,* fol. 106 *f*:

> Ses deus banieres erent grans
> Endentees molt avenans,
> De çou mie ne m'esmervel,
> L'uns en ert blans, l'autre vermel.

Syn.: see PARTI ENDENTÉ DE . . . ET DE . . .
Note: Prinet TA, pp. 4–5: 'C'est, sans doute, de *bordures endentees* qu'il s'agit, lorsque Huon de Méry parle d'"escu endenté", d'"armes endentees de felonie".' Since no tincture is specified, however—which probably would be the case if a bordure were involved—it appears more likely that an indented partition was intended.

endenté de . . . et de . . ., *vair* (?) (Fig. 4). See BORDURE ENDENTEE. *Note: Aspilogia II,* p. 180, note to item 59: '[The bordure indented in *C/Cd/Cl* 80 (59)] must be a misreading of the bordure of vair which *B* 28 gives for John's father, John FitzGeoffrey, and which appears on his own seal.'

endenté orle, *bordure indented.* See ORLE ENDENTÉ.

en deus manches de la chemise Nostre Dame, see ESCHARBOUCLE ENTRE EVANGILES EN DEUS MANCHES DE LA CHEMISE NOSTRE DAME.

en double, *forked* (*tail*). See LION RAMPANT DONT LA COUE S'ESPANT EN DOUBLE. *Syn.*: see FOURCHIÉ¹.

enerminé, *ermine* (Fig. 3). *Bl* 50: enermyné (*B* 50, see ERMINE); *SCK,* fol. 106 *e*:

> Deus autres en voit chienetees
> Qui resanblent enerminees
> A vermaus quartiers autresi;

SCT, fol. 126 *c* / *SCV,* fol. 92 *e*:

> Deus autres en voit conraees
> Qui resamblent enherminees
> A vermaus quartiers autresi.

Syn.: see ERMINE. *Note: Aspilogia II,* p. 124, note to item 50: '*Enermyne* is probably a participle meaning ermined.' In view of the fact that Gawain's arms in the *Second*

Continuation are *argent, a quarter gules,* it is clear that his son Giglain's arms merely show differencing for cadency. On this procedure, consult Gayre, *Heraldic Cadency,* chapter ii ('Cadet Differencing by Changes of Tinctures'), pp. 26–31. The modification is from argent to ermine. The exact meaning of *chienetees* in *SCK* is obscure. Comparison with *SCT/SCV,* however, where OFr. *conraees* may be translated as 'arranged' (the banners are displayed in a *conroi,* or procession), appears to rule out the possibility that this term is used here in a heraldic sense. It is, consequently, not listed in the present glossary. The *Dean Tract,* p. 26, objects to the use of this word: 'D'ermyn deit homme dire, nient enhermynee.'

en feissele, *in a small basket.* See FROMAGE EN FEISSELE.

engeignie, *angemme* (?) (Fig. 232). *TA,* v. 862: A l'engeignie de faintié. *Syn.*: see ANGEGNIES EN L'ESCU. *Note*: the following variants for this term are provided by Wimmer's critical apparatus: MS. *A*: angevine; MS. *C*: anguegine. Cf. ANGEVINE.

Engletere, *England.* See ANGLETERE.

engorgié, *gorged. TA,* vv. 996–9:

> Glouternie ot, qui vint les ambles,
> Armes de geules engoulees,
> Transglouties a granz goulees,
> Engorgiees de vilenie.

Note: the literal meaning of OFr. *engorgié* here is 'having the throat stuck, swollen'.

engoulé, *with gaping jaws. TA,* v. 1004: De glouternie ert engoulez. *Syn.*: see ENGOULÉ DE GEULES. *Note*: Goddard, pp. 131–2: 'The *gole* of a garment was the part around the throat, usually a border of fur, and *engoulé* means "provided with a *gole* or collar"'; Veyrin-Forrer, p. 176: 'Indiquent une pièce qui entre dans la gueule d'un animal: par exemple une bande engoulée à chaque extrémité dans la gueule d'un lion, ou encore la guivre qui, par définition, engoule un enfant dont on ne voit que la moitié supérieure du corps.' Stalins, item 339, suggests E. *swallowing* as the equivalent of the latter term. Boutell, p. 282, on the other hand, provides the following definition of the modern English heraldic term *engoulé*: 'pierced through the mouth'.

engoulé de geules, *with gaping jaws. TA,*
v. 997: Armes de geules engoulees. *Syn.*:
ENGOULÉ. *Note*: refers to GEULE, not GEULES,
though a pun on the latter was doubtless
intended.

engreled, see SAUTOIR ENGRESLÉ.

engreslé¹, *indented, continuous sawtooth line*
(Fig. 115). See BORDURE ENGRESLEE, ORLE
ENGRESLÉ. *Syn.*: see ENDENTÉ¹. *Note*: it was
long ago pointed out (by Nicolas in the
Gentleman's Magazine, xcvi [1826], 410–13;
see also Barron's article 'Heraldry' in the
Encyclopaedia Britannica; Prinet WR, pp.
242, 243, 255; Prinet K, pp. 348–9,
and Hope, p. 57) that the heraldic terms
indented and *engrailed* were originally
synonymous. Although certain shields in
thirteenth-century sources already show
the characteristic concave indentations
indicated by the modern term *engrailed*
(MFr. *engrêlé*), the latter term became fixed
in this meaning only subsequently to the
period under study when many other such
distinctions were also made. The term in
question is sometimes said to be derived
from OFr. *gresle* 'hail' (< OFr. *gresler* <
Germanic *grisilôn*; see, for example, the
medieval sources cited in the *OED*, s.v.
engrailed), the notion being that engrailing
resembles the pockmarks made by hail.
As can readily be seen here, however, the
earliest examples of OFr. *engreslé* in a
heraldic sense are clearly synonymous with
OFr. *endenté*. OFr. *gresle* 'lacing' (< Lat.
gracilis 'slender') has also been proposed as
the etymon of the heraldic term (*ZFSL*,
l. 346; see *FEW*, iv. 202–3) but the term
is attested only once in this sense. There is
every reason to conclude, therefore, that
OFr. *engreslé* 'indented' is a derivative of
OFr. *graisle, gresle* 'slender, sharp' (<
Lat. *gracilis*), a development based on the
pointed aspect of engrailing.

engreslé², *indented, referring to an ordinary
made up of lozenges or fusils and presenting two
continuous sawtooth edges* (Figs. 64, 84, 93,
105). See BARRE ENGRESLEE, BENDE ENGRES-
LEE, CROIS ENGRESLEE, ESTRE ENGRESLÉ,
FESSE ENGRESLEE, FESSE ENGRESLEE DE . . .
PIECES, SAUTOIR ENGRESLÉ. *Syn.*: see EN-
DENTÉ². *Note*: engrailing in the modern
sense, i.e. concave notches in the edges of
the bar, fess, saltire, etc.—as opposed to
corresponding charges made up of lozenges
or fusils conjoined—appears in several
painted shields in the period under consideration, but OFr. *engreslé* and *endenté*
were used interchangeably to refer to this
type of indentation.

en inde, *on a field of azure. K,* vv. 788–90,
836–7:

Dont moult fu defoulez li ors
De trois lyonceaus couronnez,
Ke il ot rampans en inde nez.

. . . . . .

En inde ot blanc lyon rampant,
Couronné de or, o double coue.

Syn.: see EN AZUR.

en la bende, *on the bend* (Fig. 65). See
COQUILLE EN LA BENDE, EGLE EN LA BENDE,
EGLET EN LA BENDE, ESCHALOPE EN LA
BENDE, MOLETE EN LA BENDE. *Syn.*: see
BENDE¹ (3). *Note*: see also EN LA BORDURE².

en la bende une egle, *on a bend an eaglet.*
Hg 89 [87]: en la bende trois egles (*H* 89,
see EN LA BENDE UNE EGLETE). *Syn.*: see
EGLE EN LA BENDE.

en la bende une eglete, *on a bend an eaglet.*
H 89: en la bende .iii. eglettez (*Hg* 89,
see EN LA BENDE UNE EGLE). *Syn.*: see EGLE
EN LA BENDE.

en la bende une eschalope, *on a bend an
escallop. M* 15: en la bend .iii. escallopez.
Syn.: see BENDÉ A UNE ESCHALOPE.

en la bende un lioncel, *on a bend a lioncel.*
M 64: en la bend ung leonseus.

en la bordure¹, *on the bordure* (Fig. 116).
(1) *two separate tinctures are specified for the
ordinary and its charge.* See FERS EN LA BOR-
DURE (1), LIONCEAUS EN LA BORDURE, MER-
LOZ EN LA BORDURE. (2) *only one tincture is
provided, that of the bordure.* See FERS EN LA
BORDURE (2). *Syn.*: see BORDURE¹ (2), (3).

en la bordure², *error for* EN LA BENDE. See
ESCUÇON DES ARMES DU DUC DE BOURGOGNE
EN LA BORDURE. *Note*: see BORDURE⁴.

en la boucle, see ESCHARBOUCLE EN LA
BOUCLE.

en la corniere, *in sinister chief* (Fig. 74). See
ESCUÇON OVE UN LION COURONÉ EN LA
CORNIERE, ESCUÇON OVE UN LION RAMPANT
COURONÉ EN LA CORNIERE. *Syn.*: EL SENES-
TRE QUARTIER. *Note*: refers to CORNIERE³.
See also CHIEF¹ (2) B. 1., *Note*.

en la crois¹, *on the cross*. (1) *plain cross*. See COQUILLE EN LA CROIS, COQUILLETE EN LA CROIS, ESCHALOPE EN LA CROIS, MOLET EN LA CROIS. *Syn.*: see CROIS¹ (3). (2) *cross patonce*. See JARBES EN LA CROIS. *Note*: the word *crois* always appears in another part of the same blazon, except in JARBES EN LA CROIS where the entry is defective.

en la crois², *in cross*. See LOSENGES EN LA CROIS. *Syn.*: CROIS⁴. *Note*: position only, multiple charges forming a cross.

en la crois une molete, *on a plain cross a mullet*. *M* 61: en la croys .v. molettes, see CROIS PASSANT (2). *Syn.*: MOLET EN LA CROIS. *Note*: refers to EN LA CROIS¹ (1).

en la fesse, *on the fess* (Fig. 85). See ANELET EN LA FESSE, COQUILLE EN LA FESSE, MOLELE EN LA FESSE, TOURTEL EN LA FESSE. *Syn.*: see FESSE (1) B.

en la fesse une fleur de lis, *on a fess a fleur-de-lis*. *M* 73: en la fez .iii. floure de lys. *Syn.*: see FESSE (1) B.

en la fesse un lioncel, *on a fess a lioncel rampant*. *M* 11: et en la feez .iii. leonseux. *Note*: refers to FESSE (1) B. 1.

en la fesse un molet, *on the fess a mullet*. *Hg*, Teys [93]: en la fesse troyz molés, see FESSE ET CHEVRONS.

en la geule, *in the* (*lion's*) *mouth*. See LION RAMPANT COURONÉ A LA LANGUE A UNE MANCHE EN LA GEULE DU LION A UNE ESPEE AU PONG ET AU HELT QUI TRANCHE LE LION PAR MI.

en la poitrine, *on the* (*eagle's*) *breast*. See EGLE A UN CROISSANT EN LA POITRINE.

en l'argent, *on the argent sections of a quarterly field* (*i.e. quarters 1 and 4*). The complete blazon, which is defective, reads as follows: *D* 3: [p]orte argent et gules . . . rampans en l'argent et deus toreles (?) . . . en le goules. *Note*: see EN AZUR, LIONS RAMPANZ EN LE . . ., and cf. EN LE GEULES².

en l'azur, *on a field of azure*. *C* 146: en le azure (*Cl* 146: en l'azur; *Cd* 146: in l'azure). *Syn.*: see EN AZUR. *Note*: see EN AZUR. See also EN LE . . . UNE BROIE.

en le canton une crois patee, *on a canton a cross patonce*. *Cd* 131: en les canton a crosse paté (*C* 131, see EN UN CHANTEL UNE CROIS PATEE, *Cl* 131, see CROIS PATEE EN LE CHANTEL). *Syn.*: see CROIS PATEE EN LE CHANTEL (see also EN LE QUARTIER¹). *Note*: refers to CANTON (2).

en le chantel¹, *on the canton* (Fig. 118). See CROIS PATEE EN LE CHANTEL, EN LE CHANTEL UNE QUINTEFEUILLE. *Syn.*: see EN LE QUARTIER¹. *Note*: refers to CHANTEL¹ (2) B. Hope, p. 60: 'This last term ["en le cauntel"] occurs several times in both Glover's and the Great Roll, and refers to a charge set in a corner, like that above a bend, with which it is generally associated.' Neither *chantel*, *cantel*, nor the positioning phrase *en le chantel*, *en le cantel* appears in Glover's Roll. Cf. OU CHANTEL DEVANT.

en le chantel², *in the first quarter of a quarterly field* (Fig. 26). See ESQUARTELÉ DE . . . ET DE . . . A UN LION PASSANT EN LE CHANTEL DE, ESQUARTILLIÉ DE . . . ET DE . . . A UN LION PASSANT EN LE CHANTEL DE, ESQUARTILLIÉ DE . . . ET DE . . . EN LE CHANTEL DE . . . UN MOLET, QUARTELÉ DE . . . ET DE . . . EN LE CHANTEL DE . . . UNE MOLETE, QUARTILLIÉ DE . . . ET DE . . . ET EN LE CHANTEL DE . . . OU UN MOLET. *Syn.*: see EN LE QUARTIER DEVANT. *Note*: refers to CHANTEL².

en le chantel³, *cantoned* (*i.e. in the dexter chief set off by a plain cross*) (Fig. 106). See CROIS PASSANT EN LE CHANTEL UNE MERLETE. *Note*: refers to CHANTEL³, indicating position only.

en le chantel de . . . ou une molete, *in the first quarter of a quarterly field a mullet*. See QUARTILLIÉ DE . . . ET DE . . . ET EN LE CHANTEL DE . . . OU UN MOLET. *Syn.*: EN LE CHANTEL DE . . . UNE MOLETE. *Note*: refers to EN LE CHANTEL².

en le chantel de . . . une molete, *in the first quarter of a quarterly field a mullet*. See QUARTELÉ DE . . . ET DE . . . EN LE CHANTEL DE . . . UNE MOLETE. *Syn.*: EN LE CHANTEL DE . . . OU UNE MOLETE. *Note*: refers to EN LE CHANTEL².

en le chantel une merlete, *martlet cantoned*. See CROIS PASSANT EN LE CHANTEL UNE MERLETE. *Note*: refers to EN LE CHANTEL³, indicating position only.

en le chantel une quintefeuille, *on a canton a quintfoil*. *H* 106: en le cantell quintfoyl (*Hg* 106: et en le cauntel un quintefoil). *Note*: refers to EN LE CHANTEL¹.

en le chevron, *on the chevron*. See FLEURETES EN LE CHEVRON. *Note*: refers to CHEVRON (1) B.

en le chief[1], *on the chief* (Fig. 75). See CHEVRON EN LE CHIEF, ESTOILE EN LE CHIEF[1], GASTEL EN LE CHIEF, MIREOR EN LE CHIEF, MOLETE EN LE CHIEF, MOLET EN LE CHIEF[3], ROUELE EN LE CHIEF[1]. *Syn.*: AU CHIEF, EL CHIEF, EN CHIEF[1], SOR LE CHIEF. *Note*: for a discussion of the various uses of this locution, consult Brault, 'The Chief', p. 86.

en le chief[2], *in chief* (Fig. 72). See BARRE OD UNE ESTOILE EN LE CHIEF, BARRE OD UN TOURTEL EN LE CHIEF, BARRE OVE UNE MEULE EN LE CHIEF, DANCE EN LE CHIEF, ESTOILE EN LE CHIEF, FESSE ET UNE ESTOILE EN LE CHIEF, FESSE OD UN TOURTEL EN LE CHIEF, FESSE OVE UN TOURTEL EN LE CHIEF, JUMEAUS EN LE CHIEF UN LIEPART PASSANT, JUMELES ET UN LION EN LE CHIEF PASSANT, LIEPART EN LE CHIEF A DEUS JUMELES, MEULE EN LE CHIEF, MEULET EN LE CHIEF, MOLET EN LE CHIEF[1], ROUELE EN LE CHIEF[2], TOURTEL EN LE CHIEF. *Syn.*: AL SOM, EN CHIEF[2], OU CHIEF[1]. *Note*: refers to CHIEF[2], indicating position only. Used most frequently in conjunction with one of the ordinaries featuring a horizontal line partitioning the shield into an upper and lower section (viz. bars, bars gemells, or a fess), this positioning phrase also occurs when the horizontal line is constituted by the charge itself (BASTON DE TRAVERS EN LE CHIEF, DANCE EN LE CHIEF). Cf. CHIEF[2], *Note*.

en le chief[3], *descriptive phrase referring to the chief.* See FRETÉ EN LE CHIEF. *Note*: cf. EN LE GEULES[1] and EN LE LABEL.

en le chief un liepart passant, *in chief a leopard passant.* See JUMEAUS EN LE CHIEF UN LIEPART PASSANT.

en le geules[1], *descriptive phrase referring to the gules quarters* (*i.e. quarters 2 and 3*) *of a quarterly field.* See FRETÉ EN LE GEULES. *Note*: cf. EN LE CHIEF[3], LE GEULES.

en le geules[2], *on the gules sections of the shield.* (1) *referring to alternating stripes of a barry field which are charged.* For complete blazon, see MOLETES EN LE . . . (2) *referring to alternating stripes of a barry undy field which are charged.* For complete blazon, see BESANT (1). (3) *referring to quarters 2 and 3 of a quarterly field which are charged.* See TOURELE EN LE . . . (for complete blazon, see EN L'ARGENT). (4) *referring to alternating stripes of a gyronny field which are charged.* See CROISETES

EN LE . . . *Syn.*: SOR LE GEULES. *Note*: see ES GEULES.

en le label, *on the label* (Fig. 122). *M* 38: en (G: ou) le lable. *Note*: descriptive phrase referring to BESANTÉ (5), LABEL[1]. Cf. EN LE CHIEF[3].

en le label les fleurs de lis, *label semy of fleurs-de-lis.* *Hg* 49 [50]: en le lambel les flures de lys (*H* 49, see EN CHASCUN LABEL UNE FLEUR DE LIS). *Note*: refers to LABEL[1]; *H* 49, on the other hand, refers to LABEL[2].

en le noir, see OU NOIR.

en le pre . . ., see LION PASSANT EN LE PRE . . .

en le premier quartier, *in the first quarter of a quarterly field.* See ESQUARTELÉ DE . . . ET DE . . . OVE UNE MOLETE EN LE PREMIER QUARTIER. *Syn.*: see EN LE QUARTIER DEVANT.

en le quartier[1], *on the canton* (Fig. 118). See LIEPART EN LE QUARTIER, LIEPART PASSANT EN LE QUARTIER. *Syn.*: AU QUARTIER, EL QUARTIER, EN LE CANTON, EN LE CHANTEL[1], EN UN CHANTEL, OU QUARTIER[1].

en le quartier[2], *in the first quarter of a quarterly field* (Fig. 26). For a possible use, see ESQUARTELÉ DE . . . ET DE . . . UN LION PASSANT EN LE PRE . . . *Syn.*: see EN LE QUARTIER DEVANT.

en le quartier devant, *in the first quarter of a quarterly field* (Fig. 26). See ESQUARTELÉ DE . . . ET DE . . . OVE UNE ESTOILE EN LE QUARTIER DEVANT, QUARTELÉ DE . . . ET DE . . . UN MOLET EN LE QUARTIER DEVANT. *Syn.*: EN LE CHANTEL[2], EN LE QUARTIER[2], EL PREMERAIN QUARTIER, EN LE PREMIER QUARTIER. *Note*: refers to DEVANT[1]; cf. OU QUARTIER DE.

en l'escu, *on the field.* *TC*, vv. 455, 1582: en l'escu. For other uses, see ANGEGNIES EN L'ESCU, BILLETES POUDREES EN L'ESCU, EN L'ESCU LABEL. *Syn.*: see EL CHAMP. *Note*: see BORDURE[2], *Note*.

en l'escu label, *label* (Fig. 121). *Hunbaut,* v. 2670: En l'escu au lion labiel. *Syn.*: LABEL[1].

en les espaules, *on the shoulder.* See LION RAMPANT ET EN LES ESPAULES DU LION UNE QUINTEFEUILLE. *Syn.*: EN L'ESPAULE.

en l'espaule, *on the (lion's) shoulder.* See LION ET A UNE FLEUR DE LIS EN L'ESPAULE DU LION, LION RAMPANT A UNE FLEUR DE LIS

EN L'ESPAULE DU LION. *Syn.*: EN LES ES-
PAULES.

**en les quartiers de . . ., en les quartiers
de . . .,** *in certain quarters of a quarterly field.*
See ESQUARTILLIÉ DE . . . ET DE . . . EN LES
QUARTIERS DE . . ., EN LES QUARTIERS DE . . .;
ESQUARTILLIÉ DE . . . ET DE . . . A CHASTEAUS
EN LES QUARTIERS DE . . ., A LIONCEAUS EN
LES QUARTIERS DE . . .; QUARTILLIÉ DE . . .
ET DE . . . EN LES QUARTIERS DE . . ., EN LES
QUARTIERS DE . . . *Note*: positioning phrase,
used only when the first and fourth quarters
bear a different charge from the second and
third quarters. Cf. other entries s.v. ESQUAR-
TELÉ DE . . . ET DE . . ., ESQUARTILLIÉ DE . . .
ET DE . . ., QUARTELÉ DE . . . ET DE . . .,
QUARTILLIÉ DE . . . ET DE . . .

en les quatre quartiers, *in the four 'quarters'
set off by a plain cross.* See BESANZ EN
LES QUATRE QUARTIERS, RONDEAUS EN LES
QUATRE QUARTIERS. *Syn.*: ES QUATRE QUAR-
TIERS. *Note*: positioning phrase, used only
when a cross separates identical charges.
Cf. CROIS[1] (2), ENTRE and *Note*. Cf. pre-
ceding entry. Refers to QUARTIERS[2].

en le . . . une broie, *horse-bray charging
the . . . C* 146: en le azure trois bresses d'or
(*Cl* 146: en l'azur .iii. bresser d'or; *Cd* 146:
in l'azur bresers d'or). *Syn.*: BROIE SOR
LE . . . *Note*: complete blazon provided
s.v. CHIEF[1] (2) B. 3. See also EN L'AZUR.

en lieu de, *instead of. K,* v. 321: O une fesse
en lieu de dance. For other uses, see EN
LIEU DE . . . METRE, TELS ARMES MES QU'EN
LIEU D'UNE BARRE MEINS.

en lieu de . . . metre, *to bear . . . instead of.
K,* vv. 198–9:

Car en lieu des merlos mettoit
Trois chapeaus de rosis vermelles
(W: vermeilles).

enlisté, *fimbriated* (Fig. 63). See BENDE EN-
LISTEE A DEUS BASTONS ENCOSTE.

en lonc[1], *per pale.* See DE LONC EN LONC,
PARTI DE . . . ET DE . . . EN LONC. *Syn.*: see
DE LONC. *Note*: cf. L'UN DESOUS ET L'AUTRE
DESUS (in pale).

en lonc[2], *couped, i.e. 'nourri'* (Fig. 237). See
FLEUR DE LIS EN LONC. *Note*: cf. DEMI[1] and
see FLEUR DE LIS EN LONC, *Note*.

en l'or, *on the or (yellow) stripes of a barry
field.* The complete blazon reads as follows:
BA 62: Jehan Presins, l'escu bendé d'or et

d'azur de travers a sautires (A: sautiers)
de geules (A: gueules) en l'orle [*sic*]. *Note*:
cf. parallel uses in the Bigot Roll s.v. EN
LE GEULES[2], OU NOIR, and cf. EN L'ARGENT.
Adams's note to *BA* 62 identifies the arms
in question as those of the Persijn family
and cites a seal dated 1256 as well as
the following blazon from the Armorial
du héraut Vermandois (B.N. MS. f. fr.
2249): 'fascé d'or et d'azur a sautoirs de
gueules es fasses d'or'. Adam, however,
did not suggest emending *en l'orle* to read
en l'or, a conclusion manifestly called for
by his evidence. Refers to SAUTOIRS EN L'OR.

en l'orle[1], *on the bordure* (Fig. 116). See
BESANZ EN L'ORLE. *Syn.*: see BORDURE[1]
(2), (3). *Note*: cf. BORDURE[1] (3).

en l'orle[2], *in orle.* See MERLOZ EN L'ORLE.
Syn.: see BORDURE[2].

en l'orle[3], *ghost word.* See EN L'OR.

enmi, *in the middle.* See SERPENT ENMI. *Syn.*:
EN MILIEU, OU MILIEU, PARMI[1], TOUT EN
MILIEU.

en mi, see CHEVRON EN MI, EN MI UN LIEPART,
EN MI UN LION, EN MI UN RAMPANT LION,
FAUS ESCUCEL EN MI, FESSE EN MI, TESTE DEL
DRAGON EN MI. *Note*: spelling of this word
has been varied, as is customary, according
to whether it is used as a preposition (*enmi*)
or as a prepositional phrase (*en mi*). Cf.
PARMI.

en milieu, *in the middle of the shield. Cleomadés,* vv. 11306–7: Et ot en milieu .i.
butor / . . . vert. *Syn.*: see ENMI.

en milieu ou la teste del dragon estoit,
dragon's head (Fig. 220). *Perlesvaus,* p. 252:
en mileu la ou la teste del dragon estoit.
Syn.: see CHIEF DEL DRAGON.

en milieu un butor, *bittern (a kind of heron)*
(Fig. 177). *Cleomadés,* vv. 11305–8:

Rodruars portoit l'escu d'or
Et ot en milieu .i. butor
Plus vert que n'est herbe de pré,
A nature fait et ouvré.

Note: cf. HERON.

**en milieu une egle qui ae voler faisoit
semblant,** *eagle volant* (Fig. 188). *FCT,*
vv. 4355–6:

S'ot em miliu un aigle grant
Qui de voler faisoit samblant.

Syn.: see EGLE VOLANT.

en milieu un lion, *lion rampant* (Fig. 135). *Thèbes,* v. 9040: En mi leu fist paindre un lÿon. *Syn.:* see LION[1].

en mi un liepart, *leopard* (Fig. 162). *Hunbaut,* v. 2181: Si ot d'or en mi .i. lupart. *Syn.:* see LIEPART.

en mi un lion, *lion rampant* (Fig. 135). *Fouque de Candie,* v. 2098: s'a en mi un leon; *Hunbaut,* v. 2661: S'a en mi .i. vermel lion. *Syn.:* see LION[1].

en mi un rampant lion, *lion rampant* (Fig. 135). *Renart le Nouvel,* v. 266: Ot en my un rampant lion. *Syn.:* see LION[1]. *Note:* arms of Orgueil. See Flinn, p. 260.

en or, *on a field of or.* K, v. 705: en or de inde fretté. *Syn.:* SOR L'OR (2), SOR OR.

en or vermeil, *charging a field of or. Troie,* v. 7757: en or vermeil. *Note:* cf. E. *vermeil* 'gilded silver or bronze'; cf. also TOUT A SINOPLE.

enpené, *charged with an angel's wings. TA,* vv. 1358–60:

> Et porce que trestuit estoient
> Es espaulles des anges né
> Vos di qu'il erent enpené;

v. 1378: enpenez de saluz. *Syn.:* ENPENÉ D'ELES DE MESSAGES. *Note:* in *TC,* vv. 1460–3, Beckart de Maisey's chevronny shield suggests a connection with an angel's wings:

> Ausi com angles enpennéz
> Estoit arméz d'armez vermoilles
> A chevrons d'or, et a mervoilles
> Fu de dames le jor prisiéz.

The same comparison is found in the *Roman de la Violette* (vv. 5905–9: 'Des chevaliers qui viennent samblent/ Que chou soient angele empené') which the editor of that work (p. xlvi) connects with the opening scene of *Perceval.* On the latter, consult Mario Roques, 'Les anges exterminateurs de *Perceval*', *Fin du Moyen Age et Renaissance. Mélanges de philologie française offerts à Robert Guiette* (Antwerp, 1961), pp. 1–4. The modern French heraldic term *empenné* is used only to indicate the tincture of the feathers of an arrow. The corresponding English term is *feathered, flighted,* or *penned.*

enpené d'eles de message, *charged with an angel's wings. TA,* vv. 1370–1:

> L'escu d'or a elles d'argent
> Ot enpenees de messages.

Syn.: ENPENÉ.

en rampant, *rampant.* See BENDE ENTREALEE DE DEUS COTICES LIONCEAUS EN RAMPANT ASIS AU DEHORS. *Syn.:* see RAMPANT.

en rouge, *on a field of gules.* K, vv. 220–1, 376–7:

> En sa banier trois lupart,
> De or fin estoient mis en rouge;
>
> . . . . . .
>
> Johans de la Mare une manche
> Portoit de argent en rouge ouvree.

Also vv. 429, 495, 572: en rouge.

ens, *inside.* See ENZ.

en sable, *on a field of sable.* K, vv. 128, 799: en sable.

enseigne[1], *arms. Lancelot propre,* iii. 259: Ches enseignes connois je bien; *TC,* vv. 758–9:

> Et savéz vos quex est s'ansaigne?
> Un escu d'or a la crois noire;

SCT, fol. 126 c: Que les ansaignes Gavain sont. For another use, see VRAIES ENSEIGNES. *Syn.:* ARMES. *Note:* cf. ENSEIGNIÉ.

enseigne[2], *charge or other distinctive device, but only part of a complete coat of arms.* See SANS NULE AUTRE ENSEIGNE.

enseigne[3], *war-cry uttered by a herald to identify a jousting knight. Hem,* v. 4042: 'Montauban!' escrie s'ensegne; *TC,* vv. 1228–30, 1413–14, 1858–9:

> Cil autre hiraut d'Alemaigne
> En aloient crïant l'ansaigne
> Au chevalier, en lors laingaige.
>
> . . . . . .
>
> Ains escrïent 'Priny! Priny!'
> L'ensaigne au riche duc Ferri,
>
> . . . . . .
>
> Et venoient crïent l'ansaigne
> 'Lambour', qui tant est redoutee.

Syn.: ESCRI. *Note:* use of this expression in these contexts which contain blazons suggests at least a loose connection with heraldry at this time. Many war-cries became family mottoes, and paintings of armorial bearings in the later Middle Ages frequently feature such a device placed upon a scroll below the shield, or at times above or behind the crest. OFr. *enseigne* was also used in the meaning 'banner', e.g. *K*, vv. 534–5:

Wermeille [W: vermeille], o un fer de molyn
De ermine, i [W: e] envoia se ensegne.

Cf. OFr. *baniere*. See BANIERE SON PERE A . . . POUR, *Note*.

enseignié, see TOUT ENSEIGNIÉ D'UNE MANIERE.

en som, *at the tip of a lion's tail*. See LION A LA COUE FOURCHIEE EN SOM. *Note*: refers to SOM[1]; cf. AL SOM.

en son escu, *on the field*. Des Deux Bordeors, p. 9, v. 14: en son escu; *K*, vv. 686–7, 872–3:

De goules furent trois pichier
En son escu de argent luisant;

. . . . .

En son blanc escu ot fait teindre
Un chievron rouge o trois molettes.

Syn.: see EL CHAMP.

entaillié, *carved, chiselled, cut into*. *CC*, vv. 1281–2:

Et s'i ot ou chief entailliet
Un lyonciel viermeil passant.

K, vv. 259–60, 380–4:

Baniere ot rouge, ou entallie [W: entaillie]
Ot fesse blanche engreellie.

. . . . .

Oncore i fui je conoissans
Johan de Gray, ki virree
I ot sa baniere barree,
De argent e de asur entallie,
O bende rouge engreellie.

Note: metaphorical use; cf. ENTÉ.

enté, *cut into, grafted*. See CHIEF ENDENTÉ ENTÉ D'UNE COQUILLE, CHIEF ENDENTÉ ENTÉ D'UNE MOLETE. *Note*: metaphorical use; cf. ENTAILLIÉ.

entere, see ENTIER.

entier[1], *undifferenced arms*. BA 78: Vuinant ses freres li aisnel le (A: les) porte entier (A: entires). Alemans (A: Alemant); *K*, vv. 121–4:

Cil [i.e. Nicholas de Segrave] ot la baner son pere,
Au label rouge por son frere,
Johan, ki li ainsnez estoit,
E ki entiere la portoit.

Syn.: see ARMES PLAINES[1]. *Note*: BA 78 refers to the preceding entry (*BA* 77): 'Vuinemans d'Esguiemes [A: Vuincheman d'Esquiennes], l'escu eschequeté [A: echequeté] d'or et d'azur a la bordeure de geules a .i. quartier d'ermines. Alemans [A: Alemant]'. Differencing by bordure, as exemplified here in *BA* 77, was one of the most popular modes of indicating cadency. See Gayre, *Heraldic Cadency*, chapter viii, 'Differencing by Bordure', pp. 54–8. For the arms of the Schinnen brothers, see *WB* 663, 1200; *Aspilogia II*, p. 110. On the Segrave arms, see Denholm-Young, *History and Heraldry*, pp. 142–4.

entier[2], *full, complete, referring to a charge as it appears in its normal or simple form without any adornment or modification*. See BORDURE ENTIERE, LION ENTIER, ORLE ENTIER. *Syn.*: PLAIN[2]. *Note*: cf. the following use in the *Dean Tract*, p. 28, lines 112, 117, 118: 'losenges entiers' (as opposed to 'losenges percez' [= mascles], line 113) and p. 29, lines 143–5: 'Croice entier saunz nulle diversitee qe seint George porta [= plain cross]: l'escu d'argent a un croice entre de goules saunz nulle diversitee'. For another meaning ascribed to OFr. *entier* in the *Dean Tract*, see ENTIER[3], *Note*. In so far as the cross passant may be considered to be the normal or simple form of the cross, PASSANT[2] may be regarded as a synonym of ENTIER[2]. The author of the *Dean Tract* for one, however, considered these two concepts as distinct, for he lists 'croice passaunt' and 'croice entier saunz nulle diversitee' as separate items in his list of the 'xii. maners des croices' (p. 29). Cf. the following non-heraldic use of OFr. *entier* in *Durmart*, vv. 9918–24:

Maint chevalier i a veü
Qui riches robes ont vesties,
Li un les avoient parties
Et li autre d'orfrois bendees,
Si sont tranchies et coëes.
Telz i a qui les ont entieres;
Ce ne sont mie les mains chieres.

entier[3], *plain arms (i.e. a shield of a single tincture), except*. *SCK*, fol. 95 *d*:

Un escu vermel ot entier
A un lion ranpant d'argent.

Syn.: see D'UNE COULEUR FORS. *Note*: OFr. *entier* is used with the meaning 'plain arms, i.e. shield of a single tincture' in the *Dean Tract*, p. 26, line 44: 'Le counte de Mountbiliarde d'ermyn entiere'; see also ENTIER², *Note*. For a parallel pleonasm, see ENTIEREMENT A.

entierement a, *completely, except. Sone*, vv. 13791–2:

> D'asur erent entierement
> A un aigle d'or seulement.

Syn.: D'UNE COULEUR FORS. *Note*: pleonasm; cf. ENTIER³, TOUT⁵.

entour, *in orle* (Fig. 125). See ANOZ ENTOUR, ESCHALOPES ENTOUR, MERLOZ ENTOUR, OISELEZ ENTOUR. *Syn.*: see BORDURE². For another use, see TOUT ENTOUR.

en travers, *fesswise*. See BENDES EN TRAVERS. *Syn.*: DE TRAVERS. *Note*: in *BA* 215, *en travers* is Dr. Adam-Even's misreading of *de travers*; see BASTON DE TRAVERS.

entre, *between*. See BENDE ENTRE LIONCEAUS COTICIEE, BENDE ENTRE MERLOZ, CROIS ENTRE EGLEZ, ESCHARBOUCLE ENTRE EVANGILES EN DEUS MANCHES DE LA CHEMISE NOSTRE DAME, ESTRE DE CHALENGE PAR ENTRE . . . ET . . ., FESSE ENTRE CHEVRONS, FESSE ENTRE JUMEAUS, N'AVOIR NULE AUTRE DIVERSITÉ D'ARMES ENTRE, SAUMON ENTRE DARS. *Note*: cf. PAR ENTRE. *Aspilogia II*, p. 104: 'in 5 . . . cases . . . B . . . blazons the ordinary (bend or fess) between, *entre*, the minor charges. This is the earliest example which has been observed of this use of "between".' These instances are clearly antedated, however, by the items cited above. For other locutions expressing the notion of a cross or a saltire cantoned with multiple charges, see CROIS¹ (2) and (4), EN LES QUATRE QUARTIERS, ES QUATRE QUARTIERS, SAUTOIR A ESTOILES, SAUTOIR A OISELEZ, SAUTOIR ET A ESTENCELES.

entrealé, *placed between*. See BENDE ENTREALEE DE DEUS COTICES LIONCEAUS EN RAMPANT ASIS AU DEHORS.

entreconoistre (soi), *to recognize one another's arms. Troie*, vv. 6721–8:

> Armes ont fresches e noveles,
> Heaumes, haubers, escuz e seles
> Totes d'un teint, d'une color,
> Qu'ensi plaiseit a lor seignor,

> Por ço qu'il s'entreconeüssent
> Es granz batailles ou il fussent,
> E que il fust dit e retrait,
> Saveir come il l'avreient fait;

Lancelot propre, iii. 276: Ensi nous entreconnoistrons.

entre . . . et . . . un label par reconoissance, *a label as a difference between . . . and . . . TA*, vv. 1132–3:

> S'avoit entre Hasart et li
> .I. label par reconnoisance.

en un chantel une crois patee, *on a canton a cross patonce. C* 131: in un cantell . . . un crois patee (*Cl* 131, see CROIS PATEE EN LE CHANTEL; *Cd* 131, see EN LE CANTON UNE CROIS PATEE). *Syn.*: see CROIS PATEE EN LE CHANTEL. *Note*: for synonyms of the locution *en un chantel*, see EN LE QUARTIER¹. See also EN LE CHANTEL¹, *Note*.

en une bende, *on a bend* (Fig. 65). *TA*, vv. 542–3:

> Escrit portoit son jugement
> En une bende trop eslite.

Syn.: see BENDE¹ (3).

en un en l'autre, *counterchanged*. See ROSES EN UN EN L'AUTRE. *Syn.*: see DE L'UN EN L'AUTRE¹.

en vert, *charging a field of vert. Troie*, v. 7829: D'or esmeré; *TA*, vv. 667, 1385: en vert.

environ¹, *around the shield, i.e. along the line of a bordure or an orle*. See BORDÉ ENVIRON, ORLE ENDENTÉ ENVIRON, ORLÉ ENVIRON, TREÇOIR ENVIRON. *Syn.*: see BORDURE².

environ², *around the principal charge.* (1) *referring to the tincture of the field. Troie*, vv. 8065–6:

> En son escu n'ot qu'un lion
> Mais vermeuz fu, d'or environ.

(2) *referring to the crusilly field.* See CROISILLIÉ TOUT ENVIRON.

enz, *inside. CC*, vv. 712–14, 1521:

> Escut d'or a face d'asur
> Au lionciel viermeil passant
> Portés ens ou cantiel devant.

> .   .   .   .   .   .

> Ens avoit un viermeil lyon.

erasrer, see DIASPRÉ.

ermin, *ermine* (Fig. 3). *Thèbes,* v. 6229: D'ermin. *Syn.:* see ERMINE.

ermin blanc, *ermine* (Fig. 3). *Saisnes,* p. 187, v. 4 (var.): au blanc chevron ermin. *Syn.:* see ERMINE.

ermine, *ermine* (Fig. 3). *FCT,* vv. 4882, 13819: d'ermine; *FCE,* v. 8470: d'ermines; *Saisnes,* v. 2966: hermin; *Durmart,* vv. 7279, 7323, 7328, 8413, 8548: d'ermine; *TA,* v. 2071: D'ermine; *BA* 77, 109: d'ermines; 139, 169: d'hermines; 100, 122 (A: d'ermines), 142 (A: d'ermines), 143 (A: d'ermines), 153, 203, 229, 273: d'ermine; *B/Bl* 20: d'ermyne (*Bc* 20: de heremine); *B* 130 (*Bl* 130 [134]: d'ermyne), 132 (*Bl* 132 [136]: d'ermyne), 170 (*Bl* 170 [174]: d'ermyne), 207 (*Bl* 207 [211]: d'ermyne): d'ermyn; 50 (*Bc* 50: de ermine; *Bl* 50, see ENERMINÉ), 103 (*Bl* 103: d'ermyne), 157 (*Bl* 157 [161]: d'ermyne), 208 (*Bl* 208 [212]: d'ermyne): d'ermyne; 124 (*Bl* 124 [128]: d'ermine): de ermyns; 149 (*Bl* 149 [153]: d'ermyne), 173 (*Bl* 173 [177]: d'ermyne): de hermyne; 186 (*Bl* 186 [190] [2]: d'ermyne): de hermyn; 186, 211 (*Bl* 211 [215]: d'ermyne): d'ermyn; *Ba* 62 (*B* 62, see ARGENT; *Bc* 62: de hermine; *Bl* 62: d'ermyne): de hermin; *C* 23, 102: d'ermin; 88, 92, 138, 146: d'ermine; 158: d'ermyn; *Cl* 23, 92, 102, 146, 158, Creke (new item in *Cl* [166]): d'ermine; 88: d'ermin; 138: armine; *Cd* 23, 88, 158: d'ermyn; 92, 102, 146: d'ermyne; 138: ermyne; *Cleomadés,* v. 11311: d'ermine; *Hunbaut,* vv. 2660, 2666: d'ermine; *Escanor,* v. 3570: d'ermine; *D* 14, 45, 114, 156: de ermine; 35, 115, 116, 182: d'ermine; *CP* 40, 45, 55, 78, 81, 107: d'ermine; 138: d'hermine; 143: d'ermines; *CPA* 5, 13: d'ermines; *H* 7 (*Hg* 7 [9]: d'ermine): de hermyn; 14 (*Hg* 14: d'ermine): d'armin; 22 (*Hg* 22: d'ermine): d'ermin; 29 (*Hg* 29: d'ermine): d'ermyn; 33, 51, 59, 67 (*Hg* 33 [34], 51 [53], 59: d'ermine; 67 [68]: d'erminn): d'ermyne; *M* 7: d'ermyne; 60: d'ermyn; *SCK,* fol. 87: d'ermines; *K,* vv. 195, 366, 441, 535, 783, 883: de ermine. *Syn.:* ENERMINÉ, ERMIN, ERMIN BLANC, ERMINÉ, ERMINE BLANC. *Note:* L. Foulet, in the *Glossary of the First Continuation,* pp. 85–6, s.v. *ermine,* states: 'faut-il ajouter *TV* 13819 del riche escu *d'ermine et d'or* où il s'agirait d'un des

"métaux" (or) et d'une des "fourrures" du blason, ou plutôt ne veut-on pas nous suggérer que ce précieux écu est tout or et ivoire? (Voir dans *M* le v. correspondant à *T* 13819, à savoir 18057: du riche escu *d'ivoire et d'or:* même leçon dans *A* 7993, *L* 7993, mais *D* donne, d'accord avec *TV,* *die oventür vomme schilte rich, wie schön er waz von golde und hermin zart*)?' In *Ba,* the abbreviation *er.* is used to indicate ermine; in *Bb,* the fur is tricked. Where the corresponding tinctures in *Ba/Bb* 62 provide ermine, *B* 62 reads *d'argent;* see Wagner, *CEMRA,* p. 5. *Aspilogia II,* p. 38, notes that the tincture of the ermine bend in Matthew Paris's blazon of the Warwick arms is missing ('Scutum eschekeratum d'or et d'azur [T: de or et de azure], bende . . .') and adds: 'It is possible that Matthew did not know the word for ermine and therefore left a blank.' The word ermine is found, however, in Matthew's blazon of the arms of Giffard and Hussey (*Aspilogia II,* p. 47, item 56; p. 57, item 113; on p. 7, the statement is made that 'ermine [occurs] once'). For another fur in Matthew, see MASCLÉ DE . . . ET DE . . .[1], *Note,* and VAIRIÉ DE . . . ET DE . . ., *Note.* In painted blazons, ermine is usually represented as a white fur with stylized black tails (a short vertical line with a cluster of two or three dots above it). In the Wijnbergen Roll, however, the tails are depicted as blue (Adam-Even WB, p. 56). The modern distinction between 'ermine' (white fur with black spots) and 'ermines' (black fur with white spots) dates from the fifteenth century only (Wagner, *Historic Heraldry,* p. 107, credits Nicholas Upton [*c.* 1440] with this distinction; the Bradfer-Lawrence Tract, an independent compilation about the same date [1445 or soon after], may also be cited in this connection; see Léon Jéquier, 'A propos d'hermines', *AHS,* lxvii [Annuaire, 1953], 51–8; H. S. London, 'L'hermine diversicolore dans le blason anglais', pp. 59–64 [earliest example is in Basynges' Book, *c.* 1395 (p. 59)]; idem, 'Some Medieval Treatises', p. 173). The armorial bearings of Brittany (plain ermine) from *c.* 1318 onwards are canting arms for *Ermenie* or *Hermanie,* Tristan's homeland; see Introduction. This complements the explanation provided in *Aspilogia II*, p. 172, note to item 24.

erminé, *ermine* (Fig. 3). *TC*, v. 1997: L'escu vert au chief herminei. *Syn.*: ERMINE.

ermine blanc, *ermine* (Fig. 3). *Bel Inconnu*, vv. 5921–2:

> Que i porte un escu d'azon,
> U d'ermine a un blanc lion;

FCE, v. 8119: d'ermine blanc. *Syn.*: see ERMINE. *Note*: on this expression see Horrent, *Le Pèlerinage de Charlemagne*, pp. 51–2 n. 3.

es = en les. *Note*: on this and other contractions in Old French, consult Foulet, *Petite Syntaxe*, paragraph 62.

esbochon, see ESCUÇON[1].

escaker, see ESCHEQUERÉ DE . . . ET DE . . .

escalope, *escallop*. See ESCHALOPE.

escartelé, *quarterly*. See ESQUARTELÉ DE . . . ET DE . . .

eschalope, *escallop* (Fig. 211). (1) *no position is specified. B* 26: a trois escallops (*Bl* 26: ove trois skalops); 39: trois escallops (*Bl* 39: ove trois skalops); *H* 82: ou .vi. scallopez (*Hg* 82, see OD LES ESCHALOPES); *M* 67: ou .iii. scalopes. (2) *number of escallops is specified but their position is not indicated.* See ESCHALOPES ET LA FESSE, ESCHALOPES OD LA FESSE, FESSE A UNE ESCHALOPE, FESSE OU ESCHALOPES. (3) *number of escallops and their position are not specified.* See BENDE AUS ESCHALOPES. (4) *position is specified.* A. *on a cross.* See ESCHALOPES EN LA CROIS. *Syn.*: see COQUILLE EN LA CROIS. B. *a bend engrailed between six escallops 3 and 3.* See BENDE ENGRESLEE A ESCHALOPES. C. *orle of escallops* (Fig. 212). See ESCHALOPES BORDANZ, ESCHALOPES ENTOUR. (5) *semy of escallops* (Fig. 39). See AUS ESCHALOPES, CHAMP PLEIN D'ESCHALOPES, OD LES ESCHALOPES. *Syn.*: COQUILLE, COQUILLETE. *Note*: on the escallop, see George Bellew, 'Six Marine Symbols', *Coat of Arms*, iii (1954), 22, and especially the latter's 'Escallops in Armory', *The Scallop; Studies of a Shell and its Influence on Humankind, by Eight Authors*, ed. Ian Cox (London, 1957), pp. 89–104. This volume also features an excellent study entitled 'Shell: a Word's Pedigree' by Professor Brian Woledge (pp. 9–14). K. Sneyders de Vogel, jun., 'Saint-Jacques de l'escalippe', *Neophilologus*, xxxviii (1954),

81–4, derives Old French *eschalope* and kindred terms from the Dutch equivalent *scelpe*. On this and earlier etymologies, consult Gunnar Tilander, 'Français *escalippe, escalope, escapole, escalopé*', *Studia Neophilologica*, xxvii (1955), 26–30 (revised version: 'Origem de "escalope"', *Revista de Portugal*, xxiv [1959], 115–24). In Matthew Paris, the arms of Ralph FitzNichol are blazoned: 'Scutum de gules, pentafolium d'or, bordura escal' d'argent' (Pusikan, pp. 150–1). According to *Aspilogia II*, p. 44, note to item 39: 'The orle of silver scallops is omitted in the painting.' The shield is partially erased, however, and the *bordura* may have consisted of the portion of the field semy of escallops which was not covered by the cinquefoil. Cf. *B* 150: 'Rauf le Fitz Nicole, de goules ung quintefueil de or le champ pleyn des escallopes d'argent'. See also ESCHALOPES BORDANZ.

eschalope en la bende, *on a bend an escallop.* See EN LA BENDE UNE ESCHALOPE.

eschalopes bordanz, *orle of escallops* (Fig. 212). *C* 96: 15 escallops bordeants (W: bordeantes) (*Cl* 96: as escalopes . . . bordeauntz; *Cd* 96: as escalopes . . . bourdanz). *Syn.*: ESCHALOPES ENTOUR. *Note*: see ESCHALOPE and cf. CHAMP PLEIN D'ESCHALOPES. *Aspilogia II*, p. 184, note to item 84, errs in stating that *Cl* 96 [84] 'says *six escalopes*'. The editor has misread the long *s* terminating the contraction *as* (= *aus* = MFr. *aux*) as a 6.

eschalopes en la crois, *cross semy of escallops.* *B* 193: a les escalops . . . en le croix. *Syn.*: see COQUILLE EN LA CROIS. *Note*: number of escallops not specified, but no doubt five.

eschalopes entour, *orle of escallops* (Fig. 212). *Bl* 150 [154]: od le scalops . . . entour (*B* 150, see CHAMP PLEIN D'ESCHALOPES). *Syn.*: ESCHALOPES BORDANZ.

eschalopes et la fesse, *fess between escallops.* *B* 203: a trois escaloppes . . . et la fece (*Bl* 203 [207], see ESCHALOPES OD LA FESSE). *Syn.*: see FESSE (1) D. 1. b. *Note*: cf. FESSE A UNE ESCHALOPE.

eschalopes od la fesse, *fess between escallops.* *Bl* 203 [207]: od trois escalopes . . . od la fesse (*B* 203, see ESCHALOPES ET LA FESSE). *Syn.*: see FESSE (1) D. 1. b. *Note*: cf. FESSE A UNE ESCHALOPE.

escharboucle en la boucle, *carbuncle* (Fig. 248). *Chétifs*, p. 276: .I. escharbocle i ot en la bocle. *Syn.*: see CHARBOUCLE FLEURETÉ.

escharboucle entre evangiles en deus manches de la chemise Nostre Dame, *carbuncle between gospels on the sleeves of the Virgin's shift. TA*, vv. 1272–5:

> Ot asis .i. cler escharboucle
> Entre .iiii. evangiles blanches
> Pourtrez et escriz en .ii. manches
> De la chemise Nostre Dame.

escharboucle fleureté, *carbuncle* (Fig. 248). *Cd* 58: escharbucle . . . floretté. *Syn.*: see CHARBOUCLE FLEURETÉ.

eschartelé, *quarterly.* See ESQUARTELÉ DE . . . ET DE . . .

eschelon, see A ESCHELONS.

eschequé de . . . et de . . ., *checky* (Fig. 9). *B* 7 (*Bl* 7, see ESCHEQUERÉ DE . . . ET DE . . .), 30 (*Ba* 30, see ESCHEQUERÉ DE . . . ET DE . . .; *Bb* 30, see CHEQUÉ DE . . . ET DE . . .; *Bl* 30, see ESCHEQUERÉ DE . . . ET DE . . .), 33 (*Ba* 33, see ESCHEQUERÉ DE . . . ET DE . . .; *Bb* 33, see CHEQUÉ DE . . . ET DE . . .), 50 (*Ba* 50, see ESCHEQUERÉ DE . . . ET DE . . .; *Bb* 50, see CHEQUÉ DE . . . ET DE . . .; *Bl* 50, see ESCHEQUERÉ DE . . . ET DE . . .), 175: eschequé de . . . et de . . . (*Bl* 175 [179], see ESCHEQUERÉ DE . . . ET DE . . .). *Syn.*: A ES-CHEQUIER, CHEQUÉ DE . . . ET DE . . ., CHEQUERÉ DE . . . ET DE . . ., ESCHEQUERÉ DE . . . ET DE . . ., ESCHEQUETÉ DE . . . ET DE . . ., PAR ESCHEQUIERS. *Note*: Wagner, *Historic Heraldry*, p. 46: 'The chequy coat has claims to be the oldest known to heraldry' [*c.* 1135]. On the Warenne arms alluded to by Wagner here, see C. J. Holyoake, *Coat of Arms*, iv (1956), 72, and, especially, 'The Warenne Group of Chequered Shields', *Complete Peerage*, rev. ed. by G. H. White, xii, Part I (London, 1953), appendix J; *Aspilogia II*, pp. 26–7, note to item 64.

*eschequeré de . . . et de . . ., *checky* (Fig. 9). Frequent in literary sources, e.g. *Tournoiement des Dames*, v. 198: l'escu eschequeré; *Durmart*, v. 6794: Blanche et vermelle eschequeree; *Hem*, v. 1779: Li ques? — C'est cis eschekerés; very frequent in the rolls, e.g. *Ba* 20, 30, 33, 50: eschekeré de . . . e de . . . (*B* 20, 33, 50, see ESCHEQUÉ DE . . . ET DE . . .; *B*/*Bb* 20 and *Bb* 30, 33, 50, see CHEQUÉ DE . . . ET DE . . .; *Bc* 20, 30, 33, 50:

eschequeré de . . . e de . . .; *Bl* 20: escheker de . . . et de . . .; 30, 33, 50: eschekeré de . . . e de . . .); *Bl* 7, 175 [179] (*B* 7, 175, see ESCHEQUÉ DE . . . ET DE . . .): eschekeré de . . . de . . .; *Cl* 23, 25: eschekeré de . . . e de . . . (*C* 23, 25, see CHEQUÉ DE . . . ET DE . . .; *Cd* 23, 25: eschaker de . . . et . . .); *Cl* 138, 147: eschekeré de . . . e de . . . (*C* 138, 147, see CHEQUÉ DE . . . ET DE . . .; *Cd* 138: eschekeré de . . . e . . .; *Cd* 147: escaker de . . . et de . . .); 160: eschekeré de . . . et de . . . (*C* 160, see CHEQUÉ DE . . . ET DE . . .; *Cd* 160: escheker de . . . e . . .); *H* 51: eschekeré de . . . et de . . . (*Hg* 51, see CHEQUERÉ DE . . . ET DE . . .). *Syn.*: see ESCHEQUÉ DE . . . ET DE . . . *Note*: on the arms in the *Tournoiement des Dames* (Yolent = Yonet de Dreux), see H. Petersen Dyggve, 'L'Yolent à l'écu échiqueté du "Tournoiement" de Huon d'Oisi', *Neuphilologische Mitteilungen*, xxxvii (1936), 257–61. Cf. the following vestimentary use in *Bel Inconnu*, vv. 2245–9:

> Ele estoit d'un samit vestue;
> Onques si biele n'ot sous nue.
> La pene en fu molt bien ouvree,
> D'ermine tote eschekeree,
> Molt sont bien fait li eschekier.

OFr. *eschequeré* is a derivative of OFr. *eschequier, eschaquier* (< OFr. *eschac* < Arabic *shâh* 'king' [in the locution of *shâh mât* 'the king is dead']) 'chess-board'. Matthew Paris uses the following Medieval Latin and Anglo-Norman forms: 'Roberti de Tateshale. Scutum scaccaratum auro et gules' (Pusikan, pp. 125–6; the shield has been left blank); 'Comitis de Warreni. Chekeré de auro et azuro' (Pusikan, pp. 139–40; the latter erroneously reads: *cheketé*); and 'Comitis de Warewic. Scutum eschekeratum d'or et d'azur, bende . . .' (Pusikan, pp. 141–2; Thomas de Neville, Earl of Warwick, bore an *ermine* bend, as clearly shown on the painted shield).

eschequeté de . . . et de . . ., *checky* (Fig. 9). *TA*, v. 1023: Eschequeté; *BA* 59: echeketé de . . . et de . . . (A: escheketé); 77: escheketé de . . . et de . . . (A: echeketé); 137, 138, 261 (A: echiqueté): eschequeté; *Cleomadés*, vv. 9877–9: . . . un escu noir / A .i. eschiketé sautoir / De blanc et de gueules portoit; *CPA* 13, 18, 164: echequeté de . . .

et de . . . *Syn.*: see ESCHEQUÉ DE . . . ET
DE . . . *Note*: according to Löseth, *Le Roman
en prose de Tristan*, pp. 102, 103, 112, the
arms of Palamedes, son of Esclabor, in the
Prose Tristan are 'eschiqueté d'argent et de
sable'. On these arms and their later development and adoption by Regnier Pot
in the fifteenth century, consult Max Prinet, 'Armoiries familiales et armoiries de
roman au xve siècle', *Romania*, lviii (1932),
569–73.

eschequier, *checkerboard*. *TA*, vv. 1130–1:

> Une targe, trop bien parant,
> Avoit d'un eschequier poli.

For other uses, see A ESCHEQUIER, PAR ES-
CHEQUIERS. *Note*: while the shield alluded
to in *TA* is a real checkerboard, a pun is
doubtless intended on the locutions *a eschequier, par eschequiers* 'checky'.

eschochon, see ESCUÇON.

escocheon, see ESCUÇON.

escri, *war-cry uttered by a herald to identify a
jousting knight*. *TC*, vv. 1508–10:

> Cil qui furent de moi plus pres
> Venoient escrïant 'Monjoie'.
> De tel escri ou trop grant joie;

v. 1883: escris; v. 2003: escri. *Syn.*: EN-
SEIGNE^3. *Note*: cf. ESCRIER.

escrier, *to utter a war-cry by way of identifying
a jousting knight*. Frequent in *TC*, e.g. vv.
1464–5: Uns hiraus d'armes . . . / . . . escrï-
ant: 'Vaus!' See also vv. 460, 472, 768,
902, etc. *Note*: cf. ESCRI.

***escu**^1, *shield, i.e. the field of a coat of arms*.
Literary examples only after *c.* 1250, e.g.
Hem, v. 3090: un escu; *TC*, vv. 649, 862:
L'escu; *CC*, v. 712: Escut; *K*, v. 438: L'escu,
but frequent in the rolls, e.g. *BA* 1–17,
21–3: l'escu; *C/Cl* 149: l'escue (*Cd* 149,
see ESCUÇON^3); *D* 26–185: l'escu. For other
uses, see A CROISILLES POUDRÉ A L'ESCU,
ANGEGNIES EN L'ESCU, EL ESCU, EN L'ESCU.
Syn.: CHAMP, CHAMPAIGNE, ESCUÇON^3. See
also EN AZUR, *Note*. *Note*: not to be confused with *escu* 'the whole shield or coat of
arms (not simply the field)' in the following locutions: DEVISER LA FAÇON DE L'ES-
CU, MUER SON ESCU, PORTER SIFAIT ESCU,
PORTER TEL ESCU SON PERE.

escu^2, *escutcheon* (Fig. 119). See ESCU VUIDIÉ
DU CHAMP, FAUS ESCU. *Syn.*: see ESCUÇON^1.

Note: in both instances the escutcheon is
voided, resulting in an orle. For synonyms,
then, see FAUS ESCUÇON. Cf. *P* 76 (= *B*
25, see ESCUÇON^1): a troys escus.

escu^3, *small shield consisting of the field inside
an orle* (Fig. 120). *Note*: in Grimaldi's version of Glover's Roll only; *P* 127 (= *B* 37):
un escu. Complete blazon provided s.v.
DEDENZ; see also ESCUÇON OVE UN LION
RAMPANT COURONÉ EN LA CORNIERE.

escu^4, *ghost word*. *Bl* 110 [114]: l'escu. *Note*:
error for *le gu[les]*; see *Aspilogia II*, p. 137,
note to item 114. Complete blazon provided s.v. ESQUARTELÉ DE . . . ET DE . . .
LE GEULES.

escu a breteles, *field charged with shoulder-
straps (in saltire?)*. *Des Deux Bordeors*, p. 9,
vv. 7–8:

> Ge connois monseignor Begu,
> Qui porte un escu a breteles.

Note: cf. CROISIÉ^2.

escu a quartiers, *quarterly shield* (Fig. 25).
Des Deux Bordeors, p. 9, vv. 3–4:

> Et monseignor Rogier Ertaut,
> Qui porte un escu a quartiers.

Note: cf. A QUARTIERS DE . . . ET DE . . .,
ESQUARTELÉ DE . . . ET DE . . .

escucel, *escutcheon* (Fig. 119). *TA*, v. 1945:
Escuceax de totes vertuz. *Note*: cf. FAUS
ESCUCEL. *Syn.*: see ESCUÇON^1.

escucel des armes, *escutcheon of the arms of*.
Guillaume de Dole, vv. 3159–64, 5171–2:

> Cil qui portoit un escucel
> Des armes Keu le seneschal
> En son escu bouclé d'archal
> En ot erroment grant envie.
> Il fu toz les jors de sa vie
> Assez plus fel que ne fu Keus.
>
> .   .   .   .   .   .
>
> A biaus escuciaus de ses armes
> En vesti une de samis.

Note: cf. ESCUÇON DES ARMES DE BRIENNE,
ESCUÇON DES ARMES DU DUC DE BOURGOGNE
EN LA BORDURE.

***escuçon**^1, *escutcheon* (Fig. 119). No exam-
ples in literary sources, but very frequent
in the rolls. (1) *the escutcheon is not charged*,
e.g. *BA* 19, 27: a .i. escuchon; *B* 25: trois
escocheons (*Ba* 25: a 3 escuchuns; *Bb* 25:

3 escocheuns; *Bc* 25: a treis eschuchuns; *Bl* 25: ove trois escucheons). (2) *the escutcheon is charged. D* 91: a un escuchun. For other uses, see ESCUÇON PERCIÉ, FAUS ESCUÇON. *Syn.*: ESCU², ESCUCEL, ESCUÇON OU MILIEU, ESCUÇON PAR MI, ESCUÇON VUIDIÉ, INESCO-CHON. *Note*: cf. BORDURE¹ and its synonyms, and ESCU²; see also TARGE. The following blazon is omitted by Prinet in his edition of *CP* after item 105: 'Mesire Tibaut de Mathefelon porte les armes d'or a trois es-cussons de gheules.' Cf. 'Thiébaut de Ma-tefelon': *or, an escutcheon gules* in the *Tournoi de Compiègne* ('Les chevaliers français', p. 410, item 7 [listed among the 'Limousins']). The escutcheon is usually placed in the centre of the shield (MFr. *en cœur*); thus ESCUÇON OU MILIEU and ESCUÇON PAR MI are pleonasms. Cf., however, ESCUÇON EN LA BENDE and ESCUÇON EN LA CORNIERE. In *Cleomadés*, vv. 16778–86, the ladies at the Spanish court wear green cloaks decorated with little shields bearing the arms of Spain. The little shield is first called an *escucel* (pl. *escuceaus*), then an *escuçon*:

La royne et sa fille Argente,
Et les dames dont je vous di,
Et les damoiseles aussi,
Estoient la endroit venues
En cloches vers et en sambues
A *escuciaus* de riche ouvraigne
Semez fais des armes d'Espaigne.
Li *escuchon* bien fait estoient;
Sor le vert tres bien avenoient.

Cf. the heraldic cloaks in *CC*, vv. 926–7 ('clokes des armes Huon / De Florines') and vv. 963–4 ('clokes des armes Hauwiel / De Kievraing'). See Prinet CC, pp. 163–4. I have not listed BORDURE¹ and its syno-nyms nor ESCU VUIDIÉ DU CHAMP (see VUIDIÉ¹, *Note*) as being identical in meaning with ESCUÇON¹ because, while either term may actually be used to blazon the same shield (e.g. ORLE¹ to blazon the Cleves arms which feature an escutcheon in *BA* 14), different parts of the shield are being referred to, as is evident from the tincture which follows. **escuçon²**, *small escutcheon* (Fig. 74). The complete blazon reads as follows: *Bc* 37: Huwe de Bailol, autel a un escuchun de azur a un lion de argent coroné de or. For other uses, see ESCUÇON OVE UN LION COU-

RONÉ EN LA CORNIERE, ESCUÇON OVE UN LION RAMPANT COURONÉ EN LA CORNIERE.
escuçon³, *shield, i.e. the field of a coat of arms.* The complete blazon reads as follows: *Cd* 149: Imary de Miland, sable a lion ram-pant a la quewe forché, l'eschuchon semé billetts argent (*C/Cl* 149, see ESCU¹). *Syn.*: see ESCU¹. *Note*: the author of *Cd* distin-guishes between the 'escutcheon', which designates the shield proper or field, and the 'inescutcheon', or smaller shield charging the latter, i.e. what we have termed the *escutcheon* (see INESCOCHON). This distinction is rarely made today and the most recent edition of Boutell (1963), for example, omits any mention of *inescut-cheon* (cf. 1950 ed., pp. 20, 291). See ESCUÇON VUIDIÉ, *Note*.
escuçon des armes de Brienne, *escutcheon of the arms of Brienne. CPA* 171: a l'escus-son des armes de Brienne. *Note*: refers to ESCUÇON¹. Cf. ESCUCEL DES ARMES, ESCUÇON DES ARMES DU DUC DE BOURGOGNE EN LA BORDURE.
escuçon des armes du duc de Bour-gogne en la bende, *on a bend an escutcheon of the arms of the Duke of Burgundy.* See next item.
escuçon des armes du duc de Bour-gogne en la bordure, *on a bend an es-cutcheon of the arms of the Duke of Burgundy.* The complete blazon reads as follows: *CP* 6: Li contes d'Auchoire porte les armes de gheulles a une bande d'or et a un escuchon des armes du duc de Bourgoigne en la bordure. *Note*: according to Prinet CP, p. 6 n. 2, the correct reading should be *en la bende*. On the locution, cf. ESCUCEL DES ARMES, ESCUÇON DES ARMES DE BRIENNE.
escuçon en la bende, *on a bend an escut-cheon.* See preceding item.
escuçon en la corniere, see ESCUÇON OVE UN LION RAMPANT COURONÉ EN LA CORNIERE.
escuçon ou milieu, *escutcheon* (Fig. 119). *CP* 38: a un escuchon . . . ou milieu. *Syn.*: see ESCUÇON¹.
escuçon ove un lion couroné en la corniere, *in sinister chief a small escutcheon charged with a crowned lion rampant over all.* The complete blazon reads as follows: *Bl* 37: Hugh son filz, autiel od un escuchon d'asur ove un leon d'argent coronné d'or en la cornere (*B/Ba/Bb* 37, see LION¹, *Note*;

Ba/Bc 37, see ESCUÇON², LION COURONÉ).
Syn.: ESCUÇON OVE UN LION RAMPANT COU-
RONÉ EN LA CORNIERE. *Note*: see ESCU-
ÇON OVE UN LION RAMPANT COURONÉ EN LA
CORNIERE, *Note*; LION¹, *Note*.

**escuçon ove un lion rampant couroné
en la corniere,** *in sinister chief a small
escutcheon charged with a crowned lion rampant
over all.* The complete blazon reads as
follows: *B* 37: Hugh son fitz, autiel ove ung
escochon d'azur ove ung lion rampant
d'argent coronné d'or en la corniere (*Ba/
Bb/Bl* 37, see LION¹, *Note*; *Ba/Bc* 37, see
ESCUÇON², LION COURONÉ). *Syn.*: ESCUÇON
OVE UN LION COURONÉ EN LA CORNIERE.
Note: Wagner, *Historic Heraldry*, p. 44, reads:
coroné. For *P* 127 (= *B* 37), see DEDENZ,
Note. *Autiel ove* 'the same arms, differenced
by' refers to the preceding item (*B* 36)
which reads as follows: 'John de Ballioll, de
goules ove ung faux escochon d'argent'.
John's son, Hugh, bore the same arms
(gules, an orle argent) differenced by an
escutcheon azure charged with a crowned
lion rampant argent in sinister chief over
all. The escutcheon, which is slightly
smaller than usual and which bears the
lion of Galloway (Hugh's grandfather was
Alan of Galloway), overlaps the sinister
corner of the orle. See Blair, p. 13, and
Plate IX, fig. *m* (seal dated '*c.* 1269'); see
also Brault, 'The Chief', p. 85 n. 17. *Ba* 37
('Huwe de Bailol, autel a un escuchon de
azur a un lion de argent crois [*sic*] or')
omits the positioning phrase, while *Bb* 37,
which is in trick only, erroneously centres
the escutcheon inside the orle. See *Aspilogia II*, p. 122, note to item 37; DEDENZ,
Note; ESCU³, *Note*. Compare this manner of
positioning in the sinister chief with *D* 139
(complete blazon provided s.v. CHIEF¹ [2]
B. 1., *Note*).

escuçon par mi, *escutcheon* (Fig. 119). *CP* 77:
a un escusson . . . parmi. *Syn.*: see ESCUÇON¹.

escuçon percié, *orle* (Fig. 124). *D* 130: a un
escuchun . . . percé; *M* 41: ou ung escu-
chiun percé. *Syn.*: see FAUS ESCUÇON.

escuçon vuidié, *escutcheon* (Fig. 118). The
complete blazon reads as follows: *K*, vv.
438–41:

> L'escu barré au chief palé,
> E les cornieres gyronnees,

> De or e de asur enluminees,
> O le escuchon vuidié de ermine.

Syn.: see ESCUÇON¹. *Note*: Nicolas, pp. 45
and 47, translates the line *O le escuchon
vuidié de ermine* as 'with the escutcheon
voided of ermine', an error repeated word
for word by Wright, p. 19. The author of
K makes proper use of *vuidié* 'voided,
hollowed out' in vv. 471 and 582; see
MASCLE VUIDIEE DU CHAMP and ESCU VUIDIÉ
DU CHAMP. The escutcheon in the celebrated Mortimer arms is not voided and
in other rolls *escuçon* alone is employed in
this connection (*B* 32, *C* 142, *D* 97, and
H 67); see ESCUÇON¹. The error stems from
a desire on the part of heralds to distinguish between *escuçon* 'escutcheon' (i.e.
ESCUÇON¹) and *escuçon* 'shield, i.e. the field
of a coat of arms' (see ESCUÇON³). When
writers began to designate the escutcheon
as a 'false' escutcheon, meaning a smaller
shield charging the true escutcheon or
field, its synonym *escuçon vuidié* 'orle' also
came to mean 'escutcheon'. London, 'Some
Medieval Treatises', pp. 173–4, points out
that *fauz escuchon* is used to blazon the
escutcheon in the Mortimer arms in the
Boroughbridge Roll (1322), while *faus escuchon* and *faws scochon* are also used in this
sense in Thomas Jenyns's Book (*c.* 1410)
and the Bradfer-Lawrence Tract (1445 or
soon after), respectively; see also London,
'Notes and Reflections', p. 203. London
does not mention *escuchon vuidié* in *K*, which
is the earliest attested misuse of the term,
but does cite *voide scoychion* in this sense
from the mid-fifteenth-century Dublin Roll.
On the use of this term in the *Siege of
Caerlaverock*, see Brault K, pp. 15–16.

escu vuidié du champ, *orle* (Fig. 124). *K*,
v. 582: Al rouge escu voidié du champ. *Syn.*:
see FAUS ESCUÇON. *Note*: cf. ESCUÇON¹, *Note*.
The 'escutcheon voided', i.e. orle, of the
Balliol arms is here depicted on a banner.
Champ refers to the field of the escutcheon
which is hollowed out. Cf. *P* 95 (= *B* 36;
see FAUS ESCUÇON): 'a une escuchon voidee';
127 (= *B* 37; see ESCUÇON OVE UN LION
RAMPANT COURONÉ EN LA CORNIERE): 'ove
un escuchon voidé'.

es geules, see EN LE GEULES². *Note*: *geules*
'gules' was singular, so the contraction

should not be *es* (= *en les*). See, however, CROISETES OU . . .

eslaisié, *formy, splayed.* See CROIS ESLAISIEE AUS BOUZ. *Syn.*: ESLARGI[1], FORMÉ. *Note*: *eslaisié* is the past participle of OFr. *eslaisier* 'to widen, dilate', a derivative of Lat. *exlatiare (< CL *latus* 'wide'). The related modern French heraldic term *alésé* is a derivative of *alaisié*, past participle of OFr. *alaisier* 'to widen' (< VL *allatiare < CL *latus* 'wide'), its present-day meaning ('coupled', i.e. shortened) having apparently been influenced by the use of this term in metalworking (*aléser* 'to bore out, to ream'). See *BW*[4], s.v. *aléser*.

eslargi[1], *formy, splayed.* See CROIS ESLARGIE. *Syn.*: see ESLAISIÉ.

eslargi[2], *patonce.* See CROIS ESLARGIE PAR LES BOUZ. *Syn.*: FOURCHIÉ[3], FOURCHIÉ AU KANEE, PATÉ, PATONCE. *Note*: cf. also CROIS[5].

esmerlot, *martlet.* See BENDE OD ESMERLOZ. *Syn.*: see MERLETE[1].

espani, *displayed.* See EGLE ESPANIE, EGLE ESPANIE OVE DEUS TESTES. *Syn.*: see EGLE. *Note*: for another use of this term, see SOI ESPANDRE. Prinet WR, p. 225 n. 2: 'Espani, en vieux français, est synonyme de *développé, ouvert, déployé. Displayed* a le même sens en anglais; c'est le terme héraldique qui correspond actuellement au français *éployé.*'

espart, *blossoming, open.* See FESSE DE FLEURS DE LIS ESPARZ NAISSANZ DE TESTES DE LIEPARZ. *Note*: on the semantic history of this term, consult J. Dubois and R. Lagane, '*Espardre* et *espartir*: conflit homonymique', *Français moderne*, xxxi (1963), 105–10.

espaule, *shoulder.* See LION COURONÉ UNE CROIS SOR L'ESPAULE, LION ET A UNE FLEUR DE LIS EN L'ESPAULE DU LION, LION RAMPANT A UNE FLEUR DE LIS EN L'ESPAULE DU LION, LION RAMPANT ET EN LES ESPAULES DU LION UNE QUINTEFEUILLE.

espee, *sword* (Fig. 274). *D* 111: od une espee. *Note*: the sword on the accompanying painted shield is palewise, point upward.

espee au pong et au helt qui tranche le lion par mi, see LION RAMPANT COURONÉ A LA LANGUE A UNE MANCHE EN LA GEULE DU LION A UNE ESPEE AU PONG ET AU HELT QUI TRANCHE LE LION PAR MI.

espee au quartier, *on a canton a sword. CP* 135: a une espee . . . au cartier. *Note*: see QUARTIER[1], *Note*.

esprevier, *sparrow-hawk* (Fig. 203). *TA*, v. 1829: A .i. esprevier. *Syn.*: ANOT, MOUSCHET. *Note*: falcons, hawks, and their species are indistinguishable in heraldic art (Boutell, p. 77). On the literary motif of the sparrow-hawk as a prize awarded to the most beautiful lady, consult Loomis, *Arthurian Tradition*, p. 92, and, especially, G. D. West, 'Gerbert's *Continuation de Perceval* (ll. 1528–43) and the Sparrow-hawk Episode', *BBSIA*, vii (1955), 79–87.

esprevier qui de voler ne se repose, *sparrow-hawk volant* (Fig. 204). *TA*, vv. 1724–5:

> A l'esprevier courtois et gent
> Qui de voler ne se repose.

esquartelé de . . . et de . . . , *quarterly* (Fig. 25). (1) *the quarters bear no charge. Durmart*, v. 8492: De . . . et de . . . escartelee; *BA* 253: ecartelé de . . . et de . . . ; *B/Bl* 9, 165 [169]: esquartelé de . . . et de . . . ; 54: escartelé de . . . et de . . . (*Ba* 54: esquartelé de . . . e de . . . ; *Bb* 54, see QUARTELÉ DE . . . ET DE . . . ; *Bc* 54: esquartlé de . . . e de . . . ; *Bl* 54: esquartelé de . . . et de . . .); *B* 192: esquartelé de . . . et . . . (*Bl* 192 [196]: esquartelé de . . . et de . . .); *B/Bl* 28: esquartelé de . . . et de . . . (*Ba/Bc* 28: esquartelé de . . . e de . . . ; *Bb* 28: escartellé . . . et . . .); *Bl* 19: esquartelé de . . . et de . . . (*B* 19, see QUARTELÉ DE . . . ET DE . . .); *Bc* 11: esquartelé de . . . e de . . . (*B* 11, see QUARTELÉ DE . . . ET DE . . . UN MOLET EN LE QUARTIER DEVANT; *Ba* 11, see ESQUARTELÉ DE . . . ET DE . . . UN MOLET; *Bb* 11, see QUARTELÉ DE . . . ET DE . . . UN MOLET; *Bl* 11, see ESQUARTELÉ DE . . . ET DE . . . OVE UNE ESTOILE EN LE QUARTIER DEVANT); *Bl* 142 [146], 204 [208]: esquartelé de . . . et de . . . (*B* 142, see ESQUARTILLIÉ DE . . . ET DE . . . ; 204, see QUARTELÉ DE . . . ET DE . . .); Somery [*B III* 20], *Ba/Bc*: esquartelé de . . . e de . . . (*Bb*, see QUARTELÉ DE . . . ET DE . . .); *C* 80 (*Cl/Cd* 80, see ESQUARTERÉ DE . . . ET DE . . .), 139 (*Cl* 139, see ESQUARTILLIÉ DE . . . ET DE . . . ; *Cd* 139: esquartelé . . . e . . .): escartellé de . . . et de . . . ; 117 (*Cl* 117, see ESQUARTILLIÉ DE . . . ET DE . . . ; *Cd* 117: esquartelye de . . . e . . .), 118 (*Cl* 118, see ESQUARTILLIÉ DE . . . ET DE . . . ; *Cd* 118:

esquarteley [tincture omitted] e de . . .),
119 (*Cl* 119, see ESQUARTILLIÉ DE . . . ET
DE . . .): escartellé de . . . et . . .; *Cd* 119:
esquarterlé de . . . et . . .; *D* 24, 37, 75, 84,
136, 143, 164: esquartelé de . . . et de . . .;
CP 21: escartelé de . . . et de . . .; 121: escartelé de . . . et de . . .; *Hg* 17: esquartelé
de . . . et de. . .(*H* 17, see QUARTILLIÉ DE . . .
ET DE . . .); *K*, v. 96: De . . . e de . . .
esquartelee. (2) *only the first quarter bears a
charge.* A. *the locution* EN LE QUARTIER (?) *is
used.* See ESQUARTELÉ DE . . . ET DE . . . UN
LION PASSANT EN LE PRE . . . B. *the locution*
OU QUARTIER *is used.* See ESQUARTELÉ DE
. . . ET DE . . . UNE MOLETE OU QUARTIER
DE . . . C. *the expression* DEVANT *is used.* See
ESQUARTELÉ DE . . . ET DE . . . ET DEVANT
UNE ESTOILE. D. *the locution* EN LE QUARTIER
DEVANT *is used.* See ESQUARTELÉ DE . . . ET
DE . . . OVE UNE ESTOILE EN LE QUARTIER
DEVANT. E. *the locution* EN LE PREMIER
QUARTIER *is used.* See ESQUARTELÉ DE . . . ET
DE . . . OVE UNE MOLETE EN LE PREMIER
QUARTIER. F. *the locution* EN LE CHANTEL *is
used.* See ESQUARTELÉ DE . . . ET DE . . . A
UN LION PASSANT EN LE CHANTEL DE . . .
Note: cf. EL PREMERAIN QUARTIER. G.
order of items only is used. See ESQUARTELÉ
DE . . . ET DE . . . A UNE MOLETE, ESQUARTELÉ
DE . . . ET DE . . . A UN LIONCEL RAMPANT.
(3) *the second and third quarters are fretty.*
D 131: esquartelé de . . . et de . . .
fretté; *K*, vv. 306, 308: esquartelee / . . .
E . . . fretté. *Syn.*: ESQUARTELÉ DE . . . ET
DE . . . LE GEULES, QUARTELÉ DE . . . ET DE
. . . LES QUARTIERS . . . EN LE GEULES,
QUARTILLIÉ DE . . . ET DE . . . ET LES QUAR-
TIERS DE . . ., QUARTILLIÉ DE . . . ET DE . . .
O QUARTIERS DE . . . *Note*: Despenser arms.
In both examples cited here, order of items
alone indicates which quarters are fretty;
cf. the synonyms. (4) *the four quarters bear the
same charge counterchanged.* See ESQUARTELÉ DE
. . . ET DE . . . LIEPARZ DE L'UN EN L'AUTRE,
ESQUARTELÉ DE . . . ET DE . . . LIONS DE L'UN
EN L'AUTRE. *Syn.*: ESQUARTILLIÉ DE . . . ET DE
. . . A LIEPARZ DE L'UN EN L'AUTRE, ESQUAR-
TILLIÉ DE . . . ET DE . . . A LIEPARZ DE L'UN
ET L'AUTRE. (5) *a plain cross covers the lines
which form the four quarters.* *Cd* 164: esquar-
telé de . . . e de . . . (*C*/*Cl* 164, see ESQUAR-
TILLIÉ DE . . . ET DE . . .; see also CROIS
PASSANT). *Syn.*: A QUARTIERS DE . . . ET DE

. . ., ESCU A QUARTIERS, ESQUARTELÉ DE
QUATRE COULEURS DE . . . ET DE . . . ET DE . . .
ET DE . . ., ESQUARTERÉ DE . . . ET DE . . .,
ESQUARTILLIÉ DE . . . ET DE . . ., QUARTELÉ
DE . . . ET DE . . ., QUARTERÉ DE . . . ET DE
. . ., QUARTILLIÉ DE . . . ET DE . . . *Note*: cf.
SONGIÉ DE . . . ET DE . . . The quarterly
shield dates back to the dawn of heraldry;
see *Aspilogia II*, p. 17, note to item 25,
and QUARTIERS[1], *Note*. Normally, the first
tincture specified in the blazon refers to
quarters 1 and 4, the second to quarters 2
and 3. For some early inconsistencies in
this regard, see *Aspilogia II*, p. 105. In
D 3, the blazon is defective but refers to
the quarterly coat of the King of Spain.
Greenstreet reads as follows: '[p]orte argent
et gules . . . rampans en l'argent et deus
toreles (?) . . . en le goules'. The corresponding painted shield ('Rey de Espayne')
shows a quarterly coat with traces of a lion
rampant in quarters 1 and 4. The quarters
are reversed here; the correct blazon is
provided in *WB* 1258 and *C* 6 (see ESQUAR-
TILLIÉ DE . . . ET DE . . . A CHASTEAUS EN
LES QUARTIERS DE . . ., A LIONCEAUS EN LES
QUARTIERS DE . . .; ESQUARTILLIÉ DE . . .
ET DE . . . UN CHASTEL, ET DE . . . UN
LION RAMPANT). See also the Matthew Paris
Shields in Pusikan, pp.129–30; Hauptmann,
pp. 48–9; and *Aspilogia II*, p. 51, item 72.

**esquartelé de . . . et de . . . a liepar-
deaus de l'un en l'autre,** *quarterly, leopards
counterchanged. Escanor*, vv. 3973–7:

> Li rois de Gales, qui avoit
> Le meillor cheval c'on savoit,
> Mais les armes ot granz et lees
> D'or et d'argent esquartelees
> A liepardiaus de l'un en l'autre.

Syn.: see ESQUARTELÉ DE . . . ET DE . . . A
LIEPARZ DE L'UN EN L'AUTRE. *Note*: refers
to DE L'UN EN L'AUTRE[1]. On these arms
(Llywelyn ap Gruffydd, Prince of Wales),
see Brault, 'Arthurian Heraldry', p. 86.

**esquartelé de . . . et de . . . a lieparz de
l'un en l'autre,** *quarterly, leopards counter-
changed. D* 27: esquartelé de . . . et de . . .
a quatre lepars de l'un en l'autre. *Syn.*:
ESQUARTELÉ DE . . . ET DE . . . A LIEPAR-
DEAUS DE L'UN EN L'AUTRE, ESQUARTELÉ DE
. . . ET DE . . . LIONS DE L'UN ET L'AUTRE,
ESQUARTILLIÉ DE . . . ET DE . . . A LIEPARZ

DE L'UN EN L'AUTRE, ESQUARTILLIÉ DE . . .
ET DE . . . A LIEPARZ DE L'UN ET L'AUTRE.
Note: refers to DE L'UN EN L'AUTRE[1]. Arms
of Llywelyn ap Gruffydd, Prince of Wales;
see *Aspilogia II*, p. 169, note to item 13.

esquartelé de . . . et de . . . a une molete,
quarterly, in the first quarter a mullet. D 29:
esquartelé de . . . et de . . . a une molette.
Syn.: ESQUARTELÉ DE . . . ET DE . . . A UNE
MOLETE OU QUARTIER DE . . ., ESQUARTELÉ
DE . . . ET DE . . . ET DEVANT UNE ESTOILE,
ESQUARTELÉ DE . . . ET DE . . . OVE UNE
ESTOILE EN LE QUARTIER DEVANT, ESQUAR-
TELÉ DE . . . ET DE . . . OVE UNE MOLETE EN
LE PREMIER QUARTIER, ESQUARTELÉ DE . . .
ET DE . . . UN MOLET, ESQUARTILLIÉ DE . . .
ET DE . . . EN LE CHANTEL DE . . . UN MOLET,
QUARTELÉ DE . . . ET DE . . . EN LE CHANTEL
DE . . . UNE MOLETE, QUARTELÉ DE . . . ET DE
. . . UN MOLET, QUARTELÉ DE . . . ET DE . . .
UN MOLET EN LE QUARTIER DEVANT, QUAR-
TILLIÉ DE . . . ET DE . . . UN MOLET EN LE
QUARTIER DEVANT, QUARTILLIÉ DE . . . ET DE
. . . ET EN LE CHANTEL DE . . . OU UN MOLET.

**esquartelé de . . . et de . . . a une molete
ou quartier de . . .,** *quarterly, in the first
quarter a mullet.* The complete blazon reads
as follows: *BA* 51: Reniers (A: Reiniers) de
Goisencourt, l'escu ecartelé de geules et
de noir a une molette d'or u quartier de
geules. Braibanchon. *Syn.*: see ESQUARTELÉ
DE . . . ET DE . . . A UNE MOLETE.

**esquartelé de . . . et de . . . a un lioncel
rampant,** *quarterly, in the first quarter a lion
rampant. D* 146: esquartelé de . . . et de . . .
a un leuncel rampant.

**esquartelé de . . . et de . . . a un lion
passant en le chantel de . . .,** *quarterly,
in the first quarter a lion passant. Cd* 140: es-
quartelé de . . . e de . . . a un lion passant
. . . en le cantel de . . . (*C* 140, see ESQUAR-
TELÉ DE . . . ET DE . . . UN LION PASSANT EN
LE PRE . . .; *Cl* 140, see ESQUARTILLIÉ DE . . .
ET DE . . . A UN LION PASSANT EN LE CHANTEL
DE . . .). *Syn.*: ESQUARTELÉ DE . . . ET DE . . .
UN LION PASSANT EN LE PRE . . ., ESQUAR-
TILLIÉ DE . . . ET DE . . . A UN LION PASSANT
EN LE CHANTEL DE . . . *Note*: for complete
blazons, see ESQUARTELÉ DE . . . ET DE . . .
UN LION PASSANT EN LE PRE . . .

esquartelé de . . . et de . . . endenté,
quarterly per fess indented (Fig. 28). *C* 114:
escartellé de . . . et de . . . indenté (*Cl* 114,

see ESQUARTILLIÉ DE . . . ET DE . . . ENDENTÉ;
Cd 114: eschartelé . . . e . . . endentit); 156:
escartelé de . . . et de . . . indentee (*Cl* 156,
see ESQUARTILLIÉ DE . . . ET DE . . . ENDENTÉ;
Cd 156: ebarquelé de . . . e de . . . endenté).
Syn.: ESQUARTELÉ DE . . . ET DE . . . ENDENTÉ
DE L'UN EN L'AUTRE, ESQUARTELÉ DE . . . ET
DE . . . ENDENTÉ DE L'UN ET DE L'AUTRE,
ESQUARTILLIÉ DE . . . ET DE . . . ENDENTÉ.
Note: only the horizontal line of the
quarterly field is indented. In the *Liber
Additamentorum*, Matthew Paris errs in his
depiction of the Neville arms as being
indented per pale as well as per fess (see
Aspilogia II, p. 42, note to item 31).

**esquartelé de . . . et de . . . endenté de
l'un en l'autre,** *quarterly per fess indented*
(Fig. 28). *B* 180: esquartelé de . . . et de . . .
endenté de l'un en l'autre (*Bl* 180 [184],
see ESQUARTELÉ DE . . . ET DE . . . ENDENTÉ
DE L'UN ET DE L'AUTRE). *Syn.*: see ESQUAR-
TELÉ DE . . . ET DE . . . ENDENTÉ. *Note*: refers
to DE L'UN EN L'AUTRE[2].

**esquartelé de . . . et de . . . endenté de
l'un et de l'autre,** *quarterly per fess indented* (Fig. 28). *Bl* 180 [184]: esquartelé
de . . . et de . . . endenté de l'un et de
l'autre (*B* 180, see ESQUARTELÉ DE . . . ET DE
. . . ENDENTÉ DE L'UN EN L'AUTRE). *Syn.*:
see ESQUARTELÉ DE . . . ET DE . . . ENDENTÉ.
Note: refers to DE L'UN ET DE L'AUTRE[2].

**esquartelé de . . . et de . . . et devant
une estoile,** *quarterly, in the first quarter a
mullet.* The complete blazon reads as follows: *K*, vv. 266–70:

> O le ourle endentee de noir
> Avoit baniere e longe e lee,
> De ore e de rouge esquartelee;
> De bon cendal, non pas de toyle,
> E devant une blanche estoyle.

Syn.: see ESQUARTELÉ DE . . . ET DE . . . A
UNE MOLETE.

esquartelé de . . . et de . . . le geules,
quarterly, the gules quarters are distinctive. The
complete blazon reads as follows: *Bl* 110
[114]: Hugh le Despenser, esquartelé d'argent et de gules od un bend [de sable]
l'escu [*sic*, for le gu(les)] fretté d'or (*B*
110, see QUARTELÉ DE . . . ET DE . . . LES
QUARTIERS . . . EN LE GEULES). *Syn.*: see
ESQUARTELÉ DE . . . ET DE . . . (3). *Note*: see
Aspilogia II, p. 137, note to item 114; ESCU[4].

esquartelé de . . . et de . . . lions de l'un et l'autre, *quarterly, lions passant guardant* (*i.e. leopards*) *counterchanged. C* 21: escartellé de . . . et . . . 4 leons de l'un et l'autre (*Cl* 21, see ESQUARTILLIÉ DE . . . ET DE . . . A LIEPARZ DE L'UN ET L'AUTRE; *Cd* 21, see ESQUARTELÉ DE . . . ET DE . . . A LIEPARZ DE L'UN EN L'AUTRE). *Syn.*: see ESQUARTELÉ DE . . . ET DE . . . A LIEPARZ DE L'UN EN L'AUTRE.

esquartelé de . . . et de . . . ove une estoile en le quartier devant, *quarterly, in the first quarter a mullet. Bl* 11: esquartelé de . . . et de . . . ove une estoille . . . en le quartier devant (*B* 11, see QUARTELÉ DE . . . ET DE . . . UN MOLET EN LE QUARTIER DEVANT; *Ba* 11, see ESQUARTELÉ DE . . . ET DE . . . UN MOLET; *Bb* 11, see QUARTELÉ DE . . . ET DE . . . UN MOLET; *Bc* 11, see ESQUARTELÉ DE . . . ET DE . . . [1]). *Syn.*: see ESQUARTELÉ DE . . . ET DE . . . A UNE MOLETE.

esquartelé de . . . et de . . . ove une molete en le premier quartier, *quarterly, in the first quarter a mullet.* The complete blazon reads as follows: *P* 53: Le conte de Oxenford port esquartelé d'or et de goules ove un molette d'argent en le premer quartier. *Syn.*: see ESQUARTELÉ DE . . . ET DE . . . A UNE MOLETE. *Note*: corresponds to *B* 11 (see QUARTELÉ DE . . . ET DE . . . UN MOLET EN LE QUARTIER DEVANT).

esquartelé de . . . et de . . . un lion passant en le pre . . ., *quarterly, in the first quarter a lion passant.* The complete blazon reads as follows: *C* 140: William Boyvile, escartellé d'or et sable un leon passant gulez en le pre . . . (*Cl* 140, see ESQUARTILLIÉ DE . . . ET DE . . . A UN LION PASSANT EN LE CHANTEL DE . . .; *Cd* 140: William de Boyvyle, esquartelé d'or e de sable a un lion passant de goules en le cantel d'or). *Syn.*: see ESQUARTELÉ DE . . . ET DE . . . A UN LION PASSANT EN LE CHAN-TEL DE . . . *Note*: Walford, p. 386, note *a*, states: 'So much of this coat as fol-lows *pre* is missing. When complete the conclusion was probably *premier cantell.* L[eland] has *6. cantel dor*, the 6 being, I suppose, a mistake for *en*, as the like occurs there again and again.' For the correct interpretation of '6', doubtless a mistake for *u* (= *en le*), see Prinet WR, p. 238. '*en le pre*' could be a misreading for '*en le quartier*' (*pre* = *qre* [*B* 178: 'Reinaud de

Blankmonstier, d'argent frettie d'azure: qre:']?). But see *premier* in the incipit of *H.* OFr. *chantel* is not used with *premier* during this period. Cf., however, PREMERAIN QUAR-TIER and PREMIER QUARTIER.

esquartelé de . . . et de . . . un molet, *quarterly, in the first quarter a mullet. Ba* 11: esquartelé de . . . e de . . . un molet (*B* 11, see QUARTELÉ DE . . . ET DE . . . UN MOLET EN LE QUARTIER DEVANT; *Bb* 11, see QUARTELÉ DE . . . ET DE . . . UN MOLET; *Bc* 11, see ESQUARTELÉ DE . . . ET DE . . . [1]; *Bl* 11, see ESQUARTELÉ DE . . . ET DE . . . OVE UNE ESTOILE EN LE QUARTIER DEVANT). *Syn.*: see ESQUARTELÉ DE . . . ET DE . . . A UNE MOLETE.

esquartelé de quatre couleurs de . . . et de . . . et de . . . et de . . ., *quarterly* (Fig. 25). *Lancelot propre*, iv. 104 (var.): li escuz estoit esquartelez de .iiii. coleurs de or et de azur et de argent et de sinople. *Syn.*: see ESQUARTELÉ DE . . . ET DE . . . *Note*: quarterly shields most frequently involve only *two* colours, quarters 1 and 4 being alike as opposed to 2 and 3.

esquarteré de . . . et de . . ., *quarterly* (Fig. 25). *Cl/Cd* 80: esquarteré de . . . e de . . . (*C* 80, see ESQUARTELÉ DE . . . ET DE . . .). *Syn.*: see ESQUARTELÉ DE . . . ET DE . . .

esquartillié de . . . et de . . ., *quarterly* (Fig. 25). (1) *the quarters bear no charge. B* 142: esquartilé de . . . et de . . . (*Bl* 142 [146], see ESQUARTELÉ DE . . . ET DE . . .); *Cl* 117: escartilé de . . . e de . . . (*C/Cd* 117, see ESQUARTELÉ DE . . . ET DE . . .); 118, 119 (*C/Cd* 118, 119, see ESQUARTELÉ DE . . . ET DE . . .): esquartilé de . . . et de . . .; 139: esquartilé de . . . e de . . . (*C/Cd* 139, see ESQUARTELÉ DE . . . ET DE . . .); *Hg* 5: esquartilé de . . . et de . . . (*H* 5, see QUARTELÉ DE . . . ET DE . . .). (2) *only the first quarter bears a charge.* See ESQUARTILLIÉ DE . . . ET DE . . . A UN LION PASSANT EN LE CHASTEL DE, ESQUARTILLIÉ DE . . . ET DE . . . EN LE CHANTEL DE . . . UN MOLET. (3) *the first and fourth quarters bear a different charge from that in the second and third quarters.* See ESQUAR-TILLIÉ DE . . . ET DE . . . A CHASTEAUS EN LES QUARTIERS DE . . ., A LIONCEAUS EN LES QUARTIERS DE; ESQUARTILLIÉ DE . . . UN CHASTEL, ET DE . . . UN LION RAMPANT. *Syn.*: see ESQUARTELÉ DE . . . ET DE . . ., *Note* (*D* 3); see also CHASTEL[1] (2) (*Cd* 6).

(4) *the four quartersa bear the sme charge counterchanged.* See ESQUARTILLIÉ DE . . . ET DE . . . A LIEPARZ DE L'UN EN L'AUTRE, ESQUARTILLIÉ DE . . . ET DE . . . A LIEPARZ DE L'UN ET L'AUTRE. *Syn.*: see ESQUARTELÉ DE . . . ET DE . . . A LIEPARZ DE L'UN EN L'AUTRE. (5) *a plain cross covers the lines which form the four quarters.* C 164: escartilé de . . . et . . . (*Cl* 164: eskartilé de . . . et de . . .; *Cd* 164, see ESQUARTELÉ DE . . . ET DE . . .; see also CROIS PASSANT). *Note*: in *Cd* 6, the blazon is defective, resulting in the omission of the quarterly partition. The complete entry reads as follows: 'Le roy d'Espayne, de gules .i. chasteaus d'or, pour Lion d'azure .i. lion de pourple'; refers to item (3) above; see also LION[3].

esquartillié de . . . et de . . . a chasteaus en les quartiers de . . ., a lionceaus en les quartiers de . . ., *quarterly, in 1 and 4 a castle, in 2 and 3 a lion (rampant).* Cl 6: esquartilé de . . . e de . . . a deus chastelle . . . en les quarter de . . ., a deus liunceus . . . en les quartiers de . . . (*C* 6, see ESQUARTILLIÉ DE . . . UN CHASTEL, ET DE . . . UN LION RAMPANT; *Cd* 6, see ESQUARTILLIÉ DE . . . ET DE . . ., *Note*). *Syn.*: ESQUARTILLIÉ DE . . . UN CHASTEL, ET DE . . . UN LION RAMPANT. *Note*: see also ESQUARTELÉ DE . . . ET DE . . ., *Note* (*D* 3), ESQUARTILLIÉ DE . . . ET DE . . ., *Note* (*Cd* 6). The armorial bearings of Spain are canting arms, castles for Castile, lions for León.

esquartillié de . . . et de . . . a lieparz de l'un en l'autre, *quarterly, leopards counterchanged.* Cd 21: esquartilé de . . . et de . . . a liepard de l'ung in l'authre (*C* 21, see ESQUARTELÉ DE . . . ET DE . . . LIONS DE L'UN ET L'AUTRE; *Cl* 21, see ESQUARTILLIÉ DE . . . ET DE . . . A LIEPARZ DE L'UN ET L'AUTRE). *Syn.*: see ESQUARTELÉ DE . . . ET DE . . . A LIEPARZ DE L'UN EN L'AUTRE. *Note*: refers to DE L'UN EN L'AUTRE[1].

esquartillié de . . . et de . . . a lieparz de l'un et l'autre, *quarterly, leopards counterchanged.* Cl 21: esquartilé de . . . e de . . . a leparz de l'un e l'autre (*C* 21, see ESQUARTELÉ DE . . . ET DE . . . LIONS DE L'UN ET L'AUTRE; *Cd* 21, see ESQUARTILLIÉ DE . . . ET DE . . . A LIEPARZ DE L'UN EN L'AUTRE). *Syn.*: see ESQUARTELÉ DE . . . ET DE . . . A LIEPARZ DE L'UN EN L'AUTRE. *Note*: *Aspilogia II*, p. 169, item 13, reads *escartelle* for

esquartilé and unnecessarily adds the number *quatre* before *leparz*.

esquartillié de . . . et de . . . a un lion passant en le chantel de . . ., *quarterly, in the first quarter a lion passant.* Cl 140: esquartilé de . . . e de . . . a une lion passant . . . 6 (= en le) cantel de . . . (*C* 140, see ESQUARTELÉ DE . . . ET DE . . . UN LION PASSANT EN LE PRE . . .; *Cd* 140, see ESQUARTELÉ DE . . . ET DE . . . A UN LION PASSANT EN LE CHANTEL DE . . .). *Syn.*: see ESQUARTELÉ DE . . . ET DE . . . A UN LION PASSANT EN LE CHANTEL DE . . .

esquartillié de . . . et de . . . endenté, *quarterly per fess indented* (Fig. 28). Cl 114: esquartilé de . . . et de . . . endenté (*C/Cd* 114, see ESQUARTELÉ DE . . . ET DE . . . ENDENTÉ); 156: ebartilé de . . . e de . . . endenté (*C/Cd* 156, see ESQUARTELÉ DE . . . ET DE . . . ENDENTÉ). *Syn.*: see ESQUARTELÉ DE . . . ET DE . . . ENDENTÉ.

esquartillié de . . . et de . . . en le chantel de . . . un molet, *quarterly, in the first quarter a mullet.* Hg 96: esquartilé de . . . et de . . . en le cauntel de . . . un molez (*H* 96, see QUARTILLIÉ DE . . . ET DE . . . ET EN LE CHANTEL DE . . . OU UN MOLET). *Syn.*: see ESQUARTELÉ DE . . . ET DE . . . A UNE MOLETE.

esquartillié de . . . et de . . . en les quartiers de . . ., en les quartiers de . . ., *quarterly, the first and fourth quarters are charged with the same object, the second and third with another.* Hg 92 [91]: esquartilé de . . . et de . . . en les quarteres de . . . (see GRIFON), en les quarteres de . . . (see FESSE ENGRESLEE) (*H* 92, see QUARTILLIÉ DE . . . ET DE . . . EN LES QUARTIERS DE . . . EN LES QUARTIERS DE . . .). *Syn.*: QUARTILLIÉ DE . . . ET DE . . . EN LES QUARTIERS DE . . ., EN LES QUARTIERS DE . . .

esquartillié de . . . un chastel, et de . . . un lion rampant, *quarterly, in 1 and 4 a castle, in 2 and 3 a lion rampant.* C 6: escartillé de . . . un chasteau . . ., et de . . . un leon rampant (*Cl* 6, see ESQUARTILLIÉ DE . . . ET DE . . . A CHASTEAUS EN LES QUARTIERS DE . . ., A LIONCEAUS EN LES QUARTIERS DE . . .; *Cd* 6, see ESQUARTILLIÉ DE . . . ET DE . . ., *Note*). *Syn.*: see ESQUARTILLIÉ DE . . . ET DE . . . A CHASTEAUS EN LES QUARTIERS DE . . ., A LIONCEAUS EN LES QUARTIERS DE . . .

es quatre quartiers, *in the four 'quarters' set*

off by a plain cross. See EGLES ES QUATRE QUARTIERS, LIONS ES QUATRE QUARTIERS. *Syn.*: EN LES QUATRE QUARTIERS. *Note:* cf. CROIS[1].

estachié contreval de . . . et de . . ., *paly* (Fig. 19). *Durmart,* vv. 8509–10:

Cele estachie contreval
De vair et de vermel cendal.

Syn.: see PALÉ DE . . . ET DE . . .

estachié de . . . et de . . ., *paly* (Fig. 19). *BA* 45, 101, 123, 124, 136, 256, 268: estakié de . . . et de . . . *Syn.*: see PALÉ DE . . . ET DE . . . *Note:* in *BA* 256, prepositions are omitted. The complete blazon reads as follows: 'Renax de Pressingny (A: Pressigny), l'escu contrebendé d'or et d'azur a .i. escuchon d'argent au kief estakié as cornés geronnés. Baneres (A: Banneret) et (this word omitted by A) de Toraine (A: de Torayne)'. OFr. *estachié* is the past participle of *estachier,* a derivative of OFr. *estache* 'stake' < Germanic *stakka.* See M. Dominica Legge, 'Some Notes on Anglo-Norman Vocabulary', *Studies in Medieval French Presented to Alfred Ewert in Honour of his Seventieth Birthday* (Oxford, 1961), p. 226. On the relationship between OFr. *estachier* and MFr. *attacher* 'to attach, to tie', consult *BW*[4], s.v. *attacher.*

estachié en belic de . . . et de . . ., *bendy* (Fig. 8). *CC,* vv. 962–7:

Tout en alerent par reviel,
En clokes des armes Hauwiel
De Kievraing. Bien venrai a kief
Dou deviser: d'or a un kief
Estakiet, en bellinc assis,
D'argent, de geules, ce m'est vis.

Syn.: see BENDÉ DE . . . ET DE . . .[1]. *Note:* Prinet CC, p. 164: 'Nous dirions: *d'or au chef bandé d'argent et de gueules.*' In note 3 on this page, Prinet provides the following explanation: 'Le chef est "estakiet", c'est-à-dire formé d'*estakes* juxtaposées; ces *estakes* sont placées obliquement, "en bellinc". *Estake* signifie pieu.' Adam-Even BA, p. 19, defines *estakié* in the following terms: 'palé. R. de Coucy [i.e. Delbouille's ed. of *CC*] 966, le traduit à tort par bandé.' Adam-Even is here referring to Delbouille's glossary, p. 286. Delbouille, however, who here as elsewhere in his edition merely

reproduces Prinet's definition, is correct in his interpretation, since the locution is not *estachié de . . . et de . . .* but *estachié en belic de . . . et de . . .*

estakié, see ESTACHIÉ.

estalope, see ESCHALOPE.

estant, *statant, i.e. standing, left hind leg only on the mount.* See LION RAMPANT COURONÉ ESTANT SUS UNE MOTE. *Note: estant* is the present participle of OFr. *ester* 'to stand' (< Lat. *stare*) and is not to be confused with *estant,* the present participle of OFr. *estre* 'to be' (< VL *essere*), which, however, borrowed its present participle, past participle, and imperfect indicative from this verb. Cf. DESUS (1).

esteile, estele, see ESTOILE.

estelé, *semy of mullets. TA,* v. 1270: estelé. For another use, see TOUT ESTELÉ. *Syn.*: see A MOLETES SEMÉ.

estencele[1], *small mullet* (Fig. 240). See SAUTOIR ET A ESTENCELES, TENCELE. *Syn.*: see ESTOILE.

estencele[2], *spark, i.e. a cluster of three or four small dots* (Fig. 48). See ESTENCELÉ, *Note.*

estencelé, *powdered with sparks, i.e. clusters of three or four small dots* (Fig. 48). The complete blazon reads as follows: *C* 12: Le roy de Hungrey, d'or estenzelé a deus passans d'azure (*Cl* 12: Le roy de Hongerye, de or estenzelé a deus passanz d'azur; *Cd* 12: Le roy de Hugarie, de or estenzelé de gules a .ii. passanz coroné [?]). *Syn.*: see A MOLETES SEMÉ. *Note:* see CROIS A DEUS PASSANZ, *Note,* and cf. POUDRÉ, SEMÉ. The arms of Herbert FitzMathew in Matthew Paris (Pusikan, pp. 128–9) are party gules and azure, three lions rampant or, 2 and 1; cf. *B* 78: 'Herbert le Fitz Mayhewe, party d'azur et de goulz ove trois leonseux rampants d'or'. Matthew Paris, however, adds 'totum scutum [s]cintillatum auro', a part of the blazon not executed on the accompanying painted shield (nor in Matthew's *Historia minor;* see Hauptmann, p. 30, item 72; *Aspilogia II,* pp. 50–1, note to item 71). In his article 'Scintillatum Auro. The Spark in Armory' (*Coat of Arms,* ii [1952], 111–13), H. S. London points out that the whole field of Herbert Fitz-Mathew's painted shield in the margin of Matthew Paris's *Chronica Majora* is 'spangled with little golden dots arranged in groups of three, and there can be no doubt but that those dots are what Matthew meant by *cintillatum auro*' (p. 111). London notes that the same charge is found in St. George's Roll for John de Pichford (no. 568), though both editors of this roll (C. S. Perceval in *Archaeologia*, xxxix [1864], 391–8, 418–46, and George J. Armytage in his edition of *Ancient Rolls of Arms* [as *Charles' Roll of the Reigns of Henry III. and Edward I.* (London, 1869)]) blazon the little dots as 'quatrefoils'. London further identifies *estenzelé* in *C* 12 with this charge, a theory I find plausible enough; see also *Aspilogia II*, p. 51, note to item 71 ('they were perhaps a kind of diaper'); p. 169, note to item 11. Medieval heraldic practice tolerated considerable diversity in verbal as well as pictorial blazon. *Estencelé*, like the kindred term *estencele*, was doubtless indiscriminately applied in the thirteenth century to a variety of charges ranging from clusters of small dots to miniature versions of the star-shaped or radiating figures known today as *estoiles* or *mullets*. Cf. also *Fouque de Candie*, v. 14477: 'escu a or, ou l'azur estincele', referring to the shield of the King of France. In *Aspilogia II*, p. 171, note to item 18, finally, London suggests that the semy of hearts in the modern arms of Denmark may originally have been leaves, though *WB* 1269 shows red flames.

estencelé de . . . et de . . ., *semy of mullets* (Fig. 45). *Gaidon*, v. 1070: D'or et d'azur estoit [la targe] estancelee. *Syn.*: see A MOLETES SEMÉ. *Note*: unusual instance of a field sprinkled with objects in more than one tincture. Cf. other examples provided s.v. POUDRÉ and its synonyms.

estoile, *star, i.e. estoile or mullet* (Fig. 225). *B* 75: a trois estoiles (*Ba/Bc* 75: a treis esteiles; *Bb* 75, the estoiles are tricked; *Bl* 75: od trois estoilles); 122: a trois estoilles (*Bl* 122 [126]: od trois estoilles); *K*, vv. 708, 799: o trois estoiles. For other uses, see ESQUARTELÉ DE . . . ET DE . . . ET DEVANT UNE ESTOILE, ESQUARTELÉ DE . . . ET DE . . . OVE UNE ESTOILE EN LE QUARTIER DEVANT, SAUTOIR A ESTOILES. *Syn.*: ESTENCELE[1], MOLET[1], MOLETE, MOLETE PERCIEE, ROUELE, TENCELE. *Note*: cf. (for size) ROUELE[2] and TENCELE. Though modern heraldry carefully distinguishes between the star-shaped figure with wavy rays (estoile) and that with straight rays (mullet; if pierced, this charge is sometimes referred to as rowel), these distinctions date from a period later than that under consideration here; see *Aspilogia II*, p. 129, note to item 75. As a matter of fact, there is a certain degree of confusion when blazoning or depicting these charges, the celestial object termed RAI or RAI DE SOLEIL (see also ROUELE[2]), and the flowers variously designated as ANGEMME, CINCFEUILLE, QUINTEFEUILLE, ROSE, and SISFEUILLE. See ROSE[1], *Note*.

estoile en le chief[1], *on a chief a mullet*. The complete blazon reads as follows: St. John (new item in *Bl* [110]): St. Johan, d'argent od chief de gules et deux estoiles d'or en le chief. *Syn.*: CHIEF OD UNE MOLETE, EL CHIEF UNE MOLETE, MOLETE EN LE CHIEF, MOLET EN LE CHIEF[3], ROUELE EN CHIEF[1], ROUELE EN LE CHIEF[1]. *Note*: refers to EN LE CHIEF[1].

estoile en le chief[2], *in chief a mullet*. See BARRE OD UNE ESTOILE EN LE CHIEF, FESSE ET UNE ESTOILE EN LE CHIEF, FESSE OVE UNE ESTOILE EN LE CHIEF. *Syn.*: see MOLET EN LE CHIEF. *Note*: refers to EN LE CHIEF[2].

estoile en le quartier devant, *in the first quarter a mullet*. See ESQUARTELÉ DE . . . ET DE . . . OVE UNE ESTOILE EN LE QUARTIER DEVANT. *Syn.*: see MOLET EN LE QUARTIER DEVANT.

estranges armes, *unaccustomed, different arms (as a disguise)*. *Lancelot propre*, iii. 405: si prenons tot estraignes armes. *Note*: cf. ARMES CHANGIER, DESGUISIÉ[1].

estre, *to be*. In addition to the entries provided below, various forms of this auxiliary appear in blazons found in *TC*, *CC*, and *K*, all literary texts. See LION LI CHIEF COURONÉ COUE FOURCHIEE, ORLURE DE L'ENCHAMPURE A ROSES, QUART PART. For other examples, see *TC*, vv. 1461, 1767, 1975, 2038, 3159, 3213, 3977; *CC*, vv. 1410, 1425, 1427, 1432, 1541, 1544, 1548, 1597, 1599; *K*, v. 686. For the single example of this use in a non-literary roll of arms, see ESTRE ENGRESLÉ. *Note*: cf. ESTANT.

estre croisillié, *to be crusily* (Fig. 35). *K*, vv. 249–52:

> Johans de Bar iluec estoit,
> Ke en la baner inde portoit

Deuz bars de or, e fu croissilie,
O la rouge ourle engreellie
(W: engreelie).

Syn.: see CROISELÉ.

estre de chalenge par entre . . . et . . .,
*to be the subject of a challenge, i.e. dispute over
the right to bear a certain coat of arms, between
. . . and . . . K,* vv. 353–60:

Le beau Brian le Filz Aleyn,
De courtoisie e de honnour pleyn.
I vi o baniere barree,
De or e de goules bien paree;
Dont de chalenge estoit li poinz
Par entre li e Hue Poinz,
Ki portoit tel ne plus ne meins,
Dont merveille avoit meinte e meins.

Note: on this dispute, consult Wagner,
Heralds and Heraldry, pp. 18–19, 122; Denholm-Young, *History and Heraldry*, p. 23 n.
4, *Aspilogia II*, pp. 110–11. On the legal
implications of this important passage, see
Introduction, p. 6. Godefroy, ii. 41, provides two examples of the use of this term
in this sense in 1595 and 1616. In the
Ashmolean Roll, *c.* 1334, the arms of the
knights in items 201–2 and 447–8 are said
to be *entre eux en debat* and *en debat* respectively. I am indebted to Dr. A. M. Barstow
of the University of Connecticut, who is preparing an edition of this unpublished roll,
for communicating this information to me.

estre de ses armes tel d'Angletere a . . .,
England, differenced by (literally, *to bear the
same arms as England with*). *K,* vv. 459–61:

Thomas de Langcastre estoit contes;
Se est de ses armes teus li contes,
De Engleterre, au label de France.

Syn.: see D'ANGLETERE A . . . *Note*: Nicolas,
p. 47 (followed verbatim by Wright, p. 20),
translates this passage as follows: 'Thomas
was Earl of Lancaster; this is the description
of his arms, those of England with a label
of France.' Nicolas has plainly taken *li
contes* in v. 460 to mean 'tale, story' hence
'description (i.e. blazon)'. Actually the word
is a repetition of the Earl of Lancaster's
title in the preceding verse ('Count') and the
correct translation is: 'Thomas was Earl
of Lancaster / And the latter bore England
differenced by a label of France.'

estre engreslé, *to be indented, i.e. made up of
lozenges or fusils which present two continuous
sawtooth edges* (Fig. 64). The complete
blazon reads as follows: *M* 13: Sr Robert
le Conestable port mesmes lez armes mes
la bende est engrelé d'or. *Syn.*: see EN-
DENTÉ^2. *Note*: refers to ENGRESLÉ^2. The
locution is used for differencing.

estre mis en . . ., *to charge. K,* vv. 220–2:

En sa banier trois lupart,
De or fin estoient mis en rouge,
Courant, feloun, fier, e harouge.

estreu, *stirrup.* See ESTRIER.

estre vairié de . . . et de . . ., *to be vairy*
(Fig. 4). *K,* v. 487: Vairie est de blanc e
de noir. *Syn.*: VAIRIÉ DE . . . ET DE . . .

estrier, *stirrup* (Fig. 273). *BA* 37 (A:
estrues), 134 (A: estruiers): a .iii. estriés;
177: .iii. estriers (A: estruers).

et^1, *the conjunction* 'and'. The standard particle
(sometimes written *e*) used to join together
members of a co-ordinate locution (e.g.
BENDÉ DE . . . ET DE . . ., DE L'UN ET
L'AUTRE, DESOUS ET DESOR); also used as a
separator. See Introduction. *Syn.*: AND.

et^2, see BEUF EL CHIEF.

evangile, *gospel* (Fig. 260). See ESCHAR-
BOUCLE ENTRE EVANGILES EN DEUS MANCHES
DE LA CHEMISE NOSTRE DAME.

fachon, see FAÇON.

façon, see DEVISER LA FAÇON DE L'ESCU,
DEVISER LA FAÇON DES ARMES, D'ICELE
FAÇON.

faillolé, see FALLOLÉ.

faire semblant, see EGLE QUI DE VOLER
FAISOIT SEMBLANT, EN MILIEU UNE EGLE QUI
DE VOLER FAISOIT SEMBLANT. *Note*: cf. NE
SOI REPOSER DE VOLER, SEMBLER. See also
the early fourteenth-century *Tournoiement
des Dames de Paris,* vv. 132–4, 362–4:

Un aigle trestout azure
Ens en mileu estoit assis,
Qui resambloit a estre vis;

.   .   .   .   .

Un lyon vermeil painturé
D'or el mileu estoit assis,
Qui resambloit a estre vis.

faisan, *pheasant.* See FESAN.

faisse, *fess.* See FESSE.

faissel, *demi-fess.* See FESSIEL ENCHASTELÉ DESOUS ET DESOR.

faissele, see FEISSELE.

fallolé, *decorated with an ornamental pattern. Durmart,* vv. 10000–8:

> De vert cendal fu tos covers
> Il et ses destriers ensement,
> Si ert fallolez sor argent.
> L'escu et la cote a armer
> Avoit fait mout bel falloler.
> Parmi le vert cendal paroit
> Li argens qui resplendissoit
> Cant li vens faisoit venteler
> Les fuelletes al solever.

Note: cf. DIASPRE. In v. 4648, Brun de Morois's horse is said to be covered with a red cloth (*D'unes vermelles covertures*) which is similarly ornamented: *Faillolees sor cler argent*; cf. also the following passage referring to Mordret le Petit: 'Cil covers al vermel samis / Qui sor argent est faillolés' (vv. 8418–19). In his glossary (ii. 207, 208), Father Gildea defines *faillolé* and *falloler* as 'bigarré' and 'orner de bigarrures' respectively, i.e. 'mottled'. Bearing in mind, however, the fact that *fuelletes* 'tiny leaves' (v. 10008) which move with the wind are involved, the term may be synonymous with PAPELONÉ 'scaly' or refer to the fish-scale type of diapering illustrated in Boutell, fig. 61 ('the shield of Foubert de Doure, *c.* 1180, copied from *Archaeologia Cantiana.* The arms are *Checky, a luce hauriant*; and the alternate squares are appropriately decorated with fish-scales' [p. 37]).

fanon, *gonfanon* (*i.e. flag suspended horizontally and divided into pointed or rounded tails*) (Fig. 259). *CP* 2: a .i. fanuns. *Syn.*: GONFANON. *Note*: OFr. *fanon* also had the meaning of 'maniple (the ecclesiastical vestment)' and is used in modern French heraldry in this sense. According to the *Larousse du XXᵉ siècle,* however: 'Le fanon héraldique diffère du fanon liturgique en ce que celui-ci pend au bras gauche de l'officiant, tandis que le premier est représenté comme pendant au bras droit.' The meaning of the term in *CP* is clear from the gonfanon which appears on the seals of the Counts of Auvergne since the end of the twelfth century (Prinet CP, p. 5 n. 2).

fasce, fasse, *fess.* See FESSE.

fassié, see FESSIÉ.

faus, *voided* (*i.e. with the centre of the charge hollowed out*). *Syn.*: PERCIÉ, VUIDIÉ[1], VUIDIÉ DU CHAMP.

fause crois, *cross voided* (Fig. 104). *B* 61: ung faulx crois (*Ba* 61, see CROIS PERCIEE; *Bb* 61, see CROIS VUIDIEE; *Bl* 61: ove une faux crois). *Syn.*: see CROIS PERCIEE. *Note*: canting arms for the Crevequer family; see *Aspilogia II*, pp. 50, note to item 66; 108; 109.

fause crois pomelee, *Toulouse cross* (*cross clechy, voided and botonny*) (Fig. 109). *CP* 131: a une fausse crois . . . pommelé. *Syn.*: see CROIS PATEE ET PERCIEE.

fause losenge, *mascle* (*voided lozenge*) (Fig. 87). *TA*, v. 753: fauses losenges; *BA* 45: a .iii. faisses [*sic*, for fauses] lozenges (A: lozengees); 210: a .vi. fausses lozenges; *Ba/ Bc* 8: a set fauses losenges (*B* 8, see MASCLE VUIDIEE DU CHAMP; *Bb* 8, see MASCLE²; *Bl* 8: ove sept faulses losenges); *C* 179: a trois faux losenges (*Cl* 179: a .iii. fause losenges). For another use, see POUDRÉ A FAUSES LOSENGES. *Syn.*: LOSENGE², LOSENGE PERCIEE, LOSENGE VUIDIEE, MASCLE², MASCLE VUIDIEE DU CHAMP. *Note*: for *BA* 45, see FESSE LOSENGIEE. The mascle often appears as part of a masculy field; see MASCLÉ DE . . . ET DE . . .¹, *Note.* In *TA*, the arms are those of Tort and the first meaning is doubtless that of 'false praises' (OFr. *losenge* 'praise').

fause rouele, *voided roundel* (*annulet*) (Fig. 111). *Ba* 24: a sis fauses roeles (*B* 24, see FAUS RONDELET; *Bb* 24, trick only; *Bc* 24: a sis fauses rorles; *Bl* 24: ove six fauses rouels); *Bl* 99: od six fauses roueles (*B* 99, see FAUS RONDELET). *Syn.*: see ANEL. *Note*: on this term, see London, 'The Roundel', p. 310. Refers to ROUELE³, a synonym of BESANT.

faus escu, *orle* (Fig. 124). *TA*, vv. 840, 1125: Au faus escu; *H* 28: ou ung faus eschue (*Hg* 28, see FAUS ESCUÇON). *Syn.*: see FAUS ESCUÇON. *Note*: Gayre, *Heraldic Cadency*, p. 148 n. 1: 'There is some doubt as to what a *faux escu* is. Some have held it was clearly a shield with a bordure, or an orle, round it, within which would be found the arms. Others have contended that it was a plain shield with the arms on the quarter or canton. John Woodward,

A Treatise on Heraldry, Edinburgh, 1896, Vol. II, p. 195. We incline to the latter view.' *Escu* here, however, plainly refers to ESCU². Prinet TA, p. 47: 'A plusieurs reprises, il est parlé de *faux écus*; on appelait ainsi, dans la langue héraldique du moyen âge, l'écu vidé dont la figure se confond avec ce que les modernes nomment l'*orle*.' In *TA*, v. 819, *fauz escuz* denotes Traïson's (Betrayal's) shield which is literally 'false', i.e. full of falsehood and treachery. This is also implied in vv. 840 and 1125 which refer to the arms of Mençonge (Falsehood) and Hasart (Chance) respectively. Cf. FAUS ESCUCEL. Matthew Paris, on the other hand, uses the corresponding Latin expression in the meaning 'orle' in his blazon of the Balliol arms: 'Scutum d'azuro, falsum scutum d'or, cruces d'or' (*Aspilogia II*, p. 57, item 112).

faus escucel, *orle* (Fig. 124). TA, vv. 886, 1160: A .i. faus escucel. *Syn.*: see FAUS ESCUÇON. *Note*: Prinet TA, p. 48: 'Le "faus escucel" d'Hypocrisie et celui d'Hérésie rappellent la fausseté de la vertu de l'une et des doctrines de l'autre.' Cf. FAUS ESCU, *Note*.

faus escucel en mi, *orle* (Fig. 124). TA, v. 866: A .i. faus escucel en mi. *Syn.*: see FAUS ESCUÇON.

faus escuçon, *orle* (Fig. 124). B 36: ove ung faux escochon (*Ba* 36: od un faus escuchun; *Bb* 36: od un faus escocheon; *Bc* 36: od u[n] faus escuchun; *Bl* 36: od un faus escuchon); 40: au faus escocheon (*Bl* 40: al faus escuchon); 140: ung faux escucion (*Bl* 140 [144]: od un faus escuchon); 201: ung faux escocheon (*Bl* 201 [205]: od un faus escuchon); *Ba* 38: au faus eschuchun (*Bc* 38: au faus escuchun); *C* 115: a un faux escocheon; *CP* 45: a un faus escuçon; *Hg* 28: a une faus escuchonn (*H* 28, see FAUS ESCU). *Syn.*: ESCUÇON PERCIÉ, ESCU VUIDIÉ DU CHAMP, FAUS ESCU, FAUS ESCUCEL, FAUS ESCUCEL EN MI. *Note*: Prinet WR, p. 250: 'Par "faux écusson" on entendait un écusson vidé.' On this term in the fourteenth and fifteenth centuries, see ESCUÇON VUIDIÉ, *Note*.

faus point, *voided 'point'*. TA, v. 880: A .i. faus point. *Note*: see POINT.

faus rondelet, *voided roundel (annulet)* (Fig. 111). B 24: six faux rondeletts (*Ba/Bl* 24, see FAUSE ROUELE); 99: a six faus rondlets

(*Bl* 99, see FAUSE ROUELE). *Syn.*: see ANEL. *Note*: P 88 (= B 99) reads: 'a sys anelettes'.

feissele, *small basket*. See FROMAGE EN FEISSELE.

fer¹, *horseshoe* (Fig. 264). B 118: ferrs (*Bl* 118 [122]: od fers). For other uses see BORDURE OD LES FERS, FERS EN LA BORDURE. *Syn.*: FER A CHEVAL. *Note*: here on a bordure; cf. BORDURE DE FERS A CHEVAL.

fer², *iron*. See CROCHET DE FER.

fer a cheval, *horseshoe*. See BORDURE DE FERS A CHEVAL. *Syn.*: FER¹. *Note*: here part of an orle of horseshoes; cf. FER¹.

fer de moulin¹, *cross moline* (*fer-de-moline, mill-iron, mill-rind*) (Fig. 101). BA 223, 248, 282: a .i. fer de molin; D 54: od un fer de molyn; CP 69, 126: a un fer de molin; H 22: ou ung fer de (G: ferde) molyn (*Hg* 22: a un fer de molin); 32: ou ung ferr de moulyn (*Hg* 32 [33]: a un fer de molin); K, v. 534: o un fer de molyn. *Syn.*: CROIS RECERCELEE. *Note*: cf. CROIS FOURCHIEE².

fer de moulin², *cross couped*. See FER DE MOULIN A TESTES DE SERPENZ AU FER DE MOULIN. *Syn.*: CROIS².

fer de moulin a testes de serpenz au fer de moulin, *cross gringolé* (*i.e. a cross couped with each limb ending in a pair of serpents' heads addorsed*) (Fig. 99). CP 64, 137: a un fer de molin ... a testes ... de serpens au fer de molin. *Note*: the same arms in WB 396 (fig. 39) are depicted as a cross moline. On this charge, consult Prinet CP, p. 23 n. 1 and especially p. 44 n. 4: 'Les armes données au "sire de Montfort" [i.e. Montfort-sur-Meu in Ille-et-Vilaine] par l'*Armorial* de Douët d'Arcq [i.e. *Navarre*], sont "d'argent a un fer de moulin de guelles, a testes de serpent d'or a chacune corniere du fer de moulin" (nº 743). En blason moderne, on dirait: *d'argent à la croix de gueules, gringolée d'or*.' The derivation of Fr. *gringolé* has nothing to do with *gargouille* (a suggestion made by the *Larousse du XXᵉ siècle*, s.v. *gringole*). It is rather a derivative of Middle Dutch *crink* 'curve' and akin to Modern French *dégringoler* 'to tumble down' (see *BW⁴*, s.v. *dégringoler*).

fermail, *buckle* (Fig. 246). C 163: trois fermaulx (*Cl* 163: a treis fermar; *Cd* 163: a 3 fermailes); *CP* 82: a trois fermaus.

ferreté, *cloué (ornamented with a pattern of nails)* (Fig. 46). *TC*, vv. 3213–16:

> Arméz estoit, par grant cointise,
> De riches armez a devise,
> Detranchies et ferreteies
> D'argent, de guelles bureleies.

Syn.: AUS CLAVEAUS. *Note*: cf. CLOUÉ DE POINZ EL BASTON. Refers to the arms of 'Joifroi d'Aixe', doubtless identical with 'Goiffroy d'Asse', i.e. Geoffroy III d'Esch-sur-Sûre in *WB* 526. Seal in J. Th. Raadt, *Sceaux armoriés des Pays-Bas* (Brussels, 1898–1903), i. 436.

fers en la bordure, *bordure semy of horseshoes* (Fig. 264). (1) *two separate tinctures are specified for the bordure and for the horseshoes.* *Bl* 208 [212]: od les fers . . . en la bordure. *Syn.*: BORDURE OD LES FERS. (2) *only one tincture is provided, that of the bordure.* *B* 208: et les fers en la bordure. *Note*: refers to BORDURE[1], FER[1]. Not to be confused with BORDURE DE FERS A CHEVAL.

fesan, *pheasant* (Fig. 199). *Hunbaut*, vv. 2228–9:

> Li fius le roi Urïen porte
> L'escu de gueles as faisans.

Note: arms of Yvain, knight of the Round Table. The number and position of the pheasants are not indicated, but the author was familiar with the works of Chrétien de Troyes and may have been thinking of the arms of Coguillant de Mautirec listed here s.v. FESANZ BEC A BEC.

fesanz bec a bec, *pheasants face to face* (Fig. 200). *Charrete*, vv. 5790–2:

> Et cil qui porte les feisanz
> An son escu poinz bec a bec?
> C'est Coguillanz de Mautirec.

Note: cf. the attitude of these fowl with that found in PRES A PRES UNE EGLE ET UN DRAGON.

*fesse, *fess* (Fig. 80). (1) *there is a single fess.* A. *the fess bears no charge.* Several attestations in literary sources before *c.* 1250: *Durmart*, v. 7863: a la fasse; *Fouque de Candie*, v. 14827: la fesse; *Lancelot propre*, iii. 367: a une fesse . . . moult lee; 407: a le feste; *TA*, v. 1001: A la fesse de desmesure. Very frequent in the rolls, e.g. *BA* 50: a une faisses; 106, 149–51: a une faisse; *B* 31:

ung fesse (*Ba/Bb* 31: la fesse; *Bc* 31: od la fese; *Bl* 31: ove une fesse); *CP* 9: a une fese; 18, 46: a une fesse; *K*, v. 189: O fesse; v. 299: o une fesse. *Note*: for *P* 93 (= *B/Ba/Bb* 31), see BENDE[2], *Note*. In *B/Bl* 92 and *C/Cl/Cd* 127 (Monmouth arms), the fess is over all; see CHEVRONS OD LA FESSE, *Note*. B. *the fess bears a charge.* 1. *the word* FESSE *is repeated twice, once in the locution* EN LA FESSE. *BA* 46: a .i. faisse, see COQUILLE EN LA FESSE; 105 (see COQUILLE EN LA FESSE), 131 and 159 (see MOLETE EN LA FESSE), 160 (see COQUILLE EN LA FESSE): a une faisse; *B* 127: a la fesse, see TOURTEL EN LA FESSE (*Bl* 127 [131]: od la fesse); *CP* 96: a une fesse, see ANELET EN LA FESSE; *CPA* 154: a la fasce, see MOLETE EN LA FESSE; *M* 11: ou le feez, see EN LA FESSE UN LIONCEL; 73: ou ung fez, see EN LA FESSE UNE FLEUR DE LIS. For another use, see EN LA FESSE UN MOLET (refers to FESSE ET CHEVRONS). 2. *the word* FESSE *is used only once, a locution other than* EN LA FESSE *indicating that the fess bears a charge.* *B* 119: ung fece, see FLEURÉ DE L'UN EN L'AUTRE (*Bl* 119 [123]: od une fesse, see FLEURETES DE L'UN ET L'AUTRE). For other uses, see FESSE A UN LIONCEL RAMPANT, FESSE OD UNE ROSE, FESSE OU ESCHALOPES. C. *the fess sets off a 'chief' which bears a charge.* 1. *the locution* EN CHIEF, EN LE CHIEF, *or* OU CHIEF *is used.* See FESSE A UNE DANCE EN LE CHIEF, FESSE A UNE MERLETE OU CHIEF, FESSE A UNE ROUELE EN LE CHIEF, FESSE A UN MOLET EN LE CHIEF, FESSE A UN OISELET OU CHIEF, FESSE ET UNE DANCE EN CHIEF, FESSE ET UNE DANCE EN LE CHIEF, FESSE ET UNE ESTOILE EN LE CHIEF, FESSE ET UNE ROUELE EN CHIEF, FESSE ET UN TOURTEL EN CHIEF, FESSE ET UN TOURTEL EN LE CHIEF, FESSE OVE UN TOURTEL EN LE CHIEF. *Note*: cf. FESSE A UN TOURTEL EN CHIEF, FESSE OD UN TOURTEL EN LE CHIEF, FESSE OU UN TOURTEL EN LE CHIEF (see section 2. below), and FESSIÉ D'UNE BARRE ET OU CHIEF UN LIONCEL PASSANT. 2. *a locution other than* EN CHIEF, EN LE CHIEF, *or* OU CHIEF *is used.* See FESSE AU LIONCEL PASSANT OU CHANTEL DEVANT, FESSE A UNE ESCHALOPE, FESSE A UN LIONCEL PASSANT OU QUARTIER, FESSE A UN LION PASSANT, FESSE ET A UN TOURTEL, FESSE OD UNE LOSENGE. 3. *order of items alone is used.* The complete blazon reads as follows: *Ba* 45: Willame de Evereus, de gules a une fese de argent 3 turteus de argent (*B* 45, see FESSE ET UN TOURTEL EN LE CHIEF; *Bb* 45, see FESSE ET UN TOURTEL EN CHIEF; *Bc* 45, see FESSE A UN TOURTEL EN CHIEF; *Bl* 45, see FESSE OVE UN TOURTEL EN LE CHIEF; for these two items, see section 1. above). *Note*: in FESSE AU LIONCEL PASSANT OU CHANTEL DEVANT, FESSE A UN LIONCEL PASSANT OU QUARTIER, FESSE A UN LION PASSANT, and FESSIÉ D'UNE BARRE ET OU CHIEF UN LIONCEL PASSANT, the lion or lioncel passant is actually in *dexter* chief. *Note*: see CHIEF², *Note*. D. *the fess separates multiple charges.* 1. *a positioning phrase is used.* a. *chevrons.* See CHEVRONS A LA FESSE, CHEVRONS ET UNE FESSE, CHEVRONS OD LA FESSE, CHEVRONS OU UNE FESSE, FESSE A CHEVRONS, FESSE ENTRE CHEVRONS, FESSE ET CHEVRONS, FESSE OD CHEVRONS. b. *escallops.* See ESCHALOPES ET LA FESSE, ESCHALOPES OD LA FESSE, FESSE OU ESCHALOPES, *Note* (error in MS.). c. *leopards' heads jessant-de-lis.* See FESSE DE FLEURS DE LIS ESPARZ NAISSANZ DE TESTES DE LIEPARZ, FESSE OD FLEURS DE LIS CROISSANZ HORS DE TESTES DE LIEPARZ, FESSE OU FLEURS CROISSANZ HORS DE LA TESTE DU LIEPART. d. *martlets.* See FESSE ET MERLOZ, FESSE OU MERLOZ, MERLOZ EN LE CHAMP O UNE FESSE. *Note*: see MERLETE¹, *Note*. e. *popinjays.* See FESSE A PAPEGAIS, FESSE ET PAPEGAIS, PAPEGAIS ET UNE FESSE. For another use, see PAPEGAI (2). f. *water-bougets.* See FESSE ET BOUGES. 2. *order of items alone indicates that the fess separates the charges.* The complete blazons read as follows: *B* 129: Marmaduk de Twenge, d'argent a trois papegayes de vert ung fece de goules; *C* 143: Marmaduk de Thweng, d'argent un fesse gules trois papegayes vert (*Cl*/*Cd* 143, see FESSE A PAPEGAIS). E. *the fess is cotised* (Fig. 82). See FESSE A DEUS LISTEAUS UN DESOUS L'AUTRE DESOR. F. *the fess is double-cotised* (Fig. 83). See FESSE A DEUS LISTES, FESSE ENTRE DEUS JUMEAUS, FESSE OD DEUS LISTES. (2) *there is more than one stripe designated as a fess.* *CP* 67, 88, 123: a deux fesses; *CPA* 171: a .ii. fesses; *Hg* 106: a deux fesses (*H* 106, see FESSE ET UNE DEMI FESSE); *K*, v. 393: O deus fesses. For other uses, see FESSE A UN TOURTEL EN CHIEF, FESSE OD UN TOURTEL EN LE CHIEF, FESSE OU ESCHALOPES, FESSE OU UN TOURTEL EN LE CHIEF, and cf.

FESSIEL ENCHASTELÉ DESOUS ET DESOR. *Syn.*: see BARRE¹. *Note*: in modern practice, the term *fess* (Fr. *fasce*) is usually applied to a single, broad, horizontal stripe, *bars* (Fr. *burelles*) being the designation reserved for multiples of this charge. Matthew Paris used the word whether referring to a single stripe (Pusikan, p. 123: 'Girardi et Willelmi Dodingeseles. Scutum album, .i. fesse de gules, .ii. stelle [*P*: stellae] de gules in capite'; p. 128: 'Roberti de Tuengue. Scutum album cum fessa rubea et papaginibus viridibus') or to three (Pusikan, p. 128: 'Ricardi de Grai. Scutum album, tres fesse auree [*P*: fessae aureae]'). See *Aspilogia II*, p. 7. Though he used the variants *bend, benda, bende* (Pusikan, pp. 124, 140, 141, 144) to designate the diagonal stripe, he also utilized the term *fesse* in this connection (Pusikan, p. 147: 'Willelmi de Bellocampo. Quartier d'or aū [Pusikan: anterior; *Aspilogia II*, p. 41: ante] anterior cum suo pari, alia de gules, la fesse de gules'; 'Johannis de Bassingeburne. Scutum superius de gules, leo aureus, inferius scutum de albo, fesse de gules, aves de gules'). See *Aspilogia II*, p. 41, note to item 28 (Beauchamp of Bedford). Cf. BENDE¹, *Note*. For yet another meaning of the word *fesse* in Matthew Paris, see FESSE ENDENTEE, *Note*. The fess's position over all (e.g. *B* 92) does not appear to have called for a positioning phrase; see *Aspilogia II*, p. 105; CHEVRON (1), *Note*; and cf. CHEVRONS OD LA FESSE, *Note*.

fesse a chevrons, *fess between chevrons.* *D* 88: od une fesse . . . a deus cheveruns. *Syn.*: see CHEVRON (4).

fesse a deus listeaus un desous et l'autre desor, *fess cotised* (Fig. 82). *BA* 100: a une faisse . . . a .ii. listiax . . . .i. desox (*A*: dessox) et l'autre deseure. *Syn.*: BENDE A DEUS LISTEAUS². *Note*: cf. FESSE A DEUS LISTES, FESSE OD DEUS LISTES, where the fess is double-cotised (see also FESSE ENTRE DEUS JUMEAUS). On the custom of counting from the bottom upwards, consult London, 'Some Medieval Treatises', p. 180. See also FESSIEL ENCHASTELÉ DESOUS ET DESOR. This rule is mentioned by Johannes de Bado Aureo, *Tractatus de Armis* (*c.* 1394, ed. Evan John Jones in *Medieval Heraldry* [Cardiff, 1943], p. 124), in his discussion of the plain cross: 'Et plus dubitatur de ipsa cruce quam de omnibus aliis, et propter regulam quam ponit Magister meus Franciscus, scilicet, quod semper a cono, si conus unius coloris fuerit, est incipiendum in discretione armorum; et color ille conalis est campus ipsorum armorum. Quae regula est sic intellegenda, scilicet, *Semper a cono . . . est incipiendum.* Hoc verum est si color illius coni fuerit maior et copiosior color in armis.' Cf., however, SAUTOIRS DEUS DESOR ET UN DESOUS.

fesse a deus listes, *fess double-cotised* (Fig. 83). *D* 172: od une fesse . . . a deus listes. *Syn.*: FESSE ENTRE DEUS JUMEAUS, FESSE OD DEUS LISTES. *Note*: refers to LISTE[3]. Cf. FESSE A DEUS LISTEAUS UN DESOUS ET L'AUTRE DESOR 'fess cotised'. The accompanying painted shield in the Camden Roll (no. 189) shows bars gemelles above and below the fess.

fesse a papegais, *fess between popinjays.* *Cl* 143: e une fesse . . . a treys papagays (*C* 143, see FESSE (1) D. 2.; *Cd* 143: a une fesse . . . a .iii. popayngais). *Syn.*: FESSE ET PAPEGAIS. See also PAPEGAI (2). *Note*: *Aspilogia II*, p. 187, note to item 103: '[Leland's version of Walford's Roll] gives no tincture for the popinjays, which may mean that their colour [i.e. green] was already fixed.'

fesse au lioncel passant ou chantel devant, *fess, in dexter chief a lioncel passant.* *CC*, vv. 712–14:

> Escut d'or a face d'asur
> Au lionciel viermeil passant
> Portés ens ou cantiel devant.

Syn.: FESSE A UN LIONCEL PASSANT OU QUARTIER, FESSE A UN LION PASSANT, FESSIÉ D'UNE BARRE ET OU CHIEF UN LIONCEL PASSANT.

fesse a une dance en le chief, *fess, in chief a fess dancetty.* *Cd* 170: a une fees . . . a une dame [*sic*] en le cheif (*C* 170, see FESSE ET UNE DANCE EN CHIEF; *Cl* 170, see FESSE ET UNE DANCE EN LE CHIEF). *Syn.*: FESSE ET UNE DANCE EN CHIEF, FESSE ET UNE DANCE EN LE CHIEF.

fesse a une eschalope, *fess, in chief an escallop.* *D* 152: od une fesse . . . a treis escalops. *Note*: cf. ESCHALOPES ET LA FESSE, ESCHALOPES OD LA FESSE, FESSE OU ESCHALOPES.

fesse a une merlete ou chief, *fess, in chief a martlet.* *BA* 155: a une faisse . . . a .iii. mellettes . . . u kief. *Syn.*: FESSE A UN OISELET OU CHIEF.

fesse a une rouele en le chief, *fess, in chief a mullet.* *Cl* 153: a une fesse . . . a deus rouele . . . en le chef (*C* 153, see FESSE ET UNE ROUELE EN CHIEF; *Cd* 153: a une fees . . . a une [*sic*] rowels . . . en le cheif). *Syn.*: BARRE OD UNE ESTOILE EN LE CHIEF, FESSE A UN MOLET EN LE CHIEF, FESSE ET UNE ESTOILE EN LE CHIEF, FESSE ET UNE ROUELE EN CHIEF. *Note*: refers to ROUELE EN LE CHIEF[2].

fesse a un lioncel passant ou quartier, *fess, in dexter chief a lioncel passant.* *BA* 88: a une faisse . . . a .i. lioncel (A: lionel) . . . passant u quartier. *Syn.*: see FESSE AU LIONCEL PASSANT OU CHANTEL DEVANT.

fesse a un lioncel rampant, *on a fess a lioncel rampant.* *D* 82: a une fesse . . . a treis leunceus rampant.

fesse a un lion passant, *fess, in dexter chief a lion passant.* *D* 51: od une fesse . . . a un leun passant. *Syn.*: see FESSE AU LIONCEL PASSANT OU CHANTEL DEVANT. *Note*: the accompanying painted shield shows a fess with a lion passant in dexter chief.

fesse a un molet en le chief, *fess, in chief a mullet.* *B* 138: a la fece . . . a deux molets en le cheif (*Bl* 138 [142], see FESSE ET UNE ESTOILE EN LE CHIEF). *Syn.*: see FESSE A UNE ROUELE EN LE CHIEF.

fesse a un oiselet ou chief, *fess, in chief a martlet.* *BA* 46, 60, 105 (A: oiselets), 131 (A: oiselers), 159 (A: oiselets), 160 (A: oiselets), 161 (A: oiselets): a une faisse . . . a .iii. oiselés . . . u kief. *Syn.*: FESSE A UNE MERLETE OU CHIEF.

fesse a un tourtel en chief, *bar, in chief a roundel.* *Ba* 51: a deus feses . . . a 3 turteus in chefe (*B* 51: see BARRE OVE UN TOURTEL EN LE CHIEF; *Bb* 51, see BARRE [2] A.; *Bc* 51: a deus feses . . . a treys turteus . . . en chef); *Bc* 45: a une fese . . . a treis turteus . . . en chef (*B* 45, see FESSE ET UN TOURTEL EN LE CHIEF; *Ba* 45, see FESSE [1] C. 3.; *Bb* 45, see FESSE ET UN TOURTEL EN CHIEF; *Bl* 45, see FESSE OVE UN TOURTEL EN LE CHIEF). *Syn.*: BARRE A UN MEULET EN LE CHIEF, BARRE OD UN TOURTEL EN CHIEF, BARRE OD UN TOURTEL EN LE CHIEF, BARRE OU UN TOURTEL EN LE CHIEF, BARRE OVE UNE MEULE EN

LE CHIEF, BARRE OVE UN TOURTEL EN LE
CHIEF, FESSE ET UN TOURTEL EN CHIEF,
FESSE ET UN TOURTEL EN LE CHIEF, FESSE OD
UN TOURTEL EN LE CHIEF, FESSE OU UN
TOURTEL EN LE CHIEF, FESSE OVE UN TOUR-
TEL EN LE CHIEF. *Note*: FESSE A UN TOURTEL
EN CHIEF, FESSE OD UN TOURTEL EN LE
CHIEF, and FESSE OU UN TOURTEL EN LE
CHIEF refer to FESSE (2), other locutions
cited here to FESSE (1).

fesseaus, *small fesses.* See FESSIEL ENCHAS-
TELÉ DESOUS ET DESOR.

fesse danciee, *daunce, fess dancetty* (Fig. 78).
P 91: a une fesse dauncee. *Syn.*: see DANCE.
Note: corresponds to *B* 106 (see DANCE).

**fesse de fleurs de lis esparz naissanz
de testes de lieparz,** *fess between leopards'
heads jessant-de-lis.* *K*, vv. 388–90:

> Fesse vaire ot el rouge escu,
> De trois flours de lis de or espars
> Naissans de testes de lupars.

Syn.: FESSE OD FLEURS DE LIS CROISSANZ
HORS DE TESTES DE LIEPARZ, FESSE OU
FLEURS CROISSANZ HORS DE LA TESTE DU
LIEPART. *Note*: cf. FLEUR CROISSANT HORS
DE LA TESTE DU LIEPART, FLEUR DE LIS
CROISSANT HORS DE LA TESTE DU LIEPART.
On this charge see *Aspilogia II*, pp. 119–20,
note to item 27.

fesse de travers, *fess* (Fig. 80). *Vulgate
Merlin Sequel*, p. 316: a cele fasse de travers;
TC, v. 1207: La blanche face de travers.
Syn.: see BARRE[1].

fesse endentee, *fusils conjoined in fess* (Fig.
84). *BA* 34: a .i. faisse (A: fasse) . . . endentee; 289: a une faisse . . . endentee;
D 76: od une fesse . . . endentee; *CC*, v.
1598: une fasse endentee. *Syn.*: FESSE
ENGRESLEE, FESSE ENGRESLEE DE . . . PIECES.
Note: cf. FESSIÉ DE . . . ET DE . . . Prinet CC,
p. 177: 'Par *fasce endentée* il faut entendre,
— ici comme dans d'autres textes du
moyen âge, — une fasce formée de losanges ou fusées accolées.' Matthew Paris's
blazon of the Percy arms contains the first
attested use of this expression (Pusikan,
p. 122: 'Ricardi de Perci. Scutum d'azuro
quinque fesse d'argent endentees, clausi
superius ferri argenteï'). Note that in this
blazon, each fusil is referred to as a 'fess'.
Cf. FESSE ENGRESLEE DE . . . PIECES. According to *Aspilogia II*, p. 7, this blazon is 'in-

comprehensible' (see also MASCLÉ DE . . .
ET DE . . .[1], *Note*).

fesse engreslee, *fusils conjoined in fess* (Fig.
84). *B* 41: a la fesse engrelé (*Bl* 41: od le
fesse engrelé), 115 (*Bl* 115 [119]: a la fesse
engrellé), 117 (*Bl* 117 [121]: od le fesse
engrellé), 131 (*Bl* 131 [135]: od la fesse
engrellé): ung fece engrelé; *Bl* 44: od un
fesse engrellé (*B* 44, see FESSE ENGRESLEE
DE . . . PIECES); *C* 177: un fesse engrelé (*Cl*
177: a une fesse . . . engrallé); *CPA* 162:
a la fasce engreslee; *H* 69: ou la feez
engrelee (G: engrele; *Hg* 69 [70]: od la
fesse engrelee); 92: .ii. feez engrelés (*Hg* 92
[91]: deus fesses engrelés); *M* 54: ou la
fesse engrelee; *K*, v. 260: fesse . . . engreellie.
Syn.: see FESSE ENDENTEE. *Note*: *P* 83 (= *B*
41) reads: 'ove une fesse endentee'. In *H* 92,
there is one group of fusils conjoined in
fess in quarter 2 and another in quarter 3
of the quarterly shield. On this term, consult Prinet WR, pp. 242, 253, 255; Prinet
K, pp. 348–9. The charge is said to be
canting in the Percy and Montagu family
arms; *Aspilogia II*, p. 123, note to item 41
(Percy): 'a fess of five fusils . . . has always
been the normal form. The fusils . . . may
be a pun on the idea of piercing'; p. 123,
note to item 44 (Montagu): 'The sharp-
pointed fusils may allude to the name
Mont-aigu.'

fesse engreslee de . . . pieces, *fusils conjoined in fess* (Fig. 84). *B* 44: ung fesse
engrelé . . . de trois peices (*Bl* 44, see
FESSE ENGRESLEE). *Syn.*: see FESSE ENDENTEE.
Note: the number of fusils is specified. For
these arms, see *Barons' Letter*, p. 124; *Aspilogia II*, p. 123, note to item 44.

fesse en mi, *fess* (Fig. 80). *Durmart*, v. 8497:
A la vermelle faisse en mi. *Syn.*: see BARRE[1].

fesse entre chevrons, *fess between chevrons.*
B 182: ung fece entre deus cheverons (*Bl*
182 [186], see CHEVRONS OD LA FESSE);
K, v. 47: Fesse entre deus cheverons. *Syn.*:
see CHEVRON (4). *Note*: *P* 92 (= *B* 182)
reads: 'a deux cheverons et une fesse'.

fesse entre deus jumeaus, *fess double-
cotised* (Fig. 83). *K*, v. 833: Fesse rouge entre
deuz jumeaus. *Syn.*: see FESSE A DEUS
LISTES. *Note*: refers to JUMEAUS[1] (4). Add
this locution to those listed at the end of
Brault, '*Cotice*', p. 115, as an alternative
way to blazon a fess double-cotised in the

thirteenth century without using the word *cotice* (i.e. in addition to FESSE A DEUS LISTES and FESSE OD DEUS LISTES).

fesse et a un tourtel, *fess, in chief a roundel.* CP 113: a une fesse . . . et a trois tourteaux. *Syn.*: see FESSE (1) C. 1.

fesse et bouges, *fess between water-bougets.* M 59: le fez . . . et treis bouces.

fesse et chevrons, *fess between chevrons.* Hg, Teys [93]: a une fesse et deuz cheverons, see EN LA FESSE UN MOLET. *Syn.*: see CHEVRON (4).

fesse et merloz, *fess between martlets.* Hg 83: od la fesse . . . et .vi. merlotz (H 83, see FESSE OU MERLOZ). *Syn.*: FESSE OU MERLOZ, MERLOZ EL CHAMP O UNE FESSE. *Note*: see MERLETE[1], *Note*.

fesse et papegais, *fess between popinjays.* H 35: ung fesse . . . et troys papejoyes; K, v. 571: La fesse e li trois papegaiz (W: papegai). *Syn.*: see FESSE A PAPEGAIS.

fesse et une dance en chief, *fess, in chief a fess dancetty.* C 170: un fesse . . . et un danse . . . en cheife (Cl 170, see FESSE ET UNE DANCE EN LE CHIEF; Cd 170, see FESSE A UNE DANCE EN LE CHIEF). *Syn.*: see FESSE A UNE DANCE EN LE CHIEF.

fesse et une dance en le chief, *fess, in chief a fess dancetty.* Cl 170: a une fesse . . . et une dazur [*sic*] en le chef (C 170, see FESSE ET UNE DANCE EN CHIEF; Cd 170: see FESSE A UNE DANCE EN LE CHIEF). *Syn.*: see FESSE A UNE DANCE EN LE CHIEF. *Note*: on the error (*dazur = dance* or *danse*) in Cl 170 [175], see *Aspilogia II*, p. 201, note to item 175. For the abbreviation which resembles a *6* or a *u* and actually represents *en le* in Cl and Cd, see Prinet WR, pp. 238 and 251. See also Introduction, p. 57.

fesse et une demi fesse, *fess and a demi-fess* (Fig. 81). The complete blazon reads as follows: H 106: S[r] Rauff Pipart porte d'argent ou ung feez et demy feez et le cantell d'azure, et en le cantell quintfoyl d'or (Hg 106: Rauf Pipard porte d'argent a deux fesses et le cauntel d'asur, et en le cauntel un quintefoil d'or). *Note*: Gough–Parker, p. 252: 'the term a *demi-fesse* occurs also when it is joined with a canton' (with a reference to H 106). As can be seen by the illustration of the Pipart coat in Gough–Parker, p. 91, the canton and the top bar which are of the same tincture

fuse without any line to separate them. The result is that the upper stripe is reduced about one-third. If we bear in mind that *le cantell* in H is a quarter and not a modern canton, the top bar is seen to be reduced even more to the point where *demi-fess* is a very precise description of the charge in question. Cf. FESSIEL.

fesse et une estoile en le chief, *fess, in chief a mullet.* Bl 138 [142]: od la fesse . . . et deus estoilles . . . en le chief (B 138, see FESSE A UN MOLET EN LE CHIEF). *Syn.*: see FESSE A UNE ROUELE EN LE CHIEF. *Note*: refers to ESTOILE EN LE CHIEF[2], FESSE (1) C. 1.

fesse et une rouele en chief, *fess, in chief a mullet.* C 153: un fes et deux rouells in cheif (Cl/Cd 153, see FESSE A UNE ROUELE EN LE CHIEF). *Syn.*: see FESSE A UNE ROUELE EN LE CHIEF.

fesse et un tourtel en chief, *fess, in chief a roundel.* Bb 45: a une fesse . . . et 3 [torteaux tricked] . . . in cheif (B 45, see FESSE ET UN TOURTEL EN LE CHIEF; Ba 45, see FESSE [1] C. 3.; Bc 45, see FESSE A UN TOURTEL EN CHIEF; Bl 45, see FESSE OVE UN TOURTEL EN LE CHIEF). *Syn.*: see FESSE A UN TOURTEL EN CHIEF.

fesse et un tourtel en le chief, *fess, in chief a roundel.* B 45: ove ung fesse . . . et trois torteaulx . . . en le cheif (Ba 45, see FESSE [1] C. 3.; Bb 45, see FESSE ET UN TOURTEL EN CHIEF; Bc 45, see FESSE A UN TOURTEL EN CHIEF; Bl 45, see FESSE OVE UN TOURTEL EN LE CHIEF). *Syn.*: see FESSE A UN TOURTEL EN CHIEF.

fessel, see FESSIEL ENCHASTELÉ DESOUS ET DESOR.

fesse losengiee, *ghost word.* See FAUSE LOSENGE. *Note*: the arms of the Bautersem family, which feature three mascles, are provided by WB 1178, C 179 (see FAUSE LOSENGE), and D 43 (see LOSENGE PERCIEE).

fesse od chevrons, *fess between chevrons.* D 98, 142: a une fesse . . . od deus cheveruns. *Syn.*: see CHEVRON (4).

fesse od deus listes, *fess double-cotised* (Fig. 83). D 175: a une fesse . . . od deus listes. *Syn.*: see FESSE A DEUS LISTES. *Note*: refers to LISTE[3]. The accompanying painted shield in the Camden Roll (no. 192) shows bars gemelles above and below the fess.

fesse od fleurs de lis croissanz hors de

testes de lieparz, *fess between leopards'*
heads jessant-de-lis. Hg 71 [72]: od la fesse
. . . od trois flurs de lys . . . cressant hors de
testes de lupars (H 71, see FESSE OU FLEURS
CROISSANZ HORS DE LA TESTE DU LIEPART).
Syn.: see FESSE DE FLEURS DE LIS ESPARZ
NAISSANZ DE TESTES DE LIEPARZ.

fesse od une losenge, *fess, in chief a*
lozenge. D 169: a une fesse . . . od treis
losenges. *Note*: refers to LOSENGE[1].

fesse od une rose, *on a fess a rose (i.e. a*
pierced cinquefoil). D 86: a une fesse . . . od
treis roses.

fesse od un tourtel en le chief, *bar, in chief*
a roundel. Hg 25: a deus fesses . . . od troys
tourteaux . . . en le chief (H 25, see FESSE
OU UN TOURTEL EN LE CHIEF). *Syn.*: see
FESSE A UN TOURTEL EN CHIEF.

fesse ou eschalopes, *fess between escallops.*
The complete blazon reads as follows: M
65: S[r] John de (G omits the latter word)
Seynt Lo port de gulez ou .vii. fesses
d'argent ou .iii. escaloppez (G: escallopez)
d'argent. *Syn.*: see FESSE (1) D. 1. b. *Note*:
cf. COQUILLE EN LA FESSE, FESSE A UNE
ESCHALOPE. For *.vii. fesses* read *une fesse*;
see CROIS[2], *Note*. For blazons of these arms
featuring a single fess, see Gough–Parker,
p. 236; Papworth's *Ordinary*, p. 749.

fesse ou fleurs croissanz hors de la
teste du liepart, *fess between leopards' heads*
jessant-de-lis. H 71: ou la feez . . . ou
.iii. flours . . . cresçanns hors de la test du
leopard (G: crescauns). *Syn.*: see FESSE DE
FLEURS DE LIS ESPARZ NAISSANZ DE TESTES DE
LIEPARZ. *Note*: cf. FLEUR DE LIS CROISSANT
HORS DE LA TESTE DU LIEPART.

fesse ou merloz, *fess between martlets.* H 83:
ou les feez . . . ou .vi. merlots (Hg 83, see
FESSE ET MERLOZ). *Syn.*: see FESSE ET MER-
LOZ. *Note*: see MERLETE[1], *Note*.

fesse ou un tourtel en le chief, *bar, in*
chief a roundel. H 25: ou .ii. fesses . . . ou
.iii. tourtous . . . en le chief (Hg 25, see
FESSE OD UN TOURTEL EN LE CHIEF). *Syn.*:
see FESSE A UN TOURTEL EN CHIEF. *Note*:
refers to FESSE (2).

fesse ove un tourtel en le chief, *fess, in*
chief a roundel. Bl 45: od un fesse . . . ove
trois turteaus . . . en le chief (B 45, see
FESSE ET UN TOURTEL EN LE CHIEF; Ba 45,
see FESSE [1] C. 3.; Bb 45, see FESSE ET UN
TOURTEL EN CHIEF; Bc 45, see FESSE A UN

TOURTEL EN CHIEF). *Syn.*: see FESSE A UN
TOURTEL EN CHIEF.

fesses ou eschalopes, *fess between escallops.*
See FESSE OU ESCHALOPES.

fessié, *traversed by a single horizontal stripe (a*
fess) (Fig. 80). *Durmart,* v. 8503: Tot cil
a ces escus fassiés. For another use, see
FESSIÉ D'UNE BARRE. *Note*: cf. BENDÉ[1]. The
shields in *Durmart* are borne by knights in
Giflet's retinue; the latter's arms are
blazoned *argent, a fess gules* in vv. 8496–7.

fessié de . . . et de . . .[1], *barry* (Fig. 5). *CC,*
v. 1575: Et de . . . et de . . . faissié; *CP* 43,
65, 110, 138, 145: fessié de . . . et de . . .;
124: fascé de . . . et de . . . For other uses,
see FESSIÉ DE . . . ET DE . . . A . . . PIECES,
FESSIÉ DE . . . ET DE . . . ET CONTREFESSIÉ.
Syn.: see BARRÉ DE . . . ET DE . . .[1]. *Note*: in
modern French heraldic usage, *fascé* is used
only to describe a field charged with two
or three bars, the locution *à la fasce* being
substituted when blazoning a single fess.
When there are eight or more bars, French
now prefers the term *burelé* 'barruly'. See
Veyrin-Forrer, p. 37.

fessié de . . . et de . . .[2], *lozenges conjoined*
in fess, resulting in a lozengy pattern (Fig. 16).
See FESSIÉ DE . . . ET DE . . . ENDENTÉ DE
L'UN A L'AUTRE. *Note*: cf. BENDÉ DE . . . ET
DE . . .[3], FESSE ENDENTÉ.

fessié de . . . et de . . . a . . . pieces, *barry*
(Fig. 5). *CC,* vv. 1119–20:

> Un escu avoit a cinc pieces,
> Faissiet et de vair et de geules;

CP 33: fessié de . . . et de . . . a 6 pieces.
Syn.: see BARRÉ DE . . . ET DE . . .[1]. *Note*: the
number of pieces is indicated. Prinet CC,
pp. 166–7, states that the correct reading
in *CC* should be six, not five, pieces. See also
his note 2, p. 167: 'Six est le nombre
normal des pièces d'un fascé.' Coucy arms.

fessié de . . . et de . . . endenté de l'un
a l'autre, *lozengy* (Fig. 16). *CP* 15: fascé
de . . . et de . . . endenté de l'un a l'autre.
Syn.: see LOSENGIÉ DE . . . ET DE . . .[1]. *Note*:
refers to FESSIÉ DE . . . ET DE . . .[2]; cf. BENDÉ
DE . . . ET DE . . . ENDENTÉ L'UN EN L'AUTRE.
Prinet CP, p. 9 n. 1: 'Les armes des Crespin
sont généralement constituées par un écu
fuselé . . . Le fascé endenté d'argent et
de gueules est attribué aux Crespin dans
plusieurs armoriaux [with references].'

fessié de . . . et de . . . et contrefessié, *party per pale and barry counterchanged (the tinctures of the bars are reversed as they cross the middle of the shield resulting in a party and varied field)* (Fig. 22). The complete blazon reads as follows: *CP* 38: Mesire Renaut de Prechenig porte les armes fessié d'or et d'asur et contrefescié et bandé contrebandé, au coigniet gironné et a un escuchon d'argent ou milieu. *Syn.*: BENDÉ CONTREBENDÉ DE . . . ET DE . . ., CONTREBENDÉ DE . . . ET DE . . . *Note*: these are the famous Pressigny arms noted for their difficulty in blazoning. Medieval treatises frequently cite these armorial bearings or the kindred Mortimer arms because of their complexity. Proper blazon was subject to controversy, as a matter of fact; see *Dean Tract*, pp. 25–6, vv. 19–36, and cf. BROIE SOR LE . . . See also references provided s.v. CHANTEL[4], CORNIER, and CORNIERE[1]. The Pressigny arms appear in *WB* 511, with a label in *WB* 512, and with an escutcheon gules in *WB* 513. See also Prinet CP, p. 15 n. 2, and Adam-Even BA, p. 118, notes to items 256–7. It is clear from these illustrations that *bendé contrebendé [de . . . et de . . .]* is an error here for *palé de . . . et de . . .*

fessié d'une barre et ou chief un lioncel passant, *fess, in dexter chief a lioncel passant.* *CC*, vv. 1279–82:

> Bien sai qu'il avoit escu d'or,
> D'unne bare d'asur faissiet,
> Et s'i ot ou cief entailliet
> Un lyonciel viermeil passant.

Syn.: see FESSE AU LIONCEL PASSANT OU CHANTEL DEVANT. *Note*: see BARRÉ DE . . . ET DE . . .[2], *Note*. Refers to OU CHIEF[2].

fessiel enchastelé desous et desor, *demi-fess (i.e. bar) embattled on both sides* (Fig. 58). *BA* 83: a .ii. faisseus (A: faisses) . . . encastelees desox et deseure. *Note*: the item in question is cited by London, 'Some Medieval Treatises', p. 180, as an example of the bottom-upwards system of blazoning. See also FESSE A DEUS LISTEAUS UN DESOUS ET L'AUTRE DESOR and cf. SAUTOIRS DEUS DESOR ET UN DESOUS. OFr. *fessel, fessiel* or *faissel, faissiel* 'small fess', a masculine diminutive of OFr. *fesse* (< Lat. *fascia* 'band'; cf. DEMI FESSE), occurs only

here during this period, though a related term, with an identical spelling, is well attested in Old French in the meanings 'bundle (of sticks, firewood), burden, load, etc.'. The latter is a derivative of VL **fascellum* (< Lat. *fascis* 'bundle'). Though late copies of medieval rolls of arms are hardly to be trusted in such matters as gender, it is worth noting that *encastelees* is a feminine plural, suggesting that the noun it modified may also have been of that gender and number (*fesseles*). OFr. *fessele* or *faissele* is found with the meanings 'bundle, burden, load, etc.', and it may be argued that a similar feminine form, derived, however, from OFr. *fesse* and with the meaning 'small fess', also existed in the thirteenth century. The masculine term *fusel* or *fuseau* and its feminine counterpart *fuselle* are attested in fifteenth-century heraldic sources: 'The word *fuselle* is another trap for the uninitiated who not unnaturally assume that it is the same as fusil, the elongated lozenge, fuseau or fusew in Strangways' day. Fuselle is a diminutive of the Latin *fusus*, a word which was occasionally used for a fess. According to Strangways a fuselle is a fess of half the normal width but the term was used more loosely as a synonym for bar. So in the fifteenth-century blazoned version of St. George's Roll Stoteville bears "d'argent a vj fuseaulx de gueulles" (186) and Nychol de St. Martin bears "d'argent ij fuseaulx de gueulles et v labels d'asur" (246). The thirteenth-century painted version of this roll depicts the one coat as Burely argent and gules and the other as Argent, 2 bars gules and a label azure. This latter example is particularly illuminating, for there can be no doubt that the coat attributed to St. Martin in the *General Armory*, Argent, 2 fusils in fess gules and a label of 5 points azure, is simply a misrendering of the fifteenth-century blazon' (London, 'Some Medieval Treatises', p. 179).

feste, see FESSE.

feuille de trumel, *lime-blossom leaf* (Fig. 239). *BA* 54: a .iii. fuelles de trumel.

field, see QUARTIERS[2].

first, see EGLE A UN CROISSANT EN LA POITRINE, *Note*.

fleur, *fleur-de-lis* (Fig. 235). *Ba/Bc* 63: a un flur (*B/Bb* 63, see FLEUR DE LIS; *Bl* 63: ove une flour); *Mouskés*, vv. 17408-9: A flours d'or des armes le roi / De France. For other uses, see A FLEURS, A FLEURS DE L'UN A L'AUTRE, EL CHANTEL DEVANT UNE FLEUR, FESSE OU FLEURS CROISSANZ HORS DE LA TESTE DU LIEPART. *Syn.*: see FLEUR DE LIS.

fleur croissant hors de la teste du liepart, *leopard's head jessant-de-lis*. See FESSE OU FLEURS CROISSANZ HORS DE LA TESTE DU LIEPART. *Syn.*: FLEUR DE LIS CROISSANT HORS DE LA TESTE DU LIEPART.

fleur de glaieul, *fleur-de-lis* (Fig. 235). *D* 50, 64: od treis flurs de glagel; 94: a treis flurs (G: fleurs) de glagel; 108, 182: a une flur de glagel. For other uses, see DEMI FLEUR DE GLAIEUL, FLEURS DE GLAIEUL DE L'UN EN L'AUTRE. *Syn.*: see FLEUR DE LIS. *Note*: in *D* 50, 94, 108, and 182, the corresponding painted shield shows fleurs-de-lis.

fleur de lis, *fleur-de-lis* (Fig. 235). *BA* 65: a trois fleurs de lis; 67, 68, 112, 125, 126: a .iii. fleurs de lis; 233: a fleurs de lis; *B* 27: a trois fleurs delices (*Ba/Bl* 27, see FLEU-RETE); 63: ou ung fleur de lis (*Ba/Bc/Bl* 63, see FLEUR); *EO*, v. 5005: Dedenz l'azur flours de lis d'or avoit; *Hem*, v. 4043: Cil qui porte les flours de lis. For other uses, see A FLEURS DE LIS, A FLEURS DE LIS SEMÉ, AUS FLEURS DE LIS, EN CHASCUN LABEL UNE FLEUR DE LIS, EN LA FESSE UNE FLEUR DE LIS, EN LE LABEL LES FLEURS DE LIS, LION ET A UNE FLEUR DE LIS EN L'ESPAULE DU LION, LION RAMPANT A UNE FLEUR DE LIS EN L'ESPAULE DU LION, SEMÉ DE FLEURS DE LIS. *Syn.*: FLEUR, FLEUR DE GLAIEUL, FLEURETE[1], FLEURETE DE LIS. *Note*: in two copies of Glover's Roll, the illustrations corresponding to *B/Ba* 27 feature leopards' heads jessant-de-lis; these are considered later modifications, however; see *Aspilogia II*, p. 119, note to item 27. Cf. FLEUR DE LIS CROISSANT HORS DE LA TESTE DU LIEPART. Complete blazon for *EO* provided s.v. PARTI DE . . . ET DE . . . DEDENZ LE . . . ET . . . SOR . . . In *TC*, Huart de Bazentin is mentioned, but no arms are attributed to him. The miniaturist, however, painted fleurs-de-lis on the knight's shield and horse trappings in the accompanying illumination (see Delbouille, p. xcii and Plate IV). This knight is the same

as *Cil qui porte les flours de lis* in the verse from *Hem* cited above. For the demi-fleur-de-lis, see DEMI FLEUR DE GLAIEUL and cf. FLEUR DE LIS EN LONC. The fleur-de-lis motif in architectural ornamentation has been traced to Antiquity and appears on sculptured capitals of the Chapelle Saint-Aignan in Paris *c.* 1120. For the palmette hypothesis of the origin of the charge, see Constance Garlick, 'The Fleur-de-lis of Heraldry', *Miscellanea genealogica et heraldica*, 5th ser., v (1923-5), 264-6. Sainte-Marthe, *Traité historique des armes de France et de Navarre et de leur origine* (Paris, 1673), pp. 47-8, and Louis Le Gendre, *Mœurs et coutumes des Français* (Paris, 1712), pp. 131-2, state that the earliest allusion to fleurs-de-lis as a French royal emblem appears in an ordinance of King Louis le Jeune relative to the coronation of his son Philip Augustus in 1179. Le Gendre added: 'En quel temps Louis le Jeune prit-il les Lis pour ses Armes? Il y a bien de l'apparence que ce fut quand il se croisa avec les Grands de son Royaume en 1147' (p. 132). The ordinance is alluded to by many modern authorities including the *Encyclopaedia Britannica*, s.v. *fleur de lis* (which dates it 1147), and the *Larousse du XXᵉ siècle*, s.v. *fleur*. Achille Luchaire, however, in his authoritative *Etudes sur les Actes de Louis VII* (Paris, 1885), pp. 92-3, declares that the ordinance in question is a forgery, and the date 1147 is, of course, pure conjecture. The basis for the forged document appears to be a description of the slippers, tunic, cape, etc., to be worn by Louis VIII at his coronation in 1223 found in an ordinance believed to be contemporary with this event. These are said to be *intextis per totum liliis aureis* (Théodore Godefroy, *Le Cérémonial françois*, i [Paris, 1649], p. 17). Though a single fleur-de-lis figures on a royal seal as early as that of Louis VII, the semé-de-lis shield appears only in 1223 (G. Demay, 'Le blason d'après les sceaux du moyen âge', *Mémoires de la Société nationale des antiquaires de France*, xxxvii [1877], 39-88; *Aspilogia II*, pp. 12-13, note to item 8). There is some evidence, however, that fleurs-de-lis became closely identified with French royalty, and, in particular, with Philip Augustus, before that date. Rigordus (d. *c.* 1209), in his *Gesta Philippi Augusti*, describes the royal French banner as *vexillum floribus liliorum distinctum* (Anatole de Barthélemy, 'Essai sur l'origine des armoiries féodales et sur l'importance de leur étude au point de vue de la critique historique', *Mémoires de la Société des antiquaires de l'Ouest*, xxxv [1870–1], p. 46). Giraldus Cambrensis (d. 1220), referring to the Battle of Bouvines (1214), praises 'simple little fleurs-de-lis' (*simplicibus tantum gladioli flosculis*) for having caused leopards and lions (the Plantagenets and Welfs) to flee (Marc Bloch, *Les Rois thaumaturges* [Paris, 1961], p. 230). Beginning with the reign of Louis IX, a number of variations appear, notably the disposition 2 and 1 known as France Modern (Prinet, 'Les variations du nombre des fleurs de lis dans les armes de France', *Bulletin monumental* [1911], pp. 469–88). Mystical interpretations of the three fleurs-de-lis abound, the Trinity being the most popular (Prinet, 'Les variations', pp. 480–4; *Aspilogia II*, p. 13, note to item 8). It was a non-heraldic royal emblem from Carolingian times and also symbolized the Virgin, Christ, and fertility in the Middle Ages (P. Adam-Even, 'Quelques figurations particulières de la fleur de lis et leur blasonnement', *Brabantica*, vi [1962], 215). The legend associating the fleurs-de-lis with Clovis, King of the Franks, dates only from the fourteenth century. It is first mentioned in a Latin poem written in the first half of that century by a monk at the Abbey of Joyanval (ed. Robert Bossuat in *BEC*, ci [1940], 80–101). On this poem, as well as the legend, consult F. Châtillon, 'Lilia crescunt. Remarques sur la substitution de la fleur de lis aux croissants et sur quelques questions connexes', *Revue du moyen âge latin*, xi (1955), 87–200, who provides a bibliography of earlier studies relative to this matter, including a discussion of the various explanations of the origin of the fleur-de-lis device as a royal symbol in France. *Fleurs delices* in *B* 27 is an interesting example of folk etymology (see also *flos deliciarum* in 1423; Du Cange, iii. 328). The recent hypothesis proposed by Eric Buyssens, 'Le double problème de la fleur de lis', *Archivum Linguisticum*, iii (1951),

38–44 ('l'expression française *fleur de lis* est née en France à l'époque du bilinguisme romano-germanique et sous l'influence du prestige des souverains francs' [p. 43]), is unconvincing, for the earliest example of the Old French term is to be found in a non-heraldic context in Chrétien de Troyes's *Erec*. The author refers to a damsel's complexion which he compares to the fleur-de-lis (vv. 427–8):

Plus ot que n'est la flors de lis
Cler et blanc le front et le vis.

See also *Thèbes*, vv. 8037–8:

Veïs onques tant bele chose,
Ne flor de lis ne flor de rose?

Les Lais de Marie de France, ed. J. Rychner, 'Lanval', vv. 94–6:

Flur de lis e rose nuvele,
Quant ele pert al tens d'esté,
Trespassot ele de beauté.

Other recent items of note include George Bellew, 'The Fleur de Lys', *Coat of Arms*, i (1951), 183–4; Gustav Braun von Stumm, 'L'origine de la fleur de lis des rois de France, du point de vue numismatique', *Revue numismatique*, 5ᵉ série, xiii (1951), 43–58; and Hervé Pinoteau, 'Quelques réflexions sur l'œuvre de Jean du Tillet et la symbolique royale française', *AHS*, lxx (Annuaire 1956), 2–26.

fleur de lis croissant hors de la teste du liepart, *leopard's head jessant-de-lis* (Fig. 167). *H* 37: ou deux ['.iii.' added above the line] floures de lyz . . . cressaunz hors de la teste du lepard (*Hg* 37 [38]: od troy[s] flours de lys cressans hors de testes de lupars). For another use, see FESSE OD FLEURS DE LIS CROISSANZ HORS DE TESTES DE LIEPARZ. *Syn.*: FLEUR CROISSANT HORS DE LA TESTE DU LIEPART. *Note*: cf. FESSE DE FLEURS DE LIS ESPARZ NAISSANZ DE TESTES DE LIEPARZ, FESSE OU FLEURS CROISSANZ HORS DE LA TESTE DU LIEPART. On this charge, see *Aspilogia II*, pp. 119–20, note to item 27.

fleur de lis en l'espaule du lion, *on the lion's shoulder a fleur-de-lis*. See LION ET A UNE FLEUR DE LIS EN L'ESPAULE DU LION.

fleur de lis en lonc, *fleur-de-lis coupé, i.e.* '*nourri*' (Fig. 237). *CP* 102: a trois fleurs de

lis . . . en lonc. *Note*: Prinet CP, p. 34 n. 1:
'les trois fleurs de lis ont le pied coupé,
nourri, pour employer le terme héraldique.'
The Brabantine fleur-de-lis has been
studied in detail by P. Adam-Even, 'Quelques figurations particulières de la fleur
de lis et leur blasonnement', *Brabantica*,
vi (1962), 217–20. He describes it, p. 217,
as 'caractérisée par un pied sectionné du
bout, ce qui lui donne une base trian-
gulaire'. According to Adam-Even, later
medieval rolls and treatises refer to it as
a fleur-de-lis *du pied nourry* or *à pied coupé*.
This is not to be confused with the demi-
fleur-de-lis (see DEMI FLEUR DE GLAIEUL)
which has the lower *half* removed and, in
this period, is always on a chief. Modern
French manuals, however, make no such
distinction: 'Quand elle est dépourvue de
la partie inférieure à la barrette trans-
versale, elle est dite *à pied nourri*' (Veyrin-
Forrer, p. 103). Cf. DEMI[1].

**fleur de lis espart naissant de teste
de liepart**, *leopard's head jessant-de-lis*. See
FESSE DE FLEURS DE LIS ESPARZ NAISSANZ DE
TESTES DE LIEPARZ.

fleur de lis issant, *demi-fleur-de-lis* (Fig.
236). *CPA* 10: a la fleur de lis . . . issant.
Syn.: see DEMI FLEUR DE GLAIEUL. *Note*: cf.
FLEUR DE LIS EN LONC. The charge is on
the chief.

fleur de lis tout en milieu, *fleur-de-lis in
the centre of the shield. Berte*, vv. 3222–31:

Les armes qu'il porterent li rois les devisa
D'asur, mais que de blanc un poi les
    dyaspra
Li maistres qui les fist, car on li conmanda;
Une grant fleur de lis d'or tout en mi lieu a;
A cinc labiaus de gueules l'ainsné fils le
    porta,
Le label au mainsné d'argent on besenta.
Li rois, cui Jhesus gart qui tout le mont
    forma,
Pour l'amour k'ot a aus ces armes lor
    charcha;
Des puis l'a li lignages porté et portera,
Encor le porte cil qui l'eritage en a.

Note: arms of Simon le Voier. The latter
rescues Bertha, King Pepin's bride, and is
rewarded by being knighted and named as
one of the King's counsellors; see DIASPRER.
U. T. Holmes, jun., in his edition of *Berte*,

p. 80, note to vv. 3221–4, points out the
similarity of the arms granted to Simon
and those of the Boschier family; see, however, A. Henry's criticism in the latter's
edition of *Berte*, p. 256, note to v. 3222.
Holmes says the Boschiers were 'an old
Breton family'; on the latter's arms ('d'azur
à la fleur de lis florencée d'or'), see P.
Adam-Even, 'Quelques figurations particulières de la fleur de lis et leur blasonnement', *Brabantica*, vi (1962), 216, no date
for the armorial bearings being provided,
however. It is clear (see POUR L'AMOUR
QU'OT A and cf. DROITES ARMES[2], ORLE
ENTIER, POUR AMOUR DE, and POUR
L'AMOUR DE) that Pepin was merely following the ancient royal custom of granting
the privilege of bearing his own arms or a
variation thereof to a subject as a special
mark of favour. Elsewhere Adenet uses
France Ancient (*azure, semy of fleurs-de-lis or*)
as part of the arms of Pepin's son Charlemagne (see PARTI DE . . . ET DE . . . DEDENZ
LE . . . ET . . . SOR LE). It is safe to assume
that the father, in Adenet's mind, bore a
similar coat featuring an azure field with
one or more gold fleurs-de-lis. On the
royal custom in France of granting one
or more fleurs-de-lis to favoured individuals (including the Boschier family?) and
towns, consult Mathieu, pp. 140, 167–86.
According to Mathieu, the custom dates
from the beginning of the fourteenth
century, but we see now that it may be
traced back to Adenet's day. On the
number of fleurs-de-lis in the ancient arms
of France, see M. Prinet, 'Les variations
du nombre des fleurs de lis dans les armes
de France', *Bulletin monumental* (1911),
pp. 469–88. In England, Adenet's contemporary and patron King Edward I
(see *Les Œuvres d'Adenet le Roi*, ed. A.
Henry, i [Bruges, 1951], 47, 74; Brault K,
pp. 6–7) made similar grants of the arms
of his fabled ancestors to similarly favoured
towns; see Pickford, 'The Three Crowns
of King Arthur', pp. 378–82.

fleuré, *semy of fleurs-de-lis* (Fig. 40). *Note*:
used only in the locutions FLEURÉ DE L'UN
EN L'AUTRE and FLEURÉ DE L'UNE ET DE
L'AUTRE during this period, the term
would otherwise be synonymous with
FLEURETÉ[1]. On the modern uses of the

term *flory*, see the query in *Coat of Arms*, i (1950), 38, and Louis Loynes's reply, ii (1952), 79.

fleuré de l'une et de l'autre, *fleurs-de-lis counterchanged.* H 100: florré de l'une et de l'autre. *Syn.*: see FLEURÉ DE L'UN EN L'AUTRE. *Note*: used here in conjunction with a fess.

fleuré de l'un en l'autre, *fleurs-de-lis counterchanged.* B 119: flourey de l'un en l'autre (*Bl* 119 [123], see FLEURETES DE L'UN ET L'AUTRE). *Syn.*: A FLEURS DE L'UN A L'AUTRE, FLEURÉ DE L'UNE ET DE L'AUTRE, FLEURETÉ DE L'UNE ET DE L'AUTRE, FLEURETÉ DE L'UN ET DE L'AUTRE, FLEURETÉ DE L'UN ET L'AUTRE, FLEURETES DE L'UN ET L'AUTRE, FLEURS DE GLAIEUL DE L'UN EN L'AUTRE, FLEURS DE LIS DE L'UNE A L'AUTRE.

fleurete[1], *fleur-de-lis* (Fig. 235). *Ba* 27: a treis flurettes (*B* 27, see FLEUR DE LIS; *Bc* 27: a treis flureites; *Bl* 27: ove trois floretts); *C* 154: un florette (*Cl* 154: a une florette; *Cd* 154: a une florete). For other uses, see A FLEURETES, A FLEURETES SEMÉ, BENDE OU UNE FLEURETE OU DEUS LISTEAUS, FLEURETES DE L'UN ET L'AUTRE, POUDRÉ A FLEURETES, SEMÉ DE FLEURETES. *Syn.*: see FLEUR DE LIS.

fleurete[2], *demi-fleur-de-lis* (Fig. 236). *C* 176: un florete (*Cl* 176, see CHIEF A UNE FLEURETE RECOUPEE). *Syn.*: see DEMI FLEUR DE GLAIEUL. *Note*: the charge is on the chief.

fleureté[1], *semy of fleurs-de-lis* (Fig. 40). *TA*, vv. 858–60, 1726–7:

> C'est li escuz de faus argent
> A une bende d'eresie,
> Floureté de mauvese vie.
>
> .   .   .   .   .
>
> L'escu a une passerose
> Asise sour or floreté;

D 8: floretté; *M* 4, 26, 39: fluretté. *Syn.*: A FLEURETES, A FLEURETES SEMÉ, A FLEURS, A FLEURS DE LIS, A FLEURS DE LIS SEMÉ, AUS FLEURS DE LIS, FLEURETÉ DESUS LE . . ., FLEURI, POUDRÉ A FLEURETES, SEMÉ DE FLEURETES, SEMÉ DE FLEURS DE LIS. *Note*: see also ESTENCELÉ, *Note*, and FLEURÉ. The masculine gender of *fleureté* in *TA*, v. 860, argues against reading this blazon as *bende fleuretee* 'bend ornamented with fleurs-de-lis' (cf. COTICE FLEURETEE).

fleureté[2], *ornamented with fleurs-de-lis.* See CHARBOUCLE FLEURETÉ, CROIS FLEURETEE, CROIS O BOUZ FLEURETÉS, LISTE FLEURETEE. *Note*: modern English heraldry distinguishes between a cross *flory*, whose limbs end in fleurs-de-lis, and a cross *floretty*, which has fleurs-de-lis sprouting from squared-off tips. No such distinction is drawn in French heraldry today which uses *croix fleurdelysée* to denote both kinds of crosses.

fleureté[3], *flory counterflory.* See BORDE FLEURETEE, BORDURE FLEURETEE. *Note*: the double tressure is ornamented with fleurs-de-lis pointing alternately inwards and outwards.

fleurete de lis, *fleur-de-lis* (Fig. 40). *Ogier le Danois*, v. 7348: Ben les conut as floretes de lis. *Syn.*: see FLEUR DE LIS.

fleureté de l'un et l'autre, *fleurs-de-lis counterchanged.* C 128: florettee de l'un et l'autre (*Cl* 128: fluretté de l'une e de aultre; *Cd* 128: floretté del l'un e del l'autre). *Syn.*: see FLEURÉ DE L'UN EN L'AUTRE. *Note*: used here in conjunction with a barry field.

fleureté desus le . . ., *semy of fleurs-de-lis* (Fig. 40). *Artus*, p. 130: a unes armes floretees d'argent desus l'azur. *Syn.*: see FLEURETÉ[1].

fleurete recoupee, *demi-fleur-de-lis.* See CHIEF A UNE FLEURETE RECOUPEE. *Syn.* see DEMI FLEUR DE GLAIEUL.

fleuretes de l'un et l'autre, *fleurs-de-lis counterchanged.* Bl 119 [123]: od florettes de l'un et l'autre (*B* 119, see FLEURÉ DE L'UN EN L'AUTRE). *Syn.*: see FLEURÉ DE L'UN EN L'AUTRE. *Note*: refers to FESSE (1) B. 2.

fleuretes en le chevron, *chevron semy of fleurs-de-lis.* B 148: florettz . . . en le cheveron (*Bl* 148 [152]: od florettes . . . la cheveron), see CHEVRON (1) B.

fleuri, *semy of fleurs-de-lis* (Fig. 40). *Roland*, v. 3361: Tute li freint la targe, ki est flurie; *Saisnes*, v. 2276: une targe florie; vv. 4162, 4170: sor ma targe florie; 7359: sor la targe florie; *Fouque de Candie*, vv. 64, 2625, 4884, 11670, 11896: targe florie; v. 13567: targe fleurie; v. 14256: targe flourie. *Syn.*: see FLEURETÉ[1]. *Note*: according to Ott, p. 6: '*Flori* signifie "blanc" tout d'abord quand il s'agit de *fleurs*, puis pour des choses pouvant rappeler une floraison; enfin, dans quelques cas isolés, *flori* veut dire simplement "blanc".' On the early appearance of fleurs-de-lis as a heraldic device, however, see FLEUR DE LIS, *Note*.

fleurs de glaieul de l'un en l'autre, *fleurs-de-lis counterchanged.* D 67: od le flurs (G: fleurs) de glagel de l'un en l'autre. *Syn.*: see FLEURÉ DE L'UN EN L'AUTRE. *Note*: used here in conjunction with a fess.

fleurs de lis de l'une a l'autre, *fleurs-de-lis counterchanged.* CP 124: au fleur d'asur [*sic*] de l'une a l'autre. *Syn.*: see FLEURÉ DE L'UN EN L'AUTRE. *Note*: Prinet CP, p. 41 n. 1: 'les mots "au fleur d'asur" doivent être corrigés et remplacés par "aux fleurs de lis".'

fleurs de l'un a l'autre, see A FLEURS DE L'UN A L'AUTRE.

font, *lower part of the shield (here, the field, as opposed to the chief).* CC, vv. 1316–21:

> Ses escus avoit le cief d'or,
> Et saciés qu'il avoit encor,
> El cief, une mierle de sable,
> Ce n'est ne mencongne ne fable,
> Et de geules estoit li fons,
> S'i ot trois vaironnés bastons.

Note: cf. Modern French *fond* and PIÉ².

forchié, *forked.* See FOURCHIÉ.

formé, *formy.* See CROIS FORMEE. *Syn.*: see ESLAISIÉ. *Note*: the etymology of this word has been discussed by H. S. London, 'Pattee, Patonce, and Formee', *Coat of Arms*, v (1958), no. 34, 27–8, aligning himself with Dr. Paul Adam-Even who saw in this term 'a variant of the Old French *formeus*, Latin *formosa*, beautiful (cf. the English shapely)' (p. 27). As London himself admitted, however, 'there is no obvious reason why either shaped or beautiful should denote that particular pattern' (p. 28). The latter notes in passing A. W. B. Messenger's observation that OFr. *formoir* (MFr. *fermoir*) meant a kind of chisel and that 'old chisels were shaped like the arms of a formy cross, so that the word might be interpreted as chisel-shaped'. Commander Messenger reiterated this view in a letter to the editor of the *Coat of Arms*, vii (1963), 304. Is the expression related to OFr. *lettres formees*, or *lettres de forme*, a term used to describe Gothic script from the thirteenth century onwards? The latter occurs, for example, in the fourteenth-century inventories of the library of King Charles V of France:

'Meliachin et du Cheval de fust, rimé et bien escript, en françois, de lettre *formee*, a deux coulombes. Comm.: *toute honneur.* Fin: *et plus les essauçoit.* Couvert de cuir a deux fermoirs de laton.—2 1.' (Léopold Delisle, *Recherches sur la librairie de Charles V* [Paris, 1907], IIᵉ partie, item 1138.)

fors, *except.* See D'UNE COULEUR FORS.

fors de, *with the exception of.* See NE LA PORTER DIVERSE FORS DE, N'ESTRE DIVERS DE RIEN NON FORS DE . . . SEULEMENT. *Note*: cf. FORS QUE, MES.

forse, *perhaps.* The complete blazon reads as follows: C 133: Alein de la Zouch, sable (forse gules) besantee d'or (Cl 133: Aleyn de la Zouch, de gable bezantié d'or; Cd 133: Eleyn de la Surche, de sable bessanté). *Note*: *Aspilogia II*, p. 186, note to item 94: 'The addition of *forse gules* . . . must be [herald and copyist Nicholas] Charles' emendation; it is supported by Glover's and other rolls.'

fors que, *with the exception that.* See ARMES DE PLAIN . . . FORS QU'EL QUARTIER AVOIT EGLETES PAR DESCONOISSANCE, TEL COM . . . FORS QU'AU CRESTEL EGLES AVOIT, TEL COM . . . FORS QU'EL CRESTEL EGLES AVOIT, TEL COM . . . FORS QU'EL QUARTIER EGLEZ AVOIT, TOUT DE PLAIN LES ARMES . . . FORS QU'EL QUARTIER A EGLES. *Syn.*: FORS TANT QUE, MES QUE.

fors seulement, see TOUT . . . FORS SEULEMENT.

fors tant que, *except that.* See D'UNE COULEUR FORS TANT QUE, TOUT PLAIN FORS TANT QUE. *Syn.*: see FORS QUE.

foule, see TREFEUILLE.

fourches, *gallows.* See CHEVAL FUST APENDU D'UNES FOURCHES. *Note*: modern French heraldry has a T-shaped charge termed a *potence* 'gallows', but it is a 'figure incertaine et, pour le moins, fort rare' (Veyrin-Forrer, p. 46).

fourchié¹, *forked.* See COUE FOURCHIEE¹. *Syn.*: DOUBLE, EN DOUBLE, FOURCHU.

fourchié², *forked and crossed in saltire.* See COUE FOURCHIEE². For another use, see FOURCHIÉ EN SOM. *Syn.*: see CROISIÉ².

fourchié³, *patonce.* See CROIS FOURCHIEE¹. For another use, see FOURCHIÉ AU KANEE. *Syn.*: see ESLARGI².

fourchié⁴, *fourchy, moline.* See CROIS FOURCHIEE². *Note*: cf. RECERCELÉ, RECROISELÉ.

Aspilogia II, p. 129, note to item 76: 'Cross fourchy is now generally taken to mean either a cross moline, or one similarly forked but with the eight points cut off straight.'

fourchié au kanee, *patonce.* See CROIS FOURCHIEE AU KANEE. *Syn.*: see ESLARGI[2].

fourchié en som, *forked and crossed in saltire.* See COUE FOURCHIEE EN SOM. *Syn.*: see CROISIÉ[2].

fourchu, *forked and crossed in saltire.* See COUE FOURCHUE. *Syn.*: see CROISIÉ[2]. *Note*: on the spread of *u*-type past participles in Old French, consult Pope, paragraphs 1050–4.

France, *France.* See ARMES DE FRANCE A, ARMES DU ROI DE FRANCE A, ARMES LE ROI DE FRANCE, ARMES LE ROI DE FRANCE A, DE FRANCE, DE FRANCE A.

frere, *brother.* See ARMES SON FRERE A . . . SANS.

frestel, *ghost word.* See AUTRETEL.

freté, *fretty.* *Tristan de Thomas*, v. 2202: Escu ot d'or a vair freté; *Durmart*, v. 7432: frestés; v. 8479: fretés; *TA*, v. 545: Fretee de pechiez mortiex; *BA* 2, 94, 123, 170, 180, 227, 276: freté; 60, 106: fretee; 149, 151: frettee; 195: fretté; *B/Bl* 58, 110 [114], 126 [130], 134 [138], 157 [161], 195 [199], 199 [203]: fretté; *B* 90, 96 (*Bl* 90, 96: fretté): frettey; 178: frettie; Audley [*B III* 34], *Ba/Bc*: freté; *Bb*: fretty; *C* 89: fretty (*Cl* 89: fretté; *Cd* 89, see A GEULES FRETÉ; *EO*, v. 2654: L'escu vermeill portoit freté d'argent; *D* 60, 96, 131, 141, 173: fretté; *CP* 133: freté; *CPA* 165: fretté; *H* 17, 19, 21, 43, 54: fretté (*Hg* 19, 43 [44]: frecté; 21: freté; 54 [55]: fretté); *M* 6, 20, 29, 34, 35: fretté; *K*, v. 92: frettez; vv. 308, 705; fretté. *Syn.*: FRETÉ DE . . . ET DE . . . *Note*: Gough H, p. 132, note to item 17: '[*H* 17] is corrupt here, some words [i.e. *fretté de argent*] being copied from No. 19.' According to Adam-Even, '*Tournoiement des Dames de Paris*', p. 3, *freté* is a synonym for semy in that poem. The term *freté* is also to be found in its usual meaning in the same work, however (Adam-Even, p. 6).

freté de . . . et de . . ., *fretty.* *K*, v. 315: De or e de noir fretté. *Syn.*: FRETÉ. *Note*: for complete blazon, see CHIEF O UN GASTEL. See also CHIEF UN RONDEL.

freté en le chief, *a chief fretty.* The complete blazon reads as follows: *B* 134:

Henry le Fitz Randolf, d'azure fretté d'or en le cheif. *Note*: refers to EN LE CHIEF[3], a descriptive phrase. *Bl* 134 [138] reads *fretté . . . et le chief*; see CHIEF[1] (1).

freté en le geules, *descriptive phrase referring to the gules quarters (i.e. quarters 2 and 3) of a quarterly field.* The complete blazon reads as follows: *B* 110: Hue le De Spenser, quartelé d'argent et de goules ung bend de sable les quartres fretté d'or en le goules (*Bl* 110 [114], see ESQUARTELÉ DE . . . ET DE . . . LE GEULES). *Note*: refers to EN LE GEULES[1]; see QUARTELÉ DE. . . . ET DE . . . EN LE GEULES. Cf. A GEULES FRETÉ. *P* 90 (= *B* 110) reads: 'Hugh le Despenser porte quartelee d'argent et de goules a un bende noir le goules frettee d'or.'

fretel, *ghost word.* See AUTRETEL.

fromage, *cheese. La Bataille de Caresme et de Charnage*, vv. 362–3:

> Sa baniere est de fres frommage,
> A entresaingne de matons.

Note: arms of Charnage. See Lozinski, p. 146, no. 64. For OFr. *maton* 'curdled milk', see Lozinski, p. 157, no. 96.

fromage en feissele, *cheese in a small basket.* *TA*, v. 1158: .iii. fromages en feisele. *Note*: arms of Folie. According to Prinet TA, p. 51, cheese was 'un attribut de fous que l'on retrouve ailleurs et, par exemple, sur le sceau de Pierre, fou en titre d'office de la comtesse d'Artois en 1300'. The seal in question is described in G. Demay, *Inventaires des sceaux de l'Artois et de la Picardie* (Paris, 1877), no. 2192. I am indebted to Mr. P. Baugard, directeur des Services d'Archives du Pas-de-Calais in Arras, for providing me with a photograph of this seal. The 'cheese' is depicted as a large roundel enclosed by a net or lattice (the basket?) over which is placed a cross pommé whose limbs extend to the edge of the roundel, the four knobs being slightly larger than those illustrated in Boutell, fig. 128. On the association of the fool with cheese, see Schoepperle, *Tristan and Isolt*, i. 231–3.

fuelle, see FEUILLE DE TRUMEL.

fuires, see DE FUIRES.

fust, *wooden.* See CHEVAL FUST APENDU D'UNES FOURCHES.

gable, *ghost word.* See SABLE.

gambe, *leg.* See JAMBE.

ganeles, *ghost word.* See JUMELES.

gant, *glove, gauntlet* (Fig. 256). The complete blazons read as follows: *BA* 75: Aidelames de Ramestaing, l'escu de geules a .v. gans (A: cans) d'argent; *EO*, v. 4830: L'escu portoit vermeill a trois blans gans. *Note*: Adam-Even provides no identification of the arms in *BA* 75 but in his glossary, page 20, suggests the following definition: '*gans* (75): oie (?)'. OFr. *gante, jante* 'wild goose' (cf. German *Gans* 'goose') may possibly be involved here, but OFr. *gant* 'glove' seems more likely.

gant les doiz desor, *glove with fingers upwards* (Fig. 258). *Cleomadés*, vv. 8295–8304:

En celui voiage portoit
Cleomadés, quant il s'armoit,
Armes aussi noires com meure
A .i. blanc gant les dois deseure.
Or vous dirai pourquoi avoit
Tes armes. Ce senefioit
Que il n'avoit de remanant
De s'amie que le seul gant
Que il enz ou jardin trouva
La ou li rois Crompars l'embla.

garbe, *garb.* See JARBE.

garbes en la crois, see JARBES EN LA CROIS.

Garenne, *Warenne.* See ARMES LE CONTE.

gasteaus, *gastells (i.e. roundels).* See GASTEL.

gastel, *gastell (i.e. roundel)* (Fig. 112). *C* 120: trois gastells (*Cl/Cd* 120, see GASTEL EN LE CHIEF); *D* 112: od treis gastels. For another use, see CHIEF O UN GASTEL. *Syn.*: see BESANT. *Note*: according to Harris, College of Arms MS. Arundel LXII reads *rondeaus* instead of *gasteaus* at *K*, v. 316. This is also the reading in Oxford, St. John's College MS. CLXXIV. Matthew Paris uses two forms of this word in his blazon of the Huntingfield (*Aspilogia II*, p. 40, item 23: 'a .iii. gasteus de blanc') and Siward arms (*Aspilogia II*, p. 50, item 69: 'vastellis albis'). See also BESANT, TOURTEL. On the heraldic term, see London, 'The Roundel', p. 310. *Gastel* is the Old French form of *gâteau* 'cake'. On the latter, consult *La Bataille de Caresme et de Charnage*, ed. G. Lozinski, pp. 179–80, no. 166, s.v. *wastel*.

gastel en le chief, *on a chief a gastell.* *Cl* 120: a treis gastelle . . . en le chef (*Cd* 120: a 3 casteles [*sic*] . . . en le chief; *C* 120, see GASTEL). *Syn.*: CHIEF A UN TOURTEL, CHIEF O UN GASTEL, CHIEF O UN RONDEL, MIREOR EN LE CHIEF, TOURTEL EL CHIEF. See also CHIEF[1] (2) B., TOURTEL (2).

gaune, *or.* See JAUNE.

geline, *hen* (Fig. 191). *Cleomadés*, vv. 11311–15:

Gados portoit l'escu d'ermine
A une vermeille geline
A un ourle de witecos.
Teles armes portoit Gados,
Et li witecoc erent noir.

Note: for the male of the species, see COC.

geline desus le pui, *hen statant on the mount* (Fig. 192). *BA* 64: a une ghelingue (A: ghelingne) . . . desus (A: deseure) le pui (A: piu). *Note*: the word *pui* is mentioned earlier in the same blazon. See PUI.

gemeles, *bars gemelles.* See JUMELES.

gemels, *bars gemelles.* See JUMEAUS.

gemes, *bars gemelles.* See JUMELES.

gemeus, see JUMEAUS.

gerbe, *garb.* See JARBE.

geroné, *gyronny.* See GIRONÉ DE . . . ET DE . . .

geter, see JETER.

geule, *mouth.* *TA*, vv. 748–9, 995, 2264:

A langues d'avocacïon
De geules a pledëors tretes;

.   .   .   .   .

Bendez de geules et de langues.

.   .   .   .   .

L'escu de geules et de langues.

For other uses, see ENGOULÉ DE GEULES, MANCHE EN LA GEULE DU LION. *Note*: in all the examples from *TA*, a pun on *geules* 'gules (red)' is obviously intended.

***geules**, *gules.* Several attestations in literary sources, e.g. *Troie*, v. 7469: A goles ot escu d'argent; *Gaidon*, v. 7142: de goules, *TA*, vv. 614, 1981: De geules; *Berte*, v. 3226: de gueules; *Hem*, v. 3091: De geules; *Cleomadés*, v. 717: De gueules; *K*, v. 75: de goulys; vv. 205, 356, 686, 783: de goules. Extremely frequent in the rolls where it is the only term used, e.g. *BA* 2, 108 (A: geules): gueulles; *B* 1, 4: goules; *C* 2, 4: gules; 67: de gules; 22: per le goules (see PARTI DE . . . ET DE . . ., PAR LE . . ., LE . . .); *Cd* 22: par le gules (see PARTI DE . . . ET DE . . ., PAR LE . . ., L'AUTRE . . .); *CP* 2, 4: de gueulles; 105 *bis* (see ESCUÇON[1], *Note*): de gheules. For other uses, see A GEULES FRETÉ, EN LE GEULES, LE GEULES, SOR LE GEULES, TOUT DE GEULES. *Syn.*: GEULES VERMEILLES, ROUGE, ROUGET, SINOPLE, VERMEIL, VERMEILLET, VERMEIL SINOPLE. *Note*: cf. CENDAL, ROUS. In *CP* 62, *de gheulles* is an error for *d'or*; for *CP* 131 (*de gheules* is used three times in addition to the locution *sur le gheules*), see PARTI DE . . . ET DE . . ., DE . . . SOR LE . . . ET DE . . . SOR LE . . . For another use in *Hg*, see DO[1]. This heraldic term has at times been associated with the Persian word *gul* 'rose' (see, for example, Dauzat and, especially, E. G. Lindfors-Nordin, *Jul, den hundrabladiga gúl, gulis, gueules* [Stockholm, 1955]; for a discussion of this theory, however, see K. Nyrop, '*Gueules, histoire d'un mot*', *Romania*, lxviii [1922], 559–70), but there is no evidence supporting such a derivation. The word is doubtless identical with OFr. *gole, geule* 'animal's mouth, throat'. According to *BW*[4], s.v. *gueule*: 'Au moyen âge les gueules désignaient de petits morceaux de fourrure découpés dans la peau du gosier d'un animal, particulièrement de la martre, qui servaient à orner des manteaux, surtout en forme de collet; le sens de "rouge" vient soit de la couleur naturelle de la fourrure, soit d'un rouge dû à la teinture.' As Ott, pp. 127–8, notes: 'Son évolution est ainsi assez semblable à celle de sable.' Prinet TA, p. 44 n. 2: 'Primitivement, *gueules* était un pluriel féminin (*gulae*, en latin).' Bernard of Clairvaux (d. 1153) uses *gulae* in this sense in Epist. 42, cap. 2 (Du Cange, iv. 136).

geules vermeilles, *gules (red)*. *FCE*, v. 8118: Qui de gueules vermoilles fu; v. 8471: de gueules vermoilles; *FCT*, v. 4354: Qui de gueles toz vermax fu; v. 4883: de gueles vermeilles; *Sone*, v. 9205: de gueles viermeil; v. 9867: de geulles viermaus. *Syn.*: see GEULES.

gironé de . . . et de . . .[1], *gyronny (i.e. a field divided into triangular sections, radiating around a point at the centre of the shield)* (Fig. 14). *Durmart*, vv. 8481–2:

C'est cil as armes gironees
D'or, de synoples eslevees;

BA 70, 72: gheronné de . . . et de . . ., see CROISETES OU . . .; *B* 35: gerony de . . . et de . . . (*Ba* 35: girund de . . . e de . . .; *Bb* 35: giruné de . . . et . . .; *Bc* 35: giruné de . . . e de . . .; *Bl* 35: geronné de . . . et de . . .); *C* 109: geronné de . . . et de . . . (*Cl* 109: geroun de . . . et de . . .; *Cd* 109: geroné); *D* 122: gerouné de . . . et de . . .; *Escanor*, vv. 4992–3:

D'or et de seble gironnees
Portoit li unz les armes plaines;

SCK, fol. 106 *f*: de . . . et de . . . / . . . gironées; *SCT*, fol. 126 *e* / *SCV*, fol. 93 *a*: de . . . et de . . . / gyronnees; *CP* 78, 132: gironné de . . . et de . . . *Syn.*: BENDÉ[3] (?). *Note*: OFr. *gironé* and *giron* occur frequently in twelfth-century literary texts in descriptions of tents, banners, sails, and horse trappings. The feminine substantive *gironé* is well attested in the same century in the meaning of 'skirt' as opposed to OFr. *cors* 'bodice'. Consult Goddard, pp. 102–3, s.v. *cors*, and p. 131, s.v. *gironee, giron, gironé*. According to Oswald Barron: 'Most of the earlier examples have some twelve divisions although later armory gives eight as the normal number' (*Encyclopaedia Britannica*, article 'Heraldry').

gironé de . . . et de . . .[2], *gyronny (referring here to the corners only, which are divided by a single line, per bend in the dexter corner, per bend sinister in the sinister corner* (Fig. 15). *BA* 256: geronnés; *B* 32: geroné de . . . et de . . . (*Bl* 32: geronné [de . . . et de . . .]); *C* 142: geronné; *D* 97: gerouné de . . . et de . . .; *CP* 38: gironné; *H*/*Hg* 67 [68]: geruné; *K*, vv. 439–40:

E les cornieres gyronnees,
De or e de asur enluminees.

Note: *P* 73 (= *B* 32) reads: 'gerunés'. Modern English heraldry generally blazons the subordinaries in question as 'two gyrons' (as, for example, the 'three pallets between two gyrons azure' of the Mortimer arms [Boutell, p. 58]). Since, however, *gyron* is elsewhere (p. 55) defined as 'the lower half of a canton or quarter when divided diagonally' (see also Veyrin-Forrer, p. 42: 'Le *giron* est la moitié d'un quartier'), 'two gyrons' is ambiguous since four sections are actually involved, two in each corner. In cases where the field is per pale (divided in half by a vertical line), ambiguity can be eliminated by use of the term *per pall* (Fr. *tiercé en pairle*) which describes a shield partitioned by a Y-shaped line. See Dr. Adam-Even's blazon of *WB* 511 (Pressigny): 'Tiercé en pairle, en chef palé (6) d'azur et d'or, à dextre burelé (10) d'or et d'azur, à sénestre burelé d'azur et d'or, à l'écusson d'argent sur le tout'. Later sources, confusing GIRONÉ DE . . . ET DE . . .[1] and GIRONÉ DE . . . ET DE . . .[2], at times depicted the Pressigny shield with two and sometimes even four corners gironny (i.e. GIRONÉ DE . . . ET DE . . .[1]).

glagel, see FLEUR DE GLAGEL. *Note*: the word *glagel* is a variant of OFr. *glaieul* 'sword-lily' < CL *gladiolus*, a diminutive of *gladius* 'sword'.

goboné de . . . et de . . ., *compony, gobony*. See COUPONÉ DE . . . ET DE . . .

goles, *gules*. See GEULES.

gonfanon, *gonfanon* (Fig. 259). *C* 34: un ganfanon (*Cl* 34: a un gunfanun; *Cd* 34: a une gunffanun). *Syn.*: FANON.

goute, *one of the drops of a goutté pattern* (Fig. 37). *Lancelot propre*, iii. 284: les goutes. *Note*: on the Modern English equivalent, *gout*, or *goutte*, see London, 'The Roundel', *Coat of Arms*, i (1951), 172.

gouté de . . . et de . . ., *goutté (i.e. semy of drops)* (Fig. 37). (1) *a single tincture is involved. Lancelot propre*, v. 131, 136: un escu blanc gouté de noir; 133: le blanc escu gouté de noir. For another use, see GOUTÉ MENUEMENT. (2) *two tinctures are involved. Lancelot propre*, iii. 283: gouté de . . . et de . . . *Syn.*: GOUTÉ MENUEMENT. *Note*: in *Lancelot propre*, iii. 284, the arms mentioned on the preceding page (*cel escu noir gouté d'or et d'argent*) are mentioned again but only the argent drops are said to symbolize tears (for complete reference, see SENEFIER). In the same work, v. 136 n. 2, the arms cited on this page as *argent goutté sable* ('un escu blanc gouté de noir') are described in the caption of the miniature as *.i. escu blanc*. On this symbolism, see Lot, *Etude sur le Lancelot en prose*, pp. 97–9. Curiously enough, the locution *goutté de larmes* has

come to mean a field semy of *azure* drops in modern English heraldry; see Boutell, p. 36. On the use of OFr. *gouté* in connection with wearing-apparel, consult Goddard, pp. 165, 167. The arms of the King of Denmark in *WB* 1268 are *or goutté gules, three leopards azure*, the semy pattern being described by Dr. Adam-Even as 'semé de flammes'; see CROIS A DEUS PASSANZ, *Note*.

gouté menuement, *goutté (i.e. semy of drops)* (Fig. 37). *Lancelot propre*, iii. 278: goutés menuement. *Syn.*: GOUTÉ DE . . . ET DE . . . *Note*: literally, semy of drops placed closely together in a dense pattern; cf. MENUE BURELURE DE . . . ET DE . . .

grain, *tiny lozenge* (Fig. 49). See SEMÉ DE GRAINS. *Note*: see BESANT, *Note*.

grifon, *griffin* (Fig. 221). *Horn*, v. 4485: Bien i ad conu Horn al gripun del escu; *Faits des Romains*, i. 659: peint i ot un gripphon; *D* 12: od un griffun; *H* 92: .ii. griffonns (G: griffouns; *Hg* 92 [91]: deus griffones), see EN LES QUARTIERS DE . . .; *M* 51: odve setz gryffounz. *Note*: for the term in *Faits des Romains*, consult L. F. Flutre, 'Notes sur le vocabulaire des *Faits des Romains*', *Romania*, lxv (1939), 529. See also McCulloch, pp. 122–3. Cf. the use of the word *serpent* in the following description of two such monsters at the Castle of the Griffins in *Perlesvaus*, i. 313: 'e .ii. serpens que l'on apele gripes. Il ont viaire d'omes e bes d'oiseaux e iels d'orlestes e dens de chiens e oreiles d'ane e piez de lion e coe de serpent' (see also p. 314: 'les serpenz gripes'). Cf. TESTE D'UN DRAGON CRESTÉ, *Note*. The same source (*Perlesvaus*, i. 315) refers to the griffins' young as 'lor feons', i.e. OFr. *faon* (< VL *fetonem* < Lat. *fetus* 'offspring'), a term akin to E. *fawn* 'young deer'. For an excellent discussion of the heraldic griffin, consult London, *Royal Beasts*, pp. 17–19. In *H* 92, there is one griffin in quarter 1, another in quarter 4. On this charge, see George Bellew, 'Two More Monsters', *Coat of Arms*, ii (1952), 123. The other monster (discussed on p. 124) is the phoenix. Denholm-Young, *History and Heraldry*, p. 63, commenting upon *D* 12, states: 'Among the foreigners are found the King of *Griffonie* . . . who may be fabulous.' The arms may be imaginary, but the country is not, as it was a common designation for Greece and in particular Constantinople in Old French. See Flutre, pp. 247–8, s.v. *Gré, Grec,* and p. 248, s.v. *Grece, Gresce, Gres(s)e.* An identical emblem for Greece is to be found in *HE* 16 and for Alexander the Great, associated with Greece, in the *Dean Tract,* p. 27, l. 88 ('Le roy Alexandre porta l'escu de goules ove un griffoun d'argent'); cf. also the pun *Greece = grez,* i.e. the plural of OFr. *gré* or *gret* (< Lat. *gradum* 'step') 'flight of stairs' = *crois aus degrez* 'cross Calvary' in the *Dean Tract,* p. 29; see Brault, 'The Cross', p. 221. Does this also explain *P* 19 (Grimaldi's Roll is manifestly related to the Camden Roll): 'Le roy de Grece porte d'argent ove une croice d'un pee de gules'? For another possible canting use of OFr. *gré* in the arms of Grey of Codnor, see *Aspilogia II,* p. 50, note to item 68. On the etymology, consult U. T. Holmes, jun., 'Old French *Grifaigne* and *Grifon*', *SP,* xliii (1946), 586–94.

grifon rampant, *griffin rampant* (Fig. 222). *K,* v. 397: De inde au grifoun rampant de or fin.

grifon volant, *griffin volant* (Fig. 223). *EO,* v. 4825: D'or a un noir griffon qui ert volans.

gris, *grey. TA,* v. 986: de gris. *Note:* cf. BIS.

gros, *wide, large.* See GROSSE BURELURE.

grosse burelure, *referring to a field covered with wide horizontal stripes.* See BURELÉ D'UNE GROSSE BURELURE DE . . . ET DE . . .

gules, *gules.* See GEULES.

gymeus, see JUMEAUS.

hache, *axe* (Fig. 244). *D* 15: od treis haches. For another use, see LION RAMPANT OD UNE HACHE. *Note:* the three axes here in the fictitious arms of Denmark are doubtless a pun on OFr. *danoise* 'Danish axe'; cf. the fictitious arms of the Middle and East Saxons: *gules, three seaxes barwise proper, pommels and hilts gold* (Boutell, p. 205). For other canting arms in the Camden Roll, see BARGE, *Note,* and GRIFON, *Note.*

hamade, hamaide, see HAMEDE.

hamede, *hamaide, humet* (Fig. 261). *BA* 89, 139: a .iii. hamaides; 90: .iii. haimades ou haimaides (A: hamades ou haimades). *Note:* OFr. *hamede* means a 'street-barrier, or fence', here stylized in the form of a bar couped so that the ends run parallel to the

edges of the shield. For the etymology, see *FEW,* vi. 120, s.v. **haimithi.* H. S. London and Paul Adam-Even, 'The Hamaide or Humet', *Antiquaries Journal,* xxxii (1952), 52–64, present a definitive study of the origins and use of the charge in armory. All the early examples involve three pieces, each one of which should properly be termed a hamaide. Cf. Veyrin-Forrer, p. 46: 'La *hamède* est formée de trois fasces alaisées; parfois, elle n'est que de deux pièces au lieu de trois, ce qu'il faut alors spécifier.' On this charge, see also A. W. B. Messenger, 'The Hamade', *Coat of Arms,* i (1951), 153–4, with correction in ii (1952), 120.

hanap, *cup, goblet.* See PIÉ DE HANAP. *Syn.:* COUPE.

harenc, *herring* (Fig. 213). *D* 183: od sis harangs. *Note:* see also Matthew Paris (Pusikan, p. 151): 'Roberti Harenc. Scutum de gules .iii. harenges d'argent'. On this fish, see *La Bataille de Caresme et de Charnage,* ed. G. Lozinski, p. 151, no. 79, s.v. *harenc, herenc.*

harge, *meaning obscure.* See ROSE HARGE OVE UNE ROSE.

hauriant, see AIRIANT.

helt, *hilt.* See ESPEE AU PONG ET AU HELT QUI TRANCHE LE LION PAR MI.

henap, see HANAP.

heraut, see HIRAUT.

heremine, hermine, *ermine.* See ERMINE.

herminé, *ermine.* See ERMINÉ.

heron, *heron* (Fig. 193). *M* 32: ou .iii. herouns. *Note:* cf. BUTOR.

heron paté beké (?), see HERONS PETIZ BEESTEZ.

herons petiz beestez, *membered herons (the tincture of the legs and beak is indicated)* (?). The complete blazons read as follows: *M* 32: Sr Godard Heron port d'azure ou .iii. herouns d'argent petiz beestez d'or; 33: Sr Roger Heron port d'azure ou .iii. herouns d'argent petiz beestez d'or. *Note:* cf. EGLE . . . LE BEC ET LES PIÉS. Does *petiz beestez* represent *patés* (MFr. *pattés* 'with legs') *bekés* (MFr. *becqués* 'with beaks')?

hiraudie, (1) *heralds collectively, i.e. as a class or group. TC,* vv. 1140–1:

> Que li rïos de hiraudie
> Ne pasast bien, s'i n'en fust tant.

Note: for an English equivalent, see *MED*, s.v. *heraldie*. (2) *the science of heraldry. TC*, vv. 470–9:

Li chevaliers qui s'aprestoit
Contre lui, fu de vers Hainnaut.
Adont escrïent cis hiraut.
Chascunz huia en son latin,
Et je crioie 'Bazentin'
Que je cuida que ce fust cil.
— 'Dïable vos fait si soutil',
Dist uns hiraus, 'en hiraudie.'
— 'Tais toi, mesias, Dex te maudie,
C'est Bazentins.' — 'Vos i mentéz!'

Note: ironic use (the author is arguing with another herald over the proper way to identify a knight by his war-cry). For other meanings associated with OFr. *hiraudie*, consult Tobler–Lommatzsch, iv. 1102–3, s.v. *hiraudie*.

hiraut, *herald.* Numerous attestations from the twelfth century onward. See Tobler–Lommatzsch, iv. 1103–6, s.v. *hiraut*. Chrétien de Troyes used the terms *hiraut* and *hiraut d'armes* (*Charrete*, vv. 5557 and 5537 respectively). For another use, see ROI HIRAUT. *Note*: on the etymology, see *DCELC*, ii. 902–3; *FEW*, xvi. 199–200, s.v. **heriwald*. For the English equivalent, see *MED*, s.v. *heraud*. The rise of the heralds and their functions have been studied by Wagner, *Heralds and Heraldry*, and by Adam-Even, 'Les fonctions militaires des hérauts d'armes', *AHS*, lxxi (1957), 2–33.

home crucefié, see OU MILIEU UN HOME CRUCEFIÉ QUI TOUT ESTOIT SANGLANT.

home qui estoit crucefié, *Our Lord upon the Cross* (Fig. 129). *Estoire*, p. 62: et vit l'imagene d'un homme qui estoit crucefijés dedens l'escu. Et sambloit que les mains et les piés li degoutoient de sanc. *Syn.*: OU MILIEU UN HOME CRUCEFIÉ QUI TOUT ESTOIT SANGLANT.

hors, *out of.* See FESSE OD FLEURS DE LIS CROISSANZ HORS DE TESTES DE LIEPARZ, FESSE OU FLEURS CROISSANZ HORS DE LA TESTE DU LIEPART, FLEUR DE LIS CROISSANT HORS DE LA TESTE DU LIEPART.

i, *pronoun* (= MFr. '*y*'). See TANT QUE L'ON I POUVOIT METRE.

icel, *demonstrative adjective.* See D'ICELE FAÇON.

ieuz, '*eyes*'. See D'IEUZ DE PAON.

in, *in.* See EN. *Note*: Anglicism in certain copies.

inde, *azure. Fouque de Candie*, v. 6869: Ynde; *Artus*, p. 7: inde; *Vulgate Merlin Sequel*, pp. 119, 192: ynde; p. 143: yndes; *Blancandin*, v. 2076; escuz indes; *K*, vv. 108, 347, 397, 434, 565, 705: de inde; vv. 250, 368: inde. For other uses, see EN INDE, TOUT INDE. *Syn.*: see AZUR. *Note*: on this tincture in twelfth-century literary descriptions of shields, see Bouly de Lesdain, p. 230.

indenté, *indented.* See ENDENTÉ.

inescochon, *escutcheon* (Fig. 119). *Cd* 142: an ynescochon (*C/Cl* 142, see ESCUÇON[1]). *Syn.*: see ESCUÇON[1]. *Note*: single occurrence of what appears to be a late term (*OED*: 1610). *Cd* elsewhere uses *eschouçon, eschouchon*, and *schoçon* in this sense. See ESCUÇON[1] and cf. ESCUÇON[3].

ingrelé, *indented.* See ENGRESLÉ.

inter, *between.* See CROIS ENTRE EGLEZ.

issant, *issuant.* See FLEUR DE LIS ISSANT. *Syn.*: see DEMI[1]. *Note*: cf. CROISSANT[2].

issir, *to come out of* (Fig. 256). *Charrete*, vv. 5799–5801:

Et veez vos celui qui porte
An son escu pointe une porte?
Si sanble qu'il s'an isse uns cers.

Note: in *Saisnes*, v. 2278, the lioncel in Baudouin's arms is painted in such a lifelike fashion that it appears to leap from the shield: 'Et samble que il isse de l'escu plains de vie.'

itel, *the same* (*arms*). See PORTER ITEL. *Syn.*: see AUTEL[1].

itels armes, *the same arms. Mort Artu*, p. 78: itiex armes. *Syn.*: see AUTEL[1].

itel si com, *the same* (*arms*) *as. Artus*, p. 166: itelx escu soloit il porter si com il i a oi deviser. *Syn.*: see AUTELS ARMES COM.

ivoire, *ivory. Thèbes*, v. 5513: D'yvoire; *FCM*, v. 18057: d'ivoire. *Note*: on ivory shields, consult Bouly de Lesdain, p. 233, and add *Cligés*, v. 3985: 'Un escu d'un os d'olifant' (the shield is white, see v. 3988). On the *First Continuation*, see ERMINE, *Note*.

jambe armee, *mailed leg* (Fig. 134). See JAMBES ARMEES, JAMBES ARMEES O TOUTES LES CUISSES CHASCUNE CUISSE JOINTE AUS AUTRES ET EN CHASCUNE CORNIERE SEIT UN

PIÉ, JAMBES ARMEES O TOUTES LES CUISSES ET EN CHASCUNE CORNIERE SEIT UN PIÉ.

jambes armees, *mailed legs embowed and conjoined at the thighs* (Fig. 134). *C* 17: a trois jambes armés (*Cl* 17, see JAMBES ARMEES O TOUTES LES CUISSES ET EN CHASCUNE CORNIERE SEIT UN PIÉ; *Cd* 17, see JAMBES ARMEES O TOUTES LES CUISSES CHASCUNE CUISSE JOINTE AUS AUTRES ET EN CHASCUNE CUISSE SEIT UN PIÉ). *Syn.*: JAMBES ARMEES O TOUTES LES CUISSES ET EN CHASCUNE CORNIERE SEIT UN PIÉ, JAMBES ARMEES O TOUTES LES CUISSES CHASCUNE CUISSE JOINTE AUS AUTRES ET EN CHASCUNE CUISSE SEIT UN PIÉ. *Note*: on these arms, see O. Söhring in *Archives Héraldiques Suisses*, xv (1901), 50; P. M. C. Kermode, 'Armorial Bearings of the Isle of Man', *The Ellan Vannin Magazine* (1927); letters to the editor, *Coat of Arms*, iv (1956), no. 25, 40; iv (1956), no. 27, 131; *Aspilogia II*, p. 171, note to item 19; and, especially, E. M. Kandel, 'The Trie Cassyn. An Account of the Arms of the Kingdom of the Isle of Man', *Coat of Arms*, ix (1967), 218–23.

jambes armees o toutes les cuisses chascune cuisse jointe aus autres et en chascune corniere seit un pié, *mailed legs embowed and conjoined at the thighs* (Fig. 134). *Cd* 17: a treys gambes armés o tute les quisses chekune quysse joynte a autre ben [= et en] schekune cornere seyt un pee (*C* 17, see JAMBES ARMEES; *Cl* 17, see JAMBES ARMEES O TOUTES LES CUISSES ET EN CHASCUNE CORNIERE SEIT UN PIÉ). *Syn.*: see JAMBES ARMEES.

jambes armees o toutes les cuisses et en chascune corniere seit un pié, *mailed legs embowed and conjoined at the thighs* (Fig. 134). *Cl* 17: a treys gambes armés o tutte le quisses et [en] chekun cornere seyt une pee (*C* 17, see JAMBES ARMEES; *Cd* 17, see JAMBES ARMEES O TOUTES LES CUISSES CHASCUNE CUISSE JOINTE AUS AUTRES ET EN CHASCUNE CORNIERE SEIT UN PIÉ). *Syn.*: see JAMBES ARMEES.

jambes de s'amie, *his sweetheart's legs*. *Thèbes*, vv. 6265–76:

> Un mout grant escu d'olifant
> Li aporterent dui enfant,
> Paint d'azur, a un grant chantel,
> La boucle d'or fete a neel.

Se cil qui fist l'escu ne ment,
Unne lite y ot d'orpiment
Et claviaux d'or fin trente et trois;
La guige fu toute d'orfrois.
Devant ot fet par gaberie
Paindre les jambes de s'amie,
Et delez ot un coup mout grant
Qui ne fu pas pris en fuiant.

Note: arms of Eteocles. Bouly de Lesdain, p. 203: 'la description peut à peine se citer, tant la "gaberie" en est gauloise.' L. Constans, in his edition of *Thèbes* (Paris, 1890), ii. 343, notes that Palamides in *Troie* bears the portrait of a damsel on his shield (see, however, DAMOISELE, *Note*), 'mais il n'a pas eu le mauvais goût d'Etéocle'. In his edition of the same romance Professor Guy Raynaud de Lage observes that 'on sait que ce trait s'inspire d'une fantaisie de Guillaume IX d'Aquitaine, aïeul d'Aliénor' (i. xxxvi, n. 1); 'Il y a longtemps qu'on a expliqué ces deux vers par un rappel d'une *gaberie* de Guillaume IX d'Aquitaine, connue par un passage de Guillaume de Malmesbury (éd. Bouquet, XIII, 19): "Vicecomitis cujusdam conjugem surripuit, quam adeo ardebat, ut clypeo suo simulacrum mulierculae insereret, perinde dictitans se illam velle ferre in praelio, sicut illa portabat eum in triclinio." La chose est plus piquante dans les vers de *Thèbes*. Quoi qu'il en soit, on l'a déjà fait remarquer, ce n'est guère que dans le milieu seigneurial autour d'Alinéor que ces souvenirs de son aïeul pouvaient se perpétuer et divertir' (ii. 153, note to vv. 6273–4). According to A. Jeanroy (*Les Chansons de Guillaume IX, duc d'Aquitaine* [Paris, 1913], p. ix), the anecdote is highly improbable: 'Je ne pense pas que Guillaume, malgré le sans-gêne de sa conduite, ait osé pousser le cynisme jusqu'à arborer sur ses armes le portrait d'une femme de qualité, enlevée à son légitime époux; l'idée a pu être exprimée au contraire dans une de ces facétieuses gasconnades comme nous en avons gardé quelques-unes; et l'antithèse même dont le chroniqueur nous a conservé le souvenir ne fournissait-elle pas à une pièce de ce genre un trait final tout à fait réussi?'

jarbe, *garb* (*sheaf of corn* [*i.e. wheat*]) (Fig.

228). (1) *the number of garbs is specified.*
B 16: a trois garbes (*Ba* 16: a treys garbes;
Bb 16: 3 garbes; *Bc* 16: a trey gabes; *Bl*
16: ove trois garbes); 172: trois gerbes;
C 54: trois garbes (*Cl* 54: a treys garbes;
Cd 54: a troys garbes); 84: troiz garbes
(*Cl* 84: a treys garbes; *Cd* 84: a 3 gaerbes);
137: a trois garbes (*Cl* 137: a treys garbes;
Cd 137: a .iii. garbes); *D* 167: a treis
garbes. (2) *the number of garbs is not specified
but is known. K,* vv. 113–17:

> Nicholas de Segrave o li,
> Ke nature avoit embeli
> De cors, e enrichi de cuer,
> Vallant pere ot, ki getta puer
> Les garbes e le lyon prist.

Syn.: JARBE D'AVEINE. *Note*: the Segrave
family arms are known to have featured
three garbs; see *B* 172 and *C* 137; see also
D 100, s.v. JARBE D'AVEINE. Garbs are mentioned by Matthew Paris in his blazon of
the arms of the Earl of Chester: 'Scutum
de azuro, garb' aurea' (*Aspilogia II*, p. 55,
item 100). According to Wagner, *Historic
Heraldry*, p. 47, item 24, the Comyn garbs
(*C* 84 [70]) possibly constitute canting arms,
OFr. *comin* (MFr. *cumin*) and E. *cummin* or
cumin being a dwarf plant of the carrot
family. See also *Aspilogia II*, pp. 108, 182,
note to item 70.

jarbe d'aveine, *garb* (Fig. 228). *D* 100: od
treis garbes de aveyne. *Syn.*: JARBE.

jarbes en la crois, *the cross semy of garbs.*
The complete blazon reads as follows: *Hg*
103 [104]: Willam le Latimer le fiz porte
de goules a un croys patee od les garbes de
vert sable en la croice (*H* 103: Sʳ William de
Latymer le fitz port de gulez ou ung crois
patee d'or ou le lambel d'argent). *Note*:
Gough H, p. 154, note to item 104: '[*Hg*]
is unaccountably wrong.' Refers to EN LA
CROIS¹ (2).

jaune, *or* (*yellow*). *Troie*, v. 7745: de jaune;
Erec, v. 3603: Sor l'escu qui fu tainz an
jaune; *Artus*, pp. 7, 13: jaune; *Cleomadés*,
v. 713: Dyaspré de vert et de jaune; *SCK*,
fol. 106 *e*: Gaunes; *SCT*, fol. 126 *e*: gannes;
fol. 127 *a*: gausnes; *SCV*, fol. 92 *f*: gausnes;
fol. 93 *b*: galsnes; *K*, vv. 46, 81, 158, 179,
190, 308, 329, 332, 335, 363: jaune;
vv. 247, 340, 482: jaunes. *Syn.*: see OR.
Note: see PALETÉ.

jerbe, *garb.* See JARBE.

jeter puer, *to abandon, relinquish (arms). K,*
vv. 116–17:

> Vallant pere ot, ki getta puer
> Les garbes e le lyon prist.

Note: on the practice of relinquishing arms
in the Middle Ages, consult L. Bouly de
Lesdain, 'Notes sur quelques changements
d'armoiries aux xiiᵉ et xiiiᵉ siècles',
AHS (1899), 76–82, 106–16; (1900), 1–20,
44–62. See also Mathieu, chapter v, 'Le
libre choix d'un blason et les changements
d'armoiries', pp. 187–95.

jeter sor, *to place a charge over all the others
on the shield.* See BASTON JETÉ SOR. *Syn.*:
SORJETER.

joint, *conjoined.* See CHASCUNE CUISSE JOINTE
AUS AUTRES.

jumeaus¹, *pair of stripes.* (1) *twin chevrons
(adjective)* (Fig. 68). See CHEVRONS JUMEAUS.
(2) *bars gemelles (substantive)* (Fig. 56). *H* 33:
ou .ii. gemeus (*Hg* 33 [34]: a deus jumeux);
77: ou .iii. gemeus (*Hg* 77 [76]: od trois
jumaux), see CHIEF¹ (1); *K*, v. 366: o deus
. . . jumeaus; v. 716: o deus jumeaus. For
other uses, see JUMEAUS DE L'UN EN L'AUTRE,
JUMEAUS DE L'UN ET DE L'AUTRE. *Note*:
for *H* 77, see BARRE¹ (3), *Note*. (3) *bars
gemelles, in chief a leopard.* See JUMEAUS EN
LE CHIEF UN LIEPART PASSANT. (4) *double
cotice* (Fig. 83). See FESSE ENTRE DEUS
JUMEAUS. *Syn.*: see JUMELES¹, for (2) and
(3); LISTE³, for (4). *Note*: each *pair* of stripes
is counted as one (cf. JUMEAUS²). For (3),
however, see JUMELES², *Note*.

jumeaus², *barrulets* (Fig. 56). The complete
blazon reads as follows: *M* 57: Sʳ Thomas
de Richemonde port de gules, le chef d'or
ou quatre gemeus. *Syn.*: see BARRE¹. *Note*:
each individual barrulet is counted as one
(cf. JUMEAUS¹). For a similar use of *gemelle* in
Strangways' Book (*c.* 1454), see London,
'Some Medieval Treatises', pp. 178–9. For
the exact opposite (each *liste* counts as
two), see LISTE². For the Richmond arms
which feature (as here?) *bars gemelles*, i.e.
pairs of barrulets, see next two entries
below.

jumeaus de l'un en l'autre, *bars gemelles*
(Fig. 57). The complete blazon reads as
follows: *B* 209: Roand le connestable de
Richemund, de goules a ung chief d'or

a deus gemeus de l'un en l'autre d'or (*Bl* 209 [213], see JUMEAUS DE L'UN ET DE L'AUTRE). *Syn.*: see JUMELES[1]. *Note*: a pleonasm; see DE L'UN EN L'AUTRE[3]. Refers to CHIEF[1] (1) and JUMEAUS[1] (2); cf. also BARRE[1] (3). On these arms, consult Brault, '*de l'un en l'autre*', pp. 89–90.

jumeaus de l'un et de l'autre, *bars gemelles* (Fig. 57). The complete blazon reads as follows: *Bl* 209 [213]: Rowaud le conestable de Richemond, de gules od le chief d'or od deux gymeus de l'un et de l'autre (*B* 209, see JUMEAUS DE L'UN EN L'AUTRE). *Syn.*: see JUMELES[1]. *Note*: a pleonasm; see DE L'UN ET DE L'AUTRE[3]. Refers to CHIEF[1] (1) and JUMEAUS[1] (2); cf. also BARRE[1] (3). *Aspilogia II*, p. 157, note to item 213: 'the blazon . . . seems to mean that one gemel is red on the gold chief and the other gold on the red chief. But Roald's seal displays two gemels and a chief.' See Brault, '*de l'un en l'autre*', pp. 89–90.

jumeaus en le chief un liepart passant, *bars gemelles, in chief a leopard. H* 75: ou .ii. gemeus . . . en le chef ung leopard passannt (*G*: passaunt; *Hg* 75 [77]: od trois jumaux . . . en le chef un lupart passant). *Syn.*: see LISTES A UN LIEPART. *Note*: Gough H, p. 146, note to item 77: 'In [*Hg* 75] "trois" is an error . . .' On these arms (Tregoz family), see, however, JUMELES[2], *Note.*

jumeles[1], *bars gemelles.* (1) *in combination with a chief* (Fig. 57). A. *the chief is of the same tincture as the bars gemelles and is not charged. B* 121: a trois gemelles (*Bl* 121 [125]: od trois gemels). *Note*: refers to BARRE[1] (3) and CHIEF[1] (1). B. *the 'chief' refers to position only (i.e. the upper part of the shield set off by the bars gemelles) and is of the same tincture as the field.* See JUMELES ET UN LIEPART EN CHIEF, JUMELES ET UN LION EN LE CHIEF PASSANT, JUMELES UN LION EN CHIEF PASSANT, LIEPART EN LE CHIEF A DEUS JUMELES. (2) *there is no chief. TA*, v. 840: a .ii. jumeles; *BA* 184: a .ii. jumeles; 189, 218–20: a .iii. jumelles; 216: a .iii. gemelles (*A*: ganelles); 217: a .iii. jemelles; *Escanor*, vv. 3730–1: D'un escu d'or a .iii. jumeles / D'azur, qui bien i avenoient; *TC*, v. 1477: trois gemelles; *CP* 95: a trois jumelles. *Syn.*: JUMEAUS[1] (2) and (3), JUMEAUS DE L'UN EN L'AUTRE, JUMEAUS DE L'UN ET DE L'AUTRE, JUMELETES, LISTE[2]; cf. also JUMEAUS[3]. *Note*: for a possible interpretation of OFr. *vimiele* in this light in a description of costly wearing-apparel (*Durmart*, v. 9953), see Father Gildea's note, ii. 138.

jumeles[2], *triple bars* (Fig. 59). *C* 171: trois gemells (*Cl* 171: a treis gemelle; *Cd* 171: a 3 gemes), see CHIEF[1] (1). *Note*: cf. JUMELES UN LION EN CHIEF PASSANT, JUMELES ET UN LION EN LE CHIEF PASSANT. *C/Cl/Cd* 171 are the arms of the Cresèques family known to feature three triple horizontal stripes (*Aspilogia II*, p. 201, note to item 176). In a fifteenth-century prose romance by Antoine de la Sale, the same arms are blazoned as follows: 'Le seigneur de Cresecques, d'azur a trois faisses jumelles d'or' (*Jehan de Saintré*, edd. J. Misrahi and C. A. Knudson [Paris–Geneva, 1965], p. 198, lines 28–9). Prinet WR, p. 252 n. 3, cites a nineteenth-century authority (La Chenaye des Bois) who blazons the Cresèques arms as follows: 'd'azur à deux tierces ou cresèques d'or'. Prinet wonders: '*Cresèque* serait-il un synonyme de *tierce*? Je ne crois pas l'avoir constaté ailleurs.' I note, however, its use in *Navarre* 1080: 'Le sire de Creseques, d'azur a un chief d'or a trois crequez d'or em pied'. It may be that a pun on OFr. *tiercier* 'to divide into three parts', or on one of its derivatives, was originally intended. On the etymology of the latter term, see *FEW*, xiii. 265, s.v. *tertiare* and 268, s.v. *tertius*. The mutation *ter-*, *tier-*, *tre-* > *cre-* is not uncommon in the French dialects. The modern name for Cresèques is Creques, a village situated in the vicinity of Mametz (Somme). On the family, consult the *Dictionnaire de biographie française*, ed. Roman d'Amat, ix (Paris, 1961), col. 1217. Comte Auguste de Loisne, *Dictionnaire topographique du département du Pas-de-Calais* (Paris, 1907), p. 115, lists numerous early mentions of this locality including the following: *Kerske* (1168), *Cerseca* (1174), *Kerseca* (1197), *Cresecke* (1205), *Creseka* (1223). A. Dauzat and C. Rostaing, *Dictionnaire étymologique des noms de lieux en France* (Paris, 1963), do not cite Cresèques but mention several localities, p. 226, s.v. *Crécey-sur-Tille* (Côte-d'Or) with names said to be derived from

Lat. *crixsiacum* ('Du nom d'homme gaul. latinisé *Crixsius* et suff. *-acum*'), e.g. *Creciacum* (E.-et-L., 1166), *Crisciacum* (Somme, 660), *Criciacum* (Aisne, 1156).

A very significant parallel may also be cited in this regard. The Tregoz family arms are usually said to feature two bars gemelles and in chief a leopard or lion passant; see *Aspilogia II*, pp. 136, item 113; 186, item 97; 206. There are, as a matter of fact, two bars gemelles in the painted shields of the Heralds' Roll, Dering Roll, St. George's Roll, Charles's Roll, Guillim's Roll, and in the verbal blazon of the Parliamentary Roll; see also JUMEAUS EN LE CHIEF UN LIEPART PASSANT, JUMELES ET UN LIEPART EN CHIEF, JUMELES ET UN LION EN LE CHIEF PASSANT, JUMELES UN LION EN CHIEF PASSANT, LIEPART EN LE CHIEF A DEUS JUMELES, LISTES A UN LIEPART, and LISTES A UN LION PASSANT. I have, consequently, cross-referenced these items to JUMELES[1] and LISTE[2] 'bars gemelles'. However, the drawings in both known copies of Cooke's version of Glover's Roll (i.e. the earliest version of this roll) and the verbal blazon of one of the copies of the latter and of the Falkirk Roll (*B* 109, see JUMELES UN LION EN CHIEF PASSANT; *Hg* 75 [77], see JUMEAUS EN LE CHIEF UN LIEPART PASSANT) specify three, not two, pairs of bars gemelles. Thus it may be argued that the two *jumeaus* or *jumeles* in the blazons of the Tregoz arms mean two *triple* bars. In spite of their derivation from Lat. *gemellus* (fem. *gemella*), a term meaning 'twin', French has always used these words indiscriminately whether referring to two, three, or more children born of the same birth, e.g. *deux jumelles, quatre jumeaux, les jumelles Dionne* 'twin girls, quadruplets, the Dionne quintuplets'. What lends additional support to the view that the arms in question originally at least, if not everywhere here, featured two triple bars is the name Tregoz itself. According to the *Complete Peerage*, xii. 16: 'The name comes from Troisgots: Manche, arr. St. Lô, cant. Tressy-sur-Vire.' It is not clear what three objects the bars alluded to (perhaps OFr. *gort* 'stick'? the term is only attested late [Godefroy, iv. 316]), but there is every reason to believe that triple bars were originally intended

to be canting arms for at least the first part of the surname Tregoz. Thus a heraldic parallel with the Cresèques arms now appears clearly established.

jumeles et un liepart en chief, *bars gemelles, in chief a leopard.* C 136: deux gemells et un leopard in cheif (*Cl/Cd* 136, see LIEPART EN LE CHIEF A DEUS JUMELES). *Syn.*: see LISTES A UN LIEPART. *Note*: refers to EN CHIEF[2] and JUMELES[1] (but see JUMELES[2], *Note*).

jumeletes, *bars gemelles* (Fig. 56). *Escanor*, vv. 4010–11:

> Et les portoit toutes dorees
> A .iii. jumeletes de noir.

Syn.: see JUMELES[1].

kanee, kavee, see FOURCHIÉ AU KANEE.
kene, *oak*. See CHESNE.
kenet, *kennet*. See CHIENET.
keue, *tail*. See COUE.

*****label[1],** *label* (Fig. 121). One literary source only before *c.* 1250, viz. *TA*, vv. 699, 722, 829, 864, 929, 1120, 1162, 1213: a un label; vv. 852, 939, 1649: .i. label; vv. 1095, 1728: au label; however, several examples in literature after that date, e.g. *Berte*, v. 3227: Le label au mainsné d'argent on besenta; *EO*, v. 5072: labiaus de gueules; *TC*, v. 1976: Lambiaus i a pour desparelle; *Hunbaut*, v. 2673: labiel, see TELS ARMES SANS. Very frequent in the rolls, e.g. *BA* 4, 18: au lambel; 290, 291: au lablel; *B* 2 (*Bl* 2: ove label), 9 (*Bl* 9: et un label): ung label; *C* 8: un labell (*Cl* 8: a un lambeu; *Cd* 8: a labeal); *H* 4, 11: ou ung labell (*Hg* 4, 11, see LABEL[2]); 49: ou le label, see LABEL EN CHASCUN LABEL UNE FLEUR DE LIS (*Hg* 49 [50]: od le lambel, see EN LE LABEL LES FLEURS DE LIS); 103: ou le lambel (*Hg* 103 [104], see JARBES EN LA CROIS). For another use, see EN LE LABEL. *Syn.*: EN L'ESCU LABEL, LABEL SOR, RASTEL[2]. *Note*: on this charge, see M. M., 'The Label', *Coat of Arms*, ix (1967), 165; T. R. Davies, 'The Label', pp. 306–7. Twelfth-century examples of the label are cited by Mathieu, p. 100. Matthew Paris uses *rastel* (i.e. RASTEL[2]) in this sense, reserving the term *lambel/lambellus* (i.e. LABEL[2]) for the points of the label only: 'Willelm de Valentia [*P*: Wilhelmi de Valencia], filii ejus. Similiter ut patris cum his: quinque *lambelli* de gules pendentes a superiori linea argenti, ita tamen, quod prima linea argentea sit libera, in quolibet *lambello* .iii. leopardi transeuntes' (Pusikan, p. 126); 'Ricardi de Munfichet. Scutum d'or, .iii. chevrons de gules, vel *rastel* d'azuro vel *lambel*' (*Aspilogia II*, p. 40, item 24; the word 'vel' is abbreviated by the usual symbol, an *l* with a diagonal cross stroke; Pusikan, p. 145, omits the first 'vel' and misreads the second as 'V'); 'Com' de Braib', Scut' d'or, leo gul', *rastel* d'az'; Pet' de Sabaudia. Scut' d'or, leo rubeus, *rastel* d'azur' (*Aspilogia II*, p. 53, items 80–1). *BA* 179: Dr. Adam-Even has combined two entries as follows: 'et rampant billete d'argent au lambel d'asur. Hen.' Though the blazon is defective, five distinct items are set off by the scribe on separate lines as follows:

... ent rampant billeté d'argent au ...
... ou lablel d'azur. Hen.
... rampant. Hai.
... au lablel de ...
... aston ...

According to Walford's note to *C* 61: 'The *r* of *laber* in the MS. may have been a slip for *v*.' *C* 172 reads as follows: 'Hugo de Bauçoy (le labyn vert et), d'or un crois gules resercelé un labell sable (*Cl* 172: Hugh de Bauçoy [le labiau verte], d'or a une croyz de goules recerselé a une labeu de sable; *Cd* 172: ... ge de Bauçoy [le labiau . . .] . . . a une crosse g . . .).' Walford capitalizes the first letter of the word *labyn* ('Labyn') and makes the following observation apropos of the latter: '*le labiau* L [i.e. the variant form in Leland's version]. Some partition seems omitted. Bauçay of Poitou bore, Or a cross ancre gules. *Le labyn* was probably a soubriquet, possibly for *le lambin*. In the margin is written "Ingham's cote".' Prinet WR, p. 252, however, places the words 'le labeau [*sic*, for labiau in Leland's copy] verte' in parentheses, as I have here, and adds the following explanation (note 5): 'Note corrective qui se rapporte aux derniers mots de la description, et que le copiste n'a pas comprise'. The arms are

those of the Baucey family. *H* 17, 102 omit the label. Gayre, *Heraldic Cadency*, p. 50, cites the label in *K*, v. 577, and claims that 'the usual interpretation of the Roll of Caerlaverock concerning the label in the arms of Sir Maurice de Berkeley has to be qualified. The account says:

". . . un label de asur avoit
Porce que ces peres vivoit."

This is usually translated—a label of blue he bore because his father was living. But it probably really means his fathers (grandfather and father) were living. Be that as it may, the suggestion that this refers to the label as the brisure of the eldest son, or eldest grandson, cannot be founded on this statement.' Colonel Gayre has been misled by *ses* [*sic*, not *ces*] *peres* which, though it resembles the Modern French *ses pères*, is, in actuality, a nominative *singular* (Lat. *pater* > OFr. *pere*, but 'Under the influence of the second masculine declension, *s* and *z* came to be regarded as the characteristic flexion of the nominative singular masculine' [Pope, p. 313, paragraph 805]; therefore, OFr. *ses peres* = MFr. *son père*). Note also the singular form of the verb *vivoit*.

label[2], *pendant, point (of a label)* (Fig. 123). *Berte*, v. 3226: A cinc labiaus de gueules l'ainsné fils le porta; *Cleomadés*, vv. 537–8: Et estoient d'un vert dyaspre / Li label; *Hg* 4: od le[s] lambeaux; 11: a les lambeaux (*H* 4, 11, see LAMBEL[1]). For another use, see LABEL EN CHASCUN LABEL UNE FLEUR DE LIS. *Note*: Adenet le Roi uses OFr. *label* in both meanings (see *Berte*, v. 3227, cited s.v. LABEL[1]). For three examples of LABEL[2] in Matthew Paris, see LABEL[1], *Note*; see also RASTEL[2], *Note*. Navarre 923 uses OFr. *chief* in this sense: 'M. Jehan de Clermont, semblablement a une molete d'argent sur le premier chef du lambel'.

label en chascun label une fleur de lis, *label, on each point a fleur-de-lis.* The complete blazon reads as follows: *H* 49: S[r] Thomas le counte de Loncastre porte mesmes lez armez ou le label d'azure en checun lable 3 floures de lyz d'or. *Note*: the first 'label' mentioned in this blazon refers to LABEL[1], the second (*lable*) to LABEL[2].

label en l'escu, *label.* See EN L'ESCU
LABEL.

label par reconoissance entre ... et ...,
see ENTRE ... ET ... UN LABEL PAR
RECONOISSANCE.

label sor, *label* (Fig. 121). *TA,* vv. 1592–3:

Au label de bone esperance
Portret sor debonereté.

Syn.: see LABEL[1].

labeu, *label.* See LABEL.

labin, *label.* See LABEL.

lable, *label.* See LABEL.

Ladre, *Lazarus.* See SAINT LADRE.

lambel, *label.* See LABEL.

langue, *tongue. TA,* v. 748: a langues
d'avocaïon; vv. 995, 2264: de langues.
For another use, see LION RAMPANT COU-
RONÉ A LA LANGUE A UNE MANCHE EN LA
GEULE DU LION A UNE ESPEE AU PONG ET
AU HELT QUI TRANCHE LE LION PAR MI.

langue a tranchanz, *tongue with edges.*
Roman des Eles, v. 476: A une langue a cinq
trenchans; *TA,* v. 824: A une langue a
.v. trenchanz. *Note:* on the relationship
between these two blazons, see RAMPANT,
Note.

l'autre, *the other.* See LE ..., L'AUTRE ...

l'autre moitié, *the other side, the other half*
(of a party field). Charrete, vv. 5785–7:

A cel escu vert d'une part,
S'a sor le vert point un liepart,
Et d'azur est l'autre mitiez.

Syn.: see DEMI[2].

l'azur, *the azure portion of a party field.* See
PARTI DE ... ET DE ..., PAR LE ..., LE ...

le champ plein de, *semy.* See CHAMP PLEIN
D'ESCHALOPES. *Syn.:* see POUDRÉ.

le geules, *the gules portion of a quarterly or*
a party shield. See ESQUARTELÉ DE ... ET
DE ... LE GEULES, PARTI DE ... ET DE ...,
LE ..., LE ...; PARTI DE ... ET DE ...,
PAR LE ..., L'AUTRE ...; PARTI DE ... ET
DE ..., PAR LE ..., LE ... *Syn.:* EN LE
GEULES[2].

le ..., le ..., see PARTI DE ... ET DE ...,
LE ..., LE ...

le mesme a, *the same arms, differenced by.*
Cd 88: le meme a (*C/Cl* 88, see AUTEL A).
Syn.: see AUTEL[2].

le noir, see CROISETES OU ...

lentes, see CROIS ET LIONCEAUS.

leon, *lion.* See LION.

leopard, see LIEPART.

lesance, *ghost word.* See CHARBOUCLE BE-
SANCIÉ.

l'escu, *ghost word.* See ESCU[4].

les merloz, *orle of martlets* (Fig. 125). Ba
23: lez merloz (*B/Bb* 23, see ORLE DE MER-
LOZ; *Bc/Bl* 23, see BORDURE DE MERLOZ).
Syn.: see BORDURE DE MERLETES.

letré de ... et de ..., *ornamented with*
letters, an arabesque, or other design. TA,
v. 1876: L'escu letré d'or et d'argent;
v. 1937: Letré de decrez et de lais. *Note:*
cf. DIASPRÉ (DE ... ET DE ...).

leu, *wolf.* See TESTE DE LEU.

leunces, see CROIS ET LIONCEAUS.

le vermeil, *gules (red).* See BOUCEL PAR
DESUS LE ...

levrier od le colier, *collared greyhound* (Fig.
157). *Hg* 90 [89]: a un leverer ... od le
coler (*H* 90, see LEVRIER OU LE COLIER).
Syn.: LEVRIER OU LE COLIER. *Note:* on the
heraldic greyhound, consult London, *Royal*
Beasts, pp. 39–41.

levrier ou le colier, *collared greyhound* (Fig.
157). *H* 90: ou ung leverier ... ou la
collere (*Hg* 90 [89], see LEVRIER OD LE
COLIER). *Syn.:* LEVRIER OD LE COLIER.

liepardeaus de l'un en l'autre, *leopards*
counterchanged. See ESQUARTELÉ DE ... ET
DE ... A LIEPARDEAUS DE L'UN EN L'AUTRE.
Syn.: see LIEPARZ DE L'UN EN L'AUTRE.

liepardel, *small leopard.* See LIEPARDEAUS
DE L'UN EN L'AUTRE, SEMÉ DE LIEPARDEAUS.
Syn.: see LIEPART.

liepart, *leopard* (Fig. 162). (1) *no position is*
indicated. Chanson d'Antioche, ii. 246, v. 991
(var.): uns lupars; *Troie,* v. 11360: un
liepart; *Charrete,* v. 5786: un liepart; *Aspre-*
mont, v. 2193: Trois lupars; *Durmart,* vv.
2630, 6485, 9276, 9344: a liepars; v. 7024:
al ... liupart; v. 9254: doi liepart; v. 9345:
li liepart; v. 10101: a deus liepars; v. 11143:
celui a ces liepars; vv. 11800, 13049: liepars;
v. 12370: cil a ces liepars; v. 13157: a ...
liepars; v. 13613: cil as liepars; vv. 13902,
14416: a lupars; *FCE,* v. 5091: Ou portrait
avoit un liepart; *FCT,* v. 1785: Ou portrait
avoit un lupart; *Ogier le Danois,* v. 5194:
l'escu a lupart; *TA,* v. 1701: A .i. liepart;
B 1: trois lupards (*Bl* 1: ove trois lupards);
Bl 82: a deux leopardz (*B* 82, see
LIEPART PASSANT); *Bl* 97: deus leopartz

(*B* 97, see LION PASSANT); *C* 4: a trois leopards (*Cl* 4: a treys leparde; *Cd* 4: 3 leopards); *EO*, v. 5046: L'escu de gueules; s'i ot d'or deus liepars; *D* 7: od treis leopars; *CC*, v. 1093: a un lupart; *Hunbaut*, v. 2339: Qui porte l'escu au lupart; v. 2482: Un escu porte a .i. lupart. (2) *position is indicated.* A. *in chief.* See JUMELES ET UN LIEPART EN CHIEF, LIEPART EN LE CHIEF A DEUS JUMELES, LISTES A UN LIEPART. B. *on a canton.* See LIEPART EN LE QUARTIER, QUARTIER ET UN LIEPART. C. *quarterly, leopards counterchanged.* See LIEPARZ DE L'UN EN L'AUTRE; LIEPARZ DE L'UN ET L'AUTRE. (3) *semy* (Fig. 41). See ORLE O LIEPARZ, POUDRÉ DE LIEPARZ, POUDRÉ OU LIEPARZ. For other uses, see FLEUR CROISSANT HORS DE LA TESTE DU LIE-PART, FLEUR DE LIS CROISSANT HORS DE LA TESTE DU LIEPART, FLEUR DE LIS ESPART NAISSANT DE TESTE DE LIEPART, TESTE DE SON LIEPART. *Syn.*: EN MI UN LIEPART, LIEPARDEL, LIEPART COURANT, LIEPART PASSANT, LION², LIONCEL COURANT, LIONCEL PASSANT, LION PASSANT. *Note*: *Hunbaut*, v. 2482 is part of a plagiarism of that poem contained in a rhymed version of the fabliau entitled *Chastoiement d'un père à son fils*; see Alfons Hilka, 'Plagiate in alt-französischen Dichtungen', *ZFSL*, xlvii (1925), 67. On the leopard in medieval heraldry (usually a lion passant guardant; cf., however, LIEPART RAMPANT A LA COUE FOURCHIEE, LIEPART RAMPANT OVE LA COUE FOURCHIEE), consult London, *Royal Beasts*, pp. 9–15; *Aspilogia II*, p. 134, note to item 97 (after observing that certain copies of Glover's Roll are illustrated with lions passant guardant): 'The *leopartz* of [*Bl* 97] may be a mistake, but it suggests that the pose of the head was still unimportant and that no clear distinction was drawn between a lion passant and a lion passant gardant.' Earlier studies include the latter's 'Lion Guardant or Regardant', *Coat of Arms*, ii (1953), no. 13, 194–5 (on the spelling of the modern English term *gardant* vs. *guardant*, see H. Pointer's letter to the editor and the latter's reply, *Coat of Arms*, ix [1966], 121); idem, 'Lion or Leopard?', ii (1953), no. 16, 291–2; see also pp. 305–6 ('The Royal Crest of England'), Colin Campbell's letter in iii (1954), no. 18,

72. I cite here, merely for curiosity's sake, Matthew Paris's explanation of the three leopards in the arms of the English sovereign: 'quia rex, dux et comes est' (*Historia minor*, ed. F. Madden, iii [London, 1869], 88, n. 2; Hauptmann, p. 22). Finally, according to medieval lore, the lion sur-passed the leopard in strength and courage. See *Queste*, p. 77: 'Li uns des trois passera son pere autant come li lyons passe le liepart de pooir et de hardement.' For other medieval notions and symbolism relative to the leopard, lion, and 'pard', consult McCul-loch, pp. 137–40, 150–1; Bayrav, p. 204.

liepart courant, *leopard courant* (Fig. 166). *Durmart*, v. 1279: Liepars . . . corans; *K*, vv. 220–2:

> En sa banier trois lupart,
> De or fin estoient mis en rouge,
> Courant, feloun, fier, e harouge.

Syn.: see LIEPART.

liepart courant et couroné, *crowned leopard courant* (Fig. 164). *Durmart*, vv. 1409–10:

> A deus liepars d'or eslevés,
> Corant et d'argent coronés.

Syn.: see LIEPART COURONÉ.

liepart couroné, *crowned leopard* (Fig. 163). *Durmart*, vv. 12917–18:

> A deus liepars qui sont doré
> Et si sont d'argent coroné;

Vulgate Merlin Sequel, p. 423: a .iii. liepars . . . couronés; *B* 155: ung leopard . . . coronné (*Bl* 155 [159]: od un leopard . . . coronné); *D* 42: od un leopard . . . coroné. *Syn.*: LIEPART COURANT ET COURONÉ, LIE-PART PASSANT COURONÉ, LION PASSANT COURONÉ.

liepart en chief, *in chief a leopard.* See JUMELES ET UN LIEPART EN CHIEF. *Syn.*: LION EN CHIEF PASSANT.

liepart en le chief a deus jumeles, *bars gemelles, in chief a leopard.* *Cl* 136: a un leparde . . . en le chef a .ii. gymele (*C* 136, see JUMELES ET UN LIEPART EN CHIEF; *Cd* 136: a un lepard . . . en le cheif a .ii. gemeles). *Syn.*: see LISTES A UN LIEPART. *Note*: refers to JUMELES¹, but see JUMELES², *Note*.

liepart en le quartier, *on a canton a leopard*.
B 49: ung leopard en la quartier (*Bl* 49:
od un leopard . . . en le quartier); *Bl* 58:
od un leopard . . . en le quartier (*B* 58, see
LIEPART PASSANT EN LE QUARTIER). *Syn.*:
LIEPART PASSANT EN LE QUARTIER, QUAR-
TIER ET LIEPART.

liepart passant, *leopard* (Fig. 162). *BA*
235: a .ii. liepars . . . passans (A: pasans),
237 (A: lipars); 292: a .ii. liepars passans;
B 82: a deux leopards passants (*Bl* 82,
see LIEPART); *EO*, v. 5083: deus liepars
d'or passans; *SCK*, fol. 106 *f*: Trois lupars
. . . passans; *H* 48: ou trois leopardes
passauntz (*Hg* 48 [49]: a troys lupars
passans). For other uses see JUMEAUX
EN LE CHIEF UN LIEPART PASSANT, LIE-
PART PASSANT EN LE QUARTIER. *Syn.*: see
LIEPART.

liepart passant couroné, *crowned leopard*
(Fig. 163). *BA* 40: a .ii. liepars . . . passans
coronés. *Syn.*: see LIEPART COURONÉ.

liepart passant en le quartier, *on a canton
a leopard*. *B* 58: ung leopard en la quartier
passant (*Bl* 58, see LIEPART EN LE QUAR-
TIER). *Syn.*: see LIEPART EN LE QUARTIER.

liepart rampant a la coue fourchiee,
*leopard (i.e. lion) rampant with a forked tail
crossed in saltire* (Fig. 147). *Cl* 60: au lapard
. . . raumpant a la cowe furché (*C* 60, see
LIEPART RAMPANT OVE LA COUE FOURCHIEE;
Cd 60; a liopar rampant . . . la quewe
forché). *Syn.*: LION RAMPANT A LA COUE
FOURCHIEE[2]. *Note*: refers to COUE FOUR-
CHIEE[2].

liepart rampant ove la coue fourchiee,
*leopard (i.e. lion) rampant with a forked tail
crossed in saltire* (Fig. 147). *C* 60: un leopard
rampand ove la cowe furché (*Cl/Cd* 60, see
LIEPART RAMPANT A LA COUE FOURCHIEE).
Syn.: LION RAMPANT A LA COUE FOURCHIEE[2].
Note: refers to COUE FOURCHIEE[2].

lieparz de l'un en l'autre, *leopards
counterchanged*. See ESQUARTELIÉ DE . . . ET
DE . . . A LIEPARZ DE L'UN EN L'AUTRE,
ESQUARTILLIÉ DE . . . ET DE . . . A LIEPARZ
DE L'UN EN L'AUTRE. *Syn.*: LIEPARDEAUS DE
L'UN EN L'AUTRE, LIEPARZ DE L'UN ET
L'AUTRE, LIONS DE L'UN ET L'AUTRE.

lieparz de l'un et l'autre, *leopards counter-
changed*. See ESQUARTILLIÉ DE . . . ET DE . . .
A LIEPARZ DE L'UN ET L'AUTRE. *Syn.*: see
LIEPARZ DE L'UN EN L'AUTRE.

lieu, *place*. See EN LIEU DE. *Note*: cf.
MILIEU.

lievre rampant, *hare rampant* (Fig. 158).
TA, v. 1186: a lievre rampant. *Note*:
Prinet TA, p. 49: 'le lièvre, qui s'appelle
Couard dans le *Roman de Renart*, servait au
Tournoiement d'emblème à Couardie.' See
also PALÉ DE . . . ET DE . . ., *Note*. For
other meanings associated with the hare
in the Middle Ages, consult C. K. Abra-
ham, 'Myth and Symbol: the Rabbit in
Medieval France', *SP*, lx (1963), 589–97.

*lion[1], *lion rampant* (Fig. 135). (1) *no position
indicated*. Very frequent in literary sources,
e.g. *Thèbes*, vv. 10285–6: Luisent cil escu
environ / D'or et d'argent paint a lyon;
Couronnement de Louis, v. 970: escu a lion;
Troie, 15644, 23924: al lion; *Cligés*,
v. 4741: a lyon; *Roman des Eles*, v. 479:
A lyon; *Didot Perceval*, p. 228: a deus lions;
Berte, v. 999: a un lyon; *Escanor*, v. 3696:
.i. lÿon de geules, see SOR L'OR. Very
common in the rolls, e.g. *BA* 15, 42: au
lion; *Ba* 48: a lioun (*B* 48, see LION RAM-
PANT; *Bc* 48: a lion); *Ba/Bc* 74: a lion (*B* 74,
see LION RAMPANT); *Bl* 12 (*Bc* 12: a une
lion), 88, 170 [174]: ove un leon (*B/Ba* 12,
B 88, 170, see LION RAMPANT); 18: au un
lion (*B* 18, see LION RAMPANT); 48, 74, 98,
164 [168], 196 [200]: od un leon (*B/Ba* 48,
74; *B* 98, 164, 196, see LION RAMPANT);
Cd 6:. i. lion (*C* 6, see ESQUARTILLIÉ DE . . .
UN CHASTEL . . . ET DE . . . UN LION RAMPANT;
Cl 6, see ESQUARTILLIÉ DE . . . ET DE . . .
A CHASTEAUS EN LES QUARTIERS DE . . .);
11: a .i. lion (*C* 11, see LION RAMPANT; *Cl*
11: a un lion); 73: a lion (*C/Cl* 73, see LION
RAMPANT); *H* 15: o ung leon (*Hg* 15, see
LION RAMPANT). (2) *position indicated*. A. *lions
rampant counterchanged*. See LIONS DE L'UN
ET L'AUTRE. B. *a cross cantoned with lions
rampant*. The complete blazon reads as
follows: *CPA* 151: Brian le Boeuf, de
gueules a la crois d'or a .iv. lions d'or,
see CROIS[1] (2). C. *over all*. See CHIEF A UN
LION ET A UNE FLEUR DE LIS EN L'ESPAULE
DU LION. For another use, see EN CHANTEL
DE DEVANT UN LION. *Syn.*: EN MILIEU UN
LION, EN MI UN LION, EN MI UN RAMPANT
LION, LION AMONT RAMPANT, LIONCEL,
LIONCEL RAMPANT, LION EN MI, LION ENTIER,
LIONET, LION PAR MI, LION RAMPANT, LION
RAMPANT AMONT, LION RAMPANT CONTRE-

MONT, RAMPANT LION. *Note*: cf. DEMI LION, LIEPART, LION CRESTÉ, NOBLE. 'Et as lions' in *SCT*, fol. 93 *d* / *SCV*, fol. 127 *c*, seems to indicate a field semy of lions rampant as no number is indicated; earlier in the same passage, however, Yvain's arms are blazoned as *or, two lions rampant gules*. See LION RAMPANT. On the lion as a Christ symbol, see J. Harris, 'The Role of the Lion in Chrétien de Troyes' "Yvain"', *PMLA*, lxiv (1949), 1143–63; McCulloch, pp. 137–40; Bayrav, p. 205. For a discussion of the lion in early heraldry, consult Bangert, pp. 188–91; Bouly de Lesdain, p. 199; Otto Söhring, 'Schildschmuck und Wappen, in altfranzösischen Epen', *AHS*, xv (1901), 50–1; London, *Royal Beasts*, pp. 9–15, 29–32; and R. Viel, 'La "panthère héraldique" et le "Parzifal" de Wolfram d'Eschenbach', *Archivum Heraldicum*, lxxvi (1962), 20–8, 54–7. Early blazon does not always mention the various attributes of the lion (e.g. crown, forked tail) or specify that it is rampant, as this is its normal attitude. Thus in *BA* 30 (the complete blazon reads: 'Gieres [A: Guiers] de Fauquemont, l'escu d'or a un lion de geules rampant a billetes [A: bilettes] de geules semees. Baneres [A: Banneret] et Rujers [A: Ruyer]'), 'lion rampant' alludes to a *lion rampant with a forked tail crossed in saltire* (see *WB* 619) and in *Ba* 37 ('Huwe de Bailol, autel a un escuchun de azur a un lion de argent coroné or'), *Bc* 37 ('Huwe de Bailol, autel a un escuchun de azur a un lion de argent coroné de or'), and *Bl* 37 ('Hugh son filz, autiel od un escuchon d'asur ove un leon d'argent coronné d'or en la cornere'), 'lion' refers to a *crowned lion rampant* (cf. *B* 37; see LION RAMPANT COURONÉ EN LA CORNIERE). Note also the use of the term *lion* for *lion rampant* in the following locutions: LION LI CHIEF COURONÉ COUE FOURCHIEE, LION RAMPANT COURONÉ A LA LANGUE A UNE MANCHE EN LA GEULE DU LION A UNE ESPEE AU PONG ET AU HELT QUI TRANCHE LE LION PAR MI, LION RAMPANT ET EN LES ESPAULES DU LION UNE QUINTEFEUILLE, LIONS ADOSSÉS.

lion², *lion passant guardant* (*i.e. leopard*). *C* 134: a deux leons (*Cl* 134: a deus leons; *Cd* 134: a .ii. lions). For another use, see

LIONS DE L' UN ET L'AUTRE. *Syn.*: see LIEPART. *Note*: *Aspilogia II*, p. 186, note to item 95: 'In neither version is the posture of the lions blazoned, the compiler perhaps assuming that as there were only two they must be passant'; p. 109: 'one above the other'; cf. p. 134, note to item 97. *Syn.*: see LIEPART.

Lion³, *León* (*in Spain*). See POUR LION. *Note*: the Kingdom of León was inherited by Ferdinand III of Castile in 1230, permanently uniting it to his throne.

lion a la coue fourchiee¹, *lion rampant with a forked tail* (Fig. 146). *BA* 9: a .i. lion . . . a la keue forkie; *Ba/Bb/Bc* 4: a lion . . . a la coue furché (*B* 4, see LION RAMPANT A LA COUE FOURCHIEE¹; *Bl* 4: ove un leon . . . la cowe furchee); *CP* 14: a un lion . . . a la ceue fourcie. *Syn.*: see LION RAMPANT A LA COUE FOURCHIEE¹. *Note*: refers to COUE FOURCHIEE¹.

lion a la coue fourchiee², *lion rampant with a forked tail crossed in saltire* (Fig. 147). *BA* 8: a un lyon . . . a la keue forkie. *Syn.*: see LION RAMPANT A LA COUE FOURCHIEE². *Note*: refers to COUE FOURCHIEE².

lion a la coue fourchiee en som, *lion rampant with a forked tail crossed in saltire* (Fig. 147). *TC*, vv. 1556–8:

> En celui a l'escu d'argent
> Qui porte le vermoil lyon
> A la cheue forchie en son.

Syn.: see LION RAMPANT A LA COUE FOURCHIEE². *Note*: refers to SOM¹.

lion a la coue fourchue, *lion rampant with a forked tail crossed in saltire* (Fig. 147). *CP* 119: a un lion . . . a la queue fourchue. *Syn.*: see LION RAMPANT A LA COUE FOURCHIEE². *Note*: Bruyères arms. For the tail crossed in saltire, see *WB* 26 (illustration of the painted shield on p. 62, fig. 59).

lion amont rampant, *lion rampant* (Fig. 135). *Joufroi*, vv. 2522–3:

> Li uns fu fait a dous lions
> De sinoplë amont rampanz.

Syn.: see LION¹.

lion a un colier, *collared lion rampant* (Fig. 136). *Cl* 167: a un leon . . . a une color (*C* 167, see LION COLERÉ; *Cd* 167: a un leon . . . a un colier). *Syn.*: LION COLERÉ, LION ET A UN COLIER, LION RAMPANT A UN

COLIER, LION RAMPANT OD UN COLIER.

lionceaus a une bende a deus cotices, *bend cotised between lioncels rampant. Bc* 10: a sis lionceus . . . do [*sic,* for a] une bende . . . a deus cotinces (*B/Ba/Bb* 10, see LIONCEAUS OU UNE BENDE A DEUS COTICES; *Bl* 10, see LIONCEAUS OVE UNE BENDE A DEUS COTICES). *Syn.*: see BENDE[1] (4) A. *Note*: for the ghost word in *Bc* 10, see DO[2].

lionceaus a une bende et deus cotices, *bend cotised between lioncels rampant. B* 185: six leonceux . . . a ung bend . . . et deux cotises (*Bl* 185 [189]: od six leonceux . . . a un bende . . . et deux cutices). *Syn.*: see BENDE[1] (4) A.

lionceaus a une bende les listes, *bend cotised between lioncels rampant. C* 98: 6 lionceux . . . un bend . . . les listes (*Cl* 98: a sis liuncels . . . a un bende . . . lyte; *Cd* 98: a 6 lioncs . . . a une bende . . . lyte). *Syn.*: see BENDE[1] (4) A.

lionceaus a une bende od deus cotises, *bend cotised between lioncels rampant. D* 28: od sis leuncels . . . a une bende . . . od deus cotices. *Syn.*: see BENDE[1] (4) A.

lionceaus en la bordure, *a bordure semy of lioncels rampant. CPA* 19: a lionceaux . . . en la bordure. *Note*: refers to EN LA BORDURE[1]. Cf. SEMÉ DE LIONCEAUS.

lionceaus od une bende et deus cotices, *bend cotised between lioncels rampant. Bl* 184 [188]: od six leonceux . . . od un bende . . . et deux cutices (*B* 184, see BENDE ENTRE LIONCEAUS COTICIEE). *Syn.*: see BENDE[1] (4) A.

lionceaus ou une bende a deus cotices, *bend cotised between lioncels rampant. B* 10: six lionceux . . . ou ung bende . . . a deux cotises (*Ba* 10: a siz lionceus . . . o une bende . . . a deus cotrises; *Bb* 10: au 6 lionceux . . . ou un bend . . . a deuz cotises; *Bc* 10, see LIONCEAUS A UNE BENDE A DEUS COTICES; *Bl* 10, see LIONCEAUS OVE UNE BENDE A DEUS COTICES). *Syn.*: see BENDE[1] (4) A.

lionceaus ove une bende a deus cotices, *bend cotised between lioncels rampant. Bl* 10: ove sys lyonceaux . . . ove une bende . . . a deux cutices (*B/Ba/Bb* 10, see LIONCEAUS OU UNE BENDE A DEUS COTICES; *Bc* 10, see LIONCEAUS A UNE BENDE A DEUS COTICES). *Syn.*: see BENDE[1] (4) A.

lionceaus passanz l'un contre l'autre en chief, *on a chief two lioncels passant facing* each other (Fig. 165). *CP* 109: a deux lionceaux . . . passans l'un contre l'autre en chief. *Note*: Dr. Adam-Even in his blazon for *WB* 874 uses the expression *affronté* to describe this situation ('au chef chargé de 2 lions passants affrontés'); the kindred English term *affronted* is usually reserved for describing a beast facing the observer (Boutell, p. 265). In modern English blazon, lions rampant in such a position would be termed *combattant*. Cf. COMBATRE.

lionceaus rampanz l'un desous et l'autre desus, *lioncels rampant in pale* (Fig. 89). *FCT*, vv. 4349–51:

> S'i ot deus lionciax rampans
> De sebelin, non pas molt grans,
> L'uns desoz et l'autres desus.

Note: bottom-upwards system; see FESSIEL ENCHASTELÉ DESOUS ET DESOR, *Note*.

lioncel, *lioncel rampant* (Fig. 135). (1) *no position is indicated. Troie*, vv. 7756, 23900: a leonceaus; *Fouque de Candie*, v. 3431: au leoncel; v. 4909: et au lioncel; *Gaidon*, v. 8682: a lyonciaus; v. 9415: a lyoncel; *Godefroi de Bouillon*, v. 1716: a .ii. lionchax; *Otinel*, v. 367: a .i. vert lioncel; *Fierabras*, v. 667: Quatre lionchiaus; *Aye d'Avignon*, v. 1103: .i. lioncel; *Saisnes*, v. 2277: .i. lioncel, see ISSIR; *Blancandin*, v. 1784: escu a lioncel; *Durmart*, v. 7328: a lionceas; *Lancelot propre*, iii. 402: a chel lyoncel; *TA*, vv. 1711, 1989: a .i. lioncel; *BA* 165, 166: a .iii. lionchiax; *B* 22 (*Ba* 22: a siz lionceus; *Bc* 22: a sis lionceus; *Bl* 22: .vi. leonceux), 183: a six lionceulx (*Bl* 183 [187]: od six leonceaux); 34: six lionceulx (*Bl* 34: od six leonceulx); *Ba/Bc* 77: a treis lionceus (*B/Bb* 77, see LIONCEL RAMPANT; *Bl* 77: od trois leonceux); *Bl* 78: od trois leonceux (*B* 78, see LIONCEL RAMPANT); *C* 86: a six leonceux (*Cl* 86: a sis liuncels; *Cd* 86: a 6 lioncieus); 87: a six leonceaux (*Cl* 87: a sis liuncels; *Cd* 87: a 6 lionscembl); *EO*, v. 3781: d'or a trois lionciaus bis; *CPA* 158: a .iv. lionceaux; *M* 45: ou .iii. leonceux. (2) *a bend cotised separates lioncels rampant.* See BENDE COTICIEE ENTRE LIONCEAUS, BENDE OU LIONCEAUS OU DEUS COTICES, LIONCEAUS A UNE BENDE A DEUS COTICES, LIONCEAUS A UNE BENDE ET DEUS COTICES, LIONCEAUS A UNE BENDE LES LISTES, LIONCEAUS A UNE BENDE OD DEUS COTICES, LIONCEAUS OD UNE BENDE

ET DEUS COTICES, LIONCEAUS OU UNE BENDE
A DEUS COTICES, LIONCEAUS OVE UNE BENDE
A DEUS COTICES. (3) *a cross cantoned with
lioncels rampant.* B 46: leunceus (*Ba* 46: a
4 lionceus), see CROIS[1] (2). For other uses,
see CROIS A LIONCEAUS, ESQUARTILLIÉ DE . . .
ET DE . . . A CHASTEAUS EN LES QUARTIERS
DE . . . A LIONCEAUS EN LES QUARTIERS DE . . .,
SEMÉ DE LIONCEAUS. See also locutions
beginning with the word LIONCEAUS. *Syn.*:
see LION[1]. *Note:* for the position of the three
lions rampant in *Bl* 78, see LIONCEL RAM-
PANT, *Note*, apropos of *B* 78.

lioncel courant, *lioncel courant* (Fig. 71).
See EL CHIEF DEVANT LE LIONCEL COURANT.
Syn.: see LIEPART.

lioncel couroné rampant, *crowned lioncel
rampant* (Fig. 138). *K*, vv. 789–90:

> De trois lyonceaus couronnez
> Ke il ot rampans . . .

Syn.: see LION COURONÉ.

lioncel en la fesse, *on a fess a lioncel rampant.* See EN LA FESSE UN LIONCEL.

lioncel passant, *lioncel passant* (Fig. 162).
See FESSIÉ D'UNE BARRE ET OU CHIEF UN
LIONCEL PASSANT. *Syn.*: see LIEPART.

lioncel passant ou chantel devant, *in
dexter chief a lioncel passant.* See FESSE AU
LIONCEL PASSANT OU CHANTEL DEVANT.
Syn.: LIONCEL PASSANT OU CHIEF, LIONCEL
PASSANT OU QUARTIER. *Note:* on these arms,
consult Prinet CC, pp. 162–3.

lioncel passant ou chief, *in dexter chief
a lioncel passant.* See FESSIÉ D'UNE BARRE ET
OU CHIEF UN LIONCEL PASSANT. *Syn.*: see
LIONCEL PASSANT OU CHANTEL DEVANT.

lioncel passant ou quartier, *in dexter
chief a lioncel passant.* See FESSE A UN LIONCEL
PASSANT OU QUARTIER. *Syn.*: see LIONCEL
PASSANT OU CHANTEL DEVANT. *Note:* refers
to QUARTIER[3].

lioncel rampant, *lioncel rampant* (Fig. 135).
(1) *no position indicated. FCE*, vv. 8115–16:
trois lionciaux / Rampanz; *Saisnes*, v. 641
(var.): as lionciaus rampans; *Durmart*, vv.
7324–5:

> En l'escu ot deus lionceaz
> De vermel synople rampans;

BA 66: a .iii. lionchiax . . . rampans; *B* 77:
a trois lionseux rampant (*Ba/Bl* 77, see
LIONCEL); 78: ove trois leonseux rampants

(*Bl* 78, see LIONCEL); *D* 102, 107: od sis
leuncels rampans; *SCK*, fol. 91 *c*: trois lionciaus / . . . ranpans. (2) *bend cotised between
lioncels rampant.* See BENDE ENTREALEE DE
DEUS COTICES LIONCEAUS EN RAMPANT ASIS
AU DEHORS. *Syn.*: see BENDE[1] (4) A. (3) *on
a fess a lioncel rampant.* See FESSE A UN
LIONCEL RAMPANT. (4) *on a canton.* See
QUARTIER A UN LIONCEL RAMPANT. (5) *bend
between lioncels rampant.* See BENDE A LION-
CEAUS RAMPANZ. (6) *in the first quarter of
a quarterly field.* See ESQUARTELÉ DE . . .
ET DE . . . A UN LIONCEL RAMPANT. (7)
lioncels rampant in pale (Fig. 89). See LION-
CEAUS RAMPANZ L'UN DESOUS ET L'AUTRE
DESUS. *Syn.*: see LION[1]. *Note:* in *B* 78, the
lioncels rampant are positioned, as is
customary, 2 and 1; the lower lioncel,
however, straddles the line of the party
field.

lioncel rampant couroné, *crowned lioncel
rampant* (Fig. 138). *Sone*, vv. 9868–9:

> Rampans i ot .iii. lïonchiaus,
> S'ot on cascun d'or coronné.

Syn.: see LION COURONÉ.

lioncel rampant el chantel, *in dexter chief
a lioncel rampant.* Saisnes, v. 720 (var.): Au
lioncel ranpant enz el chantel assis. *Syn.*:
EN CHANTEL DE DEVANT UN LION. *Note:*
see EL CHANTEL, *Note.*

lioncel rampant en belic, see EN BELIC,
Note.

lion coleré, *collared lion rampant* (Fig. 136).
C 167: un leon . . . collered (*Cl/Cd* 167, see
LION A UN COLIER). *Syn.*: see LION A UN
COLIER.

lion couroné, *crowned lion rampant* (Fig. 137).
Prise d'Orange, v. 955: A un lïon qui d'or fu
coronéz; *Mort Artu*, p. 269 (var.): a .ii. lions
. . . coronnés; *BA* 181, 200, 238: au lion . . .
coroné; 192: au lion . . . coronné (A:
coroné); 214, 278: a .i. lion . . . coroné;
B 3: ung lion . . . coronné (*Bl* 3: ou un
leon . . . coronné); *Ba/Bc* 37: a un lion . . .
coroné (*B* 37, see LION RAMPANT COURONÉ
EN LA CORNIERE); *CC*, vv. 1165–6: au
lyon / . . . couronné; *CP* 55, 56: a un lion
. . . couronné; *CPA* 164: au lion . . . coroné;
H 11: ou ung leon . . . coronné (*Hg* 11:
a un leon . . . coronné). For other uses, see
ESCUÇON OVE UN LION COURONÉ EN LA
CORNIERE, ESCUÇON OVE UN LION RAMPANT

COURONÉ EN LA CORNIERE. *Syn.*: LIONCEL COURONÉ RAMPANT, LIONCEL RAMPANT COURONÉ, LION RAMPANT COURONÉ, LION RAMPANT ET COURONE, LION RAMPANT ET COURONÉ.

lion couroné a une crois sor l'espaule, *crowned lion rampant shouldering a small cross* (Fig. 140). *C* 10: un lion . . . coronné . . . un crois sur l'espall (W: l'espalle) (*Cl* 10: a un lion . . . coroné . . . a un croyz . . . sur l'espaule; *Cd* 10: a ung lion . . . coroné . . . a .i. crosse . . . sur l'esspaule). *Note*: refers to CROIS³.

lion couroné la coue fourchiee, *crowned lion rampant with a forked tail crossed in saltire* (Fig. 143). *CC*, vv. 1087–90:

Couviers d'unnes armes d'argent
Au lyon de geules: fourchie
Ot la keuwe et bien fu taillie,
Et avoec cou fu couronnés.

Syn.: LION RAMPANT A LA COUE CROISIEE COURONÉ, LION RAMPANT A LA COUE CROISIEE ET COURONÉ. *Note*: refers to COUE FOURCHIEE². Cf. LION LI CHIEF ESTOIT COURONÉ COUE FOURCHIEE (refers to COUE FOURCHIEE¹).

lion couroné rampant, *crowned lion rampant*. See LION RAMPANT COURONÉ.

lion cresté, *crined lion rampant* (Fig. 137). *Saisnes*, v. 1890: Q'est cil au blanc escu au lion d'or cresté? *TA*, v. 1702: Au lïon d'or creté d'argent. *Note*: modern heraldic practice requires that the tincture of the mane be specified, as in *TA*, when it is mentioned.

lion dont dioms la coue double, *lion rampant with a forked tail* (Fig. 146). *K*, vv. 363–4:

Jaune le ot o sis bleus lyons
Dont les coues doubles dioms.

Syn.: see LION RAMPANT A LA COUE FOURCHIEE¹.

lionel, *referring to a shield which is charged with a lion*. Raoul de Cambrai, v. 5871 : l'escu lionnel; *Auberi le Bourgoing*, p. 225, v. 30: l'escu liounel.

lionel passant ou quartier, *ghost word*. See FESSE A UN LIONCEL PASSANT OU QUARTIER.

lion en chief passant, *in chief a lion passant*. See JUMELES UN LION EN CHIEF PASSANT.

lion en le chief passant, *in chief a lion*

passant. See JUMELES ET UN LION EN CHIEF PASSANT.

lion en mi, *lion rampant* (Fig. 135). *Hunbaut*, v. 2661: S'a en mi .i. vermel lion. *Syn.*: see LION¹.

lion entier, *lion rampant* (Fig. 135). *Fouque de Candie*, v. 10553: a un lion entier. *Syn.*: see LION¹. *Note*: refers to ENTIER².

lionet, *lioncel rampant* (Fig. 135). *Rigomer*, vv. 13600–1:

Deseure son escu luisant
Avoit portrais .iii. lionés.

Syn.: see LION¹.

lion et a un colier, *collared lion rampant* (Fig. 136). *CP* 114: a un lion . . . et a un collier. *Syn.*: see LION A UN COLIER.

lion et a une fleur de lis en l'espaule du lion, *lion rampant with a shoulder charged with a fleur-de-lis* (Fig. 149). *CP* 76: a un lion . . . et a une fleur de lis . . . en l'espaule du lion. *Syn.*: LION RAMPANT A UNE FLEUR EN L'ESPAULE DU LION. *Note*: the Vendôme arms feature a chief with a lion rampant over all. See CHIEF¹ (2) B., 2. For an illustration of this positioning for the fleur-de-lis, see *WB* 1147, fig. 76.

lion et la coue fourchiee, *lion rampant with a forked tail* (Fig. 146). *H* 104: ou leon . . . et le cowe fourché (*Hg* 104 [103]: a un leon . . . et la coue fourchee). *Syn.*: see LION RAMPANT A LA COUE FOURCHIEE¹.

lion li chief couroné coue fourchiee, *crowned lion rampant with a forked tail* (Fig. 142). *CC*, vv. 1549–52:

De geules au lion d'argent,
Dont li ciés estoit couronnés,
Moult estoit ricement armés;
Li lyons ot keuwe fourchie.

Syn.: LION RAMPANT COURONÉ O DOUBLE COUE.

lion par mi, *lion rampant* (Fig. 135). *Hunbaut*, v. 2667: au lion par mi. *Syn.*: see LION¹. *Note*: refers to PAR MI¹.

lion passant, *lion passant (i.e. leopard)* (Fig. 162). (1) *no position indicated*. *B* 89: le lion passant; 97: a deux leons . . . passans (*B* 97, see LIEPART); 161: a deux leons passans (*Bl* 161 [165]: od deus leons passants); *C* 130: un leon passant (*Cl* 130: a un leun . . . passant; *Cd* 130: a lion passant); 145: troiz leons passantz (*Cl* 145: a 3 lions . . . passantz; *Cd* 145: a 3 lions passant); *D* 21,

71: od deus leuns passans; 63: a treis leuns passans; *CC*, v. 1542: un lyon passant; *CP* 31, 39: a un lion . . . passant; *H* 65: ou .iii. leons passauntz (*Hg* 65 [66]: od trois leons passans); *K*, vv. 162–3:

> Rouge a passans lyons de blanc
> Trois, de un bastoun bleu surgettez;

v. 180: O treis lyouns passans; v. 379: o deuz . . . lyons passans. (2) *position is indicated by a locution.* See FESSE A UN LION PASSANT, JUMELES ET UN LION EN LE CHIEF PASSANT, JUMELES UN LION EN CHIEF PASSANT, LION PASSANT EN LE CHANTEL DE . . ., LION PASSANT EN CHIEF, LION PASSANT EN LE PRE . . ., LISTES A UN LION PASSANT. (3) *order of items alone indicates position.* A. *on an escutcheon a lion passant.* D 91: od un leun passant. B. *in chief.* CP 61: a un lion . . . passant. *Syn.*: see LIEPART. *Note*: cf. CROIS A DEUS PASSANZ, *Note*. On the confusion between the lion passant (guardant) and the leopard in early heraldry, see LIEPART, *Note*. In modern French heraldry, a lion passant is blazoned *un lion léopardé*; conversely, the locution *un léopard lionné* designates a lion rampant. According to Wagner, *CEMRA*, p. 4, *Bl* and College of Arms MS. 2 G 3 (listed as II. B by Wagner, but now renumbered I. B [see H. S. London, 'Pattee, Patonce, and Formee', *Coat of Arms*, v (1958), no. 33, 363, n. 12a; see also *Aspilogia II*, p. 89]) 'both show the lion of Hugh' le Bygot [i.e. *B* 89] "*embelief*" (i.e. in bend), though it is not so blazoned'. See also *Aspilogia II*, pp. 109; 110 n. 2; 132, note to item 89, where it is pointed out that Walford's Roll also blazons the same charge as a lion passant (see above, *C/Cl/Cd* 130). Prinet's note to *CP* 61 (p. 22 n. 1) cites a seal for Gaucher d'Autrèches in 1302 featuring 'le chef chargé d'un lion issant'; cf., however, *WB* 875: 'le chef chargé à dextre d'un lion passant'.

lion passant a teste de mouton, *lion passant (i.e. leopard) with a lamb's head.* *Cleomadés*, vv. 723–6:

> De gueules et de vert partis
> Ert li escus Bondart le Gris,
> Et i avoit d'or .i. lion
> Passant a teste de mouton.

Note: the leopard is over all.

lion passant couroné, *crowned lion passant (i.e. leopard)* (Fig. 163). *BA* 244, 281: a .ii. lions . . . passans coroné. *Syn.*: LIEPART COURONÉ, LIEPART PASSANT COURONÉ.

lion passant en chief, *in chief a lion passant (i.e. a leopard).* See LION EN CHIEF PASSANT.

lion passant en le chantel de . . ., *in the . . . quarter a lion passant (i.e. a leopard).* See ESQUARTELÉ DE . . . ET DE . . . A UN LION PASSANT EN LE CHANTEL DE . . ., ESQUARTILLIÉ DE . . . ET DE . . . A UN LION PASSANT EN LE CHANTEL DE . . . *Note*: cf. LION PASSANT EN LE PRE . . .

lion passant en le pre . . ., see ESQUARTELÉ DE . . . ET DE . . . UN LION PASSANT EN LE PRE . . .

*lion rampant, *lion rampant* (Fig. 135). (1) *no position indicated.* Very frequent in literary sources, e.g. *Durmart*, v. 6973: a un . . . lion rampant; *Lancelot propre*, v. 427: a ung lion rampant; *TA*, v. 2073: Au lïon rampant; *EO*, v. 2543: a un lyon . . . rampans; *SCK*, fol. 95 *d*: A un lion ranpant; *K*, v. 42: O un lioun rampant. Very common in the rolls, e.g. *BA* 30, 31: a un lion . . . rampant; *B* 12 (*Ba* 12: a une lion rampant; *Bc/Bl* 12, see LION[1]), 164, 170 (*Bl* 164 [168], 170 [174], see LION[1]): ung lion . . . rampant; 18 (*Bl* 18, see LION[1]), 74 (*Ba/Bl* 74, see LION[1]), 98 (*Bl* 98, see LION[1]): ung lion rampant; 48: ove ung leon rampant (*Ba/Bl* 48, see LION[1]); 88: a ung lion . . . rampant (*Bl* 88, see LION[1]); 196 (*Bl* 196 [200], see LION[1]): a ung lion rampant; *C* 11: un lion rampant (*Cl/Cd* 11, see LION[1]); 73: un leon rampant (*Cl* 73: a un lion rampant; *Cd* 73, see LION[1]); 97: 3 leons rampans (W: rampant; MS.: ramp.; *Cl/Cd* 97, see COC); *Hg* 15: a un leon rampant (*H* 15, see LION[1]). (2) *order of items alone indicates position.* A. *over all.* B 17: ung lion rampand; *C* 32: un leon rampant, see CHIEF[1] (2) B. 2. (*Cl* 32: a une lion raumpant, see CHIEF[1] (2) B. 2., *Note*; *Cd* 32: une lion rampant, see CHIEF[1] (2) B. 2., *Note*). B. *a cross cantoned with lions rampant.* *C* 150: 4 leons rampanz (W: rampant; MS.: ramp.), see CROIS[1] (2) (*Cl* 150, see CROIS A LIONS RAMPANZ; *Cd* 150, see CROIS A EGLES). (3) *position indicated by a locution.* See BENDE A LIONS RAMPANZ, BENDE ET LIONS RAMPANZ, CHIEF A LION RAMPANT.

Syn.: see LION[1]. *Note*: on *BA* 30, see LION[1], *Note*. The lion rampant gules in *B* 17 (Marshal arms) straddles the line of a field party per pale or and vert (see *Aspilogia II*, pp. 18, note to item 29; 118, note to item 17; and cf. PARTI DE . . . ET DE . . . EN LONG, *Note*). *D* 3 is largely erased, but according to Greenstreet reads: '. . . [p]orte argent et gules . . . rampans en l'argent et deus toreles (?) . . . en le goules.'

lion rampant a la coue croisiee couroné, *crowned lion rampant with a forked tail crossed in saltire* (Fig. 143). *C* 61: un leon rampant . . . la cowe croisé coronné (*Cl* 61: a un leon rampant . . . a la cowe croysé coroné; *Cd* 61: a un lion . . . a la cowe crossé coroné); 78: un leon rampant . . . la cowe croyzé coronné (*Cl*/*Cd* 78, see LION RAMPANT A LA COUE CROISIEE ET COURONÉ). *Syn.*: see LION COURONÉ LA COUE FOURCHIEE.

lion rampant a la coue croisiee et couroné, *crowned lion rampant with a forked tail crossed in saltire* (Fig. 143). *Cl* 78: a un lion . . . rampant a la bowe [*sic*] croyzé e coronee (*C* 78, see LION RAMPANT A LA COUE CROISIEE COURONÉ; *Cd* 78: a lion . . . rampant a la quwe croysé e coroné). *Syn.*: see LION COURONÉ A LA COUE FOURCHIEE. *Note*: Prinet *WR*, p. 236: 'c'est la queue qui est croisée (fourchée et passée en sautoir), et c'est le lion qui est couronné.'

lion rampant a la coue fourchiee[1], *lion rampant with a forked tail* (Fig. 146). *B* 4: ung leon rampand . . . le cowe fourchee (*Ba*/*Bb*/*Bc*/*Bl* 4, see LION A LA COUE FOURCHIEE[1]); *C* 149: un leon rampant . . . a la queue fourché (*Cl* 149: a un liun . . . raumpant a la cowe furché; *Cd* 149: a lion rampant a la quewe forché). *Syn.*: LION A LA COUE FOURCHIEE[1], LION DONT DIOMS LA COUE DOUBLE, LION ET LA COUE FOURCHIEE, LION RAMPANT DONT LA COWE S'ESPANT EN DOUBLE, LION RAMPANT ET LA COUE FOURCHIEE, LION RAMPANT OD LA COUE FOURCHIEE[1]. *Note*: in his edition of College of Arms MS. L. 14, vol. i (Glover's Roll), Armytage provides the following reading for *B* 4: 'ung leon rampand . . . le cowe le fourchee'; I have provided the reading in Wagner, *CEMRA*, p. 5.

lion rampant a la coue fourchiee[2], *lion rampant with a forked tail crossed in saltire*

(Fig. 147). *BA* 22: a .i. lion . . . rampant a la keue forkie; 23: au lion . . . rampant a la keu forqie; 26: au lion . . . rampant . . . a la keue forkie; *C* 178: un leon rampant . . . la (W: le) cowe furché (*Cl* 178: a une bende [*sic*] . . . a la cowe furché). *Syn.*: LIEPART RAMPANT A LA COUE FOURCHIEE, LIEPART RAMPANT OVE LA COUE FOURCHIEE, LION A LA COUE FOURCHIEE[2], LION A LA COUE FOURCHIEE EN SOM, LION A LA COUE FOURCHUE, LION RAMPANT OD LA COUE FOURCHIEE[2]. *Note*: Prinet *WR*, p. 255 (apropos of *bende* in *Cl* 178 [183]): 'c'est "un lion" qu'il faut lire'; see also *Aspilogia II*, p. 203, note to item 183. Rather than emend *a une bende* to *a un leon*, however, I have preferred to follow *C* 178, which provides the reading cited above, and list this item here instead of s.v. LION A LA COUE FOURCHIEE[2].

lion rampant amont, *lion rampant* (Fig. 135). *SCU*, fol. 197 *b*:

> A un lyon, mien escïent,
> Rampant amont et trestout noir.

Syn.: see LION[1].

lion rampant a un colier, *collared lion rampant* (Fig. 136). *Hg* 88 [86]: a un leon rampant . . . a un color (*H* 88, see LION RAMPANT OD UN COLIER). *Syn.*: see LION A UN COLIER.

lion rampant a une fleur en l'espaule du lion, *lion rampant with a shoulder charged with a fleur-de-lis* (Fig. 149). *BA* 128: a .i. lion . . . rampant a une fleur de lis en l'espaule du lion. *Syn.*: LION ET A UNE FLEUR DE LIS EN L'ESPAULE DU LION.

lion rampant contremont, *lion rampant* (Fig. 135). *Guillaume de Dole*, v. 70: Au lïon rampant contremont; *Escanor*, vv. 5001–5:

> Ses compainz r'avoit armes beles,
> Toutes blanches auques noveles;
> Mais sor le blanc par conoissance
> Ot .iii. lionz d'une samblance
> De geules rampanz contremont.

Syn.: see LION[1].

lion rampant couroné, *crowned lion rampant* (Fig. 138). *Artus*, p. 67: au lion rampant coroné; p. 307: a un lion rampant coroné; *BA* 17, 158: a .i. lion . . . rampant coroné; 73: au lion . . . rampant coroné; 52: au lion . . . rampant coronné; 64: a .i. lion . . . rampant coronné; 239: a .i. lion

... coronné (A: coroné) ... rampant; 277, 293: a .iii. lions ... rampant (A, in both cases: rampans); 285: au lion ... rampant coronné (A: coroné); *C* 43 (*Cl* 43: a un liun raumpant ... coronee; *Cd* 43: a lion rampant ... crounnet), 59 (*Cl* 59: a une leon ... rampant coroné; *Cd* 59: a ... lion ... rampant coroné): un leon rampant ... coronné; 99: un leon rampant ... coronné (*Cl*/*Cd* 99: a un lion raumpant ... coroné); *D* 33, 49, 77: a un leun rampant ... coroné; 59: a treis leuns rampans ... coroné; *H* 8: ung leon rampaunt ... coronné (*Hg* 8 [7]: a un leon rampant ... coronné). *Syn.*: see LION COURONÉ.

lion rampant couroné a la langue a une manche en la geule du lion a une espee au pong et au helt qui tranche le lion par mi, *crowned lion rampant langued grasping a maunch in its mouth with a sword pommelled and hilted cutting the lion in half* (Fig. 139). *BA* 284: a .i. lion rampant ... coroné ... a le (A: la) langhe ... a une manche ... en le geule du lyon (A: en la goule de lyon) a une espee ... au pong et au heurt ... quy trenche le lion par my. *Note*: Tranchelion arms. See TRANCHIER.

lion rampant couroné en la corniere, *crowned lion rampant in sinister chief.* See ESCUÇON OVE UN LION RAMPANT COURONÉ EN LA CORNIERE.

lion rampant couroné estant sus une mote, *crowned lion rampant statant on a mount* (Fig. 141). *Cl* 49: a une lion ... coroné ... estant sus une mote (*C* 49, see LION RAMPANT COURONÉ SUS UNE MOTE: *Cd* 49: a une lyon ... coroné ... estant sus une mote). *Syn.*: LION RAMPANT COURONÉ SUS UNE MOTE.

lion rampant couroné o double coue, *crowned lion rampant with a forked tail* (Fig. 142). *K*, vv. 836–7:

> En inde ot blanc lyon rampant,
> Couronné de or, o double coue.

Syn.: LION LI CHIEF COURONÉ COUE FOURCHIEE.

lion rampant couroné sus une mote, *crowned lion rampant statant on a mount* (Fig. 141). *C* 49: un leon rampant ... coronné sous un mote (W: mole) (*Cl*/*Cd* 49, see LION RAMPANT COURONÉ ESTANT SUS UNE MOTE). *Syn.*: LION RAMPANT COURONÉ ESTANT SUS UNE MOTE.

lion rampant dont la coue en double s'espant, *lion rampant with a forked tail.* See LION RAMPANT DONT LA COUE S'ESPANT EN DOUBLE.

lion rampant dont la coue s'espant en double, *lion rampant with a forked tail* (Fig. 146). *K*, vv. 335–6:

> Jaune, o un noir lyoun rampant,
> Dont la coue en double se espant.

Syn.: see LION RAMPANT A LA COUE FOURCHIEE[1]. *Note*: refers to COUE FOURCHIEE[1].

lion rampant et courone, *crowned lion rampant* (Fig. 138). Sone, vv. 14937–9:

> Escu d'or au lÿon rampant.
> Et si avoit couronne grant,
> Qui de riches geules estoit.

Syn.: see LION COURONÉ.

lion rampant et couroné, *crowned lion rampant* (Fig. 138). *K*, vv. 128–9:

> O un lyoun de argent en sable
> Rampant, e de or fin couronné.

Syn.: see LION COURONÉ.

lion rampant et en les espaules du lion une quintefeuille, *lion rampant with a shoulder charged with a cinquefoil* (Fig. 148). *H* 46: ou ung leon raumpantt ... et en les espaules (G: le sespaules) du lyon ung quintfoil (*Hg* 46 [47]: a un leon rampant ... en les espaules del leon un quintefoile).

lion rampant et la coue fourchiee, *lion rampant with a forked tail* (Fig. 146). *H* 66: ou ung leon rampaunt ... e la cowe fourché (*Hg* 66, see LION RAMPANT OD LA COUE FOURCHIEE[1]). *Syn.*: see LION RAMPANT A LA COUE FOURCHIEE[1]. *Note*: refers to COUE FOURCHIEE[1].

lion rampant od la coue fourchiee[1], *lion rampant with a forked tail* (Fig. 146). *D* 123: a un leun rampant ... od la cue furché; *Hg* 66 [67]: a un leon rampant ... od la coue fourché (*H* 66, see LION RAMPANT ET LA COUE FOURCHIEE); Brewes [31]: a un leon rampant ... od la coue forchee. *Syn.*: see LION RAMPANT A LA COUE FOURCHIEE[1]. *Note*: refers to COUE FOURCHIEE[1].

lion rampant od la coue fourchiee[2], *lion rampant with a forked tail crossed in saltire* (Fig. 147). *D* 22: a un leun rampant ... od la couwe furché. *Syn.*: see LION RAMPANT A LA COUE FOURCHIEE[2]. *Note*: refers to COUE FOURCHIEE[2].

lion rampant od un colier, *collared lion rampant* (Fig. 136). *H* 88: o le leon ramphaunt . . . od ung collour (*Hg* 88, see LION RAMPANT A UN COLIER). *Syn.*: see LION A UN COLIER.

lion rampant od une hache, *lion rampant holding an axe in its paws* (Fig. 145). *D* 13: a un leun rampant . . . od une hache. *Note*: the Royal Arms of Norway since 1283; see *WB* 1275 (Plate VIII). On the date of these arms, see P. Warming, 'L'apparition de la hache dans les armes de Norvège', *Archivum Heraldicum*, lxviii (1954), 38-40; *Aspilogia II*, p. 35, note to item 100.

lion recoupé, *demi-lion rampant* (Fig. 144). *C* 146: un leun recoupé (*Cl/Cd* 146; see CHIEF A UN LION RECOUPÉ). For another use, see CHIEF A UN LION RECOUPÉ. *Syn.*: see DEMI LION. *Note*: the demi-lion is on the chief; see CHIEF[1] (2) B. 3.

lions adossés, *lions rampant addorsed* (Fig. 150). *BA* 154: a .ii. lions . . . adossés. *Syn.*: LIONS RAMPANZ DOS A DOS. *Note*: lions rampant addorsed and combattant originated in Oriental art where they were primitively part of the Tree of Life motif. See Emile Mâle, *L'Art religieux du XIIe siècle en France* (Paris, 1928), chapter ix, part IV.

lions de l'un et l'autre, *lions passant guardant (i.e. leopards) counterchanged.* See ESQUARTELÉ DE . . . ET DE . . . LIONS DE L'UN ET L'AUTRE. *Syn.*: see LIEPARZ DE L'UN EN L'AUTRE.

lions es quatre quartiers, *cross cantoned with lions rampant.* *CP* 20: a quatre lions . . . es quatre quartiers, see CROIS[1] (2). *Syn.*: see CROIS[1] (2).

lions rampanz dos a dos, *lions rampant addorsed* (Fig. 150). *D* 44: a deus leuns rampans . . . dos a dos. *Syn.*: LIONS ADOSSÉS.

lions rampanz en le . . ., see EN L'ARGENT.

lions rampanz on the quarters of the field, *cross cantoned with lions rampant.* Chevreuse (addition in *Cd* [110]); the complete blazon reads as follows: N. de Cheverouse, ar. a crosse g. .iiii. lions rampant on the + of the feld. *Syn.*: see CROIS[1] (2). *Note*: *Aspilogia II*, p. 189, note to item 110, interprets the latter part of the blazon as follows: 'on the cross of the field', and provides the following comment: 'The latter coat, with the lions on

instead of beside the cross, is otherwise unknown.'

lis, see FLEUR DE LIS, FLEURETE DE LIS.

liste[1], *cotice, used in a pair, one on either side of a bend* (Fig. 61). See LIONCEAUS A UNE BENDE LES LISTES. For another use, see LISTE FLEURETEE; cf. also BENDE A LISTES. *Syn.*: see COTICE (1); cf. also COTICIÉ.

liste[2], *bars gemelles* (Fig. 56). See LISTES A UN LIEPART, LISTES A UN LION PASSANT. *Syn.*: see JUMELES[1]. *Note*: see CHIEF[2], *Note*. Each *liste* refers to a pair of bars gemelles, i.e. counts as two. Cf. JUMEAUS[2] and see JUMELES[2], *Note*.

liste[3], *double cotice* (Fig. 83). See FESSE A DEUS LISTES, FESSE OD DEUS LISTES. *Syn.*: JUMEAUS[1] (4).

liste[4], *bordure* (Fig. 114). *FCE*, v. 8465: Qui a l'escu au listes d'or. *Syn.*: see BORDURE[1]. *Note*: Foulet, *Glossary of the First Continuation*, does not mention this term but defines the related expression *liter* as 'tout bordé d'or' (p. 167); see LISTÉ. For the corresponding verse in MS. T of the same work (*FCT*, v. 4877), see BORDÉ[1]. For non-heraldic uses of OFr. *listé* in descriptions of shields, consult Schirling, pp. 23-4; Bouly de Lesdain, p. 204.

listé, *with a bordure (or stripe).* *FCE*, v. 8122: tot lité d'or; *TA*, v. 1160: A .i. faus escucel listé; vv. 1500, 2071: escu listé. *Syn.*: see BORDÉ[1]. *Note*: mention is made of OFr. *listé* as early as the *Roland* (e.g. v. 3150: 'D'or est la bucle e de cristal listet') where it appears that a border was intended. Foulet, *Glossary of the First Continuation*, p. 167, defines *liter* as 'tout bordé d'or'. This is the meaning ascribed by Bouly de Lesdain to several early examples of *escu listé* and *targe listee* which he does not, however, consider to be heraldic shields: 'Cette liste ne paraît être autre chose qu'une armature métallique entourant l'écu pour en maintenir les ais; quelques sceaux au XIIe siècle montrent des écus dont cette bordure forme l'unique ornementation.' See also Schirling, pp. 23-4. Goddard, p. 154, on the other hand, provides early examples of OFr. *listé* in descriptions of wearing-apparel where the meaning is clearly 'striped' and our examples of *liste* in its various acceptations in classic blazon also have this sense; cf.

DE BENDES PAR MI LISTÉ, LISTÉ DE . . . ET DE . . .

listeaus un desous et l'autre desor, *cotices, one above and the other below* (Fig. 82). See FESSE A DEUS LISTEAUS UN DESOUS ET L'AUTRE DESOR. *Syn.*: see COTICE (1); cf. also COTICIÉ. *Note*: the singular of OFr. *listeaus* is *listel*.

listé de bendes par mi, see DE BENDES PAR MI LISTÉ.

listé de . . . et de . . ., *traversed by multiple stripes. Fouque de Candie*, v. 5521: Et li escuz d'azur et d'or listez; *TA*, vv. 886–7:

> A .i. faus escucel listé
> D'avarice et d'ipocreisie.

Syn.: see A BENDES BENDÉ.

liste fleuretee, *cotice ornamented with fleurs-de-lis* (Fig. 77). See BENDE A LISTES FLEURE-TEES. *Note*: refers to FLEURETÉ[2] and LISTE[1]. Cf. BENDE A LISTES.

listel, *cotice, used in a pair, one on either side of a bend or a fess.* See BENDE A DEUS LISTEAUS[1], BENDE A DEUS LISTEAUS[2], BENDE OU FLEURETES OU DEUS LISTEAUS. *Syn.*: see COTICE (1); cf. also COTICIÉ. *Note*: LISTEL is the only term used to designate a *fess* cotised; see BENDE A DEUS LISTEAUS[2]. All other terms refer to a *bend* cotised (see COTICE [1]). For a fess double-cotised, see FESSE A DEUS LISTES, FESSE ENTRE DEUS JUMEAUS, FESSE OD DEUS LISTES.

listes a un liepart, *bars gemelles, in chief a leopard.* The complete blazon reads as follows: *D* 93: Munsire Johan Tregoz, l'escu d'or od deus listes de gules a un leopard de gules. *Syn.*: see JUMEAUS EN LE CHIEF UN LIEPART PASSANT, JUMELES ET UN LIEPART EN CHIEF, JUMELES UN LION EN CHIEF PASSANT, LIEPART EN LE CHIEF A DEUS JUMELES, LISTES A UN LION PASSANT. *Note*: refers to LISTE[2], but see JUMELES[2], *Note*.

listes a un lion passant, *bars gemelles, in chief a lion passant (i.e. a leopard).* The complete blazon reads as follows. *D* 181: Munsire Henri Tregoz, l'escu d'azur od deus lystes d'or a un leun passant d'or. *Syn.*: see LISTES A UN LIEPART. *Note*: refers to LISTE[2], but see JUMELES[2], *Note*.

lité, see LISTÉ.

loier, *strap, bend* (Fig. 60). *TA*, v. 1000: A .i. loier de glouternie. *Syn.*: see BENDE[1]. *Note*: see COTICE, *Note*.

l'on, see DES COURONES TANT QUE L'ON I POUVOIT METRE.

lonc, long, see DE LONC, DE LONC EN LONC, EN LONC.

l'or, see SOR L'OR.

loriol, see ORIOL.

losenge[1], *lozenge* (Fig. 86). *BA* 135, 169: a .x. losenges; *Ba* 21: a sept losenges (*B/Bl* 21, see MASCLÉ DE . . . ET DE . . .[1]; *Bb* 21, see MASCLE[1]; *Bc* 21, see LOSENGIÉ DE . . . ET DE . . .[1]); *CP* 34: a dix losanges; 52: a dix losenges. For other uses, see A LOSENGES, A LOSENGES DE . . . ET DE . . . LOSENGIÉ, FAUSE LOSENGE, FESSE OD UNE LOSENGE, LOSENGE PERCIEE, LOSENGES EN LA CROIS. *Syn.*: MASCLE[1]. *Note*: compare, for size, GRAIN. Lozenges are frequently conjoined. For early examples of isolated lozenges, however, see Félix Brassart, 'Le blason de Lalaing', *Souvenirs de la Flandre wallonne*, viii (1877–8), 36–8; see also Robert of Stockport's seal *c.* 1260, Blair, Plate VIII *m.* According to *BW*[4], OFr. *losenge* was first used in heraldry and is derived from Germanic **lausa* 'flagstone'. The Modern French word is feminine when used in a heraldic sense. As a masculine geometrical term, it is first attested in the fourteenth century. On the later distinction between lozenge and fusil, consult Roger F. Pye, 'A Return to First Principles. II. Lozenge and Fusil', *Coat of Arms*, vii (1962), 60–2. See also letters to the editor in vii (1962), 173, and vii (1963), 259. For another word for lozenge in Matthew Paris (*quarterium*), see MASCLÉ DE . . . ET DE . . .[1].

losenge[2], *mascle (voided lozenge)* (Fig. 87). *H* 58: ou .vii. losengez (G: lozenges; *Hg* 58 [60], see LOSENGE PERCIEE). *Syn.*: see FAUSE LOSENGE. *Note*: the mascles in the arms of William de Ferrers of Groby appear on his seal in 1301 (*Barons' Letter*, p. 113); see also MASCLE VUIDIEE DU CHAMP (*K*, v. 471). Matthew Paris blazons the masculy shield of the Earl of Winchester as 'Scutum gules, losenges d'or' (Pusikan, p. 141), a use corresponding, therefore, with LOSENGE[2]. His description of the shield borne by the Earl of Kent, however, involves LOSENGE[1]. See MASCLÉ DE . . . ET DE . . .[1], *Note*.

losenge perciee, *mascle (voided lozenge)* (Fig.

87). (1) *number is specified*. D 43: od treis losenges percé. (2) *number is not specified*. See OD LES LOSENGES PERCIEES, OD LOSENGES PERCIEES. *Syn.*: see FAUSE LOSENGE. *Note*: on these arms (i.e. D 43, Bautersem), see *Aspilogia II*, p. 203, note to item 184.

losenges a la crois, *ghost word*. See LOSENGES EN LA CROIS.

losenges en la crois, *lozenges conjoined in cross* (Fig. 105). BA 133: a .vi. lozenges . . . en le crois (A: a le croix). *Syn.*: see CROIS ENDENTEE[1].

losenge vuidiee, *mascle* (Fig. 87). The complete blazon reads as follows: P 59: Le conte de Wynchestre porte de goules ove sept losenges d'or voidés. *Syn.*: see FAUSE LOSENGE. *Note*: corresponds to B 8 (see MASCLE VUIDIEE DU CHAMP).

losengié a losenges de . . . et de . . ., see A LOSENGES DE . . . ET DE . . . LOSENGIÉ.

losengié de . . . et de . . .[1], *lozengy* (Fig. 16). *Durmart*, v. 8452: De . . . et de . . . losengie; v. 8463: Tot cil as escus losengiés; *TA*, vv. 720–1: losengiees / De . . . et de . . .; vv. 814–15: losengiee / De . . . et de . . .; v. 839: Losengié de fauses noveles; vv. 926–7: losengiez . . . / De . . . et de . . .; vv. 1550–1: losengié / De . . . et de . . .; vv. 1564–5: Losengié de . . . / Et de . . .; vv. 1644–5: losengiez / De . . . et de . . .; v. 1712: Losengié de veraie gloire; v. 2059: cel losengié; *BA* 204: lozengié de . . . et de . . . (A: losengie); 245: losengié de . . . et de . . . (A: lozengie); *Bc* 21: losengés de . . . e de . . . (*B/Bl* 21, see MASCLÉ DE . . . ET DE . . .[1]; *Ba* 21, see LOSENGE[1]; *Bb* 21, see MASCLE[1]); *TC*, v. 2118: l'escu losengié; *CC*, vv. 1199–1200: Un escut portoit losengiet / D'or et de geules; *Sone*, vv. 14287–8: De couvretures losengies / De noir et de blanc entaillies; v. 14443: Ce losengier. *Syn.*: A LOSENGES, A LOSENGES DE . . . ET DE . . . LOSENGIÉ, BENDES LOSENGIEES DE . . . ET DE . . ., FESSIÉ DE . . . ET DE . . . ENDENTÉ DE L'UN A L'AUTRE, MASCLÉ DE . . . ET DE . . .[2]. *Note*: cf. BENDÉ DE . . . ET DE . . . ENDENTÉ L'UN EN L'AUTRE.

losengié de . . . et de . . .[2], *ghost word*. See FESSE LOSENGIEE.

loup, *wolf*. See LEU.

lozence, *ghost word*. See CHARBOUCLE BESANCIÉ.

lucet, *pike* (Fig. 214). B 108: a trois lucies (*Bl* 108 [112]: od trois lucés). *Syn.*: see LUZ. *Note*: for P 111 (= B 108), see LUCET AIRIANT. OFr. *lucet* is a diminutive of *luz*; see *FEW*, v. 436, s.v. *lucius*. The heraldic pike is depicted as facing upwards.

lucet airiant, *pike* (Fig. 214). The complete blazon reads as follows: P 111: Richard Lucy port de goules ove trois lucés ayrantz d'argent. *Syn.*: see LUZ. *Note*: corresponds to B 108 (see LUCET). Cf. BARS SINANZ. Boutell, p. 79, lists *hauriant* as one of the terms used to denote the position of various fish and defines it as follows: 'palewise with the heads upwards, as if rising to the surface for breathing'. The earliest attestation for the word in the *OED* (v. 122) is 1572 and it is said to be derived from Lat. *haurientem* < *haurire* 'to draw (water, etc.)'. Orthographical variants cited by the *OED* include *haurient, hariant, hauriant*, and *eirant*, the latter spelling said to be erroneous but illustrated by an example dated 1587: 'charged with foure leuses heads eirant'. The *MED*, Part E–F, p. 45, s.v. *eirond*, cites the following example from Randle Holme's Book (*c.* 1460; see *CEMRA*, pp. 101–2): 'A beryth synobyll .vi. loucys eyronde of sylvyr' and provides this explanation in the wake of the *OED*: 'Ultimately from L. *haurient*—drinking, swallowing (OD *haurient*); probably from AF *heiraunt*, a secondary variant of *hoiraunt*'. Tobler–Lommatzsch, ii. 255, however, lists the following use, drawn from the mid-fourteenth-century French crusade epic *Baudouin de Sebourg* (ii. 339, vv. 976–7), of the Middle French verb *airier* 'to come out in the air' (doubtless formed on OFr. *air* 'air'):

Adés gaite Gaufroi pour savoir s'il ira
Airier le corps de lui, ou s'il s'eslongera.

This French verb, then, not Lat. *haurire*, explains the heraldic term *airiant*. The *h* in the modern English term, on the other hand, may have resulted from an attempt to link this word with the presumed Latin source; for another possible example of false learned etymology, cf. *crois patee* (see CROIS PATEE ET PERCIEE, *Note*).

l'un contre l'autre, *facing each other* (Fig. 165). See LIONCEAUS PASSANZ L'UN CONTRE L'AUTRE EN CHIEF.

l'un desous et l'autre desus, *one below, the other above* (*i.e. in pale*) (Fig. 89). See LIONCEAUS RAMPANZ L'UN DESOUS ET L'AUTRE DESUS. *Note:* cf. EN LONC[1] (per pale), UN DESOUS ET L'AUTRE DESOR.

l'un en l'autre, *pleonasm.* See BENDÉ DE . . . ET DE . . . ENDENTÉ L'UN EN L'AUTRE, PARTI DE . . . ET DE . . . L'UN EN L'AUTRE. *Syn.:* see DE L'UN EN L'AUTRE[2].

lunete, *crescent* (Fig. 224). *Gerbert's Continuation,* v. 4177: A trois lunetes. *Syn.:* CROISSANT[1]. *Note:* cf. the canting arms of Roger de Cressy in Matthew Paris (Pusikan, p. 147: 'Scutum aureum, lune [P: lunae] de gules'): the painted shield shows three crescents gules. In modern French heraldry, *lunel* 'small moon' is an arrangement of four crescents in the form of a quatrefoil, *lune* is a crescent with a human profile, and *pleine lune* is a full moon (see Veyrin-Forrer, p. 97).

lupart, see LIEPART.

luz, *pike* (Fig. 214). *C* 108: troiz luz (*Cl* 108: a treis luz; *Cd* 108: a 3 luz); *D* 79, 99: od treis luz. *Syn.:* LUCET, LUCET AIRIANT. *Note:* on the etymology of OFr. *luz*, see *FEW,* v. 436, s.v. *lucius*; Schwan–Behrens, *Grammaire de l'ancien français,* paragraphs 70, 198. The fish is discussed in *La Bataille de Caresme et de Charnage,* ed. G. Lozinski, p. 155, no. 92, s.v. *lus, luz.*

lytteg, see LISTEL.

mace, *ghost word.* See MANCHE.

macle, maclé de . . . et de . . ., see MASCLE, MASCLÉ DE . . . ET DE . . .

madame sainte Marie, *the Virgin* (Fig. 131). *Brut,* vv. 9293–6:

Dedenz l'escu fu par maistrie
De ma dame sainte Marie
Purtraite e peinte la semblance,
Pur enur e pur remembrance.

Syn.: NOSTRE DAME. *Note:* King Arthur's arms; see Introduction.

Mahomet, *Mohammed* (*here regarded as a pagan deity*). *Gaufrey,* vv. 3011–12:

Va ferir Malachar en la targe doree,
Ou l'image Mahom estoit d'or painturee.

Note: on this deity, consult W. W. Comfort, 'The Saracens', *PMLA,* lv (1940), 640, and note 45.

Mahomet el senestre quartier, *in sinister chief Mohammed* (*here regarded as a pagan deity*). *Chétifs,* p. 276: Mahomes estoit pains el senestre quartier.

maillet, *hammer, mallet* (Fig. 262). *CP* 62: a trois maillés; *CPA* 62: a .iii. maillets. *Syn.:* MARTEL.

main, *hand.* See MEIN.

mais, see MES.

malet, *mullet.* See MOLET.

manche[1], *maunch* (Fig. 269). *Fouque de Candie,* v. 2099: une manche; vv. 10527, 10949: .ii. manches; *Durmart,* v. 8532: le . . . manche; *TA,* v. 1565: a une manche; v. 2070: Et celi qui porte la manche; *BA* 175: a une mance (A: mace); 255: a .i. manche; *B* 62: ou ung manche (*Ba* 62: a la manche; *Bb* 62: a manche; *Bc* 62: a la manche; *Bl* 62: ove le manche); 91 (*Bl* 91: ove le maunche), 146 (*Bl* 146 [150]: ove une manche): ung manche; 120: a la manche (*Bl* 120 [124]: od la manche); Creke, *Cl* [166]: a une manche, *Cd*: a une mawnche; *D* 125: od une manche; *Escanor,* v. 4086: sour le blanc la mance vermeille; v. 4123: a une mance toute blanche; *H* 34: od .iii. maunches (*Hg* 34 [35]: od la maunche); 41 (*Hg* 41 [42]: od la maunche), 70 (*Hg* 70 [71]: od la manche): ou la maunche; 64 (*Hg* 64 [65]: od la maunche): ou le (G: la) maunche; 41, 70: ou la maunche; 64: ou le (G: la) maunche; *K,* v. 376: une manche; v. 420: o la . . . manche; v. 550: o la manche; v. 560: la manche. *Note:* on the tincture of the maunch in *B/Ba/Bb/Bc/Bl* 62 (argent in *B* 62, ermine in the other copies), consult *CEMRA,* p. 5; *Aspilogia II,* p. 126, note to item 62 ('ermine . . . is correct'). Gough H, p. 136, note to item 35: '[*H* 34] has 3 maunches, which is an error.' On the significance of the arms of Robert de Tony 'ki bien signe / Ke il est du Chevaler au Cigne' (*K,* vv. 421–2), see *Aspilogia II,* p. 25, note to item 57; Brault K, pp. 16–18. The Tony arms appear among the Matthew Paris Shields and are blazoned in the following terms: 'Scutum d'or, manche de gules' (Pusikan, p. 146). The heraldic maunch is a curious relic of a twelfth-century fashion in long, detachable sleeves. See Goddard, pp. 11–13, 156–63. There are many allusions in medieval romances to knights bearing or displaying a damsel's sleeve as a love token, e.g. *Erec*, vv. 2084–7:

> La ot tante vermoille ansaigne,
> Et tante guinple et tante *manche*,
> Et tante bloe, et tante blanche,
> Qui par amors furent donees.

Other early examples are provided by Adam-Even, '*Roman de Troie*', p. 21. In *Sone*, sleeves are attached to five lances by Countess Ydain, one white (v. 10725), one green (v. 10731), one blue (v. 10733: *ynde*), one red (v. 10735: *viermeille*), and one gold (v. 10737). The symbolism of these tinctures is explained in vv. 10938–41, 10979–88, 11011–19, 11043–51, and 11082–11115, respectively, e.g. blue: 'c'est emperïaus coulour' (v. 11015). In the *Chevalier à la Manche*, the hero asks his lady for a favour ('U guimple u mance, pour porter / En armes pour moi conforter', vv. 135–6) and she accedes to his request by giving him a white sleeve. He attaches it to his helmet but also begins carrying a shield 'De geules a mances d'argent' (vv. 272, 1633). Throughout the poem, he is thereafter referred to as the Knight of the Maunch. The shield is specifically mentioned in vv. 537, 703, and 1036–7 ('L'escu as mances'; 'Cieus qui portoit l'escu as mances'; 'escu / A le mance'). Cf. CHAPEL DE ROSES. On this charge in heraldry, which in spite of its romantic history and graceful design is considered a 'monstrosity' by certain persons, see George H. Viner, 'The Maunch', *Coat of Arms*, i (1950), 14; see also letters to the editor from E. A. Scholes, p. 102, G. R. Bellew and R. C. Gale, p. 136, and B. C. Trappes-Lomax, i (1951), 175.

manche², *sleeve* (Fig. 131). See ESCHARBOUCLE ENTRE EVANGILES EN DEUS MANCHES DE LA CHEMISE NOSTRE DAME.

manche en la geule du lion, *lion rampant grasping a maunch in its mouth*. See LION RAMPANT COURONÉ A LA LANGUE A UNE MANCHE EN LA GEULE DU LION A UNE ESPEE AU PONG ET AU HELT QUI TRANCHE LE LION PAR MI.

maniere, see D'UNE MANIERE.

marel, see MARTEL.

Marie, see MADAME SAINTE MARIE.

marlete, *martlet*. See MERLETE.

marteaus, *hammers, mallets*. See MARTEL.

martel, *hammer, mallet* (Fig. 262). (1) *no position indicated*. C 124: trois martells (*Cl* 124: a treis martelle; *Cd* 124: a 3 marels); *CP* 83: a trois marteaus. (2) *on a chief*. See CHIEF A UN MARTEL. *Syn.*: MAILLET.

martel en belic, *hammer bendwise* (Fig. 263). See CHIEF A UN MARTEL EN BELIC.

mascle¹, *lozenge* (Fig. 86). *Bb* 21: 7 mascles (*B/Bl* 21, see MASCLÉ DE . . . ET DE . . .¹; *Ba* 21, see LOSENGE¹; *Bc* 21, see LOSENGIÉ DE . . . ET DE . . .¹). For another use, see MASCLE VUIDIEE DU CHAMP. *Syn.*: LOSENGE¹. *Note*: OFr. *mascle*, *macle* (< Germanic **maskila*, diminutive of **maska* 'mesh') is attested at the end of the thirteenth century with the meaning 'mesh (of a fishnet), link (of chain mail)'. See Godefroy, v. 60; *FEW*, xvi. 540, s.v. **maskila*.

mascle², *mascle (voided lozenge)* (Fig. 87). *Bb* 8: a set mascles (*B* 8, see MASCLE VUIDIEE DU CHAMP; *Ba/Bl* 8, see FAUSE LOSENGE). *Syn.*: see FAUSE LOSENGE.

masclé de . . . et de . . .¹, *lozengy* (Fig. 16). *B* 21: masculee . . . et de . . . (*Ba* 21, see LOSENGE¹; *Bb* 21, see MASCLE¹; *Bc* 21, see LOSENGIÉ DE . . . ET DE . . .¹; *Bl* 21: masclee de . . . et de . . .); 94 (*Bl* 94: masclee de . . . et de . . .), 173 (*Bl* 173 [177]: masclé de . . . et de . . .): masculé de . . . et de . . .; 132: masculy de . . . et de . . . (*Bl* 132 [136]: masclé de . . . et de . . .); *Bl* 133 [137]: masclé de . . . et de . . .; *C* 144: masculee de . . . et de . . . (*Cl* 144: maclé de . . . et de . . .; *Cd* 144: masclé de . . . e de . . .); *D* 126: masclé de . . . et de . . .; *H* 93: masclé de . . . et de . . . (*Hg* 93 [92]: mascli [*sic*] de . . . et de . . .); *M* 22: masklee de . . . et de . . .; *K*, v. 272, 775, 783: masclé de . . . e de . . . *Syn.*: see LOSENGIÉ DE . . . ET DE . . .¹. *Note*: this term later came to mean masculy, i.e. mascles conjoined so as to form a field of voided lozenges, and, consequently, a synonym of POUDRÉ A FAUSES LOSENGES. During this period, as a matter of fact, the mascle often appears as part of a masculy field; see FAUSE LOSENGE and its synonyms and cf. OD LES LOSENGES PERCIEES, OD LOSENGES PERCIEES. On the meaning here, consult Prinet WR, p. 236, and Prinet K, pp. 350–1. Matthew Paris's blazon of the arms of the Earl of Kent (Pusikan, pp. 142–

3: 'Losenga media maskele, de albo et azuro, alia quarteria de gules') has long puzzled scholars; see, for example, *Aspilogia II*, p. 7 ('incomprehensible') and p. 39, note to item 16 ('unintelligible'); cf. also FESSE ENGRESLEE, *Note*. The confusion stems from the word *maskele* which, when associated with *masclé de . . . et de . . .* in such blazons as *B* 21: 'Le conte de Kent, masculee verree et de goules', leads us to believe that the two expressions are identical. *Maskele* in Matthew Paris is neither 'lozengy' nor 'masculy', however, but a derivative of Lat. *maculare* (> Fr. *maculer*) 'to spot'. If we eliminate the first comma, the meaning of Matthew Paris's blazon becomes clear: 'the middle lozenges spotted (i.e. to resemble the fur = vair) argent and azure, the other lozenges (*quarteria*) gules'. Though the 'middle lozenges' are left blank on the accompanying shield (cf. Hauptmann, p. 26, no. 42; Table 2, fig. 25; *Aspilogia II*, p. 39, note to item 16), two renderings of the same arms in the *Historia Minor* (Hauptmann, p. 29, nos. 68, 70; Table 3, fig. 44) show a pattern of spots (actually a diminutive undy line [Hauptmann, p. 35, calls it bell-shaped ('Glockenform')]; cf. the Aumale shield corresponding to Pusikan, p. 150; see also Hauptmann, Table 3, fig. 49) arranged in horizontal rows. *Maskele* in Matthew Paris, therefore, is a synonym for *variatus*. See VAIRIÉ DE . . . ET DE . . ., and cf. ERMINE, *Note*. The *s* in *maskele* resulted perhaps from contamination with OFr. *masclé*, but Matthew Paris does not seem to have known the technical meaning of this word.

masclé de . . . et de . . .², *lozengy in bend* (Fig. 17). *C* 75: masculy de . . . et de . . . (*Cl* 75: maclé de . . . e de . . .; *Cd* 75, see CHASTELÉ²). *Syn.*: BENDÉ DE . . . ET DE . . . ENDENTÉ L'UN EN L'AUTRE. *Note*: arms of Bavaria. Prinet WR, p. 236: 'Rien n'indique ici que le losangé (ou plutôt fuselé) soit en bande.' *Aspilogia II*, p. 178, note to item 48: 'The arms have regularly been borne as fusilly bendways.' In the *Dean Tract*, p. 27, the same arms are blazoned as follows: 'Le duc de Beyvre porte l'escu masclee d'argent et d'azeure, et si est la masclure en belif.' For an illustration of these arms, see *WB* 595, fig. 134.

mascle du champ vuidiee, *mascle* (*voided lozenge*). See MASCLE VUIDIEE DU CHAMP.

mascle vuidiee du champ, *mascle* (*voided lozenge*) (Fig. 87). *B* 8: a six mascles . . . voydés du champ (*Ba/Bl* 8, see FAUSE LOSENGE; *Bb* 8, see MASCLE²); *K*, vv. 470-1: De armes vermeilles ben armés / O mascles de or del champ voidies. *Syn.*: see FAUSE LOSENGE. *Note*: refers to MASCLE¹. *P* 59 (= *B* 8) reads: 'ove sept losenges . . . voidés' (complete blazon provided s.v. LOSENGE VUIDIEE).

masculé de . . . et de . . ., see MASCLÉ DE . . . ET DE . . .

mastin, *mastiff* (Fig. 168). *Garin le Loherain*, v. 470: En son escu fu .i. mastin escriz. For another use, see CHIEF DE MASTIN. *Note*: arms of Godin, a Saracen chieftain. Cf. CHIENET, LEVRIER OD LE COLIER, LEVRIER OU LE COLIER.

mastin rechignié, *mastiff with bared teeth* (Fig. 170). *TA*, v. 703: A .i. rous mastin rechignié.

meesme, see MESME.

mein, *hand* (*dexter*) (Fig. 133). *TA*, vv. 1120-1:

A .i. label de males meins
Atachié a faus seremens;

D 148: a treis meyns. *Syn.*: MEIN DESOR, MEIN PAR MI, OUVERTE MEIN. *Note*: in his edition of the Camden Roll, Greenstreet blazons the charges in question on the accompanying painted shield (no. 164) as 'three dexter hands'.

mein crochue, *grasping hand*. *TA*, v. 929: A .i. label de meins crochues. *Note*: arms of Larrecin (Larceny). In Modern French, *avoir les mains crochues* still means 'to be light-fingered, rapacious'.

mein desor, *hand* (Fig. 133). Bel Inconnu, vv. 2058-60:

D'un samit blanc con flors de rains
Furent les mains et bien ouvrees
Et deseur le cendal posees.

Syn.: see MEIN. *Note*: refers to MEIN PAR MI.

mein ouverte, *open hand*. *TA*, v. 1990: A meins overtes de largesce. *Syn.*: see MEIN.

mein par mi, *hand* (Fig. 133). Bel Inconnu, v. 2057: Par mi ot unes blances mains; v. 2062: Et mains blances par mi avoit. *Syn.*: see MEIN. *Note*: refers to MEIN DESOR.

meins, *less.* See TELS ARMES MES QU'EN LIEU D'UNE BARRE MEINS.

meisme, see MESME.

mellete, *martlet.* See MERLETE.

meme, see MESME.

menu, *small.* See next items. *Syn.*: PETIT.

menue burelure de ... et de ..., *barruly* (Fig. 5). *Cl* 33: a une menue burlure de ... e de ... (*Cd* 33: a une menue burlure ... e de ...; *C* 33, see BURELÉ D'UNE MENUE BURELURE DE ... ET DE ...). *Syn.*: BURELÉ D'UNE MENUE BURELURE DE ... ET DE ...

menue burule, *barruly.* See BURELÉ D'UNE MENUE BURELURE DE ... ET DE ...

menuement, see GOUTÉ MENUEMENT.

mer, *sea.* See BAR DE MER, DAUFIN DE MER.

mere, *sea.* See MER.

merle, *martlet.* See BORDURE DE MERLES. *Syn.*: see MERLETE[1].

merle el chief, *on a chief a martlet. CC,* vv. 1316–18:

Ses escus avoit le cief d'or,
Et saciés qu'il avoit encor,
El cief, une mierle de sable.

Syn.: OISELET AU CHIEF.

merlet, *martlet.* See BENDE ET MERLEZ, BENDE OU MERLEZ.

merlete[1], *martlet* (Fig. 195). See BENDE A MERLETES, BENDE ET MERLETES, BENDE OU MERLETES, BORDURE DE MERLETES, CROIS PASSANT EN LE CHANTEL UNE MERLETE, MERLETE OU CHIEF, ODVE LES MERLETES. *Syn.*: ESMERLOT, MERLE, MERLET, MERLOT, OISEL, OISELET. *Note*: when there was a bend or fess between the martlets, early heralds normally utilized a positioning phrase and indicated the number of birds (e.g. *BA* 194: Robers [A: Robert] de Juin, l'escu d'argent a une bende [A: bande] de geules a .vi. oiselés de geules. Mansel; see BENDE A OISELEZ). The shield may actually show an orle of martlets, however (e.g. *BA* 91: Morel de Harvaing, l'escu d'or a une bende [A: bande] de geules a .vi. mellettes de geules. Hennuyer; in a note, Dr. Adam-Even refers to 'L'orle de merlettes' on a contemporary seal) and *CP* 18 prefers to designate the arrangement as a *bordure* (= orle) of martlets, without specifying the number of birds (see BORDURE D'OISELEZ). Cf. POUDRÉ, *Note*. The martlet is one of the most controversial

charges in heraldry. Recent discussions include those in letters to the editor, *Coat of Arms*, ii (1952), 39, and iv (1956), 40–1. The martlet is a swallow, often but not always depicted without legs from the earliest times, and later usually without legs or beak. Matthew Paris, for example, shows the martlets on the shield of John de Bassingbourne without legs; the Furnival martlets, on the other hand, do have legs and feet, as do those on the Pembroke shield illustrating the *Historia Minor* (Hauptmann, Table 6, fig. 98). On the other hand, there are no feet on the sparrow-hawks in the arms of Robert Muschet in the Matthew Paris Shields (see MOUSCHET; Wagner, *CEMRA*, Plate I). Martlets are generally associated with the fictitious arms of Edward the Confessor, but the thirteenth-century carved and painted shield with his arms in Westminster Abbey bears doves with feet (C. W. Scott-Giles, *Heraldry in Westminster Abbey*, rev. ed. [London, 1961], pp. 6–7). For additional illustrations, consult J. G. O. Whitehead, 'The Arms of the Confessor', *Coat of Arms*, viii (1965), 266–71. On the origins of these arms, see H. C. Curwen, 'Some Notes on a Penny of Edward the Confessor', *Coat of Arms*, v (1959), 184–5. There are no feet, however, on the martlets illustrating the earliest French roll (see Adam-Even WB, p. 56), nor on those illustrating Glover's Roll. The French martlet is not a swallow but a duckling, according to Veyrin-Forrer, p. 114: 'La *cannette* représente la canne ou le canard; si elle est dépourvue de bec et de pattes, elle devient une *merlette*'; D'Haucourt–Durivault, p. 82, speaks of a *merle* 'blackbird' in this connection, but also of a *martinet* 'swift' (p. 112). According to H. S. London in *Chambers' Encyclopaedia*, new edn., vii (London, 1963), 35, heraldry 'standardized, if it did not invent [this] conventionalized bird'. The elimination of the feet (and later the beak) in depictions of the martlet may have been purely conventional. The *OED* (vi. 193, s.v. *martlet[2]*) states that the martlet was at times represented without feet 'by accident or caprice, or with symbolical intention' but does not incline to any one of these explanations. It does, however, suggest that the heraldic bird was identified with the swift 'which has short legs'. The medieval bestiaries do not mention anything unusual about the blackbird (Lat. *merula*, OFr. *merle*), but at least one early collection claims that the swallow (Lat. *hirundo*) is so named 'because it takes its food not sitting but while *haerundo*, "remaining", in the air' (McCulloch, pp. 96–7, 174–5). According to Johannes de Bado Aureo, *Tractatus de Armis* (c. 1394, ed. Evan John Jones in *Medieval Heraldry* [Cardiff, 1943], p. 122), martlets are painted without feet to symbolize the fact that those who bear them in arms are noble but 'without foundation', that is lack means of subsistence (*fundamento carent seu substantia*), and must, consequently, dwell at the courts of kings or lords. Surely the latter notions, together with the one favoured by certain manual-writers that the legs were omitted because the swallow was believed to be incapable of perching on the ground, are to be rejected. If an explanation must be provided I suggest that it may have been the result of a misunderstanding of OFr. *coupé* 'covered with feathers, tufted' (see Gunnar Tilander, *Glanures lexicographiques* [Lund, 1932], p. 55: 'la petite geline a piez cupez'), for the martlet's legs, even when its feet are omitted, are generally depicted as tufted. I know of no examples of *merlette a pié coupé*, but cf. *cane coupee a pié* 'martlet' in *Navarre* 868: 'M. Briant de Lannion, d'argent a un chief de gueules a trois canes noires cupié a pié, et a bec de gueules a trois roses d'argent au chef' (the latter blazon, however, may also be read: *cupié a pié et a bec*, i.e. 'with feet and beak cut off'). Cf., finally, *Roland*, v. 1491: *piez a copiez* (referring to a horse); see Jenkins' note to this verse. A bird with tufted feet is designated as *pattu* in Modern French, e.g. *poule pattue*, *pigeon pattu*; see *Larousse du XXe siècle*, s.v. *pattu*.

merlete², *error for* MOLETE. *CP* 48: a trois merlettes. *Note*: on this error, see Prinet *CP*, p. 18 n. 2 and p. 23 n. 4, referring to *Navarre* 699 (*moletes* instead of *merletes*). See also Adam-Even *CPA*, p. 3.

merlete ou chief, *in chief a martlet*. See FESSE A UNE MERLETE OU CHIEF. *Syn*.: OI-SELET OU CHIEF. *Note*: refers to OU CHIEF¹.

merlot, *martlet* (Fig. 195). (1) *bend between martlets*. See BENDE ENTRE MERLOZ, BENDE ET MERLOZ, BENDE OD MERLOZ, MERLOZ ET BENDE, MERLOZ ET UNE BENDE. (2) *bend indented between martlets*. See MERLOZ A UNE BENDE ENGRESLEE, MERLOZ ET UNE BENDE ENGRESLEE. (3) *cross cantoned with martlets*. See CROIS A MERLOZ. (4) *fess between martlets*. See FESSE ET MERLOZ, FESSE OU MERLOZ, MERLOZ EL CHAMP O UNE FESSE. (5) *in orle* (Fig. 125). See BORDURE DE MERLOZ, BORDURE DE MERLOZ PORALEE TOUT ENTOUR, LES MERLOZ, MERLOZ BORDANZ, MERLOZ EN L'ORLE, MERLOZ ENTOUR, OD LES MERLOZ, MERLOZ, ORLE DE MERLOZ, ORLE OF MERLOZ. *Note*: cf. MERLOZ EN LA BORDURE. (6) *semy*. See A MERLOZ, POUDRÉ DE MERLOZ. *Note*: cf. MERLOZ EN LA BORDURE. *Syn*.: see MERLETE¹. *Note*: in *K*, vv. 198–9 ('Car en lieu des merlos mettoit / Trois chapeaus de rosis vermelles'), *merlos* refers to the orle of martlets in the arms of the Earl of Pembroke which are cited in vv. 171–3 (see BORDURE DE MERLOZ PORALEE TOUT ENTOUR).

merloz a une bende engreslee, *bend indented (i.e. fusils conjoined in bend) between martlets*. *C* 95: siz merloz . . . un bend engrelé (*Cl* 95: a sis merlor . . . a une bend . . . engralé; *Cd* 95, see MERLOZ ET UNE BENDE ENGRESLEE). *Syn*.: MERLOZ ET UNE BENDE ENGRESLEE.

merloz bordanz, *orle of martlets* (Fig. 125). *C* 57 (*Cl* 57: a merloz . . . bordeand; *Cd* 57: a merloz . . . bordeand), 129 (*Cl* 129: a merlor . . . bordiauz; *Cd* 129: a merloz . . . bourdanz): a merloz . . . bordeans; 91: a merlos . . . bordeans (*Cl* 91: a merlor . . . bordeanz; *Cd* 91: a merlon . . . bordeanz). *Syn*.: see BORDURE DE MERLETES. *Note*: on the blazon in *C/Cl/Cd* 129 (Fauconberge arms), see ANOZ ENTOUR, *Note*.

merloz el champ o une fesse, *fess between martlets*. *K*, vv. 320–1:

Sis merlos de or el rouge champ
O une fesse en lieu de dance.

Syn.: see FESSE ET MERLOZ. *Note*: see MERLETE¹, *Note*.

merloz en la bordure, *bordure semy of martlets*. *B* 135: merlots . . . en le bordur (*Bl* 135 [139]: merlotz . . . en la bordure).

Note: refers to BORDURE[1]; not to be confused with BORDURE DE MERLETES (refers to BORDURE[2]).

merloz en l'orle, *orle of martlets* (Fig. 125). *Bc* 56: od merloz . . . en l'urle (*B/Bb* 56, see ORLE OF MERLOZ; *Ba* 56, see OD MERLOZ); *Bl* 186 [190]: od merlots . . . en le urle (*B* 186, see ORLE DE MERLOZ). *Syn.*: see BORDURE DE MERLETES. *Note*: refers to EN L'ORLE[2].

merloz entour, *orle of martlets* (Fig. 125). *B* 197: les merlotts . . . entour. *Syn.*: see BORDURE DE MERLETES.

merloz et bende, *bend between martlets*. *K*, v. 374: Sis merlos e bende vermeille. *Syn.*: see BENDE A MERLETES.

merloz et une bende, *bend between martlets*. *Bl* 141 [145]: od six merlotz . . . et une bende; 143 [147], 145 [149]: od six merlotz . . . et un bende (*B* 141, 143, 145, see BENDE ENTRE MERLOZ). *Syn.*: see BENDE A MERLETES.

merloz et une bende engreslee, *bend indented (i.e. fusils conjoined in bend) between martlets*. *Cd* 95: .6. merloz . . . e une bende ingrelé (*C/Cl* 95, see MERLOZ A UNE BENDE ENGRESLEE). *Syn.*: MERLOZ A UNE BENDE ENGRESLEE.

mes, *but, except*. See AUTEL MES, MESMES LES ARMES MES, TELS (ARMES) QUE . . . MES POUR DESCOMPAROISON, TOUT . . . MES SOR LE . . . PAR CONOISSANCE. *Note*: cf. FORS DE, FORS QUE.

mesme[1], *the same (arms)*. See ARMES CELES MESMES A, CELES MESMES A, CEZ MESMES ARMES A, DE MESME, DE MESME A, DE MESME LE TAINT, LE MESME A, MESMES ARMES, MESMES AVUEC, MESMES LES ARMES MES, MESMES LES ARMES OD, MESMES LES ARMES OU, MESMES PORTER ARMES, PORTER MESME, SOIES ARMES MESMES. *Syn.*: see AUTEL[1].

mesme[2], *the same (tincture)*. See DEL MESME.

mesmes armes, *the same arms*. Mort Artu, pp. 12, 15: unes meïsmes armes. *Syn.*: see AUTEL[1].

mesmes avuec, *the same arms, differenced by*. The complete blazon reads as follows: *B* 112: Nicholas son filz, mesmes oveque la labell goulez. *Syn.*: see AUTEL[2].

mesmes les armes mes, *the same arms, differenced by*. The complete blazon reads as follows: *M* 13: Sr Robert le Conestable

port mesmes lez armez (G: armes) mes la bende est engrelé d'or. *Syn.*: see AUTEL[2].

mesmes les armes od, *the same arms, differenced by*. *Hg* 49 [50]: mesmes les armes od (*H* 49, see MESMES LES ARMES OU). *Syn.*: see AUTEL[2].

mesmes les armes ou, *the same arms, differenced by*. *H* 49: mesmes lez armez (G: armes) ou (*Hg* 49 [50], see MESMES LES ARMES OD); *M* 30: mesmes les armes ou; 39: mesmes lez armes ou. *Syn.*: see AUTEL[2].

mesmes porter armes, *to bear the same arms*. Lancelot propre, iii. 407: li rois meismes porta armes. *Syn.*: see AUTEL[1].

mes que, *with the exception that*. Lancelot propre, iii. 395: si port l'escu que il porta a la daraine assamblee mais qu'il i ait une bende blanche de bellic. For other uses, see ARMES TELS COM . . . MES QUE, TELS ARMES . . . MES QUE, TELS ARMES MES QU'EN LIEU D'UNE BARRE MEINS. For another use, see DEVISER[2]. *Syn.*: see FORS QUE.

message, *angel*. See ENPENÉ D'ELES DE MESSAGE. *Note*: cf. ANGELOT.

metre[1], *to bear*. See EN LIEU DE . . . METRE. *Syn.*: PORTER.

metre[2], *to place upon*. See TANT QUE L'ON I POUVOIT METRE. *Note*: cf. SEIR, SEOIR.

meule en le chief, *in chief a roundel*. See BARRE A UNE MEULE EN LE CHIEF, BARRE OVE UNE MEULE EN LE CHIEF. *Syn.*: see TOURTEL EN CHIEF. *Note*: on OFr. *moele*, *meule* 'millstone (here, a synonym for roundel)', consult H. Stanford London, 'The Roundel', p. 311; London, 'Notes and Reflections, II', pp. 270–1; *Aspilogia II*, p. 130, note to item 83: 'Originally they may have been shown as millstones, but all known representations of the arms show roundels.' Cf. MEULET PERCIÉ, MEULETE PERCIEE.

meulet en le chief, *in chief a roundel*. See BARRE A UN MEULET EN LE CHIEF. *Syn.*: see TOURTEL EN LE CHIEF.

meulete perciee, *annulet* (Fig. 111). *Cl* 116: a treis molette . . . percés (*C/Cd* 116, see MEULET PERCIÉ). *Syn.*: see ANEL. *Note*: Aspilogia II, p. 196, note to item 145: 'This is an instance of *meulette* "little millstone", used for a roundel.'

meuletes od un chevron, *chevron between roundels*. *Bl* 179 [183]: a trois molettes . . . od un cheveron (*B* 179, see CHEVRON ET

TOURTEAUS). *Syn.*: CHEVRON ET TOURTEAUS. *Note*: refers to CHEVRON (2). *Aspilogia II*, p. 150, note to item 183: 'here, too, as in *B* 83 [see BARRE A UN MEULET EN LE CHIEF], [*Bl*] uses "molettes" for roundels. [*B*] emends the blazon to torteaux.' On the position of the charges, see *Aspilogia II*, p. 104.

meulet percié, *annulet* (Fig. 111). *C* 116: a trois mullets (W: mullettes) percees (*Cl* 116, see MEULETE PERCIEE; *Cd* 116: 3 mouletts . . . perceys). *Syn.*: see ANEL. *Note*: Walford, note *b*: 'In the margin is *anulettes* [*sic*, the MS. actually reads *anuletts*] credo; which is probably correct. See Roll temp. Hen. III, p. 5.' The Plessis arms do indeed feature annulets, but *anelete perciee* or *anelet percié* would be a pleonasm. On the heraldic term *meule* of which *meulet* and *meulete* are diminutives, see MEULE EN LE CHIEF, *Note*.

mi, see EN MI, PAR MI. *Syn.*: MILIEU.

mierle, *martlet*. See MERLE EL CHIEF.

milieu, *middle*. See CROIS EL MILIEU, EN MILIEU, OU MILIEU, PAR LE MILIEU.

mi parti de . . . et de . . ., *party per pale* (Fig. 21). *Perlesvaus*, p. 111: mi partiz de . . . et de . . .; *Lancelot propre*, iv. 186: mi parti de . . . et de . . .; 186, 187, 264: l'escu mi parti; v. 5: mi parties de . . . et de . . .; 431: my parties de . . . et de . . .; *Vulgate Merlin Sequel*, p. 195: mi parties de . . . et de . . .; p. 266: mi parti de . . . et de . . .; p. 404: mi partie de . . . et . . .; *Artus*, p. 7: mi parti de maintes diverses colors; p. 13: mi partie de . . . et de . . .; p. 62: mi parties de . . . et de . . .; p. 67: mi parti le champ de . . . et de . . .; *TA*, vv. 1996–7:

Et orent armes mi parties
De beauté et de courtoisie;

SCU, fol. 185 *b*: Cil a la cote mi partie; *Bataille des VII Arts*, v. 340: Une baniere mi partie; *CP* 131: mi party de . . . et de . . . (complete blazon provided s.v. PARTI DE . . . ET DE . . ., DE . . . SOR LE . . . ET DE . . . SOR LE . . .). *Syn.*: see PARTI DE . . . ET DE . . . *Note*: cf. PARTIR DE . . . ET DE . . . For a discussion of the evolution of the meaning of this expression, see PARTI DE . . . ET DE . . ., *Note*.

mireor, *mirror* (here a synonym for roundel) (Fig. 112). *Roman des Eles*, v. 478: al

mirëor; *TA*, v. 670: A .i. mirëor; vv. 826, 1086, 1721: au mirëor; vv. 863, 1022, 2530: au miroër. For another use, see MIREOR EN LE CHIEF. *Syn.*: see BESANT. *Note*: Prinet TA, p. 51: 'Les *miroirs* sont très communs; on les a choisis de préférence à d'autres ustensiles, parce que leur rôle est de refléter. Ils reflètent les qualités, les caractères.' On the relationship between the *Roman des Eles* and *TA*, see RAMPANT, *Note*. London, 'The Roundel', p. 311: '*myrrours* . . . occur in the first version of Glover. In the slightly later second version the myrrours have been omitted. . . . Myrrour calls for no particular comment, nor is there any apparent reason for the choice of the word'; *Aspilogia II*, p. 154, note to item 199: 'no other instances have been noticed.'

mireor en le chief, *on a chief a mirror (i.e. a roundel)*. *Bl* 195 [199]: od trois myrrours . . . en le chief. *Syn.*: see GASTEL EN LE CHIEF. *Note*: '[*B* 195] omits the bezants [i.e. 'myrrours'], probably by inadvertence.'

moele, *millstone* (here a synonym for roundel) (Fig. 112). See MEULE. *Syn.*: see BESANT. *Note*: since all examples are in the plural, *moeles*, or *meules*, could also represent *moelez*, i.e. the plural of the masculine form *moelet*, or *meulet*; see, for example, MEULET PERCIÉ. The arms in question, however, are those of Nicholas de Moels or Mules, a name derived from Meulles in Calvados, France (*Aspilogia II*, p. 130, note to item 83), so *moeles* was doubtless intended.

moins, *less*. See MEINS.

moitié, see L'AUTRE MOITIÉ. *Syn.*: PART. *Note*: cf. DEMI².

mole, *ghost word*. See LION RAMPANT COURONÉ SUS UNE MOTE.

molet¹, *mullet* (Fig. 225). *C* 82: trois mulletts (W: mulletes) (*Cl* 82, see MOLETE; *Cd* 82: a 3 moulets); *M* 36: ou trois moletz. For other uses, see ESQUARTELÉ DE . . . ET DE . . . UN MOLET, ESQUARTILLIÉ DE . . . ET DE . . . EN LE CHANTEL DE . . . UN MOLET, MOLET EN LA CROIS, MOLET EN LE CHIEF¹, QUARTELÉ DE . . . ET DE . . . UN MOLET, QUARTELÉ DE . . . ET DE . . . UN MOLET EN LE QUARTIER DEVANT, QUARTILLIÉ DE . . . ET DE . . . ET EN LE CHANTEL DE . . . OU UN MOLET. For another use, see MOLET PERCIÉ. *Syn.*: see ESTOILE.

molet², *roundel.* See MEULET EN LE CHIEF, MEULET PERCIÉ. *Syn.*: see BESANT.

molete¹, *mullet* (Fig. 225). (1) *no position is indicated. BA* 96, 147: a une molette; *Cl* 82: a treys molette (*C/Cd* 82, see MOLET¹); *D* 161: od treis molettes; *TC*, v. 901: une moleste; *CP* 48: a trois merlettes [*sic*, see MERLETE²]; *CPA* 4: a la molette; *M* 7: ou deux molettes; 31: ou .iii. moletez. (2) *position is indicated.* A. *a locution is used.* See CHIEF ENDENTÉ D'UNE MOLETE, CHIEF OD UNE MOLETE, CHEVRON O MOLETES, CHEVRON OD MOLETES, EL CHIEF UNE MOLETE, EN LA CROIS UNE MOLETE, ESQUARTELÉ DE . . . ET DE . . . A UNE MOLETE, ESQUARTELÉ DE . . . ET DE . . . A UNE MOLETE OU QUARTIER DE . . ., QUARTELÉ DE . . . ET DE . . . EN LE CHANTEL DE . . . UNE MOLETE. (3) *semy* (Fig. 45). See A MOLETES SEMÉ, MOLETES EN LE . . . B. *order of items alone is used. D* 129: od une molette (the mullet is in sinister point of the chief; for complete blazon, see CHIEF¹ [2] B. 1., *Note* [3]). *Syn.*: see ESTOILE. *Note*: on this charge, see Gil Baudrand-Massière, 'Molettes ou étoiles percées', *Nouvelle Revue Héraldique*, N.S., i (1946–7), 77–80; *Aspilogia II*, p. 182, note to item 67: 'straight-rayed stars'.

molete², *roundel* (Fig. 112). See MEULETES OD UN CHEVRON. *Syn.*: see BESANT.

molete en chief, *in chief a mullet. TC*, vv. 896–901:

> Mes iex tornai a si bone eure
> Que je vi tout a descovert
> Un chevalier d'armes couvert
> D'or fin a un çaintour vermoil,
> Et si porte par desparoil
> Une moleste d'or en chief.

Syn.: see MOLET EN LE CHIEF¹. *Note*: in an accompanying miniature in the Oxford MS. (see Delbouille, Plate VII, min. 7), the knight in question, Conrad Werner of Hattstatt, is depicted as bearing a saltire with the mullet placed in chief, squarely between the arms of the saltire. See also *WB* 615 (and fig. 146). Delbouille, p. lxxiv, however, states that the mullet is placed in *dexter* chief ('chargé en chef [à dextre] d'une molette'). Delbouille adds that the mullet is of the field ('du champ'), which is a correct translation of the text but

impossible, as it calls for a gold charge on a gold field. In the miniature, the mullet appears to be of the same tincture as the saltire (i.e. gules), but Adam-Even in *WB* 615 blazons it sable. Cf. Delbouille, p. xxvi.

molete en la bende, *on a bend a mullet. BA* 286: a une molette . . . en le bende (A: en la bendee), see BENDE A DEUS LISTEAUS¹.

molete en la fesse, *on a fess a mullet. BA* 131, 159: a .iii. molettes . . . en le faisse; *CPA* 154: a .ii. molettes . . . en la fasce.

molete en le chief, *on a chief a mullet. H* 102: ou .ii. moletties . . . en le chef, see CHIEF¹ (2) A. (*Hg* 102, see MOLET EN LE CHIEF³). *Syn.*: see ESTOILE EN LE CHIEF¹.

molete en le premier quartier, see ESQUARTELÉ DE . . . ET DE . . . UNE MOLETE EN LE PREMIER QUARTIER.

molet en la crois, *on a plain cross a mullet. H* 72: ou .v. molets . . . en la crois (*Hg* 72 [73]: od .v. molez . . . en la croyz), see CROIS¹ (3). *Syn.*: EN LA CROIS UNE MOLETE.

molet en le chief¹, *in chief a mullet.* See FESSE A UN MOLET EN LE CHIEF. *Syn.*: ESTOILE EN LE CHIEF², MOLETE EN CHIEF, ROUELE EN CHIEF², ROUELE EN LE CHIEF².

molet en le chief², *in chief a roundel.* See MEULET EN LE CHIEF.

molet en le chief³, *on a chief a mullet. Hg* 102: od deux molez . . . en le chef, see CHIEF¹ (2) A. (*H* 102, see MOLETE EN LE CHIEF). *Syn.*: see ESTOILE EN LE CHIEF¹.

molet en le quartier devant, *in the first quarter a mullet.* See QUARTELÉ DE . . . ET DE . . . UN MOLET EN LE QUARTIER DEVANT. *Syn.*: DEVANT UNE ESTOILE, EN LE CHANTEL DE . . . OU UN MOLET, EN LE CHANTEL DE . . . UNE MOLETE, ESTOILE EN LE QUARTIER DEVANT, MOLETE OU QUARTIER DE . . . See also MOLET¹, MOLETE¹, and cf. MOLETE OU QUARTIER.

molete ou quartier, *on a canton a mullet. BA* 135: a une molette . . . u quartier, see QUARTIER¹ (2); 141: a .i. molette . . . u quartier, see QUARTIER¹ (2). *Note*: refers to OU QUARTIER¹.

molete ou quartier de . . ., *in the first quarter a mullet.* See ESQUARTELÉ DE . . . ET DE . . . A UNE MOLETE OU QUARTIER DE . . . *Syn.*: see MOLET EN LE QUARTIER DEVANT.

molete perciee¹, *pierced mullet* (Fig. 226). *BA* 81: a .i. molette . . . perchie. *Syn.*: see ESTOILE.

molete perciee[2], *annulet* (Fig. 111). See MEULETE PERCIEE.

moletes en le . . ., *semy of mullets* (Fig. 45). The complete blazons read as follows: *BA* 95: Gilles de Busengnies, l'escu bendé de geules (A: gueules) et de vair a molettes (A: molette) d'or en le (A: en) gueules. Hennuyer, see EN LE GEULES[2] (1); 157: Gherars (A: Gherart) de Busingnies, l'escu bendé de geules et de vair a molettes d'or en le geules (A: en gueules). Hanuiers (A: Hainnuier), see EN LE GEULES[2] (1). *Syn.*: see A MOLETES SEMÉ. *Note*: refers to BENDÉ DE . . . ET DE . . .[2].

molin, see MOULIN.

mote, *mount* (Fig. 141). See LION RAMPANT COURONÉ ESTANT SUS UNE MOTE, LION RAMPANT COURONÉ SUS UNE MOTE. *Syn.*: PUI. *Note*: in a letter to the editor of the *Coat of Arms*, iii (1954), 36–7, H. S. London provides details concerning this charge which is very common in Swiss heraldry, less common in Italy, less still in southern Germany, almost unknown elsewhere.

mouchet, *sparrow-hawk*. See MOUSCHET.

moulin, *mill*. See FER DE MOULIN.

mouschet, *sparrow-hawk* (Fig. 203). *Syn.*: see ESPREVIER. *Note*: Matthew Paris only (Pusikan, p. 151): Roberti Muschet, scutum d'azuro et tres muschetz (P: muchetz; *Aspilogia II*, p. 44, item 41: muschet) d'or. On the etymology, see *BW*[4], s.v. *émouchet*: 'Cette désignation de "petite mouche" vient de ce que l'émouchet est plus petit que le faucon et que l'épervier.'

mouton, *lamb*. See TESTE DE MOUTON.

muer son escu, *to change one's arms (as a disguise)*. Perlesvaus, p. 198: trop souvent mue son escu. *Syn.*: CHANGIER SES ARMES. *Note*: cf. ARMES MUER. On this observation by Gawain concerning Perceval's habit of changing his arms, consult Nitze, ii. 224, note to line 510 and see ARMES CHANGIER, *Note*.

mule, see OREILLE D'UNE MULE.

muschet, *sparrow-hawk*. See MOUSCHET.

myrrour, *mirror*. See MIREOR.

naissant, *jessant*. See FESSE DE FLEURS DE LIS ESPARZ NAISSANZ DE TESTES DE LIEPARZ. *Syn.*: CROISSANT[2]. *Note*: in modern usage, *naissant* is synonymous with *issant* in French

and *issuant* in English, though the latter tends to restrict *naissant* to living creatures.

n'avoir nul autre taint desous, *to have no other tincture underneath* (?). *Troie*, vv. 7815–16:

> D'or bruni ert sis escuz toz;
> N'aveit nul autre teint desoz.

Note: the reading *desus* 'on, upon (the shield)' is tempting (cf. SOUS = SUS) but is ruled out by the rhyme. The author probably meant that the shield was tinctured gold through and through, not simply on the outside surface. Cf. Isolt's remark apropos of Tristan's shield after the Dragon Episode in *Le Roman de Tristan par Thomas* (ed. J. Bédier, i [Paris, 1902], 119): '"Par foi, dame," dit Isolt, "jamais le sénéchal n'a porté cet écu; il a été fait depuis peu, et il est doré à l'intérieur comme au dehors; ce n'est point la coutume de ce pays."'

n'avoir nule autre diversité d'armes entre, *to have no other difference between*. *Queste*, p. 140: et estoient li un covert de blanches armes et li autre de noires, ne nule autre diversité d'armes n'avoit entr'ax.

ne, *negative particle*. See NE LA PORTER DIVERSE FORS DE, NE SOI REPOSER DE VOLER, N'ESTRE DIVERS DE RIEN NON FORS DE . . . SEULEMENT.

neir, *sable* (*black*). See NOIR.

ne la porter diverse fors de, *the same arms, differenced by*. *K*, vv. 345–7:

> Patrik de Dunbar, fiz le conte,
> Ne la portoit par nul aconte
> Fors de une label de inde diverse.

Syn.: see AUTEL[2].

ne pas estre seul, see CEZ CHOSES.

ne soi reposer de voler, see ESPREVIER QUI DE VOLER NE SOI REPOSE. *Note*: cf. FAIRE SEMBLANT, SEMBLER.

n'estre divers de rien non fors de . . . seulement, *the same arms, differenced by*. *K*, vv. 100–1:

> Ne estoit diverse de rien noun,
> Fors de un label vert soulement.

Syn.: see AUTEL[2].

Noble, *Noble* (*animal character* [*a lion*] *in the*

'*Roman de Renart*'). The complete blazon reads as follows: *TA*, vv. 614–17:

De geules estoit ses escuz
Plus vermeilles que nus sinoples;
Par mi rampoit misires Nobles
A une queue bobenciere.

Note: cf. LION[1]. Arms of Bobance (Pride); see Flinn, pp. 259–60. Cf. BRUN.

***noir**, *sable* (*black*). Very frequent in literary sources, e.g. *Cligés*, v. 4556: unes noires; *Tristan de Béroul*, v. 4015: noire; *Durmart*, v. 8492: de noir; *Perlesvaus*, p. 251: l'escu . . . noirs; *Bataille des VII Arts*, v. 39: noir; *EO*, vv. 2656, 4818: noir; *Escanor*, v. 3600: noir; *K*, vv. 190, 349: noire. Very common in the rolls, e.g. *BA* 6, 51: de noir; *B* 14: noir; *Ba* 56: noirs (*Bb* 56, see SABLE; *Bc* 56: noirs); *Bl* 3: noir (*B* 3, see SABLE); *Cl* 1: peyr [*sic*] (*C/Cd* 1, see SABLE); *CP* 14, 24: noir; *CPA* 17: de noir. For other uses, see OU LES NOIR, POURPRE NOIR, TOUT NOIR. *Syn.*: see SABLE. *Note*: in *Perlesvaus*, p. 38, mention is made of a knight riding a black horse 'e avoit escu autretel'. For the emendation *peyr* > *neyr* (= *noir*) in *Cl* 1, consult Prinet WR, p. 225. *Aspilogia II*, p. 167, substitutes *espany* (see EGLE A DEUS TESTES, *Note*).

non, *negative particle*. See N'ESTRE DIVERS DE RIEN NON FORS DE . . . SEULEMENT.

Nostre Dame, *the Virgin*. See CHEMISE NOSTRE DAME. *Syn.*: MADAME SAINTE MARIE.

Nostre Seigneur, *Our Lord*. See ARMES A NOSTRE SEIGNEUR, ARMES NOSTRE SEIGNEUR. *Syn.*: NOSTRE SIEUR.

Nostre Sieur, *Our Lord. Aye d'Avignon*, vv. 2736–7:

En l'escu de son col ot paint .i. gent miracle,
Ainssi con Nostre Sire resuscita saint Ladre.

Syn.: NOSTRE SEIGNEUR.

nul, *any*. See SANS NULE AUTRE DESCONOIS-SANCE, SANS NULE AUTRE ENSEIGNE.

nul autre taint desous, see N'AVOIR NUL AUTRE TAINT DESOUS.

nule autre diversité d'armes entre, see N'AVOIR NULE AUTRE DIVERSITÉ D'ARMES ENTRE.

o besanz, see BANIERE O BESANZ.

od croiseles, *crusily* (Fig. 35). *Bl* 174 [178]: od croiseles (*B* 174, see CROISELE). *Syn.*: see CROISELÉ.

od croiselez, *crusily* (Fig. 35). *Bl* 140 [144]: od croiselez (*B* 140, see CROISELÉ). *Syn.*: see CROISELÉ.

od croisilles, *crusily* (Fig. 35). *Bl* 175 [179]: od croisilles (*B* 175, see CROISELETÉ). *Syn.*: see CROISELÉ.

od les couwes, *semy of choughs* (?) (Fig. 32). The complete blazon reads as follows: *Hg* 91 [90]: Otes de Casenan porte d'or od les couwes de sable (*H* 91: Hotes de Sassenau port d'or ou lez pies de sable). *Syn.*: OU LES PIES. *Note*: Gough H, p. 150, note to item 90, established that the knight in question was Otho de Casa Nova, the latter being a Latinized form of Casenave, the modern Cazeneuve in Gascony. According to Gough: 'The arms are not intelligibly blazoned.' The word *pie* 'magpie (a bird of the crow family)' in the corresponding blazon (*H* 91), however, suggests that *couwe* may be a form of OFr. *choe, choue* 'owl' but also, more loosely, 'any bird of the crow family'. It is this meaning which yielded E. *chough*, now distinguished heraldically from the crow only by its red beak and legs. The original charge may have been an owl, however, for 'Cassenau' and 'Sassenau' (as Gough correctly points out the words should be written) suggest a pun on Gallo-Latin *cavannus* 'owl' (> Fr. *chouan, chat-huant*).

od les croisilles, *crusily* (Fig. 35). *Hg* 99 [100]: od les croisilles (*H* 99, see OU LES CROISELETES). *Syn.*: see CROISELÉ.

od les croissanz, *semy of crescents* (Fig. 34). *Hg* 85: od les cressanz (*H* 85, see OU LES CROISSANZ). *Syn.*: OU LES CROISSANZ. *Note*: the arms in question (William de Rithre, or Rye) are known to have featured three crescents (Gough H, p. 148, note to item 85).

od les eschalopes, *semy of escallops* (Fig. 39). *Hg* 82: od les schalops (*H* 82, see ESCHA-LOPE [1]). *Syn.*: see A COQUILLES SEMÉ.

od les losenges perciees, *masculy* (Fig. 18). *D* 119: od les losenges . . . percés. *Syn.*: OD LOSENGES PERCIEES, POUDRÉ A FAUSES LO-SENGES. *Note*: see MASCLÉ DE . . . ET DE . . .[1], *Note*.

od les merloz, *orle of martlets* (Fig. 125). *D* 132, 135: od les merloz. *Syn.*: see BOR-

DURE DE MERLETES. *Note*: the accompanying painted shields (nos. 146, 149) show
an orle of martlets.

od les tourteaus, *bezanty* (Fig. 29). *Hg* 9
[8]: od les tourteaux (*H* 9, see BESANTÉ).
Syn.: see BESANTÉ.

od merloz, *orle of martlets* (Fig. 125). *Ba* 56:
od merloz (*B* 56: Patrik de Chaurcy, burelé
d'argent et de goules [*sic*, no orle of mart-
lets]; *Bb* 56, see ORLE OF MERLOZ). *Syn.*:
see BORDURE DE MERLETES.

odve les merletes, *orle of martlets* (Fig. 125).
M 79: odve lez merleste. *Syn.*: see BORDURE
DE MERLETES.

oeil, *'eye'*. See D'IEUZ DE PAON OEILLETÉ.

oeille passant, *ewe passant* (Fig. 156). The
complete blazon reads as follows: *Cleomadés*, vv. 627–8:

> Li uns portoit armes vermeilles
> A .ii. blanches passans oueilles.

Note: Comte de Marsy, p. 202: 'M. P. Paris,
dans une note mise en marge du manu-
scrit, avait rappelé que ces armes étaient
celles de Béarn. C'en sont en effet les
pièces, mais non les émaux, Béarn portant
d'or à deux vaches de gueules.' Comte de
Marsy persisted in Paulin Paris's error by
translating OFr. *oeille*, *oueille* as 'cow',
whereas the term is plainly related to
MFr. *ouaille* (< Late Latin *ovicula*) 'sheep'
(used only in the plural today and figura-
tively to designate the pastor's 'flock', i.e.
parishioners). Cf. VACHE.

oeilleté, *semy of 'eyes'* (*i.e. the markings on a
peacock's tail*). *TA*, v. 1894: d'euz de paon
oilleté. *Syn.*: D'IEUZ DE PAON OEILLETÉ.

oeilleté d'ieuz de paon, see D'IEUZ DE
PAON OEILLETÉ.

of, *the English preposition*. See ON THE QUAR-
TERS OF THE FIELD, ORLE OF MERLOZ.

oiseaus, *martlets*. See OISEL.

oisel, *martlet*. See DANCE EN BELIC A OI-
SEAUS. *Syn.*: see MERLETE[1].

oiselet, *martlet* (Fig. 195). *CP* 33: a un oi-
selet. For other uses, see BENDE A OISELEZ,
BORDURE D'OISELEZ, CHEVRON A OISELEZ,
SAUTOIR A OISELEZ. *Syn.*: see MERLETE[1].

oiselet au chief, *on a chief a martlet*. *CP* 12:
a trois oiselés . . . au chief. *Syn.*: MERLE EL
CHIEF. *Note*: refers to CHIEF[1] (2) A. ('the
word CHIEF is used twice, one of which is

in the locution AU CHIEF'), though the blazon is actually elliptical here.

oiselet ou chief, *in chief a martlet*. See
FESSE A UN OISELET OU CHIEF. *Syn.*: MERLETE
OU CHIEF. *Note*: refers to OU CHIEF[1].

oiselez entour, *orle of martlets* (Fig. 125).
BA 186: a l'oiselés [MS. *sic*, for as oiselés]
. . . entor. *Syn.*: see BORDURE DE MERLETES.

oiset, *ghost word*. See BORDURE D'OISELEZ.

olifant, *elephant* (Fig. 155). *EO*, v. 4828:
Armes ot bleues a deus blans olifans; *Cleomadés*, v. 8665: a .i. noir olifant. *Note*: OFr.
olifant also had the meaning 'ivory horn',
a sense often associated with Roland's
famous horn in the Middle Ages (see *BW*[4],
s.v. *éléphant*). Cf. COR. In both instances
here, however, the arms are those of fictitious Saracen kings (Abilant and Pri-
monus) whose realms ('Persia' and
'Chaldea') were traditionally associated
with elephants. According to medieval
lore: 'The Persians and Indians place
wooden towers on them and fight with
javelins as if from a wall' (McCulloch,
p. 116; bibliography in notes 58 and 59).
On the elephant and its tower, see William
S. Heckscher, 'Bernini's Elephant and
Obelisk', *Art Bulletin*, xxix (1947), 158–65;
Dorothy Neave, 'Old French *chastel* / *tour*
"Elephant's War-Tower"', *Romania*,
lxxxviii (1967), 253–8. See also the arms
of the City of Coventry (Boutell, p. 71).

on, see L'ON.

ondé de . . . et de . . ., *barry undy* (Fig. 7).
BA 83, 84, 250, 252, 283: ondé de . . . et
de . . .; *B* 111: oundé de . . . et de . . . (*Bl*
111 [115]: oundé de . . . et de . . .); 159:
undé de . . . et de . . . (*Bl* 159 [163]: undé
de . . . et de . . .); *Bl* 93, 112 [116]: oundé
de . . . et de . . . (*B* 93, see DE . . . ET DE . . .[1]);
C 113: undee de . . . et de . . . (*Cl* 113: undé
de . . . e de . . .; *Cd* 113: undé . . . e . . .);
D 124, 174: undee de . . . et de . . .; *H*/*Hg*
13: undé . . . et de . . . *Syn.*: DE . . . ET
DE . . .[1], ONDOIÉ DE . . . ET DE . . . *Note*: the
term is apparently first attested in Matthew
Paris's blazon of the Basset arms: 'Scutum
album [*sic*, for aureum] undé de gules'
(Pusikan, p. 148). The expression, however, is normally followed by co-ordinated
prepositions (*de . . . et de . . .*) and Lat. *unde*
(= *undae*) 'waves' may have been intended.
On the form of the line and the modern

distinction between *wavy* and *nebuly*, consult Roger F. Pye, 'A Return to First Principles. IV', *Coat of Arms*, vii (1963), 295.

ondé de lonc de . . . et de . . ., *paly undy* (Fig. 20). *B* 210: oundee de long de . . . et de . . . (*Bl* 210 [214]: oundé de long de . . . et de . . .); *D* 185: undee de lung de . . . et de . . . *Note:* Gernon arms. *Aspilogia II*, p. 157, note to item 214: 'The arms are perhaps intended as a pun on the name Gernons, whiskers or beard'; see also p. 108. OFr. *gernon*, however, did not mean beard (= OFr. *barbe*), but moustache, the hair on or on either side of a man's upper lip.

ondoié de . . . et de . . ., *barry undy* (Fig. 7). *CP* 37, 120: ondoié de . . . et de . . .; *CPA* 160: ondoié de . . . et a . . . *Syn.:* see ONDÉ DE . . . ET DE . . .

*****or,** *or* (*yellow*). Very frequent in literary sources, e.g. *Thèbes*, v. 2989: a or; *Ille et Galeron*, v. 410: d'or; *Enéas*, v. 4457: D'or; *Tristan de Thomas*, v. 2182: d'or; *Cligés*, v. 4741: d'or; *Escoufle*, v. 1136: d'or; *Didot Perceval*, pp. 228, 231: d'or; *Joufroi*, v. 408: A or; *EO*, vv. 976, 2542: d'or; *CC*, vv. 712, 965: d'or; *K*, vv. 50, 60: de or; v. 55: de fin or; v. 86: De or fyn. Extremely frequent in the rolls where it is the only term used, e.g. *BA* 2, 4: d'or; *B* 1, 3: d'or; *D* 5, 13: de or; *CP* 1, 2, 105 *bis* (see ESCUÇON[1], *Note*): d'or; *M* 1, 4: d'or. For other uses, see EN L'OR, EN OR, SOR L'OR. *Syn.:* DORÉ, JAUNE, OR VERMEIL, SAFRIN. *Note:* cf. DORER, PALETÉ. Bouly de Lesdain, p. 231 n. 3, lists 41 heraldic or quasi-heraldic mentions of *or* in twelfth-century French literature. Matthew Paris alternates between *aureus* and *d'or*, and in one instance provides the agglutinated form *dor* (Pusikan, p. 145: 'Scutum *de dor* cheveruns cum bordura de gules'). In *C* 58 ('Le countee de Cleve, gules un escocheon d'argent un carbuncle de flurté'), emendation of the second last word from *de* to *d'or* is supported by *Cl/Cd* 58. *D* 1, 2, 5, and 6 are found in partially erased blazons. According to Prinet's notes, *d'or* in *CP* 60, in one of the two mentions of *CP* 119, and in one of the three mentions of *CP* 131 is in error. Gough H, p. 140, note to item 48: '[*H* 47] seems to be incorrect.' The first *or* in *Hg* 2 is an error for *argent* (see Gough H,

p. 130, note to item 2). For *do* in *H* 25, see DO[1].

oreille, (*serpent's*) *ear*. Complete blazon provided s.v. SERPENT.

oreille d'une mule, *mule's ear*. *Cassidorus*, ii. 597: En ce que la dame ert en tel point, li est venuz uns varlez devant, et li dist: 'Dame, la hors a un chevalier, qui est de toutes armes armez, et dist qu'il veult a vous parler.—Dis tu voir?' dist elle. 'Voirement dis je voir,' dist il, 'a toutes ces enseignes qu'il a en son escu .ii. oreilles d'une blanche mule, et ou pic de l'escu li pent la queue, si que bien le puet on veoir, et avec tout ce maine il la mule ainsi mehaignie aprés lui en destre.' *Note:* the lady in question is the wife of the Duke of Lorraine; the varlet is announcing the arrival of her lover who, on an earlier occasion, manhandled her and cut off her mule's ears and tail (ii. 592: 'et ot la queue et les oreilles coupees'). The lover's shield, therefore, bears the symbol of her humiliation. The source of this episode has been discussed by J. Neale Carman in his review article entitled 'New Light on *Le Roman de Cassidorus*', *RPh.*, xxi (1967), 220.

oriol, *oriole* (Fig. 197). *TA*, v. 674: A l'oriol de niceté.

orle[1], *bordure* (*border outlining the edge of the shield*) (Fig. 114). *BA* 14, 202: a l'orle; *EO*, vv. 4836–8:

Et Danemons ses fieus teles avoit,
Mais que une ourle qui les descounoissoit
I ot de gueules qui bien y avenoit.

For other uses, see EN L'ORLE[1], ORLE ENDENTÉ, ORLE ENDENTÉ ENVIRON, ORLE ENGRESLÉ, ORLE ENTIER, ORLE O LIEPARZ. *Syn.:* see BORDURE[1]. *Note:* cf. ORLÉ, ORLURE DE L'ENCHAMPURE A ROSES. The word is usually but not always masculine in Old French, a gender it has retained in the modern idiom. According to Wagner, *Historic Heraldry*, p. 111, E. *orle* 'voided escutcheon' assumed its present-day meaning only in the sixteenth century. H. S. London, 'Notes and Reflections', pp. 203–4, outlines the history of the terms *orle, false scocheon, voided scocheon* (see also his 'Some Medieval Treatises', pp. 173–4) and adds (p. 204): 'I have not found the word orle used either for a voided scocheon or for a broad tressure before the middle or latter half of the sixteenth century, e.g. in Gerard Legh's *Accedence of Armorie*, 1564, fo. 68.' On the same page, London observes that he has found the term orle used in the meaning of BORDURE[1] in the fifteenth century, a usage which our examples antedate by two centuries. See also ESCUÇON[1], *Note*.

orle[2], *in orle* (Fig. 125). See MERLOZ EN L'ORLE, ORLE DE MERLOZ, ORLE DE POIRES, ORLE DE WITECOCS, ORLE OF MERLOZ. *Syn.*: see BORDURE[2]. *Note*: cf. EN L'ORLE[1].

orle[3], see EN L'ORLE[3].

orlé, *with a bordure. Enéas*, v. 4457: D'or fu toz li escuz orlez; *EO*, v. 5161: et ert d'azur orlés; *CC*, vv. 1544–5: Et s'estoit li escus ourlés / De geules. Bien iert acesmés. *Syn.*: see BORDÉ[1]. *Note*: Prinet CC, p. 179: 'Comme les hérauts de son temps, il se sert du mot *ourlé*, là où nous employons le mot *bordé*.'

orle de merloz, *orle of martlets* (Fig. 125). *B* 23 (*Ba* 23, see LES MERLOZ; *Bb* 23: un urle d' [a martlet is tricked]; *Bc/Bl* 23, see BORDURE DE MERLOZ), 186: ung urle dez merlotts (*Bl* 186 [190], see MERLOZ EN L'ORLE). *Syn.*: see BORDURE DE MERLETES.

orle de poires, *orle of pears* (Fig. 230). *Cleomadés*, v. 738: A .i. ourle de verdes poires.

orle de witecocs, *orle of woodcocks* (Fig. 207). *Cleomadés*, v. 11313: A un ourle de witecos.

orlé d'une enbordure par conoissance, see ORLÉ PAR CONOISSANCE D'UNE ENBORDURE.

orle endenté, *bordure indented* (Fig. 115). *EO*, vv. 975–6, 2535–47:

Armes ot verdes a une orle endentee
D'or, et estoit de gueules besentee.

. . . .

'Biaus niés,' dist Namles, 'demain serez portans
Mes droites armes, car tieus est mes commans.'
Et dist Ogiers: 'De ce sui moult joians,
Moult en doi estre envers vous mercians
Quant si preudons m'est ses armes carchans;
Ne les lairai tant com serai vivans
Car je ne sai armes si acesmans
K'armes qui sont d'or qui est reluisans.
A un lyon de sable qu'est rampans,

Encore y a chose moult avenans:
L'ourle endentee de gueules flamboians;
L'endentee ourle ne m'iert pas demorans,
A l'orle entiere les arai a tous tans';

TC, v. 1998: L'orle . . . endenté; *K*, v. 266: O le ourle endentee. For another use, see ORLE ENDENTÉ ENVIRON. *Syn.*: see BORDURE ENDENTEE. *Note*: refers to ENDENTÉ[1] and ORLE[1]. Comte de Marsy, pp. 194–5: 'Dans les notes qui suivent son texte, M. Scheler dit, en parlant de l'*orle endentée*: "Je ne saisis pas exactement le sens des deux vers qui suivent, d'où il paraît résulter que la bordure endentée accuse un degré de chevalerie inférieur, et qu'Ogier exprime la résolution de se rendre un jour digne de porter la bordure entière. Il y a ici une question de science héraldique que je laisse à d'autres à élucider." Je suis presque aussi embarrassé que le savant éditeur des *Enfances Ogier*, mais je crois cependant qu'il faut comprendre ce passage, en supposant que Naimes veut laisser entendre que la valeur de son neveu le lui rendra plus cher, resserrera les liens de sa parenté, et en fera en quelque sorte son fils. Ce ne sont pas les rangs de chevalerie que marquent les brisures, mais les degrés de parenté et, dans nos poèmes, ils se simplifient d'autant plus que l'on se rapproche du chef de la famille.' On this passage, consult Henry, iii. 351, note to *EO*, v. 2535, cited above, s.v. DROITES ARMES[2], *Note*. Ogier differences his arms from those of his uncle Naimes by bearing a full border instead of an indented one. Cf. FLEUR DE LIS TOUT EN MILIEU, *Note*.

orle endenté environ, *bordure indented* (Fig. 115). *EO*, vv. 5028–9:

Mais il y ot, pour descomparison,
Ourle de gueules endenté environ.

Syn.: see BORDURE ENDENTEE. *Note*: see DROITES ARMES[2], *Note*, and POUR DESCOMPAROISON.

orle engreslé, *bordure indented* (Fig. 115). *K*, v. 252: O la rouge ourle engreellie (W: engreelie). *Syn.*: see BORDURE ENDENTEE. *Note*: refers to ENGRESLÉ[1] and ORLE[1].

orle entier, *bordure* (Fig. 114). *EO*, v. 2547: A l'orle entiere les arai a tous tans (complete blazon provided s.v. ORLE EN-

DENTÉ). *Syn.*: see BORDURE[1]. *Note*: refers to ENTIER[2] (full, not indented) and ORLE[1].

orlé environ, *with a bordure.* Guillaume, v. 372: D'or fu urlé environ a desmesure. *Syn.*: see BORDÉ[1].

orle of merloz, *orle of martlets* (Fig. 125). The complete blazons read as follows: *Bb* 56: Patric de Chevres, barry argent et gules an urle of [a martlet tricked] sable (*B* 56: Patrik de Chaurcy, burelé d'argent et de goules [*sic*, no orle]; *Ba* 56, see OD MERLOZ; *Bc* 56, see MERLOZ EN L'ORLE). *Syn.*: see BORDURE DE MERLETES. *Note*: Chaworth arms.

orle o lieparz, *bordure semy of leopards.* *K*, v. 247: A rouge ourle o jaunes lupars. *Note*: refers to LIEPART (3).

orlé par conoissance d'une enbordure, *with a bordure as a difference.* Durmart, vv. 7863–5:

> L'escu vert a la fasse blanche,
> Si ert orlez par connissance
> D'une vermelle enbordeüre.

Syn.: see BORDÉ[1]. *Note*: refers to PAR CONOISSANCE[2].

orlure, *bordure* (Fig. 114). *FCE*, v. 8113: A orleüre. *Syn.*: see BORDURE[1]. *Note*: corresponds to *FCT*, v. 4347 (see BORDURE[1]).

orlure de l'enchampure a roses, *bordure semy of heraldic roses.* *K*, vv. 341–4:

> Cele au conte de Laönois
> Rouge o un blanc lyoun conois,
> E blanche en estoit le ourleüre
> A roses de l'enchampeüre.

Note: Wright, p. 15, translates the last two verses as follows: 'And the border was white, / With roses of the field.' In other words, *enchampeüre = champ* 'field'. In *H* 23, however ('Le counte Patrik porte de gulez ou ung leon d'argent ou le bordure d'argent de roses'), the same arms are blazoned without any indication of tincture for the roses which are, consequently, proper. I conclude that *K* omits any indication of tincture for the same reason, and that *enchampeüre*, which is nowhere else attested, means 'edge of the shield', i.e. that part of the shield covered by the bordure. *Laönois*, erroneously translated as 'Lennox' by Nicolas, pp. 210–11, and Wright, p. 14, was correctly identified with Lothian, the southern part of Scotland, by Sir Iain

Moncreiffe in *Coat of Arms*, ii (1952), 39. For this toponym and its Arthurian associations (King Loth and Tristan), see Flutre, s.v. *Leoneis*, and West, s.v. *Loënois*[1].

or vermeil, *or (yellow).* Troie, v. 7746: de fin or vermeil. For another use, see EN OR VERMEIL. *Syn.*: see OR.

ou[1] = **en le.** *Syn.*: EL. *Note*: it is difficult at times to determine whether *u* represents *ou*, i.e. the contraction for *en le*, or an abbreviation for the same locution. The former appears in the Bigot Roll, the latter in Walford's Roll (see Prinet WR, pp. 238 n. 3, 251.

ou[2], *with.* Separator appearing in several rolls. For another use, see AUTEL OU.

ou[3], *where (equivalent of MFr. 'où').* Bel Inconnu, vv. 5920–2:

> Un chevalier i ai veü
> Que i porte un escu d'azon,
> U d'ermine a un blanc lion;

SCT, fol. 126 *c* / *SCV*, fol. 92 *e*: Deus grandes blanches en i voit / Ou deus quartiers vermax avoit; *TC*, v. 3977: Ou li bar d'or estoient point; *K*, vv. 259–60, 482, 575–8:

> Baniere ot rouge, ou entallie
>   (W: entaillie)
> Ot fesse blanche engreellie.
>
> · · · · · ·
>
> Jaunes ou le egle verde estoit.
>
> · · · · · ·
>
> Baniere ot vermeille cum sanc,
> Croissillie o un chievron blanc,
> Ou un label de asur avoit,
> Por ce que ses peres vivoit.

For other uses, see CHIEF OU OT UNE COQUILLE, EN MILIEU OU LA TESTE DEL DRAGON ESTOIT. *Note*: the corresponding Latin form *ubi* appears in Matthew Paris (e.g. Pusikan, p. 124: 'Hugonis Dispensatoris. Album ubi benda nigra, aliud gules a or freté').

ou[4], *the conjunction 'or'.* The complete blazons read as follows: *BA* 28: Li sires (A: Le sire) de Drestre (A: Diestre), l'escu d'or a 2 bastons noirs de (Travers) [*sic*, A: de travers] ou triers (A: tu ers). Baneres et Rujers (A: Banneret et Ruyer); 90: Gerars de le (A: de la) Hamaide, l'escu d'or a .iii. haimades ou haimaides (A: hamades ou haimades) au lablel (A: lalbel) d'azur besandé (A: bezandé) d'argent. Flamens. *Note*: actually not part of the blazon, this conjunction serves to indicate hesitation on the part of the scribe as to the proper spelling of a word.

ou chantel devant, *in dexter chief* (Fig. 73). See FESSE AU LIONCEL PASSANT OU CHANTEL DEVANT. *Syn.*: EL CHANTEL, EL CHANTEL DEVANT, OU CHIEF², OU QUARTIER², OU QUARTIER DEVANT.

ou chief¹, *in chief* (Fig. 72). See BASTON DE TRAVERS OU CHIEF, MERLETE OU CHIEF, OISELET OU CHIEF. *Syn.*: see EN LE CHIEF². *Note*: refers to CHIEF².

ou chief², *in dexter chief* (Fig. 73). See FESSIÉ D'UNE BARRE ET OU CHIEF UN LIONCEL PASSANT. *Syn.*: see OU CHANTEL DEVANT. *Note*: refers to CHIEF³.

oueille passant, *ewe passant.* See OEILLE PASSANT.

ouisse, *hind, doe* (Fig. 159). *BA* 5, 85: a une ouisse. *Syn.*: BISSE. *Note*: according to Adam-Even, p. 20, *BA* 5 provides the same arms as *C* 65 (Adam-Even's note actually reads: 'le Walford Roll Nº 57 donne les mêmes armes: *d'or à une byse de gules*', but he is referring to Prinet WR, p. 247, no. 57); see BISSE. In his glossary, p. 20, Adam-Even suggests a connection with OFr. *oueille*, but the latter means 'ewe', not 'hind'. See OEILLE PASSANT. OFr. *ouisse* is nowhere else attested, to my knowledge, and may be an orthographical slip for OFr. *bisse*. On the Tierstein arms (= *BA* 5, *C* 65), consult *Aspilogia II*, p. 192, note to item 120.

ou les croiseletes, *crusily* (Fig. 35). *H* 99: ou lez croiselettes (*Hg* 99 [100], see OD LES CROISILLES). *Syn.*: see CROISELÉ.

ou les croissanz, *semy of crescents* (Fig. 34). *H* 85: ou lez cressaunts (G: cressauntz; *Hg* 85, see OD LES CROISSANZ). *Syn.*: OD LES CROISSANZ.

ou les pies, *semy of magpies* (Fig. 43). *H* 91: ou lez pies (*Hg* 91 [90], see OD LES COUWES). *Syn.*: OD LES COUWES. *Note*: see OD LES COUWES, *Note*.

ou milieu, *in the middle of the shield.* See ESCUÇON OU MILIEU. *Syn.*: see ENMI.

ou milieu un home crucefié qui tout estoit sanglant, *Our Lord upon the Cross proper* (Fig. 129). *Queste*, p. 33: ou mileu un

home crucefié qui toz estoit sanglenz. *Syn.*: HOME QUI ESTOIT CRUCEFIÉ.

ou noir, *charging the sable sections of the shield* (1) *referring to a gyronny field.* See CROISETE OU . . . (2) *referring to alternating stripes of a barry field.* See QUINTEFEUILLES OU . . .

ou quartier¹, *on the canton* (Fig. 118). See MOLETE OU QUARTIER. *Syn.*: EN LE QUARTIER¹.

ou quartier², *in dexter chief* (Fig. 73). See FESSE A UN LIONCEL PASSANT OU QUARTIER. *Syn.*: see OU CHANTEL DEVANT.

ou quartier de . . ., *in the . . . quarter (of a quarterly field).* See ESQUARTELÉ DE . . . ET DE . . . A UNE MOLETE OU QUARTIER DE . . *Syn.*: see MOLET EN LE QUARTIER DEVANT. *Note*: though only a tincture is specified and thus either quarter 1 or 4 could be involved, in actuality the first quarter is indicated.

ou quartier devant, *in dexter chief* (Fig. 73). See COC OU QUARTIER DEVANT. *Syn.*: see OU CHANTEL DEVANT.

ouvert, *open.* See MEIN OUVERTE, OUVERTE MEIN.

ouverte mein, *open hand.* *TA*, v. 1649: .i. label d'overtes meins. *Syn.*: see MEIN. *Note* arms of Largesce.

ovec, *with.* See AVUEC.

paillié, *diapered* (Fig. 51). The complete blazon reads as follows: *B* 57: Phelip Marmion, de veiree ove la fece pailé (*B* 57: Philip Marmyon, de veer od la fesse de pailé). *Syn.*: DIASPRÉ. *Note*: cf. *Navarre* 173 'Le sire de Clere, d'argent a une fesse de paellé'. The field is either green or blue the diapering gold. Adam-Even WB, p. 56 'Le *paillé* (Nº 414, etc.), spécial à la Normandie, est ici une simple diaprure d'or sans l'aigle et le lion qui en seront presque l'essentiel par la suite.' H. S. London pointed out, however, that 'Sir Philip Marmion's own seal in 1265 represents the *paillé* by a row of five contiguous annulets enclosing small roses or cinquefoils' (*Aspilogia II*, p. 161; see also pp. 106; 126, note to item 57; and, especially, appendix 1, pp. 160–3, which is a discussion of this design). OFr. *palie, paile* is a derivative of Lat. *pallium* 'cloak' and originally meant 'rich, ornamental cloth'. It is this sense which yielded the term under discussion here. As early as the thirteenth century, however, OFr. *paile* became specialized in the meaning 'fine cloth to cover a coffin' and this usage gave us E. *pall* and MFr. *poêle*. Major T. R. Davies, in a letter to the editor, *Coat of Arms*, ix (1966), 117, points out: 'Heraldically it was treated as a "Fur" and often used with a colour, not with a metal charge.' For the modern distinction between Fr. *diapré* and *paillé*, see Veyrin-Forrer, pp. 20–1: 'Quand le diapré n'est pas du même émail que le champ ou la pièce qu'il orne, il devient un *meuble*, et, à ce titre, il faut le blasonner, bien qu'il n'ait pas de forme fixe ni précise; dans ce cas de très bons héraldistes disent *paillé* au lieu de *diapré*, ce qui évite toute confusion.' Cf. PALETÉ.

pal, *pale, pile* (Fig. 88). *CPA* 9: a .iii. pals; 163: a .ii. pans [*sic*, for paus]. *Syn.*: BASTON[2], PEL, PELET, PILE. *Note*: cf. PEUS RECOUPÉS DEUS . . . UN. Modern usage distinguishes between the vertical stripe known as the pale and the wedge-shaped pile, whereas medieval practice confused both ordinaries. Thus Matthew Paris used the Latin equivalent of 'pales' to blazon a shield showing piles for the Earl of Huntington (Pusikan, p. 144: 'Scutum aureum, tres pali [Pusikan: palli] aurei [*sic*, for gules]'). On the pale–pile confusion, consult Roger F. Pye, 'A Return to First Principles. I. The Pile', *Coat of Arms*, vii (1962), 4–6; see also letters to the editor, pp. 85, 86, 172.

palé de . . . et de . . ., *paly* (Fig. 19). *B* 32: palé [de . . . et de . . .] (*Bl* 32: palé [de . . . et de . . .]); 14, 171: palé de . . . et de . . . (*Bl* 14, 171 [175]: palé de . . . et de . . .); *C* 7 (*Cl* 7: palé de . . . e de . . .; *Cd* 7, see PALÉ DE . . . ET DE . . . PIECES), 24 (*Cl/Cd* 24: palé de . . . e de . . .), 26 (*Cl* 26: palé de . . . et de . . .; *Cd* 26: palé de . . . e de . . .), 52 (*Cl/Cd* 52: palé de . . . e de . . .), 90 (*Cl* 90: palé de . . . e de . . .; *Cd* 90: pallé . . . e . . .), 176 (*Cl* 176: palé de . . . et de . . .), 179 (*Cl* 179: palé de . . . et de . . .): paly de . . . et de . . .; 131: palee de . . . et . . . (*Cl* 131: palé de . . . e de . . .; *Cd* 131: pallé de . . . e de . . .); 142: palee [de . . . et de . . .] (*Cl* 142: palé [de . . . et de . . .]); 180: palé de . . . et de . . . (*Cl* 180: palé de . . . et de . . .); *D* 6, 30, 32, 40, 43, 48, 57,

115, 162: palé de . . . et de . . .; 73: paslé de . . . et de . . .; *TC*, v. 1082: Cil qui porte l'escu palé; *Cleomadés*, v. 719: L'escu d'or palé de vermeill; *CP* 9, 84, 105, 115: pallé de . . . et de . . .; *CPA* 6: palé de . . . et de . . .; *H* 29: pallé de . . . et de . . . (*Hg* 29: palee de . . . et de . . .); 67: palee [de . . . et de . . .] (*Hg* 67: palé [de . . . et de . . .]); 84: palee de . . . [et] de . . . (*Hg* 84: palé de . . . et de . . .); 89: palee de . . . et de . . . (*Hg* 89 [87]: pallee de . . . et de . . .); *Hg* 59: palé de . . . et de . . . (*H* 59, see DE . . . ET DE . . .[2]); *K*, vv. 253–4: palee / De argent e de asur . . .; v. 438: palé [de . . . e de . . .]. *Syn.*: DE . . . ET DE . . .[2], DE LONG EN LONG BENDÉ, ESTACHIÉ CONTREVAL DE . . . ET DE . . ., ESTACHIÉ DE . . . ET DE . . ., PALÉ DE . . . ET DE . . . PIECES. *Note*: cf. PEUS RECOUPÉS DEUS . . . UN. As is evident here, *palé de . . . et de . . .* is often used where modern practice requires listing the number of pallets; see Prinet WR, p. 228 n. 3; cf. BASTON[2], PAL, PEL, PELET, PILE, PEUS RECOUPÉS DEUS . . . UN. In *H* 59, the field is *paly or and gules*, though the term is omitted; see DE . . . ET DE . . .[2]. Is *pale* in *TA*, vv. 1186–7 ('L'escu pale a lievre rampant / Portoit, qui estoit fet de tremble)', a pun on this word? On these arms (Couardie), see LIEVRE RAMPANT, *Note*.

palé de . . . et de . . . pieces, *paly of . . .* (*the number of pieces, i.e. stripes, is indicated*) (Fig. 19). The complete blazon reads as follows: *Cd* 7: Le roy d'Aragon, palé d'or et de gules 8 p. (*C/Cl* 7, see PALÉ DE . . . ET DE . . .). *Syn.*: see PALÉ DE . . . ET DE . . .

paleté, *gold-spangled* (Fig. 52). *SCT*, fol. 93 *d* / *SCV*, fol. 127 *c*: A l'escu qu'il voit paleté. *Note*: in the same work, the field of Yvain's shield is said to be *or* (yellow); see JAUNE. OFr. *paleté* corresponds to MFr. *pailleté*. The dots we have used to illustrate this tincture are merely conjectural. This is, of course, the conventional way of representing gold in the system which, according to Oswald Barron (see Introduction, p. 1), was introduced in 1600.

pans, *ghost word*. See PAL.

paon, *peacock*. See D'IEUZ DE PAON OEILLETÉ, ROUE DE PAON. *Note*: on the heraldic peacock, consult George Bellew, 'Heraldic Birds', *Coat of Arms*, ii (1953), 253.

papegai, *popinjay* (*parrot*) (Fig. 201). (1) *alone on the field. TA,* vv. 672–3:

A. iiii. papegais d'argent,
Qui chantent de joliveté;

Escanor, v. 3712: L'escu d'or a .v. papegauz. (2) *fess between popinjays.* The complete blazon reads as follows: *B* 129: Marmaduk de Twenge, d'argent a trois papegayes de vert ung fece de goules (*Bl* 129 [133], see PAPEGAIS ET UNE FESSE). For other uses, see FESSE A PAPEGAIS, FESSE ET PAPEGAIS. *Note:* popinjays are mentioned by Matthew Paris in his blazon of the Thweng arms (Pusikan, p. 128: 'Scutum album cum fessa rubea et papaginibus [the editor indicates that *papagallis* is also possible; the MS. reads *papag*'] viridibus'). Prinet TA, p. 49 (apropos of the arms of Cointise [Prettiness, Grace]): 'Il faut l'imagination d'un poète pour trouver de la "joliveté" au cri d'un perroquet!' The fact remains, however, that the alleged beauty of the parrot's song was a medieval commonplace. María Rosa Lida de Malkiel, 'Arpadas lenguas', *Estudios dedicados a D. Ramón Menéndez Pidal,* ii (Madrid, 1950), 227–52, cites nine examples from medieval Spanish and Portuguese literature in this regard. On the confusion of *papelart* and *papegai,* see PAPELART, *Note.*

papegais et une fesse, *fess between popinjays. Bl* 129 [133]: ove trois papelays . . . et une fesse (*B* 129, see PAPEGAI [2]). *Syn.:* see PAPEGAI (2). *Note:* refers to FESSE (1) D. 1. e.

papelart, *sanctimonious person, hypocrite. Chanson d'Antioche,* ii. 246, v. 991: En l'escu de son col ot paint uns papelart. *Note:* I am indebted to Professor Philippe Ménard of the University of Toulouse for bringing this curious shield to my attention. In his edition (ii [Paris, 1848], 246 n. 1), Paulin Paris states: 'Papelart, var.: Beleart. E. *uns lupars.* A. F. Baelart. B. Je ne trouve pas *baielart,* ou *bailart,* dans les Glossaires. J'entends Papelart, *papegai* ou perroquet.' The translation of this epic by the Marquise de Sainte-Aulaire (*Chroniques des croisades. La Chanson d'Antioche composée au XIIe siècle par Richard le Pèlerin, renouvelée par Graindor de Douai au XIIIe siècle* [Paris, 1862], p. 386) follows Paulin Paris's suggestion when it renders the verse in ques-

tion as follows: 'Sur l'écu qu'il a au col on a peint un perroquet.' This is the shield of Corbaran, the adversary of the Count of Normandy. If the reading is authentic and the poem is to be dated about 1185, this is an earlier use of the term *papelart* than has heretofore been noted (*c.* 1220 in Dauzat, s.v. *papelard;* same date in *BW*[4], s.v. *lard*). In a private communication to me dated 29 November 1969, Professor Lewis A. M. Sumberg of the University of Kentucky informs me that the word *papelart* appears only in MS. B.N. f. fr. 12558 (early fourteenth century), but that the latter generally provides the most reliable text. He conjectures that Graindor substituted this term for the word *papion* which he found in his source, the poem by Richard le Pèlerin, but could not understand. Sumberg identifies the latter with the *papiones* 'beasts (hyenas?) who eat ravenously and furtively' of Jacques de Vitry. According to *BW*[4], *papelard* 'contient peut-être l'anc. verbe *paper* "manger goulûment", lat. *pappāre,* dit ainsi parce que le faux dévot mange le lard en cachette . . ., ou bien est un dér. d'un anc. verbe **papeler* "bavarder", attesté encore dans les patois sous les formes élargies *papeloter, papelauder* et appuyé par l'anc. fr. *papeter* "babiller"'. For a more convincing explanation (Lat, *papalem* > OFr. *papel* 'representative, adherent of the Pope'+the pejorative suffix -*ard*), see V. Frederic Koenig, 'On the Etymology of Old French *papelard*', *RPh.,* xxii (1969), 492–7: '[*Papelart*] served primarily to designate hypocritical clerics and [was] primarily associated with the orders credited with ultramontane ties' (p. 497). In the *Roman de la Rose* (*c.* 1236), *Papelardie* wears a hair shirt and holds a psalter (*Le Roman de la Rose par Guillaume de Lorris et Jean de Meun,* ed. Ernest Langlois, ii [Paris, 1920], vv. 407–40); see Ménard, pp. 162, 530, 542.

papelay, see PAPEGAIS ET UNE FESSE.

papeloné, *scaly* (*an ornamental pattern resembling fish scales*) (Fig. 53). *BA* 286: papellonné; *CC,* v. 1167: Un escu vi papellonné. *Note:* Prinet CC, p. 168 n. 4, observes that *Navarre* 951 uses the locution *decoupé sor* to describe the same arms as those in *CC*, v. 1167 ('d'argent decouppé sur gueules'). Cf. also the following passage in the fourteenth-century *Tournoiement des Dames de Paris*, vv. 84–6:

> Elle est d'azur a l'aigle d'or,
> De sinople tres bien bordee,
> D'argent menu papeillonnee.

Adam-Even WB, introduction, p. 56, provides the following description: 'Le *papelonné* (N° 1038, etc.) est formé de rangées de croissants juxtaposés, les vides étant garnis de pièces rappelant les mouchetures d'hermines.' London, however, in *Aspilogia II*, appendix II, p. 166, has argued that the term was synonymous with *diaspré*. Whatever the case may be, *papeloné* appears to be akin to *papillon* 'butterfly' and *papillote* 'spangle, ornament', and *papelonné* in modern French heraldry means 'scaly' (Veyrin-Forrer, p. 56). Cf. FALLOLÉ.

par, see DE PAR.

par conoissance[1], *as a distinctive device*. See TOUT . . . MES SOR LE . . . PAR CONOISSANCE.

par conoissance[2], *as a difference*. See ORLÉ PAR CONOISSANCE D'UNE ENBORDURE. *Syn.*: see PAR DESCONOISSANCE.

par desconoissance, *as a difference*. See ARMES DE PLAIN FORS QU'EL QUARTIER AVOIT EGLETES PAR DESCONOISSANCE. *Syn.*: PAR CONOISSANCE[2], PAR DESPAREIL, PAR RECONOISSANCE ENTRE . . . ET . . ., POUR DESCOMPAROISON, POUR DESPAREILLE. *Note*: cf. AUTEL[2].

par despareil, *as a difference*. *TC*, vv. 896–901:

> Mes iex tornai a si bone eure
> Que je vi tout a descovert
> Un chevalier d'armes couvert
> D'or fin a un çaintour vermoil,
> Et si porte par desparoil
> Une moleste d'or en chief.

Syn.: see PAR DESCONOISSANCE.

par desparoil, *as a difference*. See PAR DESPAREIL.

par desus le . . ., *on, over the* . . . See BOUCEL PAR DESUS LE . . . *Syn.*: see SOR.

par entre, *between*. See ESTRE DE CHALENGE PAR ENTRE . . . ET . . . *Note*: cf. ENTRE.

par eschequiers, *checky* (Fig. 9). *Thèbes*, vv. 5286–8:

> Sor son hauberc ot conoissance
> De colors de dous pailes chiers
> Et entailliez par eschequiers.

Syn.: see ESCHEQUÉ DE . . . ET DE . . . *Note*: these arms, borne by Melampus who carries a shield party gules and argent (see DEMI . . . ET DEMI . . .), are noted by Wagner, *Heralds and Heraldry*, p. 13 (see also appendix A, p. 121); cf. the checky arms of Waleran, Count of Meulan and Lord of Worcester, and those of his maternal uncle Ralph, Count of Vermandois, cited by Wagner, pp. 14–15. The verses here refer to the edition of *Thèbes* by L. Constans. Verses 5287–8 evidently do not appear in the base manuscript followed by Professor G. Raynaud de Lage who omits them in his edition (after v. 5512).

par le . . ., l'autre . . ., see PARTI DE . . . ET DE . . . PAR LE . . ., L'AUTRE . . .

par le . . ., le . . ., see PARTI DE . . . ET DE . . . PAR LE . . ., LE . . .

par le milieu, see CROIS PAR LE MILIEU.

par les bouz, *at the tips (referring to a cross patonce)*. See CROIS ESLARGIE PAR LES BOUZ. *Syn.*: AUS BOUZ.

par mi[1], *in the middle (of the shield)*. See BENDE PAR MI DE BELIC, DE BENDES PAR MI LISTÉ, ESCUÇON PAR MI, LION PAR MI, MEIN PAR MI, PAR MI RAMPER. *Syn.*: see ENMI.

par mi[2], *through the middle*. See ESPEE AU PONG ET AU HELT QUI TRANCHE LE LION PAR MI.

parmi, *preposition*. See PARMI LE VERT. *Note*: on the spelling of this word, see EN MI, *Note*.

parmi le vert, *here and there in, or through, the vert*. *Durmart*, vv. 10005–8:

> Parmi le vert cendal paroit
> Li argens qui resplendissoit
> Cant li vens faisoit venteler
> Les fuelletes al solever.

par mi ramper, *to be rampant*. *TA*, v. 616: Par mi rampoit misires Nobles; v. 704: Par mi rampoit Bruns sans pitié. *Note*: cf. RAMPANT.

par reconoissance entre . . . et . . ., see LABEL PAR RECONOISSANCE ENTRE . . . ET . . . *Syn.*: see PAR DESCONOISSANCE.

part, (1) *one side, one half (of a party shield)*. See D'UNE PART. *Syn.*: MOITIÉ. *Note*: see

DEMI[2]. (2) *a canton or quarter* (Fig. 117). See QUART PART. *Syn.*: see CHANTEL[1]. *Note*: Matthew Paris uses the Latin equivalent in the meaning '(upper and lower) half of the shield [as sectioned off by a fess]': 'Haimonis Pecche. Scutum album, cheverunes de gules scilicet pars superior et inferior' (Pusikan, p. 148).

parti de . . . et de . . ., *party per pale* (Fig. 21). *FCA*, vv. 802–3: Ses escuz estoit d'or partiz / Et d'azur de riche façon; *Roman de la Violette*, vv. 2874–5: En l'escu k'il avoit parti / D'or et d'asur; *Roman des Eles*, v. 473: partis de lecherie; *Perlesvaus*, pp. 79, 404: parti de . . . e de . . .; p. 189: parti de . . . et de . . .; *Lancelot propre*, iii. 407: parti de . . . et de . . .; *TA*, v. 993: Parti d'outrage et de delices; vv. 1126–7: Que parti ot double chaance / De rencontres et d'envïaus; vv. 1554–5: parti / D'oreisons et d'obedïence; vv. 1811–12: partie / De largesce et de cortoisie; vv. 1984–5: parti / De proesce et de corteisie; *BA* 183: parti de . . . et de . . .; *B* 17, 78: party de . . . et de . . . (*Bl* 17, 78: party de . . . et de . . .); *Bl* 107 [109] (the complete blazon reads as follows): Johan de Courtenay, party les armes le comte de Garenne et de vert deux barres d'argent sur le tout; *C* 101: party de . . . et . . . (*Cl/Cd* 101, see PARTI DE . . . ET DE . . . EN LONC; *D* 9: parté de . . . et de . . .; *Cleomadés*, v. 723: De gueules et de vert partis; *H* 3: party de . . . et de . . . (*Hg* 3: parti de . . . et de . . .). *Syn.*: DEMI . . . ET DEMI . . ., MI PARTI DE . . . ET DE . . ., PARTI DE . . . ET DE . . . EN LONC. *Note*: cf. D'AUTRE PART, DE . . . ET DE . . .[3], DEMI[2], D'UNE PART, L'AUTRE MOITIÉ, PARTIR DE . . . ET DE . . ., SONGIÉ DE . . . ET DE . . . On the connection between *Roman des Eles* and *TA*, see RAMPANT, *Note*. As Prinet *TA*, p. 44, observes: 'Des grandes partitions, le poète ne paraît connaître que le *parti* ou le *mi-parti* (qu'il ne distingue pas).' Prinet refers here to the modern distinction between impalement (Fr. *partition*) and dimidiation (Fr. *mi-partition*). In the latter case, usually involving the arms of two families joined together by marriage (the husband's appearing on the dexter side, the wife's on the sinister), only one half of each shield cut down the middle vertically is shown. Impalement, on the other hand, is an arrangement whereby the whole coat, or as much of it as possible, appears on the appropriate half of the shield. Dimidiation is attested in the twelfth century (seal of Robert of Pinkney; see Blair, pp. 8, 10; Plate VI *f*) and became widespread in the latter part of the thirteenth on women's arms (Blair, p. 22). Impalement, which appears in the fourteenth century (Blair, pp. 22–3; Hope, p. 23), eventually supplanted this practice, except in a few isolated cases (see Boutell, p. 133). An example of marshalling is provided below, s.v. PARTIR DE . . . ET DE . . . Early blazon uses the term *parti de . . . et de . . .* and *mi parti de . . . et de . . .* synonymously. Thus in the *Perlesvaus*, both expressions refer to the same knight (see MI PARTI DE . . . ET DE . . .). Moreover, in the black letter editions of this work, published in 1516 and 1523 respectively, whose source is believed to be a manuscript belonging to the best group (see Nitze, ii. 24–42), 'li Partiz Chevaliers' (p. 79) is referred to as the 'Chevalier My Party' (see Table of Proper Names, i. 419). Nitze's designation of this character as the 'Motley Knight' (i. 419) refers to the parti-coloured dress of the professional jester in the Middle Ages (*OED*, s.v. *motley*). For an illustration of the vestimentary use of this term, see ENTIER[2], *Note*. On the position of the lion in *B* 17 (Marshal arms), see LION RAMPANT (2) A. and *Note*, and cf. PARTI DE . . . ET DE . . . EN LONC, *Note*. For *Bl* 107 [109], see *Aspilogia II*, p. 136, note to item 109. In *TC*, v. 1995 ('Parti des armes de Douai'), *parti de . . .* means 'ornamented with', not 'party' (Delbouille's glossary, p. 176: 'doté de, garni de').

parti de . . . et de . . ., dedenz le . . . et . . . sor le . . ., *party per pale (position of the charges is specified)* (Fig. 21). *EO*, vv. 5004–6:

Armes parties d'or et d'azur portoit,
Dedenz l'azur flours de lis d'or avoit
Et demi aigle noire sor l'or seoit.

Syn.: see PARTI DE . . . ET DE . . ., LE . . ., LE . . ., PARTI DE . . . ET DE . . ., PAR LE . . ., L'AUTRE . . ., PARTI DE . . . ET DE . . ., PAR LE . . ., LE . . .; cf. PARTI DE . . . ET DE . . ., DE . . . SOR LE . . . ET DE . . . SOR LE . . . *Note*: arms of Charlemagne. On this coat, consult L. Carolus-Barré and P. Adam-

Even, 'Les armes de Charlemagne dans l'héraldique et l'iconographie médiévales', *Mémorial d'un voyage d'études de la Société nationale des antiquaires de France en Rhénanie* (*juillet 1951*) (Paris, 1953), pp. 289–308. The passage in question is cited on p. 289.

parti de . . . et de . . ., de . . . sor le . . . et de . . . sor le . . ., *party per pale (counter-colouring is specified)* (Fig. 21). The complete blazon reads as follows: *CP* 131: Li vicontes de Burniquet porte les armes mi party d'argent et de gheules a une fausse crois partie d'or et de gheules, pommelé, (d'or et) de gheules sur l'argent et d'or sur le gheules.

parti de . . . et de . . . endenté l'un en l'autre, *party per pale indented* (Fig. 24). *BA* 211, 224: party de . . . et de . . . endenté l'un en l'autre; 213: parti de . . . et de . . . endenté l'un en l'autre. *Syn.*: see PARTI ENDENTÉ DE . . . ET DE . . . *Note*: refers to ENDENTÉ[1].

parti de . . . et de . . . en lonc, *party per pale* (Fig. 21). *Cl* 101: party de . . . e de . . . en lunge (*C* 101, see PARTI DE . . . ET DE . . .; *Cd* 101: party de . . . e de . . . en lung). *Syn.*: see PARTI DE . . . ET DE . . . *Note*: Marshal family arms. The party palewise lion rampant is evidently an error: 'it should be all gules' (*Aspilogia II*, pp. 105; 196, note to item 143; cf. also LION RAMPANT, *Note*).

parti de . . . et de . . ., le . . ., le . . ., *party per pale (position of the charges is specified)* (Fig. 21). The complete blazon reads as follows: *C* 22: Le countee de Poiteres, party d'azure et de gulez, l'azure poudré a floretts d'or, le gulez poudré a turells d'or (*Cl* 22, see PARTI DE . . . ET DE . . ., PAR LE . . ., LE . . .; *Cd* 22, see PARTI DE . . . ET DE . . ., PAR LE . . ., L'AUTRE . . .). *Syn.*: see PARTI DE . . . ET DE . . ., DEDENZ LE . . . ET . . . SOR LE . . .

parti de . . . et de . . ., par le . . ., l'autre . . ., *party per pale (position of the charges is specified)* (Fig. 21). The complete blazon reads as follows: *Cd* 22: Le conte de Poisters, party azure et de gules, par le gules poudré a tupelles d'or, l'autre poudré a flouretes d'or (*C* 22, see PARTI DE . . . ET DE . . ., LE . . ., LE . . .; *Cl* 22, see PARTI DE . . . ET DE . . ., PAR LE . . ., LE . . .). *Syn.*: see PARTI DE . . . ET DE . . ., DEDENZ LE . . . ET . . . SOR LE . . .

parti de . . . et de . . ., par le . . ., le . . ., *party per pale (position of the charges is specified)* (Fig. 21). The complete blazon reads as follows: *Cl* 22: Le counte de Poyters, party d'azure de goule, per le goule poudré a turelles d'or, l'azur poudré a flurettes d'or (*C* 22, see PARTI DE . . . ET DE . . ., LE . . ., LE . . .; *Cd* 22, see PARTI DE . . . ET DE . . ., PAR LE . . ., L'AUTRE . . .). *Syn.*: see PARTI DE . . . ET DE . . ., DEDENZ LE . . . ET . . . SOR LE . . .

parti endenté de . . . et de . . ., *party per pale indented* (Fig. 24). *B* 4: party endentee de . . . et de . . . (*Bl* 4: party endenté de . . . et de . . .). *Syn.*: ENDENTÉ[4], PARTI DE . . . ET DE . . . ENDENTÉ L'UN EN L'AUTRE. *Note*: banner of Simon de Montfort; see *Aspilogia II*, p. 18, note to item 30; p. 115, note to item 4. On this device, consult Denholm-Young, *History and Heraldry*, pp. 44–5 (where it is erroneously referred to, however, as '*party per pale Argent and Gules*'); see also the *Dean Tract*, p. 27: 'La Banere q'apent al Counte de Leycestre endenté d'argent et de goules'. *CEMRA*, p. 4, omits the word *party* ('Le Comte de Leycestr' de gules ove un leon blank la cowe furchee et la baner' endenté d'or et de gules') which Wagner provides, however, in his *Historic Heraldry*, p. 35 ('Le Comte de Leycester de gules ove un leon blank la cowe furchee et la banner party endenté d'or et de gules'); see also *Aspilogia II*, p. 115, item 4.

partir de . . . et de . . ., *to impale*. *Artus*, p. 62: et por la grant amor qui estoit entre le neveu et les oncles, li partirent il lor armes de noir et de vermeil. *Note*: cf. PARTI DE . . . ET DE . . . The arms are those of Plares and of Madoc le Noir, the nephew and brother, respectively, of Raolais, the Red Knight of Estremores. They both should have borne plain sable, the author tells us, but out of love for Raolais (whose arms were plain gules), their shields were party sable and gules. On the terminology of marshalling, see PARTI DE . . . ET DE . . ., *Note*.

pas, see NE PAS ESTRE SEUL.

passant[1], *passant (i.e. passing by, in a walking attitude, as opposed to rampant, the normal attitude)*. See LIEPART PASSANT, LIEPART PASSANT COURONÉ, LIONCEAUS PASSANZ L'UN CONTRE L'AUTRE EN CHIEF, LIONCEL PASSANT, LION PASSANT, LION PASSANT A TESTE

DE MOUTON, LION PASSANT COURONÉ, OEILLE PASSANT. *Note*: cf. COURANT.

passant², *plain (referring to a cross with limbs extending to the edge of the shield)*. See CROIS PASSANT. *Syn.*: PLAIN². *Note*: see ENTIER², *Note*. The origin of the term *passant* in this sense is not known. Walford, in note *b*, p. 389 of his edition of *C*, suggests: 'It may have been equivalent to the Passion cross, i.e. the Latin cross', but OFr. *passant* is surely unrelated to the term Passion. Gough–Parker, p. 447, states that it is 'thought to be the equivalent of *throughout*, but probably means rather *over all*'. I lean toward the former explanation. The definition 'croix passant = cross patonce' in *Aspilogia II*, glossary, p. 228, is an error (see, for example, the correct reference to a plain cross on p. 198, note to item 156). According to the latter, p. 109, finally: '*passant* is apt to be omitted when there are other charges.'

passant³, *ghost word*. See CROIS A DEUS PASSANZ, LION PASSANT, *Note*.

passant⁴, *salient* (?). See LION PASSANT, *Note*.

passant oeille, *ewe passant*. See OEILLE PASSANT.

passerose, *hollyhock* (Fig. 237). *TA*, v. 1726: a une passerose. *Note*: the Modern French equivalent is *rose trémière*.

passeur, *ghost word*. See CROIS PASSEUR.

paté, *patonce*. See CROIS PATEE, CROIS PATEE ET PERCIEE, CROIS PERCIEE ET PATEE ET BOITⁿONEE. *Syn.*: see ESLARGI².

pate beké (?), see HERON PATÉ BEKÉ (?).

patonce, *patonce*. See CROIS PATONCE. *Syn.*: see ESLARGI².

paus, see PAL.

pees, see PIÉ.

peir, see NOIR.

pel, *pale, pile* (Fig. 88). *Bl* 124 [128] (*B* 124, see PELET), 158 [162] (*B* 158, see PILE): od trois peus; *C* 81: troiz peuz (*Cl/Cd* 81: a treys peuz); *TC*, v. 862: L'escu d'or a trois piés de guelle; *CP* 79: a trois peus (P: paus); 109: a trois peus; *M* 10: et ung penn [*sic*, for peus?]. For another use, see PEUS RECOUPÉS DEUS . . . UN. *Syn.*: see PAL. *Note*: on the Brechin arms (*C/Cl/Cd* 81) which feature three piles meeting in base, consult *Aspilogia II*, p. 181, note to item 64. Greenstreet, apropos of *M* 10, states: 'The word "penn" in the roll evidently means a pennon, which

is now considered, by many, to be the object originally intended to have been represented by the device in heraldry which we are accustomed to call a pile' (p. 228). See, however, PAL, *Note*. OFr. *pel* (the form *peus* may represent either a nominative singular or an oblique plural) is a regular development from Lat. *palum* 'stake'. *Aspilogia II*, glossary, p. 229, suggests a connection between *peus, peuz*, and Fr. *piece*, but this is an error as is the form *peces*, mentioned in this connection on the same page, which is not attested at this time to my knowledge. For the orthography, cf. *P* 73 (see PEUS RECOUPÉS DEUS . . . UN).

pelet, *pallet* (*i.e. small pale, pile*) (Fig. 90). *B* 124: a trois pelés (*Bl* 124 [128], see PEL). *Syn.*: see PAL. *Note*: cf. PEUS RECOUPÉS DEUS . . . UN. *P* 115 (= *B* 124) reads: 'paalé de goules et d'or'.

pelote, *roundel* (Fig. 112). See BARRE OD UNE PELOTE. *Syn.*: see BESANT. *Note*: on this term, consult London, 'The Roundel', p. 311. The Modern English equivalent is *pellet*.

pel recoupé, see PEUS RECOUPÉS DEUS . . . UN.

penart, *bird's wing, here part of a vol, i.e. two wings joined together at the base* (Fig. 176). See POIVRE CHAUT O LES PENARZ. *Note*: other examples of this heraldic term are provided by Godefroy, vi. 82, s.v. *pennart*.

penn, *pile*. See PEL, PEUS RECOUPÉS DEUS . . . UN.

perche de daim, *stag's attire, or antler* (Fig. 173). *C* 64: 3 perch de daimes (*Cl* 64: a .iii. perche de deym; *Cd* 64: a .iii. perches de deym). *Note*: Württemberg arms; see Prinet WR, pp. 246–7, who refers to *bois de cerf*. The Modern French equivalent is *une ramure* (Veyrin-Forrer, p. 121: 'sa position paraît être en fasce, l'extrémité à senestre.' C. R. Humphery-Smith and Michael G. Heenan, 'The Royal Heraldry of England', *Coat of Arms*, vi (1961), 348, blazon these arms: 'Or, three stag's attires fessways in pale sable'). *Aspilogia II*, glossary, p. 229, links *perche de deym* with Fr. *perchant* 'perching', but this is an error, OFr. *perche* 'antler' being plainly derived from Lat. *pertica* 'stick'. OFr. *perche* in this sense appears in Marie de France's 'Guigemar' (*Les Lais de Marie de France*, ed. J. Rychner, p. 8, v. 92: 'Perches de cerf out en la teste'; see Ernst Bormann, *Die Jagd in den altfranzösischen Artus- und Abenteuer-Romanen* [Marburg, 1887], p. 62).

percié, *pierced, voided (referring to a hollowed-out charge).* See CROIS PATEE PERCIEE, CROIS PERCIEE, CROIS PERCIEE ET PATEE ET BOU-TONEE, ESCUÇON PERCIÉ, LOSENGE PERCIEE, MEULET PERCIÉ, MEULETE PERCIEE, MOLETE PERCIEE. *Syn.*: see FAUS.

pere, *father.* See ARMES A SON PERE, ARMES DE SON PERE A, ARMES LE ROI SON PERE O, ARMES SON PERE A, ARMES SON PERE OD, ARMES SON PERE OU, AUTELS ARMES COM SON PERE, AUTRETEL COM SON PERE, BANIERE SON PERE A . . . POUR, PORTER DE PAR SON PERE, PORTER TEL ESCU SON PERE. *Note*: literary characters do not simply inherit arms; they bear their father's coat out of a sense of loyalty and devotion: 'Onques la connoissance ne voust changier, kar tele la porta ses peres' (*Perlesvaus*, p. 404).

per le . . ., le . . ., see PARTI DE . . . ET DE . . ., PAR LE . . ., LE . . .

pers, *azure (blue).* TC, v. 2062: L'escu varié au baston pers. *Syn.*: see AZUR. *Note*: in v. 2039, the same arms featured a *baston d'azur*. To the bibliography cited in Delbouille's note to this verse, add Harri Meier, 'Ein dunkles Farbwort', *Wort und Text. Festschrift für Fritz Schalk*, edd. Harri Meier and Hans Schommodau (Frankfurt am Main, 1963), 101–10, and the comments in J. H. R. Polt's review of the latter work in *RPh.*, xviii (1965), 329.

petit, *small.* See BESANTÉ DE PETIZ BESANTEAUS. *Syn.*: MENU. *Note*: cf. HERONS PETIZ BEESTEZ.

petite croisete, *crosslet* (Fig. 100). TC, vv. 3159–62:

> De toutes armez paréz fu,
> Ainsi vermoilles comme feu,
> A deus bar d'or et a croissetes
> Petites, asséz joiïetez.

Syn.: see CROISELE.

peus, *pales.* See PEL.

peus recoupés deus . . . un, *pallets couped 2 (of one tincture) and 1 (of another)* (Fig. 15). The complete blazon reads as follows: *P* 73: Roger Mortymer port d'azure ove troys barres d'or ove trois pens [*sic*, for peus] recopez deux d'azure un d'or

ove les cornors gerunés ove un escuchon d'argent. *Note*: cf. PAL, PALÉ DE . . . ET DE . . . Corresponds to *B* 32 (see PALÉ DE . . . ET DE . . .); cf. the diminutive form PELET. The blazon is awkward here since it does not indicate the tinctures of the gyronny corners. Also, in modern blazon the spaces between the vertical stripes would not be regarded as pallets, but as part of the field, which has already been blazoned azure. The expression '2 and 1', consequently, would not be used. The latter, moreover, is not to be confused with the positioning phrases DEUS DESUS ET UN DESOUS and DEUS ET UNE.

peyr, see NOIR.

pichier, *pitcher* (Fig. 271). *K*, v. 686: De goules furent trois pichier.

pie, *magpie* (Fig. 194). See OU LES PIES. *Syn.*: COUWE. *Note*: see OD LES COUWES, *Note*.

pié¹, *foot. Cleomadés*, v. 734: Et ot blans piés, see SERPENT. For other uses, see EGLE . . . LE BEC ET LES PIÉS, EN CHASCUNE CORNIERE SEIT UN PIÉ, PIÉ DE HANAP. *Note*: cf. HERONS PETIZ BEESTEZ, PUI.

pié², *base (of the shield)* (Fig. 2). *Bel Inconnu*, v. 330: li piés. *Note*: cf. CHIEF¹, FONT.

piece, *piece.* (1) *the number of stripes is indicated.* See BENDÉ DE . . . PIECES DE . . . ET DE . . ., DE . . . PIECES BARRÉ DE . . . ET DE . . ., FESSIÉ DE . . . ET DE . . . A . . . PIECES, PALÉ DE . . . ET DE . . . PIECES. (2) *the number of fusils is indicated.* See FESSE ENGRESLÉ DE . . . PIECES. *Syn.*: POINT.

pieces de . . . et de . . ., *barry* (Fig. 5). The complete blazons read as follows: *Hg* 16: Henri le Gray porte .vi. pieces d'argent et d'asur (*H* 16, see BARRÉ DE . . . ET DE . . .¹); 36 [37]: John de Grey porte .vi. pieces d'asur et d'argent od le baston de goules (*H* 36, see BARRÉ DE . . . ET DE . . .¹); 60 [61]: Reinaud de Gray porte .vi. pieces d'argent et d'asur od le lambel de goules (*H* 60: Sr Raignald de Gray port .vi. peces d'argent et d'azur ou le lable de gulez). *Syn.*: see BARRÉ DE . . . ET DE . . .¹.

pié de hanap, *foot (and stem) of a cup or goblet.* TA, v. 1095: Au label de piez de henas.

piés, *pales.* See PEL.

pile, *pile* (Fig. 91). *B* 158: a trois piles d'or (*Bl* 158 [162], see PEL). *Syn.*: see PAL.

piler, *pillar, column* (Fig. 270). *BA* 55: a .iii. pilirs (A: piliers).

plain¹, *undifferenced* (*arms*). See ARMES PLAINES, DE PLAIN, TOUT DE PLAIN LES ARMES . . . FORS QU'EL QUARTIER A EGLES, TOUT PLAIN FORS TANT QUE. *Syn.*: DROIT², ENTIER¹.

plain², *full, complete, referring to a charge as it appears in its simple or normal form without any adornment or modification* (*here a cross with limbs extending to the edge of the shield*). See CROIS PLAINE. *Syn.*: ENTIER², PASSANT². *Note*: see also CROIS¹.

plain³, *plain* (*arms*), *i.e. of a single tincture.* Escanor, v. 3761: plaines. *Syn.*: see ARMES PURES SANS NULE AUTRE DESCONOISSANCE. *Note*: complete blazon provided s.v. PLAINES ARMES.

plaines armes, *plain arms, i.e. shield of a single tincture.* Escanor, vv. 3755–63:

Et il estoit costume adonques
Que nus nouviaus chevaliers onques
Le premier an qu'armes eüst
Tant fust hauz hon ne tant seüst,
N'osast porter c'une semblance
D'armes sanz autre connissance,
Plaines si conme de vermeil,
De noir ou de tel apareil
Qu'en plaines armes doit avoir.

Syn.: see ARMES PURES SANS NULE AUTRE DESCONOISSANCE.

plein, *full.* See LE CHAMP PLEIN DE, TOUT PLEIN. *Syn.*: see POUDRÉ.

plus, see SANS PLUS.

point¹, *piece* (*referring to one of a number of stripes*). *K*, vv. 353–9:

Le beau Brian le Filz Aleyn,
De courtoisie e de honnour pleyn,
I vi o baniere barree,
De or e de goules bien paree;
Dont de chalenge estoit li poinz
Par entre li e Hue Poinz,
Ki portoit tel ne plus ne meins.

For another use, see BARRÉ DE . . . POINZ DE . . . ET DE . . . *Syn.*: PIECE.

point², *point, an ornament resembling the head of a nail* (Fig. 46). *TA*, v. 754: A .iiii. poinz. For other uses, see CLOUÉ DE POINZ EL BASTON, FAUS POINT. *Syn.*: CLAVEL. *Note*: cf. FERRETÉ.

poire, *pear.* See ORLE DE POIRES.

poisson, *fish. TA*, v. 1386: A .i. poison.

poitrine, *breast.* See EGLE A UN CROISSANT EN LA POITRINE.

poivre chaut o les penarz, *hot pepper volant. Bataille des VII Arts*, vv. 35–9:

. . . et Balsamon,
Qui avoit escrit .i. saumon
Sor son escu, entre .ii. dars,
D'un poivre chaut o les pennars,
Plus noir que coille de provoire.

Note: Paetow translates this passage as follows:

. . . and Balsamon,
Who had inscribed a salmon
On his shield, between two dace,
With a hot pepper volant,
Blacker than charcoal.

The same editor conjectures (p. 40, note to line 35) that Balsamon was a poet 'who had a reputation in or about Orleans' about the time this work was written, i.e. the second quarter of the thirteenth century.

pomelé, *botonny* (Fig. 109). See FAUSE CROIS POMELEE. *Syn.*: BOUTONÉ. *Note*: cf. CROIS PATEE ET PERCIEE.

pong, *handle, grip* (*referring to a sword*). See ESPEE AU PONG ET AU HELT QUI TRANCHE LE LION PAR MI. *Note*: often confused with OFr. *pon* (< Lat. *pugnum*) 'pommel (i.e. the knob at the end of the grip)', the term under consideration here is derived from Lat. *pomum* 'fruit'.

popayngai, *popinjay.* See PAPEGAI.

poralé, *in orle.* See BORDURE DE MERLOZ PORALEE TOUT ENTOUR.

porpre, *purpure* (*purple*). See POURPRE.

porte, *door, gate* (Figs. 255, 256). *Charrete*, v. 5800: une porte (complete blazon provided s.v. CERF); *Cleomadés*, v. 11310: Vermeill a une blanche porte.

porter, *to bear.* Used frequently in the rolls of arms and thirteenth-century French literature to introduce a blazon, e.g. *B* 1: Le roy d'Angleterre porte goules trois lupards d'or. *Syn.*: METRE¹.

porter autrement que, *to bear a different coat of arms. K*, vv. 196–200:

Rauf le Filz Guillieme autrement
Ke cil de Valence portoit;
Car en lieu des merlos mettoit
Trois chapeaus de rosis vermelles
    (W: vermeilles),
Ki bien avient a mervellez.

Note: verse 196 is missing in MS. Cotton Caligula A. XVIII.

porter de par son pere, *to bear arms on behalf of one's father.* Perlesvaus, p. 179: Je le port, fet il, de par mon pere.

porter itel, *to bear the same arms.* Perlesvaus, p. 186: itel le porta son pere. *Syn.*: see AUTEL[1].

porter mesme, *to bear the same arms.* B 133: Thomas le Fitz William port mesme. *Syn.*: see AUTEL[1]. *Note*: Aspilogia II, p. 141, note to item 137: '[B 133] is in error in making Thomas bear the same arms as [B 132, see MASCLÉ DE . . . ET DE . . .[1]], i.e. *lozengy ermine and gules*.'

porter sifait escu, *to bear the same arms.* Durmart, v. 13172: Sifait escu porte mes fiuz. *Syn.*: see AUTEL[1].

porter tel, *to bear the same arms.* K, v. 359: Ki portoit tel ne plus ne meins. *Syn.*: see AUTEL[1]. *Note*: complete blazon provided s.v. POINT.

porter tel escu son pere, *to bear the same arms as one's father.* Durmart, v. 9717: Tel escu porta vostre pere. *Syn.*: see ARMES A SON PERE.

porter tels armes, *to bear the same arms.* Lancelot propre, iv. 291: portoit tiels armes. *Syn.*: see AUTEL[1].

porter tels armes sans, *to bear the same arms, without.* Hunbaut, v. 2673: Qui tels [armes] san(le) labiel porte. *Syn.*: AUTEL SANS. *Note*: cf. AUTEL[2].

poudré, *powdered, semy. Syn.*: LE CHAMP PLEIN DE, POUDRÉ EN L'ESCU, SEMÉ, SEMENCIÉ. *Note*: when the accompanying preposition is *a*, the latter usually but not always follows POUDRÉ (e.g. A CROISILLES POUDRÉ A L'ESCU); all other prepositions always do so. Cf. SEMÉ. On the positioning of the charges, see BORDURE[2], *Note*. In addition to phrases with *poudré* and *semé*, early blazon also indicated powdering by using locutions beginning with the preposition *a*, e.g. A EGLEAUS, A FLEURETES, the preposition *od*, e.g. OD LES ESCHALOPES, OD LES TOURTEAUS, and the preposition *ou*, e.g. OU LES CROISSANZ, OU LES PIES. See also ANGEGNIES EN L'ESCU, DES COURONES TANT QUE L'ON I POUVOIT METRE, ESTENCELÉ, LIONCEAUS EN LA BORDURE, TOUT ENVIRON, TOUT PLEIN, and cf. BESANTÉ, BILLETÉ, CROISELÉ, and their synonyms.

poudré a cercles, *semy of castles* (Fig. 31). *C* 29: poudré a circle (*Cl* 29b: pudré a circle; *Cd* 29b: pudré cerele. *Syn.*: see CHASTELÉ[1]. *Note*: *circle* is evidently an error for *toureles, chasteaus*, or one of their variant forms; Prinet WR, p. 230: 'Circle est-il pour turelles ou pour chastels? Je ne sais.' *Aspilogia II*, p. 174, note to item 31: 'it should be *chasteles*, castles . . . Robert II's s. Philip, d. 1298 v.p., charged the label with silver roundels and it was perhaps a knowledge of this fact which led to the misinterpretation . . .'

poudré a croiseles, *crusily* (Fig. 35). *Ba* 55: a cruseles . . . poudré (*B* 55, see CROISELÉ; *Bb* 55, see SEMÉ A CROISELES; *Bc* 55, see A CROISILLES POUDRÉ A L'ESCU); *C* 108: poudré a croisell (*Cl/Cd* 108, see POUDRÉ A CROISILLES); 110: poudré a croisel (*Cl* 110, see POUDRÉ A CROISILLES; *Cd* 110, see SEMÉ DE CROISILLES). *Syn.*: see CROISELÉ.

poudré a croisilles, *crusily* (Fig. 35). *Cl* 2: poudré a croysyle (*C* 2, see CROISELÉ; *Cd* 2: poudré a crosyle); 29a: pudré a croisile (*Cd* 29a: pudré a croysile); 108 (*C* 108, see POUDRÉ A CROISELES; *Cd* 108: poudré a crosyl), 110 (*C* 110, see POUDRÉ A CROISELES; *Cd* 110, see SEMÉ DE CROISILLES): poudré a croisil; Acre, *Cl* [14]: poudré a croysille, *Cd*: poudré a croysile. *Syn.*: see CROISELÉ. *Note*: cf. A CROISILLES POUDRÉ A L'ESCU.

poudré a fauses losenges, *masculy* (Fig. 18). *C* 100: poudré a faux losengez (*Cl* 100: poudré a fause losenge; *Cd* 100: poudré a fause lozengs). *Syn.*: see OD LES LOSENGES PERCIEES. *Note*: see MASCLÉ DE . . . ET DE . . .[1], *Note*.

poudré a fleuretes, *semy of fleurs-de-lis* (Fig. 40). *C* 8: poudré a florets (*Cl* 8: poudré a florettes; *Cd* 8, see SEMÉ DE FLEURS DE LIS); 22: poudré a floretts (W: florettes) (*Cl* 22, see POUDRÉ O FLEURETES; *Cd* 22: poudré a flouretes); 29: poudré a florets (W: floretes) (*Cl/Cd* 29b: pudré a florette); *Cl* 5: poudré a flurette (*C* 5, see SEMÉ DE FLEURETES; *Cd* 5, see SEMÉ DE FLEURS DE LIS). *Syn.*: see FLEURETÉ[1]. *Note*: Aspilogia II, p. 167, item 2 needlessly emends *Cl* 5 [2] to read *semé de floretes* as in *C* 5.

poudré a toureles, *semy of castles* (Fig. 31). *C* 18: poudré turells (*Cl* 18: poudré a turelle; *Cd* 18, see POUDRÉ A TOURETES);

22: poudré a turells (*Cl* 22: poudré a turelles; *Cd* 22: poudré a tupelles). *Syn.*: see CHASTELÉ[1].

poudré a touretes, *semy of castles* (Fig. 31). *Cd* 18: poudré a turetes (*C/Cl* 18, see POUDRÉ A TOURELES). *Syn.*: see CHASTELÉ[1].

poudré a tupelles, see POUDRÉ A TOURELES.

poudré d'eglez, *semy of eaglets* (Fig. 38). *C* 151: poudré de eglets (W: egletes) (*Cl* 151: poudré d'eglé; *Cd* 151, see CROIS ENTRE EGLEZ). *Syn.*: see A EGLEAUS SEMÉ.

poudré de lieparz, *semy of leopards* (Fig. 41). *Hg* 51 [53]: poudré de lupars (*H* 51, see POUDRÉ OU LIEPARZ). *Syn.*: see SEMÉ DE LIEPARDEAUS.

poudré de merloz, *semy of martlets* (Fig. 44). *Hg*, Valence [98]: poudré de merlos. *Syn.*: A MERLOZ.

poudré de roses, *semy of heraldic roses* (Fig. 47). *Hg* 23: poudré de roses, see BORDURE[1] (3) (*H* 23, see BORDURE DE ROSES). *Syn.*: see SEMÉ DE ROSES.

poudré en l'escu, see BILLETES POUDRÉ EN L'ESCU. *Syn.*: see POUDRÉ.

poudré o fleuretes, *semy of fleurs-de-lis* (Fig. 40). *Cl* 22: poudré o flurettes (*C/Cd* 22, see POUDRÉ A FLEURETES). *Syn.*: see FLEURETÉ[1].

poudré ou lieparz, *semy of leopards* (Fig. 41). *H* 51: poudré ou leopars (*Hg* 51 [53], see POUDRÉ DE LIEPARZ). *Syn.*: see SEMÉ DE LIEPARDEAUS.

pour amour de, (*to bear another person's arms*) *as a sign of love for* (*him*). *Lancelot propre,* iv. 104 (var.): Et des lors en avant porta misire Ywain l'escu de sinople a la bende blanche pur amur de Lancelot qui lo portoit blanc a .i. bende vermeille de bellic. *Syn.*: POUR L'AMOUR DE, POUR L'AMOUR QU'OT A.

pour descomparoison, *as a difference.* See TELS (ARMES) QUE . . . MES POUR DESCOMPAROISON. *Syn.*: see PAR DESCONOISSANCE.

pour despareil, *as a difference. TC,* vv. 1974–6:

A ses armez bien le cognois:
D'argent sont a la crois vermoille,
Lambiaus i a pour desparelle.

Syn.: see PAR DESCONOISSANCE.

pour l'amour de, (*to bestow one's own arms upon someone, or to bear another person's arms*) *as a sign of love for* (*him*). *Perlesvaus,* p. 289: Sire, fait ele, je voil que vos portez hui .i.

armes vermeiles que je vos baillerai por l'amor de moi; p. 292: La mainnee baila le jor lo roi Artu .i. bloues armes autresi comme d'azur, si li proia e requist qu'il les portast por s'amor; p. 301: Lancelot ot .i. escu vert, que il porta por l'amor dou chevalier qui fu ocis por lui aidier en la forest; *Artus,* p. 62: qui ne portoit nule fiee armes se noires non. Et por la grant amor qui estoit entre le neveu et les oncles li partirent il lor armes de noir et de vermeil. *Syn.*: see POUR AMOUR DE. *Note:* cf. DROITES ARMES. Mathieu, pp. 142–60, discusses at length the conditions under which a person was entitled to bear another's arms in the Middle Ages. These include the transfer of arms by bequest, as in the case of a family which is dying out, the bearing of identical arms by persons living in different countries, and the assumption of the coat of a vanquished adversary. Another important category (pp. 153–5) involved arms borne as a sign of submission or gratitude. Chapter iv (pp. 167–86), finally, concerns the granting and differencing of arms for various reasons, notably the latter. In the illustration of one of the manuscripts of the *Chronica Majora,* Matthew Paris provides two shields for Otto IV on the occasion of his election as Emperor in 1199: (1) or, a double-headed eagle sable, for the Empire; and (2) England dimidiating the Empire. Under the latter shield the scribe wrote: 'Scutum mutatum pro amore regis Anglie' (*Aspilogia II,* p. 60, item 5). On these arms, see *Aspilogia II,* p. 15, note to item 21. OFr. *amour* does not necessarily imply affection and may at times have the legal or political connotation of 'allied'. On this concept, consult G. F. Jones, 'Friendship in the *Chanson de Roland*', *MLQ,* xxiv (1963), 88–98; see also, by the same author, *The Ethos of the Song of Roland* (Baltimore, 1963), pp. 36–45. Adam-Even BA, p. 73, note 108, cites the antonymous locution *pour la hayne de* in Jacques de Hemricourt (fourteenth century), where it refers to differencing. Cf. also J. Frappier, '*D'amors, par amors*', *Romania,* lxxxviii (1967), 433–74.

pour l'amour qu'ot a, (*to bestow one's own arms upon someone*) *as a sign of love for* (*him*). *Berte,* vv. 3216–31:

Et Symons passe avant, mie ne s'oublia
Et il et si doi fill chascuns s'agenoilla;
Constance et ses deus filles nule n'i demora,
Chascune s'agenoille, envers le roi clina;
Chascuns de Damedieu le roi en mercia.
La devient si home, chascun en foi baisa;
Les armes qu'il porterent li rois les devisa
D'asur, mais que de blanc un poi les
   dyaspra
Li maistres qui les fist, car on li conmanda;
Une grant fleur de lis d'or tout en mi lieu a;
A cinc labiaus de gueules l'ainsné fils le
   porta,
Le label au mainsné d'argent on besenta.
Li rois, cui Jhesus gart qui tout le mont
   forma,
Pour l'amour k'ot a aus ces armes lor
   charcha;
Des puis l'a li lignages porté et portera,
Encor le porte cil qui l'eritage en a.

Syn.: see POUR AMOUR DE. *Note*: for a discussion of these arms, see CHARGIER SES
ARMES A, FLEUR DE LIS TOUT EN MILIEU.

pour Leon, *for León.* See POUR LION.

pour Lion, *for León.* The complete blazon
reads as follows: *Cd* 6: Le roy d'Espayne,
de gules .i. chasteaus d'or, pour Lion
d'azur .i. lion de pourple. *Note*: refers to
LION[2]. Defective blazon, since no mention
of a quarterly partition is provided.

pourpre, *purpure (purple).* *Troie,* vv. 7816–
17: N'aveit nul autre teint desoz, / Mais
de porpre ert coverz desus, see POURPRE
NOIRE; *C* 6: purpr (W: purpur) (*Cl* 6,
see AZUR; *Cd* 6: de pourple) (*H* 1: de
purpre (*Hg* 1: de pourpre); *M* 46,
64: de purpure. *Syn.*: POURPRE NOIRE,
POURPRIN. *Note*: Matthew Paris uses the
Latin equivalent of this term in his blazon
of the arms of Spain (as in *C* 6): 'leo de
purpura' (Pusikan, p. 129). Many authorities reject the authenticity of purpure as
a tincture. The *Larousse du XXe siècle,* s.v.
pourpre, provides the following explanations: 'La plupart des héraldistes n'ad-
mettent point le *pourpre* comme couleur
régulière, parce qu'il n'a pas de couleur
propre mais qu'il est composé du mélange
égal des quatre autres, disent les uns,
ou que c'est un argent altéré par le
temps, disent les autres. C'est un émail
mitoyen, et que l'on a employé tantôt

comme émail et tantôt comme métal.' Cf.
Veyrin-Forrer, p. 17: 'le pourpre ne peut
pas se distinguer du gueules. . . . D'après
Foras, on ne trouverait cet émail dans les
armes d'aucune famille authentiquement
ancienne.' On this tincture, however,
consult C. R. Humphery-Smith, 'Purpure',
Coat of Arms, iv (1956), 19–20. After listing
or, azure, argent, gules, sable, and vert,
the author of the *Dean Tract,* p. 25, states:

> . . . pluys sount nulles
> Forsqe purpre soulement:
> De cele penserocount poy de gent.

pourpre noire, *purpure (purple).* *Troie,* v.
7819: La porpre ert neire a grans labeaus.
Syn.: see POURPRE.

pourprin, *purpure (purple).* *Fouque de Candie,*
vv. 1716, 2797, 7073: confanon porprin;
v. 2143, 2521, 5090, 11598: gonfanon
porprin; *K*, v. 42: O un lioun rampant
purprin. *Syn.*: see POURPRE.

pouvoir, see TANT QUE L'ON I POUVOIT
METRE.

pre . . ., see EN LE PRE . . .

premerain, see PREMERAIN QUARTIER. *Syn.*:
see DEVANT[1].

premerain quartier, *the first quarter of
a quarterly field.* See EL PREMERAIN QUARTIER.
Syn.: see DEVANT[1].

premier, see PREMIER QUARTIER. *Syn.*: see
DEVANT[1].

premier quartier, *the first quarter of a
quarterly field.* See EN LE PREMIER QUARTIER.
For another possible use, see EN LE PRE
. . . *Syn.*: see DEVANT[1].

prendre, *to assume arms.* *K*, v. 117: le lyon
prist. *Note*: complete blazon provided s.v.
JETER PUER.

pres a pres une egle et un dragon, *eagle
preying on (?) a dragon* (Fig. 186). *Charrete,*
vv. 5777–9:

> Et veez vos celui aprés,
> Qui an son escu pres a pres
> A mise une aigle et un dragon?

Note: J. Frappier, in his translation of this
romance (*Le Chevalier de la Charrette* [*Lancelot*] [Paris, 1962], p. 179), suggests a side-
by-side arrangement: 'Et voyez-vous après
celui qui côte à côte a mis sur son écu une
aigle et un dragon?' It may be idle to
speculate on the disposition of charges in

fictitious arms, but it seems more likely that the author intended the eagle and the dragon to be depicted as though in combat (cf. FESANZ BEC A BEC, SERPENT ENMI), or with the eagle pouncing, preying, or trussing on (i.e. devouring) the dragon. On the latter attitudes of the eagle, consult Boutell, p. 76.

prime les, *ghost word.* The complete blazon reads as follows: *CP* 62: Mesire Simon de Mailli porte les armes d'or a trois maillés de gheules, prime les [*sic*] de gheulles, a une bordure dantelee de gheules. *Note*: Prinet CP, p. 22 n. 2: 'Je ne sais ce que signifient les mots "prime les de gheules".' Dr. Adam-Even has cleared up this mystery by showing that *prime les* is an error for the proper name Preuilly; see *CPA* 62 *bis*.

propres armes, see SES PROPRES ARMES.

pui, *mount* (Fig. 192). The complete blazon reads as follows: *BA* 64: Li (A: Le) conte de Huiniberghe, l'escu de geules (A: gueules) a .i. lion burelé d'argent et d'azur rampant coronné (A: coroné) d'or a .i. pui (A: piez) vert et a une ghelingue (A: ghelingne) noire desus (A: deseure) le pui (A: piu) vert. Alemant. *Syn.*: MOTE.

pur, *plain arms, i.e. shield of a single tincture.* Sone, vv. 13213–14:

> Et si a blanques couvretures,
> De tout autre rien erent pures.

For other uses, see ARMES PURES SANS NULE AUTRE DESCONOISSANCE, TOUT PUR. *Syn.*: D'UNE COULEUR, D'UN SEUL TAINT, ENTIER[3], ENTIEREMENT, SANS AUTRE TAINT, SANS CONOISSANCE NULE, SANS NULE AUTRE DESCONOISSANCE, SIMPLE, TOUT[1], TOUT D'UNE COULEUR, TOUT D'UN TAINT, TOUT PUR. *Syn.*: see ARMES PURES SANS NULE AUTRE DESCONOISSANCE.

purpure, see POURPRE.

qre, *meaning obscure.* The complete blazon reads as follows: *B* 178: Reinaud de Blankmonstier, d'argent frettie d'azure: qre: [*sic*]. *Note*: cf. *M* 6: Sr Richard de Blamminstr' porte d'argent fretté de gules. Evidently an abbreviation of some sort. Armytage prints the first letter as a lower-case *q* with a horizontal stroke through the minim.

quartelé de . . . et de . . ., *quarterly* (Fig.

25). (1) *the quarters bear no charge. B* 19 (*Bl* 19, see ESQUARTELÉ DE . . . ET DE . . .), 204 (*Bl* 204 [208], see ESQUARTELÉ DE . . . ET DE . . .): quartelé de . . . et de . . .; *Bb* 54: quartely . . . and . . . (*B/Ba/Bc/Bl* 54, see ESQUARTELÉ DE . . . ET DE . . .); Somery [*B III* 20], *Bb*: quartely . . . et . . . (*Ba/Bc*, see ESQUARTELÉ DE . . . ET DE . . .); *H* 5: quartellé de . . . et de . . . (*Hg* 5, see ESQUARTILLIÉ DE . . . ET DE . . .); *M* 12: quartelé de . . . [et] de . . .; 15: quartelé de . . . et de . . . (2) *the first quarter bears a charge.* See QUARTELÉ DE . . . ET DE . . . EN LE CHANTEL DE . . . UNE MOLETE, QUARTELÉ DE . . . ET DE . . . UN MOLET, QUARTELÉ DE . . . ET DE . . . UN MOLET EN LE QUARTIER DEVANT. (3) *quarters 2 and 3 are fretty.* See QUARTELÉ DE . . . ET DE . . . LES QUARTIERS . . . EN LE GEULES. *Syn.*: see ESQUARTELÉ DE . . . ET DE . . .

quartelé de . . . et de . . . en le chantel de . . . une molete, *quarterly, in the first quarter a mullet.* The complete blazon reads as follows: *M* 56: Sr Richard de Perreres port quartelé (MS.: quart'e; G: quartilé) d'argent et de sable en la cantel d'argent .vii. molettez de gulez. *Syn.*: see ESQUARTELÉ DE . . . ET DE . . . A UNE MOLETE. *Note*: refers to EN LE CHANTEL[2]. For *.vii. molettez* read *une molette*; see CROIS[2], *Note.* For blazons of these arms featuring a single mullet, see Papworth's *Ordinary*, pp. 990, 1040.

quartelé de . . . et de . . . les quartiers . . . en le geules, *quarterly, the gules quarters are distinctive. B* 110: quartelé de . . . et de . . . les quartres . . . en le goules (*Bl* 110 [114], see ESQUARTELÉ DE . . . ET DE . . . LE GEULES). *Syn.*: see ESQUARTELÉ DE . . . ET DE . . . (3). *Note*: complete blazon provided s.v. FRETÉ EN LE GEULES.

quartelé de . . . et de . . . un molet, *quarterly, in the first quarter a mullet.* The complete blazon reads as follows: *Bb* 11: Le c. d'Oxenford, quartelé de gules et or un (a mullet is tricked) argent (*B* 11, see QUARTELÉ DE . . . ET DE . . . UN MOLET EN LE QUARTIER DEVANT; *Ba* 11, see ESQUARTELÉ DE . . . ET DE . . . A UN MOLET; *Bc* 11, see ESQUARTELÉ DE . . . ET DE . . . [1]; *Bl* 11, see ESQUARTELÉ DE . . . ET DE . . . OVE UNE ESTOILE EN LE QUARTIER DEVANT). *Syn.*: see ESQUARTELÉ DE . . . ET DE . . . A UNE MOLETE.

quartelé de . . . et de . . . un molet en

le quartier devant, *quarterly, in the first quarter a mullet.* B 11: quartelé de . . . et de . . . ung molet . . . en le quartier devant (*Ba* 11, see ESQUARTELÉ DE . . . ET DE . . . UN MOLET; *Bb* 11, see QUARTELÉ DE . . . ET DE . . . UN MOLET; *Bc* 11, see ESQUARTELÉ DE . . . ET DE . . . [1]; *Bl* 11, see ESQUARTELÉ DE . . . ET DE . . . OVE UNE ESTOILE EN LE QUARTIER DEVANT). *Syn.*: see ESQUARTELÉ DE . . . ET DE . . . A UNE MOLETE.

quarter, see QUARTIER.

quarteré de . . . et de . . ., *quarterly* (Fig. 25). Appears only in Matthew Paris: 'De Berners. Quarteré d'or et viridi, auro ante' (Pusikan, p. 133). *Syn.*: see ESQUARTELÉ DE . . . ET DE . . .

quartier¹, *canton, quarter (upper dexter quarter of the shield set off from the field by a line and a different tincture)* (Fig. 117). (1) *the canton bears no charge. Durmart,* v. 7433: A un . . . quartier; v. 8409: Al . . . quartier; *Lancelot propre,* iii. 279: a .i. . . . quartier; *TA,* vv. 1646, 1893: A un cartier; *BA* 77, 203, 219, 271: a .i. quartier; 171: a un quartier; B 147 (*Bl* 147 [151]: et un quartier), 173 (*Bl* 173 [177]: od un quartier): ung quartier; 124: ung quartre (*Bl* 124 [128]: a un quartier); 159: a ung quartier; *Bl* 105: od quartier (*B* 105, see CANTON); *EO,* v. 5095: Armes ot blanches a un vermeill quartier; *D* 35, 48, 115, 116, 133: od le quartier; *SCK,* fol. 106 *e* / *SCT,* fol. 126 *c* / *SCV,* fol. 92 *e* (Gawain): quartiers; (Giglain): A . . . quartiers; *CP* 17, 66: a un quartier; 134: et a un cartier; *CPA* 5: a un quartier; 13: au quartier; *H* 54: o quartier; *Sone,* vv. 9046, 9153, 9205: au quartier. (2) *the canton bears a charge.* A. *the word* QUARTIER *is used twice, one of which is in the locution* AU QUARTIER, EN LE QUARTIER, *or* OU QUARTIER. *BA* 135, 141: a .i. quartier, see MOLETE OU QUARTIER; *B* 49: ung quartier (*Bl* 49: od un quartier), see LIEPART EN LE QUARTIER; 58: ung quartier, see LIEPART PASSANT EN LE QUARTIER (*Bl* 58: od un quartier, see LIEPART EN LE QUARTIER). For another use, see ESPEE AU QUARTIER. B. *the word* QUARTIER *is used once, order of items indicating that the canton is charged with the object which is named next.* See QUARTIER A UNE CROISSANTE, QUARTIER A UN LIONCEL RAMPANT, QUARTIER ET UN LIEPART. C. *the word* QUARTIER *is used once*

in the locution EL QUARTIER. See EL QUARTIER. *Syn.*: see CHANTEL¹. *Note: CP* 135 (Mesire Hue de Touart porte celles armes a une espee d'argent au cartier) is elliptical, the term for quarter (*cartier*) appearing in the preceding blazon (*CP* 134: Li vicontes de Touart porte les armes d'or au fleur de lis d'asur semees et a un cartier de gheules); see paragraph (2) A. (reference to ESPEE AU QUARTIER).

quartier², *the first quarter of a quarterly shield* (Fig. 26). See EL PREMERAIN QUARTIER, EN LE PREMIER QUARTIER, EN LE QUARTIER². Cf. ESQUARTELÉ DE . . . ET DE . . . (2), OU LE QUARTIER DE. *Syn.*: see CHANTEL².

quartier³, *the dexter chief, set off by the horizontal line of a fess.* See FESSE A UN LIONCEL PASSANT OU QUARTIER. *Syn.*: see CHANTEL DEVANT.

quartier⁴, *sinister chief* (Fig. 2). See EL SENESTRE QUARTIER. *Syn.*: CORNIERE³. *Note*: refers to position only. Cf. DEVANT³.

quartier⁵, *one of four 'quarters' set off by a plain cross.* See QUARTIERS². *Note*: cf. CHANTEL³.

quartier⁶, *ghost word.* See CROIS ET LIONCEAUS. *Note*: error for *quatre.*

quartier a une croissante, *on a canton a crescent.* D 155: od le quarter . . . a une cressante. *Note*: refers to QUARTIER¹.

quartier a un lioncel rampant, *on a canton a lion rampant.* D 153: od le quarter . . . a un leuncel rampant. *Note*: refers to QUARTIER¹.

quartier devant¹, *the first quarter of a quarterly shield* (Fig. 26). See QUARTELÉ DE . . . ET DE . . . UN MOLET EN LE QUARTIER DEVANT. *Syn.*: see CHANTEL². *Note*: Matthew Paris uses this expression, but the fourth quarter is also implied: 'Willelmi de Mandevilla. Ad quatre quartiers, quartier devant d'or cum suo pari' (Pusikan, p. 145; see also p. 147: 'Willelmi de Bellocampo. Quartier d'or anterior cum suo pari, alia de gules, la fesse de gules'). Cf. QUARTIERS¹, *Note.*

quartier devant², *the dexter chief without any line or different tincture setting off this section of the shield from the rest of the field* (Fig. 2). See COC OU QUARTIER DEVANT. *Syn.*: see CHANTEL DEVANT.

quartier et un liepart, *on a canton a leopard.* K, v. 81: Quartier rouge e jaune lupart. *Note*: refers to QUARTIER[1].

quartiers[1], *quarters (referring to two or more quarters of a quarterly field)*. (1) *the second and third quarters are distinctive*. See FRETÉ EN LE GEULES, QUARTELÉ DE . . . ET DE . . . LES QUARTIERS . . . EN LE GEULES, QUARTILLIÉ DE . . . ET DE . . . ET LES QUARTIERS DE . . .; QUARTILLIÉ . . . ET DE . . . O QUARTIERS DE. *Syn.*: see ESQUARTELÉ DE . . . ET DE . . . (3). (2) *the first and fourth quarters are charged with the same object, the second and third with another object*. See ESQUARTILLIÉ DE . . . ET DE . . . A CHASTEAUS EN LES QUARTIERS DE . . . A LIONCEAUS EN LES QUARTIERS DE . . .; QUARTILLIÉ DE . . . ET DE . . ., EN LES QUARTIERS DE . . ., EN LES QUARTIERS DE . . . For other uses, see A QUARTIERS DE . . . ET DE . . ., ESCU A QUARTIERS. *Note*: Bouly de Lesdain, pp. 193–5, discusses the expressions *escu a quartiers* and *escu de quartier*, frequent in twelfth-century texts (he cites over fifty examples), and states that while most editors consider the terms to refer to quarterly shields, he is not happy with this interpretation. While hinting in a note (p. 193 n. 4) that Hermann Suchier's suggestion ('bouclier divisé par des bandes de fer en quatre cases') deserves more attention than it has been accorded, he admits that it is difficult to reconcile this interpretation with such locutions as *bliaut de quartier, lance de quartier*, and a banner which is *portraite de quartier*, all of which are attested in contemporary literary sources. See also EN LE PRE . . . In addition to making use of *quartier devant*, its Gallo-Latin equivalent *quartier anterior*, and *quatre quartiers* (see QUARTIER DEVANT[1]), Matthew Paris utilized Lat. *quarterium* in the meaning 'lozenge' (Pusikan, p. 142: 'alia quarteria de gules'; complete blazon provided s.v. MASCLÉ DE . . . ET DE . . .[1]).

quartiers[2], *'quarters' set off by a plain cross (the cross is cantoned with four charges)*. See BESANZ EN LES QUATRE QUARTIERS, EGLES ES QUATRE QUARTIERS, LIONS ES QUATRE QUARTIERS, LIONS RAMPANZ ON THE QUARTERS OF THE FIELD, RONDEAUS EN LES QUATRE QUARTIERS.

quartillié de . . . et de . . ., *quarterly* (Fig. 25). (1) *the quarters bear no charge*. H 17: quartillé de . . . et de . . . (2) *the four quarters bear the same charge*. See QUARTILLIÉ DE . . . ET DE . . . OU LES ROSES EN UN EN L'AUTRE. (3) *the first quarter bears a charge*. See QUARTILLIÉ DE . . . ET DE . . . ET EN LE CHANTEL DE . . . OU UN MOLET. (4) *the second and third quarters are distinctive*. See QUARTILLIÉ DE . . . ET DE . . . O QUARTIERS DE . . . (5) *the first and fourth quarters are charged with the same object, the second and third with another object*. See QUARTILLIÉ DE . . . ET DE . . . EN LES QUARTIERS DE . . ., EN LES QUARTIERS DE . . . *Syn.*: see ESQUARTELÉ DE . . . ET DE . . .

quartillié de . . . et de . . . en les quartiers de . . ., en les quartiers de . . ., *quarterly, the first and fourth quarters are charged with the same object, the second and third with another*. H 92: quartilé de . . . et de . . . en lez quarters de . . . (see GRIFON), en lez (G: les) quarters de . . . (see FESSE ENGRESLEE) (*Hg* 92 [91], see ESQUARTILLIÉ DE . . . ET DE . . . EN LES QUARTIERS DE . . ., EN LES QUARTIERS DE . . .). *Syn.*: ESQUARTILLIÉ DE . . . ET DE . . . EN LES QUARTIERS DE . . ., EN LES QUARTIERS DE . . .

quartillié de . . . et de . . . et en le chantel de . . . ou un molet, *quarterly, in the first quarter a mullet*. H 96: quartilé de . . . et de . . . et en le cantel de . . . ou ung moleit (*Hg* 96, see ESQUARTILLIÉ DE . . . ET DE . . . EN LE CHANTEL DE . . . UN MOLET). *Syn.*: see ESQUARTELÉ DE . . . ET DE . . . A UNE MOLETE. *Note*: refers to EN LE CHANTEL[2].

quartillié de . . . et de . . . et les quartiers de . . ., *quarterly, the second and third quarters are distinctive*. *Hg* 54 [55]: quartilé de . . . et de . . . et le quarter de . . . (*H* 54, see QUARTILLIÉ DE . . . ET DE . . . O QUARTIERS DE . . .). *Syn.*: see ESQUARTELÉ DE . . . ET DE . . . (3). *Note*: the second and third quarters are fretty.

quartillié de . . . et de . . . o quartiers de . . ., *quarterly, the second and third quarters are distinctive*. H 54: quartillé de . . . [et] de . . . o quarter de . . . *Syn.*: see ESQUARTELÉ DE . . . ET DE . . . (3). *Note*: the second and third quarters are fretty.

quartillié de . . . et de . . . ou les roses en un en l'autre, *quarterly with roses counterchanged*. H 86: quartillé de . . . et de . . . ou lez (G: les) roses en ung en l'autre.

quartires, *four*. The complete blazon reads as follows: *B* 46: William Dakigny, d'azur ove la croix d'or et quartires leonceus d'or (*Ba* 46: Baudwin Dakeni, d'azure a la croiz d'or a 4 lionceus de or; *Bb* 46: Baudwin Dakeni, B [= azure] a crosse et 4 [a lion rampant is tricked] or). *Note*: refers to CROIS[1] (2). See *Aspilogia II*, p. 124, note to item 46.

quart part, *canton* (Fig. 117). *K*, v. 248: De ermine estoit la quart pars. *Syn.*: see CHANTEL[1].

que, see FORS QUE, MES QUE.

queue, *tail.* See COUE.

quevron, *chevron.* See CHEVRON.

qui, *which.* See EGLE QUI DE VOLER FAISOIT SEMBLANT, EN MILIEU UNE EGLE QUI DE VOLER FAISOIT SEMBLANT, ESPEE AU PONG ET AU HELT QUI TRANCHE LE LION PAR MI, ESPREVIER QUI DE VOLER NE SE REPOSE, HOME QUI ESTOIT CRUCEFIÉ, OU MILIEU UN HOME CRUCEFIÉ QUI TOUT ESTOIT SANGLANT.

quintefeuille, *cinquefoil* (Fig. 234). *B* 70: a trois quintefueiles (*Ba* 70: a treys quintefoile; *Bb* 70, see CINCFEUILLE; *Bc* 70: a treys quintefoils; *Bl* 70: od trois quintefoilles); 118 (*Bl* 118 [122]: od la quintefoill): ung quintefoile; 149, 197, 206 (*Bl* 149 [153]: od une quintefoill; 197 [201]: od un quintefoill; 206 [210]: od un quintefoille): ung quintefueile; 150: ung quintefueil (*Bl* 150 [154]: od un quintefoill); *C* 96 (*Cl* 96: a un quintefoyl; *Cd* 96, see CINCFEUILLE): un quintefoil; 129 (*Cl* 129: a une quintefoil; *Cd* 129, see CINCFEUILLE): un quintefoile; 110: 3 quintefoiles (*Cl* 110: e treis quintefoile; *Cd* 110, see CINCFEUILLE); 111: trois quintefoiles (*Cl* 111: a treys quintefoile; *Cd* 111, see CINCFEUILLE); 162: trois quintefoyles (*Cl* 162: a treys quintefoile; *Cd* 162, see CINCFEUILLE); *D* 66: od une quintefoille; 103: od une quintefoile; 150: a treis quintefoiles; 163: od treis quintefoiles; *CP* 143: a trois quintefueilles; *CPA* 174, 175: a .iii. quintefeuilles; *H* 10: ou .iii. quintfoils (*Hg* 10: a trois quintefoiles); 24: ou ung quintfoyl (*Hg* 24: a un quintefoile); *M* 2: ou la quintefoil; *K*, v. 54: En asur quintfullez trois. For other uses, see EN LE CHANTEL UNE QUINTEFEUILLE, LION RAMPANT ET EN LES ESPAULES DU LION UNE QUINTEFEUILLE. *Syn.*: see CINCFEUILLE. *Note*: see SISTEFEUILLE, *Note*.

quintefeuilles ou, *semy of cinquefoils on the . . . (referring to alternating stripes)* (Fig. 33).

BA 103: as quintefeuilles . . . u noirs; 104: as quintefuelles . . . u noir (A: quintefeuilles). *Note*: see OU NOIR and BENDÉ DE . . . ET DE . . .[2].

rai, *cinquefoil* (Fig. 234). *CP* 90, 91: a trois roies. *Syn.*: see CINCFEUILLE. *Note*: Prinet CP, p. 30 n. 2: 'On employait souvent le mot *rais* pour désigner les quintefeuilles.' Dr. Adam-Even, blazoning the same arms as *CP* 91 in the Wijnbergen Roll, describes these objects as 'angemmes', i.e. six-petalled flowers (*WB* 407). Cf. SISFEUILLE. OFr. *rai* is the same as the term which follows and is derived from Lat. *radius*. On the confusion between OFr. *rai* '(sun) ray' and *raie, roie* 'line', consult *BW*[4], s.v. *raie*.

rai de soleil, *sun in his splendour* (Fig. 227). *B* 87: ung rey de soleil (*Bl* 87: od une rey de soleil); *D* 78: od un ray de solail. *Syn.*: ROUELE[2]. *Note*: on the De la Haye arms in early blazon, consult London, 'Notes and Reflections', p. 270; *Aspilogia II*, p. 131, note to item 87: 'a star-like charge, which was commonly represented as a many-rayed mullet . . .' See also ANGEGNIES EN L'ESCU, *Note*. The human features sometimes given to this charge are a late-fifteenth- or early-sixteenth-century innovation; see *Aspilogia II*, pp. 93; 131, note to item 87. See also ANGEGNIES EN L'ESCU, *Note*. Meliador, the hero of the romance which bears his name, is known as *Le Chevalier au Soleil d'or*. On his arms (*azure, a sun in his splendour or*) and the possible connection with the sunburst badge of the later Plantagenets, see A. H. Diverres, 'Froissart's *Meliador* and Edward III's Policy towards Scotland', *Mélanges offerts à Rita Lejeune*, ii (Gembloux, 1969), 1408.

rampant, *rampant.* *BA* 179, 179 *ter*: rampant (blazon is defective); *D* 3: rampans (blazon is defective). For other uses, see EN MI UN RAMPANT LION, GRIFON RAMPANT, ESCUÇON OVE UN LION RAMPANT COURONÉ EN LA CORNIERE, LIEPART RAMPANT A LA COUE FOURCHIEE, LIEPART RAMPANT OVE LA COUE FOURCHIEE, LIEVRE RAMPANT, LION AMONT RAMPANT, LIONCEAUS RAMPANZ L'UN DESOUS ET L'AUTRE DESUS, LIONCEL COURONÉ RAMPANT, LIONCEL RAMPANT, LIONCEL RAMPANT COURONÉ, LIONCEL RAMPANT EL CHANTEL, LIONCEL RAMPANT EN BELIC, LION

COURONÉ RAMPANT, LION RAMPANT, LION RAMPANT A LA COUE CROISIEE COURONÉ, LION RAMPANT A LA COUE CROISIEE ET COURONÉ, LION RAMPANT A LA COUE FOURCHIEE, LION RAMPANT AMONT, LION RAMPANT A UN COLIER, LION RAMPANT A UNE FLEUR EN L'ESPAULE DU LION, LION RAMPANT CONTREMONT, LION RAMPANT COURONÉ, LION RAMPANT COURONÉ A LA LANGUE A UNE MANCHE EN LA GEULE DU LION A UNE ESPEE AU PONG ET AU HELT QUI TRANCHE LE LION PAR MI, LION RAMPANT COURONÉ EN LA CORNIERE, LION RAMPANT COURONÉ ESTANT SUS UNE MOTE, LION RAMPANT COURONÉ O DOUBLE COUE, LION RAMPANT COURONÉ SUS UNE MOTE, LION RAMPANT DONT LA COUE S'ESPANT EN DOUBLE, LION RAMPANT ET COURONE, LION RAMPANT ET COURONÉ, LION RAMPANT ET EN LES ESPAULES DU LION UNE QUINTEFEUILLE, LION RAMPANT ET LA COUE FOURCHIEE, LION RAMPANT OD UN COLIER, LION RAMPANT OD UNE HACHE. *Syn.*: AMONT RAMPANT, EN RAMPANT, RAMPANT AMONT, RAMPANT CONTREMONT. *Note*: cf. PAR MI RAMPER. OFr. *ramper* had the meaning 'to climb up'; the present-day meaning of this French verb ('to creep, to crawl') is first attested in 1487 (see *BW*[4], s.v. *ramper*). In *TA*, v. 823, Traïson (Betrayal) bears a shield 'A .iiii. rampones rampanz'. This is a pun using OFr. *ramposne* 'insult' as an imaginary charge. Huon de Méry states in v. 822 ('Molt fu bien par Raoul descris') that he borrowed this and other ideas from Raoul de Houdenc. Prinet TA, p. 52, identifies the work in question as Raoul's *Roman des Eles*, where a sensual person (*li lechieres*) is said to bear a shield 'A quatre rampunes rampans' (*Roman des Eles*, v. 475). The identification was first made by M. Grebel, *Le Tournoiement Antechrist, par Huon de Méry, in seiner literarhistorischen Bedeutung* (Leipzig, 1885), p. 90. Other heraldic borrowings from Raoul de Houdenc are listed here s.v. LANGUE A TRANCHANZ, LION[1], MIREOR, and PARTI DE . . . ET DE . . .

rampant amont, *rampant*. See LION RAMPANT AMONT. *Syn.*: see RAMPANT.

rampant contremont, *rampant*. See LION RAMPANT CONTREMONT. *Syn.*: see RAMPANT.

ramper par mi, see PAR MI RAMPER.

rasteaus, *rakes*. See RASTEL[1].

rastel[1], *rake* (Fig. 272). *C* 41: troiz rastells

(*Cl* 41, see RASTELE; *Cd* 41, see CHASTEL[2]). *Syn.*: RASTELE. *Note*: cf. LABEL[1], *Note*. According to Prinet WR, p. 234, and *Aspilogia II*, p. 177, note to item 43, there are two (not three) rakes in the Rethel arms. The latter adds: 'They are generally drawn without handles.'

rastel[2], *label* (Fig. 121). *Syn.*: see LABEL[1]. *Note*: see the examples in Matthew Paris provided s.v. LABEL[1], *Note*. See also Du Cange, vii. 21, s.v. *rastellum*[3], citing a document dated *c.* 1280: 'In contrasigillo est quidam leo rampans cum quodam rastello super spatulas, et alibi cum quodam rastello quinque lambellorum.'

rastele, *rake* (Fig. 272). *Cl* 41: a treis rastelle (*C* 41, see RASTEL[1]; *Cd* 41, see CHASTEL[2]). *Syn.*: RASTEL[1].

recercelé, *moline*. See CROIS RECERCELEE. *Syn.*: RECROISELÉ. *Note*: cf. CROIS FOURCHIEE[2], FER DE MOULIN. The term also means 'curly' and is a commonplace in descriptions of a popular male hair-do of the eleventh and twelfth centuries; see A. Roncaglia, 'L'*Alexandre* d'Albéric et la séparation entre chanson de geste et roman', *Chanson de Geste und höfischer Roman. Heidelberger Kolloquium 30. Januar 1961* (Heidelberg, 1963), pp. 38–40; Ménard, p. 537.

rechigné, *teeth bared*. See MASTIN RECHIGNIÉ.

reconoissance, *difference*. See ENTRE . . . ET . . . UN LABEL PAR RECONOISSANCE. *Syn.*: see DESCONOISSANCE[2].

reconoistre, *to recognize* (*arms*). Cligés, v. 1834: Et les escuz bien reconurent; v. 2043: Por son escu qu'il reconoissent; *Durmart*, v. 7429: As armes le reconissoient; *Perlesvaus*, p. 195: il ne le reconoist mie. *Syn.*: CONOISTRE (1).

recoupé, *halved, couped*. See FLEURETE RECOUPEE, LION RECOUPÉ, PEUS RECOUPÉS DEUS . . . UN. *Syn.*: see DEMI. *Note*: in *K*, vv. 838–9 ('Mes ne croi pas ke il la rescoue / Ke iluec ne li soit recoupee'), the author has just blazoned John de Cromwell's arms which feature a crowned lion rampant double-queued. *Recoupee* refers to the lion's double tail ('But I don't believe he will bring it [i.e. the tail] away / Without being cut short there'). Wright, p. 32, translates this ironic passage effectively: 'But I believe he will not bring it away /

Without being curtailed [i.e. in the primitive sense "docked, clipped" (referring to an animal's tail)] there.'

recroiselé, *moline.* See CROIS RECROISELEE. *Syn.:* RECERCELÉ. *Note:* cf. CROIS FOUR-CHIEE², FER DE MOULIN.

rei, *king.* See ROI.

renouveler armes, *to change arms (as a disguise). Perlesvaus,* p. 294: je voil renoveler vos armes. *Syn.:* see ARMES CHANGIER.

reposer, *to rest, to stop doing something.* See SOI REPOSER DE VOLER.

resusciter, *to resurrect.* See NOSTRE SIEUR, SAINT LADRE.

rey de soleil, *sun in his splendour.* See RAI DE SOLEIL.

rien, *thing (but here part of a negative locution = nothing).* See N'ESTRE DIVERS DE RIEN NON FORS DE . . . SEULEMENT. *Note:* OFr. *rien* was a feminine noun.

roge, see ROUGE.

roi, *king.* See ARMES LE ROI, ARMES LE ROI AVUEC, ARMES LE ROI D'ANGLETERE A, ARMES LE ROI SON PERE A.

roi d'Angletere, *King of England.* See ARMES LE ROI D'ANGLETERE A.

roi de France, *King of France.* See ARMES LE ROI DE FRANCE, ARMES LE ROI DE FRANCE A.

roie¹, *cinquefoil.* See RAI.

roie², *stripe (bar?)* (Fig. 54). *Lancelot propre,* iii. 413: la campaigne estoit blance a grandes roies vermeilles. Si en fu la campaigne de blanc cordoan et les roies d'escarlate d'un drap vermeil d'Engleterre. Ne quanque on em portoit a cel tans n'estoient les covertures se de cuir non ou de drap, ce tesmoignent li conte, porce que plus enduroient. *Syn.:* BARRE¹ (?). *Note:* arms of King Yder.

roi hiraut, *king of arms. TC,* v. 1012: li rois hiraus; v. 2666: les rois hiraut. *Note:* cf. HIRAUT. In *TC,* vv. 1015, 1019, a lady addresses a herald as 'Rois'. See also *TC,* v. 1017: Li rois Maigniens. On the proper name Adenet le Roi, believed to be an indication of the poet's function as king of arms at the court of Count Guy of Flanders, consult Comte de Marsy, p. 183; *Les Œuvres d'Adenet le Roi,* ed. Albert Henri, i (Bruges, 1951), 53, 55. See also Brault K, pp. 6–7.

rondeaus en les quatre quartiers, see CROIS PASSANT A RONDEAUS EN LES QUATRE QUARTIERS ET EN CHASCUN RONDEL UN

CROISIÉ, CROIS PASSANT A RONDEAUS EN LES QUATRE QUARTIERS ET EN CHASCUN RONDEL UNE CROISILLE. *Syn.:* BESANZ EN LES QUATRE QUARTIERS. *Note:* There is one bezant in each 'quarter' (i.e. QUARTIER⁵). For the singular form, see RONDEL.

rondel, *roundel* (Fig. 112). *K,* v. 311: De or fin o trois rouges rondeaus. For other uses, see CHIEF O UN RONDEL, FAUS RONDELET, RONDEAUS EN LES QUATRE QUARTIERS. *Syn.:* see BESANT.

rondelet, *roundel (but here voided = annulet).* See FAUS RONDELET. *Syn.:* see ANEL, BESANT.

rose¹, *heraldic rose* (Fig. 47). *Bel Inconnu,* vv. 1711–13:

Ses escus a argent estoit,
Roses vermelles i avoit,
De sinople les roses sont;

BA 193, 240: a .iii. roses; *B* 114: a trois roses (*Bl* 114 [118]: od trois roses); *CP* 130: a une rose; *CPA* 130: a une rose; *H* 79: ou .vi. roses (*Hg* 79: od .vi. roses); *Hg* 38 [39]: od troys roses (*H* 38, see CROISELETE). For other uses, see BORDURE DE ROSES, FESSE OD UNE ROSE, ORLURE DE L'ENCHAMPURE A ROSES, POUDRÉ DE ROSES, QUARTILLIÉ DE . . . ET DE . . . OU LES ROSES EN UN EN L'AUTRE. *Syn.:* see CINCFEUILLE. *Note:* cf. PASSEROSE. The heraldic rose has no stem or leaves and was often confused with the cinquefoil or sexfoil. See *Aspilogia II,* p. 137, note to item 118; 141, note to item 134; ESTOILE, *Note.*

rose², *heraldic rose slipped* (Fig. 241). *C* 46: ove 3 roses (*Cl/Cd* 46: une rose, see SOR CHASCUN ROSIER UNE ROSE, CHASCUN ROSIER). *Note:* Rapperswil arms. See Prinet WR, pp. 237–8.

rose³, *heraldic rose, but here part of a chaplet* (Fig. 233). See CHAPEL DE ROSES.

rose⁴, *ghost word.* See ROSE HARGE OVE UNE ROSE.

rose harge ove une rose, *meaning obscure.* The complete blazon reads as follows: *C* 46: Le countee de Rummesvile, d'or trois roses harges ove 3 roses vert (*Cl/Cd* 46, see ROSIERS SOR CHASCUN ROSIER UNE ROSE CHASCUN ROSIER). *Syn.:* ROSIERS SOR CHASCUN ROSIER UNE ROSE CHASCUN ROSIER. *Note:* Walford, p. 382 n. *f:* 'This reading is evidently erroneous: probably for *roses harges* should be read *roses charges.'* Cf. CHARGIER SES ARMES A. The word could also be a misreading of OFr. *chascun*; see the synonymous locutions in *Cl/Cd* 46.

roses en un en l'autre, *heraldic roses counterchanged.* See QUARTILLIÉ DE . . . ET DE . . . OU LES ROSES EN UN EN L'AUTRE.

rosete, *small heraldic rose.* See A ROSETES, A ROSETES SEMÉ, SEMÉ DE ROSETES. *Syn.*: see CINCFEUILLE.

rosier, *stem of a heraldic rose slipped* (Fig. 241). See ROSIERS SOR CHASCUN ROSIER UNE ROSE CHASCUN ROSIER. *Syn.*: ROSIERE.

rosiere, *stem of a heraldic rose slipped* (Fig. 241). *Cl* 46: sur chekune roser une rose chekune roser verte (*C* 46, see ROSE HARGE OVE UNE ROSE; *Cd* 46: sur chekune rosser ver une rose checkune rosere verte). *Syn.*: ROSIER. *Note*: complete blazons for *Cl/Cd* 46 provided s.v. ROSIERS SOR CHASCUN ROSIER UNE ROSE CHASCUN ROSIER.

rosiers sor chascun rosier une rose chascun rosier, *heraldic roses slipped* (Fig. 241). *Cl* 46: Le counte de Rampsvile, d'or a treis rosers sur chekune roser une rose chekune roser verte (*C* 46, see ROSE HARGE OVE UNE ROSE; *Cd* 46: Le conte Rampsshroyke, or a 3 rosers sur chekune rosser ver une rose chekune rosere verte). *Syn.*: ROSE HARGE OVE UNE ROSE. *Note*: cf. ROSIERE. Prinet WR, p. 237: 'Voilà une description peu élégante et incomplète; nous dirions : *d'or à trois roses de . . . tigées de sinople.*' Rapperswil family arms; *Aspilogia II*, p. 179, note to item 54: 'The blazon . . . is incompréhensible.'

rossignol, *nightingale* (Fig. 196). *TA*, v. 1723: A .iiii. roussignous; v. 2550: au roussignol.

roué, *ornamented with a wheel-like or flowery design.* See TOUT ROUÉ.

roue de paon, *peacock's tail* (Fig. 198). *Durmart*, v. 8484: A cele rue de paon. *Note*: refers to the outspread tail of a peacock in his pride.

rouele¹, *rowel (mullet)* (Fig. 225). *C* 135: 3 rouells (*Cl* 135: a .iii. ronelle [*sic*]; *Cd* 135: .iii. roueles); 180: un rouell (*Cl* 180: a une rouel). For other uses, see ROUELE EN CHIEF, ROUELE EN LE CHIEF. *Syn.*: see ESTOILE. *Note*: in *C/Cl* 180, the rowel is on a canton.

rouele², *sun in his splendour* (Fig. 227). *C* 132: a ruell (*Cl* 132: a ruell; *Cd* 132: a une ruel). *Syn.*: RAI DE SOLEIL. *Note*: De la Haie arms.

The chief difference between ROUELE¹ and ROUELE² is the size of the charge. Cf. TENCELE. Other distinctions such as the number of rays (the modern mullet or rowel usually has five, the estoile and sun as many as twenty-four) or their shape (the estoile and sun have wavy rays) are not necessarily found in the period under consideration. Thus the De la Haie arms may show a sun with straight rays. On the other hand, only a mullet or rowel is sometimes found pierced, though the piercing may not be noted in the verbal description.

rouele³, *roundel.* See FAUSE ROUELE. *Syn.*: see BESANT.

roulé de . . . et de . . ., *concentric rings of alternating tinctures covering the whole field* (Fig. 11). The complete blazon reads as follows: *B* 188: Rauf de Gorges, roelé d'argent et d'azur (*Bl* 188 [192]: Rauf Gorges, roelé d'argent et d'azur). *Note*: Armytage, note to item 188: 'A tricking of this appears in the margin in which the "Roele", or "Gurge", is drawn in circles, and not spirally as usual.' On this term, consult London, 'The Roundel', p. 311; *Aspilogia II*, p. 152, note to item 192: 'This fits the blazon "roele" from the Old French *roel* or *roele*, a wheel or disk, better than the spiral form, although the latter was preferred in later times. Both forms represent a whirlpool, Latin *gurges*.' See also p. 93.

rouele en chief¹, *on a chief a rowel (mullet).* *C* 159: deux rouells . . . en cheif (*Cl/Cd* 159, see ROUELE EN LE CHIEF¹). *Syn.*: see ESTOILE EN LE CHIEF¹.

rouele en chief², *in chief a rowel (mullet).* See FESSE ET UNE ROUELE EN CHIEF. *Syn.*: see MOLET EN LE CHIEF¹.

rouele en le chief¹, *on a chief a rowel (mullet).* *Cl* 159: a deus roueles . . . en le chef (*C* 159, see ROUELE EN CHIEF¹; *Cd* 159: a deus ruelles . . . en le cheif). *Syn.*: see ESTOILE EN LE CHIEF¹.

rouele en le chief², *in chief a rowel.* See FESSE A UNE ROUELE EN LE CHIEF. *Syn.*: see MOLET EN LE CHIEF¹.

rouge, *gules (red).* *Thèbes*, v. 5514: Et demi rouge conme sanc; *Cligés*, v. 4816: Li chevaliers au roge escu; *Méraugis*, v. 1939: Le roge escu; *Estoire*, p. 48: rouge; *Artus*, p. 62: de rouge; *Sone*, v. 13428: le rouge; *K*, vv. 51, 59, 81, 92, 96, 122, 162, 168,

188, 194, 202, 247, 252, 255, 259, 318, 320, 332, 338, 342, 379, 384, 388, 394, 417, 498, 582, 708, 833, 873, 883: rouge; v. 173: de rouges; v. 268: de rouge; vv. 311, 366: rouges. For another use, see EN ROUGE. *Syn.*: see GEULES.

rouget, *gules* (*red*). See TOUT ROUGET.

rous, *russet red*. *TA*, v. 703: A .i. rous mastin rechignié. *Note*: cf. GEULES.

rowel, *rowel*. See ROUELE.

rue, see ROUE.

*sable, *sable* (*black*). Literary examples only after *c.* 1250, e.g. *Mouskés*, v. 22036: de sable; *EO*, v. 2543: de sable; *Escanor*, v. 4992: de seble; *CC*, v. 1318: de sable; *K*, vv. 86, 180: de sable. Attested only once in a French roll, viz. *CPA* 10: de sable, but very frequently in English rolls, e.g. *B* 3 (*Bl* 3, see NOIR), 110: de sable; 9 (*Bl* 9, see NOIR), 192: sable; *Bb* 56: sable (*Ba*/*Bc* 56, see NOIR); *C* 1, 3: sable; *Cl* 3, 28: de sable; 133: de gable [*sic*]; *D* 2, 18: de sable; *H*/*Hg* 11, 18: de sable; *M* 38, 39: de sable. For another use, see EN SABLE. *Syn.*: NOIR, SEBELIN. *Note*: term derived from the fur of the animal of the same name. Matthew Paris mentions the word only once, in his blazon of the Earl of Lincoln's arms: 'benda nigra, que [P: quae] gallice sable dicitur' (Pusikan, p. 144). *Hg* 17 and 103 are errors (see Gough H, pp. 132, note to item 7; 154, note to item 104).

safrin, *or* (*yellow*). *K*, vv. 41–2:

Baner out de un cendal safrin,
O un lioun rampant purprin.

Syn.: see OR.

saiccour, *ghost word*. See SAUTOIR.

Sainte Eglise, see ARMES DE SAINTE EGLISE.

sainte Marie, see MADAME SAINTE MARIE.

saint Ladre, *Lazarus*. *Aye d'Avignon*, vv. 2736–7:

En l'escu de son col ot paint .i. gent
  miracle,
Ainssi con Nostre Sire resuscita saint
  Ladre.

saltier, see SAUTOIR.

s'amie, see JAMBES DE S'AMIE.

sanglant, see OU MILIEU UN HOME CRUCEFIÉ QUI TOUT ESTOIT SANGLANT.

sanglier, *boar* (Fig. 151). *Note*: no early examples. According to Adam-Even, 'Ro-

man de Troie', p. 21, mention is made of arms featuring a boar's head in *Fouque de Candie*, v. 6818. See, however, Schultz-Gora's note in iii. 207–8. In *Thèbes*, v. 785 ('Et Thideüs l'ot d'un senglier'), the skin of a boar is worn as a protective outer garment. Note, however, the boars in the arms of Morris de Powis in the early-fourteenth-century *Fouke Fitz Warin* (ed. Louis Brandin [Paris, 1930], p. 34): 'Morys se arma mout richement e prent le vert escu a deus senglers d'or batu; d'argent fust la bordure ou flours de lys d'asure' (see also pp. 6, 80). For Tristan's arms, which, in an early German source, feature a boar, see Introduction, p. 20.

sans, *without*. See ARMES SON FRERE A . . . SANS, AUTEL SANS, PORTER TELS ARMES SANS.

sans autre conoissance, *plain* (*arms*), i.e. *shield of a single tincture*. *Escanor*, v. 3760: sanz autre connissance. *Syn.*: see ARMES PURES SANS NULE AUTRE DESCONOISSANCE. *Note*: complete blazon provided s.v. PLAINES ARMES.

sans autre taint, *plain* (*arms*), i.e. *shield of a single tincture*. *Enéas*, vv. 4450–1:

La targe en ert tote vermoille,
Sanz autre taint, de sa nature;

Mort Artu, p. 75: sanz autre taint; p. 78 (var.): sains autre taint; *Guiron le Courtois* (cited by Lathuillère, p. 240): escu a or sains autre taint. *Syn.*: see ARMES PURES SANS NULE AUTRE DESCONOISSANCE. *Note*: for the variant reading corresponding to *Mort Artu*, p. 78, lines 9–10 (*.i. escu blanc sans autre taint* instead of *un escu blanc a trois bendes de bellic vermeilles*), see Sommer, vi. 250. For the arms of Guiron le Courtois, see Introduction, p. 35.

sans conoissance nule, *plain* (*arms*), i.e. *shield of a single tincture*. *Mort Artu*, p. 8: sanz connoissance nule. *Syn.*: see ARMES PURES SANS NULE AUTRE DESCONOISSANCE.

sans nule autre desconoissance, *plain* (*arms*), i.e. *shield of a single tincture*. See ARMES PURES SANS NULE AUTRE DESCONOIS-SANCE. *Syn.*: see PUR. *Note*: cf. SANS NULE AUTRE ENSEIGNE where the field features three pallets. See also *Tournoiement des Dames de Paris*, vv. 1576–7:

Couvert de couverture d'or,
Sans nisune autre connoissance.

sans nule autre enseigne, *without any other charge.* TC, vv. 862–3:

> L'escu d'or a trois piés de guelle
> Porte sans nule autre ansaigne.

Note: refers to ENSEIGNE². Cf. SANS NULE AUTRE DESCONOISSANCE alluding to a shield of a single tincture.

sans plus, *alone.* See CROIS SANS PLUS. *Syn.*: SEUL. *Note*: pleonasm.

saumon, *salmon* (Fig. 215). TC, v. 1739: li dui saumont; v. 3170: a deus saumons.

saumon entre dars, *salmon between dace.* Bataille des VII Arts, vv. 36–7: .i. saumon / Sor son escu, entre .ii. dars. *Note*: complete blazon provided s.v. POIVRE CHAUT O LES PENARZ.

sautoir¹, *saltire* (Fig. 92). TA, v. 658: A .i. sautëoir; vv. 928, 1020, 1087: A .i. sautoir; BA 48, 49, 153 (A: sautor), 162, 163: a .i. sautoir; B 59: ou un saltier (Ba 59: a sautur; Bb 59: a saltier; Bc 59: a sautur; Bl 59: od un saut'); 100: ung saultoir (Bl 100: od un sautor); C 66: un saultoir (Cl 66: a un sautour; Cd 66: a un saiccour); 79 (Cl 79: a une sautour; Cd 79: a une saltoier), 107 (Cl 107: a une sautor), 166 (Cl 166: a un sautour; Cd 166: a une saulter): un sautour; D 56, 129, 168, 179: a un sautur; 58: od un sautur; TC, v. 899: a un çaintour; Cleomadés, v. 9878: a .i. . . . sautoir; CC, v. 1526: au . . . sautoir; CP 78: et au sautoir; K, v. 712: O un sautour. *Note*: cf. CROISIÉ², ESCU A BRETELES. In *Navarre* 129, the arms of the saltire are referred to as *bras*. For saltires cantoned with multiple charges, see SAUTOIR A ESTOILES, SAUTOIR A OISELEZ, SAUTOIR ET A ESTENCELES. Cf. ENTRE and *Note*.

sautoir², *small saltire* (Fig. 94). BA 32: a .v. sautors. For other uses, see SAUTOIRS DEUS DESOR ET UN DESOUS, SAUTOIRS EN L'OR. *Note*: the modern French heraldic term for this charge is *flanchis*.

sautoir a estoiles, *saltire cantoned with mullets.* BA 241: a .i. sautoir . . . a .iii. [*sic*, for .iiii.] estoiles. *Syn.*: SAUTOIR ET A ESTENCELES. *Note*: Averton family arms; see WB 504 and SAUTOIR ET A ESTENCELES.

sautoir a oiselez, *saltire cantoned with martlets.* BA 162: a .i. sautoir . . . a .iii. (A: .ii.) oiselés; 163: a .i. sautoir . . . a .iiii. oiselés (A: oiselets).

sautoir endenté, *saltire indented* (Fig. 93). Bl 79: od un salter engrellé (B 79, see SAUTOIR ENGRESLÉ). *Syn.*: SAUTOIR ENGRESLÉ. *Note*: see SAUTOIR ENGRESLÉ, *Note*.

sautoir engreslé, *saltire engrailed* (*indented*) (Fig. 93). B 79: ung sautoir . . . engrelé (Bl 79, see SAUTOIR ENDENTÉ); C 112: un sautour engrellé (Cl 112: et un sautor engrallé; Cd 112: a saulter engreled); D 68: a un sautour engraslé; H 73: ou le sautre . . . engrelee (Hg 73 [74]: od le sautoir . . . engrelee); M 72: ou le sauter (G: sautour) . . . engrelé; K, v. 328: Au sautour . . . engreellie. *Syn.*: SAUTOIR ENDENTÉ. *Note*: while this charge could, theoretically, be made up of lozenges or fusils in saltire (see ENGRESLÉ²), I have not found the latter form in the period under consideration.

sautoir et a estenceles, *saltire cantoned with mullets.* CP 127: a un sautoir . . . et a quatre estancelles. *Syn.*: SAUTOIR A ESTOILES. *Note*: Averton family arms.

sautoirs deus desor et un desous, *small saltires 2 and 1.* BA 47: a .iii. sautoirs . . . .ii. deseur et .i. desox. *Note*: refers to SAUTOIR². The top-downwards system of counting was uncommon in medieval blazon; see FESSE A DEUS LISTEAUS UN DESOUS ET L'AUTRE DESOR, *Note*.

sautoirs en l'or, *small saltires charging the or stripes of a barry field* (Fig. 94). Complete blazon provided s.v. EN L'OR. *Note*: refers to SAUTOIR². When alternating stripes of a barry field are fretty, the result is an identical pattern; see A GEULES FRETÉ.

sautoirs en l'orle, *ghost word.* See SAUTOIRS EN L'OR.

scalop, schalop, schalope, *escallop.* See ESCHALOPE.

schabucle, see CHARBOUCLE BESANCIÉ.

schekune, see EN CHASCUNE CORNIERE SEIT UN PIÉ.

scheveron, see CHEVRON.

schoçon, see ESCUÇON.

sebelin, *sable* (*black*). FCT, vv. 4349–51:

> S'i ot deus lionciax rampans
> De sebelin, non pas molt grans,
> L'uns desoz et l'autres desus.

Syn.: see SABLE. *Note*: Foulet, *Glossary of the First Continuation*, p. 272: 's'agit-il de la

couleur? ou la fourrure elle-même inter-
vient-elle?'

seble, see SABLE.

Seigneur, see NOSTRE SEIGNEUR. *Syn.*: SIEUR.

seir, *to be placed.* See SEIT. *Syn.*: SEOIR. *Note*:
seir is a variant form of OFr. *seoir*. Cf.
METRE[2].

seit, *is placed.* See EN CHASCUNE CORNIERE
SEIT UN PIÉ. *Syn.*: SEOIT. *Note*: third person
singular indicative present of SEIR.

sellé, *saddled.* See CHEVAL SELLÉ.

semblance, see D'AUTRE SEMBLANCE. *Syn.*:
SEMBLANT[1].

semblant[1], see D'UN SEMBLANT, D'UN SEM-
BLANT TAINT. *Syn.*: SEMBLANCE.

semblant[2], see FAIRE SEMBLANT. *Note*: cf.
SEMBLER.

sembler, *to appear, to seem.* See VOLER. *Note*:
cf. FAIRE SEMBLANT, NE SOI REPOSER DE
VOLER.

semé, *semy.* (1) *the preposition* A *is used.* See
A BILLETES SEMÉ, A COQUILLES SEMÉ, A
CROISELES SEMÉ, A CROISETES SEMÉ, A
EGLEAUS SEMÉ, A FLEURETES SEMÉ, A FLEURS
DE LIS SEMÉ, A MOLETES SEMÉ, A ROSETES
SEMÉ. (2) *the preposition* DE *is used.* See SEMÉ
DE BESANZ, SEMÉ DE BILLETES, SEMÉ DE
CROISETES, SEMÉ DE CROISILLES, SEMÉ DE
FLEURETES, SEMÉ DE FLEURS DE LIS, SEMÉ
DE GRAINS, SEMÉ DE LIEPARDEAUS, SEMÉ DE
LIONCEAUS, SEMÉ DE ROSETES, SEMÉ DE
TENCELES, SEMÉ DE TREFLES. *Syn.*: see
POUDRÉ. *Note*: the term designating the
charge with which the field is scattered
always comes immediately *after* the words
semé de; when the preposition *a* is used, the
charge is named after the latter but *before*
the word *semé*. The charge which is
sprinkled is, as a rule, of the same tincture
throughout. For an exception, see ESTEN-
CELÉ DE . . . ET DE . . . On the use of OFr.
freté 'semy', see FRETÉ, *Note.* On powdered
or semy fields, consult Roger F. Pye,
'A Return to First Principles. III. Semy',
Coat of Arms, vii (1963), 206–8. Wearing-
apparel of various kinds was often ornamented with coats of arms and OFr. *semé*
was evidently used in describing such
cloth; see ESCUÇON[1], *Note.* This is the case
for SEMÉ DE LIEPARDEAUS, SEMÉ DE LION-
CEAUS, and SEMENCIÉ D'EGLES.

semé de besanz, *bezanty* (Fig. 29). *EO,*
vv. 4819–21:

Androines ot armes moult acesmans
Qui erent verdes semees de besans,
Li besant erent d'or qui ert flamboians.

Syn.: see BESANTÉ.

semé de billetes, *billety* (Fig. 30). *Cd* 149:
semé billetts (*C/Cl* 149, see BILLETÉ). *Syn.*:
see BILLETÉ[1].

semé de croisetes, *crusily* (Fig. 35). *CP* 48,
63: semé de croisettes. *Syn.*: see CROISELÉ.

semé de croisilles, *crusily* (Fig. 35). *Cd*
110: semé croissill (*C* 110, see POUDRÉ
A CROISELES; *Cl* 110, see POUDRÉ A CROI-
SILLES). *Syn.*: see CROISELÉ.

semé de fleuretes, *semy of fleurs-de-lis* (Fig.
40). *C* 5: semé de [a fleur-de-lis tricked]
(*Cl* 5, see POUDRÉ A FLEURETES; *Cd* 5, see
SEMÉ DE FLEURS DE LIS). *Syn.*: see FLEURETÉ[1].
Note: *C* uses only *fleurete* to designate the
fleur-de-lis; see *C* 154 (un florette), 176
(florete, see FLEURETE[2]); see also *C* 8
(poudré a florets), 22 (poudré a floretts),
29 (poudré a florets); cf., finally, *C* 11 (un
borde floretté), 58 (un carbuncle . . .
flurté), 128 (florettee de l'un et l'autre).

semé de fleurs de lis, *semy of fleurs-de-lis*
(Fig. 40). *Cd* 5: semé flour de lis (*C* 5, see
SEMÉ DE FLEURETES; *Cl* 5, see POUDRÉ A
FLEURETES); 8: semé flor de lis (*C/Cl* 8, see
POUDRÉ A FLEURETES). *Syn.*: see FLEURETÉ[1].

semé de grains, *bezanty* (Fig. 29). *CP* 90:
semé de grains. *Syn.*: see BESANTÉ. Prinet CP,
p. 30 n. 2, cites *Navarre* 326–8 which provides the same Patry family arms with this
feature blazoned 'grenetés d'or'. Cf. PALETÉ.

semé de liepardeaus, *semy of leopards*
(Fig. 41). *CC,* v. 1886: Semé de lupardiaus
d'or fin. *Syn.*: POUDRÉ DE LIEPARZ, POUDRÉ
OU LIEPARZ. *Note*: see SEMÉ, *Note.*

semé de lionceaus, *semy of lioncels rampant*
(Fig. 42). *CC,* v. 1879: D'or semé de noirs
lionciaus. *Syn.*: cf. LIONCEAUS EN LA BOR-
DURE. *Note*: see SEMÉ, *Note.*

semé de rosetes, *semy of heraldic roses* (Fig.
47). *Cd* 51: semé rossetets. *Syn.*: A ROSETES,
A ROSETES SEMÉ, POUDRÉ DE ROSES. *Note*:
on this blazon, see *Aspilogia II,* p. 181, note
to item 61.

semé de tenceles, *semy of mullets* (Fig. 45).
CP 125: semé de tencelles. *Syn.*: see A
MOLETES SEMÉ. *Note*: cf. ESTENCELÉ. Prinet
CP, p. 41 n. 2: 'Le mot *tencelles* paraît être
ici pour *estencelles,* nom qui désignait les

étoiles, les molettes et autres petites figures pourvues de rayons.' See ESTENCELE[1]. Adam-Even in *WB* 440 describes the same Hotot family arms as 'étoilé'.

semé de trefles, *semy of trefoils* (Fig. 50). *CP* 128: semé de trefles. *Syn.*: TREFLÉ.

semencié d'egles, *semy of eaglets* (Fig. 38). *CC*, v. 1863: Tous semenciés d'aigles dorés. *Syn.*: see A EGLEAUS SEMÉ. *Note*: see SEMÉ, *Note*.

semiax, *ghost word.* See ANEAUS DE L'UN EN L'AUTRE.

senefiance, *meaning, symbolism (of a shield or of a coat of arms). Lancelot propre*, v. 403: Si estoit li escus plus noirs que meure et el milieu, ou la boucle devoit estre, avoit painte une royne d'argent et devant li avoit paint .i. chevalier qui estoit a genouls aussi comme s'il criast merchi. Et cil qui laiens estoient ne sorent pas la senefiance de l'escu fors seulement Lancelos et la fille le roy Pelles; *Estoire*, pp. 264–5: Et neporquant li dragons avoit moult grant senefiance en soi, car ensi se senefioit li rois Artus et sa poissanche. Et la flambe qu'il jetoit parmi la goule hors senefioit la grant martire de gent et la grant ochision qui fu faite al tans le roy Artu. Et la keue qui estoit toute tortice senefie la grant traison de sa gent par qui il fu puis trais qui se revelerent contre lui par Mordret son fils qu'il engendra en sa seror la feme al roy Loth; p. 376: Et gardés que vous faites une grant baniere blance et qu'il i ait une crois vermeille sans plus. Et autresi auront tout li prince qui i venront. Et si ne sauront ja mot li un de l'autre por coi il ont ce fait. Et i aura moult grant senefiance; *Blancandin*, vv. 2769–72:

> Fait sont par granz senefïances
> De deus princes les connoissances.
> L'une est blanche comme cristal,
> Et l'autre d'un vermeil cendal.

Note: cf. SENEFIER. In *Durmart*, vv. 4507–12, the act of displaying a vanquished adversary's shield is said to symbolize this conquest:

> La senefïance savrés
> Des escus dont vos demandés:
> Mesire a trestos cealz conquis
> Dont li escu sunt la sus mis;
> Quant il a chevalier vencu,
> La sus en fait pendre l'escu.

senefier, *to represent, to symbolize (something upon a shield). Lancelot propre*, iii. 284: li noirs senefie duel et les goutes d'argent senefient larmes. For another use, see GANT LES DOIZ DESOR. *Note*: cf. *Durmart*, vv. 4494–6:

> Aprés nos dites par amor
> Que senefïent cil escu
> Qui sont a ces creteaz pendu.

For the reply, see SENEFIANCE, *Note*.

senestre, *sinister, i.e. the left side of the shield from the point of view of the bearer but referring here to the sinister chief* (Fig. 2). See MAHOMET EL SENESTRE QUARTIER. *Note*: the sinister side doubtless connotes evil in the shield borne here by the Saracen king, Cornumaran (*Chétifs*, p. 276).

seoir, *to be placed.* See PARTI DE . . . ET DE . . ., DEDENZ LE . . . ET . . . SOR LE . . . *Syn.*: SEIR. *Note*: cf. METRE[2].

seoit, see SEOIR. *Syn.*: SEIT. *Note*: third person singular indicative present of SEOIR.

serpent, *serpent* (Fig. 217). *Méraugis*, v. 1939: au noir serpent; *EO*, v. 2656: Portoit l'escu d'or a un noir serpent; *Cleomadés*, vv. 727–34:

> Armes portoit moult desguisees
> Sormans li Rous, mais devisees
> Les vous arai assez briement:
> L'escu d'or a .i. vert serpent
> Portoit, et ot eles vermeilles
> Li serpens, et bleues oreilles;
> Et ot aussi la teste bleue,
> Et ot blans piés et noire keue.

For another use, see TESTE DE SERPENT. *Syn.*: SERPENT ENMI.

serpent enmi, *serpent. TA*, vv. 568–9:

> .I. dëablel et .i. sarpent
> Vi combatre enmi la baniere.

Syn.: SERPENT. *Note*: cf. FESANZ BEC A BEC, *Note*; PRES A PRES UNE EGLE ET UN DRAGON, *Note*.

ses, see SON[1].

ses propres armes, *his own arms, his proper arms. K*, vv. 480–3:

> Si ne faisoit pas malement
> Kant ses propres armes vestoit,
> Jaunes ou le egle verde estoit.
> Se avoit non Rauf de Monthermer.

Syn.: SOIES ARMES MESMES. *Note*: in the preceding verses, the author states that Ralph de Monthermer also bore the arms of Lady Gloucester, widow of Gilbert de Clare. Cf. ARMES A DROIT, DROITES ARMES.

seul, *single, alone. Lancelot propre*, iii. 147: l'escu a une seule bende; 165: chil a la seule bende; 421: a une seule aigle. For other uses, see CEZ CHOSES, D'UN SEUL TAINT, NE PAS ESTRE SEUL, TOUT SEUL. *Syn.*: SANS PLUS.

seulement, *only. Sone*, v. 13792: a un aigle d'or seulement. For other uses, see N'ESTRE DIVERS DE RIEN NON FORS DE . . . SEULEMENT, TOUT . . . FORS SEULEMENT.

si, see ITEL SI COM.

Sieur, see NOSTRE SIEUR. *Syn.*: SEIGNEUR. *Note*: OFr. *sieur* 'was either formed on *sire* or reduced from dialectal *signeur*' (Pope, paragraph 600; the derivation of the Old French forms *sire* and *seigneur* is also discussed by Miss Pope under this heading).

sifait, *the same (arms)*. See PORTER SIFAIT ESCU. *Syn.*: see AUTEL[1].

simple, *plain (arms), i.e. shield of a single tincture.* See ARMES SIMPLES. *Syn.*: see ARMES PURES SANS NULE AUTRE DESCONOISSANCE.

sinant, *addorsed.* See BARS SINANZ. *Syn.*: see ADOSSÉ.

sinople, *gules (red). Erec*, v. 2100: de sinople; *Charrete*, v. 5957: armes de sinople taintes; *Partonopeu*, v. 6901: de sinople; *Bel Inconnu*, v. 1713: De sinople; v. 2061: Ses escus a sinople estoit; *Fouque de Candie*, v. 10553: escu de synople; *FCA*, v. 805: de sinople; *FCE*, vv. 8116, 8122: de sinople; *FCT*, v. 4358: De sinople; *Perlesvaus*, pp. 84, 142, 197, 207: de sinople; *Durmart*, vv. 1408, 10100: sinople; vv. 7432, 9253: de synople; v. 8482: de synoples; *Lancelot propre*, iii. 174, 176, 309, 367, 402: de sinople; 407: de synople; iv. 88, 93, 220: de synople; 104 (var.) (2): de sinople; *Mort Artu*, p. 103: de synople; *Artus*, p. 67: de synople; p. 307: de sinople; *TA*, vv. 614–15:

De geules estoit ses escuz
Plus vermeilles que nus sinoples;

vv. 1268, 2073: de sinople; *Joufroi*, v. 899: a sinople; v. 2523: De sinople; *Atre périlleux*, v. 6017: De l'escu a sinnople taint; *Hunbaut*, v. 2180: Escu ot de sinople paint. For

other uses, see SOR SINOPLE, TOUT A SINOPLE, VERMEIL SINOPLE. *Syn.*: see GEULES. *Note*: on this colour consult Ott, pp. 143–4. The shift in meaning of this term from red to green has misled many scholars; see, for example, G. Perrie Williams, *Bel Inconnu*, p. 212: 'vert (blason)', and B. Woledge, *Atre périlleux*, p. 299: 'couleur verte'. According to Comte de Marsy, p. 185 n. 2, the earliest recorded use of *sinople* in its present-day meaning in French heraldry is in 1415. See also '.iii. papegauz de sinoble' (three green popinjays) in the fifteenth-century blazon of the Vermandois Roll quoted by London, 'Some Medieval Treatises', p. 180. Godefroy, x. 678, cites an example of OFr. *sinople* 'green' in the poem entitled 'Le Joli Buisson de Jonece' by Froissart (d. 1400); the *FEW*, xi. 650, adds a reference to Jehan Maillart's romance *Le Comte d'Anjou* (1316). Neither passage, however, offers conclusive evidence that the word in question means green, not red. *Le Comte d'Anjou*, vv. 2735–8:

Si me fai faire un char molt noble,
D'or et d'azur et de synoble,
Garni de cinc si fors chevaux
Que ne lez tieigne mons ne vaux;

'Le Joli Buisson de Jonece', vv. 1405–10:

Ce buisson dont je vous pourpos
Avoit une coulour tres propre,
Qui n'estoit mies de sinopre,
D'or ne d'argent ne de noir pur,
Ançois se traioit sus l'azur,
Cler et fin et resplendissant.

On the other hand, the meaning 'green' is twice attested in heraldic blazons in *Le Miroir des Nobles de Hesbaye*, a chronicle by Jacques de Hemricourt dated 1353–98 (*Œuvres de Jacques de Hemricourt*, edd. C. de Borman and A. Bayot, i [Brussels, 1900], paragraphs 244, 720; see L. Bouly de Lesdain, 'L'héraldique dans Hemricourt', *Revue du Nord*, iv [1913], 325). The author, who was burgomaster of Liège, also used the synonym *vert* in another passage of the same work (paragraph 205). The shift in meaning occurred therefore—at least in one source—in the second half of the fourteenth century. It would appear, then, that in the following passage in *SCU*, fol. 152, *vermeille* and *synople* are synonymous, though this seems rather curious:

> Tant y avoit targe vermeille
> A or, a synople, a argent.

It is surely significant, finally, that the term *sinople* was not used in either meaning by the compilers of rolls of arms before the fourteenth century, all the examples cited above being drawn from literary sources. The emergence of *sinople* as a new term for 'green' in French blazon may be due in part to rivalry between *vert* and *vair* which could be homonymic in Old French. 'The earliest example of *sinople* "green" in Old French may be found in the Tournoi d'Ardres (1377), Paris, Bibliothèque nationale, MS. fonds français 32753, fol. 161, nos. 2 and 10' (Barstow, p. 533, s.v. VERT).

Sire, see SIEUR. *Note*: OFr. *sire* is the nominative form of *sieur*.

sisfeuille, *sixfoil* (Fig. 242). *B* 130: trois six-fueilles (*Bl* 130, see SISTEFEUILLE). *Syn.*: SISTEFEUILLE. *Note*: see ANGEGNIES EN L'ESCU; RAI, *Note*.

sistefeuille, *sixfoil* (Fig. 242). *Bl* 130 [134]: od trois sixtefoilles (*B* 130, see SISFEUILLE). *Syn.*: SISFEUILLE. *Note*: this term is made up of an ordinal number *siste* + *feuille*. Cf. *cincfeuille / quintefeuille*; *trefeuille*, *trefle / tiercefeuille*.

sixtefoille, see SISTEFEUILLE.

skalop, see ESCHALOPE.

soies armes mesmes, *his own arms*, *his proper arms*. Lancelot propre, iii. 214: .i. escu vermeil et les soies armes meismes que il avoit quant ele le prinst. *Syn.*: SES PROPRES ARMES. *Note*: cf. ARMES A DROIT, DROITES ARMES. Here Lancelot bears a red shield as a disguise; 'his own arms', mentioned earlier, are *argent, three bends gules*.

soi espandre en double, *to spread out in a fork*. See LION RAMPANT DONT LA COUE S'ESPANT EN DOUBLE. *Note*: see FOURCHIÉ[1]. Cf. ESPANI, past participle of the kindred Old French verb *espanir*.

soi reposer de voler, *close, said of a bird standing on the ground with wings folded*. See ESPREVIER QUI DE VOLER NE SE REPOSE.

soleil, *sun*. See RAI DE SOLEIL.

som[1], *tip (of a lion's tail)*. See LION A LA COUE FOURCHIEE EN SOM. *Note*: cf. BOUT. OFr. *som* is a derivative of Lat. *summum*.

som[2], *chief*. See AL SOM. *Syn.*: CHIEF[2]. *Note*: refers to position only.

son[1], *his*. See ARMES A SON PERE, ARMES DE SON PERE A, ARMES DE TEL APAREIL, ARMES LE ROI SON PERE O, ARMES SON FRERE A . . . SANS LE LABEL, ARMES SON PERE A, ARMES SON PERE OD, ARMES SON PERE OU, AUTELS ARMES COM SON PERE, AUTRETEL COM SON PERE, BANIERE SON PERE A . . . POUR, EN SON ESCU, ESTRE DE SES ARMES TEL D'ANGLE-TERE A, PORTER DE PAR SON PERE, PORTER TEL ESCU SON PERE, SES PROPRES ARMES, TESTE DE SON LIEPART.

son[2], *tip (of a lion's tail)*. See SOM[1].

songié de . . . et de . . ., *meaning obscure*. The complete blazon reads as follows: *BA* 6: Le comte (A: conte) Sauvage, l'escu songié d'argent et de noir. Allemans. *Note*: Adam-Even identifies this person as Conrad Wildgraf and points out that according to Conrad of Mure's *Clipearius Teutonicorum* the arms were *quarterly argent and sable*. In his glossary, p. 20, however, Adam-Even, referring to *BA* 6, defines *songié* as 'parti'.

sor, *on, upon*. See ASIS SOR, BASTON JETÉ SOR LE . . ., DE . . . SOR LE . . . ET DE . . . SOR LE . . ., LION COURONÉ A UNE CROIS SOR L'ESPAULE, PARTI DE . . . ET DE . . ., DEDENZ LE . . . ET . . . SOR LE . . . *Syn.*: DEDENZ, EN, PAR DESUS LE . . . *Note*: for the rule forbidding metal on metal and colour on colour, see above, p. 18 n. 4, and CROIS[1], *Note*. The *Dean Tract*, p. 27, remarks apropos of the arms of Jerusalem: 'Et si avient malement colour d'or en argent.' Cf. *Sone*, vv. 14940–1 (see above, p. 22 n. 3): 'De coi mains hons s'esmierveilloit, / Pour coi geules deseur l'or sont.'

soralé de bende o un eglel, *on a bend over all an eaglet*. *K*, vv. 253–6:

> Guillemes de Grantson palee
> De argent e de asur, suralee
> De bende rouge o trois eigleaus
> Portoit de or fin bien fais e beaus.

Syn.: see EGLE EN LA BENDE.

sor argent[1], *on a field of argent*. Durmart, vv. 8419, 10002: sor argent. *Syn.*: see EN ARGENT.

sor argent[2], *meaning obscure.* See TOUT A SINOPLE.

sorargenté, *argent (white). SCK,* fol. 106 *f*/ *SCT,* fol. 126 *d*/*SCV,* fol. 92 *f* (Agravain): Sorargentees. *Syn.*: see ARGENT.

sor azur, *on a field of azure (blue). TA,* v. 1719: sour azur. *Syn.*: see EN AZUR.

sor blanc, *on the argent quarters of a quarterly shield. K,* v. 307, see BASTON JETÉ SOR.

sor chascun rosier une rose, *on each stem a heraldic rose.* See ROSIERS SOR CHASCUN ROSIER UNE ROSE CHASCUN ROSIER.

sorjeté d'un baston, *bend over all* (Fig. 62). *K,* vv. 162–3:

Rouge a passans lyons de blanc
Trois, de un bastoun bleu surgettez.

Note: cf. BASTON JETÉ SOR.

sorjeté o une dance, *daunce over all* (Fig. 79). *K,* vv. 565–6:

De inde coulour (W: colour) de or billetee,
O une dance surgetté.

sor l'argent, *on a field of argent (white). CC,* vv. 1601: sur l'argent, see LABEL SOR LE . . . *Syn.*: see EN ARGENT.

sor l'azur, *on a field of azure (blue). CP* 40: sor l'asur, see BROIE SOR LE . . .

sor le blanc, *on a field of argent (white). Escanor,* v. 4086: Sour le blanc la mance vermeille; v. 5003: sor le blanc. *Syn.*: see EN ARGENT.

sor le chief, *on the chief.* See CHEVRON SOR LE CHIEF. *Syn.*: see EN LE CHIEF[1].

sor le geules, *on the gules half of a party shield.* See PARTI DE . . . ET DE . . ., DE . . . SOR LE . . . ET DE . . . SOR LE . . . *Syn.*: EN LE GEULES[2].

sor l'espaule, *shouldering.* See LION COURONÉ A UNE CROIS SOR L'ESPAULE.

sor le tout, *over all.* See BARRE SOR LE TOUT.

sor le vert, *on a field of vert (green). Charrete,* v. 5786: S'a sor le vert point un liepart.

sor l'or, (1) *on the or (yellow) section of a party shield. EO,* v. 5006: sor l'or, see PARTI DE . . . ET DE . . ., DEDENZ LE . . . ET . . . SOR LE . . . (2) *on a field of or (yellow). Escanor,* v. 3696: .i. lyon de geules sour l'or. *Syn.*: see EN OR.

sor or, *on a field of or (yellow). TA,* v. 1269: sor or; v. 1727: sour or. *Syn.*: see EN OR.

sorplus, *remaining charges, what needs to be added to complete the blazon. Hem,* vv. 1070–1:

Et se tu veus sonner ce cor,
Le surplus t'en deviserai.

Note: cf. CEZ CHOSES.

sor sinople, *on a field of gules (red). Durmart,* v. 9346: Sor synople.

sous = sus, see LION RAMPANT COURONÉ SUS UNE MOTE. *Note*: OFr. *sous* 'under' and *sus* 'on, upon', though orthographically confused at times, were, of course, two distinct terms.

sur, *on, upon.* See SOR.

sus, *on, on top of.* See ASIS SUS, LION RAMPANT COURONÉ ESTANT SUS UNE MOTE, LION RAMPANT COURONÉ SUS UNE MOTE. *Syn.*: see DESUS. *Note*: cf. SOUS.

taint[1], *colour, tincture.* Appears frequently in literary texts during the period in question; also OFr. *taindre, teindre* 'to colour'. E.g. *K,* v. 70: Baniere avoit en asure teinte; vv. 872–3:

En son blanc escu ot fait teindre
Un chievron rouge o trois molettes.

For other uses, see D'UN SEUL TAINT, N'AVOIR NUL AUTRE TAINT DESOUS, SANS AUTRE TAINT, TOUT D'UN TAINT. *Note*: consult Max Prinet, 'Le "taint" des écus', *Mélanges de philologie et d'histoire offerts à M. Antoine Thomas par ses élèves et ses amis* (Paris, 1927), pp. 347–54: '. . . le *taint* des écus n'est autre chose que la couche de peinture dont les écus étaient recouverts' (p. 354). This term may at times refer to more than one tincture on the shield; see DE MESME LE TAINT. Verse 70 is missing in MS. Cotton Caligula A. XVIII.

taint[2], *tinctured.* See D'UN SEMBLANT TAINT. *Syn.*: COULEURÉ. *Note*: past participle of the verb *taindre* 'to tincture, to colour'. More than one tincture is involved here.

tant, see FORS TANT QUE, TOUT PLAIN FORS TANT QUE.

tant que l'on i pouvoit metre, see DES COURONES TANT QUE L'ON I POUVOIT METRE.

targe, *shield* (?). *D* 10: od treis targes. *Note*: cf. ESCUÇON[1]; for another explanation of this term, see BARGE, *Note*.

tel, *the same.* See ARMES DE TEL APAREIL,
ESTRE DE SES ARMES TEL D'ANGLETERE A,
PORTER TEL, PORTER TEL ESCU SON PERE.

tel avuec, *the same arms, differenced by.* B 2:
teile ovecque (*Bl* 2, see AUTEL OVE). *Syn.*:
see AUTEL².

tel com, *the same arms, differenced by.* CC,
vv. 1519–21:

> Bien sai qu'escu brullé avoit
> Tel com Joffroi de Lesegnon:
> Ens avoit un viermeil lyon.

For another use, see ARMES TELS COM . . .
MES QUE. *Syn.*: see AUTEL².

**tel com . . . fors qu'au crestel egles
avoit,** *the same arms, but the canton semy of
eaglets.* SCV, fol. 92 e:

> Lors rechoisi iluec bien pres
> Les banieres Gaherïés
> Qui sont teles, por voir le cont,
> Com les monseignor Gavain sont
> Fors qu'as crestiax aigles avoit
> De coi chascune bien paroit.

Syn.: see ARMES DE PLAIN . . . FORS QU'EL
QUARTIER AVOIT EGLETES PAR DESCONOIS-
SANCE.

**tel com . . . fors qu'el crestel egles
avoit,** *the same arms, but the canton semy of
eaglets.* SCT, fol. 126 c–d:

> Lors rechoisi iluec bien pres
> Les banieres Gaherïés
> Qui sont teles, por voir le cont,
> Com les monseignor Gavain sont
> Fors qu'es crestiax aigles avoit
> De coi chascune bien paroit.

Syn.: see ARMES DE PLAIN . . . FORS QU'EL
QUARTIER AVOIT EGLETES PAR DESCONOIS-
SANCE.

**tel com . . . fors qu'el quartier eglez
avoit,** *the same arms, but the canton semy of
eaglets.* SCK, fol. 106 e:

> Dont recoisi iluec bien pres
> Les banieres Gaherïés
> Qui sont teles, por voir le cont,
> Com les monsegnor Gavain sont
> Fors qu'es quartiers aiglés avoit
> Gaunes dont cascuns bien paroit.

Syn.: see ARMES DE PLAIN . . . FORS QU'EL
QUARTIER AVOIT EGLETES PAR DESCONOIS-
SANCE.

tels armes, see PORTER TELS ARMES. *Syn.*:
see AUTEL¹.

tels armes a, *the same arms, differenced by.*
The complete blazons read as follows: *CPA*
10: Messire Jacques de Sainct Pol porte
telles armes a la fleur de lis de sable issant;
K, vv. 459–62:

> Thomas de Langcastre estoit contes;
> Se est de ses armes teus li contes,
> De Engletere, au label de France,
> E ne vuel plus mettre en sousfrance
> (W: sousfrance).

Syn.: see AUTEL².

tels armes com, *the same arms as.* Perlesvaus, p. 126: tex armes comme vostre escu;
Lancelot propre, v. 263: armés de teles armes
comme Belyas estoit; 268: armes toutes
teles lez unes comme lez autres.

tels armes com . . . mes que, see ARMES
TELS COM . . . MES QUE.

tels (armes) . . . mes que, *the same arms,
differenced by.* EO, vv. 4836–8 (complete blazon provided s.v. DESCONOISTRE), 5071–4:

> Et Danemons ses fieus teles avoit,
> Mais que une ourle qui les descounoissoit
> I ot de gueules qui bien y avenoit;
>
> . . . .
>
> Tes armes ot li quens Hues dou Mans,
> Mais que labiaus de gueules bien seans
> I ot, car l'uns ert l'autre apartenans
> Et ert l'uns l'autre de cuer forment amans;

Cleomadés, vv. 629–30:

> Li autres teles les portoit,
> Mais que labiaus bleus i avoit.

Syn.: see AUTEL².

**tels armes mes qu'en lieu d'une barre
meins,** *the same arms, differenced by one bar
less.* K, vv. 72–81:

> Acompainiez a cel gent
> Thomas de Moultone se fu,
> Ky avoit baner e escu
> De argent, o treis barres de goulys.
> Ses armes ne furent pas soules
> D'esiente en le apparellement;
> Kar teles ot resemblantment
> Johans de Langcastre entre meins,
> Mes ke en lieu de une barre meins,
> Quartier rouge e jaune lupart.

Note: cf. AUTEL².

tels (armes) que . . . mes pour descomparoison, *the same arms, differenced by.* *EO*, vv. 5023–9:

Quels armes ot Charlos, li fieus Charlon,
Deviserai, car ce me samble bon.
Teles, dont j'ai fait la devision,
K'ot li rois Charles o le flori grenon
Portoit Charlos ses fieus, la ot raison;
Mais il y ot, pour descomparison,
Ourle de gueules endenté environ.

Syn.: see AUTEL². *Note*: Henry, p. 360, note to *EO*, v. 5028: '*Descomparoison* : "distinction, différenciation"; *pour desc.* "pour les distinguer"'.

tels armes sans, *the same arms, without . . .* See PORTER TELS ARMES SANS. *Syn.*: AUTEL SANS.

tencele, *small mullet.* See SEMÉ DE TENCELES. *Note*: cf. ESTOILE, RAI DE SOLEIL, ROUELE² for size of charge.

tenebres, *clouds.* *TA*, vv. 939–40: .i. label / De tenebres; v. 2868: Sor l'escu de tenebres peint. *Note*: arms of Gawain and Pluto respectively.

teste, *head.* See CORNEILLE, EGLE A DEUS TESTES, EGLE A UNE TESTE, EGLE DE DEUS TESTES, EGLE ESPANIE OVE DEUS TESTES, FESSE DE FLEURS DE LIS ESPARZ NAISSANZ DE TESTES DE LIEPARZ, FESSE OU FLEURS CROISSANZ HORS DE LA TESTE DU LIEPART, FLEUR DE LIS CROISSANT HORS DE LA TESTE DU LIEPART, SERPENT. *Syn.*: CHIEF⁴.

teste d'aune a la teste couronee d'une courone, *meaning obscure, except that the bird's (?) head is crowned.* *Cleomadés*, vv. 712–17:

Garsianis portoit l'escu
Dyaspré de vert et de jaune
A une noire teste d'aune;
Et la teste estoit coronnee
D'une coronne a point ouvree
De gueules, qui bien i seoit.

Note: the term is listed in Tobler–Lommatzsch, i. 676, with no definition. *Aune,* however, may be a variant of OFr. *ane* 'female duck' (Godefroy, i. 287, s.v. *ane,* lists the form *aulne*), in which case the device was probably intended as a pun on the name *Garsianis* (= OFr. *gars* > MFr. *jars* 'gander'). See also ANOZ ENTOUR, *Note.*

teste del dragon, *dragon's head* (Fig. 220). *Perlesvaus*, p. 253 (4): la teste del dragon. For another use, see EN MILIEU OU LA TESTE DEL DRAGON ESTOIT. *Syn.*: see CHIEF DEL DRAGON.

teste del dragon en mi, *dragon's head* (Fig. 220). *Perlesvaus*, p. 251: Il voit le Chevalier au Dragon monté. . . . Il vit l'escu a son col, qui molt estoit granz et noirs et hisdex. Il voit la teste del dragon enmi, qui gitoit feu et flanbe a grant esploit, si laide et si orrible que tote la chanpaige en put. *Syn.*: see CHIEF DEL DRAGON.

teste de leu, *wolf's head* (Fig. 175). *Cleomadés*, v. 9882: A trois testes blanches de leu.

teste de liepart, *leopard's head.* See FESSE DE FLEURS DE LIS ESPARZ NAISSANZ DE TESTES DE LIEPARZ, FESSE OD FLEURS DE LIS CROISSANZ HORS DE TESTES DE LIEPARZ, FESSE OU FLEURS CROISSANZ HORS DE LA TESTE DU LIEPART, FLEUR DE LIS CROISSANT HORS DE LA TESTE DU LIEPART. *Note*: cf. TESTE DE SON LIEPART.

teste de mouton, *lamb's head.* See LION PASSANT A TESTE DE MOUTON.

teste de serpent, *serpent's head* (Fig. 99). See TESTES DE SERPENZ AU FER DE MOULIN.

teste de son liepart, *the head of the leopard (on his shield).* *Hem*, vv. 3358–9:

Et mesire Guis l'a feru
En la teste de son lupart.

Note: Henry, p. 140, refers to Prinet CC, p. 165, who describes the Sorel family arms which feature a leopard; Henry observes, however, that the author may have meant a leopard on the knight's helmet.

teste du liepart, see TESTE D'UN LIEPART.

teste d'un dragon cresté, *crested dragon's head* (Fig. 220). *Perlesvaus*, p. 237: et a par dehors la teste d'un dragon cresté, qui gite feu et flanbe toutes les eures que il velt. *Note*: cf. CHIEF DEL DRAGON. Nitze, i. 434, defines *cresté* here as 'rampant'; he also defines the verb *crester*, used on p. 315 in connection with a griffin, as 'to rear up, rise threateningly'. Let us first examine the latter expression which is found in the Castle of the Griffins episode. This castle has a dungeon with a cistern defended by a lion and two griffins. Lancelot slays the lion and eludes the griffins with the help of a hunting-dog (*brachet*) to which the monsters are curiously partial: 'Tantos con eles [i.e. *les gripes* 'the griffins', here viewed as females; see Nitze's note to line 7396 in ii. 331] l'oïrent venir, eles se drechent en piez, e se *cresterent* conme serpent, e jeterent tel fu e si grant flambe parmi les goles que tote la cisterne en esclarci; e virent a la clarté de lor flamme le brachet venir. Tantost con eles l'ont choisi, eles le prenent e portent avec lor feons, si en mainent la graignor joie dou mont' (i. 314–15). The locution *soi drecier en piez* 'to rise, to stand up' immediately precedes *soi crester* here which has misled Nitze into believing that the expressions are synonymous. While the context does not rule out this possibility, other examples of the verb plainly show that it rather describes the griffin's crest or comb which, like that of the dragon and of the serpent in medieval lore, was believed to bristle or stand erect when the monster became angry (see Godefroy, ii. 368, s.v. *crester*; Tobler–Lommatzsch, ii. 1037–8, s.v. *crester*).

testes de serpenz au fer de moulin, *on (each point of) the fer-de-moline a pair of serpent's heads (cross gringolé)* (Fig. 99). See FER DE MOULIN A TESTES DE SERPENZ AU FER DE MOULIN.

the, see QUARTIERS².

tiercefeuille, *trefoil* (Fig. 243). *BA* 295: a .iii. tierches feuilles (A: feulles). *Syn.*: TRANLINE, TREFEUILLE, TREFLE. *Note*: cf. TREFLÉ. For a description of the trefoils in the Wijnbergen Roll (they are pierced in the centre), see Adam-Even WB, p. 56. See also SISTEFEUILLE, *Note*.

tigre, *heraldic tiger* (Fig. 174). *TA*, v. 941: A .i. tigre de cruauté. *Note*: on one of the peculiar attitudes of the tiger in heraldry, consult C. R. Humphery-Smith, 'The Tiger and the Mirror', *Coat of Arms*, iv (1957), 318–20. Additional medieval lore concerning this animal is provided by McCulloch, pp. 176–7, and, especially, in the latter's article, 'Le tigre au miroir: la vie d'une image de Pline à Pierre Gringoire', *Revue des sciences humaines*, cxxx (1968), 149–60.

tilleul, tilluel, *lime-blossom*. See TRUMEL.

tor, torele, torete, tortel, see TOUR, TOURELE, TOURETE, TOURTEL.

tortue, *tortoise* (Fig. 218). *TA*, v. 742: A la tortue de tors fez. *Note*: arms of Tort (Wrong).

tot, see TOUT.

tour, *tower* (= *castle*) (Fig. 251). *BA* 254: a une tor. *Syn.*: see CHASTEL¹.

tourele, *tower* (= *castle*) (Fig. 251). See POUDRÉ A TOURELES. *Syn.*: see CHASTEL¹.

tourele en le . . ., *tower* (= *castle*) *charging the . . .* (Fig. 251). *D* 3: et deus toreles (?) . . . en le . . . *Note*: though the blazon is defective, the arms are known to be those of Spain (*quarterly Castile and León*); complete blazon provided s.v. EN L'ARGENT.

tourete, *tower* (= *castle*) (Fig. 251). See POUDRÉ A TOURETES. *Syn.*: see CHASTEL¹.

tourteaus, *torteaux*. See TOURTEL.

tourtel, *torteau* (Fig. 112). (1) *alone on the field*. *TA*, v. 1006: a .iii. torteaus; v. 2013: A .iii. tourteaus; *BA* 33: a .x. tortiax; 87: a .iii. tortiax; *CP* 11: a sept tourtiaus; 94: a trois torteaus; 105: a sept tourteaus; *CPA* 159: a .iii. tourteaux; *H* 110: ou .iii. tourtaus (*Hg* 110 [111]: od troys torteaux). (2) *on a chief*. *Ba* 64: 3 turteus (*B/Bc* 64, see CHIEF A UN TOURTEL; *Bb* 64, the torteaux are tricked; *Bl* 64, see TOURTEL EL CHIEF). (3) *in chief*. *Ba* 45: 3 turteus, see FESSE (1) C. 3. (*B* 45, see FESSE ET UN TOURTEL EN CHIEF; *Bb* 45, see FESSE A UN TOURTEL EN CHIEF). For other uses, see TOURTEL EN CHIEF, TOURTEL EN LE CHIEF. (4) *chevron between torteaux*. See CHEVRON ET TOURTEAUS. (5) *on a fess*. See TOURTEL EN LA FESSE. (6) *semy* (Fig. 29). See OD LES TOURTEAUS. *Syn.*: for (1) to (5), see BESANT; for (6), see BESANTÉ. *Note*: Matthew Paris provides the Latin equivalent of OFr. *tourtel* 'round bread' in this sense in the following blazon: 'Nicholaus de Moles. Similiter [= similar to the Lusignan arms] et .iii. turtelli superius' (Pusikan, p. 127). The bread in question is discussed by Lozinski in his edition of *La Bataille de Caresme et de Charnage*, p. 177, no. 158, s.v. *tortel*. In *TA*, tincture is not indicated.

tourtel el chief, *on the chief a torteau*. *Bl* 64: od trois turteux . . . el chief (*B/Bc* 64, see CHIEF A UN TOURTEL; *Ba* 64, see TOURTEL [2]; *Bb* 64, the torteaux are tricked). *Syn.*: see GASTEL EN LE CHIEF.

tourtel en chief, *in chief a torteau*. See BARRE OD UN TOURTEL EN CHIEF, FESSE A UN

TOURTEL EN CHIEF, FESSE ET UN TOURTEL EN CHIEF, FESSE OU UN TOURTEL EN CHIEF. *Syn.*: MEULE EN LE CHIEF, MEULET EN LE CHIEF, TOURTEL EN LE CHIEF. See also PE-LOTE. *Note*: refers to EN CHIEF².

tourtel en la fesse, *on a fess a torteau*. B 127: et trois torteux . . . en la fesse (*Bl* 127 [131]: a trois torteus . . . en la fesse), see FESSE (1) B. 1.

tourtel en le chief, *in chief a torteau*. See BARRE OD UN TOURTEL EN LE CHIEF, BARRE OU UN TOURTEL EN LE CHIEF, BARRE OVE UN TOURTEL EN LE CHIEF, FESSE ET UN TOURTEL EN LE CHIEF, FESSE OD UN TOURTEL EN LE CHIEF, FESSE OU UN TOURTEL EN LE CHIEF, FESSE OVE UN TOURTEL EN LE CHIEF. *Syn.*: see TOURTEL EN CHIEF. *Note*: refers to EN LE CHIEF².

tout¹, *plain arms, i.e. shield of a single tincture*. See TOUT BLANC¹, TOUT DE GEULES, TOUT D'OR, TOUT DORÉ, TOUT INDE, TOUT NOIR, TOUT ROUGET, TOUT VERMEIL¹. *Syn.*: see ARMES PURES SANS NULE AUTRE DESCONOIS-SANCE.

tout², *plain arms (i.e. shield of a single tincture) except (that)*. See TOUT . . . A, TOUT . . . FORS SEULEMENT, TOUT . . . MES SOR LE . . . PAR CONOISSANCE. *Syn.*: see D'UNE COULEUR FORS. *Note*: pleonasm; cf. TOUT A SINOPLE.

tout³, *whole (adj.)*. See JAMBES ARMEES O TOUTES LES CUISSES CHASCUNE CUISSE JOINTE AUS AUTRES ET EN CHASCUNE CORNIERE SEIT UN PIÉ, JAMBES ARMEES O TOUTES LES CUISSES ET EN CHASCUNE CORNIERE SEIT UN PIÉ.

tout⁴, *all (here describing both sections of the party field)*. See SOR LE TOUT. The complete blazon reads as follows: *Bl* 107 [109]: Johan de Courtenay, party les armes le comte de Garenne et de vert deux barres d'argent sur le tout. *Note*: cf. the modern heraldic expressions *over all* and *sur le tout*.

tout⁵, *completely, all (adv.)*. See OU MILIEU UN HOME CRUCEFIÉ QUI TOUT ESTOIT SAN-GLANT, TOUT BLANC², TOUT DORÉ², TOUT D'UNE COULEUR, TOUT D'UN TAINT, TOUT EN MILIEU, TOUT ENSEIGNIÉ D'UNE MANIERE, TOUT ENTOUR, TOUT ENVIRON, TOUT ESTELÉ, TOUT PLEIN, TOUT ROUÉ, TOUT SEUL, TOUT VERMEIL². *Note*: pleonasm; cf. ENTIER³, EN-TIEREMENT A. There is a similar pleonastic use of the Latin equivalent in Matthew Paris; see London, 'Scintillatum Auro',

p. 111: 'It is tricked per pale *gules* and *asur*, and below is this: *tres leones rampansz unus in quartero rubeo alius in quartero azurino tercius in pede et totum scutum cintillatum auro*. If we ignore the last five words we are left with the arms: Per pale gules and azure, three lions or, and that is precisely the coat painted by Matthew Paris in the *Historia Anglorum* for Herbert FitzMatthew.' London's reading of this blazon is more accurate than that of Pusikan who normalized the words *rampansz* (p. 128: *rampantes*; *Aspilogia II*, p. 50, item 71: *rampanz*) and *cintillatum* (p. 129: *scintillatum*; *Aspilogia II*: *scintillatum*) and added *d'auro* after *rampantes* (p. 128). Furthermore, the plate in Pusikan shows two words above the dexter half of the shield: the abbreviation for *gules* (*gul'*) and what appears to be *aiscū* or *aiseū*. Pusikan mentions neither word, but London, in *Aspilogia II*, p. 51, note to item 71, explains plausibly enough that 'The dexter half was tricked "aureum", but that was carefully and almost completely erased and "gules" superscribed'. Note, finally, that the word for azure at the top of the shield is written *azur*, not *asur* as in London, 'Scintillatum Auro', p. 111.

tout . . . a, *plain arms (i.e. shield of a single tincture) except*. See TOUT BLANC A, TOUT DORÉ A. For another use, see TOUT A SINOPLE. *Syn.*: see D'UNE COULEUR FORS.

tout a sinople, *meaning obscure*. SCU, fol. 152 *a*: Tout a sinople sor argent. *Note*: doubtless refers to TOUT², but it is not clear which tincture predominates in this blazon, red (*sinople*) or white (*argent*). Perhaps gilded silver is intended; cf. EN OR VERMEIL.

tout autel, *with the same arms*. Lancelot propre, v. 431: et un escu tout autel. *Syn.*: see AUTEL¹.

tout autel a, *with the same arms, differenced by*. Lancelot propre, v. 427: a unes armes blanches et ung escu tout autel a ung lion rampant vermeil. *Syn.*: see AUTEL².

tout blanc¹, *plain argent (white)*. Cligés, v. 3988: Tote fu blanche s'armeüre; Saisnes, v. 1131: Toute ert de blanche soie; Fouque de Candie, v. 2320: Totes ses armes sunt blanches come nois; Durmart, v. 5026: totes blanches; vv. 5048, 5763,

8365: tos blans; *Gerbert's Continuation,* vv. 4182–3: un escu porte / Tout blanc; *Lancelot propre,* iii. 118, 121: tout blanc; 299: tous blans; iv. 215, 359: tous blans; 215: toute blanche; 233, toutes blanches; v. 126: tot blanc; 319: toutes blances; *Mort Artu,* p. 78; toutes blanches; *Sone,* v. 1381: toutes blanches. *Note*: refers to TOUT[1].

tout blanc[2], *argent (referring to the tincture of a charge).* *Gerbert's Continuation,* v. 4177: A trois lunetes totes blanches; *Escanor,* v. 4123: A une mance toute blanche. *Note*: refers to TOUT[5].

tout blanc a, *argent (referring to the tincture of a field bearing a charge).* *Escanor,* vv. 3650–1:

Ses armes furent totes blanches
A un vermeil demi lyon.

Note: refers to TOUT[2].

tout de geules, *plain gules (red).* The complete blazon reads as follows: *H* 56: S[r] Eumenious de la Brett porte tout (G: toute) de gulez (*Hg* 56 [57]: Edmund de la Brette porte tut de goules). *Syn.*: TOUT ROUGET, TOUT VERMEIL[1]. *Note*: on the arms in question, see TOUT ROUGET, *Note.*

tout de plain les armes . . . fors qu'el quartier a egles, *the full coat, but the canton semy of eaglets.* The complete blazon reads as follows: *Escanor,* vv. 5578–80:

Icil qui porte tot de plain
Les armes monseingnor Gavain
Fors qu'el quartier a aigles blanches.

Syn.: see ARMES DE PLAIN . . . FORS QU'EL QUARTIER AVOIT EGLETES PAR DESCONOIS-SANCE. *Note*: arms of Gaheriet.

tout d'or, *plain or (yellow).* *Troie,* v. 7815: D'or bruni ert sis escuz toz. *Syn.*: TOUT DORÉ[1].

tout doré[1], *plain or (yellow).* *Durmart,* v. 1821: Ses armes sunt totes dorees. *Syn.*: TOUT D'OR.

tout doré[2], *or (referring to the tincture of a field bearing a charge).* *Durmart,* v. 7431: tos frez dorés; v. 7731: totes dorees; *Escanor,* v. 4010: toutes dorees.

tout d'une couleur, *plain arms, i.e. shield of a single tincture.* *Fouque de Candie,* v. 9981: Ses armes sunt vermoilles, totes d'une color; *Mort Artu,* p. 8: Et Lancelos commença a regarder les deus escuz as deus chevaliers et vit qu'il estoient tuit ver-

meill comme feus sanz connoissance nule. Et il estoit coustume a cel tens que nus chevaliers nouviaus ne portast le premier an qu'il receüst l'ordre de chevalerie escu qui ne fust tout d'une color; et se il autrement le fesoit, ce estoit contre son ordre. *Syn.*: see ARMES PURES SANS NULE AUTRE DESCONOISSANCE.

tout d'un taint, *plain arms, i.e. shield of a single tincture.* *Mort Artu,* p. 33: toutes d'un taint. *Syn.*: see ARMES PURES SANS NULE AUTRE DESCONOISSANCE. *Note*: cf. the expression *tout d'un taint* 'all the same colour (for recognition)' in *Troie,* v. 6723 ('Totes d'un teint') ; see D'UNE COULEUR.

tout en milieu, *in the middle of the shield.* See FLEUR DE LIS TOUT EN MILIEU. *Syn.*: see EN MI.

tout enseigné d'une maniere, *all bearing the same arms.* *Lancelot propre,* v. 175: il estoient tout enseigné d'une maniere.

tout entour, *in orle.* See BORDURE DE MER-LOZ PORALEE TOUT ENTOUR. *Syn.*: see BORDURE[2].

tout environ, *pleonasm.* See CROISILLIÉ TOUT ENVIRON.

tout estelé, *semy of mullets* (Fig. 45). *TA,* v. 1377: Touz estelez. *Syn.*: see A MOLETES SEMÉ.

tout . . . fors seulement, *plain arms (i.e. shield of a single tincture) except.* *Vulgate Merlin Sequel,* p. 388: toutes blances fors seulement une bende en belic de fin or. *Syn.*: D'UNE COULEUR FORS. *Note*: refers to TOUT[2].

tout inde, *plain azure (blue).* *Blancandin,* v. 3350: toz indes. *Note*: refers to TOUT[1].

tout . . . mes sor le . . . par conoissance, *pleonasm.* The complete blazon reads as follows: *Escanor,* vv. 5001–5:

Ses compainz r'avoit armes beles
Toutes blanches auques noveles
Mais sor le blanc par conoissance
Ot .iii. lionz d'une samblance
De geules rampanz contremont.

Note: refers to TOUT[2]. Cf. AUTEL[2].

tout noir, *plain sable (black).* *Cligés,* v. 4617: Noire fu s'armeüre tote; *Didot Perceval,* p. 173: toutes ses armes estoient . . . noires; *Perlesvaus,* p. 55: totes noires; *Lancelot propre,* iii. 231: toutes noires . . . tout noir. *Note*: refers to TOUT[1].

tout plain fors tant que, *undifferenced arms, except that.* TA, vv. 938–41:

> Murtrice ot son escu tot plein,
> Fors tant qu'il i ot .i. label
> De tenebres parant et bel,
> A .i. tigre de cruauté.

Note: refers to PLAIN[1]. Cf. TOUT PLEIN.

tout plein, *full.* TA, vv. 655–9:

> Qui portoient l'escu tot plein
> De vanterie et de desdaing
> Bien connëu en totes places
> A .i. sautëoir de menaces,
> A l'angevine de dangier.

Note: the locution is probably a pun on PLAIN[1]; cf. POUDRÉ, TOUT PLAIN FORS TANT QUE.

tout pur, *plain arms, i.e. shield of a single tincture.* Blancandin, vv. 3350–1:

> Escuz ont toz indes, vermax
> Et totes lor ensaignes pures.

Syn.: see ARMES PURES SANS NULE AUTRE DESCONOISSANCE. *Note:* according to Adam-Even, 'Tournoiement des Dames de Paris', p. 3, the same expression was also used in the meaning 'undifferenced arms', as in 'Des armes le roi toutes pures' (Tournoiement des Dames de Paris, v. 174).

tout roué, *ornamented with a wheel-like or flowery design.* Blancandin, vv. 3305–6:

> Por ce que d'Inde erent venu
> Furent tuit roé lor escu.

Note: Bouly de Lesdain, p. 196: 'La "targe roée" ne compte qu'un fort petit nombre de mentions. Rien n'indique exactement ce qu'il faut entendre sous ce nom; comme il est souvent question, dans les textes, de "draps roés" des recherches dirigées de ce côté permettraient sans doute de préciser le sens du mot.'

tout rouget, *plain gules (red).* The complete blazon reads as follows: K, vv. 261–2:

> Mes Eumenions de la Brette
> La baner ot tout rougette.

Syn.: see TOUT DE GEULES. *Note:* Prinet K, p. 350: 'Les armes de la maison de Lebret ou d'Albret présentent cette rare particularité de ne renfermer aucune figure; elles sont *de gueules purement*.'

tout seul, *pleonasm.* See BENDE TOUTE SEULE.

tout vermeil[1], *plain gules (red).* Enéas, vv. 4450–1:

> La targe en ert tote vermoille,
> Sanz autre taint, de sa nature;

Perceval, v. 872: toutes vermeilles; Lancelot propre, iii. 260: unes toutes vermeilles; iv. 308: toutes vermeilles; Mort Artu, p. 8: tuit vermeill; p. 22: unes toutes vermeilles; p. 36: toutes vermeilles; Joufroi, v. 991: totes vermeilles. *Syn.:* see TOUT DE GEULES.

tout vermeil[2], *gules (referring to the tincture of a charge).* SCK, fol. 106 e: Et tos vermaus com rose en mai; SCT, fol. 126 d / SCV, fol. 92 e: Et toz vermax com rose en mai; Escanor, v. 4957: A .iii. aigles totes vermeilles. *Note:* refers to TOUT[5].

tranchant, *cutting edge.* See LANGUE A TRANCHANZ.

tranchier, *to cut.* See ESPEE AU PONG ET AU HELT QUI TRANCHE LE LION PAR MI. *Note:* the Tranchelion arms are variously depicted (see Adam-Even BA, p. 120). Our illustration (Fig. 139) shows the sword as found on a seal dated 1540 (Paris, Archives nationales, Pièces originales, tome 2874, dossier 60774, pièce 10), which suggests that here *tranchier par mi* means 'to cleave lengthwise'.

tranline, *trefoil* (Fig. 243). CC, vv. 1205–7:

> Escu de geules a deus bars
> Portoit, et s'i avoit encor
> Assis tranlines de fin or.

Syn.: see TIERCEFEUILLE. *Note:* on this term, consult Delbouille, p. 291.

travers, see DE TRAVERS, EN TRAVERS.

treçoir, *tressure* (Fig. 126). The complete blazon reads as follows: CC, vv. 1524–9:

> Lors vint ou renc, a coer hardi,
> Sires Hues de Rumegny,
> Couviers d'or au viermeil sautoir;
> De vert y avoit un trecoir,
> Et pour faire l'escu plus gent
> Y ot cinq cokilles d'argent.

Syn.: TREÇOIR ENVIRON, TREÇON. *Note:* according to Prinet CC, pp. 175–6, the Rumigny family arms show the saltire placed over the tressure, not vice versa as the order of items suggests here. On this charge in heraldry, see Wagner, *Historic*

Heraldry, p. 113, and Robert Saunders, 'An Unusual Tressure', *Coat of Arms*, iii (1954), 13–14. According to Godefroy, viii. 61, s.v. *tresseor*: 'La langue du blason a le mot trescheur, sorte d'orle étroit représentant une tresse' (cf. also, s.v. *tressoir*: 'orle étroit représentant une tresse'). Rather than a braid, however, the tressure is more likely a stylized hair-ribbon, another meaning of the Old French word listed by Godefroy; cf. *TA*, vv. 1830–2 (apropos of Courtoisie's banner):

> D'un treçoir ma dame Amistié
> Et de .ii. fresiaus d'Alïance
> L'ot Amours lïé a sa lance.

It belongs, therefore, to the group of heraldic terms of vestimentary origin. This is also the interpretation to be given to TREÇON. On these terms, which are akin to OFr. *trece* 'tress, braid', consult Goddard, pp. 215–20, and *FEW*, xiii (1965), 262–5, s.v. **trichia*.

treçoir environ, *tressure* (Fig. 126). *EO*, v. 5133: A un trechoir . . . environ. *Syn.:* see TREÇOIR.

treçon, *tressure*. See DOUBLE TREÇON. *Syn.:* see TREÇOIR. *Note:* on the etymology of this term, consult *FEW*, xiii (1965), 262.

trefeuille, *trefoil* (Fig. 243). The complete blazon reads as follows: *M* 44: Sʳ Walter de Lyle port d'or ou ung cheveron de gulez .iii. foulez de gulez ou ung label d'azure. *Syn.:* see TIERCEFEUILLE. *Note:* the MS. reads *iij foulez*, i.e. *trefoulez* or *tiercefoulez* 'semy of trefoils', or 'three leaves'. Cf. Barstow, pp. 325–7.

trefle, *trefoil*. See SEMÉ DE TREFLES. *Syn.:* see TIERCEFEUILLE.

treflé, *semy of trefoils* (Fig. 50). *CP* 41, 42: treflé. *Syn.:* SEMÉ DE TREFLES. *Note:* cf. TIERCEFEUILLE.

tretel, *ghost word*. See AUTRETEL.

triers, *ghost word*. See BASTON DE TRAVERS.

trompe, *trumpet* (Fig. 275). *D* 106: od deus trumpes; 178: a deus trumpes. *Note:* Trumpington family arms; cf. the canting arms (*gules, two trumpets in pile or*) of Dareines (= OFr. *araine* 'brass trumpet') in Matthew Paris (Hauptmann, p. 27; *Aspilogia II*, p. 25, item 58).

troncené de . . . et de . . ., *compony, gobony*. See TRONÇONÉ DE . . . ET DE . . .

tronçoné de . . . et de . . ., *compony, gobony* (Fig. 12). *TC*, vv. 2219–20:

> A celle bende troncenee
> D'argent et d'azur enlistee;

v. 2245: Celui au baston troncenei; *CP* 26: a une bande tronçonnee d'argent et d'azur. *Syn.:* see COUPONÉ DE . . . ET DE . . . *Note:* in both *TC* and *CP*, the bend compony argent and azure is a feature of the arms of Renaud de Trie.

trumel, *lime-blossom*. See FEUILLE DE TRUMEL. *Note:* this form is a variant of OFr. *tilleul, tilluel < VL *tiliolus < *tilius < CL tilia*.

tu ers, *ghost word*. See BASTON DE TRAVERS.

tupelles, *ghost word*. See POUDRÉ A TOURELES.

u = ou, see OU.

un, see DE L'UN A L'AUTRE, DE L'UNE A L'AUTRE, DE L'UN EN L'AUTRE, DE L'UNE ET DE L'AUTRE, DE L'UN ET DE L'AUTRE, DE L'UN ET L'AUTRE, EN UN EN L'AUTRE, L'UN EN L'AUTRE, UN DESOUS ET L'AUTRE DESOR, PEUS RECOUPÉS DEUS . . . UN.

undé de . . . et de . . ., *barry undy*. See ONDÉ DE . . . ET DE . . .

un desous et l'autre desor, *one below and the other above*. See FESSE A DEUS LISTEAUS UN DESOUS ET L'AUTRE DESOR. *Note:* cf. DESOUS ET DESOR.

unes, *the feminine plural form of the indefinite article 'un'*. See CHEVAL FUST APENDU D'UNES FOURCHES. *Note:* on this Old French form, consult Foulet, *Petite Syntaxe*, para. 87.

urle, see ORLE.

vache, *cow* (Fig. 154). *Escanor*, v. 3641: a .ii. vaches. *Note:* complete blazon provided s.v. COR. Cf. OEILLE PASSANT, *Note*.

vair, *vair* (Fig. 4). *Tristan de Thomas*, v. 2182: Escu ot d'or a vair freté; *Saisnes*, v. 2823 (var.): Et Berarz le feri desor la targe vaire; *Tristan de Béroul*, v. 4017: L'autre connois as armes vaires; *Durmart*, v. 8510: De vair; *BA* 95, 157: de vair; 201–3: vers; *B* 13, 25: de verre (*Bc* 13, 25: de ver; *Bl* 13, 25: de veer); 120: de veirre (*Bl* 120 [124]: de veer); *Ba* 13: de vere; 21: de vare; 25: de ver; 28: de vair; *Bc* 21, 28: de ver (*B/Bb* 21, 28, see VAIRIÉ; *Bl* 21, 28: de veer); 47: verre (*B/Ba/Bb* 47, see

VAIRIÉ); *Bl* 47, 57, 95, 176 [180]: de veer; 201 [205] (*B* 201, see VAIRIÉ): veyr; *C* 24 (*Cl/Cd* 24: de veyr), 26 (*Cl* 26: de veyr; *Cd* 26: de veire): de veir; 48: de veyre (*Cl* 48: de veyr; *Cd* 48: de vere); 50 (*Cl* 50: de veyr; *Cd* 50: veyr), 126 (*Cl/Cd* 126: de veyr), 144 (*Cl* 144: de veyr; *Cd* 144: de vaier), 152 (*Cl/Cd* 152: de veyr), 155 (*Cl/Cd* 155: de veyr), 175 (*Cl* 175: de veyr): de veire; *Cl* 176: de veyr (*C* 176, see VAIRIÉ); *Cl/Cd* 63: de veyr (*C* 63, see VAIRIÉ); *Escanor*, v. 3575: vair; v. 3597: vers; *D* 30, 32, 48, 73, 126: de veir; *TC*, v. 2089: vair; *CC*, vv. 1120, 1230: de vair; *Hunbaut*, v. 2269: ver; *CP* 65, 121, 132: de vair; 109: vaires; *CPA* 9, 165: de vair; 163: vaires; *H* 71: de veire (*Hg* 71 [72]: de veir); 76 (*Hg* 76 [88]: de veir): de verre; 105 (*Hg* 105: de veir): de veere (G: de verre); *M* 12, 16, 59, 68, 78: de verre; 62, 63: verre; *K*, vv. 207, 393: de vair; v. 388: vaire; v. 691: vair. *Syn.*: VAIRIÉ, VAIRONÉ. *Note*: cf. VAIRIÉ DE . . . ET DE . . . *P* 63 (= *B* 13) reads: 'veré d'argent et d'azure'. OFr. *vair* (< Late Latin *varius*; see Manfred Bambeck, 'Lexikalisches und Etymologisches', *ZRPh.*, lxxvii [1961], 328) was used in a variety of meanings, as an adjective to indicate 'blue-grey, mottled, spotted, and other similar patterns', as a noun to designate horses and other animals with such markings; and as a noun and adjective to refer to the skin of a kind of squirrel, or wearing-apparel lined or ornamented with such costly fur (*FEW*, xiv [1958], 182–6, s.v. *varius*). In the Latin *Clipearius Teutonicorum*, the adjective *varius* and the substantive *variamina* sometimes mean vair, i.e. the fur (e.g. in the arms of Freiburg), at other times barry (e.g. Thuringia). For Matthew Paris's use of Lat. *variatus*, see VAIRIÉ DE . . . ET DE . . . As can be seen by comparing the Old French heraldic term *vair* with the next two items, it is sometimes difficult to distinguish between this word and its synonyms, and, moreover, these may even be mistaken for OFr. *vert* 'green' (see VERT). At any rate, this fur is attested in the twelfth century in its present-day stylized form (e.g. arms of William de Guines on a seal dated before 1177; see Bouly de Lesdain, p. 210; *Aspilogia II*, p. 176, note to item 39, also refers to a seal

of Arnold II de Guines dated 1186). The arms referred to here featured a field vairy or and azure, not vair, but while different tinctures may have been involved, the design was essentially what it is today. Vair is a term now restricted to an argent and azure pattern, vairy to any other combination of tinctures. For the period under consideration here, OFr. *vair* apparently had its present-day restricted use (i.e. only for argent and azure), a meaning also shared by *vairié*. On the other hand, OFr. *vairié de . . . et de . . .* was used for various combinations of tinctures *including* argent and azure.

vairié, *vair* (Fig. 4). *BA* 284: vairie; *B* 21: verree (*Ba/Bb/Bc/Bl* 21, see VAIR); 28 (*Ba/Bc/Bl* 28, see VAIR), 47 (*Ba* 47: verré; *Bb* 47: verry; *Bc/Bl* 47, see VAIR): de verree; 57: de veiree; 95: de vairree; 176: varriee; 201: varree (*Bl* 57, 95, 176 [180], 201 [205], see VAIR); *Bb* 13 (*B/Ba* 13, see VAIR), 28: verry; 21, 25 (*B/Ba/Bc/Bl* 25, see VAIR): varry; *C* 63: veiree (*Cl/Cd* 63, see VAIR); 176: de verry (*Cl/Cd* 176, see VAIR). *Syn.*: see VAIR.

vairié de . . . et de . . ., *vairy* (Fig. 4). (1) *the tinctures are argent and azure*. *BA* 86, 149–51, 196: vairié de . . . et de . . .; *B* 139: vairré de . . . et de . . . (*Bl* 139 [143]: verree de . . . et de . . .); *D* 61, 128, 136: verré de . . . et de . . .; 117: verrez de . . . et de . . .; 145: verrés de . . . et de . . . (2) *other combinations of tinctures*. *BA* 243: vairié de . . . et de . . .; *B* 15: verree de . . . et de . . . (*Ba* 15: veré de . . . e de . . .; *Bb/Bl* 15: verré de . . . et de . . .; *Bc* 15: veré de . . . e de . . .); *C* 37: veiré de . . . et de . . . (*Cl* 37: veyré de . . . et de . . .; *Cd* 37: veiré de . . . e . . .); *C* 66 (*Cl/Cd* 66: veiré de . . . e de . . .), 161 (*Cl* 161: veyré de . . . e de . . .; *Cd* 161: wer de . . . e de . . .): veiré de . . . et . . .; *D* 69, 72, 138, 147, 154: verré de . . . et de . . .; *TC*, v. 2038: D'or et de guelles fu vairiéz; v. 2062 (referring to the same arms [Bauffremont]): L'escu varié; *CP* 79: vairés de . . . et de . . .; 140: vairié de . . . et de . . .; *CPA* 173: vairié de . . . et de . . .; *H/Hg* 101: verré de . . . et de . . . *Syn.*: ESTRE VAIRIÉ DE . . . ET DE . . . *Note*: cf. VAIR. In Matthew Paris, the Latin equivalent *variatus* is used, on the one hand, with the tinctures argent and azure (Pusikan, p. 150: 'Comitis d'Aubemarle. Scutum de gules, crux variata de albo et azuro'), and, on the other, with or and gules (Pusikan, p. 126: 'Comitis de Ferrariis. Scutum variatum auro et gules'; p. 140: 'Comitis de Ferreres. Scutum variatum auro et gules'). For a synonym of Lat. *variatus* in this sense in Matthew Paris, see MASCLÉ DE . . . ET DE . . .[1], *Note*; for another fur, see ERMINE, *Note*. For a possible synonym in Walford's Roll, see ENDENTÉ DE . . . ET DE . . .

vairon, *sea-perch, sea-wolf* (*a kind of fish*) (Fig. 216). *Bataille de Caresme et de Charnage,* vv. 297–301:

Et li chevestres et li frains
Et li poitraus et li lorains
Des armes le conte de Bar;
Sa baniere fu d'un osbar,
A entresaigne de vairons.

Syn.: see BAR. *Note*: Lozinski, p. 103: 'L'étendard de Quaresme est orné de *vairons,* genre de petits poissons (v. 301): c'est un jeu de mots avec le terme héraldique *vair.* Le harnais de sa monture est aux armes du comte de Bar (v. 299); ici, le poète trouve un auxiliaire précieux dans la science héraldique : en effet, le blason du Barrois était : "d'azur, semé de croix recroisetées au pied fiché d'or, à deux *bars* adossés de même brochant sur le tout".' On the fish in question, consult Lozinski, p. 178, no. 162. On page 41, Lozinski observes: 'Le "comte de Bar" (v. 299) fournit une date-limite trop éloignée pour qu'on puisse la prendre en considération : le Barrois fut érigé en duché en 1354.' These arms, however, are ascribed to the Count of Bar by the middle of the thirteenth century. For Matthew Paris's drawing of the arms of Count Henry II of Bar, see Hauptmann, p. 28 (no. 57) and Table 2, fig. 36; see also *WB* 519 and fig. 94. For OFr. *osbar,* another kind of fish used here as a banner, consult Lozinski, p. 160, no. 111.

vaironé, *vair* (Fig. 4). The complete blazon reads as follows: *CC,* vv. 1315–21:

De Casteillon ot non Gautiers.
Ses escus avoit le cief d'or,
Et saciés qu'il avoit encor,
El cief, une mierle de sable,
Ce n'est ne mencongne ne fable,

Et de geules estoit li fons,
S'i ot trois vaironnés bastons.

Syn.: see VAIR. *Note*: on the arms in question, see Prinet CC, pp. 171–2. As far as the term *vaironé* itself is concerned, Prinet explains: '[Le poète] sait que le blason des Châtillon renferme trois pals de vair; mais s'il disait "trois pals de vair", il aurait quatre syllabes; or il lui en faut six; il dit donc "trois vaironnés bastons", inventant une épithète et appliquant abusivement aux pals un terme dont il connaît bien le sens propre et qu'il emploie, ailleurs, pour désigner de véritables bâtons héraldiques' (pp. 178–9). It should be noted, however, that *vaironé* is elsewhere attested as a synonym for OFr. *vair* in a non-heraldic sense; see *FEW,* xiv (1958), 183, s.v. *varius.*

***vermeil,** gules.* Used only in literary contexts, e.g. *Thèbes,* v. 5033: un escu vermeill; *Troie,* v. 8066: vermeuz; *Erec,* v. 2084: vermoille ansaigne; v. 5849: Armé d'unes armes vermoilles; *Aquin,* v. 69: escu vermail; *Faits des Romains,* i. 659: vermelz; *Gerbert's Continuation,* v. 4176: unes armes vermeilles; *Lancelot propre,* iii. 147, 150: vermeille; *Queste,* pp. 7, 74: vermeilles; *EO,* vv. 2654, 4830: vermeill; *Hem,* v. 1124: vermeil; *Escanor,* vv. 3596, 3651: vermeil; v. 3485: le vermeil (see BOUCEL PAR DESUS LE . . .); *TC,* v. 454: vermoillez; *CC,* vv. 713, 1282: viermeil; *K,* vv. 47, 478: vermaus; v. 199: vermelles (W: vermeilles); v. 534: wermeille (W: vermeille). For other uses, see EN OR VERMEIL, GEULES VERMEILLES, OR VERMEIL, TOUT VERMEIL, VERMEIL SINOPLE. *Syn.*: see GEULES. *Note*: cf. ENTIER[3]. On the expression *tourner le vermeil de l'escu* 'to leave a lord's service', see J. Fox, 'Two Borrowed Expressions in the *Charroi de Nîmes*', *MLR,* l (1955), 315–17; *FEW,* xiv. 289.

vermeillet, *gules. K,* v. 183: vermellettis; v. 299: vermellette. *Syn.*: see GEULES.

vermeil sinople, *gules* (*red*). *Durmart,* v. 4666: vermel sinople; v. 7325: De vermel synople. *Syn.*: see GEULES.

vert, *vert* (*green*). *Troie,* vv. 7745, 7878: De vert; *Cligés,* vv. 4557, 4715: verz; v. 4669: Les armes verz; *Charrete,* v. 5785: A cel escu vert d'une part; *Durmart,* v. 7863: vert; v. 10000: De vert; *Otinel,* v. 367:

vert; *Fouque de Candie*, vv. 10407, 10552:
verz; vv. 12415, 14727: vert; *Huon de
Bordeaux*, v. 1106: Les escus vers; *Blancandin*, v. 5330: uns vers escus; *Perlesvaus*, pp. 126, 190, 191, 199, 201 (and var.),
208, 301: vert; pp. 128–30: Chevaliers
au Vert Escu; p. 129: Chevalier au
Vert Escu; p. 201 (var.): verde; p. 404:
de vert; *Lancelot propre*, v. 18: unes vers;
Artus, p. 7: vert; *Vulgate Merlin Sequel*,
p. 120: de vert; *TA*, v. 1828: Ensaigne
avoit d'un vert cendé; *Joufroi*, v. 2525: de
verz colors; *BA* 1, 4, 36, 45, 64 (2), 76, 93,
108, 123, 124, 127, 173, 181, 282, 294: vert;
214, 231, 239, 280: de vert; *B* 17 (*Bl* 17:
de vert), 129 (*Bl* 129 [133]: vert), 142 (*Bl*
142 [146]: de vert): de vert; *B/Bl* 170 [174]:
vert; *Bl* 107 [109]: de vert; *C* 13, 46, 101,
119, 143, 167, 172, 179: vert; 128: de
vert; *Cl/Cd* 46: verte; 101: de vert; *Cl* 13,
128, 167, 179: de vert; 119: de verte; 172:
verte; *Cd* 13: de verte; 46: ver; 119: vert;
128, 167: de ver; *EO*, vv. 975, 4820, 5083:
verdes; v. 5132: vert; *D* 77: de vert; *TC*,
v. 1997: vert; *Cleomadés*, vv. 537, 713, 723,
730, 11307: vert; v. 738: verdes; *CC*,
v. 1527: de vert; *CP* 29: vers; 68, 80: vert;
79, 124, 141: de vert; *CPA* 146: vert; *H/Hg*
3, 41 [42], 95: de vert; *H* 35: de vert; *Hg*
103 [104]: de vert; *Sone*, v. 13421: Plus
estoit vers que papegais; vv. 13427, 13543:
vert; v. 13439: de viert; v. 13519: li vers;
K, v. 101: vert; vv. 482, 559, 803: verde.
For other uses, see EN VERT, PARMI LE VERT,
SOR LE VERT. *Note*: the Old French heraldic
term *sinople* never means green in the period
under consideration here; see SINOPLE. *Hg*
103 [104] is an error; see Gough H, p. 154,
note to item 104.

vidé, *voided*. See VUIDIÉ.

vivre, *fess dancetty* (Fig. 78). See VUIVRE DE
TRAVERS EL CHIEF.

voidé, *voided*. See VUIDIÉ.

volant, *volant (flying)*. See EGLE VOLANT,
GRIFON VOLANT. *Note*: cf. VOLER.

voler, *to fly*. Charrete, vv. 5818–20:

Ou vos veez ces deus arondres
Qui sanblent que voler s'an doivent,
Mes ne se muevent . . .

For other uses, see EGLE QUI DE VOLER
FAISOIT SEMBLANT, EN MILIEU UNE EGLE QUI
DE VOLER FAISOIT SEMBLANT, ESPREVIER QUI
DE VOLER NE SE REPOSE. *Note*: cf. VOLANT.

vrai, *true, correct (arms)*. Lancelot propre, iii.
273, 275: vraies enseignes; 273: enseignes
vraies. *Syn.*: DROIT[1]. *Note*: cf. DROITES ARMES,
SES PROPRES ARMES, SOIES ARMES MESMES.

vuidié[1], *voided*. See CROIS VUIDIEE, ESCUÇON
VUIDIÉ, LOSENGE VUIDIEE, VUIDIÉ DU CHAMP.
Syn.: see FAUS. *Note*: in the Bradfer-
Lawrence Tract, written *c*. 1445, the
English substantive *voide* is used as a syno-
nym for ESCUÇON[1]; see London, 'Some
Medieval Treatises', p. 173.

vuidié[2], *an improper use*. See ESCUÇON VUIDIÉ.

vuidié du champ, *voided*. See ESCU VUIDIÉ
DU CHAMP, MASCLE VUIDIÉ DU CHAMP. *Syn.*:
see FAUS.

vuivre de travers el chief, *on a chief
a fess dancetty*. BA 205: a une vuivre (A:
vuive) . . . de travers el (A: es) kief. *Note*:
modern French heraldry has retained
the adjective *vivré* which is derived
from OFr. *vuivre* (also attested as *wivre,
guivre*, etc.) < LL *wipera < CL *vipera*
'serpent'. The Modern French term is
the equivalent of E. *dancetty*, an adjective
used to designate a sawtooth line. Cf.
BASTON DE FUIRES, DANCE. For the heraldic
monster referred to in French heraldry as
a *guivre, vivre*, or *vouivre*, see Veyrin-Forrer,
p. 116, and cf. E. *wivern, wyver,
wyvern* (Boutell, p. 81; Plate VII, 12). See
also Georgine E. Brereton, 'Viper into
Weasel (A Note on a Line in Chaucer's
Melibee)', *Medium Ævum*, xxvii (1958),
173–4. This serpent is not to be confused
with OFr. *guivre, vivre, vuivre, wivre* 'weever,
sting-fish' (MFr. *vive*), a kind of marine
fish. On the latter, consult *La Bataille de
Caresme et de Charnage*, ed. G. Lozinski,
p. 150, no. 75.

witecoc, *woodcock*. See ORLE DE WITECOCS.
Note: on this fowl, see *La Bataille de Caresme
et de Charnage*, ed. G. Lozinski, p. 180, no.
167.

wivre, *fess dancetty*. See VUIVRE DE TRAVERS
EL CHIEF. *Syn.*: see DANCE.

yeux, *'eyes'*. See D'IEUZ DE PAON OEILLETÉ.

ynescochon, *escutcheon*. See INESCOCHON.

TABLE III

COATS OF ARMS IDENTIFIED BY NAME

N.B. The orthography used here is the modern form provided by the Index of Proper Names of *Aspilogia II*, by Flutre, or by scholars in the notes to the editions and studies cited in this book. A case could be made for indexing certain names below in the alternate category (e.g. Charlemagne, a historical personage, has fictitious arms; on the other hand, Roger Ertaut may actually have lived). Others could properly have appeared on both lists (e.g. the King of Scotland in *Escanor*). For further identification of the literary characters, consult Flutre and West. See also Ernest Langlois, *Table des noms propres de toute nature compris dans les chansons de geste imprimées* (Paris, 1904).

I. HISTORICAL PERSONAGES AND PLACES

Acre, 129
Ainghien, *see* Enghien
Aixe, Asse, *see* Esch
Albret, d', 54
Albret, Amanieu d', 29, 33, 54, 282, 283
Alexander the Great, 218
Alsace, 123
Alsace, Basse-, 124
Angevin, Bernard, 106
Annandale, *see* Brus
Ap Adam, John, 12
Aquitaine, Eleanor of, wife of Louis VII, King of France, and Henry II, King of England, 19, 174
— William IX, Duke of, 22, 220
Aragon, King of, 27, 253
— Ramon Berengar IV, King of, 27
Archat, Richard, 14
Argentine, 152
Armenia, Lesser, 11, 36–7, 116, 154, 160
Arms, King of, 45
Artois, Count of, 141
— Philip of, 261
— Robert II, Count of, 149, 261
Aspremont, Joffroi d', 168–9
Aubigny, Elie d', 251
Aumale, 240
— Earl of, 10, 155, 286
Aunou, 174
Autrèches, Gaucher d', 232
Auvergne, Count of, 200

Auxerre, Count of, 190
Averton, 272

Badeham, *see* Ap Adam
Badlesmere, Bartholomew de, 177, 205
Balliol, 191, 201
— Alexander de, 175, 191
— Hugh de, 165, 190–1, 228
— John de, 191
Balsamon, 260
Bar, Count of, 286
— Henry II, Count of, 114, 286
— John of, 114, 198–9
Bardolf, Hugh, 176
Basseger, *see* Châtillon-Bazoches
Basset, 146, 162, 248
— Philip, 165
Bassingbourne, John de, 203, 241
Baucey, Hugh de, 224
Bauffremont, 285
Baugé, 22
Bautersem, 206, 237
Bavaria, 240
— Duke of, 141, 240
Bazentin, Huart de, 209
— war-cry of Huart de, 219
Béarn, 248
Beauchamp, Robert de, 29
— Walter de, 163, 242
— William de, 169, 203, 265
Beaumont, 167

8223374   U

II. FICTITIOUS AND LEGENDARY CHARACTERS AND PLACES, SAINTS, DIVINE BEINGS, ETC.

PRINTED IN GREAT BRITAIN
AT THE UNIVERSITY PRESS, OXFORD
BY VIVIAN RIDLER
PRINTER TO THE UNIVERSITY

74376